AMERICAN COURT SYSTEMS

AMERICAN COURT SYSTEMS

Readings in Judicial Process and Behavior

SECOND EDITION

EDITED AND WITH INTRODUCTORY ESSAYS BY

Sheldon Goldman
University of Massachusetts at Amherst

Austin Sarat
Amherst College

Longman
New York & London

American Court Systems: Readings in Judicial Process and Behavior, second edition

Longman Inc., 95 Church Street, White Plains, N. Y. 10601

Associated companies:
Longman Group Ltd., London
Longman Cheshire Pty., Melbourne
Longman Paul Pty., Auckland
Copp Clark Pitman, Toronto
Pitman Publishing Inc., New York

Executive editor: David Estrin
Production editor: Dee Amir Josephson
Text design: Jill Francis Wood
Cover design: Susan J. Moore
Production supervisor: Judi Stern

Library of Congress Cataloging-in-Publication Data

American court systems: readings in judicial process and behavior/edited and with introductory essays by Sheldon Goldman, Austin Sarat.
     p.   cm.
  Bibliography: p.
  Includes index.
  ISBN 0-582-28602-6
  1. Courts—United States. 2. Judicial process—United States.
3. Judges—United States—Attitudes.
  KF8700.A7A46 1989
  347.73′1′09—dc19   87-28942
  [347.307109]   CIP

ISBN 0-582-28602-6

94 93 92 91 90 89 9 8 7 6 5 4 3 2

Table of Contents

Preface to the Second Edition

The first edition of this book was published over a decade ago. Our objective in preparing this book of readings remains what it was then—to present to the student, within a broad dispute-processing framework, some of the best materials available to illuminate various facets of American courts. However, our task has been much more difficult now because the judicial politics and the law and society literature has expanded tremendously since we prepared the first edition and the quantity and quality of the relevant work has meant that of necessity a number of major contributors and major contributions to our understanding of courts could not be included in this volume. But we hope that the richness of what we *have* included will whet the appetites of students and stimulate them to explore further.

Like the first edition, we include introductory essays to each of the fifteen chapters that not only set the stage for the readings that follow but also aim to complement those selections so that the student is given an overall view of the judicial process. There are, however, some topics that are not covered such as the police and law enforcement, the technical issues of judicial administration, and the prison and parole systems. These subjects deserve separate extensive treatment, but were we to have included them this book would have become unmanageable. Also, these topics do tend to diverge from our central concerns.

The basic structure of the first edition remains in this edition although some chapter topics were collapsed for the new edition. Of the 64 selections in this book, 21 are carried over from the first edition. Like the first edition, our perspective on the judicial process is to focus on courts as dispute-processing institutions. "Dispute" is the basic unit of analysis.

Although we worked together on the entire manuscript and share responsibility for its contents, we would like to thank several scholars for their helpful comments and suggestions. The first edition benefited substantially from the views of Professors Lawrence Baum, Jonathan Casper, David Danelski, Joel Grossman, William McLauchlan, and Harold Spaeth. This edition was helped by the comments of Professors Malcolm Feeley, Burton Atkins, and, once again, Lawrence Baum. We wish to thank David Estrin, political science editor at Longman, and his predecessor Irv Rockwood for their encouragement to undertake a second edition and for their enthusiastic support for the project. We are also appreciative of the work of Victoria Mifsud in obtaining permissions from authors and publishers and the overall supervision and coordination by managing editor Dee Josephson. We also thank Dan Dunlop who helped with proofreading. Finally, we are grateful to the authors and publishers of the works we have included for allowing us to reprint them.

Austin Sarat
Sheldon Goldman

Introduction

Alexis de Tocqueville, perhaps the most perceptive of all commentators on American social life, noted early in the nineteenth century what he believed to be a distinctive tendency of Americans to transform almost every important political question into a legal question. The spirit of American democracy is, according to Tocqueville, the spirit of spontaneity, energy, creativity, and perhaps even anarchy. Tocqueville saw in the early experience of America the potential for great achievement and, at the same time, the possibility of great peril. He looked to law and to its spirit to provide a guiding, stabilizing, and limiting force, a force that would channel the vitality of American life into creative paths. Particularly important in this role would be the part played by courts and judges. What is remarkable about American courts, Tocqueville noted, is that judges are invested with the power and responsibility to supervise the contests of a majoritarian political system, to protect an essentially democratic polity and society from the excesses of democracy. Courts are unique among political and social institutions in that they embody the spirit of reason and reasoned judgment. They provide a forum in which the strength of argument rather than the strength of numbers is decisive.[1]

Tocqueville's observations about the special character of American courts have been echoed throughout the nineteenth and twentieth centuries, but not always with Tocqueville's spirit of admiration. Our judicial system has been variously criticized for being irresponsible, abusing its power, failing to uphold the central tenets of democracy, and being costly and inefficient.[2] Recently, for example, sociologist Nathan Glazer advanced the argument that we have developed an "Imperial Judiciary"—that is, that courts and judges now have so much power, play so much of a role in regulating the way Americans conduct their lives, that they pose a threat and a challenge to the vitality of our political system. Too much power, wrote Glazer, has moved from the elected, representative branches of government to the largely nonelective judiciary. Furthermore, he argued that the judicial system is no less political than are the other branches of government. Judges use their positions to carry out specific policy preferences rather than to provide neutral judgment. They do so without being accountable for their actions.[3]

Whether the power of American courts is too great or whether it is appropriate and necessary to the maintenance of democratic politics, there can be little doubt that courts have played and continue to play a major role in shaping and influencing political and social life in the United States. Perhaps more than in any other nation, courts in this country have been and remain a barometer of the morals, problems and aspirations of the citizenry.

Glazer's position is important in that it represents a wide variety of contemporary concerns about the operation of American courts. These concerns have developed in recent years along

1

with the increase in the number of things subject to government regulation. The law now regulates and prescribes standards for what we wear, what we eat, how we conduct our business dealings, how we educate our children and are educated ourselves, and most other aspects of our daily lives.[4] As the scope of law has expanded, so have the activities of the American judiciary. Whereas most courts, particularly at the lower levels, were once largely concerned with settling narrowly drawn conflicts between private parties, courts in the 1980s were often concerned with the broadest issues of public policy—for example, school desegregation, environmental pollution, and the rights of people on welfare.[5] In dealing with these issues the courts have been doing more than simply making declarations of the legal rights of the particular parties involved in the litigation. Because of their apparent perception of governmental agencies as being unable or unwilling to satisfactorily implement such judicial declarations, judges, in a number of legal areas affecting large numbers of people, have become increasingly involved in devising detailed positive plans for enforcing the law as they determine it. For example, in recent years there have been a number of school desegregation cases where judges, finding that local officials have been unable or unwilling to draw up satisfactory plans to desegregate urban school districts, have themselves drawn up such plans. They have gone beyond simply deciding whether districts are illegally segregated and have attempted to devise remedies that in practice tell communities how their schools should be organized. This positive kind of judicial policy-making has raised questions in the minds of many people—questions as to whether it is fair for judges rather than the elected representatives of the citizenry to make such decisions and, even more importantly, whether judges are competent to decide such complex issues of public policy.

Other critics maintain that the major problem with contemporary courts is not that judges are engaged in policy-making, but that the policy made is unjust.[6] This criticism, often from the political left, suggests that American courts are simply tools of an inegalitarian social order and that they are used as an instrument to repress the legitimate political grievances of the poor and the powerless. These criticisms, focusing as they do on questions of fairness, competence, and justice, have placed the courts at the center of strident political controversy about the nature of American politics and law.

The major issues of American political life, perhaps even more so today than in Tocqueville's time, frequently find their way into court. Abortion, the conduct of the police and the rights of criminals, obscenity, the powers of the President, the way we conduct and finance elections—these and other issues are argued in American courts. We know that courts are important in our lives, but it is fair to say that most of us are not sure why they are or how they came to be that way or what difference it makes that courts are so important. An underlying assumption in this book is that the fact that our courts are active and frequent makers of public policy makes a great deal of difference in the quality of American life. It makes a difference in terms of the nature and quality of our democracy and of our private lives as well. It makes a difference because courts are distinctive types of institutions; they operate in ways that are quite unlike the ways in which other political and social institutions operate. Our concern in this book is to try to understand how courts operate and why they operate as they do, and to compare, although more often implicitly than explicitly, their operation with the workings of other public institutions (such as legislatures and administrative agencies) and private institutions (such as marriage counseling and labor arbitration). We do this in the context of what, for lack of a better term, might be called the *political sociology of the judicial process*.

What this means is that we are concerned with the institutional characteristics of courts. We ask what courts are, what they do, and what effect their activities have. It also means that we believe that one cannot understand courts and their role in American life without understanding what makes them distinctive—that is, without having some sense of their relation to and place in the range of public and private institutions that deal with important social and political issues.[7]

What do American courts do? The most direct, if not the simplest, answer is that courts hear lawsuits; they decide cases in which two or more individuals, organizations, or government officials argue about their rights, obligations, and responsibilities under the law. A lawsuit is a particular type of dispute. A dispute may be defined as a particular set of behaviors marked by competition, aggression, and more or less open displays of hostility that may focus on material or nonmaterial values.[8] Thus it might be said that courts hear disputes, that is, that what courts do is to try to decide between or among those who have some disagreement, misunderstanding, difference, or conflict. Disagreements might involve, for example, who should pay for the damage in an automobile accident, whether money must be paid for an appliance that is defective, whether a father can exclude his child from his will, whether a student has to wear his hair in a particular way, or whether the police can legally search a car stopped for a traffic offense.[9] These types of events or disputes are the source of the material upon which courts work. Yet, as we will suggest in Part One, these kinds of disputes do not have to end up in court. People, when they have a disagreement or problem, generally can do many things to deal with it without resorting to law or using the courts. However, it is only in the course of deciding a dispute between two parties that a court can make a broad public policy decision. Thus, the dispute that was actually heard and decided by the Supreme Court in the abortion decision of *Roe* v. *Wade*[10] involved one woman and the district attorney of one city.

What courts do is to hear and decide disputes. Another way of putting this is to say that courts are a particular kind of dispute-processing institution.[11] When we say that courts process disputes, we mean to caution against the widespread belief that a court decision represents the last word in a dispute. Most people think that when a decision is handed down by a court, it puts an end to the particular problem in dispute. Thus if two people go to court to get a divorce, we may have the impression that the granting of the divorce terminates their relationship; in fact, it may simply move the relationship to a new phase. Instead of fighting over who should do what in the house or fighting over money, the former spouses may continue to argue, but now they argue about visiting rights for the children, about the things that each one says to former friends, or about how to treat each other in public. Rarely do the actions or decisions of courts fully terminate the social problems that are brought before them. Think about the experience of northern cities that have, in recent years, been ordered to desegregate their schools. In some cities the court decision ordering desegregation did not resolve the issue of where children should go to school, to say nothing of the more enduring interracial problems. In fact, at times the court decisions increased feelings of racial hostility and racial conflict. Whether the disputes that courts hear involve only the two parties who bring the case or whether they have broader ramifications, court decisions are rarely the final events or the last words in a dispute.

The role of courts is to process disputes, not to end them—to render a decision informing citizens of their legal rights. To say that courts do not end disputes is not to say that what they do is insignificant. The conflicts and disputes that come to court are seldom simple.[12] To bring a case to court requires a substantial investment in time and money, an investment that ensures that people whose disputes are decided have an intense commitment to their cause that will not easily dissipate once a court decision has been made. Decisions may serve only, as in the divorce example, to alter the nature of the dispute that gave rise to the lawsuit. Just as judges react to the presentation of facts and evidence in the course of a lawsuit, so do the individuals involved in a suit react to the operations of the court. Judicial decisions may represent the legal termination of a dispute but they may not reach the underlying problem. This is generally true when, as in the United States, courts do not process disputes with an eye toward reconciling the disputants. In most cases a judge is concerned only with what is desirable from the perspective of law or public policy, not what will restore harmony to the relations of the litigants.

To say that courts process disputes is not to suggest that they can or will process any and all disputes. American courts do not actively seek out the disputes with which they deal. Instead it may be said that our courts are passive and reactive.[13] They wait for disputes to be brought to them. If a citizen is involved in a dispute in which he or she is entitled to some help or remedy, the courts will be able to do nothing unless the citizen initiates a lawsuit. Courts do not set their own agendas. However, courts are able to exert some control over the cases they hear by selecting among those that are brought to them. Only disputes that are framed as a contest over legal rights and responsibilities and for which there are remedies specified by law are eligible for judicial action.[14] However, this restriction is one that is, except in its broadest outline, growing increasingly less significant. Given the vast reach and high level of inclusiveness that characterizes modern legal systems like our own, almost any dispute can be so framed as to give it the form of a contest over legal rights and responsibilities. This has led to what some analysts consider the overburdening of American courts. It is this easy transformation of disputes to cases that leads us to view the sociological category of "dispute" rather than the legal category of "case" as the appropriate unit for understanding the functions of judicial systems. To talk about cases is to talk about the ritualized and stylized presentation of disputes rather than about any distinctive, substantive subtype of social conflict. It is not unimportant, as we shall see, that courts require disputes to take the form of cases but not so important and fundamental as to alter the fact that courts process essentially the same kinds of disputes that are processed by a wide range of public and private institutions. This book is organized to enable us to trace the way in which disputes are translated into cases and the way in which cases are translated into judicial decisions. In short, we believe that the best way to understand what courts do is to examine how and why they process disputes as they do.

There are three important categories of disputes that provide the bulk of the work of American courts.[15] The first is what we will call the *private dispute*. Private disputes are defined by the absence of any initial participation by public authorities. For example, when a husband and wife quarrel, when two automobiles collide, when two businessmen disagree about the terms of a contract, these events are likely to give rise to private disputes. Such disputes may occur in public places or they may involve competing interpretations of public norms, but they remain private so long as the government is not a party. These types of disputes arise more or less spontaneously in the normal course of social life. Because they arise out of purely private relations, they are also typically processed and managed without the intervention of government. Most private disputes are unknown to anyone except those who are immediately involved; they are most often dealt with within the general context of ongoing relationships or through an ad hoc and temporary framework of bargaining and negotiation.[16] Yet these kinds of disputes may vary in intensity to the extent that the intervention of outside parties may be required to help structure and interpret the dispute. Private disputes typically have the widest range of options insofar as their processing is concerned.

The two other types of disputes with which American courts most often deal are public in that both involve the participation of some agency of government as a disputant.[17] The first of these categories, which we will call the *public-initiated dispute*, occurs when government seeks to enforce norms of conduct or to punish individuals who breach such norms. These kinds of public disputes arise as governments attempt to control and channel social behavior through the promulgation of binding legal norms. Such attempts at control cannot proceed solely in the abstract, that is, government cannot rely simply on the promulgation of norms to ensure that citizens will conduct themselves in accordance with governmental desires. Enforcement is necessary. The most appropriate model of the public-initiated dispute is the ordinary criminal case in which the state or some official acting on its behalf seeks to use the courts to determine whether a particular breach of legal norms has occurred and whether sanctions ought to be applied. The public-initiated dispute is distinctive in that it always involves and is governed by the law of the entire community. These kinds of disputes are public in terms of both their participants and their substantive bases. This means that, at least formally, dispute processing must occur in a public forum. However, not all public-initiated disputes are resolved or processed by means of judicial action. A variety of informal devices ranging from the warnings that a policeman may give to a speeder to the prosecutor's decision not to proceed with a criminal case to the practice of plea bargaining, may be employed to deal with breaches of public norms.[18] Furthermore, there is evidence to suggest that many disputes that involve such breaches are not brought to the attention of public authorities. For example, the husband who beats his wife may have committed a breach of public norms. However, their dispute remains private unless and until a complaint is lodged with law enforcement authorities.[19] Viewed from the perspective of all of the disputes that might involve a breach of public norms, the percentage of public-initiated disputes is rather small; however, from the perspective of the judiciary such disputes are of major quantitative and qualitative importance.

A third type of dispute that frequently finds its way into American courts is what might be called the *public defendant dispute*. Unlike the public-initiated dispute, in this type the government participates as a defendant. These kinds of disputes typically involve challenges to the authority of some government agency or challenges of the propriety of some government action, challenges that may be initiated by a private individual or organization. In these types of cases courts are called upon to review the action of other branches of government. This is the kind of judicial quality control that Tocqueville recognized as characteristic of our constitutional system and that Nathan Glazer believes has gone too far in the modern age. Public defendant disputes often involve claims that the government has not abided by its own rules or followed procedures that it has prescribed. For example, parents of school children in racially segregated public schools might claim that public school officials violated the Constitution's guarantee of equal protection of the laws. Or a landowner might complain of being wrongfully denied a property tax exemption to which the landowner believes entitled under a city's zoning regulations. Public defendant disputes generally come to court only after the aggrieved party has failed to remedy his or her grievance either through the political process or through remedy procedures provided by the offending government agency. Public defendant disputes provide an especially important staple of the business of American courts, even though such disputes make up a significantly smaller number of the cases on any court's docket than do either private- or public-initiated disputes. Their importance lies in the fact that they provide the courts with an opportunity to affirm the rule of law, to ensure that the government will act according to its own rules and that such rules conform to the most basic principles of constitutional government.

Private-initiated, public-initiated, and public defendant disputes constitute the workload of American courts. However, dispute processing in America does not typically result in an easy or uniform flow of disputes into the judicial system. American courts are expensive, slow, and difficult to use. Their decisional style, that is, their tendency to focus narrowly on particular elements of law and the compatibility of social action and legal norms, means that as dispute-processing institutions, they may be more costly and inefficient than other, comparable institutions. In the United States courts are part of an innumerable array of individuals and institutions that perform dispute-processing functions. Such individuals and institutions range from marriage counselors and religious or community leaders to organized mediation and arbitration services. All employ wide-ranging techniques and procedures for dealing with disputes.[20]

To understand what courts do, how they operate, and what their role is in American life, it is necessary to determine what distinguishes courts from other dispute-processing institutions, that is, to establish standards for judging whether or not and to what extent courts function in a distinctive manner and to apply those standards in judging the performance of American courts. Ultimately our concern is evaluative. We want to be able to measure the performance of courts against those standards of performance which give courts special claim to authority and a legitimacy in American life.

Four aspects of the judicial process seem particularly important in establishing the standards necessary to understand and judge how courts operate: the ways in which courts acquire their business, the types of people who participate in the judicial process, the way in which judicial decisions are made, and the nature of the results produced by those decisions. First, as we have already suggested, courts, unlike other dispute-processing institutions, are reactive. Judges can, in theory, act only when they are called upon to do so by parties with no official connection to the judiciary. Legislative institutions, in contrast, do not wait nor do they need to wait for problems to be brought to their attention. They can and frequently do undertake to define and investigate situations before those situations give rise to problems. In this sense they are able to set their own agenda. The judiciary is passive; courts do not seek out disputes. "When it is called upon to repress a crime, it punishes the criminal; when a wrong is to be redressed, it is ready to redress it; when an act requires interpretation, it is prepared to interpret it; but it does not pursue criminals, hunt out wrongs or examine evidence of its own accord."[21]

The passivity of courts is itself a product of America's commitment to individualism, that is, it is a product of a value system that stresses the importance of personal privacy and self-sufficiency. The passivity of courts places the burden on citizens to recognize and define their own needs and problems and to decide which of those needs and problems require legal judgment. As sociologist Donald Black puts it, this method of acquiring cases ". . .assumes that each individual will voluntarily and rationally pursue his own interests. . . ."[22] The courts are indifferent to those problems or disputes that citizens fail to notice or wish to ignore. The reactive nature of the courts has the further effect of narrowing and isolating problems. Since disputes are processed on a case-by-case basis, it is difficult for many disputants or other participants in the judicial system to perceive underlying patterns and common problems.[23] Furthermore, the reactive nature of courts ensures that they deal with disputes after injuries have occurred and problems have matured. This in turn ordinarily limits the ability of courts to become important agents of basic social change.

Accompanying and part of the liberal underpinnings of the manner in which courts get their cases is an ideological commitment to equal protection of the law that determines the types of people who participate. Courts are, in theory, different from other kinds of dispute-processing institutions because they are available to all citizens. Any citizen having a dispute for which there is a potential legal remedy should be able to use the courts. Unlike other dispute-processing institutions that are available only to specific kinds or groups of people (for example, religious tribunals), courts are public in the broadest sense. Furthermore, they allow for the participation of a peculiar mix of ordinary citizens and legal experts. Judicial processing of disputes involves both the application of legal knowledge and the interpretation of factual events. Thus, there is a division of labor in which disputants and jurors on the one hand and lawyers and judges on the other play equal roles. Participants in court proceedings bring diverse interests and skills to a forum in which their skills are, in theory, equally valued.

A third element that distinguishes courts from other dispute-processing institutions is the way in which decisions are made. Courts are *legal* institutions. Their role in the political and social system is to interpret and apply law—to use legal norms to process disputes. Furthermore, their legitimacy is thought to be dependent on their tie to such norms. Unlike other branches of American government that may claim to derive their authority through the electoral process, courts claim distinctive competence in matters of law. Judicial interpretation of legal norms is expected to be neutral, that is, those making judicial decisions are expected not to base their interpretation of legal norms on their own private interests or policy preferences. Their decisions are expected to be governed by legal principle and not by political pragmatism.[24] Judges are not supposed to do what is best for the disputants; instead they are charged to do right in accord with *legal* definitions of what is right. In practice, however, it is clear that the process of interpreting and applying law is quite complex. Laws are ambiguous and rules of interpretation are themselves open to interpretation. No two cases are exactly alike. Yet judges are expected to decide cases on the basis of the facts insofar as they can be established and specific legal rules and principles insofar as they can be determined and reasonably applied. To the extent that judges do not fulfill this expectation they abandon their distinctive claim as dispute processors, and courts become indistinguishable from other dispute-processing institutions.

The fourth and final distinguishing characteristic of courts is the nature of the results of their activity. Simply put, those results are expected to be impartial. Equal justice requires that the merits of fact and law, rather than the characteristics of the disputants, determine the result. The results of judicial decision making differ from the results of decision making by other branches of government to the extent that they do not favor particular types or categories of litigants. Furthermore, the results of court decisions ought to have a special claim on the individuals or groups involved in disputes. By providing a neutral and unbiased forum, the courts invite good sportsmanship; they invite people to submit to a process of judgment that is fair, and expect that their decisions will be accepted by those who lose as well as by those who win.

We believe that in order to understand American court systems it is necessary to deal with the issues of access, participation, decision making, and result. This book is organized to facilitate the examination of the evidence that suggests the extent to which courts operate in a distinctive manner. It is about the ways that the disputes that occur in society find their way into courts, the ways that they are transformed into cases, the ways that cases become court decisions, and the ways that decisions affect the environments in which courts operate. We have selected readings that address concerns relevant to the politics of the judicial process and that we believe provide a key to understanding and assessing the role of courts in American life.

NOTES

1. Alexis de Tocqueville, *Democracy in America*, Vol. 1 (New York: Vintage Books, 1954), Chaps. 6 and 8.
2. See, for example, Henry S. Commager, *Majority Rule and Minority Rights* (New York: Peter Smith, 1943); Herbert Wechsler, "Toward Neutral Principles of Constitutional Law," *Harvard Law Review* 73 (1959), 1–35; and Leonard Downie, *Justice Denied* (New York: Praeger, 1971).
3. Nathan Glazer, "Toward an Imperial Judiciary?," *The Public Interest* 41 (1975), 104–123. Also see Raoul Berger, *Government by Judiciary* (Cambridge, Mass.: Harvard University Press, 1977).
4. This expansion is discussed and criticized by Thomas Ehrlich in "Legal Pollution," *New York Times Magazine*, February 8, 1976.
5. Compare Francis Laurent, *The Business of a Trial Court* (Madison: University of Wisconsin Press, 1959) and Donald Horowitz, *The Courts and Social Policy* (Washington: Brookings Institution, 1977).
6. See, for example, Howard Zinn, "The Conspiracy of Law," and Edgar Friedenberg, "The Side Effects of the Legal Process," in *The Rule of Law*, edited by Robert Paul Wolff (New York: Simon and Schuster, 1971), pp. 15–53. See also Mark Tushnet, "Truth, Justice and the American Way," *Texas Law Review*, 57 (1979), 1307 and David Kairys, ed., *The Politics of Law* (New York: Pantheon Books, 1982).
7. Council on the Role of Courts, *The Role of Courts in American Society* (St. Paul: West Publishing, 1984).
8. Vilhelm Aubert, "Competition and Dissensus," *Journal of Conflict Resolution* 7 (1963), 25.
9. William Felstiner, Richard Abel and Austin Sarat, "The Emergence and Transformation of Disputes," *Law and Society Review* 15 (1980–81), 631.
10. 410 U.S. 113 (1973). Also Austin Sarat, "Abortion and the Courts," in *American Politics and Public Policy*, ed. Allan P. Sindler (Washington: Congressional Quarterly, 1982).
11. Richard Abel, "A Comparative Theory of Dispute Institutions in Society," *Law and Society Review* 8 (1974), 229.
12. Even those involving relatively little in the way of tangible resources may present

complex legal and factual problems. See Barbara Yngvesson and Patricia Hennessey, "Small Claims, Complex Disputes," *Law and Society Review* 9 (1975), 219–274.

13. See Donald Black, "The Mobilization of Law," *Journal of Legal Studies* 2 (1973), 128.

14. The standards courts use in selecting the cases they hear are discussed in David Rohde and Harold Spaeth, *Supreme Court Decision Making* (San Francisco: W.H. Freeman, 1976), pp. 9–20.

15. See Lawrence Friedman, "The Functions of Trial Courts in the Modern World," paper presented to the Conference on the Sociology of the Judicial Process, Bielefeld, Germany, 1973.

16. Austin Sarat, "Alternatives in Dispute Processing: Litigation in a Small Claims Court," *Law and Society Review* 10 (1976), 339–375.

17. We recognize that there may be some blurring of these categories since government officials or agencies are often involved in what appear to be private disputes. This occurs when the government is not trying to enforce or is not being held accountable to a public norm. The government, for example, may seek to enforce the terms of a contract with someone doing work for it or it may seek to recover damages done to government property. Nevertheless, we think it most useful to categorize disputes along a public-private dimension.

18. See James Eisenstein and Herbert Jacob, *Felony Justice* (Boston: Little, Brown, 1977).

19. Elizabeth Pleck, *Domestic Tyranny* (New York: Oxford University Press, 1987).

20. Austin Sarat and Joel B. Grossman, "Courts and Conflict Resolution," *American Political Science Review* 69 (1975), 1200.

21. Tocqueville, op. cit., note 1, pp. 103–104.

22. Black, op. cit., note 13, p. 138.

23. See Stuart Scheingold, *The Politics of Rights* (New Haven: Yale University Press, 1974).

24. See Wechsler, op. cit., note 2.

PART ONE

From Social Order to Legal Order

CHAPTER 1

Courts and Their Alternatives

"Tell me how you got here," asked the interviewer. "Well, it is a long and not happy story," answered the rather plump, middle-aged man seated in a large, noisy courtroom in New York City. "At first I didn't know what to do. I wasn't even sure that there was a problem, let alone something worth going to court about. I talked to my wife about it and eventually we decided to call and see if we couldn't get it fixed or get our money back." The "it" in this man's description was a used television set; the problem was that it had a faulty picture tube.

"I bought the set without really paying too much attention. We needed to replace our old one and it was cheap so I figured that we were getting a good deal. It wasn't until a few days after we had it at home that the picture began to fade out. You'd have it on for a few minutes and then it would lose the picture. Well, eventually I called the store and talked with the salesman. He said that he was sorry but that all sales were final and that there was no guarantee. We talked for a while and finally he said that he would take it up with his boss and get back to me. I never heard from him. After much trying I managed to contact his boss, who gave me pretty much the same story. Now I didn't want to cause trouble for this guy, but what good is a television set if you can't watch it? After thinking a bit I called the Better Business Bureau. They are always advertising on the radio and when I told my brother what was going on he suggested that they might be able to do something. Well, I guess they talked to the guy who owns the store and asked him to do something. They called back to tell me that there was nothing they could do but record the complaint and advise people not to buy from him. I was pretty upset and disgusted. I didn't want to buy another TV, but I didn't know what I could do. I'd pretty much made up my mind to forget the whole thing when my brother told me that I should go to court. I didn't want to make a federal case out of it. But, when I found out that I could go to small claims court and not have to pay a lawyer or miss work, I decided to sue."[1]

In this man's story we have a rather typical profile of the process whereby individuals translate disputes into lawsuits. This process is characterized by several distinct stages.[2] First, there is the stage of "recognition," that is, of coming to understand that there is a problem. This stage is, of course, just the beginning, but it is, in some ways, the most important stage. Most people do not relish trouble, problems, or conflict; most of us have an ingrained inability to distinguish from among all the events of daily life those which are, in fact, troublesome. This reluctance and inability to identify trouble stems in part from a desire to think of our lives as relatively comfortable and rewarding. The theory of cognitive dissonance, developed by psychologists, indicates the tendency of most people to try to minimize or ignore conflicts or problems that might disturb their psychic tranquility.[3] Furthermore, people are generally reluctant to take on the role of troublemaker, to risk the stigma of appearing to cause trouble for someone else even though that other person may be directly responsible for the trouble.[4] It is only after an individual decides to shoulder this burden that the processing of a dispute begins.

In the second stage of the process, a decision is made whether to "lump it."[5] This decision occurs after an individual acknowledges the existence of trouble; it involves a calculation as to whether the benefits of seeking to deal with the trouble are outweighed by the costs of doing so.[6] The choice is between accepting a loss and risking a greater loss (the original loss compounded by the time and energy invested in pursuing a remedy) in seeking to solve the problem. Yet the decision whether to initiate action to deal with the problem is not totally an unemotional one. As law professor Arthur Leff suggested, "spite," as much as any other variable that figures into the calculus of costs and benefits, is what spurs much disputing and dispute-processing behavior.[7] An individual, once feeling aggrieved, may act simply out of a desire to complicate the life of the individual responsible for the injury.

Once an individual recognizes the problem and decides to do something about it, dispute processing can commence. The kind of unpleasantness that is part of this process is, from the perspective of the judiciary, both the source and the object of action. The job of American courts is to provide a means of managing such unpleasantness. However, in any society, there is a wide variety of institutions or mechanisms for dealing with disputes, of which the courts are just one.

The simplest and most frequently employed remedies do not require third-party intervention. As in the case of the man with the broken television set, an individual faced with a problem involving another individual or organization typically begins the process of dealing with that problem by dealing directly with the other party. There may be an informal contact in which all that transpires is the exchange of information; that is, the aggrieved party notifies the other party that trouble exists. Frequently, such notification prompts remedial action. Yet the form of such action may itself become the subject of discussion. Should the set be repaired, a replacement be provided, or money returned? This is the classic bargaining situation: a problem is acknowledged to exist and some degree of responsibility is conceded. There are, however, frequent occasions in which neither occurs; the putative defendant refuses to admit that trouble exists or, having done so, refuses to take responsibility. Two-person dispute processing is likely to be successful only when both parties perceive a need for settlement. The process of negotiation may itself be understood as attempting to foster such a perception when it is absent in one of the parties.[8] Quite often one party desires a solution, but the other does not. The latter party may not care or may hope to gain by inaction or may simply be intransigent. Generally, it is only after attempts to deal directly with the other party have failed that third parties (such as judges, mediators, arbiters) will be called in. When two people find that they cannot settle a dispute between themselves, they may seek some other respected person, someone with no stake in the dispute, to listen to their problem and give them advice. The way in which this third-party intervention may occur is highly variable.

This variability is important because the organization and structure of third-party intervention affects the way people deal with their problems. Third parties, which, like umpires at sporting events, are positioned in anticipation of conflict, facilitate both the perception of trouble when it occurs and its resolution. Such remedy systems regularly supervise the execution of potentially troublesome events. This is exemplified by the supervision by the National Labor Relations Board of elections in which workers decide whether they wish to be represented by a labor union. Should trouble occur, or questions arise about the propriety of someone's performance or about the interpretation of an event, these kinds of remedy systems will already have at hand information gathered in the course of their normal monitoring activity that can provide the basis for settlement. These kinds of third parties are already present before disputes occur. They do not have to be called in. The dispute does not have to be explained to them because they have already observed it. Furthermore, the very positioning of these third parties with regard to relationships and situations prior to the occurrence of trouble facilitates its identification and declaration by expressing, in a symbolic way, the expectation that trouble is a normal part of those relationships and situations. In baseball, the positioning of umpires at every base indicates a general expectation that disputes will occur regularly and that judgments will be required regularly. The fact that such an expectation exists means that people will feel less hesitant about making a fuss than they would if third parties had to be sought out and informed about the problem.

When disputants have to seek out third parties, the significance of their declaration of trouble is magnified both in their minds and in the minds of others. Reactive procedures force the troubled party to come forward in a visible way, to step out of the normal trend of the troubled relationship.[9] They also impose costs special to each case by requiring that the parties involved in a problem describe and interpret the transaction or the context in which the problem developed. Courts, as a third-party dispute institution, thus deter the declaration of trouble by emphasizing its disruptive effects and manage the trouble by placing the burden of fact-finding and interpretation on the parties themselves.[10]

Different third parties see disputes in different ways. Whether any disagreement is seen and dealt with as an isolated incident or as part of a pattern of similar incidents may influence whether disputants will seek one or another kind of third-party help. Third parties who operate in a private and informal manner generally mediate disputes; that is, they see any single dispute in a broad context. They try to shape trouble, problems, or conflict into disagreements and to restore order by getting the parties to come to an agreement.[11] Public, formal alternatives, like courts, attempt to transform personal problems into disputes over questions of fact or over competing interpretations of rights and rules; they try to produce a more limited version of the dispute and render verdicts that are in conformity with those rights and rules—verdicts that the parties may or may not find agreeable. As a result, parties who desire to retain control over the ultimate resolution of their problem will try to avoid third-party remedy systems that are public and formal.[12] When a dispute is brought to court, the parties are, in essence, agreeing to abide by a decision before they know what that decision is.

The way in which third-party remedy systems account for the emergence of trouble in a relationship also influences the way people will deal with that trouble. Those which try to settle troubles by determining whether someone violated a social norm and by assigning causal or moral responsibility will not be attractive to people who have long-standing personal relationships. These people will generally see greater ambivalence in the evolution and continuance of their trouble than such a settlement procedure recognizes. Typically, in a marital dispute, the spouses may find it difficult to accurately trace the blame. So complex is their relationship that there are no clear causes of any single dispute. Furthermore, when remedy systems focus on the question of responsibility, they may exacerbate the original trouble that needed to be settled. Relationships can best survive the trauma of an open declaration of trouble if the procedure invoked to deal with that trouble places it in the context of the complex moral history of the parties' relationship and thus serves to obscure partially whatever particular incident gave rise to the present trouble.

The resolution of troubles in public by formal remedy systems like courts generally has formal institutionalized precedent value. Decisions in one case become the basis for subsequent decisions in similar cases; this means that when the "judge" attempts to resolve a particular trouble in the present, that "judge" must fashion a settlement with an eye toward what other parties in future cases may make of it.[13] For example, when parties bring problems to court they lose control over the context in which their problems are perceived. Present problems are placed in a context of the past and the future, which may be entirely divorced from the needs and interests of the parties themselves. Furthermore, their troubles become important to a wider audience.[14] Their problems are played out before a public that is interested because of the bearing the decision may have on the future adjudication of its own problems. The court forces litigants to present their problems in such a way as to give them meaning in the context of a past and future with which judges must deal and in such a way that outside parties can read its meaning for themselves and their problems. A settlement that occurs in private is, in contrast, relieved of this burden of publicity; the parties are under no obligation to be "other directed" in their interpretation of their own problems.

By choosing to employ different third-party remedy systems, the parties to a troubled relationship express different things about themselves and their interactions. People who employ private, informal alternatives, which promote negotiation and compromise, acknowledge some potential community of interest. Their choice implies that they recognize that there is more to their relationship than the trouble itself. It further signifies that they have greater trust in each other than in the type of normative systems that usually govern public, formal procedures. When the parties choose a public, formal alternative, they express a shared belief in the reasonableness of the intervener and in the validity of the normative system that is represented.[15] They express greater faith in the reasonableness and ability of the third party to make distinctions between them than in their own ability to come to a mutually satisfactory agreement. When parties have had no prior relationship, and when they expect none to develop in the future, they have no basis for believing in their mutual reasonableness and ability to compromise. When they have had prior relations, the kind of context that makes compromise feasible is more likely to be present.[16]

One cannot accurately understand the way in which courts function or the way in which disputes are processed and sometimes translated into lawsuits without taking account of the alternatives that are available to disputants. Furthermore, like the man with the broken television set, most people move reluctantly, if at all, into third-party arenas and especially reluctantly into courts. To understand this reluctance it is necessary to understand the structure and operation of third-party dispute-processing institutions, which compete with courts for society's dispute-processing business. The readings in this chapter facilitate such an understanding.

NOTES

1. This man was interviewed as part of a research project on small claims courts. See Austin Sarat, "Alternatives in Dispute Processing: Litigation in a Small Claims Court," *Law and Society Review* 10 (1976), 339.

2. For a discussion of these stages see William Felstiner, Richard Abel and Austin Sarat, "The Emergence and Transformation of Disputes," *Law and Society Review* 16 (1980–81), 631.

3. See Leon Festinger, *A Theory of Cognitive Dissonance* (Evanston, Ill.: Row, Peterson, 1957).

4. Austin Sarat, "The Emergence of Disputes," in *A Study of the Barriers to the Use of Alternative Methods of Dispute Resolution* (South Royalton, Vt.: Vermont Law School, 1984). See also Kristin Bumiller, "Victims in the Shadow of the Law," *Signs* 12 (1987), 421.

5. For a discussion of the costs of "lumping it," see Richard Danzig and Michael Lowy, "Everyday Disputes and Mediation in the United States," *Law and Society Review* 9 (1975), 675.

6. Frank Gollop and Jeffrey Marguart, "A Microeconomic Model of Household Choice: The Household As A Disputant," *Law and Society Review* 15 (1980–81), 611.

7. Arthur Leff, "Ignorance, Injury and Spite," *Yale Law Journal* 80 (1970), 1. See also Sally Merry and Susan Silbey, "What Do Plaintiffs Want? Reexamining the Concept of Dispute," *Justice System Journal* 9 (1984), 151.

8. See Philip Gulliver, *Neighbors and Networks* (Berkeley: University of California Press, 1971).

9. Donald Black, "The Mobilization of Law," *Journal of Legal Studies* 2 (1973), 125.

10. Marc Galanter, "Adjudication, Litigation and Related Phenomena," in *Law and the Social Sciences*, Leon Lipson and Stanton Wheeler, eds. (New York: Russell Sage Foundation, 1986).

11. Sally Merry, "The Social Organization of Mediation in Nonindustrial Societies," in *The Politics of Informal Justice*, Vol. 2, ed. Richard Abel (New York: Academic Press, 1982). In general, see Christine B. Harrington, *Shadow Justice* (Westport, Conn.: Greenwood 1985).

12. Martin Shapiro, "Courts," in *The Handbook of Political Science*, Vol. 5, Fred Greenstein and Nelson Polsby, eds. (Reading, Mass.: Addison-Wesley, 1975), pp. 321–371.

13. Martin Shapiro, "Toward a Theory of Stare Decisis," *Journal of Legal Studies* 1 (1972), 125.

14. See Lynn Mather and Barbara Yngvesson, "Language, Audience and the Transformation of Disputes," *Law and Society Review* 15 (1980–81), 775.

15. See Merry and Silbey, op. cit., note 7.

16. On the importance of the prior relationship among disputants, see Sarat, op. cit., note 1, and Donald Black, "The Social Organization of Arrest," *Stanford Law Review* 23 (1971), 1087.

What Courts Do and Do Not Do Effectively

Council on the Role of Courts

Evolution of Courts and Our Thinking About Them

Every inquiry into the nature and efficacy of social institutions must consider, even if only glancingly, their historical and intellectual underpinnings. For social institutions do not exist in a void, abstract and prior to the concerns of the society in which they are found, nor has any society itself been conjured up from thin air. So we cannot hope to understand what courts are doing, what they are equipped to do, and, especially, what they ought to do, unless we attend, though briefly, to their origins and evolution, in practice and thought.

Dispute Resolving. Of all the possible and actual functions of courts, the anthropological and historical literature suggest that the courts emerged institutionally to resolve quarrels that threatened the peace of the community. As Carl J. Friedrich has put it: "The settlng of disputes is the primordial

internal function which a political order has to perform, antedating the making of rules and the application of such rules in administrative work."[1]

In communities without a formal political order, we may posit that every man, family, or clan had a "state of nature right" to redress wrongs done to one of them. We know that a single act of killing by a hot-headed individual often led to a blood feud that spread geographically and persisted over time.[2] It may not be entirely fanciful to suggest that, except in societies whose rulers came to the fore by warding off attack by outsiders, the need to suppress the free exercise of this desire to repay one killing with another gave birth to the political ruler, whose first duty was to settle disputes. Careful studies of African tribes during the twentieth century have lent credence to this view. Thus the relatively recent action of a Ugandan tribe that had never had a leader: for the express purpose of at last being able to settle quarrels, the tribe sought out a ruler from a neighboring clan known for its chiefs.[3]

Certainly this dispute-resolving function was central to the leadership of Great Britain, the society with which we have the most direct concern. Before the twelfth century, the center of British political activity was local; the people knew no nation-state in the modern sense. Such courts as existed represented the crude and self-interested justice of the nobles, who exercised the power to put down insurrection and to settle disputes among serfs and vassals in order to consolidate their own role as petty sovereigns. This was more social disorder than social order, however, for the nobles warred on each other. Until the kings established royal courts and substituted public sanctions and a system of compensation for blood feuds, violence and warfare were the norm.

. . . Judges began to search for rules of law that would justify their decisions for one litigant or the other.

Law Ascertaining.   That judges make law as they go about searching for rules to apply to cases before them seems obvious enough to us now, but to the medieval mind it was a perplexing matter that has cast a shadow into our own time. Though King James I would insist from 1608 on that the king was superior to the law and hence could promulgate new law, his predecessors had supposed, at least since 1215, that they were bound by law. Magna Carta, say Pollock and Maitland, "means this, that the king is and shall be below the law."[4] In short, the law—the body of rules that in time would become the common law—was superior and prior to conscious human creation by kings and judges hearing cases. The law simply *was*, and it was the function of judges to ascertain it, not to make it up.

For several centuries, the theory of law thus developed at odds with its practice. Judges held that they were merely discovering pre-existing law, even as they grandly created an immense body of common law dealing with subjects unknown to their ancestors, and even as other courts, such as those of chancery (equity), grew up along-

side them to temper the rigidities of the common law.

This notion that the courts have but one function—to resolve disputes by applying pre-existing law—passed into fundamental American belief via Montesquieu, who articulated clearly the great principle of the separation of powers. He believed that each of the three branches of government should be confined to its proper sphere. Writing in the early eighteenth century he admired above all the English system, which, he believed (probably mistakenly), had separated the legislative, executive, and judicial branches. If separation of powers were truly observed, Montesquieu said, the judges would pose no threat: "[T]he national judges are no more than the mouth that pronounces the words of the law, mere passive beings, incapable of moderating either its force or rigor."[5]

The Constitutional Convention studied Montesquieu; to him the first three articles of the Constitution owe their general structure. His theory provided the way around the dilemma of judicial law-making: in ascertaining the rules to apply to a particular case, the courts would but interpret the laws given by others. In *The Federalist Papers* (No. 78), Alexander Hamilton argued that

> the judiciary, from the nature of its functions, will always be the least dangerous to the political rights of the Constitution; because it will be least in a capacity to annoy or injure them. The executive not only dispenses the honors but holds the sword of the community. The legislature not only commands the purse but prescribes the rules by which the duties and rights of every citizen are to be regulated. The judiciary, on the contrary, has no influence over either sword or the purse; no direction either of the strength or of the wealth of the society, and can take no active resolution whatever. It may truly be said to have neither FORCE nor WILL but merely

judgment; and must ultimately depend upon the aid of the executive arm even for the efficacy of its judgments. . . . The interpretation of the laws is the proper and peculiar province of the courts.

This summary forms the core of the conventional wisdom about state and federal courts in our own time. Putting aside that Hamilton was speaking of the federal judiciary and that the thorny question of federal common law jurisdiction would not arise explicitly for half a century, the nub of his argument is that which any school child can recite: rule-making is for legislators; when they decide cases, courts are merely interpreting.

This textbook view, still devoutly held by many, shades the truth considerably. Though law-making troubled the early judges and they frequently created extravagant fictions (e.g., assigning imaginary leases to imaginary parties, allegations of which could not be denied) to persuade themselves or others that they were not deviating from the ancient customs, the courts virtually from the outset were making law in the course of deciding cases. This troubled our ancestors because law was not supposed to be created by human agency, not even by legislation; it continues to trouble us, now that law creating is acceptable, because making law is presumed to be the office of the legislator alone.

Law Declaring. Despite the textbook theory, Anglo-American courts have always been rule-making institutions. The types of disputes that the common law and equity courts heard gave birth to an immense corpus of rules governing every manner of private relations. In time these rules became unexceptionable, and many fields of law down to the present day are articulated largely at the hands of the judges. Nor ought

this to seem peculiar. To be sure, there is a logical distinction between settling quarrels and announcing rules. When the source of the rule is statutory and the statute's import is unclear in the particular dispute that it is invoked to settle, the court could refrain from filling in the gap—either by declaring for the defendant or by giving a decision for the plaintiff that has no precedential value. . . . Few would disagree that in deciding a case a court should articulate a rule or principle on which its decision is based. Such, at any rate, has been our tradition: for centuries courts, like legislatures, have been in the business of defining the nature of remediable injury—ineluctably, as long as the judicial function includes deciding disputes that, because of changed conditions or creative claiming, raise novel legal questions resulting in recognition of novel legal rights.[6]

The American Experience

A written constitution and a federal system distinguish American political and judicial history from that of most other common law jurisdictions. In spelling out limitations on the power of government, the Constitution preordained that issues which in other countries would be labeled political would in America be resolved in court. A complex system of government, with branches that overlap both jurisdictionally and territorially, also ensures that disputes will arise among the branches and between the states and the central government. Together, these conditions imply at a minimum that the courts will accrete power because they are empowered to decide who may decide and who may act—one person or another? the people or the state? a state or the federal government? the legislature or the executive? the other branches or the courts? Moreover, because the Constitution's most significant limitations are couched in phrases of majestic obscurity, the courts sooner or later must also intervene in important and potentially explosive cases involving civil rights and liberties. And, at a maximum, the American constitutional tradition could be taken to empower the courts not merely to settle quarrels but to bring about social order and social justice.

These farther reaches of judicial role (farther, that is, from the role of deciding disputes) were not necessarily apparent from the outset. They developed over the course of our history. As Professor James Willard Hurst (from whose work much of the discussion in this section is drawn) has noted, in the early years the courts were much distrusted, and legislatures were the governmental branch most closely identified with "the law." As Hurst says: "The courts did not fully capture popular imagination as the type and model of 'the law' until after 1875."[7] Into the 1890s, the judiciary, especially at the appellate level, was the agency most responsible for the creation of law in the states. "People came to regard appellate courts primarily as lawgivers, rather than as agencies to secure the best adjustment in the particular case."[8] Just how far the courts were prepared to play the former rather than the latter role became manifest in their frequent refusal "to dispose of the whole case [and their willingness] to see a given lawsuit wind its laborious way upward on successive appeals, as successive appeals were brought to the front by the logic of nice procedure and the meticulous observance of the limitations of the record."[9] Eventually, this philosophy led to a large increase in the number of appellate cases, leading the states to grant appellate courts more discretionary control over their dockets and the courts to view procedure more as a means to dispose of cases than to continually declare the law.

. . .

What did the courts actually do throughout this long stretch from the mid-nineteenth to the mid-twentieth centuries? If recent statistics are vague, all the more so are figures for the greatest part of our history. Yet it does seem possible to conclude "that judges had their widest influence on the disposition of people's disputes by exerting background pressure for the parties to settle cases by negotiation."[10] Judicial disposition of cases probably peaked in the early years of the twentieth century; until then most disputes could go only to courts if the disputants desired an official resolution of their differences. With the rise of administrative agencies and commercial arbitration, the number of cases coming to court probably declined, at least for a while, beginning in the 1920s.[11]

. . .

The courts also began to play a more active role in policy-making, as legislatures from 1880 on began to reassert their authority to enact statutes that broadly reshaped both public and private relations. This role was especially apparent in the federal courts, which, importantly, policed state laws that seemed to restrict the free flow of interstate commerce. But this role of overseeing and enforcing national policy was not limited to state encroachments on commerce; as Congress began to legislate actively from the 1930s on and as administrative agencies began to play an increasingly significant role in law-making, the courts were required to legitimate the shift from common law to legislative and administrative law. From the vantage point of mid-century, Hurst supposed that "the most profound social function which the courts served, through the simple fact that they were available to hear and decide disputes, was the strength that this imparted to popular confidence in law in the United States—that is, to the legitimacy of government."[12]

What, then, of changes in court role since 1950?

1. Both federal and state courts have seen a significant increase in caseloads.
2. The mix of cases coming into state courts has altered significantly. A lower proportion of commercial cases appears on the dockets, the greater proportion being tort, domestic relations, and public law cases.
3. Among the public law cases, a relatively new type—the extended impact case—has arisen in sufficient numbers to worry many observers.
4. Among the private law cases, both routine and non-routine cases have proliferated.
5. The routine administrative, largely non-adversary cases include such matters as debt collection, probate, and no-fault divorces.
6. The non-routine cases include suits concerning "ongoing relationships" —for example, child-parent and student-teacher cases.
7. Though precise measurement is difficult, a growing number of cases are "diverted" to or initiated in various alternatives to the traditional adversary process. These include forms of arbitration and mediation, both within and without the courts.

As this list suggests, the courts have scarcely moved away from their traditional role of resolving disputes. Nevertheless, the courts have evidently extended their other roles as well. Law declaration and policy-making loom large. For example, significant areas of common law emerged transformed at the hands of courts in the post-World War II period—most notably, the numerous changes in tort law that greatly increased the scope of liability of private corporations for mishaps with their products and of public and private institutions for defects in their services. During this same period, the federal courts, perhaps leading society as a whole, began to take far more seriously than ever before issues of individual and group civil rights and civil liberties. In this arena, *Brown* v. *Board of Education*[13] is the benchmark from which stemmed innumerable cases that, in the context of a seeming dispute between two or more parties, permitted the courts to address broad issues of social justice and community peace. Not that they had not done so in decades past; only now they were doing so more frequently and with arguably greater impact.

A related development has been the extensive scrutiny of administrative decisions and actions. As administrative bodies have extended their writ into more and more corners of American life, so the courts have sought to scrutinize their behavior to ensure compliance with basic norms of due process in rule-making and enforcement. One effect has been to expand the category of persons permitted to bring suit against allegedly errant agencies. These cases have attracted the most attention when litigants have sought, often successfully, to challenge basic methods by which such public institutions as prisons, hospitals, and schools operate. Building on principles of due process, a number of courts have sought to impose novel remedies that seem to put the courts in the business of administration.

This latter class of cases, sometimes called "extended impact" or "public law" actions, suggests that judicial role depends as much on social setting as on legal theory and that as times change the functions of courts change. As recently as the late 1960s, the major "structural change" cases in which the courts had been involved were those of school desegregation and legislative reapportionment. Complex and controversial as the consequences of these decisions were, they were based on the straightforward propositions that people of different races ought not be treated differently in law and that each citizen's vote should count equally.

Within a very few years, by the early 1970s, a few courts began to probe the operations of state-run institutions by the far more flexible standards of the due process clause. To the objections of a large chorus of critics who deny the courts' ability to issue remedial decrees in such cases, the courts have responded that the conditions in the prisons and hospitals under scrutiny were so brutal as to defy any permissible rationale. In short, the extended impact cases (which we examine in greater detail below) point to the courts' adaptability: matters that doubtless could be resolved better elsewhere move to courts by default.

Not all of the judicial forays into social policy were self-propelled: much of the federal caseload stemmed from issues raised by the vast outpouring of federal legislation from the mid-1960s. Born of necessary political compromise for the most part (and sometimes of sheer hasty law-making), much of the new federal law was vague. Like the antitrust statutes that have permitted the courts to make most of that law in common law-like fashion, recent enactments in many areas have given the courts virtually a free hand in making important social policy.[14]

LENSES FOR VIEWING THE COURTS

.   .   .

History permits us to construct two sets of lenses through which to view the functions of courts. One is that of the "traditionalist," who sees courts as a particular kind of institution. The traditionalist attempts to describe courts by looking closely to discern their special attributes and characteristics. The other set of lenses is that of the "adaptationist," who takes a longer view that permits inspection of courts in the social firmament.

The two views do not conflict in every respect. For example, neither "school" believes that courts are free to act as autonomous and self-propelled social troubleshooters reaching out to find disputes no party has brought to them. Both place high value on basic elements of procedural due process. They do not differ in their choices about the nature or kinds of disputes that should be in or out of the courts. However, some traditionalists, who begin by agreeing that extended impact cases raising constitutional issues belong in the courts, develop objections to the remedial measures the courts take in some of those cases. In their view, the court should not engage in long-term monitoring of institutions such as schools, prisons, or hospitals, should not attempt to negotiate detailed plans, and should not engage in administering those institutions. Their objections to the courts' remedial activities in these cases lead these observers to revise their initial appraisal of the suitability for court treatment of such cases; they urge that these claims be handled by means other than the judicial process. The adaptationists disagree, asserting that the courts must take these cases and that they have the institutional wherewithal to structure appropriate remedies.

While not rejecting either social or historical influences, the traditionalist view stresses the importance of examining the courts' role in relation to what courts are and how they function. Traditionalists want to know what is distinctive about a court as a governmental institution. They ask what functions are being confided to courts and whether the demands of the various functions are compatible with each other. From this perspective, they undertake to learn what the judicial attributes are, and what, everything else being equal, a court is best equipped to do. They worry that society may be assigning courts too broad a repertoire of functions, functions that require the invocation of different processes and different skills by judges and the administrators who surround them. It follows from the traditionalist that courts cannot be altered beyond certain limits and still be recognizable as courts.

By contrast, the adaptationist view looks at courts in historical perspective and stresses their social setting, their continuously changing functions, and their constant interaction with other institutions, legislatures and executive agencies in particular. Those espousing the adaptationist view do not assert that the capacity of courts is unlimited, but they attach little or no importance to identifying the essential characteristics of courts and insist that whatever the limitations are they have not yet been reached. To know whether courts work effectively, according to the adaptationist approach, we must also know whether other institutions work effectively, and to what degree the various social institutions work together effectively. Thus, if judges were to make rulings in certain cases that the rest of society would repudiate, the courts would not be supposed to act effectively. But if the rulings are supported, then courts will be seen to be effective, no matter what objections the traditionalists raise. This is true even if these other institutions do not immediately support courts. Over time, the force of judicial rulings may bring the rest of society along.

Brown v. *Board of Education*, the most influential and best known Supreme Court decision of our time, is a good example of this phenomenon. *Brown* certainly was not incompatible with the traditionalist view, nor has it been rejected by those who espouse this more orthodox view of the role of courts. Yet its initially narrow focus quickly ignited a vision of equality much harder to contain, and its influence on American life has been pervasive. For the adaptationists it was fitting and proper that courts helped enlarge this vision; their concern was what contribution the law could make. For some traditionalists, at least, the enlargement of *Brown's* initial ruling, to encompass such ends as assuring a numerical balance of races in public schools, proved far more troublesome.

.   .   .

The Traditionalist View: Courts as Dispute-Resolvers

The traditionalist response to the questions just raised emphasizes the uniqueness of courts as adjudicators of disputes and seeks to define the appropriate limits of court function within the traditional boundaries of the adversary process. This view assumes that the capacity of courts to decide disputes is relatively fixed in the "nature" of adjudication, and its proponents see serious problems of legitimacy should the courts fail to adhere to these norms.

In this view, courts are reactive institutions, best suited to hear bipolar disputes pitting one party against another. The parties ought to control the proceedings, which should be adversary and sharply-focused (i.e., they should not be theoretical disputes but rooted in real injuries or threats of injuries). The disputes should be such that the courts can resolve them by applying some articulable standards or principles and affording an appropriate and viable remedy. Cases posing routine or repetitive issues, treading on the established decision-making authority of other institutions, or threatening to intrude unnecessarily into ongoing relationships do not belong in the courts. Likewise, cases that call on judges to determine "social" or "legislative" facts (e.g., predictions about future behavior), rather than the reconstruction of historical facts, require special justification.

To proponents of the traditionalist view, a more open-ended notion of courts leads to vast difficulties. They argue that if courts are indeed chameleon-like, if they can "take any form or adopt any procedure" without incurring substantial institutional costs, then they can look forward to a virtually unlimited agenda of human controversies. No conceptual boundaries will separate their domain from that of all other decision-makers and problem solvers. For that very reason, a limitless flexibility of judicial form and process is not credible: we simply do not submit all social controversies and problems to judges, nor should anyone be understood to argue that it would be sensible to do so.

The Adaptationist View

Critics of the traditionalist view assert that the implications of drawing the line according to a model of strictly limited functions would lead to profound results. They argue that if strictly applied, the traditionalist adjudicatory view might exclude cases that would be handled by no other institution, including most structural reform or extended impact cases in which the judgments of legislators and administrators are challenged in court.

According to these critics, our history demonstrates that courts are capable of "dynamic adaptation".[15] Subject only to the relatively flexible constraints of due process, "courts can take any form or adopt any procedure."[16] Any "rigid institutional adherence to any ideal of 'courtness' is wholly rejected."[17]

Citing nineteenth-century cases calling for equitable remedies to correct chronic conditions, proponents of the "dynamic adaptation" view assert that extended impact cases are not unique in their demand that the courts devise flexible remedies. The change lies not in procedures or concepts but in

plaintiffs and defendants: different types of institutions are now under siege, and the political interests that they represent are unused to being hailed into court. The judicial responses are thus time-honored and only appear to be different from those that the courts have undertaken to give in the past.

The adaptationists reject fears of nonlegitimacy.[18] In extended impact cases the public might conclude that the courts have over-reached. But that is a political, not a legal, concern. Members of the public who distrust the recent trend of some courts do so not because of disagreement with procedures and capacities but because of disagreement over results. But one group or another has always criticized judicial outcomes. For the adaptationist, the crucial question is whether other public institutions have failed to address a pressing social problem. If the courts can tackle a problem consistent with due process, and in an efficient and effective manner, no theory of "courtness" need stand in their way.

Pushed to the limit, the adaptationist approach views courts as the hub of a complex civil justice network of systems that order private and public relationships. The adaptationists stress that historically courts have served to resolve conflicts and also to act as social "controllers" or "orderers." In this light, courts can be regarded as institutions that can change form, or at least procedures, to reflect the prevailing social demand for these two functions.[19]

Under the latter approach to judicial role (one by no means antithetical to many traditionalists), disputes that threaten the social fabric in some way are appropriate to resolution by courts if some judicial process is likely to be serviceable in mending the tear. In other words, judicial effectiveness depends on pragmatic experimentation, not on a theoretical analysis of the essential characteristics of courts as an institution distinct from other governmental entities. Indeed, courts need not be limited to hearing cases which they "do best." By this view, what courts *should* do is a question distinct from what courts can do most effectively, and the answer to the latter question ought not be the definitive answer to the former. Among the types of cases courts might be expected to hear, in this view, are these:

1. Disputes not susceptible to resolution by private ordering; e.g., disputes among strangers and those involving irreconcilable claims about principles.
2. Disputes that should not be settled privately because society has an important stake in governing them by authoritatively imposing public standards; e.g., disputes arising between parties who are significantly unequal in resources for bargaining, or involving one party significantly dependent on the other, or resulting in a privately agreed-upon solution that imposes unacceptable costs on others or that violates established norms of public policy.
3. Disputes that permit courts to create "bargaining endowments" by setting standards in a few cases, thereby facilitating the private system of bargaining and settlement.
4. Cases that recognize and will encourage the airing of grievances that society ought to be interested in articulating.

Clearly, the traditionalist and adaptationist views clash. They disagree most strongly on two points: (1) the remedial powers of courts in extended impact cases; and (2) the degree to which the judge must be devoted to the formal norms of the adversary system. Re-

conciling these differences will be difficult, perhaps impossible to the satisfaction of everyone. That is why a debate rages and will continue to rage about the role of courts.

JUDICIAL ATTRIBUTES

The Nature of Judicial Cases

The attributes of courts are largely determined, in the traditionalist view, by the nature of the matters that are thought properly to come before them—i.e., when disputants asserting claims based on legal entitlement ask the court to take jurisdiction to determine the facts and apply the law. Therefore, we begin the analysis of the attributes of courts by examining the nature of judicial cases.

Trouble is the human lot. Neither the world around us nor the societies in which we live can be arranged to spare us sorrow or grant us every wish. Perhaps some people live contentedly or at least without airing a grumble, but they are few. Most people much of the time can articulate a host of *problems*. These can be abstract, in the sense that they do not affect the person contemplating them. Thus "they're having a big problem with hurricanes in Hawaii," recited by a newscaster in New England; or "racism is quite a problem in South Africa," stated phlegmatically by one with no political, moral, financial, or emotional stake in the affairs of that troubled country.

When the problem does somehow affect the individual, it can become a *grievance*. Many grievances are diffuse, complaints against the world or the perversity of human nature: "The flooding on this highway is awful"; "inflation is killing me"; "I can't breathe in here, there's so much smoking going on." Such grievances can be the basis for a request for action: "Somebody ought to do something about it." But grievances do not, in this posture, attract the attention of a court because no one person or group of persons is being blamed. Intuitively it is clear that a petition to a court to "stop all this smoking in America" presents a non-justiciable issue.

A grievance may become focused on a person or group. "The state highway engineers did a lousy job grading this road"; "the Fed's monetary policy is asinine"; "that person there is blowing smoke in my face." By requesting action against a person thought to be causing the trouble, the aggrieved person can make his grievance into a *claim* or a *complaint*: "The engineers ought to regrade the road (or pay me for the damage done to my car)"; "the Fed should be made to alter its policy"; "you ought to stop blowing smoke in my face." Still, this is too premature a stage for judicial intervention, since the parties complained against could agree with their accusers and right the wrongs.

If, however, the one against whom the complaint is lodged does not respond satisfactorily, a *dispute* is born. It is this dispute that becomes eligible for treatment in a variety of ways ranging from conciliation to third-party determination to legislation. The dispute is not necessarily the sort that should be heard in court. For judicial intervention depends, among other things, on whether it is a *legal dispute*, and that rests at bottom on whether the aggrieved party has a *legal entitlement*. Not every such person has. The citizen has no legal right to impress his views of economic policy on the Federal Reserve Board. A restaurant patron may have no legal right to prevent another patron from smoking. For a court to entertain a case, the assertion of entitlement must rest on a legal rather than political, moral, or spiritual basis.

An assertion of legal right ordinarily will permit a court to hear a dispute ("ordinarily,"

because a statute might specifically deny jurisdiction to hear the particular subject, as, for example, federal courts are denied jurisdiction to hear veterans' claims). Even if the court has jurisdiction, it will not necessarily decide to hear it. Other threshold characteristics must be satisfied: a dispute must be "ripe," "concrete," and "non-trivial." But if these characteristics are present, a court must take the case.

With this much both traditionalists and adaptationists largely agree. The difference between them lies far less in how a case arrives in court than in what the court does to it after it is there. On any view, cases must be brought in by contending parties; the courts do not reach out into the community to bring before them disputes they would like to hear. It is at this point—how the courts operate on the cases that come before them—that serious controversy has emerged.[20]

On the traditionalist view, a court is not any institution that someone cares to label with that name. Courts have particular tasks to perform, and institutions that do not undertake them, or that undertake different tasks (like those of administrative agencies and legislatures), are not courts—a principle that by the name of "separation of powers" is deeply rooted in the first three articles of the Constitution. But because courts in the United States come in a huge variety of forms and undertake multiple functions, it is not practicable to attempt a definition, even on the traditionalist view, by looking to their ultimate goals.... Instead, the nature of courts must be understood by examining how they deal with the types of cases just defined as proper for them.

Following the logic of a dispute (opposing parties contending over a claim of right), the traditionalist sees as the characteristic court function a process called *adjudication*. Among the principles that constitute this process, narrowly defined, are party participation and control, sharp focus, reasoned decisions and, if the matter is important, review by a collegial court for error. Once a matter is reviewed, another operating principle requires finality.

Adjudication need not be defined narrowly. . . . At its broadest, adjudication consists of all that a court does with a matter once jurisdiction is established. The traditionalist analysis holds, however, that underlying the broader conception of adjudication is the process that permits a judge actually to *decide* a case. Traditionalists assert that as central as adjudication is to our understanding of how courts operate, it is by no means the only thing that courts do. Indeed, much of the actual time of judges is spent undertaking a variety of other functions, encouraging mediation and prodding the parties to settle. To the adaptationists, courts legitimately perform in a variety of different modes; no single process, rigidly defined, stands out.

Nevertheless, all observers agree that courts do adjudicate. as narrowly defined. Most agree also that many other judicial functions are carried out in the "shadow" of adjudication. That is, other forms of dispute resolution are shaped by the power of judges to adjudicate a dispute to a final disposition. Because on any view adjudication is, therefore, *a* central method of operating, we will begin our examination of judicial functioning by taking a close look at the essential characteristics of adjudication as a process for reaching a decision.

Essential Characteristics of Adjudication

Operating Principles

Party Participation and Control. What is it that distinguishes adjudication from such closely similar processes as arbitration,

mediation, and consultation and from such clearly disparate ones as administration and legislation? A signal criterion is *control*. "The distribution of control among the procedural group participants is the most significant factor in characterizing a procedural system."[21] In all decision processes, two crucial control variables stand out: (1) control over the decision, and (2) control over the process. Control over decisions is "measured by the degree to which any one of the participants may unilaterally determine the outcome of the dispute"; control over process "refers to control over the development and selection of information that will constitute the basis" for the action taken.[22]

The distribution of control determines whether the resulting process is bilateral bargaining (in which the disputing parties have complete control over the selection and presentation of information and together exercise sole control over the final outcome) or the kind of inquisitorial model popularly identified in the United States with legislative committee hearings (in which the activist decision maker has complete authority to develop and present information and to dictate the outcome). Allocating a large degree of process control to the contending parties and decision control to an impartial third party yields arbitration when the third party is private or adjudication when the third party is a judge.[23] In the view of the late Lon Fuller, the "distinguishing characteristic of adjudication lies in the fact that it confers on the affected party a peculiar form of participation in the decision, that of presenting proofs and reasoned arguments for a decision in his favor."[24]

Sharp Focus. Fuller maintained that adjudication demands a high "burden of rationality not borne by any other form of social ordering"[25] and that the institutional framework in which adjudication functions converts whatever is submitted into a claim of right.[26] The rationality that adjudication summons up and the concomitant claim of right sharpen the focus of the controversy. The spotlight shines intensely on a relatively narrow inquiry—the questions that flow immediately out of the dispute—and the factfinder is not required to cast a wide glance at tangential concerns implicated in a broad social problem. The judge is supposed to decide the questions presented, not related matters that a legislator might take up. Although historical or social context may be important in understanding the origin of the dispute, the judge treats the symptoms rather than the underlying causes. His decree runs, for example, against those who committed a particular act of unlawful discrimination, not against racial hatred; against the immediate actors, not against remote causes.

.   .   .

Reasoned Decision. The judge's decision must be responsive to the case presented. In Fuller's terms, adjudication requires "strong responsiveness": not only must the decisionmaker attend to the parties' arguments, but "that decision ought to proceed from and be congruent with those proofs and arguments."[27]

Whenever the litigants do not question the rule that supports the claim of right, strong responsiveness can be expected. Many disputes, however, center not only on facts but on the meaning, reach, and validity of the underlying right. When the parties' arguments for a reinterpretation of a rule or for the promulgation of a new one do not appreciate the consequences to others of a change in the rule, a judge is not bound to respond as strongly to the parties' arguments and proofs.[28]

Finality. Because the judgement is (or ought to be) strongly responsive to the parties'

arguments and proofs, the court's decision should be conclusive (subject to review for legal error by an appellate court). Once adjudicated, the dispute is almost always put to rest as far as the law is concerned and can be enforced by sanctions. This is the principle of *res judicata*: the parties may not renew their controversy in another court. To some extent, in fact, even other parties may rely on the findings of the court (*collateral estoppel*). To a much lesser degree, the legal rules enunciated by the courts are also final (*stare decisis*); they serve as binding precedent on inferior courts within a jurisdiction, until overturned by legislation or in a subsequent decision after the grounds for the rule have evaporated.

.   .   .

The Adversary Process. The American judicial system is praised and condemned for using an adversary process. Supporters claim for it several virtues. It is implicit to some degree in party participation and control, assuring that the parties can tell their stories, assert their interests, and present their witnesses and evidence. Because the parties know what they want the court to determine, adversary process helps narrow and focus the dispute. It also allows exposure of mistakes and lies through crossexamination and argument. A well-known accolade is that the adversary system "combats the normal human tendency to judge too swiftly in terms of the familiar that which is not fully known."[29]

Detractors maintain that the adversary system too highly values winning. Precisely because it does underwrite party participation, it frequently leads to excess partisanship and can frustrate the search for truth, as advocates ignore and distort salient facts and attempt to confuse rather than clarify in argument. Other rules of procedure, such as exclusionary rules of evidence, uphold the primacy of values other than truth (e.g., confidentiality, preservation of ongoing relationships, freedom from coercion), and the result contributes to the limitation of full truth-getting. Consequently, the adjudicatory approach to problems frequently is piecemeal and directed to symptoms rather than causes. The adversary process often flounders in excesses of adversariness; indeed, sometimes it enhances rather than abates contentiousness.

Another consequence of the adversary process is high costs and delay. Because the parties control the gathering and submission of information to the fact-finder, they can manipulate the system to harass each other. Even if no evil was intended, the usual lack of judicial direction often unduly prolongs the proceedings. A related, though external factor, is the self-interest of lawyers in joining battle and maintaining conflict: since their basis of remuneration is the time they expend and the difficulty of the matter presented, they have at minimum an unconscious motivation to see legal difficulties where none may exist.[30] Other factors also add to cost and delay; for example, constitutional requirements, such as the right of either party to a jury in most civil suits, make the judicial process too cumbersome and costly for many everyday disputes.

Finally, critics assert that the judicial process tends toward winner-loser decisions that produce winner-take-all ("zero-sum") outcomes. Although many cases are structured so as to force a judge who will be strongly responsive to the parties' arguments and proofs to decide for one party or the other (e.g., whether or not to issue an injunction), it ought to be borne in mind that considerable leeway exists for at least hidden compromise in determining legal claims. Sometimes the law expressly allows for it (for example, in states that follow the rule of comparative negligence, the jury must

decide the proportion of fault attributable to the plaintiff and reduce his award accordingly); more often, perhaps, a judge can pick and choose among the various issues presented in the case to achieve a balance required by fairness in light of the uncertainties that attend the proofs. To what degree judges engage in such balancing is unknown; it would be fruitful to explore the issue further.

Whether or not the advantages outweigh the disadvantages, many entities other than courts have adopted the adversary process. Trial-type adversary procedures are widely used in activities ranging from administrative agency proceedings to labor arbitrations. Thus this originally distinctive attribute of courts is now, rightly or wrongly, thought to be transferable to mechanisms far removed from the courts and the judicial process.

A Broader View of Adjudication

The foregoing discussion set forth the traditionalist view of court functioning, a view that stems from the characteristics of adjudication. From this view arises a particular conception of the judicial function, that of the judge whose obligation is to apply rules as perceived rather than to conceive and implement social policy outside given rules, if that means, in a particular case, that some injustice will be done. In short, by the lights of the traditionalist's lens, the judge's duty is to ensure that the formal norms of the adversary system are properly observed.

To the adaptationist, this role of the judge has a critical flaw: it is incapable of dealing with a central shortcoming of the party-controlled adversary system—the lack of adequate representation. To the traditionalist, it is no business of the judge to ensure that a party's lawyer acts smarter than he is. No matter how the client suffers, the duncical lawyer who fails to make evidentiary objections or to cross-examine thoroughly will get no assistance from the judge. Likewise, the party without a representative will find no solace from the bench: the judge does not fill in for absent counsel, and an absent party will justify the court in entering a default judgment.

Adaptationists argue that the judge need not be the passive instrument of justice prescribed in the traditionalist canon. They note that "the tendency of modern American procedure is away from the extreme position which would render the judge a passive umpire."[31] Judges, they insist, can actively seek to do justice: "By encouraging participation, scrutinizing uncontested petitions, restricting access to creditors, and taking advantage of the availability of publicly compensated attorneys, courts are increasingly equipped to overcome the handicaps [imposed on unrepresented parties]."[32]

Judicial activism need not be limited to traditional two-party cases in which one party does not appear or appears with inadequate counsel. The adaptationist views with approval the ability of judges to "reach out for the information needed to alert them to the possible impact of their decisions on individuals not before the court."[33] They are aided in doing so by various techniques, such as class action procedures, through which "courts are more likely to see both the significance of the claims of a plaintiff and the consequences of imposing liability upon a defendant, and thus are more likely to arrive at a substantively just conclusion. Through class action procedures, moreover, the interests of absentees . . . are given representation in the litigative process, and thus are more likely to be given their due."[34]

Similarly, both in extended impact cases and in cases involving ongoing relations (e.g., families) the courts, it is argued, can serve a "backup" role, prodding the parties to reach an optimal solution to the problems presented, despite the formal obstacles in court processes to the task of reordering complex relationships and institutions. "The court's role is to make sure that issues are addressed and choices made, not to make those choices itself."[35] If these types of cases represent the outer limits of judicial capacity, adaptationists do not shrink from the difficulties but see in the courts the only institution willing to lend time and energy in the search for a solution to the many real-world dilemmas that confront us. The adaptationist refuses to be limited by a formal theory of adjudication, and finds comfort in the ability of courts to adapt their processes to take on social grievances left festering by somnolent political institutions. In so doing, courts have begun to borrow from other techniques.

. . .

NOTES

1. C. Friedrich, *Man and His Government: An Empirical Theory of Politics* 423 (1963). Friedrich notes that "[t]he modern view has tended to assign to it third place, and to see the judiciary as the main form of it."

2. See M. Bloch, *Feudal Society* 126ff. [1961]: "In the eleventh century a dispute between two noble houses of Burgundy, begun one day during the vintage season, went on for thirty years, and in the course of it one of the parties had lost more than eleven men." *Id.* at 127.

3. L. Mair, *Primitive Government* 58 (1970).

4. F. Pollock & F. Maitland, *The History of English Law Before the Time of Edward I* 173 (Milsom ed. 1968 rev.).

5. *The Spirit of the Laws* 70, 73 (Ency. Brit. Great Books, 1970).

6. See Lieberman, "The Relativity of Injury," 7 *Phil. & Pub. Affairs* 60 (Fall 1977).

7. J.W. Hurst, *The Growth of American Law: The Law Makers* 85 (1950).

8. *Id.* at 102.

9. *Id.* at 103.

10. J.W. Hurst, supra note 8, at 118.

11. *Id.* at 176.

12. *Id.*

13. 347 U.S. 483 (1954).

14. See e.g., Schuck, "The Graying of Civil Rights Law: The Age Discrimination Act of 1975," 89 *Yale L.J.* 27 (1979)

15. Cavanagh & Sarat, "Thinking About Courts," 14 *L. & Soc'y' Rev.* 371, 411 (1980).

16. *Id.*

17. *Id.*

18. A concern voiced, e.g., by Glazer, "Towards an Imperial Judiciary?", 41 *The Pub.Int.* 104 (1975).

19. M. Shapiro, *Courts: A Comparative and Political Analysis* Ch. 1, esp. at 17 (1981).

20. Opinions vary, of course, on just how and where these views diverge. Abram Chayes, for example, whose earlier writing gave shape and substance to the adaptationist view, recently offered the following clarification:

    > I bear some responsibility for this confusion, I suppose, for in my earlier article I spoke of the decree as "[t]he centerpiece of the emerging public law model." Even then, however, I think I sketched out a broader conception. In any event, further reflection has confirmed me in the view that the nature of the controversy, the sources of the governing law, and the consequent extended impact of the decision—rather than the form of relief—are what really differentiate public law from private law adjudication. Chayes, "The Supreme Court, 1981 Term—Foreword: Public Law Litigation and the Burger Court," 96 *Harv.L.Rev.* 4, 58, (1982).

21. Thibaut & Walker, "A Theory of Procedure," 66 *Calif.L.Rev.* 541, 546 (1978).

22. *Id.*

23. *Id.* at 546–47. See also Thibaut, Walker, LaTour & Houlden, "Procedural Justice as Fairness," 26 *Stan.L.Rev.* 1271, 1273–75 (1974).

24. Fuller, "The Forms and Limits of Adjudication," 92 *Harv.L.Rev.* 353, 364 (1978).

25. *Id.* at 367.

26. *Id.* at 369. . . .

27. See, e.g., Justice Brandeis's concurrence in *Ashwander v. Tennessee Valley Authority*, 297 U.S. 288 (1936).

28. Eisenberg, "Participation, Responsiveness, and the Consultative Process: An Essay for Lon Fuller," 92 *Harv.L.Rev.* 410, 413 (1978). As examples, see, *Erie R.R. Co.* v. *Tompkins*, 304 U.S. 64 (1938) and *MacPherson* v. *Buick Motor Co.*, 217 N.Y. 382, 111 N.E. 1050 (1916).

29. Fuller, supra n. 24.

30. See Johnson, "Lawyers' Choice: A Theoretical Appraisal of Litigation Investment Decisions," 15 *L. & Soc'y Rev.* 567 (1980–1981).

31. F. James, *Civil Procedure* 7 (1965).

32. Cavanagh & Sarat, *supra* note 15, at 393.

33. *Id.* at 381.

34. Note, "Developments in the Law: Class Actions," 89 *Harv.L.Rev.* 1318, 1353 (1976).

35. Diver, "The Judge as Political Powerbroker: Superintending Structural Change in Public Institutions," 65 *Va.L.Rev.* 43, 92 (1979).

Alternatives to Formal Adjudication

Austin Sarat

In the United States during the 1980s there has been lively debate about the role of courts. Some believe that Americans have become too eager to litigate, to turn to courts for the resolution of a multitude of complicated personal and social problems, and it is felt that the courts have all too eagerly welcomed these new demands. Courts, it is said, have engineered a rights revolution and have become involved in problems that exceed their institutional capacities and overburden their limited resources. For those sympathetic to this argument, the search for, and development of, alternatives to formal adjudication is necessary to reduce the burdens on courts and to provide mechanisms the institutional design of which is better suited for the provision of effective redress.

But not everyone believes in, or subscribes to, the theory of the litigation explosion and its associated crisis in the courts. (Galanter, 1983) Those skeptical of this view acknowledge that there has indeed been an increase in the rate at which cases are filed in courts.

They argue, however, that this does not represent a change in the frequency with which grievances are brought to court, but rather an increase in the rate at which grievances are experienced and acknowledged. Americans are no more litigious than they have ever been. There is simply more to litigate about. To suggest that those who litigate are acting inappropriately is, in fact, to blame the victims and to fail to come to terms with the sources and roots of their victimization.

The skeptics remind us that most disputes—that is, most potential lawsuits—never get to court, and they suggest that courts play a residual role in dispute resolution. Moreover, they argue that the filing of a lawsuit tells us very little about what courts actually do, because the vast majority of those suits will be settled without any court action at all. Formal adjudication is the tip of the iceberg, both in terms of the disputes that could be brought to court and in terms of the cases that are actually filed. Finally, the skeptics claim that the capacities of courts to resolve effectively the disputes that are formally adjudicated is underestimated by many critics of courts. (Cavanagh and Sarat, 1980) Adjudication is, in this view, both useful and effective for most of the disputes that are brought to it. As a result, the skeptics question the urgency and necessity of the movement to create alternatives to formal adjudication and the need to channel disputes to such alternatives.

. . .

ALTERNATIVES TO FORMAL ADJUDICATION: TECHNIQUES AND PROCESSES

Alternatives to formal adjudication can be approached in several ways. One way highlights the distinction between those alternatives involving third–party intervention as against bi-lateral dispute processing, in which the parties manage their own conflict. Another distinguishes between those that are in some way connected to state power and those that are not. Yet another emphasizes the formality or informality of the procedures that are utilized. Still others emphasize the political dimensions of dispute processing, contrasting alternatives, on the one hand, that, like adjudication itself, employ a specialized discourse and a relatively closed private setting and thus allow third parties to define the operational content of the dispute, with, on the other hand, those employing more generalized discourse in an open setting to allow the parties themselves, as well as their allies and supporters, to retain control of their dispute and its definition. There is, of course, no right way to divide up and speak about the world of alternatives to formal adjudication. Each of these approaches has its advantages; each emphasizes a somewhat different aspect of the alternatives that are surveyed.

Perhaps the most common alternative to formal adjudication is in many ways the least recognized and least recognizeable. This alternative involves *unilateral action* on the part of a potential disputant to avoid voicing a grievance or complaint or to avoid making a claim. This alternative, variously called "lumping it," "endurance," "avoidance," and "denial," stops the disputing process before it begins. It occurs when people self–consciously refuse to define some event or transaction in their lives as troubled or problematic. This occurs at the stage of problem recognition and is, in many ways, the predominant, or modal response to potential disputes. Social life is, for the most part, inert. The world as it is, fraught with problems and difficulties, is perceived to be the world as it has to be. People invest substantial energy in resisting attempts to define events within life as either injurious or blameworthy. It is almost always easier to endure the familiar than to seek redress or compensation.

. . .

If these barriers are overcome and a claim is made, a second alternative to formal adjudication—*bilateral bargaining and negotiation*—may be employed. Bilateral negotiation can be implicit and indirect, or it may be relatively formal and direct. It occurs within a framework of norms and expectations about how reasonable people ought to behave, how responsibility ought to be assessed and what constitutes fair and equitable compensation for wrongs and injuries. These expectations both shape and reflect legal norms and the patterns of formal adjudication. They are, at the same time, autonomous from and often resistant to, those norms and patterns. Bilateral dispute processing may be more or less embedded in a common folk culture, which exerts as much or more influence than the legal culture.

Bilateral dispute processing is likely to continue throughout the course of a dispute. Invocation or intervention of third parties seldom ends, although it significantly alters, the negotiation phase. We must recognize the overlapping quality of alternatives to formal adjudication and the way in which the various mechanisms of, and strategies for, processing disputes interpenetrate. It would be inaccurate to assume that there are rigid boundaries between dispute–processing techniques, that when one is invoked others are abandoned. There is no neat pattern in the way dispute processing occurs. Choices are tentative and revocable. What happens in the process of negotiation structures the way in which triadic processes are employed, just as the expectation or threat of resort to those processes influences the negotiation process itself.

The content and form of bilateral negotiation is, of course, highly varied. It is difficult for an outsider to know the extent to which disputants bargain over norms and facts, whether negotiation is highly ritualized or ad hoc, and whether the negotiation process is oriented toward compromise or toward establishing the conditions under which one or another of the parties will feel comfortable and secure enough to concede or surrender. Indeed, even what is most central to the process of bilateral negotiation—namely, the fact that the parties themselves retain control over the final outcome—may be blurred through the intervention of allies and supporters and the use of intermediaries, such as lawyers. Bilateral dispute processing is, then, in many ways the most idiosyncratic and difficult to understand of the various alternatives to adjudication.

Perhaps the most prominent type of bilateral dispute processing is plea bargaining in criminal courts. Plea bargaining is, of course, one example of the overlap and interpenetration of dispute-processing mechanisms, since it generally occurs only after a criminal case has been formally initiated. Like other types of bilateral negotiation, plea bargaining is highly varied in its application. It can focus on an exchange of a plea of guilty for a reduction in the number and seriousness of criminal charges or for an agreed-upon and more lenient sentence recommendation. Judges may be more or less actively involved in trying to facilitate agreement. Moreover, because local norms and conventions often dictate the range of appropriate punishments for different offenses, bargaining may focus on the question of what was done rather than on what should be done about it. Thus, when fixing the type of offense requires rather precise knowledge of the circumstances and conditions surrounding a crime, what is most at issue is what type of offense was committed. Bargaining may take the form of an exchange of information rather than a succession of offers and demands, an exchange designed to produce an agreed-upon definition of the offense so that a rather standardized response can be applied.

.   .   .

Third-party, *triadic*, alternatives to formal adjudication are both less common and easier to understand than either the unilateral or bilateral type. Each triadic dispute-processing institution has its own special set of participants, perhaps a different set of rules, and a distinctive style. Each alternative provides its own kind of "justice"; some proceed without reference to general rules known and articulated in advance; others operate according to such rules. Some provide a process of judgment in which it is the status of the parties in dispute, or the preferences of the third party that determine the outcome; others require impartiality. Courts, for example, generally emphasize greater procedural regularity than do other dispute–processing institutions. Furthermore, while adjudicative decision-making is, as we have seen, supposed to encompass the marshaling of reasons and justifications by an impartial arbiter, triadic processes do not always produce reasoned decisions and equitable results.

The structure of a third-party dispute-processing institution has an important influence on the way the dispute is presented; indeed, it may alter the basic nature of the dispute itself. This is as true in moving from informal to more formal means of conflict resolution as it is in moving from trial to appellate courts. Finally, any particular institution has inherent some limitations on the available remedies and thus indirectly on the nature of the settlement that is possible. Participants have to agree to play by the rules of the institution; often this requires that they redefine their interests, goals and strategies.

The third-party technique that displays the greatest family resemblance to adjudication is arbitration. Like adjudication, arbitration seems to produce a result on the basis of some principle; unlike adjudication, it need not establish that principle in advance. Arbitration is, in general, although it need not be, entered into voluntarily. Often arbitration provisions are written into contracts as a way of avoiding the need to resort to formal adjudication, should disagreements arise.

The arbitration process is similar to adjudication in that each party has the opportunity to present its "case" to the arbiter, who is most often a subject-matter specialist rather than a generalist trained in law. Some believe that the tailor-made expertise of the arbiter gives arbitration a major advantage over adjudication in technically complex disputes. Arbitration procedures are supposed to be less formal and more flexible than those used in formal adjudication and it is argued that as a result arbitration is speedier and simpler. At least in theory, arbitration places considerably less emphasis on adversariness and on the establishment of guilt or responsibility. As in adjudication, the arbiter is assumed to be neutral and impartial. Nevertheless, the arbiter may, with agreement of the parties, undertake some independent fact-finding and, in such instances, render decisions on grounds which go beyond those that are established or presented by the parties themselves.

Another type of triadic dispute processing that is much less like adjudication is mediation. Mediation differs from both adjudication and arbitration in that the third party is not empowered to enter a binding decision. Instead, the mediator attempts to bring about an agreement between the parties by listening to each side, trying to identify areas of common concern and building on those areas by proposing solutions in areas of disagreement. In mediation the disputants thus have control over the process and the results. A successful mediation is one in which the parties are enabled to reach an agreement that they were, or would have been, unable to reach bilaterally and that is truly satisfactory to both parties, so that they are willing to comply with it even in the absence of coercion or threat. Although the third party in mediation is supposed to be neutral and unbiased, mediators are encouraged to actively shape proposals and develop conditions out of which an agreement might arise. Finally, mediation is ad hoc in the sense that the mediator is bound by neither abstractly stated and codified normative principles nor by previously mediated agreements.

There is an important danger to any discourse about alternatives to formal adjudication that proceeds as this one has. This danger, roughly equivalent to the danger of . . . [traditionalist] definitions of adjudication, is the danger of the ideal type, the danger of relying on abstract, ahistorical descriptions of complex social processes. With respect to both arbitration (Kritzer and Anderson, 1983) and mediation (Merry, 1982) there is some suggestion that many of their advertised differences from formal adjudication are not realized in practice. Arbitration, especially in commercial disputes, has become increasingly formal and rule-bound, increasingly lawlike in its procedures. This again demonstrates the power of adjudication as a model for dispute processing. Mediation, on the other hand, despite its advertised emphasis on voluntariness and on the retention of its control by the disputants, has been found to be highly coercive and often unfair or inequitable in the results it produces, especially in situations in which there are significant power differentials between the parties or in which it is used as an adjunct to more formal processes.

We have to this point talked about alternatives to adjudication in terms of the number of parties most directly involved as participants, but there are, as suggested above, several other ways in which we can talk about them. One approach (Sarat and Grossman, 1975) emphasizes both *the level of formality of adjudication and its alternatives* (that is, the presence or absence of a specialized third-party role, specialized rules of evidence and procedure, written records, and established channels of appeal) and *their connection to the established governmental apparatus* (that is, whether the coercive power of the state can be used to enforce their decisions).

In this view, the first type of third-party dispute-processing alternative to adjudication is *informal and private*. The adjusters of disputes in a private, informal setting do not have any formal connection with the state, although in some cases they may have to be licensed by the state or by a quasi-public organization of professionals that exercises a delegated licensing function. The third party may be chosen because the individual has status, position, respect, power or money. Or the party may simply be the designated agent of an organization set up to handle specific. disputes. The technique of bringing disputes to a private, informal third party may be the choice of both disputants or of one but not the other party to a conflict. Or it may be the result of private norms or expectations of a subcultural group which "require" that disputes be settled, as much as possible, within the group.

Private, informal dispute resolution is found in the United States in religious and ethnic communities, in the work of trained professionals such as marriage counselors, in various commercial relationships, and even in large shopping malls. In all of these settings private, informal dispute processing is based on the assumption that the parties to a dispute will agree about what matters are in dispute and will trust the person called upon to act as a judge.

.   .   .

Third-party processing of disputes also proceeds through *public, informal* methods. These methods involve the informal intervention by agents of the state to solve disputes. Such dispute processing is utilized to complement the needs of public, formal institutions by reducing their operating burdens through the delegation of discretion to actors whose behavior in working out disputes is less often guided by standardized norms or procedures than by role-relevant routines. Dispute treatment in this context reflects not only official norms of substance and procedure but also, within broad limits, the organizational commitments of the public agents involved.

Avoidance of procedural regularity in the pursuit of more immediate and more efficient conflict resolution is also characteristic of plea bargaining, the practices in the early juvenile courts, and the pretrial conference, which has come to play an increasing role in facilitating the settlement of civil suits in the United States. In the case of plea bargaining the defendant is induced to settle his "conflict with the law" through an informal, bargaining process. Thus, plea bargaining may be less like other third-party mechanisms in which the roles of judge and adversary are clearly separated than the kind of dyadic negotiation that generally begins before resort to adjudication. The public prosecutor becomes the "dispute settler" and has virtually complete discretion as to whether to prosecute or on what charge. He has available both the coercive power of the state (in the form of a probable guilty verdict if the case goes to trial) and the discretion to work out an acceptable compromise.

Mediating toward a compromise is also in the prosecutor's interest. It reduces the risk of (too many) acquittals, and it gives better control of the outcome. The prosecutor's role becomes managerial and bureaucratized in place of the formality of court adjudication of guilt or innocence. The prosecutor becomes the manager of a ritualized conflict-resolution ceremony. While in some ways the handling of guilty pleas resembles the resolution of private, informal disputes, it is much less open-ended. The prosecutor is a public official designated to resolve such conflicts, and the defendant cannot simply drop out of the relationship.

The thread connecting all public, informal methods of dispute resolution is their proximity to the formal arena of the courts and to third-party adjudication by a judge (Harrington, 1985), and their reliance on private bargaining within this context. There are no formal rules, but a set of norms and mutual expectations gives these processes some structure. Indeed, in some cases, the process by which informal settlements are reached (plea bargaining is the best example) has become bureaucratized. A relatively small group of actors is involved in any one jurisdiction, regularized relationships and mutual dependencies develop, and the needs of the bureaucracy for compromise and accommodation frequently predominate.

Unlike private, informal alternatives, which act to deflect disputes from formal processes before they are carried into litigation, these examples, although not all, of public, informal processes act to deflect disputes from formal processes only after the process of litigation has been initiated. In a sense, these devices do not act as alternatives to such formal adjudication; they function instead to reduce it from a highly conflictual process to one in which all that is sought is certification of an informally agreed–upon solution.

A third category—*private formal* alternatives—involves dispute settlers who remain private actors but carry out their functions in accord with certain agreed-upon and standardized procedures. They are more likely to act as judges than mediators, although role definitions may be fluid. Such formal but private tribunals are found within the confines of organizations or associations, professional groups, and within certain subcultural groups. These tribunals exist to settle conflicts between group members, conflicts that cannot be settled informally, but that, for some reason, the parties are reluctant to move into the public arena. Where group membership is conditioned by a voluntary or imposed acceptance of certain norms or a code of conduct, the enforcement of such norms will typically be handled at several levels within the group. Those breaches that cannot be settled or sanctioned informally will usually have to be settled by more formal means. Although the rules and procedures followed by such tribunals may bear some resemblance to those of the courts, those rules and procedures remain private and often diverge substantially from those employed in the public sector.

.   .   .

Private, formal dispute–processing devices employ courtlike procedures for settling disputes between group members. Decision-makers are not agents of the state but may be regarded by group members as possessing some sort of jural authority based on the stipulation of a prior contract or on delegated state authority. Compliance may be purely voluntary, as in the case of a religious court, or induced by potential sanctions (loss of license, loss of hospital privileges for a doctor, and the like) or the ultimate threat of a spillover into the public courts, with greater potential consequences.

The final type of dispute–processing mechanism includes adjudication in courts. This type is both *public and formal*. The rules that govern access and establish the procedural framework of these bodies are variables of critical importance. What kinds of disputes are to be decided, who can bring these disputes, and what kinds of solutions are possible are among the most important determinants of the involvement of public, formal mechanisms in defining, managing, and interpreting conflict. In contrast to private, informal mechanisms, the "rules" for decision in courts do not come from the parties themselves. Their sources are many —statutes, prior decisions governed by the rule of precedent, and evolving policy considerations responsive to current demands.

Unlike other dispute-processing institutions, those that are both public and formal generally require, either explicitly or implicitly, that parties in dispute be represented by legal specialists, people who claim unique knowledge of the procedural and substantive rules governing access to, and the operation of, public, formal institutions. These specialists act on behalf of the parties to shape and structure the issues presented to these institutions and the way in which the issues are perceived and handled by them. Legal specialists play a critical role in influencing and determining the conditions under which courts and similar types of adjudicative institutions become involved in conflict management and in defining the goals and objectives of litigation.

. . .

This way of talking about alternatives to formal adjudication has recently been criticized for overemphasizing the discontinuity of dispute-processing institutions, for artificially separating those institutions from their social context, and for not being useful in helping to explain differences in outcomes typically associated with different types and styles of dispute processing (Yngvesson and Mather, 1983). Critics suggest attention be given to the social accessibility of such institutions and the nature of the language and procedures that they employ. In this view, the significant differences between the various dispute-processing institutions are the extent to which they are open and accessible or closed and inaccessible to informal audiences and participants and the extent to which they rely on specialized language and procedures. Institutions that are closed and inaccessible and those that rely on specialized language and procedures concentrate and centralize power and stratify the disputing process much more than those that are open and rely on generalized discourse.

The value of this way of thinking is that it alerts us to the power and control dimensions of dispute processing—that is, to the extent to which particular techniques and approaches confer control over the dispute on specialists or officials or allow continuing control on the part of disputants. In this view, formal adjudication, because of its relative inaccessibility and its specialized language and procedure, would be seen as a disempowering way for individuals to deal with disputes, while mediation would be seen as keeping power in the hands of the disputants.

THE FUTURE OF ADJUDICATION AND ITS ALTERNATIVES

However one chooses to describe and discuss formal adjudication and its alternatives, it is clear that during the 1980s in the United States, there is considerable dissatisfaction with the former and considerable energy being devoted to the development and encouragement of the latter. Whether because of doubts about the competence and effectiveness of courts in resolving the kind of complex social policy disputes that now seem so much a part of the American judicial process, or out of sense that courts are all too often violating and ignoring the essential attributes of adjudication, many observers now seem to feel that there is a serious crisis in the courts. For them the preferred solution is often to encourage the development of or greater reliance on alternatives to adjudication, and to divert particularly troublesome cases from formal adjudication to one or another of those alternatives. . . .

Those who support the further development and encouragement of alternative dispute resolution believe that it will not only alleviate the problems of courts but also that it will make justice more accessible, efficient, and effective (Council on the Role of Courts, 1984). For them, formal adjudication should be even more of a last resort than it has been in the past; for them, public policy ought to be devoted to the efficient allocation of disputes among various dispute-processing techniques with an eye to insuring the best fit between the demands of different kinds of cases and the resources and capacities of those techniques. The crisis of the courts provides, in this view, an opportunity to assess the proper role of courts and of adjudication and to take steps to bring both back within the bounds of that role.

In the final analysis, it seems unlikely that the nature and role of formal adjudication will soon undergo significant alteration. Formal adjudication plays and will continue to play a secondary, but major, part in the dispute-processing apparatus of American society. The primary, if not the most significant, part will continue to be played by the least visible and least manipulable processes of unilateral and bilateral adjustment. The energy devoted to the proliferation of non-adjudicative third-party mechanisms will not, it seems, much alter this basic pattern of disputing and dispute processing.

REFERENCES

Ralph Cavanagh and Austin Sarat, "Thinking About Courts," *Law and Society Review*, 14 (1980).

Council on the Role of Courts, *The Role of Courts in American Society*, (St. Paul, 1984).

Marc Galanter, "Reading the Landscape of Disputes," *U.C.L.A. Law Review*, 31 (1983).

Nathan Glazer, "Toward An Imperial Judiciary," *The Public Interest*, 41 (1975).

Christine B. Harrington, *Shadow Justice* (Westport, Conn., 1985).

Herbert Kritzer and Jill Anderson, "The Arbitration Alternative" *Justice System Journal* 8 (1983).

Sally Merry, "The Social Organization of Mediation in Nonindustrial Societies" in Richard Abel, ed., *The Politics of Informal Justice* (New York, 1982).

Austin Sarat and Joel Grossman, "Courts and Conflict Resolution" *American Political Science Review*, 69 (1975).

Barbara Yngvesson and Lynn Mather, "Courts, Moots and the Disputing Process" in Keith Boyum and Lynn Mather, eds., *Empirical Theories About Courts* (New York, 1983).

CHAPTER 2

Litigation in Trial and Appellate Courts

In 1976 Thomas Ehrlich, former dean of the Stanford Law School, wrote that America was suffering from "legal pollution." As Ehrlich put it, "We have far too many laws; we rely too heavily on law as an instrument of social change; we depend too much on courts, legislatures and administrative agencies to resolve our woes." Speaking specifically about courts, Ehrlich cited statistics describing a pattern of rapid growth in the number of cases that have been brought into both the state and federal judicial systems in recent years.[1]

While there is no doubt that the caseload of American courts has increased in recent years, it is by no means clear that America is suffering from a litigation explosion.[2] Being involved in litigation is an experience not shared by the vast majority of the American people.[3]

It is important as we try to understand the nature of the demands made on courts that we not confuse an increased volume of cases brought to court with a litigation crisis.[4] Increased numbers of cases may reflect an expansion of the rights recognized by, and within, our legal order. It may signify the fact that barriers to access to justice have been removed.[5] As the scope of law expands, as more legal rights and remedies are created, the amount of litigation increases as a result of the new opportunities for court action.[6] As new rights are created, litigation may be necessary to clarify how those rights will be defined and understood by the courts. Furthermore, the creation of new rights may direct the attention of organized interest groups to the judiciary. Interest groups may come to perceive litigation as a viable strategy for stimulating group mobilization to achieve the groups' political goals.[7]

Increases in the number of cases on the dockets of courts may also be related to decreases in the costs of litigation. Litigation is a relatively expensive way of processing disputes. A substantial investment of time and money is required to bring and sustain a lawsuit. However, in recent years numerous attempts have been made to reduce or redistribute such costs through such devices as the provision of free legal services. As a result of the reduced costs, the amount of litigation may have increased, because people who formerly were unable to afford to bring disputes to court are now able to do so, and because those already able to afford litigation are simply able to afford more of it.[8]

Thus, it seems that one can identify three generic factors that may explain litigation. The first is what we call social development. Variation in the amount of litigation is a function of changes in the level of complexity, differentiation, and scale of the society in which courts operate.[9] Increased reliance on courts to process disputes results from changes in the nature of typical social relationships that appear to accompany processes of social development and changes in the structure of society. In less developed societies individuals have relatively stable and enduring contacts with a limited range of other individuals. Disputes in such settings are easier to resolve informally. The framework of trust and the context of ongoing relationships generally found in such societies mean that resort to supposed impartial third parties can be avoided.[10] As a result, courts play a less important role in processing disputes.

In more complex, industrialized societies individuals generally have a wider range of social relationships, but this expansion is accompanied by a diminution in their depth and intensity. Relationships typically are of a more transitory nature; disputes often occur between strangers, between people who have nothing more in common than the dispute itself. Under such circumstances informal dispute processing is impractical. The social development argument suggests that courts will play a more important role in dispute processing in developed societies than in underdeveloped societies because of the proliferation of impersonal relationships. We are not suggesting that courts replace other dispute-processing mechanisms in developed societies, but rather that their share of society's dispute-processing business increases.

The second factor that explains why disputes are translated into demands for judicial services is subjective cost/benefit calculations on the part of disputants. The decision to employ courts to process disputes is for some disputants a relatively objective, well-thought-out decision. For others, however, the decision to go to court may be an act that has value because of its cathartic effect, even though it may not produce tangible, material benefits.[11] Those who use the court frequently tend to use it for more clearly instrumental purposes than do those who are occasional users.[12] The major distinction between those who use courts and those who use other mechanisms to process disputes may be less attitudinal than financial. As a general rule, the costs of using various dispute-processing institutions rise as one moves from informal, private institutions to formal, public institutions.

Since courts process disputes by clearly declaring who is entitled to what from whom, disputants must calculate a "risk" factor and weigh what they might lose against the possible benefits of doing nothing or of using different devices for dispute processing. Thus, courts encourage settlements that might not otherwise occur by conveying to disputants the idea that they have more to gain by trying to reach an informal settlement of differences, a settlement that allows them to exercise some control over the result.[13]

A third factor is that legislatures and courts are creating more legally actionable rights and remedies. The greater the reach and scope of the legal system, the higher its litigation rate will be. An expanded scope of law increases litigation by implicitly, if not directly, expanding the jurisdiction of the courts. The creation of new legal rights is likely to stimulate litigation designed to vindicate or protect those rights. This sequence is illustrated by the "criminal rights explosion" of the 1960s, in which the creation of new rights stimulated further litigation, which in turn produced new rights, which required further litigation. Because judicial dispute processing must proceed in accordance with the law, courts and legislatures are able to alter the amount of litigation by creating or changing law.

The readings that follow each provides a distinctive perspective from which to view the demands made on courts. Zemans suggests that litigation, no matter what its volume, can and should be understood as a political act and as a form of political participation. Miller and Sarat demonstrate that no matter how substantial the caseloads of American courts they continue to play a relatively small role in dealing with society's dispute-processing business. Engel describes the uneven pattern of demands made on courts in one Illinois county, and he indicates that there are substantial cultural barriers that discourage litigation of particular types of disputes. He also provides evidence on the impact of social development in altering the relationship of court and community. That relationship is further explored by Atkins and Glick in their discussion of state supreme courts. The chapter concludes with a selection by Marc Galanter, which reviews existing studies of litigation and concludes that there is no litigation crisis in the United States.

NOTES

1. Thomas Ehrlich, "Legal Pollution," *New York Times Magazine*, February 8, 1976.
2. See Lawrence Friedman, "The Six Million Dollar Man: Litigation and Rights Consciousness in Modern America," *Maryland Law Review* 39 (1980), 691; see also Marc Galanter, "The Day After the Litigation Explosion," *Maryland Law Review* 46 (1986), 3.
3. Barbara Curran and Francis Spaulding, *The Legal Needs of the Public* (Chicago: American Bar Foundation, 1974).
4. Friedman, *op. cit.*, note 2 and Galanter, *op. cit.*, note 2.
5. Mauro Cappelletti and Bryant Garth, *Access to Justice*, Vol. I (Amsterdam: Sijthoff and Noordhoff, 1979).
6. Karen Orren, "Standing to Sue: Interest Group Conflict in the Federal Courts," *American Political Science Review* 70 (1976), 723.
7. Stuart Scheingold, *The Politics of Rights* (New Haven: Yale University Press, 1974). See, also Lee Epstein, *Conservatives in Court* (Knoxville: University of Tennessee Press, 1985).
8. On the importance of cost see Lawrence Friedman, "Legal Rules and the Process of Social Change," *Stanford Law Review* 19 (1967), 786. See also David M. Trubek *et al.*, "The Costs of Ordinary Litigation," *UCLA Law Review* 31 (1983), 72.
9. For a useful discussion of the social development approach see Stephen Daniels, "Ladders and Bushes: The Problem of Caseloads and Studying Court Activities Over Time," *American Bar Foundation Research Journal 1984* (1984), 751.
10. Richard Abel, "A Comparative Theory of Dispute Institutions in Society," *Law and Society Review* 8 (1974), 217.
11. See Arthur Leff, "Ignorance, Injury and Spite," *Yale Law Journal* 80 (1970), 1.
12. Marc Galanter, "Why the 'Haves' Come Out Ahead: Speculations on the Limits of Legal Change," *Law and Society Review* 9 (1974), 95.
13. Marc Galanter, "The Radiating Effects of Courts," in *Empirical Theories About Courts*, eds. Keith Boyum and Lynn Mather (New York: Longman, 1983).

Legal Mobilization: The Neglected Role of the Law in the Political System

Frances Kahn Zemans

POLITICAL BEHAVIOR AND THE PUBLIC-PRIVATE DICHOTOMY

The study of individual participation in the polity (that is, action directed from citizen to the state), has essentially ignored the legal system altogether. This fact reflects both the ancestry of the political participation literature (in voting studies) and the traditional distinction between law and politics. Participation research has been oriented to "public" policy and outcomes; it implicitly requires a political consciousness, an awareness of entry into the political arena and a desire for an effect beyond one's personal life space.

A definition of political activity which relies upon the public motivation of the actor may be attractive by virtue of its clarity and simplicity, but it would exclude much of what we traditionally think of as political activity. Attempts to use the political system to gain personal or group advantage may be criticized for failure to consider the general good, but these attempts are certainly not

dismissed as private or apolitical and therefore beyond the legitimate concerns of those attempting to explain the authoritative distribution of social valuables. Indeed a central question in American political thought has been the maintenance of a public spirit. . . . The dominant American ideology responds to this concern with an underlying faith that the public good will most likely be achieved through an aggregation of the assertion of narrower interests. . . .

The very nature of the judicial process blurs the public-private distinction that pervades the political science literature. In a common law system in which the rules are said to emerge in large measure out of an aggregation of cases brought for consideration, the initiation of individual demands (and not merely outcomes) is central to the development of the law. In this common law system, with its commitment to *stare decisis*, each case has the potential to influence all subsequent similar cases. This process has been described as

> one in which the classification changes as the classification is made. The rules change as the rules are applied. More important, the rules arise out of a process which, while comparing fact situations, creates the rules and then applies them (Levi, 1948, pp. 3–4).

"Legal Mobilization: The Neglected Role of the Law in the Political System," Frances K. Zemans. *American Political Science Review*, Vol. 77, No. 3, 1983. Reprinted with permission of author and publisher.

The point is that courts are essentially reactive institutions, so rules "change as they are applied" in response to claims made. Within the limits of jurisdictional rules that structure participation, individual litigants actually set the agenda of the judicial branch of government.

In addition, of course, there are the more unusual cases that begin as private matters of personal interest to the claimant and that, by virtue of the court's response to them, are transformed into significant new policy. A prominent example is the case of Clarence Gideon, the ne'er-do-well Florida convict sentenced to prison without the benefit of counsel in his felony defense (*Gideon* v. *Wainwright*, 372 U.S. 335, 1963). Within a few short years of that decision, the extent of criminal defense and the role and financial burden of the state in providing it had been revolutionized.

The more general point is that individual choice and demands on public authority by invoking legal rights are closely interwoven with the making of public policy without any requisite involvement by a collectivity or any necessity for a public consciousness. However, even recognition of the importance of privately motivated individual cases to the development of the law ties their political role to a requisite contribution to rule making. A much broader conceptualization is necessary if the full magnitude of the political role of the law is to be appreciated.

.   .   .

LEGAL MOBILIZATION AS POLITICAL PARTICIPATION

Political participation is implied in the very notion of democracy. Whether characterized as serving the protection or maximization of interest, providing for self-rule, or as a means of self-realization of one's humanity, political participation has been and continues to be central to democratic theory (Arendt, 1959; Bachrach, 1967; Dahl, 1961; Fanon, 1965). Although these various roles are surely not mutually exclusive, neither are they necessarily mutually dependent. More important to the concerns expressed here, each of these goals is potentially available through legal activity and, it might be argued, more so than from traditionally acknowledged modes of political participation. For unlike other governmental structures, the legal system is structured precisely to promote individual rather than collective action. Although that surely limits the precipitousness of change that is likely to occur, it also means that the individual citizen does not require the imprimatur of an annointed group to have access to government authority. The legal system, limited as it is to real cases or controversies involving directly injured or interested parties, provides a uniquely democratic (as opposed to republican) mechanism for individual citizens to invoke public authority on their own and for their benefit. The bulk of this activity takes place among private citizens who, in the process of invoking legal norms, employ the power of the state and so become state actors themselves.

In this way the legal system can be considered quintessentially democratic, although not necessarily egalitarian if the competence and the means to make use of this access to governmental authority is not equally distributed. Despite neglect by political science, the fact is that the share of the output of the political system that individuals receive is in part determined by the extent to which they mobilize the law on their own behalf. The reliance of some of the distribution of social valuables upon individual assertions of public authority is ultimately democratic, for it mitigates some of the problems inherent in representative government, including the limits of collective action and the difficulty of measuring intensity of subjective interest. If the dispersion of power provides protection from tyranny, then the potential for every individual to mobilize the law can play an important role in democratic governance.

Without diminishing either the rule-making role of the courts or the importance of collective action in politics, scholarly neglect of the citizenry's mobilization of the law has contributed to a wide-spread failure to recognize the centrality of individual demands to the very implementation process that determines the benefits that citizens actually receive from their government.... Black's (1973) work, "The Mobilization of Law," is an important exception. Black, however, defines law as the equivalent of "governmental social control," and its mobilization as "the process by which a legal system acquires its cases." These definitions are at once too broad and too narrow. The first is too broad because it does not distinguish law from government power; thus it would, for example, include as an act of law the burglary of a psychiatrist's office to obtain Daniel Ellsberg's case file. Although that perspective may be highly recommended by virtue of its avoidance of many of the most complex questions that have historically plagued jurisprudential thought, it is a conceptualization that distorts the common understanding of law as a framework within which governmental actors can operate legitimately, setting limits on governmental power. The definition is too narrow because it is unidirectional and fails to recognize the interactive nature of the law. Finally, although Black has done more than anyone to call attention to legal mobilization as a meaningful area of study, he defines mobilization far too formalistically and so fails to encompass the breadth of its role in the distribution of governmental power among the citizenry.

Although defining mobilization as "the process by which a legal system acquires its cases" seems rather all-encompassing, Black goes on to make the direct involvement of public actors a prerequisite to the transformation of an incident or situation into a "case." In the criminal system this means involvement by the police, in the civil system the actual filing of a case in court. The attractiveness of this definition is its relative ease of operationalization. Yet an understanding of cases even so defined is itself necessarily dependent upon knowledge about those potential cases which do not enter the formal system and why they do not. Further, and more closely related to the role of the legal system as a mechanism for participatory democracy, an individual that invokes the law on his or her own behalf *without* direct assistance from the formal mechanism assumes the role of governmental actor. This form of mobilizing public authority is indeed worthy of inquiry. In addition, it can be argued that successful legal mobilization may be substantially more efficient than the interposition of police, prosecutors, and courts in the implementation of the law.

A more useful formulation of legal mobilization is provided by Lempert (1976) as "the process by which legal norms are invoked to regulate behavior" (p. 173). This definition includes the earliest stages of the mobilization process when, in Eastonian terms, desires or wants are transformed into demands, when the public authority inherent in legal norms is first asserted by the citizen in this participatory act. From this perspective legal mobilization is not dependent upon the use of particular formal structures. Most important, it does not exclude individual action and implicitly recognizes the central role that mere knowledge and assertion of legal norms have in the distribution of public policy. The individual citizen can be a true participant in the governmental scheme as an enforcer of the law without representative or professional intermediaries.

The model of political participation that underlies this conceptualization includes an active role for the citizenry in both the making and the implementation of public policy. In contrast, the more traditional perspective on citizen participation in governance has been oriented almost exclusively to policymaking. Verba and Nie (1972, p. 3) for example, are interested in democratic participation as "processes of influencing governmental policies, not carrying them out." Consistent with that view, the crucial question with respect to the relationship between the citizen and the state has been how the preferences of the citizens of a society are aggregated into a social choice. Further, according to Verba and Nie, it is "through participation [that] the goals of the society are set in a way that is assumed to maximize the allocation of benefits in a society to match the needs and desires of the populace" (p. 4). However, no such assumption is warranted. For although they claim that "the relevant consequence of participation for the individual citizen is what he gets from the government" (p. 9), along with other students of participation they fail to acknowledge that what one gets is not the same as allocation, for the latter is only the apportionment or designation of government benefits, and not their actual distribution. Although what one gets is most certainly *related* to governmental allocative decisions, to a substantial degree what citizens *receive* from the government is dependent upon the demands they make for their entitlements and upon participation in the policy-implementation as well as the policy-making process. In particular, what the populace actually receives from government is to a large extent dependent upon their willingness and ability to assert and use the law on

their own behalf. Yet legal mobilization as political demand has been virtually ignored by the literature that purports to be concerned with who gets what.

Verba and Nie's definition of political participation ("activities by private citizens aimed at influencing actions of government personnel") does not necessarily exclude legal activity, and the mode of participation they denote as "citizen-initiated contacts" would seem to incorporate legal contacts. Yet when it comes to their data analysis, they, like others, are particularly interested in attempts to influence governmental policy decisions and in collectively oriented outcomes. In reporting the correlations among campaign activity, communal activity, and voting they assert:

> What may hold [these] modes of activity together is that all involve some political consciousness, some awareness of and concern about issues that transcend the individual's most narrow life space. But parochial participation can take place in the absence of such general concern with political matters (Verba & Nie, 1972, p. 71).

Although such a characterization might reasonably exclude the bulk of legal activity from the main arena of political participation, it is inappropriate on two different counts. First, it substantially narrows the purview of political participation as it has been variously conceptualized in the theoretical literature; second, it fails to take cognizance of the particular difficulty in characterizing public versus private issues in a legal system that is structured to generate rules out of an incremental aggregation of individual (largely "private") cases, and through which the implementation of public policy often proceeds. As a result it fails to acknowledge the importance of citizen-initiated demands to the actual distribution of social valuables.

LAW AS POTENTIAL — RIGHTS AS CONTINGENT: THE CITIZEN'S ROLE IN ENFORCEMENT

"Law," according to Samuel Johnson, "supplies the weak with adventitious strength" (Boswell, 1791, 1969, p. 498). In other words, law confers power. In Dahl's (1961) words, the "mantle of legality" conferred on private citizens provides them with power previously unavailable to them. Any new authoritative rule, whether statute, judge-made common law, or administrative regulation, merely provides opportunities. As an essentially reactive process, the legal system fits an entrepreneurial market mode; it is structured so that by invoking the law private citizens play a social role in its enforcement. Whatever rights are conferred are thus contingent upon the factors that promote or inhibit decisions to mobilize the law.

Ironically it has been sociologists rather than political scientists who have recognized that the legal process makes the individual a participant in governance rather than an object of government. Selznick's study of the law of employment and Nonet's study of the administration of the state workmen's compensation laws by the Industrial Accident Commission in California both document the legalization of the administrative process; i.e., enforcement agencies progressively become passive recipients of privately initiated claims with an increasing orientation to the settlement of disputes. Although on one hand that development may have the effect of diverting public policy goals inherent in the enabling legislation, it has the advantage of making legalized policy responsive to individual circumstances (Selznick, 1969).

Nonet found that the social welfare model, in which government is actively to provide service and distribute benefits, is by itself unable to accomplish the intended ends; in the agency he examined, legalization actually facilitated the transformation of welfare policy into secure rights (Nonet, 1969, p. 263). In the process, private citizens become active agents of the growth of the law; instead of a passive object of the state, the citizen is the demander of rights and status. Nonet's conclusion that the law was liberating, freeing the injured employee from dependence upon agency and industry notions of his interests, sounds curiously like Fanon's arguments about the liberation and self-realization that come from participation in politics. In both cases citizens transform themselves from objects to willful participants.

Participation and the distribution of demands in any entrepreneurial scheme depend upon resources, skill, aggressiveness, and rights consciousness, none of which is evenly distributed in society. Because virtually all legal rights in the United States depend upon the citizen to initiate the legal process, the distribution of such resources and access to them are critical. It is here that organized groups play a central role in an otherwise individualized system, for as with other forms of political participation, they can provide the resources to support the assertion of individual claims. For example, Nonet found that the union played this important role in facilitating the claims of their members for workmen's compensation (Nonet, p. 9), even though such a role lay outside the union contract. There is also evidence from other contexts that similar support for the assertion of individual claims is forthcoming from more informal networks. Friends, relatives, employers, co-workers, and neighbors all play a part in increasing awareness of the legal nature of problems and thus the availability of legal remedies. . . . In addition they provide guidance in the search for and selection of legal assistance. . . .

Such citizen participation in the legal

process is typically assumed to be central to private but not public law; however, that distinction is clearer in theory than in practice. Although it is true that the state is authorized to enforce public law on its own initiative, and that in private law that right is granted exclusively to private citizens (Black, 1973, p. 128), the evidence indicates that the state only rarely exercises that authority because in general the legal system is structured to respond to citizen-initiated complaints. Both the growth of the criminal law and the creation of specialized administrative structures have an impact upon legal mobilization, but it is largely by virtue of the shifting of a substantial proportion of the costs to the polity. Although this has the effect of making it cheaper and less complicated for an individual to make a claim , the cases pursued by government still depend largely upon complaints from outside, that is, on active participation by the citizenry.

Reliance upon citizen–initiated complaints undermines the ability of government agencies to set their own agendas as authorized by their enabling legislation. Although they can and do select among cases for particular attention, agencies are bound to respond to complaints. As a result, any enforcement agenda–setting attempted by a governmental agency depends upon the affected citizenry's demands for implementation. Agencies would often like to concentrate their efforts on exposing and pursuing serious and continuous offenders, being less concerned with individual aberrations. However, a system that is dependent upon individual complainants cannot easily discriminate among these cases. Legal mobilization and the initiation of complaints with public authorities is thus dependent on complainant–related variables rather than offender–related variables. To the extent that the bulk of the complaints are individualized,

the agency's work becomes substantially particularized.

.   .   .

The importance of citizen mobilization of the law to its enforcement is further reflected in the continuing debate over Congressional and judicial authorization of private causes of action. A citizen has the right to file a private lawsuit in the courts either to secure compliance directly or to seek damages for injuries suffered by virtue of noncompliance. Proponents of a strong enforcement effort often do not want to rely on suits by private citizens as the only mechanism to force compliance. Indeed it has been noted that "the very origins of administrative agencies lay in dissatisfaction with private litigation as an undemocratic mechanism for social choice and control" (Stewart & Sunstein, 1982, p. 1294). Despite the documented pervasive reliance of regulatory agencies on citizen-complainants (Kagan, 1978), the authorization to bring complaints (and suits if necessary) against violators constitutes a grant of substantial control to the agency, at least insofar as there is virtually unlimited discretion *not* to pursue a case. The option of a private cause of action thus limits an agency's enforcement monopoly. The continuing debate and the criticisms of private rights of action as usurpations of legislative authority that "may engender overenforcement of regulatory statutes" (Fein, 1981, p. 23) reflect how seriously mobilization of the law is taken as a tool of policy implementation.

.   .   .

CONCLUSION

Defining legal mobilization as the act of invoking legal norms to regulate behavior is purposively broad enough to include the earliest stage of legal activity; in the simplest case, a particular behavior is demanded by verbal appeal to the law. The law is thus mobilized when a desire or want is translated into a demand as an assertion of one's rights. At the same time that the legitimacy of one's claim is grounded in rules of law, the demand contains an implicit threat to use the power of the state on one's own behalf. This is most definitely not to argue that a legal mobilization framework provides a complete analytic scheme for understanding the law and its place in the polity; that would be both presumptuous and inaccurate, for surely it is not the case that the law affects actual behavior only via citizen demands. Much of the impact of the law results from voluntary compliance that stems from both an obligation to obey and a fear of sanction; i.e., a great deal of citizen behavior is self-regulated, with law providing a backdrop of state-imposed parameters. By contrast, actual legal mobilization occurs only when there is an active demand based on legal norms. Although it must be preceded by a perceptual stage in which a given incident or situation is conceptualized first as calling for a response, and second as actionable in the law, it is not until the law is actually invoked that participation occurs.

. . .

The selective focus here has been on the sorely neglected interactive nature of the law. More specifically, it has been argued that the governmental power inherent in the law is used by the citizen actively and individually to participate in the political system in order to receive part of the authoritative distribution of valuables. Law is of course not the panacea of the powerless, but by its very nature it does lend its legitimacy and the power of the state to whomever has the ability and willingness to use it (Thompson, 1975).

An interactive view of the law that acknowledges the universal availability of govern-ment power to the citizenry has important implications for socialization in a democratic society. Neglect of legal mobilization as a form of political participation is both a result and a part of the skew in political socialization toward the obligation of the citizen to obey the law. Such an orientation to the law is unidirectional (from state to citizen), and presents the law as merely a mechanism for social control. It does not in any way endorse an active, assertive participatory citizenry that is central to a democratic society. An interactive approach to the law dictates the promotion of a legally competent citizenry as essential if public aims are to be realized in a system in which the implementation of public policy is highly dependent upon mobilization of the law by individual citizens. It is time for researchers to broaden their scope and not to be bound by respondents' awareness of the "political" nature of their acts. To do otherwise causes us to remain victims of the traditional view that separates law and politics and leaves unexplored an important area of interaction between citizens and the state.

REFERENCES

Arendt, H. *The human condition*. Garden City, N.Y.: Doubleday, 1959.

Bachrach, P. *The theory of democratic elitism*. Boston: Little Brown, 1967.

Black, D. The mobilization of law. *Journal of Legal Studies*, 1973, *2*, 125–129.

Boswell, J. *Life of Samuel Johnson*. London: Oxford University Press, 1969 (Originally published, 1791.)

Dahl, R. *Who governs?* New Haven, Conn.: Yale University Press, 1961.

Fanon, F. *The wretched of the earth*. New York: Grove Press, 1965.

Fein, B.E. Receding U.S. judicial influence marked by rulings in 1980–81 term.

National Law Journal, August 17, 1981, p. 23.

Kagan, R.A. *Regulatory justice*. New York: Russell Sage Foundation, 1978.

Lempert, R.O. Mobilizing private law: an introductory essay, *Law and Society Review*, 1976, *2*, 173–189.

Levi, E.H. *An introduction to legal reasoning*. Chicago: University of Chicago Press, 1948.

Nonet, P. *Administrative justice*. New York: Russell Sage Foundation, 1969.

Selznick, P. *Law, society, and industrial justice*. New York: Russell Sage Foundation, 1969.

Stewart, R.B., & Sunstein, C.R. Public programs and private rights. *Harvard Law Review*, 1982, *95*, 1193–1322.

Thompson, E.P. *Whigs and hunters*. New York: Pantheon, 1975.

Verba, S., & Nie, N. *Participation in America*. New York: Harper & Row, 1972.

Grievances, Claims, and Disputes: Assessing the Adversary Culture

Richard E. Miller
Austin Sarat

INTRODUCTION

What is the origin of disputing? How do disputes develop? At what rate are different problems transformed into disputes? These questions are rarely addressed (but see Felstiner *et al.*, 1981), despite the centrality of the study of disputes in the sociology of law and the growing body of empirical work about the disputing process (Abel, 1980: 813). The emphasis of the dispute processing perspective has been on the linkage between law and legal institutions and a broader array of dispute processing mechanisms. But this perspective has limited our understanding of disputing as a social process.

. . .

Disputes begin as *grievances*. A grievance is an individual's belief that he or she (or a group or organization) is entitled to a resource which someone else may grant or deny. People respond to such beliefs in various ways. They may, for example, choose to "lump it" so as to avoid potential conflict

"Grievances, Claims, and Disputes: Assessing the Adversary Culture," Richard Miller and Austin Sarat. *Law and Society Review*, Vol. 15, No. 3–4, 1981. Reprinted by permission of the Law and Society Association.

(Felstiner, 1974). They may redefine the problem and redirect blame elsewhere. They may register a *claim* to communicate their sense of entitlement to the most proximate source of redress, the party perceived to be responsible. As Nader and Todd (1978: 14) suggest,

> The grievance or preconflict stage refers to a circumstance or condition which one person...perceives to be unjust, and the grounds for resentment or complaint.... The grievance situation...may erupt into conflict, or it may wane. The path it will take is usually up to the offended party. His grievance may be escalated by confrontation; or escalation may be avoided by curtailing further social interaction....

Consumers, for example, make claims when they ask retailers to repair or replace defective goods. Claims can be rejected, accepted, or they can result in a compromise offer.

If the other party accepts the claim in full and actually delivers the resource in question in a routine manner ("Yes, we'll repair your new car; just bring it in"), there is no dispute. Outright rejection of a claim ("The car was not defective; it broke down because of your misuse") establishes an unambiguous dispute; there are now two (or more) parties with conflicting claims to the same resource. A compromise offer ("We'll supply the parts if you will pay for the labor") is a partial rejection of the claim, which initiates negotiation, however brief, and thus constitutes a dispute. A delayed reaction by the claimee construed by the claimant as resistance is considered to be a rejection of the claim. Encountering difficulty in obtaining satisfaction of an ostensibly accepted claim also creates a dispute. *A dispute exists when a claim based on a grievance is rejected either in whole or in part.* It becomes a civil legal dispute when it involves rights or resources which could be granted or denied by a court.

.   .   .

DISPUTING AND THE ADVERSARY SOCIETY

The manner and rate at which disputes are generated is sometimes taken as an indicator of societal "health." This view is most characteristic of the work of historians writing after World War II (see particularly Hofstadter, 1948; Hartz, 1955). They presented a picture of American society as a stable balance between conflict and calm, a society in which all disputes were resolved within a framework of consensus. Some may question the validity of that picture as a description of *any* period in American life (see Potter, 1971; Bell, 1976), but the experience of the last two decades has certainly undermined both the social basis upon which the balance of conflict and calm may have existed...and its viability as an ideology or a system of legitimizing beliefs.... We increasingly hear the voices of those who perceive and fear the growth of an "adversary society" (e.g., Rehnquist, 1978), a society of assertive, aggressive, rights-conscious, litigious people ready and eager to challenge

each other and those in authority (see Huntington, 1975; Nisbet, 1975, Kristol, 1979). Images of our allegedly unprecedented assertiveness, of the ingenious ways which we have found to fight each other, flow through the popular culture, from *New Yorker* cartoons about children threatening to sue their parents for forcing them to drink their milk to palimony suits against celebrities.

There is, of course, another view of contemporary American society, a view which suggests that we are, in fact, relatively uncontentious and even passive (see Steele, 1977: 675; Sarat, 1977: 448–454; Nader and Serber, 1976). Americans are said to be reluctant to admit that their lives are troubled and conditioned to accept circumstances and treatment which are far from ideal.... Since our institutions respond slowly, inefficiently, and reluctantly, we learn not to complain, not to pursue our grievances or claim our rights. Even when we do, we find that appropriate institutions do not exist (Nader, 1980). As our society becomes ever more complex and expansive, it becomes easier to avoid conflict or to ignore it merely by moving on (Felstiner, 1974). People unable or unwilling to assert their rights or defend their interests may be easily victimized by self-interested organizations seeking to perpetuate a social and economic status quo (Nader and Serber, 1976). Proponents of this view typically question the adequacy of existing political, social, and economic arrangements to achieve justice.

It is ultimately both an empirical question and a matter of definition as to whether ours is a society of rights consciousness and conflict, or one of acquiescence and equilibrium. Arguments about the level and consequences of conflict in American society, to the extent that they are based on data at all, are often rooted in comparative analyses (e.g. Ehrmann, 1976) or cyclical interpretations of history (Potter, 1971). But there is another approach which might be employed to describe and assess levels of conflict in the United States. Lempert (1978: 98, 135) has suggested that the occurrence of particular types of conflict can be measured against a pre-established baseline. The baseline might be a measure of the number of transactions of a particular type, the number which result in injury, or the number which result in grievances and the making of claims. For example, the level of conflict about the quality of medical care might be measured by comparing the quantity of medical service—e.g., visits to doctors—to the amount of conflict generated by such services—e.g., the number of medical malpractice suits. Malpractice suits might also be compared to some measure of medical ineptitude such as rates of unnecessary or unsuccessful surgery. The baseline approach seeks to identify the realization of a social condition—e.g., conflict—against its potential.

We employ such an approach to describe and analyze the generation of disputes in American society. This paper presents a conceptual map of the process of dispute generation and develops empirical estimates of the incidence of grievances, claims, and disputes.... The data are neither fully comprehensive[1] nor the most appropriate for testing the adversary society argument, but they are relevant to, and illustrative of, the central themes in that argument.

SAMPLE AND METHODOLOGY

Data for this article are derived from a telephone survey of households conducted as part of the Civil Litigation Research Project.... That project was designed to explore the contribution of courts to civil dispute processing and to describe and explain patterns of investment in disputing and dispute processing. The survey was administered in January, 1980, to approximately 1,000 randomly selected households in each of five federal judicial districts: South Carolina, Eastern Pennsylvania, Eastern Wisconsin, New Mexico, and Central California.

The survey sought to identify the occurrence in the general population of civil disputes of the type that might be brought to the courts or nonjudicial alternatives. Our approach was to focus on three stages of the

[1] To forestall misinterpretation of the data obtained from our Household Screening Survey, it is appropriate to set forth clearly and openly what is not claimed or intended. The survey *does not constitute a definitive estimate of households' incidence rates of all grievances, claims, and disputes*, for at least the following reasons:

[a] The role of the survey in the CLRP's research design was to identify civil legal disputes which could be processed bilaterally and which involved a household member acting as a private individual in a nonbusiness capacity. (These disputes were the subject of lengthy followup interviews, which were also administered to other disputants sampled from court records and nonjudicial third-party institutions.) Therefore, the survey did not cover a definitive list of possible problem areas for individuals and ignored the problems of groups, organizations, or other collectivities. Restricting our focus to civil legal disputes eliminated many kinds of troublesome experiences. Intra-household conflicts were ignored; few such conflicts (at least at the present time) are resolved by the courts. Problems with business or rental property, difficulties in collecting fees for professional services, and problems encountered on behalf of businesses, professions, or organizations generally, were excluded by the restriction to private, non-business problems.

[b] Disputes in which courts *must* play some role, such as suits for divorce or estate settlements, were excluded because they could not be bilateral disputes.

[c] The survey was conducted in five judicial districts. Even though these districts were chosen for their geographic and demographic diversity, they are not a random sample of the nation.

[d] Additional biases include ignoring households and individuals without telephones and relying on one person to report the experiences of all in the household.

disputing process: grievances, claims, and disputes. In the grievance stage an injurious experience is perceived as a problem, and some other party is blamed for it. While recognition of problems and attribution of causes are in theory separate activities, we are unable, because of our retrospective research design, to treat them as such. Respondents were asked whether anyone in their household had experienced one or more of a long list of problems within the past three years and, if so, about how that problem was handled. Where possible the interviewer tried to establish whether a household was significantly *at risk* of a particular type of grievance.[2] In addition, for most problems they were asked whether that problem involved $1,000 or more. This threshold served as an operational definition of the kind of "middle-range" disputes which were the exclusive preoccupation of the Civil Litigation Research Project.

About 40 percent of households sampled reported at least one grievance for which the time frame and amount at issue criteria were met. Those who reported a grievance were asked whether they had sought redress from the allegedly offending party, indicating that the claims stage had been reached. Finally, we inquired about the result of that claim. Did the parties reach an agreement? If so, was there any difficulty involved? An unre-

solved claim or one resolved only after initial resistance was overcome was recorded as a dispute.

Supplementary questions sought information about the timing, nature, and results of reported disputes. Respondents were also asked whether either side had used a lawyer or had sought assistance from some other third party. They were asked if they had any prior relationship with the opposing party and, if so, whether that relationship had been changed by the dispute.

.   .   .

DESCRIBING THE STRUCTURE OF CONFLICT: GRIEVING, CLAIMING, AND DISPUTING

Grieving

Disputes emerge out of grievances. Consequently we look first to the incidence of grievances to establish the baseline potential for disputes. There is, however, a conceptual problem. Grievances are composed of concrete events or circumstances which are relatively objective, but they are also composed of subjective perceptions, definitions, and beliefs that an event or circumstance is unwarranted or inappropriate. . . . Individuals may react differently to the same experience. One buyer of a defective good may find it unacceptable and remediable; another may regard the bad purchase as "inevitable" and "lump it" or write it off to experience. According to our definition, the first individual has a grievance; the second does not. Grievance rates reflect both the occurrence of certain events and a willingness by the participants to label those events in a particular way. Care must be taken to avoid confusion between the expressed rate of grievances among our survey respondents (as well as the claims and dispute rates which flow from it) and the degree of injury which they may be said to have suffered.

---

[2] Households differ in both degree and type of exposure to risks of grievances, depending upon the amount and the kinds of interaction they have with the outside world. People who do not rent, for example, cannot have landlord-tenant problems: they are not in a relationship from which such problems could arise. The more a person drives a car, the higher the risk of an auto accident, all else being equal. We ascertained the following kinds of risks: owning real property, owning a home built within the last five years, holding a mortgage, having recent home repair work, renting a home or apartment, being divorced, and owning property jointly with someone outside the household.

The survey began by asking about the occurrence of 33 types of problems. These have been aggregated into nine general categories.... The first line in Table 1 shows the percentage of households reporting grievances of each type.[3] Slightly over 40 percent of the households in our sample had some middle-range grievance within the three-year period surveyed; approximately 20 percent reported two or more different grievances. We cannot say whether this number is high or low, since there is no baseline of potential grievance-generating events or relationships against which to compare that number. However, two things can be said. First, experiencing significant grievances is by no means a rare or unusual event. Smaller grievances no doubt occur more often, larger ones less frequently. Second, the incidence of middle-range grievances provides a substantial potential for conflict.

The range of reported grievance experience varies considerably. On the low end, 6.7 percent of the households surveyed reported a grievance arising out of the payment or collection of debts, while 17.1 percent of the households which rented had experienced grievances in dealing with landlords. The range and distribution of grievances reported in Table 2 is quite similar to what has been found in other studies, both in the United States and abroad (cf. Curran, 1977; Sykes, 1969; Abel-Smith et al., 1973; Cass and Sackville, 1975). Grievances involving racial, sexual, age, or other discrimination in employment, education, or housing were reported by 14 percent of the households. It is likely that the level of discrimination grievances has risen in recent years as a result of increased public awareness and sensitivity to this type of problem, although we cannot confirm this with longitudinal data. At the same time, public attention to the problem of discrimination may have produced a decline in instances of discriminatory behavior. Here again we recognize the problematic relationship between experience and perception in the generation of grievances and the evaluation of grievance rates.[4]

Claiming

Given the perception that some event or circumstance is unacceptable and remediable, we can ask how assertive those who experience grievances are in seeking a remedy. Possible responses, as previously mentioned, range from avoidance (Felstiner,

---

[3] The household was the aggrieved party in most cases for several reasons. Fully twenty-two of the thirty-three specific problems for which we probed were household grievances by their nature; eight could involve a grievance both of and against the household; and three involved grievances against the household. This apparent bias largely reflects our focus on disputes arising from members acting in a private non-business capacity. It also reflects our methodological expectation that seems to have been accurate. For example, 2.8 percent of the households reported some property damage or personal injury other than auto accidents "through the fault of someone else" which involved over $1,000. In contrast, only 0.5 percent reported that a household member had "been accused of injuring anyone or of damaging someone else's property, either accidentally or on purpose."

[4] One reason for this relatively high grievance rate may be that the survey was careful to remind respondents both of a number of potentially illegal discriminatory grounds ("...race, sex, age, handicaps, union membership") and of discriminatory actions ("Have you or anyone in your household been denied a job or promotion or lost a job because of discrimination? ...had any problems with working conditions or harassment, or being paid less?...had any other employment problem because of discrimination? ...any problem with discrimination in schooling or education? ...in buying or renting housing? ...any other problems of discrimination because of race, sex, age or anything else?").

TABLE 1
Grievances, Claims, and Outcomes: Rates by Type of Problem[a]

	All Grievances		Torts		Consumer		Debt		Discrimination		Property		Government		Post-Divorce		Landlord	
Grievances[b] (Percents of Households)	41.6%	(5147)	15.6%	(5147)	8.9%	(5147)	6.7%	(5147)	14.0%	(5147)	7.2%	(3798)[c]	9.1%	(5147)	10.9%	(1238)[c]	17.1%	(2293)[c]
Claims (Percents of Terminated Grievances)	71.8	(2491)	85.7	(559)	87.3	(303)	94.6	(151)	29.4	(595)	79.9	(193)	84.9	(240)	87.9	(51)	87.2	(307)
Disputes: (Percents of Claims)																		
a. No Agreement	32.0		2.6		37.1		23.9		58.0		32.1		40.7		37.7		55.0	
b. Agreement After Difficulty	30.6		20.9		37.9		60.6		15.5		21.8		41.4		49.3		26.7	
c. Dispute	62.6	(1768)	23.5	(467)	75.0	(263)	84.5	(142)	73.5	(174)	53.9	(154)	82.1	(203)	87.0	(45)	81.7	(267)
Lawyer Use[d] (Percent of Disputes)	23.0	(1100)	57.9	(107)	20.3	(197)	19.2	(120)	13.3	(128)	19.0	(84)	12.3	(163)	76.9	(39)	14.7	(218)
Court Filing[d] (Percent of Disputes)	11.2	(1093)	18.7	(107)	3.0	(197)	7.6	(119)	3.9	(128)	13.4	(82)	11.9	(159)	59.0	(39)	7.3	(218)
Success of Claims (Percent of Claims)																		
a. No Agreement (0)	32.0		2.6		37.1		23.9		58.0		32.1		40.7		37.7		55.0	
b. Compromise (1)	34.2		85.4		15.2		23.5		11.3		9.7		18.3		35.5		10.3	
c. Obtained Whole Claim (2)	33.8		11.9		47.7		52.6		30.7		58.3		41.0		26.8		34.6	
	100.0		100.0		100.0		100.0		100.0		100.0		100.0		100.0		100.0	
d. Success Scale Mean[e]	1.02	(1782)	1.09	(479)	1.11	(265)	1.29	(142)	0.73	(174)	1.26	(154)	1.00	(203)	0.89	(45)	0.80	(267)

[a] Observations were weighted by the population of each judicial district so that the five samples could be combined. Weights were calculated to preserve the actual number of observations. Numbers in parentheses are the total upon which the reported proportions are based. The miscellaneous "other" category (see Appendix 1) is included in the "all grievances" column but omitted as a separate item from this and subsequent tables (3.5 percent of households reported an "other" grievance).

[b] Proportions are of households reporting one or more grievances of each type.

[c] These are proportions and numbers of households at risk. Households at risk of property problems are those owning their own home, apartment, or land within the three-year period (73.8 percent of all households). Households at risk of post-divorce problems were the 24.0 percent of all households which had a divorced member. The 44.2 percent of households which rented within the three years were at risk of landlord problems.

[d] The number in these rows differ slightly due to missing data.

[e] The success of claims was scaled 0, 1, or 2: 0 if no agreement was reached, 1 if the agreement was a compromise, and 2 if the entire claim was met.

57

1974), through repair without direct confrontation, registering a claim, to a demand for monetary compensation. Unless a claim is made, a dispute cannot occur. Other responses, such as avoidance, may be accompanied by feelings of bitterness or resentment which could lead to later conflict.

The second line of Table 1 shows that claiming is a frequent response to middle-range grievances. Apart from discrimination problems, there is considerable uniformity in behavior across problem types. The range of claiming fluctuates between 79.9 percent (real property) and 94.6 percent (debts). While most of the problems are substantial, . . . there is, nevertheless, considerable variation between problem types in stakes, situations, and the configuration of the parties. This variation makes the uniformly high claiming rates all the more significant.

The one exception to this pattern is found among discrimination grievants, of whom only 29.4 percent made a claim. This finding is not entirely surprising. Curran reports virtually the same proportion of job discrimination grievants "taking some action" (1977: 137). There are several explanations for this anomaly. First, it may be that remedies for discrimination are less available and accessible than those for other types of problems. The evidence is mixed. Remedial devices such as equal opportunity commissions are not recent developments. . . . Indeed, a review of specialized nonjudicial dispute processing agencies in the five geographic areas covered by our survey found that for discrimination problems there are "many alternatives available with low access costs". . . . The assertion that a lack of available mechanisms for processing rejected claims may explain many cases where grievances are lumped or endured (Nader, 1980) is challenged by this finding. But, availability is not accessibility;

just because mechanisms exist does not mean that they are, in fact, attractive to, or usable by, people seeking redress. This seems especially true in the discrimination area where available mechanisms have been found to be inefficient and ineffective (Crowe, 1978).

Perhaps people do not make claims unless they feel confident that something can be done should the claim be accepted. Perhaps a lack of assertiveness has more to do with the substance of the problem itself. In discrimination situations it seems easier for those who believe that they have been unfairly denied a job or home just to keep on looking. Securing a job or home is likely to be much more pressing and important than filing a claim for something which is made undesirable by the very act that generates the grievance. "I need a job, and who would want to work there anyway" would not be an inexplicable response. For this reason, the survey asked whether discrimination grievants who made no claim had nonetheless registered a complaint without asking for anything, and we found that an additional 26.6 percent had done so.

Furthermore, there may be some stigma attached to the grievance itself or to the act of assertion. Victims, for example, may blame themselves for the unfair treatment. In discrimination grievances, especially, victory may turn into defeat. Those who are assertive, even if vindicated, are branded as troublemakers. Furthermore, grievants may be uncertain about the fit between their own perceptions and definitions of grievances and those embodied in statutes or otherwise recognized in their community. Indeed, both the law and popular expectations in this area of relatively new rights appear unsettled. Many who experience discrimination problems are, as a result, uncertain whether their grievance constitutes a sustainable claim.

Whatever the explanation for the low

claiming rate for discrimination problems, what remains striking in our data is uniformity, not variation. Our data indicate the existence of a widespread readiness to seek redress of substantial injuries. Contrary to what some believe, Americans are assertive when the stakes are substantial—able and willing to seek redress from wrongdoers.

The Incidence of Disputes

When a claim is made, the allegedly offending party may accept responsibility and accede to the demand for redress. If this happens there is no dispute. Claims are made and promptly satisfied. But resistance may be engendered, responsibility denied. Even if responsibility is accepted, unacceptable levels of redress may be offered. Resistance to accepting responsibility or providing redress establishes adversarial interests.

Table 1 reveals that among the 1768 claims made by respondents experiencing grievances almost two-thirds (62.6 percent) were rejected or resisted and thus resulted in disputes. These disputed claims are almost equally divided between those which were completely rejected and produced no agreement—32 percent of all claims (Table 1, Row 3a)—and those in which initial resistance gave way to some agreement about responsibility and remedy—30.6 percent (Row 3b). The dispute rate of 62.6 percent is subject to many interpretations. We do not have trend data. (Indeed, to our knowledge, ours is the first attempt to collect and report data of this kind.) It seems, however, safe to say that among middle-range grievances, adversarial relations result in a substantial majority of situations in which claims are made. Whether this is too high or too low, conducive to a healthy social life or deleterious in and of itself, we leave for others to decide.

While problem-specific variation is some-what greater in disputing than in claiming, here again we are struck by the patterned uniformity among six of the eight problems. Putting aside torts and property matters, the incidence of disputing varied only from a low of 73 percent in discrimination claims to a high of 87 percent in those arising in response to post-divorce problems, with over 80 percent of claims to landlords, former spouses, debtors, creditors, or government agencies leading to disputes. Tort claims are least likely to be contested. This reflects, we believe, a highly institutionalized and routinized system of remedies provided by insurance companies, and the well-established customary and legal principles governing behavior in this area.

The Role of Lawyers and Courts

The language of rights and remedies is preeminently the language of law. One might logically ask where, in all of this, the law and legal institutions play a role. There is relatively little empirical work on the role of lawyers and courts in disputing (see Curran, 1977; Mayhew and Reiss, 1969; Friedman and Percival, 1976; Sarat and Grossman, 1975; McIntosh, 1981). An assessment of the role of law, legal institutions, and legal services in the development of, or response to, conflict requires us to confront the problem of baselines. We agree with Lempert's (1978: 95) comments about the methodology needed for evaluating the dispute resolution role of courts, and would extend his suggestion to the role of lawyers as well.

> A fundamental problem is to develop a measure of judicial involvement in community dispute settlement that can vary over time.... For most purposes, the base should relate to the number of occasions on which the court might be asked to settle disputes.

The ideal base is probably the number of cognizable disputes arising within a court's jurisdiction. At any point in time, the degree to which a court is functioning as a community dispute settler could be measured by the percentage of such disputes brought to it for resolution. Unfortunately, information on disputes that are not officially processed is seldom available over time.

Our survey covers only one point in time, but we are able to estimate the rates at which lawyers and courts are used in relation to the number of reported disputes in our sample. Thus we can provide an empirical estimate of the rate of direct participation of lawyers and courts in these middle-range disputes.[5]

Examining Table 1 (Row 4), we find that relatively few disputants use a lawyer's services at all. Lawyers were used by less than one-fourth of those engaged in the disputes we studied. There are, however, two significant exceptions to the pattern. The role of lawyers is much more pronounced in post-divorce and tort problems.... In the former, the involvement of lawyers is a function of the fact that many of these problems, e.g., adjustment in visitation arrangements or in alimony, *require* court action. In the latter, the contingent fee system facilitates and encourages lawyer use.

Few disputants (11.2 percent) report taking their dispute to court. Excluding post-divorce disputes, where court action is often required, that number is approximately 9 percent. These findings do not mean that courts or lawyers play a trivial role in middle-range disputes. Claims are made,

[5] We recognize, of course, that lawyers and courts do more than process such disputes; much of their activity is administrative or aimed at dispute prevention. We also recognize that the role of lawyers and courts may be very different in small or large disputes than it is in the area of middle-range disputes. Nevertheless, our data provide a first, albeit tentative and limited, overview of their role in those disputes.

avoided, or processed at least in part according to each party's understanding of its own legal position and that of its opponent; that understanding reflects both the advice that lawyers provide and the rights and remedies which courts have in the past recognized or imposed....

The Success of Claims

Overall, 68 percent of those who made a claim eventually obtained part or all of what they originally sought. This is roughly comparable to the results of previous research.... Those who claim may do so because they are confident their claims are justified. Indeed, the modal pattern among middle-range grievances is for claims to be made, disputes to result, and agreements to be reached. Claimants who reached an agreement after some difficulty—and so had disputes—were more successful than claimants reporting no difficulty reaching an agreement. Fully two-thirds (66.1 percent) of the first group obtained their whole claim, while only a little over one-third (39.7 percent) of the second got all they asked for. Conflicts, disputes, and difficulties are often engendered by the desire for, and are necessary in order to obtain, complete satisfaction.

Some important specific variations do, of course, show up in the results of claims. Virtually no tort claimants (26 percent) were unable to reach an agreement, but note that, of the 97.3 percent of tort claimants recovering something, very few obtained all of their original claim. One might expect tort claims to be inflated for negotiating purposes, an expectation reinforced by the low proportion reporting any difficulty reaching an agreement. This pattern also suggests an acceptance by claimants of insurance companies' valuations of damage, perhaps reflecting a reluctance to dispute with such organizations.

Court Filings	50
Lawyers	103
Disputes	449
Claims	718
Grievances	1000

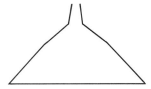

FIGURE 1A.   A Dispute Pyramid: The General Pattern (No. per 1000 Grievances)

	Tort	Discrimination	Post-Divorce
Court Filings	38	8	451
Lawyers	116	29	588
Disputes	201	216	765
Claims	857	294	879
Grievances	1000	1000	1000

Tort	Discrimination	Post-Divorce

... Courts
... Lawyers
... Disputes
... Claims
... Grievances

FIGURE 1B.   Dispute Pyramids: Three Deviant Patterns (No. per 1000 Grievances)

While most tort claims resulted in a compromise agreement, other claims were much more likely to have all-or-nothing outcomes. To some extent this reflects the nature of many problems. For example, property disputes involving permission to build are not amenable to compromise. Some opposing parties were unlikely to offer anything: more than half of all discrimination (58.0 percent) and tenant (55.0 percent) claimants failed to obtain any redress at all. Such claimants are apparently in a particularly weak bargaining position and also may lack effective recourse to any third-party remedy system. We shall take up this point again.

Summary

We can visualize the process of dispute generation through the metaphor of a pyramid (see Figure 1A). At the base are grievances, and the width of the pyramid shows the proportions that make the successive transitions to claims, disputes, lawyer use, and litigation. Figure 1B presents three contrasting patterns—the disputing pyramids for torts, post-divorce, and discrimination grievances.

Torts show a clear pattern. Most of those with grievances make claims (85.7 percent), and most claims are not formally resisted (76.5 percent result in immediate agreement). As a result, disputes are relatively rare (23.5 percent of claims). Where they occur, however, lawyers are available, accessible, and are, in fact, often employed (57.9 percent). Moreover, the same can be said for the employment of courts (at least in comparison with other problems). The overall picture is of a remedy system that minimizes formal conflict but uses the courts when necessary in those relatively rare cases in which conflict is unavoidable.

The pattern for discrimination grievances is quite different. Seven of ten grievants make no claim for redress. Those who do are very likely to have their claim resisted, and most claimants receive nothing. Only a little more than one in ten disputants is aided by a lawyer, and only four in a hundred disputes lead to litigation. The impression is one of perceived rights which are rarely fully asserted. When they are, they are strongly resisted and pursued without much assistance from lawyers or courts. Of course, we do not know how many of these or any other grievances would be found meritorious in a court of law. Nonetheless, as perceived grievances, they are a source of underlying tension and potential social conflict.

Post-divorce problems engender high rates of grievances, claims, and disputes, and are characterized by frequent use of lawyers and courts. As a result, almost half of all grievances lead to court involvement. While the court's activity in many, possibly most, of these cases is more administrative than adjudicative, this is, at least formally, the most disputatious and litigious grievance type we have measured.

Dispute pyramids could be drawn for the other types of problems, but they would all be quite similar: high rates of claims (80 to 95 percent of grievances), high rates of disputes (75 to 85 percent of claims), fairly low proportions using a lawyer (10 to 20 percent of disputants), and low litigation rates (3 to 5 percent of disputants). Indeed, the most striking finding in these descriptive data is again the general uniformity of rates at each stage of the disputing process across very different types of middle-range grievances.

. . .

REFERENCES

Abel, Richard L. (1980) "Redirecting Social Studies of Law," 14 *Law & Society Review* 805.

Abel-Smith, Brian, Michael Zander, and Rosiland Brooke (1973) *Legal Problems and the Citizen: A Study in Three London Boroughs*. London: Heinemann.

Bell, Daniel (1976) *The Cultural Contradictions of Capitalism*. New York: Basic Books.

Cass, Michael and Ronald Sackville (1975) *Legal Needs of the Poor*. Canberra: Australian Government Publishing Service.

Crowe, Patricia Ward (1978) "Complainant Reactions to the Massachusetts Commission Against Discrimination," 12 *Law & Society Review* 217.

Curran, Barbara A. (1977) *The Legal Needs of the Public: The Final Report of a National Survey*. Chicago: American Bar Foundation.

Ehrmann, Henry (1976) *Comparative Legal Cultures*. Englewood Cliffs, NJ: Prentice-Hall.

Felstiner, William L. F. (1974) "Influences of Social Organization on Dispute Processing," 9 *Law & Society Review* 63.

Felstiner, William L. F., Richard L. Abel, and Austin Sarat (1981) "The Emergence and Transformation of Disputes: Naming, Blaming, Claiming. . . ," 15 *Law & Society Review* 631.

Friedman, Lawrence M. and Robert V. Percival (1976) "A Tale of Two Courts: Litigation in Alameda and San Benito Counties," 10 *Law & Society Review* 267.

Hartz, Louis (1955) *The Liberal Tradition in America*. New York: Harcourt, Brace.

Hofstadter, Richard (1948) *The American Political Tradition*. New York: Alfred A. Knopf.

Huntington, Samuel (1975) "The Democratic Distemper," 41 *Public Interest* 9.

Kristol, Irving (1979) "The Adversary Culture of Intellectuals," in S. M. Lipset (ed.), *The Third Century*. Stanford: Hoover Institution Press.

Lempert, Richard O. (1978) "More Tales of Two Courts: Exploring Changes in the 'Dispute Settlement Function' of Trial Courts," 13 *Law & Society Review* 91.

Mayhew, Leon H. and Albert J. Reiss, Jr. (1969) "The Social Organization of Legal Contacts," 34 *American Sociological Review* 309.

McIntosh, Wayne (1981) "150 Years of Litigation and Dispute Settlement," 15 *Law & Society Review* 823.

Nader, Laura (1980) (ed.) *No Access to Law: Alternatives to the American Judicial System*. New York: Academic Books.

Nader, Laura and David Serber (1976) "Law and the Distribution of Power," in L. Coser and O. Larsen (eds.), *The Uses of Controversy in Sociology*. New York: Free Press.

Nader, Laura and Harry F. Todd, Jr. (eds.) (1978) *The Disputing Process: Law in Ten Societies*. New York: Columbia University Press.

Nisbet, Robert (1975) *The Twilight of Authority*. New York: Oxford University Press.

Potter, David (1971) "Changing Patterns of Social Cohesion and the Crisis of Law Under a System of Government by Consent," in E. Rostow (ed.), *Is Law Dead?* New York: Simon and Schuster.

Rehnquist, William (1978) "The Adversary Society," mimeo, text of a speech at the University of Miami.

Sarat, Austin (1977) "Studying American Legal Culture: An Assessment of Survey Evidence," 11 *Law & Society Review* 427.

Sarat, Austin and Joel B. Grossman (1975) "Courts and Conflict Resolution: Problems in the Mobilization of Adjudication," 69 *American Political Science Review* 1200.

Steele, Eric H. (1977) "Two Approaches to Contemporary Dispute Behavior and Consumer Problems," 11 *Law & Society Review* 667.

Sykes, Gresham M. (1969) "Legal Needs of the Poor in the City of Denver," 4 *Law & Society Review* 255.

The Oven Bird's Song: Insiders, Outsiders, and Personal Injuries in an American Community

David M. Engel

INTRODUCTION

Although it is generally acknowledged that law is a vital part of culture and of the social order, there are times when the invocation of formal law is viewed as an *anti*-social act and as a contravention of established cultural norms. Criticism of what is seen as an overuse of law and legal institutions often reveals less about the quantity of litigation at any given time than about the interests being asserted or protected through litigation and the kinds of individuals or groups involved in cases that the courts are asked to resolve. Periodic concerns over litigation as a "problem" in particular societies or historical eras can thus draw our attention to important underlying conflicts in cultural values and changes or tensions in the structure of social relationships.

In our own society at present, perhaps no category of litigation has produced greater public criticism than personal injuries. The popular culture is full of tales of feigned or exaggerated physical harms, of spurious whiplash suits, ambulance-chasing lawyers,

"The Oven Bird's Song: Insiders, Outsiders, and Personal Injuries in an American Commuity," David M. Engel. *Law and Society Review*, Vol. 18, No. 4, 1984. Reprinted by permission of the Law and Society Association.

and exorbitant claims for compensation. . . .

To the mind agitated by such concerns, Sander County (a pseudonym) appears to offer a quiet refuge. In this small, predominantly rural county in Illinois, personal injury litigation rates were low in comparison to other major categories of litigation and were apparently somewhat lower than the personal injury rates in other locations as well. Yet Sander County residents displayed a deep concern with and an aversion toward this particular form of "litigious behavior" despite its rarity in their community.

Those who sought to enforce personal injury claims in Sander County were characterized by their fellow residents as "very greedy," as "quick to sue," as "people looking for the easy buck," and as those who just "naturally sue and try to get something [for] . . . life's little accidents." One minister describing the local scene told me, "Everybody's going to court. That's the thing to do, because a lot of people see a chance to make money." A social worker, speaking of local perceptions of personal injury litigation, particularly among the older residents of Sander County, observed: "Someone sues every time you turn around. Sue happy, you hear them say. Sue happy." Personal injury plaintiffs were viewed in Sander County as people who made waves and as troublemakers. Even members of the community who occupied positions of prestige or respect could not escape criticism if they brought personal injury cases to court. When a minister filed a personal injury suit in Sander County after having slipped and fallen at a school, there were, in the words of one local observer:

> [A] lot of people who are resentful for it, because...he chose to sue. There's been, you know, not hard feelings, just some strange intangible things....

How can one explain these troubled perceptions of personal injury litigation in a community where personal injury actions were in fact so seldom brought? The answer lies partly in culturally-conditioned ideas of what constitutes an injury and how conflicts over injuries should be handled. The answer is also found in changes that were occurring in the social structure of Sander County at the time of this study and in challenges to the traditional order that were being raised by newly arrived "outsiders." The local trial court was potentially an important battleground in the clash of cultures, for it could be called on to recognize claims that traditional norms stigmatized in the strongest possible terms.

.   .   .

INJURIES AND INDIVIDUALISM

For many of the residents of Sander County, exposure to the risk of physical injury was simply an accepted part of life. In a primarily agricultural community, which depended on hard physical work and the use of dangerous implements and machinery, such risks were unavoidable. Farmers in Sander County told many stories of terrible injuries caused by hazardous farming equipment, vehicles of different kinds, and other dangers that were

associated with their means of obtaining a livelihood. There was a feeling among many in Sander County—particularly among those from a farming background—that injuries were an ever-present possibility, although prudent persons could protect themselves much of the time by taking proper precautions.

It would be accurate to characterize the traditional values associated with personal injuries in Sander County as individualistic, but individualism may be of at least two types. A rights-oriented individualism is consistent with an aggressive demand for compensation (or other remedies) when important interests are perceived to have been violated. By contrast, an individualism emphasizing self-sufficiency and personal responsibility rather than rights is consistent with the expectation that people should ordinarily provide their own protection against injuries and should personally absorb the consequences of harms they fail to ward off.

It is not clear why the brand of individualism that developed over the years in Sander County emphasized self-sufficiency rather than rights and remedies, but with respect to personal injuries at least, there can be no doubt that this had occurred. If the values associated with this form of individualism originated in an earlier face-to-face community dominated by economically self-sufficient farmers and merchants, they remained vitally important to many of the long-time Sander County residents even at the time of this study. For them, injuries were viewed in relation to the victims, their fate, and their ability to protect themselves. Injuries were not viewed in terms of conflict or potential conflict between victims and other persons, nor was there much sympathy for those who sought to characterize the situation in such terms. To the traditional individualists of Sander County, transforming a personal injury into a claim against someone else was an attempt to escape responsibility for one's own actions. The psychology of contributory negligence and assumption of risk had deep roots in the local culture. The critical fact of personal injuries in most cases was that the victims probably could have prevented them if they had been more careful, even if others were to some degree at fault. This fact alone is an important reason why it was considered inappropriate for injured persons to attempt to transform their misfortune into a demand for compensation or to view it as an occasion for interpersonal conflict.

Attitudes toward money also help explain the feelings of long-time residents of Sander County toward personal injury claimants. While there might be sympathy for those who suffered such injuries, it was considered highly improper to try to "cash in" on them through claims for damages. Money was viewed as something one acquired through long hours of hard work, not by exhibiting one's misfortunes to a judge or jury or other third party, even when the injuries were clearly caused by the wrongful behavior of another. Such attitudes were reinforced by the pervasive sense of living in what had long been a small and close-knit community. In such a community, potential plaintiffs and defendants are likely to know each other, at least by reputation, or to have acquaintances in common. It is probable that they will interact in the future, if not directly then through friends and relatives. In these circumstances it is, at best, awkward to sue or otherwise assert a claim. In addition, in a small community one cannot hide the fact of a suit for damages, and the disapproving attitudes of others are likely to be keenly felt. Thus, I was frequently assured that local residents who were mindful of community pressures generally reacted to cases of personal injury, even those that might give rise to liability in tort, in a "level-headed" and

"realistic" way. By this it was meant that they would not sue or even, in most cases, demand compensation extrajudicially from anyone except, perhaps, their own insurance companies.

Others had so internalized this value system that they followed its dictates even when community pressures did not exist. A doctor told me that one of his patients was seriously burned during a trip out of state when an airline stewardess spilled hot coffee on her legs, causing permanent discoloration of her skin. This woman refused to contact a lawyer and instead settled directly with the airline for medical expenses and the cost of the one-week vacation she had missed. Regarding the possibility of taking formal legal action to seek a more substantial award, she said simply, "We don't do that." This same attitude may help to explain the apparent reluctance of local residents to assert claims against other potential defendants from outside Sander County, such as negligent drivers or businesses or manufacturers.

Thus, if we consider the range of traditional responses to personal injuries in Sander County, we find, first of all, a great deal of self-reliant behavior. Injured persons typically responded to injuries without taking any overt action, either because they did not view the problem in terms of a claim against or conflict with another person or because membership in a small, close-knit community inhibited them from asserting a claim that would be socially disapproved. Some sought compensation through direct discussions with the other party, but such behavior was considered atypical. When sympathy or advice was sought, many turned to friends, neighbors, relatives, and physicians. The County Health Department, the mayor, and city council representatives also reported that injured persons occasionally sought them out, particularly when the injuries were caused by hazards that might endanger others. In such cases, the goal was generally to see the hazard removed for the benefit of the public rather than to seek compensation or otherwise advance personal interests.

.   .   .

LAWYERS AND LOCAL VALUES

Sander County attorneys reported that personal injury cases came to them with some regularity, although they also felt that many injury victims never consulted an attorney but settled directly with insurance companies for less than they should have received. When these attorneys were consulted, it was by people who, in the opinion of the attorneys, had real, nonfrivolous grievances, but the result was seldom formal legal action. Most personal injury cases were resolved, as they are elsewhere (Ross, 1970), through informal negotiation. Formal judicial procedures were initiated primarily to prod the other side to negotiate seriously or when it became necessary to preserve a claim before it would be barred by the statute of limitations. The negotiating process was, of course, strongly influenced by the parties' shared knowledge of likely juror reaction if the case actually went to trial. Thus, plaintiffs found negotiated settlements relatively attractive even when the terms were not particularly favorable.

But expectations regarding the outcome of litigation were probably not the only reason that members of the local bar so seldom filed personal injury cases. To some extent Sander County lawyers, many of whom were born and raised in the area, shared the local tendency to censure those who aggressively asserted personal injury claims. One attorney, for example, described client attitudes toward injury claims in the following terms: "A lot of people are more conducive to

settlement here just because they're attempting to be fair as opposed to making a fast buck." Yet this same attorney admitted that informal settlements were often for small amounts of money and were usually limited to medical expenses, without any "general" damages whatever. His characterization of such outcomes as "fair" suggests an internalization of local values even on the part of those whose professional role it was to assert claims on behalf of tort plaintiffs.

The local bar was widely perceived as inhospitable to personal injury claimants, not only because there were few tort specialists but because Sander County lawyers were seen as closely linked to the kinds of individuals and businesses against whom tort actions were typically brought. Although plaintiffs hired Sander County attorneys in 72.5 percent of all non-tort actions filed locally in which plaintiffs were represented by counsel, they did so in only 12.5 percent of the tort cases. One lawyer, who was frequently consulted by potential tort plaintiffs, lived across the county line in a small town outside of Sander County. He told me, "I get a lot of cases where people just don't want to be involved with the, they perceive it to be the hierarchy of Sander County. . . . I'm not part of the establishment."

Thus, even from the perspective of insurance company personnel and attorneys, who were most likely to witness the entry of personal injury cases into the formal legal system in Sander County, it is clear that the local culture tended in many ways to deter litigation. And when personal injury cases were formally filed, it usually was no more than another step in an ongoing negotiation process.

Why was the litigation of personal injury cases in Sander County subjected to disapproval so pervasive that it inhibited the assertion of claims at all stages, from the moment injuries occurred and were perceived to the time parties stood at the very threshold of the formal legal system? The answer, I shall argue, lies partly in the role of the Sander County Court in a changing social system and partly in the nature of the personal injury claim itself.

THE USE OF THE COURT

In the recent literature on dispute processing and conflict resolution, various typologies of conflict-handling forums and procedures have been proposed. Such typologies usually include courts, arbitrators, mediators, and ombudsmen, as well as two-party and one-party procedures such as negotiation, self-help, avoidance, and "lumping it" (see, e.g., typologies in Abel, 1973; Felstiner, 1974; Steele, 1975; Nader and Todd, 1978; Black and Baumgartner, 1983; Galanter, 1983). Analyses of these alternative approaches incorporate a number of variables that critically affect the ways in which conflict is handled and transformed. Such variables include, among others, procedural formality, the power and authority of the intervenor, the coerciveness of the proceedings, the range and severity of outcomes, role differentiation and specialization of third parties and advocates, cost factors, time required, the scope of the inquiry, language specialization, and the quality of the evidence that will be heard. When variables such as these are used to analyze various approaches to conflict resolution, the result is typically a continuum ranging from the most formal, specialized, functionally differentiated, and costly approaches to the most informal, accessible, undifferentiated, and inexpensive. The court as a forum for dispute processing and conflict resolution is typically placed at the costly, formalistic end of such continua.

Yet common sense and empirical investigations consistently remind us that trial courts rarely employ the adjudicative procedures that make them a symbol of extreme formalism. Very few of the complaints filed in courts are tried and adjudicated. Most are settled through bilateral negotiations of the parties or, occasionally, through the efforts of a judge who encourages the parties to reach an agreement without going to trial. This was true of the Sander County Court, as it is of courts elsewhere, and it applied with particular force to the relatively infrequent personal injury complaints that were filed in Sander County. Adjudication on the merits was extremely rare. In my sample only one of fifteen personal injury cases went to trial, and the judges and lawyers to whom I talked confirmed the generality of this pattern. Yet the court did play a crucial role in the handling of personal injury conflicts. It did so by providing what was perhaps the only setting in which meaningful and effective procedures of any kind could be applied. To understand why this was so, we must examine some distinctive characteristics of the relationships between the parties in the personal injury cases that were litigated in Sander County.

Among the relative handful of personal injury cases filed in the Sander County Court, almost all shared a common feature: the parties were separated by either geographic or social "distance" that could not be bridged by any conflict resolution process short of litigation. In at least half of the fifteen personal injury cases in the sample, the plaintiff and the defendant resided in different counties or states. These cases were evenly split between instances in which the plaintiff, on the one hand, and the defendant, on the other hand, was a local resident. In either situation, geographic distance meant that the parties almost certainly belonged to different communities and different social networks. Informal responses by the injured party, whether they involved attempts to negotiate, to mediate, or even to retaliate by gossip, were likely to be frustrated since channels for communication and shared value systems and acquaintance networks were unlikely to exist. This is reflected in the disproportionate presence of parties from outside the county on the personal injury docket.

A more elusive but no less significant form of distance was suggested by interviews with the parties as well as by the court documents in several personal injury cases. In these cases, it became apparent that "social distance," which was less tangible but just as hard to bridge as geographic distance, separated the parties even when they were neighbors.

Social distance could take many forms in Sander County. In one personal injury case, the plaintiff, who lived in one of the outlying towns in Sander County, described himself as an outsider to the community although he had lived there almost all his life. He was a Democrat in a conservative Republican town; he was of German extraction in a community where persons of Norwegian descent were extremely clannish and exclusive; he was a part-time tavernkeeper in a locality where taverns were popular but their owners were not socially esteemed; the opposing party was a "higher up" in the organization for which they both worked, and there was a long history of "bad blood" between them.

.   .   .

Social distance also played a part in an action brought by a woman on behalf of her five-year-old daughter, who had suffered internal injuries when a large trash container fell on her. The little girl had been climbing on the trash container, which was located in back of an automobile showroom. The plaintiff and her husband were described by their adversaries as the kind of people who were constantly in financial trouble and always trying to live off somebody else's money. The

plaintiff herself stated frankly that they were outsiders, in the community, ignored or avoided even by their next-door neighbors. As she put it, "Everybody in this town seems to know everybody else's business...but they don't know you."

Her socially marginal status in the community precluded any significant form of nonjudicial conflict resolution with the auto dealer or the disposal company, and the matter went to the Sander County Court, where the $150,000 lawsuit, was eventually settled for $3,000. Since initiating the lawsuit, the plaintiff had become a born again Christian and, from her new perspective on life, came to regret her decision to litigate. The little money they had obtained simply caused her to fight with her husband, who sometimes beat her. She came to believe that she should not have sued, although she did feel that her lawsuit had done some good. After it was concluded, she observed, signs were posted near all such trash containers warning that children should not play on them.

In my interviews with local residents, officials, community leaders, and legal professionals, I presented the fact situation from this last case (in a slightly different form, to protect the privacy and identity of the original participants) and asked them how similar cases were handled in the segments of the community with which they were familiar. From our discussion of this matter there emerged two distinct patterns of behavior which, the interviewees suggested, turned on the extent to which the aggrieved party was integrated into the community. If the parents of the injured child were long-time residents who were a part of the local society and shared its prevailing value system, the consensus was that they would typically take little or no action of any sort. Injuries, as we have seen, were common in a rural community, and the parents would tend to blame themselves for not watching the child more carefully or, as one interviewee put it, would "figure that the kid ought to be sharp enough to stay away" from the hazard. On the other hand, if the parents of the injured child were newcomers to the community, and especially if they were factory workers employed in the area's newly established industrial plants, it was suggested that their behavior would be quite different. One union steward assured me that the workers he knew typically viewed such situations in terms of a potential lawsuit and, at the least, would aggressively seek to have the auto dealer and the disposal company assume responsibility for the damages. Others described a kind of "fight-flight" reaction on the part of newcomers and industrial blue collar workers. One particularly perceptive minister said, "Those . . . that feel put down perceive everything in the light of another putdown and I think they would perceive this as a putdown. See, nobody really cares about us, they're just pushing us around again. And so we'll push back." He also noted, however, that it was equally likely that aggrieved individuals in this situation would simply move out of the community—the "flight" response.

There was, then, some agreement that responses involving the aggressive assertion of rights, if they occurred at all, would typically be initiated by newcomers to the community or by people who otherwise lacked a recognized place in the status hierarchy of Sander County. Such persons, in the words of a local schoolteacher, would regard the use of the court as a "leveler" that could mitigate the effects of social distance between themselves and the other side. Persons who were better integrated into the community, on the other hand, could rely on their established place in the social order to communicate grievances, stigmatize what they viewed as deviant behavior, press claims informally, or, because they felt comfortable enough psychologically and financially, to simply absorb the injury without any overt response whatever.

. . .

The picture of the Sander County Court that emerges from this brief overview of personal injury cases differs substantially from that which might be suggested by conventional typologies of conflict resolution alternatives. In processual terms litigation, although rare, was not strikingly different from its nonjudicial alternatives. It was characterized by informal negotiation, bargaining, and settlement in all but the extremely infrequent cases that actually went to trial. Yet these processes occurred only as a result of the filing of a formal legal action. Because of the distance separating the parties, nonjudicial approaches, even with the participation of lawyers, sometimes failed to resolve the conflict. Resorting to the Sander County Court could vest socially marginal persons with additional weight and stature because it offered them access to the levers of judicial compulsion. The very act of filing a civil complaint, without much more, made them persons whom the other side must recognize, whose words the other side must hear, and whose claims the other side must consider. The civil trial court, by virtue of its legal authority over all persons within its jurisdiction, was able to bridge procedurally the gaps that separated people and social groups. In a pluralistic social setting, the court could provide, in the cases that reached it, a forum where communication between disparate people and groups could take place. In so doing, it substituted for conflict-handling mechanisms which served the well-integrated dominant group but which became ineffective for persons who were beyond the boundaries of the traditional community.

The communication that the court facilitated could, however, give rise to anger and frustration. Plaintiffs often viewed the process negatively, because even when they went to court they could not escape the rigid constraints imposed by a community unsympathetic to claims for damages in personal injury cases. Thus, the plaintiff whom I have described as a Democrat in a Republican town told me that the experience of filing and settling a personal injury claim was "disgusting...a lot of wasted time." Low pretrial settlements were, not surprisingly, the rule.

Defendants viewed the process negatively because they were accustomed to a system of conflict resolution that screened out personal injury cases long before they reached the courthouse. Even though settlements might turn out to be low, defendants resented the fact that personal injuries had in the first place been viewed as an occasion to assert a claim against them, much less a formal lawsuit. Being forced to respond in court was particularly galling when the claimant turned out to be a person whom the core members of the community viewed with dislike or disdain.

In short, the Sander County Court was able to bridge gaps between parties to personal injury cases and to promote communication between those separated by social or geographic distance. It did so, however, by coercion, and its outcomes (particularly when both parties resided in the community) tended to exacerbate rather than ameliorate social conflict. In the court's very success as a mechanism for conflict resolution we may, therefore, find a partial explanation for the stigmatization of personal injury litigation in Sander County.

THE PRESERVATION AND DESTRUCTION OF A COMMUNITY

The social and economic life of Sander County had undergone major changes in the years preceding this study, and the impact of those changes on the world view of local residents and on the normative structure of the community as a whole was profound. Small single family farms were gradually giving way to larger consolidated agricultural operations owned by distant and anonymous persons or corporations. The new and sizeable manufacturing plants, together with some of the older local industries, now figured importantly in the economic life of Sander County and were the primary reasons why the population had become more heterogeneous and mobile.

These changes had important implications for traditional concepts of individualism and for the traditional relationships and reciprocities that had characterized the rural community. Self-sufficiency was less possible than before. Control over local lives was increasingly exercised by organizations based in other cities or states (there were even rumors that local farmlands were being purchased by unnamed foreign interests). Images of individual autonomy and community solidarity were challenged by the realities of externally-based economic and political power. Traditional forms of exchange could not be preserved where individuals no longer knew their neighbors' names, much less their backgrounds and their values. Local people tended to resent and perhaps to fear these changes in the local economic structure, but for the most part they believed that they were essential for the survival of the community. Some of the most critical changes had been the product of decisions made only after extensive deliberations by Sander County's elite. The infusion of new blood into the community— persons of diverse racial, ethnic, and cultural backgrounds—was a direct result of these decisions. The new residents were, in the eyes of many old-timers, an "alien element" whose introduction was, as in rural Japan, grudgingly recognized as "absolutely necessary" to preserve the well-being of the community.

The gradual decay of the old social order and the emergence of a plurality of cultures and races in Sander County produced a confusion of norms and of mechanisms for resolving conflict. New churches were established with congregations made up primarily of newcomers. Labor unions appeared on the scene, to the dismay and disgust of many of the old-timers. New taverns and other social centers catered to the newer arrivals. Governmental welfare and job training programs focused heavily (but not exclusively) on the newcomers. Newcomers frequently found themselves grouped in separate neighborhoods or apartment complexes and, in the case of blacks, there were reported attempts to exclude them from the community altogether. The newcomers brought to Sander County a social and cultural heterogeneity that it had not known before. Equally important, their very presence constituted a challenge to the older structure of norms and values generated by face-to-face relationships within the community.

PERCEPTIONS OF CONTRACT AND PERSONAL INJURY CLAIMS

The reaction of the local community to the assertion of different types of legal claims was profoundly affected by this proliferation of social, cultural, and normative systems. The contrast between reactions to claims based on breaches of contract and those based on personal injuries is especially striking. Contract actions in the Sander County Court were nearly ten times as numerous as personal injury actions. They involved, for the most part, efforts to collect payment for sales, services, and loans. One might expect that concerns about litigiousness in the community would focus upon this category of cases, which was known to be a frequent source of court filings. Yet I heard no complaints about contract plaintiffs being "greedy" or "sue happy" or "looking for the easy buck." Such criticisms were reserved exclusively for injured persons who made the relatively rare decision to press their claims in court.

In both tort and contract actions, claimants assert that a loss has been caused by the conduct of another. In contractual breaches, the defendant's alleged fault is usually a failure to conform to a standard agreed upon by the parties. In personal injury suits, the alleged fault is behavior that falls below a general societal standard applicable even in the absence of any prior agreement. Both are, of course, long-recognized types of actions. Both are "legitimate" in any formal sense of the word. Why is it, then, that actions to recover one type of loss were viewed with approval in Sander County, while far less frequent actions to recover the other type of loss were seen as symptomatic of a socially destructive trend toward the overuse of courts by greedy individuals and troublemakers? The answer appears to lie in the nature of the parties, in the social meanings of the underlying transactions, and in the symbolism of individuals and injuries in the changing social order.

Most of the contract litigation in Sander County involved debts to businesses for goods and services. Typically, the contracts that underlie such debts are quite different from the classic model of carefully considered offers and acceptances and freely negotiated exchanges. Yet many townspeople and farmers in the community saw such obligations as extremely important. . . . They were associated in the popular mind with binding but informal kinds of indebtedness and with the sanctity of the promise. Long-time Sander County residents viewed their society as one that had traditionally been based on interdependencies and reciprocal exchanges among fellow residents. Reliance upon promises, including promises to pay for goods and services, was essential to the maintenance of this kind of social system. One farmer expressed this core value succinctly: "Generally speaking, a farmer's word is good between farmers." Another farmer, who occasionally sold meat to neighbors and friends in his small town, told me:

> We've done this for 20 years, and I have never lost one dime. I have never had one person not pay me, and I've had several of them went bankrupt, and so on and so forth. I really don't pay any attention to bookkeeping or what. I mean, if someone owes me, they owe me. And you know, I've never sent anybody a bill or anything. I mean, sooner or later they all pay.

In these interpersonal exchanges involving people well known to one another there was, it appears, some flexibility and allowance for hard times and other contingencies. On the other hand, there was a mutual recognition that debts must ultimately be paid. When I asked a number of people in the community about a case in which an individual failed to pay in full for construction of a fence, the typical reaction among long-time residents was that such a breach would simply not occur. Of course, breaches or perceptions of breaches did occur in Sander County and the result could be, in the words of one farmer, "fireworks." I was told stories of violent efforts at self-help by some aggrieved creditors, and it was clear that such efforts were not necessarily condemned in the community. A member of the county sheriff's department observed that small unpaid debts of this kind were often viewed as matters for the police:

> We see that quite a bit. They want us to go out and get the money. He owes it, there's an agreement, he violated the law. . . . You see, they feel that they shouldn't have to hire an attorney for something that's an agreement. It's a law, it should be acted upon. Therefore, we should go out and arrest the man and either have him arrested or by our mere presence, by the sheriff's department, a uniformed police officer, somebody with authority going out there and say, hey, you know, you should know that automatically these people give the money and that would be it. So therefore they wouldn't have to go to an attorney. Boy, a lot of people feel that.

Other creditors, particularly local merchants, doctors, and the telephone company, brought their claims not to the police but to the Sander County Court. In some cases, contract plaintiffs (many of whom were long-time residents) appeared to litigate specifically to enforce deeply felt values concerning debt and obligation. As one small businessman explained:

> I'm the type of a person that can get personally involved and a little hostile if somebody tries to put the screws to me. . . . I had it happen once for $5 and I had it happen once for $12. . . . I explained to them carefully to please believe me that it wasn't the money, because it would cost me more to collect it than it'd be worth, but because of the principle of it that I would definitely go to whatever means necessary, moneywise or whatever, to get it collected. And which I did.

Even those creditors for whom litigation was commonplace, such as the head of the local collection agency and an official of the telephone company, shared the perception that contract breaches were morally offensive. This view appeared to apply to transactions that were routinized and impersonal as well as to the more traditional exchanges between individuals who knew each other well. As the head of the collection agency said, "When you get to sitting here and you look at the thousands of dollars that you're trying to effect collection on and you know that there's a great percentage of them you'll never get and no one will get, it's gotta bother you. It's gotta bother you." Certainly, business creditors felt none of the hesitancy of potential tort plaintiffs about asserting claims and resorting to litigation if necessary. Equally important, the community approved the enforcement of such obligations as strongly as it condemned efforts to enforce tort claims. Contract litigation, even when it involved "routine" debt collection, differed from tort litigation in that it was seen as enforcing a core value of the traditional culture of Sander County: that promises should be kept and people should be held responsible when they broke their word.

CONCLUSION

In Sander County, the philosophy of individualism worked itself out quite differently in the areas of tort and contract. If personal injuries evoked values emphasizing self-sufficiency, contractual breaches evoked values emphasizing rights and remedies. Duties generated by contractual agreement were seen as sacrosanct and vital to the maintenance of the social order. Duties generated by socially imposed obligations to guard against injuring other people were seen as intrusions upon existing relationships, as pretexts for forced exchanges, as inappropriate attempts to redistribute wealth, and as limitations upon individual freedom.

These contrasting views of contract and tort-based claims took on special significance as a result of the fundamental social changes that Sander County had experienced. The newcomers brought with them conceptions of injuries, rights, and obligations that were quite different from those that had long prevailed. The traditional norms

had no doubt played an important role in maintaining the customary social order by reinforcing longstanding patterns of behavior consistent with a parochial world view dominated by devotion to agriculture and small business. But the newcomers had no reason to share this world view or the normative structure associated with it. Indeed, as we shall see, they had good reason to reject it. Although they arrived on the scene, in a sense, to preserve the community and to save it from economic misfortune, the terms on which they were brought into Sander County—as migrant or industrial workers—had little to do with the customary forms of interaction and reciprocation that had given rise to the traditional normative order. The older norms concerning such matters as individual self-sufficiency, personal injuries, and contractual breaches had no special relevance or meaning given the interests of the newcomers. Although these norms impinged on the consciousness and behavior of the newcomers, they did so through the coercive forces and social sanctions that backed them up and not because the newcomers had accepted and internalized local values and attitudes.

Indeed, it was clear that in the changing society of Sander County, the older norms tended to operate to the distinct disadvantage of social outsiders and for the benefit of the insiders. Contract actions, premised on the traditional value that a person's word should be kept, tended to involve collection efforts by established persons or institutions against newcomers and socially marginal individuals. Such actions, as we have seen, were generally approved by the majority of Sander County residents and occurred with great frequency. Personal injury actions, on the other hand, were rooted in no such traditional value and, although such claims were infrequent, they were usually instituted by plaintiffs who were outsiders to the community against defendants who occupied symbolically important positions in Sander County society. Thus, a typical contract action involved a member of "the establishment" collecting a debt, while the typical personal injury action was an assault by an outsider upon the establishment at a point where a sufficient aggregation of capital existed to pay for an injury. This distinction helps to explain the stigmatization of personal injury litigation in Sander County as well as its infrequency and its ineffectiveness.

Yet personal injury litigation in Sander County was not entirely dysfunctional for the traditional social order. The intrusion of "the stranger" into an enclosed system of customary law can serve to crystallize the awareness of norms that formerly existed in a preconscious or inarticulate state (See Fuller, 1969: 9–10 and Simmel, 1908/1971). Norms and values that once patterned behavior unthinkingly or intuitively must now be articulated, explained, and defended against the contrary values and expectations of the stranger to the community.

In Sander County, the entry of the stranger produced a new awareness (or perhaps a reconstruction) of the traditional normative order at the very moment when that order was subjected to its strongest and most devastating challenges. This process triggered a complex response by the community —a nostalgic yearning for the older world view now shattered beyond repair, a rearguard attempt to shore up the boundaries of the community against alien persons and ideas (compare Erikson, 1966), and a bitter acceptance of the fact that the "stranger" was in reality no longer outside the community but a necessary element brought in to preserve the community, and therefore a part of it.

Local responses to personal injury claims reflected these complexities. In part, local

residents, by stigmatizing such claims, were merely defending the establishment from a relatively rare form of economic attack by social outsiders. In part, stigmatization branded the claimants as deviants from the community norms and therefore helped mark the social boundaries between old-timers and newcomers. Because the maintenance of such boundaries was increasingly difficult, however, and because the "alien element" had been deliberately imported into the community as a societal act of self-preservation, the stigmatization of such claims was also part of a broader and more subtle process of expiation (to borrow Yamaguchi's [1977] term), a process reminiscent of rituals and other procedures used in many societies to deal with problems of pollution associated with socially marginal persons in the community (Douglas, 1966; Turner, 1969; Perin, 1977: 110–15).

Local residents who denounced the assertion of personal injury claims and somewhat irrationally lamented the rise in "litigiousness" of personal injury plaintiffs were, in this sense, participating in a more broadly based ceremony of regret that the realities of contemporary American society could no longer be averted from their community if it were to survive. Their denunciations bore little relationship to the frequency with which personal injury lawsuits were actually filed, for the local ecology of conflict resolution still suppressed most such cases long before they got to court, and personal injury litigation remained rare and aberrational. Rather, the denunciation of personal injury litigation in Sander County was significant mainly as one aspect of a symbolic effort by members of the community to preserve a sense of meaning and coherence in the face of social changes that they found threatening and confusing. It was in this sense a solution— albeit a partial and unsatisfying one—to a problem basic to the human condition, the problem of living in a world that has lost the simplicity and innocence it is thought once to have had. The outcry against personal injury litigation was part of a broader effort by some residents of Sander County to exclude from their moral universe what they could not exclude from the physical boundaries of their community and to recall and reaffirm an untainted world that existed nowhere but in their imaginations.

REFERENCES

Abel, Richard L. (1973) "A Comparative Theory of Dispute Institutions in Society," 8 *Law & Society Review* 217.

Black, Donald and M.P. Baumgartner (1983) "Toward a Theory of the Third Party," in K. Boyum and L. Mather (eds.), *Empirical Theories About Courts*. New York: Longman.

Douglas, Mary (1966) *Purity and Danger*. London: Routledge & Kegan Paul, Limited.

Erikson, Kai T. (1966) *Wayward Puritans*. New York: John Wiley & Sons.

Felstiner, William L.F. (1974) "Influences of Social Organization on Dispute Processing," 9 *Law & Society Review* 63.

Fuller, Lon L. (1969) "Human Interaction and the Law," 14 *American Journal of Jurisprudence* 1.

Galanter, Marc (1983) "Reading the Landscape of Disputes: What We Know and Don't Know (And Think We Know) About Our Allegedly Contentious and Litigious Society," 31 *UCLA Law Review* 4.

Nader, Laura and Harry F. Todd, Jr. (1978) "Introduction: The Dispute Process—Law in Ten Societies," in L. Nader and H. Todd, Jr. (eds.), *The Disputing Process—Law in Ten Societies*. New York: Columbia University Press.

Perin, Constance (1977) *Everything in Its Place*. Princeton: Princeton University Press.

Ross, H. Laurence (1970) *Settled Out of Court*. Chicago: Aldine Publishing Co.

Simmel, Georg (1908/1971) "The Stranger," in D. Levine (ed.), *On Individuality and Social Forms: Selected Writings*. Chicago: University of Chicago Press.

Steele, Eric H. (1975) "Fraud, Dispute and the Consumer: Responding to Consumer Complaints," 123 *University of Pennsylvania Law Review* 1107.

Turner, Victor W. (1969) *The Ritual Process*. Chicago: Aldine Publishing Co.

Yamaguchi, Masao (1977) "Kingship, Theatricality, and Marginal Reality in Japan," in R. Jain (ed.), *Text and Context: The Social Anthropology of Tradition*. Philadelphia: Institute for the Study of Human Issues.

Environmental and Structural Variables as Determinants of Issues in State Courts of Last Resort

Burton M. Atkins
Henry R. Glick

A considerable body of research published in the last several years has demonstrated the important effects of socioeconomic and political diversification upon political processes and policy outputs. Yet little research has been conducted on the impact of environmental differences on judicial processes and policy. This is not to suggest, however, that the linkage between environmental conditions and courts has been totally ignored. On the contrary, most models of the judicial processes make some reference to this linkage, and the systems model in particular underscores the effects of the flow of demands and conflict from the environment towards the judicial system. However, while reference is often made to these relationships, the literature is still devoid of empirical research that systematically examines the impact of environment upon judicial action. To remedy this omission, the

"Environmental and Structural Variables as Determinants of Issues in State Courts of Last Resort," Burton M. Atkins and Henry R. Glick. Reprinted from *American Journal of Political Sciences*, Vol. 20, No. 1, February 1976. Copyright © 1976 by the University of Texas Press. By permission of authors and the publisher.

present study will offer a comparative examination of the relationship between socioeconomic and political conditions within the fifty American states, on the one hand, and issues decided by state courts of last resort on the other.

Our focus is upon issues resolved by state supreme courts, since the types of controversies that political institutions confront is an important component among the factors that determine the types of policies courts make. While processes that determine which issues will be considered and which will be ignored are important for all institutions, they are particularly relevant for courts, since whether or not judicial action will be invoked is greatly dependent upon the types of demands and conflicts brought to them by participants and processes beyond the institution itself. This is not to suggest, of course, that appellate courts cannot exercise any discretion over the types of issues they will resolve. However, the discretion exercised is normally negative rather than positive, with the parameters of the issue universe set by actors often far from the courtroom. Thus, since courts are passive rather than active policymakers, the characteristics of the socioeconomic and political environment which generate demands and conflicts may be particularly important predictors to the kinds of issues resolved by judicial institutions.

We are choosing state supreme courts as the focus of the study, given their important role as courts of last resort within state political systems. While the powers and roles of these courts vary somewhat, they are nevertheless analogous to the United States Supreme Court in terms of their functional relationship with the political system. By examining these courts, we can also tap the comparative dimension and take advantage of the socioeconomic and political diversity among the fifty states.

By selecting these systemic characteristics as our independent variables, we are not necessarily implying that contextual variables are either the only or most important predictors of issues found in state courts of last resort; nor need we specify that certain levels of statistical explanations will be achieved. Rather, we posit the general hypothesis that contextual variables establish parameters within which judicial policymaking occurs, and our goal is to determine what portion of the variance can be accounted for by socioeconomic and political environments. Moreover, by examining the impact of these forces we can draw upon several cognate bodies of research being conducted by political scientists and begin to examine whether or not the forces that shape public policy within the fifty states have a similar impact upon judicial decisionmaking.

RESEARCH DESIGN

The Dependent Variables

State supreme court decisions filed with full opinions during 1966–67 formed the data base for this study. Since considerable varia-

tion exists in the number of decisions rendered each year by state supreme courts, two criteria were used to determine how many decisions from each court would be coded. If the total number of decisions on the merits was less than one hundred, all cases were included in the data set; however, if the N for a court was considerably larger, a sample was taken so that at least one hundred cases were included. This procedure created a data set of 4,974 cases, with a mean for each state of 99.8.

An important feature of many state supreme courts that distinguishes them from the United States Supreme Court is that they generally decide an enormous variety of issues, many of which hardly ever appear at all in Supreme Court decisions. Besides criminal appeals, found frequently in most state courts of last resort, economic controversies such as wills, trusts, estates, contract disputes, and real estate litigation constitute a large proportion of decisions on the merits. Other issues found frequently in state supreme courts are divorce, motor vehicle accident, and personal injury suits. The coding format used to collect these data obviously had to be sufficiently flexible to capture the range of litigation found in fifty courts of last resort, yet when data collection was completed, the code sheet provided for more than fifty categories of issues.

In order to facilitate data analysis, these categories were reduced to five. The first includes criminal appeals with or without a concomitant constitutional claim. Civil rights litigation, defined as cases raising questions under the First and Fourteenth Amendments of the federal Constitution, or similar provisions in state constitutions, were coded in a second category. Though relatively uncommon in state courts, civil rights issues are an important component of the decisions rendered by the United States Supreme Court, and thus provide a basis of policy comparison between the state courts of last resort and their federal counterpart.

A third category contains cases that raise issues concerning regulation and redistribution of economic resources. For the most part, cases in this category are tax appeals or appeals from state regulatory agencies and commissions in which the supreme courts review decisions associated with the redistribution of wealth, implicitly requiring the court to balance the ethic of governmental intrusions into the business sector against the ethic associated with a free marketplace. As with civil liberties and rights, these issues parallel those found frequently in the United States Supreme Court.

The last two categories include private litigation, cases in which both parties are individuals, as opposed to corporations, criminal defendants, or state agencies. On the assumption that some judges may view questions concerning the distribution of economic resources as more important than noneconomic problems, these cases were separated on the basis of whether or not an economic dispute was involved. Private economic settlements include various claims associated with contests over wills, trusts, estates, landlord-tenant controversies, and disputes over property titles and sales. The primary distinction between private economic and private noneconomic litigation is that the former directly involves conflict over control of economic resources, whereas the latter, while often involving money, does not necessarily stem from economic conflicts. Among the private noneconomic conflicts are personal liability suits, wrongful death actions, and malpractice suits.

Cases that could not be identified as belonging in any of the above categories were omitted from the data analysis since they lacked any apparent common dimension. Of the original 4,974 cases, approximately 81% (4,045) were retained. The distribution of these issues in state supreme courts is reported in Table 1.

Environmental Variables

State environmental characteristics . . . measuring six aspects of state socioeconomic and political settings [are employed]. Also employed to measure state characteristics are two policy factors. . . . Since courts share policymaking with legislatures and administrative agencies, the types of decisions made by the these branches of state government help to shape the types of issues involved in court litigations. For our purposes, therefore, the public policy orientation of the state is conceptualized as one of the contextual variables accounting for variations among issues found in court decisions.

Political Characteristics. These are measured by two factors, one labeled Professionalism-Local Reliance, and the other, Competition-Turnout. The factor scores are based on an original set of 53 items which measure participation and party competition, characteristics of the legislative, executive, and judicial branches of the states, and individual and mutual aspects of the state, local, and intergovernmental fiscal structures. Professionalism-Local Reliance primarily concerns salaries of judges and legislators, legislative staff budgets, and local tax effort. Competition-Turnout primarily concerns measures of gubernatorial election turnout and one-party domination. . . .

Socioeconomic Characteristics. The industrialization factors taps economic and occupational activity and has the proportion of the population engaged in manufacturing and the value added per capita by manufacturing loading highly on it. Affluence, the second factor, is heavily regional along a North-South axis. States loading high on the

TABLE 1
Issues in State Supreme Courts (Percent of Caseload)

State	Criminal	Civil Liberty	Economic Regulation	Private Economic	Private Noneconomic
Alabama	24.5	1.1	16.0	23.4	21.3
Alaska	41.9	0.0	4.8	22.6	14.5
Arizona	48.5	1.0	4.1	20.6	7.2
Arkansas	19.6	2.1	10.3	37.1	14.4
California	44.8	4.2	13.5	9.4	6.3
Colorado	18.6	2.1	17.5	22.7	9.3
Connecticut	20.9	2.3	22.1	14.0	8.1
Delaware	26.1	5.7	19.3	13.6	12.5
Florida	36.0	0.0	8.0	6.0	2.0
Georgia	21.2	2.0	16.2	24.2	3.0
Hawaii	14.9	4.5	16.4	31.3	1.4
Idaho	21.6	1.0	6.2	32.0	14.4
Illinois	57.3	1.0	13.5	3.1	5.2
Indiana	71.7	1.0	6.1	4.0	4.0
Iowa	29.3	3.0	13.1	24.2	9.1
Kansas	33.3	1.0	9.1	32.3	13.1
Kentucky	20.2	0.0	10.2	21.2	22.2
Louisiana	53.5	2.0	8.1	15.2	9.1
Maine	45.5	0.0	14.8	17.0	9.1
Maryland	5.0	5.0	20.0	41.0	15.0
Massachusetts	18.6	4.9	20.6	34.3	16.7
Michigan	24.4	4.4	21.1	25.6	16.7
Minnesota	40.0	4.0	2.0	29.0	19.0
Mississippi	15.6	2.1	4.2	19.8	20.8
Missouri	50.0	3.0	11.0	17.0	15.0

State					
Montana	27.1	2.1	10.4	19.8	17.7
Nebraska	32.0	3.0	13.0	23.0	13.0
Nevada	43.3	0.0	9.3	18.6	11.3
New Hampshire	14.1	0.0	9.8	28.3	25.0
New Jersey	28.3	1.0	13.1	18.2	13.1
New Mexico	48.0	2.0	4.1	29.6	9.2
New York	23.4	2.1	9.6	26.6	11.7
North Carolina	40.0	1.0	5.0	27.0	21.0
North Dakota	12.1	0.0	15.5	20.7	29.3
Ohio	23.7	2.1	32.0	14.4	17.5
Oklahoma	45.9	0.7	6.4	20.3	11.1
Oregon	33.0	1.0	9.3	22.7	14.4
Pennsylvania	34.3	2.0	13.1	17.2	15.2
Rhode Island	22.0	1.0	18.0	24.0	20.0
South Carolina	22.2	0.0	9.1	34.3	23.0
South Dakota	27.4	0.0	9.6	26.0	15.1
Tennessee	26.5	1.0	14.3	38.8	11.2
Texas	52.0	0.5	6.0	25.0	7.5
Utah	26.3	0.0	12.6	26.0	15.8
Vermont	28.0	0.0	4.0	33.3	17.2
Virginia	28.7	3.2	13.8	25.5	20.2
Washington	45.7	1.1	12.0	17.4	9.8
West Virginia	16.7	0.0	9.3	27.8	24.1
Wisconsin	29.0	3.2	8.6	24.7	18.3
Wyoming	23.5	0.0	4.4	26.5	25.0
	$\bar{X} = 31.12$	$\bar{X} = 1.70$	$\bar{X} = 11.60$	$\bar{X} = 23.12$	$\bar{X} = 14.30$
	SD = 13.52	SD = 1.55	SD = 5.85%	SD = 8.25	SD = 6.15
	CV = 43%	CV = 91%	CV = 50%	CV = 35%	CV = 43%

positive end of this dimension are characterized by high education and generally are indicative of modern, affluent cultures.

Public Policy Factors. . . . The first factor is Welfare-Education, and separates states on the basis of amount of welfare payments, the likelihood of high school pupils to remain until graduation, and student success on nationwide examinations. The second factor is Highway-Natural Resources, and is characterized by measures of rural highway mileage and highway expenditures, measures of fish and wildlife services and expenditures for natural resources. Since the political conflicts that flow to the judiciary are essentially one component of the distribution of conflicts in the environment, these measures are useful in assessing the relationship between issues decided by the state courts of last resort and the policy orientation of other institutions within the state . . . .

Method of Analysis

Multiple regression models were used to examine the relationship between environmental variables and the issues decided by state supreme courts. The first model tests the total effects of environmental variables upon the distribution of issues and assumes a linear effect of the independent variables on each of the issue categories. This model hypothesizes that much of the variation in issues decided by state supreme courts can be accounted for by the state's environmental characteristics which shape the conflicts requiring political and judicial resolution. Moreover, it is hypothesized that criminal law, civil liberties, and government economic regulation decisions will be positively related to economic development and political competition, positively related to expenditures on health and welfare services,

but negatively related to expenditures on Highways-Natural Resources. Private litigation, both economic and noneconomic, should occur most frequently in states low on Affluence and Industrialization, low on Professionalism and Competition, low on Welfare, but high on Highways-Natural Resources.

These hypotheses, however, do not presume that there is a direct correspondence between socioeconomic and political conditions on the one hand, and issues resolved by state courts on the other; numerous processes can divert certain types of controversies from the judicial system and thereby skew the distribution of issues. Insofar as a state supreme court is concerned, one particularly important variable is whether or not the court system of which it is a part contains an intermediate appellate court.

Intermediate appellate courts are usually established to reduce the case load of courts of last resort. In practice, however, the effect of intermediate appellate courts is not so much to reduce the case load as it is to redistribute the types of issues decided by the court of last resort. Cases not raising fundamental issues are left to the intermediate appellate court, thus allocating the supreme court's time more effectively by reserving their attention to issues perceived to be more critical to the political system. The second regression model tests for effects of the state intermediate appellate courts upon the distribution of issues decided by courts of last resort by adding Court System as a dummy variable to the equation, with a value of zero when no intermediate appellate court exists, and a value of 1 when the intermediate appellate court does exist.

For the purposes of this study, criminal law issues were analyzed in a third regression model. While we have hypothesized that the distribution of criminal cases decided by state supreme courts is a function of environmental variables and the court structure, one would obviously expect that the amount of criminal litigation would be a reflection of the number of cases prosecuted by the state. Since information on the number of prosecutions was not available, a measure of reported crime in the states was used as a surrogate and added as a separate variable in the regression equation.

The final regression model tested for an interaction effect between crime rate and the presence or absence of an appellate court upon the distribution of criminal law cases decided by state supreme court. This was done because the continued increase of criminal litigation in state and federal judicial systems, recognized as placing severe strains upon the legal systems, has spawned attempts to shield state supreme courts from routine criminal appeals. One tactic often used to divert criminal appeals is to create an intermediate appellate court between trial and supreme courts. Thus, the joint effects of high crime rates and intermediate appellate courts were added to the stepwise model as a separate interaction term.

RESULTS OF REGRESSION ANALYSIS: MODEL 1

The data in Table 2 report the contribution of each of the three pairs of indicators as well as the explanatory power of all six. The correlation between each environmental component and each issue, it should be observed, is the R between the two factors comprising the dimension and each issue. For example, the R representing the relationship between economic conditions and civil liberties decisions (.20) is the multiple correlation between affluence and industrialization, on the one hand, and civil liberties decisions on the other. Likewise, the

R respresenting the relationship between the political dimension and civil liberties decisions (.31) reflects the multiple correlation of each of the two dimensions within that environmental descriptor and that issue. Since the two dimensions within each environmental component are uncorrelated, there is no statistical redundancy within this multiple correlation. Also reported in Table 2 are the regression coefficients for each environmental dimension. Finally, at the bottom of each column are the R and statistical significance for each model. These data show that no one set of environmental factors is primarily responsible for the variance on the issues, although the economic descriptors are marginally stronger correlates with private litigation and government economic regulation suits.

Another basis for comparing the relative effects of the environmental indicators is their explanatory contribution in the regression equations. Table 2 shows that affluence is the most important variable affecting civil liberties, private economic, and private noneconomic litigation, whereas industrialization is the most important predictor of economic regulation controversies, and almost as important as affluence in the civil liberties equation.

Additional information concerning the impact of environmental variables is provided by the multiple R for all six factors in the Model 1 equations. These correlations range from a low of .21 for criminal law to .60 for private noneconomic suits. While the average amount of explained variance in the five equations is not very high, the data do indicate that environmental variables are an important component in the configuration of processes that shape issues decided by state courts of last resort. Yet the fact that the multiple R's vary as much as they do, especially among issues that are fairly comparable, such as private economic and pri-

TABLE 2
Regression Coefficients of Six Environmental Variables on State Supreme Court Decisions

	Civil Liberties					Private Suits (Noneconomic)					Private Suits (Economic)				
	Model 1			Model 2		Model 1			Model 2		Model 1			Model 2	
	R	b	Beta	b	Beta	R	b	Beta	b	Beta	R	b	Beta	b	Beta
Economic Component	.20					.35					.34				
Affluence		.81	.33	.95	.39		-6.63	-1.01	-6.19	-.94		-5.31	-.58	-4.93	-.54
Industrialization		-.85	-.33	-.80	-.33		1.52	.23	1.70	.26		.12	.01	.27	.03
Political Component	.31					.29					.29				
Professionalism		.71	.30	.96	.41		.78	-.12	.02	.003		-.48	-.05	.21	.02
Competition		.00	.00	-.01	.00		.87	.14	.81	.12		-1.92	.22	-1.98	-.22
Policy Component	.25					.21					.20				
Highways		-1.04	-.45	-1.20	-.52		4.28	.68	3.77	.60		3.56	.41	3.12	.35
Welfare		-.20	-.08	-.46	-.19		2.85	.45	2.01	.32		3.56	.41	2.84	.32
Court System				-1.37	-.28				-4.46	-.34				-3.82	-.21
	R = .40			R = .47		R = .60			R = .67		R = .44			R = .47	
	p = .27			p = .162		p = .003			p = .001		p = .15			p = .14	

Economic Regulation

	Model 1			Model 2	
	R	b	Beta	b	Beta
Economic Component	.47				
Affluence		2.46	.406	3.76	.619
Industrialization		3.53	.581	2.56	.421
Political Component	.26				
Competition		-.918	-.158	-.952	-.164
Professionalism		-1.86	-.316	-1.43	-.243
Policy Component	.42				
Highways		-2.82	.487	-3.09	-.533
Welfare		-.922	-.158	-1.36	-.234
Court System				-2.34	-.195
	R = .575			R = .598	
	p = .008			p = .009	

Criminal Law

	R	Model 1 (Environmental)		Model 2 (Court Structure)		Model 3 (Crime Rate)		Model 4 (Interaction)	
		b	*Beta*	*b*	*Beta*	*b*	*Beta*	*b*	*Beta*
Economic Component	.16								
Affluence		2.11	.146	.379	.026	-6.21	-.43	-6.175	-.42
Industrialization		-.520	-.036	-1.22	-.085	-1.68	-.11	-1.626	-.11
Political Component	.19								
Competition		2.56	.186	2.82	.204	4.62	.33	4.265	.33
Professionalism		.937	.067	-2.19	-.157	-3.10	-.22	3.11	-.22
Policy Component	.13								
Highways		-1.61	-.117	.358	.015	1.23	.08	1.25	.09
Welfare		1.55	-.112	1.70	.123	4.00	.29	3.92	.28
Court System				17.32	.608	14.56	.51	13.57	.47
Crime Rate						.158	.45	.155	.44
Crime Rate × System								9.56	.03
		R = .210		R = .551		R = .63		R = .63	
		p = .925		p = .03		p = .006		p = .01	

vate noneconomic controversies, not only indicates substantial differences in the impact of environment from one issue to the next, but also suggests redundancy among the independent variables. Part of the problem stems from the fact that while each pair of factors comprising an environmental component is uncorrelated...there are several high interdimensional correlations. For example, ... Professionalism is correlated .72 with Industrialization, Competition .67 with Affluence, and Competition .70 with Welfare. This multicollinearity is not damaging to the analysis so long as we are aware of the relative importance of each environmental component. However, the problem is compounded when several of the independent variables have higher correlations among themselves than they have with the dependent variables.... [I]n Table 3 the zero order correlations between the factors and issues, shows that this is indeed the case. As a result of these patterns, the magnitudes, and especially the signs of the regression coefficients in the equations, are affected, thus obscuring potentially important relationships in the data.

Some of this ambiguity can be removed by more closely examining the zero order correlations between the environmental characteristics and issues. While these data cannot show the unique contributions made by each variable, they will show any patterns between environmental conditions and issues in the supreme courts unencumbered by the multicollinearity in the regression equations. While none of the relationships in Table 3 are strong, several patterns do emerge. Private litigation is more likely to appear in less affluent, less industrialized, and less politically diversified states. The appearance of these decisions is also negatively correlated with high expenditures for welfare policies (a positive correlate of affluence and industrialization), and positively related to high

expenditures for highways and natural resources (a negative correlate of industrialization but a positive correlate of affluence). In other words, supreme courts within more rural, and politically undifferentiated states tend to decide greater proportions of private litigation. By contrast, civil liberties and government economic regulation decisions appear in states that score higher on affluence, economic development, and political professionalism. Criminal appeals do not show any strong correlations with any of the environmental characteristics.

While our research design is not longitudinal, the data do suggest that the emergence of conflicts in supreme court decisions may be hierarchical. In other words, the fact that environmental diversification is related to the appearance of certain issues in supreme courts does not imply that other litigation is not appearing at all in the state judicial system. Rather, it would seem that as political and economic diversification generates alterations in the universe of litigation, supreme courts restructure their decisional priorities to meet changing demand patterns. Thus, supreme courts within rural, less affluent, and less politically competitive states are not relegated to secondary status because they decide substantial portions of private litigation. Since their role is determined in part by the types of conflict generated by the environment, these courts of last resort would naturally decide few civil rights or economic regulation cases until economic and political diversification develops to the point where it generates litigation that would have de facto priority in the supreme courts. This developmental process would have the effect of "bumping" private litigation from the court of last resort to some lower court. Once we presume that courts of last resort resolve issues perceived to be of fundamental importance within a political system, it follows that the appearance of

TABLE 3
Zero Order Correlations, Environmental Factors by Issues

	Criminal Appeals	Civil Liberties	Economic Regulation	Private Economic	Private Noneconomic
Affluence	.15	.11	.11	−.27	−.30
Industrialization	.07	.16	.46	−.20	−.18
Professionalism	.08	.30	.25	−.19	−.28
Competition	.17	.02	.03	−.22	−.02
Welfare	.13	.14	.16	−.17	−.11
Highways-Natural Resources	−.01	−.21	−.39	.11	.17

larger proportions of civil liberties, criminal law, and particularly economic regulation cases may be indicative of judicial systems which have remained attuned to changing patterns of demands entering the political system from the differentiated political and socioeconomic environment.

Besides reflecting changing patterns in the environment, the distribution of issues resolved by supreme courts also indicates, in some instances, how certain groups perceive the benefits of judicial action. For example, it is well recognized that civil rights groups avoided southern supreme courts and sought judicial remedies in federal courts instead. Similarly, other groups, particularly business or labor litigants, might avoid a certain supreme court because of perceived bias in its prevailing ideology. Thus the appearance of groups in court decisions may be closely related to the types of decisions made by supreme courts.

EFFECTS OF INTERMEDIATE APPELLATE COURTS: MODEL 2

Since economic and political development is associated with an increase in litigation, intermediate appellate courts would presumably be established in states having complex socioeconomic and political structures. To test this hypothesis, Table 4 compares the mean factor scores of states with and without intermediate appellate courts. As anticipated, the characteristics of the states do differ. In particular, states with intermediate appellate courts tend to score high on Professionalism, high on Industrialization, and low on Highways-Natural Resources (a negative correlate of economic development).

The fact that the establishment of intermediate appellate courts is related to socioeconomic and political diversification suggests a certain restructuring of issues in supreme courts with an appellate court below. In particular, it would be expected that supreme courts with the appellate court below would decide fewer cases involving personal justice, these having been siphoned away by the lower appellate court, and would decide larger proportions of criminal law, civil liberties, and government economic regulation cases.

The regression coefficients for the Court System variable entered into the equations for each issue show the effect of intermediate appellate courts upon the distribution of issues. Some of the results are startling. The negative signs of the coefficients indicate that the appearance of four of the issues is

TABLE 4
Mean Factor Scores by Type of Court System

	States with Intermediate Appellate Court	States Without Intermediate Appellate Court
Professionalism	.561	−.310
Competition	−.271	.173
Welfare-Education	−.121	.084
Highways-Natural Resources	−.528	.322
Affluence	−.172	.092
Industrialization	.455	−.250

inversely related to the presence of an intermediate appellate court. However, supreme courts with intermediate appellate courts below are not necessarily deciding fewer cases, since the sign and magnitude of the regression coefficient for Court System on criminal appeals (17.32) shows that the existence of an intermediate appellate court is associated with substantial increases of criminal decisions rendered by the supreme court. The effect of intermediate appellate courts on the appearance of criminal law decisions is also apparent in the substantial increment of the R from .210 to .551 when that variable is added to the regression equation. The empirical significance of the marked increase in criminal litigation decided by supreme courts with intermediate appellate courts below is difficult to ascertain without data on the flow of litigation at all tiers of the state judicial systems. In other words, it is impossible to ascertain whether or not these court systems have so much criminal litigation that the intermediate appellate courts cannot effectively shield the supreme court from them, or whether or not the appearance of these cases represents a policy by the supreme courts to devote their attention to criminal law cases. In either event, the data do show that some supreme courts, by necessity or design, are functioning primarily as criminal courts of last resort.

Some evidence concerning the environmental conditions that transform some state supreme courts into de facto criminal courts of last resort can be obtained by adding the Crime Rate variable and the interaction term representing the joint effects of crime rate and the presence or absence of an intermediate appellate court to the regression equations. The results show that the addition of Crime Rate (Model 3) increases the multiple R to .63. More importantly, however, the new regression coefficient indicates that while Crime Rate is an important predictor to the percentage of criminal appeals decided by a state supreme court, Court System remains the most critical variable in the regression equation. However, the Model 4 equation shows that the interaction term does not add substantially to the explained variance, and that Court System and Crime Rate remain as important determinants of criminal appeals.

It thus appears that one reason why large numbers of criminal appeals are resolved by supreme courts with intermediate appellate courts below is that the environment within which these judicial systems operate generates considerable criminal litigation. Although the data are not currently available, it may be that intermediate appellate courts in the very same states are also besieged with criminal appeals, and thus can only minimally shield the court of last resort. This suggests, in turn, that although a court may have certiorari discretion, a device that seeks to allow the court reasonable initiative over which issues it will decide, environmental stress may dictate the parameters within which the discretion is exercised. Though intermediate appellate courts are created to restore the initiative within courts of last resort beleaguered by litigation, our data suggest that their presence may not have the intended effect when environmental conditions effectively set the agenda for the court of last resort. It seems that supreme courts may remain sensitive to environmental stress only at the cost of deferring the resolution of certain issues to courts below.

CONCLUSIONS

The data reported in this study demonstrate that environmental variables are important predictors to the types of issues resolved through state supreme court decisions. Court System, it has been shown, is an important structural variable shaping the distribution of issues as they emerge in state courts of last resort. Although our emphasis has been upon the effects of the environmental variables, the fact that the presence or absence of an intermediate appellate court affects the distribution of issues on supreme courts suggests the need to incorporate additional court system variables into models seeking to account for the types of conflicts found in courts of last resort. By examining aggregate relationships between judicial decisions and environmental conditions, we naturally by-pass some of the more subtle relationships between courts and other governmental institutions and environmental conditions that bear upon the types of issues resolved by supreme courts. . . .

Reading the Landscape of Disputes

Marc Galanter

INTRODUCTION

Whether or not America has experienced a "litigation explosion," or is suffering from "legal pollution," or is in thrall to an "imperial judiciary," there has surely been an explosion of concern about the legal health of American society. A battery of observers has concluded that American society is over-legalized. According to these commentators, government, at our urging, tries to use law to regulate too much and in too much detail. Our courts, overwhelmed by a flood of litigation, are incapable of giving timely, inexpensive and effective relief, yet simultaneously extend their reach into areas beyond both their competence and legitimacy. A citizenry of unparalleled contentiousness exercises a hair trigger readiness to invoke the law, asking courts to address both trifles unworthy of them and social problems beyond their grasp. In short, these observers would have us believe that we suffer from too much law, too many lawyers, courts that take

on too much—and an excessive readiness to utilize all of them. As a convenient label for this whole catalog of ills, I borrow the term "hyperlexis" from one of these observers. This article will examine one component of the hyperlexis syndrome—the alleged high rates of disputing and litigation—in the context of current research. I shall then offer a few reflections on the hyperlexis perspective.

The "Hyperlexis" Explosion

The assertion that we engage in too much disputing and litigation implies two determinations: first, ascertainment of how much we have, and, second, establishment of how much is too much. What are the data from which such determinations can be made?

Until recently there have been few attempts to measure the amount of contention and litigation. Although court statistics have been compiled for management use, they are incomplete. We have no established indicators like the Gross National Product or the rate of index crimes—indicators that are themselves fraught with all sorts of problems.

Typically the evidence cited for the litigation explosion consists of:

1. The growth in filings in federal courts;
2. The growth in size of the legal profession;
3. Accounts of monster cases (such as the AT & T and IBM antitrust cases) and the vast amounts of resources consumed in such litigation;
4. Atrocity stories—that is, citation of cases that seem grotesque, petty or extravagant: A half-million dollar suit is filed by a woman against community officials because they forbid her to breast-feed her child at the community pool; a child sues his parents for "mal-parenting" a disappointed suitor brings suit for being stood up on a date; rejected mistresses sue their former paramours; sports fans sue officials and management, and Indians claim vast tracts of land; and
5. War stories—that is, accounts of personal experience by business and other managers about how litigation impinges on their institutions, ties their hands, impairs efficiency, runs up costs, etc.

Even if these statistics and accounts establish that we have a great deal of litigation, how do we know it is too much? This evidence draws its polemical power from the implicit comparison to some better past or some more favored place. Pervading these reports is a fond recollection of a time when it wasn't so—federal courts had fewer cases, there were fewer lawyers, people with outlandish claims were properly inhibited or chastened by upright lawyers, and managers could carry out their duties without fear of being sued. In this golden pre-litigious era, problems which were not solved by sturdy self-reliance or stoic endurance were addressed by vigorous community institutions. Not only was our own past more favored but, it

is often noted, other societies of comparable advancement and amenity have fewer lawyers and less litigation. Japan, in particular, is viewed as exemplary. Its few lawyers and scarce litigation are thought to betoken a state of social harmony conducive to high productivity and prosperity.

. . .

Compared to What?

How can we tell whether the amount of disputing and litigation...is too much—or too little? In part this depends on our reading of the meaning of disputes and lawsuits—are they evils which inevitably detract from social well-being? Or do they, some of them anyway, contain the seeds of vindication, justice, even social improvement? Such judgements could be applied to any quantity of disputes. But even if individual disputes or lawsuits may be harmless or even beneficent, having too many of them may be a bad thing. But how many are too many? Are we to measure this by the capacity of courts or other institutions? But how do we know *they* are the right size? We might instead measure the value of disputing by its measurable effects, but as we shall see this is a daunting and untried endeavor. As noted earlier, much of the literature expressing concern about the litigation explosion finds a standard, at least implicitly, by comparing the present situation to our own national past or to more favored lands abroad.

Then and Now. Unfortunately for purposes of comparison, we have almost no data from earlier points in our own history that are comparable to our contemporary survey evidence. Hence we have only a dim picture of what the lower layers of the dispute pyramid used to be like. But there is one kind of evidence that we can compare across time—data on the number of cases brought in the courts. By combining this with population figures we can derive a litigation rate for various populations and see if this rate has increased over time. This procedure has a number of infirmities if we are using it to estimate the disputatious or contentious character of the population. For example, are all the cases counted really disputes or contests, and how comparable are the figures from time to time as recording systems change, jurisdictions are altered, etc. Again, our rate does not reflect the portion of disputes that comes before agencies other than regular courts—administrative agencies, zoning boards, licensing bodies, small claims courts, justices of the peace and others—whose number and identity have changed over time. Thus our rates tell us about the use of the regular courts rather than about the entire use of official third party dispute institutions. This is troubling because we don't know how much changes in rates reflect changes in the population of dispute institutions and the flow of traffic among them, and how much reflects changes in the tendency to litigate in the broad sense of taking disputes to governmental third parties. Nevertheless, let us see what litigation rates tell us.

Federal courts handle only a tiny fraction of all the cases filed in the United States. In 1975 there were approximately 7.27 million cases (civil, criminal, and juvenile) filed in state courts of general jurisdiction and about 160,000 in the federal district courts. There has been a dramatic rise in federal court filings in recent decades. Filings in the district courts increased from 68,135 in 1940 to 89,112 in 1960, and to 198,710 in 1980. From 1940 to 1960, the absolute rise barely kept pace with population growth, but from 1960 to 1980 there was a pronounced per capita increase in filings from 0.5 per thousand population to 0.9 per thousand.

These higher rates of filings are frequently cited as evidence of feverish litigiousness. But other evidence provides little support for the notion that these are linked with desperate congestion and crushing caseloads. David Clark's revealing analysis of federal district court activity from 1900 to 1980 shows a dramatic reduction in the duration of civil cases from about three and a half years at the beginning of the century to 1.16 years in 1980. The number of cases terminated per judge has been steady since World War II and remains considerably lower than in the inter-war period. Not only has the increase in judges kept up with the caseload, but there has been a massive increase in the support staff. While the average number of cases terminated per judge was approximately the same in 1980 as in 1960, the total employment of the federal judiciary rose during that period from 27.7 for every million people to 65.6 per million.

However, there has been a striking growth of appeals in federal courts. The rate at which those eligible to press appeals have exercised that right has risen, especially in criminal cases. The number of appeals filed in the federal courts of appeal almost quintupled from 1960 to 1980, while the number of judges nearly doubled. Understandably, it is the Supreme Court, whose filings during this period more than doubled, and the courts of appeal that are the provenance of much of the imagery of catastrophic overload.

Federal courts aside, the official statistics on the work of the courts are not readily usable for the purpose of measuring trends over time. Fortunately a number of scholars have in the past decade developed a technique of sampling the work of courts at intervals and using these successive portraits to give us a picture of the change in the work of these courts over time. These studies provide us with a periodic measure of the resort to the courts. The longest series of measurements of this type is from the very comprehensive work of McIntosh, tracing the work of the St. Louis Circuit Court since 1820.

. . . [F]ilings in that court have grown more than twenty-seven times from the 1820's to the 1970's, but the litigation rate in the 1970's is about half of what it was during the early nineteenth century. There has been a long slow rise in the per capita use of the court since the beginning of the present century.

. . . [T]here have been recent increases in most localities in the per capita filing of civil cases. The pattern in federal courts is more accentuated, but these rates are not marked by abrupt and extreme departures from past patterns. In several instances overall litigation rates have been higher in the past. Indeed, the glimpse of the remote past we get from McIntosh suggests sustained periods at much higher levels than we now have. What we know of law in the even more remote colonial past suggests that our predecessors were less reluctant to go to court. In Accomack County, Virginia, in 1639 the litigation rate of 240 per thousand was more than four times that in any contemporary American county for which we have data. In a seven year period, 20% of the adult population appeared in court five or more times as parties or witnesses. In Salem County, Massachusetts, about 11% of the adult males were involved in court conflicts during the year 1683. "[M]ost men living there had some involvement with the court system and many of them appeared repeatedly."

To understand the meaning of the recent trend to higher per capita filings, we have to examine the kinds of cases that are filed and what happens once they come to the courts. These filing statistics treat cases as interchangeable units, but cases are of different sizes and shapes. Some represent hotly contested disputes; others (like most divorce or debt or probate cases) are seeking administrative confirmation of a resolution, a claim, or some action taken. Some represent a major involvement by a court in which a judge actually decides the controversy; others represent little more than registration at the court. We have no figures on the quantum of contest or of judicial decision in these cases, but we can try to refine our picture by indirect evidence.

Over the past century there has been a pronounced shift in the make-up of the cases being brought to regular trial courts in the United States. There has been a shift from civil to criminal in the work of these courts. On the civil side, there has been a shift from cases involving market transactions (contract, property, and debt collection) to family and tort cases.

. . .

There was a corresponding decline in the portion of the caseload composed of commercial, contract, and property matters. . . .

Not only has there been a shift in the pattern of cases coming into the courts, there have been changes in what has transpired once they are filed. The available evidence requires more detailed analysis than space or time allows, so let me confine myself to a few general observations. First, it is evident that in all these courts most cases for the entire span of time in question have been disposed of without a full adversary trial. Voluntary dismissal (presumably the result of settlement) and uncontested judgement are the most common dispositions recorded in these courts. There is not evidence to suggest an increase in the portion of cases that runs the whole course. Several studies suggest that while litigation rates have risen, there has been a decline in the per capita rate of contested cases. Similarly, there has been a decline in the per capita rate of cases eliciting written opinions from state supreme courts.

One measure of the change in disposition patterns is the diminishing percentage of cases that go to trial. While federal court filings have risen dramatically, the percentage of cases reaching trial has diminished. (Note that this is a measure of the number of trials begun, not of trials completed: many cases are settled after trial has begun.) Similarly, from the early 1960's to 1980—a period of increased filings and larger jury awards—the number of jury trials actually held fell in both Cook County and San Francisco County.

There have been other changes in the character of what courts do. Less of their work is the direct, decisive resolution of individual disputes; more of it is routine administration and supervised bargaining. Courts contribute to the settlement of disputes less by imposing authoritative resolutions and more by pattern setting, by distribution of bargaining counters, and by mediation. Courts produce effects that radiate widely: rulings on motions, imposition of sanctions and damage awards become signals and sources of counters used for bargaining and regulation in many settings. The portion of cases that run the whole course has declined. But for the minority of matters that run the full course, adjudication is more protracted, more elaborate, more exhaustive, and more expensive. The process is more rational in the sense that it is free of antiquated and arbitrary formalities. Concealment is discouraged; litigants have access to more information. It is open to evidence of complicated states of facts and responsive to a wider range of argument.

. . .

Litigation concerning areas previously untouched by the courts mirrors a massive extension of governmental concern into areas of life which until recently were unregulated by the state (as in the great proliferation of environmental, health, safety and welfare regulation) or where regulation was not closely linked with the application of legal principles. As many activities and relationships not earlier subject to governmental control have become the subject of legislative and administrative concern, they have come before the courts as well. J. Willard Hurst points out that "[o]nly limited and episodically selected aspects of these reaches of statute and administrative law come into litigation at all." Although the judicial role in shaping public policy is overshadowed, there has been an extension of judicial oversight and the consequent legalization of whole areas of government activity that were not previously thought needful of close articulation with legal principles. These include large sections of the criminal justice system including police, prisons and juvenile justice, and other institutions dealing with dependent clients, such as schools, mental hospitals, and welfare agencies.

If a smaller proportion of the population are direct participants in contested adjudication, more people have what they perceive to be legal problems and they increasingly use lawyers to deal with them. The number of lawyers has increased much faster than the population. There were approximately 114,000 lawyers in 1900 (just over 150 per million). Through much of this century, the number of lawyers grew more slowly than the population and their relative presence declined. The proportion of lawyers in 1900 was surpassed only in 1955. Since then there has been a sharp increase in the number of lawyers. In 1960 there were about 286,000 lawyers; by 1980 this had doubled and there were over 250 lawyers per million. From 1960 to 1978 the portion of national income contributed by legal services increased by fifty percent—from six-tenths of one percent in 1960 to nine-tenths of one percent in 1978. There is some indication that legal expenses form an increasing portion of operating expenses for many businesses. For example, the president of a Chicago bank reported that the bank's legal expenses rose from 2% of net income in 1971 to 5% in 1976.

.   .   .

Thus litigation proliferates. It becomes more complex and refined, but at the same time most of it is truncated, decomposing into bargaining and mediation, or adminis- tration. Courts and big cases are more visible. For many in the society courts occupy a larger part of the symbolic universe even when their relative position in the whole governmental complex diminishes. Cost and remoteness remove the courts as an option in almost all disputes for almost all individuals. When courts are available, they may be found flawed. But courts are ever present as promulgators of symbols of en- titlement, enlivening consciousness of rights and heightening expectations of vindication.

Elsewhere, Perhaps.   Local differences in recording practices, differences in the juris- diction of courts and other tribunals, and differences in what is recorded as a case all add to differences in substantive law, making comparison of litigation across societies extremely treacherous. The figures in Table 2, below, must be taken with appropriate caution. They suggest great variation in litigation rates. These are rates for the ordinary courts, so the variation they show may be amplified or diminished by control- ling for the handling of similar disputes in other forums. To varying degrees, most industrialized states have curtailed the juris- diction of ordinary courts, diverting routine and/or sensitive matters into special courts or tribunals. Since the proceedings in such tribunals are often analytically indistinguish- able from litigation in court, these figures may tell us about the location rather than about the amount of adjudicative disputing in society. At the least we get an indication of

the very different uses to which the ordinary civil courts are put in various societies. I have also included some data on the number of judges and the number of lawyers. . . .

. . . [T]he United States rate of per capita use of the regular civil courts in 1975 was just below 44 per thousand. This is in the same range as England, Ontario, Australia, De- nmark, New Zealand, somewhat higher than Germany or Sweden, and far higher than Japan, Spain or Italy. It is difficult to know what to make of these rates until we sup- plement them with data about recording practices and about the other forums and tribunals which handle disputes in each of these societies. Given the serious problems of comparison, it would be foolhardy to draw any strong conclusions about the relative contentiousness or litigiousness of popula- tions from these data.

The contrasts in other parts of the legal system are as striking as are differences in litigation rates. The United States has many more lawyers than any other country—more than twice as many per capita as its closest rival. In contrast, the number of judges is relatively small. The ratio of lawyers to judges in the United States is the one of highest anywhere; the private sector of the law industry is very large relative to the public institutional sector. (Perhaps this has some connection with the feeling of extreme overload expressed by many American judges.)

If the figures themselves are inconclusive, does examination of our legal culture sug- gest that Americans are particularly given to litigation? Those who report on the litigation explosion credit Americans with a hair trig- ger readiness to file suit. Yet the survey evidence we have examined, the high rates of settlement, and personal experience sug- gest a picture quite different than in notably litigious societies. . . .

One comparison with a less litigious

TABLE 2
Judges, Lawyers and Civil Litigation in Selected Countries

Country	Judges		Lawyers		Civil Cases	
	Source & Date	Number per Million*	Source & Date	Number per Million*	Source & Date	Number per 1000*
Australia	C 1977	41.6	F 1975	911.6[a]	D 1975	62.06[b] [Western Australia only]
Belgium	E 1975	105.7	B 1972	389.7	E 1969	28.31[c]
Canada	H[d] 1970	59.3	G 1972	890.1[e]	M 1981–2	46.58[f] [Ontario only]
Denmark					E 1970	41.04g
England/Wales	H[d] 1973	50.9	H[h] 1973	606.4[i]	H 1973	41.1[j]
France	H[d] 1973	84.0	H[h] 1973	206.4	L 1975	30.67[k]
Italy	H[d] 1973	100.8	H[h] 1973	792.6	H 1973	9.66[j]
Japan	J 1974	22.7	R 1973	91.2[l]	T 1978	11.68[m]
Netherlands	E[d] 1975	39.8	B 1972	170.8	E 1970	8.25[n]
New Zealand	P 1976	26.8	O 1975	1081.3[o]	Q 1978	53.32[p]
Norway	R c.1977	60.8[q]	R c.1977	450.0	U 1976	20.32[r]
Spain	K 1970	31.0	B 1972	893.4	K 1970	3.45[s]
Sweden	H[d] 1973	99.6	H[h] 1973	192.4	H 1973	35.0[j]
United States	A, I, N 1980	94.9[v]	V 1980	2348.7[w]	1975	c.44.0[t]
W. Germany	H[d] 1973	213.4	H[h] 1973	417.2	S 1977	23.35[u]

NOTES:

* Unless noted otherwise, all population data taken from WORLD POPULATION 1979 (Washington, D.C.: U.S. Dept. of Commerce, Bureau of the Census, 1980).

[a] Disney, *et al.*, *supra* at 78, define lawyers as: practicing barristers, principal solicitors in private practice, solicitors employed by principal solicitors, and persons admitted as lawyers who are employed by government, by corporations or by other private organizations primarily for the purpose of providing legal services. This definition excludes judges, court officials, law professors and law book publishers.

[b] Figure based on filings in local courts, District Court and first instance bankruptcy, divorce and other proceedings filed in the Supreme Court of Western Australia. Western Australia's population in 1975 was 1,146,700 as reported in *Year Book Australia: No. 66, 1982.*

[c] Figure based on the number of cases brought in 1969 in civil courts; Magistrates' Courts, Courts of First Instance, Commercial Courts, Courts of Appeal, Courts of Cassation. All courts except Magistrates' Courts (15.78 cases brought per 1,000 population) hear both cases of first instance and appeals.

[d] Johnson, *et al.*, *supra* at 9-1, attempt to measure "career judges." They explain, "the functions of a judge vary considerably among the judicial systems embraced in this study. . . . While part-time judges and 'honorary judges' (generally law assessors) are common in some of. . .[the nations studied], they are rare in the United States. As much as possible, every attempt has been made to control for these particular variations by deleting 'honorary judges' from our manpower totals, and by combining part-time judgeships into equivalent full-time positions."

[c] Law Society membership includes retired, non-active, those in business, government, court officials; some may be members of more than one society.

[f] Figure based on filings in the Family Courts, County and District Courts, Small Claims Courts, Surrogate Court and Supreme Court. The total may be inflated by an admixture of appeals in the docket of the Supreme Court. Ontario's population in 1981 was 8,664,600 as reported in *The World Almanac and Book of Facts, 1983.*

[g] Figure based on cases brought before the District Courts and High Courts as courts of first instance.

[h] Johnson, *et al.*, *supra*, delete the judiciary and certain members of the profession not performing an advocacy or representational function, such as government and corporate employees whose possession of a law degree is only incidental. Counted are the private lawyers available to represent clients for a fee, the state prosecutors, salaried lawyers or private attorneys paid by government to handle criminal cases or to assist individual citizens with non-criminal legal problems.

[i] Includes 27,379 solicitors and 2,485 barristers.

[j] Figure based on judicial filings per 1,000 population.

[k] Figure based on civil cases, family matters, landlord-tenant cases, garnishments and orders to pay filed in the Tribunaux

d'instance and Tribunaux de grande instance. France's population in 1975 was 52,655,800, as reported in the *Annuaire statistique de la France, (1981)*. Calculation based on continental French data only.

l Lawyers registered with the bar association.

m Figure based on ordinary litigation cases, administrative cases, conciliation cases, domestic cases, executions, auctions, bankruptcies, provisional attachments, collection and compromise cases received by the Summary and District Courts, but does not include non-penal fines. Including the latter brings the rate to 13.18. Japan's population in 1978 was 114,898,000, as reported in the *Japan Statistical Yearbook, (1982)*.

n Based on contentious civil proceedings heard by the Supreme Court, Court of Appeals, Regional Courts and District Courts in 1970.

o Members of New Zealand Law Society holding practicing certificates.

p Figure based on civil cases filed in the Magistrates' Courts, the Supreme Court as a court of first instance, domestic proceedings and divorce petitions.

q This figure does not include members of mediation councils, which exist in each municipality. Disputes must be brought before the councils before going to court. Council members are often not lawyers.

r Figure based on cases *disposed of* by Conciliation Boards (71,490) and City and District Courts (10,318).

s Total number of first instance civil cases filed per 1,000 population.

t Estimate explained in text, *infra*.

u Figure based on cases received in the Municipal, District and Administrative Courts. The latter court has jurisdiction over cases with a public authority as defendant.

v Figure based on state and federal totals including 354 associate or assistant state judges. Figure does not include 263 part-time federal magistrates, 22 combination federal magistrates, 6,022 part-time state judges and magistrates, and 105 non-judicial state magistrates. When these judges are included the figure is 123.25. The U.S. Census of 1980 reported a population of 226,504,825.

w The U.S. Census of 1980 reported a population of 226,504,825.

SOURCES:

A. ADMINISTRATIVE OFFICE OF THE UNITED STATES COURTS, *Management Statistics for the United States Courts*, at 13, 129 (1980).

B. AMERICAN BAR FOUNDATION, *International Directory of Bar Associations*, 3d ed. Chicago: American Bar Foundation, at 5, 28, 35 (1973).

C. BARWICK, Sir Garfield, "The State of the Australian Judicature," 51 AUSTRALIAN L.J. 480, app. A (1977).

D. COMMONWEALTH BUREAU OF CENSUS & STATISTICS, *Statistics of Western Australia, Social, 1975*. Canberra: Commonwealth Bureau of Census and Statistics, Western Australia Office, 1976, Tables 44, 54 (1975).

E. COUNCIL OF EUROPE, *Judicial Organization in Europe*. London: Morgan-Grampian, Ltd., at 19, 33, 104, 105 (1975).

F. J. DISNEY, J. BASTEN. P. REDMOND & S. ROSS, LAWYERS, Sydney: The Law Book Company Limited, at 79 (1977).

G. P. EGAN, ed., *The Canadian Law List*. Ontario: Canada Law Book Limited, at 384 (1972).

H. E. JOHNSON, JR., S. BLACK, A. DREW, W. FELSTINER, E. HANSEN & G. SABAGH, Comparative Analysis of the Statistical Dimensions of the Justice Systems of Seven Industrial Democracies. A report submitted to the National Institute for Law Enforcement and Criminal Justice (1977).

I. JUDICIAL CONFERENCE OF THE UNITED STATES, *The Federal Magistrates System: Report to the Congress by the Judicial Conference of the United States*. Washington, D.C., at 25 (1981).

J. M. MCMAHON, *Legal Education in Japan*, 60 A.B.A. J. 1376, 1379 (1974).

K. J. MERRYMAN & D. CLARK, COMPARATIVE LAW: WESTERN EUROPEAN AND LATIN AMERICAN LEGAL SYSTEMS New York: Bobbs-Merrill Co., Inc., at 486, 497, tables 7.1, 7.13 (1978).

L. MINISTERE DE LA JUSTICE [France], *Compte general de la justice civile et commerciale, Tome II*, Paris: La Documentacion Francaise, tables Part 2: IV, VI, XIV, XV, XXV, XXVIII (1979).

M. MINISTRY OF ATTORNEY GENERAL [Ontario], *Court Statistics Annual Report, Fiscal Year 1981–1982*. Toronto: Ministry of Attorney General, Province of Ontario (1982) (1982).

N. NATIONAL COURT STATISTICS PROJECT, *State Court Organization, 1980*. Williamsburg, Va.: National Center for State Courts, tables 1, 3-25 (1982).

O. New Zealand Dep't of Statistics, *New Zealand Official Yearbook 1976* (81st Annual Ed. 1976).

P. New Zealand Dep't of Statistics, *Justice Statistics 1976*, at 15 (1978).

Q. New Zealand Dep't of Statistics, *Justice Statistics 1977–1978, Part A* table 4, at 29, 58, 88 (1980).

R. C. RHYNE, LAW AND JUDICIAL SYSTEMS OF NATIONS, Washington, D.C.: World Peace Through Law Center, at 388, 543–46 (1978).

S. STATISTICHES BUNDESAMT [Federal Republic of Germany], *Statistiches Jahrbuch 1980 fur die Bundesrepublik Deutschland*. Wiesbaden: Statistiches Bundesamt, tables 15.4.1, 15.4.5, 15.7.1 & 15.9 (1980).

T. STATISTICS BUREAU, PRIME MINISTER'S OFFICE [Japan], *Japan Statistics Yearbook, 1982*, Tokyo: Japan Statistical Association, 1982, tables 482, 483, 484 (1982).

U. STATISTIK SENTRALBYRA [Norway] n.d. *Sivilretts-Statistik 1976* (Civil Judicial Statistics 1976), Oslo: Statistik Sentralbyra, table 10.

V. U.S. DEPARTMENT OF LABOR, BUREAU OF LABOR STATISTICS, *Labor Force Statistics Derived From the Current Population Survey: A Datebook, Vol. 1*, Washington, D.C.: U.S. Department of Labor, Bureau of Labor Statistics, table B-20 (1982).

society merits closer examination because it is often made as part of the diagnosis of American hyperlexis. The American situation is juxtaposed with that of Japan, which appears in contrast as a peaceful garden that has remained uncorrupted by the worm of litigation. The Japanese have few lawyers, few judges and a low rate of litigation. It strikes many outsiders as a society that is free of the appetite to transform grievances into adversary contests. Social harmony promotes, and is reinforced by, the resolution of disputes through conciliatory means. In this view the small number of lawyers and judges in Japan reflects the low level of demand for their services, which in turn reflects an inbred cultural preference for harmonious reconciliation and disapproval of the assertiveness and contentiousness that are associated with litigation.

In assessing this "cultural" explanation for Japan's low litigation rates, we should recall (from table 2) that the Dutch, Spanish and Italian rates may be even lower. Few observers have associated Italian society with lack of contentiousness! This suggests that we should be wary of assuming that litigation rates are directly reflective of cultural preferences. How else might they be explained?

Professor John Haley provides a reading of the Japanese scene that argues the inadequacy of the classic view of Japan as anti-litigious. Haley contends that the much-cited preference for conciliation in Japan reflects the deliberate constriction of adjudicative alternatives by successive Japanese regimes. Summarizing Henderson's research, Haley recounts that:

> Tokugawa officialdom had constructed a formidable system of procedural barriers to obtaining final judgment in the Shogunate's courts. The litigant was forced each step of the way to exhaust all possibilities of conciliation and compromise and to proceed

> only at the sufferance of his superiors.... Conciliation was coerced...not voluntary. Yet...litigation still increased.

Modern statutes providing for formal conciliation were not "the product of popular demand for an alternative to litigation more in keeping with Japanese sensitivities." Rather "they reflected a conservative reaction to the rising tide of lawsuits in the 1920's and early 1930's and a concern on the part of the governing elite that litigation was destructive to a hierarchical social order based upon personal relationships." Mandatory conciliation brought about not a decrease in litigation, but an even greater increase in the number of cases channeled in the formal process, now enlarged to include additional remedial tracks.

The real check on Japanese litigation is the deliberate limitation of institutional capacity: the number of courts and lawyers is kept small. Haley asserts that maintenance of a small judicial plant in Japan reflects a government policy of restricting access to judicial remedies.

> [T]he number of judges in Japan has grown but little for the entire period from 1890 to the present. Thus as the population has grown the ratio of judges to the population has declined from one judge to 21,926 persons in 1890 to...one judge to 56,391 persons in 1969.

Of course many jobs done by lawyers in the United States are done by non-lawyers in Japan—and practically everywhere else. The small number of lawyers in Japan, however, reflects not an aversion to law, but a severe constriction of opportunities to enter the profession. There is a single institute from which graduates may enter bench, bar or prosecution. Places are limited to about 500 per year. Haley notes that "the number *per capita* of Japanese taking the judicial examination in 1975 was slightly higher than that of Americans taking a bar examination; ...in the United States, 74% passed, compared to 1.7% in Japan." In sum, the low rate of litigation in Japan evidences not the preferences of the population, but deliberate policy choices by political elites.

The Japanese comparison proves less revealing than appears at first glance, not least because the society is so vastly different than our own. But we may learn more about our supposed litigiousness from a society much more similar to ours. Dr. Jeffrey FitzGerald, an Australian researcher, has replicated in the State of Victoria the Civil Litigation Research Project's household survey—the basis for the analysis of Miller and Sarat. This affords a remarkable opportunity to compare the whole dispute pyramid, not just imponderable litigation rates. FitzGerald asked about the same types of problems as did CLRP and found Australians to be overall "more frequent perceivers of 'middle range' grievances than their American counterparts." He found an overall similarity in the shape and structure of the disputing pyramids in the two countries— that is, the extent to which different kinds of grievances gave rise to claims, in which claims gave rise to disputes, and disputes to consultation of lawyers. Overall, the Australian pyramid was more "bottom-heavy" "with more claims and fewer appeals to courts per 1,000 grievances." In other words, "Australians are substantially more likely to complain of troubles than are their U.S. counterparts and somewhat more likely to engage in an actual dispute."

The role of lawyers in the maturation of disputes is different. In Australia, 19% of the instances in which a lawyer was consulted in a grievance did not mature into a dispute. The US figure is 24%. In other words, American lawyers are more likely to dampen

disputes. At the same time they are more likely to invoke a court—at least by filing. Americans are twice as likely to take middle range disputes to court. Thus, American lawyers are involved in more "lumping it" as well as in going to court more. But "going to court" may mean something different in Australia. From what we have seen about settlement rates in the United States, we know that filing suit is often part of negotiation, so the meaning of this difference in filings is not clear. But it at least suggests that the way the negotiation game is played in Australia is different and that lawyers can conduct it without playing the court card. It also may reflect differences in the state of the law (more settled), in the organization of the profession (divided), and in fee arrangements (no contingency).

FitzGerald's research reminds us of the dissociation between litigation and other levels of disputing, so that we cannot take the former as representative of the larger whole. It points to the need to explore the way in which grievances are transformed into disputes and lawsuits. It also suggests that these processes are not explainable either by global and pervasive cultural traits, or by characteristics of individual disputants. As in the American study, education, income, occupation and ethnicity seem to explain little of the variation in grievance rates. In both countries "by far the most powerful explanatory factor" for the career of the dispute was the type of grievance involved. In other words, what happens depends on institutionalized ways of handling different kinds of disputes, not on broader cultural propensities to dispute.

.   .   .

CONCLUSION

In the course of this quick tour of disputing and litigation in the United States, I have tried to suggest a reading of the landscape that differs radically from the "litigation explosion" reading. This "contextual" reading differs in its view of the source and career of disputes and in its view of their significance. It does not view contemporary litigation as an eruption of pathological contentiousness or a dangerous and unprecedented loosening of needed restraints or the breakdown either of a common ethos or of community regulation. Instead, I see contemporary patterns of disputing as an adaptive (but not necessarily optimal) response to a set of changing conditions. There have been great changes in the social production of injuries as a result of, among other things, the increased power and range of injury-producing machinery and substances. There has been a great increase in social knowledge about the causation of injuries and of technologies for preventing them; there has been a wide dissemination of awareness of this knowledge to an increasingly educated public. There is an enhanced sense that harmful and confining conditions could be remedied. At the same time more of the interactions in the lives of many are with remote entities over which there are few direct controls. Government is used more to regulate these remote sources of harm and to assuage previously unremedied harms. Legal remedies become available to large segments of the population who earlier had little occasion to use the law. It may be easier to mobilize social support for disputing. In the light of all these changes, the pattern of use is conservative, departing relatively little from earlier patterns.

But overshadowing the change in actual disputing patterns are changes in the symbolic aspects of the system. There is more law, and our experience of most of it is increasingly indirect and mediated. Even while most disputing leads to mediation or bargaining, rather than authoritative disposition

by the courts, the courts occupy a larger portion of the symbolic universe and litigation seems omnipresent.

Is more and more visible litigation the sign and agent of the demise of community? This view of litigation as a destructive force, undermining other social institutions, strikes me as misleadingly one-sided. If litigation marks the assertion of individual will, it is also a reaching out for communal help and affirmation. If some litigation challenges accepted practice, it is an instrument for testing the quality of present consensus. It provides a forum for moving issues from the realm of unilateral power into a realm of public accountability. By permitting older clusters of practice to be challenged and new ones tested and incorporated into the constellation it helps to "create a new paradigm for the establishment of stable community life." If we relinquish the notion of community as some unchanging and all-encompassing *gemeinschaft* in favor of the multiple, partial and emergent community that we experience in contemporary urban life, we need not regard litigation as an antagonist of community.

I have argued that, like disputes themselves, knowledge about disputes is the product of interpretive acts, informed by the preconceptions and values of the observer. If so, the contextual response is as much an act of interpretation as the hyperlexis response. Obviously, I think that the former is more adequate than the latter. If interpretation is inevitable, how can one be superior to another? This shouldn't be much of a puzzle for lawyers. We are in the business of assessing competing interpretations. We know that just because *something* can be said for one reading of a matter, it is not automatically a toss-up between that and some other view.

I have argued that the hyperlexis reading of the dispute landscape displays the weakness of contemporary legal scholarship and policy analysis. We have seen the announcement of general conclusions relevant to policy on the basis of very casual scholarly activity. The information base was thin and spotty; theories were put forward without serious examination of whether they fit the facts; values and preconceptions were left unarticulated. Portentous pronouncements were made by established dignitaries and published in learned journals. Could one imagine public health specialists or poultry breeders conjuring up epidemics and cures with such cavalier disregard of the incompleteness of the data and the untested nature of the theory? If the profession's claim to expertise in such matters as disputes and litigation is to be taken seriously, it will need to adopt ground rules to require more respectful touching of the data bases. It will have to recognize that the collection of data and the development of coherent and tested theories for interpreting it are an inescapable collective responsibility of a group that purports to proffer expert opinions about the arrangements of public life. The career of the "litigation explosion" literature does not offer much reassurance that the legal profession and legal education are prepared to exercise such responsibility.

CHAPTER 3

Plea Bargaining and Civil Settlement in Trial Courts

American courts are reactive institutions; that is, they become involved in dispute processing at the initiative of parties who are not members of the judiciary. Yet bringing a dispute to court, filing a lawsuit, doesn't generally mean bringing that dispute to trial. Most lawsuits are resolved through some form of negotiation between the parties.[1] Litigation is, in this regard, continuous with efforts at settlement. It simply moves the parties to another arena.[2] Moreover, American courts deploy a variety of techniques, some of which they control directly and some of which are controlled externally, to encourage the settlement of disputes without a judicial decision.[3] Active judicial management of civil cases and plea bargaining are two such techniques considered in this chapter. In the reading by Galanter, he places both those techniques in the frame of an argument about what he calls "the decomposition of adjudication."

Disputes between the state and any of its citizens over alleged violations of the criminal law begin with the decision to arrest.[4] This decision is of substantial interest and importance but it is rather remote from the interests of someone concerned with the activities of American courts. It is remote because between arrest and appearance in court are several screening stages that substantially reduce the number of criminal cases reaching the courts.[5] One might imagine a progressively smaller number of cases flowing through a funnel until one reaches the theoretical end, the formal trial.

The two most important screening decisions that reduce the number of criminal cases reaching court are the prosecutor's decision to charge and the defendant's decision whether to waive the right to a formal trial by pleading guilty.[6] There are other screening stages such as indictment by a grand jury, arraignment, and pretrial or motion hearings, but none are as significant or as obvious as the charging and pleading decisions.

The prosecutor is a public official who is given the responsibility for deciding which suspects arrested by the police should be formally charged with having committed a crime and what the charges should be. In making decisions, the prosecutor considers two basic questions. First, is there a reasonable probability of the suspect's factual guilt? Second, is there enough legally admissible evidence to establish guilt in a trial? If the answer to either of these questions is no, then, at least in theory, the prosecutor ought not to charge a suspect with a crime.[7] Given that the reason for an arrest may have little or nothing to do with the task of enforcing the criminal law, what frequently happens is that the prosecutor is faced with the necessity of releasing many of those arrested. The police arrest people for a variety of reasons, such as harassment of "undesirables," protective detention of drunks, or merely to allow disputants time to cool their tempers. Thus prosecutors may have neither the necessary evidence nor the inclination to charge.

The considerations that influence the charging decision may have less to do with the evidence of a suspect's guilt than is generally assumed. Five such influences should be noted. First, prosecutors, especially in large cities, typically carry a heavy work load, or at least they perceive their work load to be burdensome. They believe that they have more cases to handle than they can reasonably process in an efficient and effective way. To the extent that this is true, prosecutors have an incentive to be lenient in cases where the evidence is not strong—that is, to use the decision not to charge as a way of maintaining control over their own work load.

A second influence affecting the decision to charge is the prosecutor's need or desire to achieve a high conviction rate. This is often assumed to be an extremely important part of a prosecutor's professional orientation. We think, however, that its importance may be overestimated. To the extent that a concern for maintaining a high conviction rate *does* influence the prosecutor, it may lead to a refusal to charge in cases in which there may be enough evidence to go to trial but not enough evidence to make conviction a sure thing.

A third influence on the charging decision is the expressed interest of criminal court judges regarding the disposition of particular kinds of criminal cases. Judicial resources are scarce and judges frequently communicate to prosecutors the manner in which they desire to expend them—that is, the kinds of cases they think ought to be emphasized. Thus, prosecutors may not charge people who are arrested for committing the kinds of offenses that judges believe to be trivial or insignificant.

The prosecutor's sense of "substantive justice" is a fourth influence on the charging decision.[8] Prosecutors may use their power to charge as a way of imposing sanctions on those who they believe deserve punishment. They may do so even though they may not believe that a case can be made in court or even though they are confident that no guilty plea will be forthcoming. In this sense the charging decision is the prosecutor's way of dealing with people who may be factually but not legally culpable for violating the criminal code. The charging decision, by threatening a suspect with trial and by establishing a formal record of prosecution, imposes sanctions even on those who the prosecutor knows cannot be convicted.

Finally, prosecutors may charge in anticipation that a suspect will plead guilty even in cases in which the prosecutor does not believe there is sufficient evidence to convict. Each of these influences may also be important in encouraging prosecutors and judges to dismiss cases even after the initial charging decision. Each of the five influences is as important as the official determination of factual or legal guilt. The reading by Cole, which is based on a case study of a prosecutor's office, illustrates several of these points.

Once an individual is charged with a serious crime, the commission of which the prosecutor believes can be proven in court, all that stands between the suspect and a formal trial is the decision whether to claim innocence or to plead guilty. In most American courts the overwhelming majority of criminal cases are terminated by a plea of guilty. This perhaps indicates, first, that the charging decisions made by prosecutors are so accurate that those who are in fact innocent tend to be screened out of the judicial process without being charged.

Second, the high percentage of criminal cases terminated by guilty pleas may result from the particular cost/benefit calculations of individuals charged with crimes. The costs of going to trial include lawyers' fees, time that may or may not have to be spent in jail, uncertainty, and the risk of incurring a more severe penalty than would be imposed should the individual voluntarily acknowledge guilt. Each defendant must decide whether the chances of success at trial are worth incurring such costs.[9]

Third, it is often argued that the high incidence of guilty pleas is a direct result of "bargain justice." This phrase implies that no one in the criminal justice system has an incentive to pursue cases through to trial. Prosecutors seek a rapid and certain disposition of cases and attempt to reduce the workload for both the prosecutor and the judge. They may do so by offering concessions to those accused of crimes in return for confessions of guilt. These concessions typically take the form of reduced or dropped charges or promises to recommend leniency in sentencing. It should be recognized that guilty pleas do not necessarily result from an explicit process of bargaining between prosecutor and defendants. Bargaining can take place tacitly with no direct exchange of concessions. A plea of guilty may be entered in anticipation of a leniency recommendation or a dropped charge.

As both the Heumann and Feeley articles point out, it is important to recognize that the high incidence of guilty pleas is not a recent phenomenon. It is not simply a result of the pressures of heavy caseloads but reflects instead the kind of calculations that defendants have always had to make about the costs and benefits of protesting their innocence. Some believe (see the reading by Schulhofer) that those calculations need not always lead to a bargained plea of guilty. They challenge the view that plea bargaining is inevitable or desirable.

In criminal cases the regulation of demands is largely controlled not by the judges but rather by the prosecutors and defendants. In contrast, in civil litigation the role of the judge in diverting cases from court is frequently more direct. As in the criminal process, many civil cases are not filed with any expectation that they will proceed to a formal trial. Filing a lawsuit may simply be a strategic device designed to promote or facilitate out-of-court settlements. In this sense there is a specifiable level of natural "fall-out" that will occur between the filing and the disposition stages in civil litigation. As in the criminal process, most civil cases never go to trial.

In order for a dispute to be processed by a court, it must meet certain formal qualifications. First, it must involve an actionable legal right and an available legal remedy. However, given the wide scope of legal regulation in America today, almost any dispute can be framed as a contest over legal rights. Second, a dispute must fall within the court's geographic or subject-matter jurisdiction. Third, the parties must have standing to sue, that is, their dispute must be real, must involve a recognizable conflict of interest and a direct and substantial injury to one of the parties. Traditionally courts have allowed litigants to sustain actions to protect their own personal or property rights. These and other formal requirements provide courts with limited, but nevertheless useful, ways in which they may avoid hearing particular disputes or particular categories of disputes. The requirements are useful to courts precisely because they are broad and flexible; they allow judges wide latitude in deciding which cases will or will not be heard.

One of the many factors that determine which cases persist and go to trial is the pretrial conference. The pretrial conference is of relatively recent vintage and is not employed by all courts or in all civil cases.[10] In some states it is a formal requirement for particular kinds of cases, but in most courts its use is informal and at the discretion of the judge. During pretrial conferences the judge meets with lawyers for both parties and seeks to promote a mutually satisfactory settlement. The judge may suggest what, if anything, a case is "worth" or may try to narrow the differences between the parties in such a way as to increase the likelihood that they themselves will reach settlement. The pretrial conference is only one of a variety of tools judges can use to manage civil cases and guide them toward settlement. The selection by Judith Resnik provides an overview of those tools and assesses the impact of judicial management for the role of the judge.

NOTES

1. David M. Trubek et al., "The Costs of Ordinary Litigation," *UCLA Law Review* 31 (1983), 72.

2. Marc Galanter, "The Radiating Effects of Courts," in *Empirical Theories About Courts*, eds. Keith Boyum and Lynn Mather (New York: Longman, 1983).

3. See Marc Galanter, "The Emergence of the Judge as a Mediator in Civil Cases," *Judicature* 69 (1986), 256.

4. Wayne Lafave, *Arrest: The Decision to Take a Suspect into Custody* (Boston: Little, Brown, 1965), and Jerome Skolnick, *Justice Without Trial* (New York: Wiley, 1966).

5. By "screening stages" we mean the major occasions when cases once filed in a criminal court are disposed of, resolved, or diverted.

6. See James Eisenstein and Herbert Jacob, *Felony Justice* (Boston: Little, Brown, 1977) and James Eisenstein, Roy B. Flemming, and Peter F. Nardulli, *The Contours of Justice* (Boston: Little, Brown, 1988).

7. Frank Miller, *Prosecution: The Decision to Charge a Suspect with a Crime* (Boston: Little, Brown, 1970). Also see John Hagan, "The Parameters of Criminal Prosecution," *Journal of Criminal Law and Criminology* 65 (1974), 536 and Celesta A. Albonetti, "Prosecutorial Discretion: The Effects of Uncertainty," *Law & Society Review* 21 (1987), 291.

8. Malcolm M. Feeley, *The Process is the Punishment* (New York: Russell Sage, 1979).

9. Donald Newman, *Conviction: The Determination of Guilt or Innocence Without Trial* (Boston: Little, Brown, 1966). Also see Arthur Rosett and Donald Cressey, *Justice by Consent: Plea Bargains in the American Courthouse* (Philadelphia: Lippincott, 1976); John Klein, *Let's Make a Deal* (Lexington, Mass.: Lexington Books, 1976); Milton Heumann, *Plea Bargaining: The Experiences of Prosecutors, Judges, and Defense Attorneys* (Chicago: University of Chicago Press, 1978); Lynn M. Mather, *Plea Bargaining or Trial?* (Lexington, Mass.: Heath, 1979); and Malcolm M. Feeley, *Court Reform on Trial: Why Simple Solutions Fail* (New York: Basic Books, 1983).

10. Maurice Rosenberg, *The Pretrial Conference and Effective Justice* (New York: Columbia University Press, 1964). See also J. Skelly Wright, "The Pretrial Conference," *Federal Rules Decisions* 18 (1962), 141 and John Paul Ryan, Allan Ashman, Bruce D. Sales, and Sandra Shane-DuBow, *American Trial Judges: Their Work Styles and Performance* (New York: Free Press, 1980), chap. 8.

Adjudication, Litigation and Related Phenomena

Marc Galanter

THE LITIGATION PROCESS: ATTRITION, ROUTINE PROCESSING, BARGAINING AND SETTLEMENT

In America the greatest majority of disputes which are taken to an adjudicative forum are disposed of (by abandonment, withdrawal or settlement) without full-blown adjudication and often without any authoritative disposition by the court. In fact, of those cases that do reach a full authoritative disposition by a court, a large portion do not involve a contest. They are uncontested either because the dispute has been resolved (as in divorce) or because only one party appears.... Over 30 per cent of cases in American courts o. general jurisdiction are not formally contested. The predominance of uncontested matters in American courts is long-standing....

Many cases are withdrawn or abandoned because invocation of the court served the initiator's purpose of harassment, warning or

"Adjudication, Litigation, and Related Phenomena," by Marc Galanter. Taken from Law and the Social Sciences (New York: Russell Sage Foundation), edited by Leon Lipson and Stanton Wheeler. Copyright © 1986 Russell Sage Foundation. Reprinted by permission of Russell Sage Foundation.

delay. Police may make an arrest or file charges for reasons of control with no intention of pursuing prosecution.... The invocation of official adjudicatory institutions does not necessarily express either a preference or an intention to pursue the dispute in official forums, to secure the application of official rules, or to obtain an adjudicated outcome. The official system may be invoked (or invocation may be threatened) in order to punish or harass, to demonstrate prowess, to force an opponent to settle, or to secure compliance with the decision of another forum....

The master pattern of American disputing is one in which there is invocation (actual or threatened) of an authoritative decision-maker countered by a threat of protracted or hard-fought resistance, leading to negotiated or mediated settlement in the anteroom of the adjudicative institution. Adversary conflict is replaced by maneuver with an eye to negotiation—the imposition of arbitral judgment is replaced by mediation.

Plea-Bargaining

The best known instance of this pattern is the processing of criminal cases in the United States. The term "plea bargaining" is employed popularly and here to refer to a whole family of patterns of processing criminal cases. These may involve protracted explicit bargaining or tacit reference to established understandings. Feeley (1979: 462) observes that:

> discussions of plea bargaining often conjure up images of a Middle Eastern bazaar, in which each transaction appears as a new distinct encounter, unencumbered by precedent or past association. Every interchange involves higgling and haggling anew, in an effort to obtain the best possible deal. The reality of American lower courts is different. They are more akin to modern supermakets, in which prices for various commodities have been clearly established and labeled in advance.
>
> .   .   .

Agreement may take the form of submission to an abbreviated trial in which formal rules of evidence are suspended and a finding of guilt is foreordained. . . . Or, more commonly, it takes the form of an agreement about the charges brought against the accused, about the sentence to be imposed, about subsequent behavior, restitution, or the like.

These non-trial dispositions account for some 80 or 90 percent or more of criminal dispositions in almost every American jurisdiction. . . . Local styles differ as to the stage of the process. . . and the role of the judge. The judge may be passive, merely ratifying deals arranged by the parties: he may actively participate in plea discussions; or he may be dominant, orchestrating the whole process. . . .

Attempts to eliminate the negotiation element demonstrate the vital role of these processes to the local criminal justice culture. Abolition of the prevalent species of negotiated disposition lead to a shift to others. . . .

Where plea bargaining was once viewed as disreputable it has won considerable respectability, because of its perceived contribution to facilitating the work of the courts. . . . It is also credited with leading to dispositions preferable to the outcomes produced by trial. Thus the United States Supreme Court has observed that plea bargaining "can benefit all concerned." *Blackledge* v. *Allison*, 430 U.S. 63, 71 (1976). Similarly, judicial participation in the process has become more respectable and there are calls for more judicial supervision to insure "equal plea bargaining opportunities." (California Law Review 1971)

Civil Settlement

Similarly, most civil cases in American courts are settled. That is, they terminate in an outcome agreed upon by the parties, sometimes formally ratified by the court, sometimes only noted as settled, and sometimes (from the court's viewpoint) abandoned. The settlement process may begin before filing of suit, for example, a great majority of automobile injury claims are settled before filing. . . . Of those claims that become lawsuits, settlement is the prevalent mode of disposition of most commercial cases as well as tort cases. . .and in the overwhelming majority of family cases, (although in the latter case, the result takes the form of a decree in which one party apparently prevails over the other). Settlement has been the prevalent pattern in the United States for at least half a century. . . .

Just as "plea bargaining" on close inspection encompasses a cluster of distinct patterns, the umbrella term "settlement" encompasses a whole family of related but distinct phenomena. It includes bilateral negotiation among the parties. . .prior to or after filing, more or less articulated to moves in the judicial arena. It also includes participation by third parties—outside mediators, officials, even judges. American judges in recent decades have increasingly accepted the notion that courts should actively promote settlements.

Judges may participate pursuant to a formal judicial responsibility to supervise the settlement (as in class actions, stockholders derivative suits, bankruptcy reorganization cases, where minors are parties, and so forth). There is a growing body of legal doctrine about the way in which courts are obliged to exercise these responsibilities... Judges may also participate indirectly where the form of the proceeding requires that the bargain struck by the parties be ratified by the court and embodied in a decree—as in divorce cases.... Judges may also participate in settlement negotiations in the absence of any formal requirement that they supervise the settlement or ratify its results. American trial judges employ a variety of techniques to promote settlement, including voluntary and mandatory conferences, meetings and consultations with the parties individually, together and serially. The proferring of settlement formulas and various other techniques of active brokering are utilized by at least some judges.

The participation of American judges in active promotion of settlements is increasing and increasingly respectable. The primary rationalization (like that for endorsement of plea bargaining) is that this departure from the adjudicative model is necessary to preserve the forum from unbearable pressures of caseload. But judges also justify active participation on the ground that such efforts provide greater satisfaction to litigants, repair relations between contesting parties, and avoid untoward results in particular cases Thus, one Federal judge in Pittsburgh, trying a suit that threatened the existence of the Westinghouse corporation, sought to avoid a decision based on contract norms and pressed the parties to settle explaining:

> The fiscal well-being, possibly the survival of one of the world's corporate giants is in jeopardy. Likewise, the future of thousands of jobs.
>
> Any decision I hand down will hurt somebody and because of that potential damage, I want to make it clear that it will happen only because certain captains of industry could not together work out their problems so that the hurt might have been held to a minimum. (*New York Times*, February 11, 1977: D-1, D-10)
>
> Solomon-like as I want to be, I can't cut this baby in half. (*New York Times*, February 17, 1977: 57) (Quoted in Macaulay 1977: 516)

Indeed, many judges accept the notion that settlement promotes more just results than would be produced by full-blown adjudication. Thus one veteran federal judge told a training session for new federal judges that:

> One of the fundamental principles of judicial administration is that, in most cases, the absolute result of a trial is not as high a quality of justice as is the freely negotiated, give a little, take a little settlement. (Will: FRD)

There appears to be some increase in the portion of cases that are settled, but this is a surmise and remains to be tested, controlling for types of cases. There is no evidence that increased judicial participation in the settlement process brings about more settlements....

But we cannot conclude that these judicial efforts do not have other effects. Is it the same cases that get settled? At the same stage? And on comparable terms? With what effects on the currency of endowments or bargaining counters to be used in other cases? And what perceptions of the process by the participants?

. . .

Which cases manage to survive the winnowing process and end up being fully adjudicated? (1) Perhaps the single most common type is the case where a party needs the judicial declaration—as in divorce or probate proceedings. In such cases there is typically no contest or, if there was a contest, it has been settled between the parties before securing a judicial ratification of it. (2) Another very frequent kind of frequently adjudicated case is one which is "cut and dried" and can be processed cheaply and routinely, as in most collection cases where frequently the defendant does not appear. In both these types the element of contest is minimal.

Other cases are adjudicated because of a premium placed on having an external agency make the decision. (3) Thus an insurance company functionary may want to avoid responsibility for a large payout. . . . A prosecutor may prefer that charges against the accused in an infamous crime be dismissed by the court rather than by his office. . . . (4) Or there may be value to an actor in showing some external audience (a creditor or the public) that no stone has been left unturned. (5) Or external decision may be sought where the case is so complex or the outcome so indeterminate that it is too unwieldy or costly to arrange a settlement. . . . (6) Settlement may be unappealing because the "settlement value" is insufficient. Ross (1970) describes as the "lawyer's gamble" the personal injury case in which damages are high but liability sufficiently doubtful to preclude a large settlement. Similarly accused criminals facing mandatory sentences may find the available bargains unattractive. (7) Even when the bargain is acceptable in itself, it may be spurned because of the effect that accepting it would have on the bargaining credibility of a player in future transactions.

A litigant or lawyer may want to display his commitment and thus enhance his credibility as an adversary in future rounds of play. . . .

Finally, a party may want to adjudicate in order to affect the state of the law. (8) Some parties—typically recurrent organizational litigants—are willing to invest in securing from a court a declaration of "good law" (or avoiding a declaration of "bad law") even where such a decision costs far more than a settlement in the case at hand. . . since such a declaration will improve its position in series of future controversies. (9) Or parties may seek not furtherance of their interests, but vindication of fundamental value commitments—for example, the organizations which have sponsored much church-state litigation in the United States. . . . Players whose conflict is about value differences rather than about interest conflicts are less likely to settle. (10) Related to this is the special case of government bodies whose notion of "gain" is often problematic and who may seek from courts authoritative interpretations of public policy (i.e., redefinitions of their notion of gain.) . . .

. . . .

THE ELABORATION AND DECOMPOSITION OF ADJUDICATION

Full-blown adversary adjudication becomes more rare as it becomes more refined and elaborate. In its appointed precincts, we find vast amounts of negotiation "in the shadow of the law," routine administrative processing, abbreviated forms of adjudication. . . the settlement conference, the "preliminary hearing". . ."informal administrative hearings". . .and active mediation on the part of officials clothed with arbitral powers.

How can we account for the attenuation and abandonment of adjudicative modes? The most prevalent explanation is that these distortions result from massive caseloads that prevent institutions from conducting affairs the way they are supposed to. Plea bargaining then is the result of the immense crush of criminal cases; and settlements of civil and administrative matters are induced by the long delays and high costs.

A series of incisive analyses have demolished the notion that non-trial dispositions in criminal cases are a recent response to pressures of caseload...

Of course, caseload pressures may have been connected with the origins of plea-bargaining patterns and they certainly affect the process. And caseload may affect the bargains that are struck. For example, Feeley (1979: 254) found heavy caseload strongly related to charge reductions in felony cases. Extremes of congestion may be associated with more lenient disposition.... Similarly, more crowded dockets and consequent longer delays presumably increase the discounts that defendants can command in settling civil claims.

Caseload may be connected with settlement in another way. A higher volume of transactions creates channels of communication among regular participants: more occasions for establishing trust, exchanging reciprocities and communicating about what cases are worth, what factors are to be taken into account, may rationalize dealings by reducing the amount of learning needed on any single occasion.

A rival explanation attributes the settlement to fundamental strategic considerations rather than to temporary institutional conditions. In this "strategic" view, all of the participants, seeking to achieve their goals while avoiding risks, find full-blown adjudication inexpedient. Judges want to achieve "appropriate" dispositions while managing the flow of cases. Most lawyers find trials distasteful: they may bring little financial gain, they disrupt his practice, require extensive preparation and expose him to risks of losing or revealing lack of expertise.... If trial offers parties hope of complete victory or vindication, it involves additional cost, protracted delay and a risk of losing all. For the criminal defendant, choosing trial means more time before resolution, and a substantial probability of more severe sentencing.... One recent study showed "that individual judges, regardless of sentencing philosophy, systematically sentenced jury defendants more heavily than ...defendants who had pled guilty or elected a bench trial." (Uhlman and Walker 1980: 339) The pull of these strategic inclinations is suggested by the tenacity with which systems of arranged dispositions survive attempts to abolish them.... Where "bargaining" is eliminated it is by standardizing the terms of arranged disposition, not by increasing the number of trials....

Reports from other settings point to the centrality of the striving of participants to maintain control and avoid untoward risks....

The decomposition of adjudication into bargaining may be accompanied by the simplification and vulgarization of authoritative legal learning. Refined legal standards are replaced by formulae like "three times specials"... or by the typifications employed by the criminal court regulars who deal with "heavy hitters," "pros" and "nuisance cases".... These typifications of people and events, which cut across legal categories and emphasize qualities relevant to disposition, suggest that bargaining may extend as well as attenuate the range of issues considered relevant. Bargaining about criminal dispositions may apply norms about first offenders, youth, seriousness, family responsibility, and so forth, that are institutionalized in the local legal culture, but not in the higher law. Similarly, negotiation in civil cases may take into account a range of norms that are excluded from authoritative decision by the court. . . .

REFERENCES

Feeley, Malcolm M. (1979). Pleading Guilty in Lower Courts, 13 *Law & Society Review* 461–66.

Kagan, Robert A., Bliss Cartwright, Lawrence M. Friedman, and Stanton Wheeler (1977) "The Business of State Supreme Courts, 1870–1970," 30 *Stanford Law Review* 121–156.

Macaulay, Stewart (1977) "Elegant Models, Empirical Pictures, and the Complexities of Contract," 11 *Law & Society Review* 507–528.

Ross, H. Laurence (1970) *Settled Out of Court: The Social Process of Insurance Claims Adjustment.* Chicago: Aldine.

Uhlman, Thomas M. and N. Darlene Walker (1980) "'He Takes Some of My Time; I Take Some of His': An Analysis of Judicial Sentencing Patterns in Jury Cases," 14 *Law and Society Review* 323–341.

Will, Hubert L., Robert R. Merhige, and Alvin B. Rubin (1977) "The Role of the Judge in the Settlement Process," 75 *Federal Rules Decisions* 203–36.

The Decision to Prosecute

George F. Cole

This paper is based on an exploratory study of the Office of Prosecuting Attorney, King County (Seattle), Washington.... An open-ended interview was administered to one-third of the former deputy prosecutors who had worked in the office during the ten-year period 1955–1965. In addition, interviews were conducted with court employees, members of the bench, law enforcement officials, and others having reputations for participation in legal decision-making. Over fifty respondents were contacted during this phase. A final portion of the research placed the author in the role of observer in the prosecutor's office. This experience allowed for direct observation of all phases of the decision to prosecute so that the informal processes of the office could be noted. Discussions with the prosecutor's staff, judges, defendant's attorneys, and the police were held so that the interview data could be placed within an organizational context.

The primary goal of this investigation was to examine the role of the prosecuting attorney as an officer of the legal process within the context of the local political system.... By focusing upon the political and social linkages between these systems, it is expected that decision-making in the prosecutor's office will be viewed as a principal ingredient in the authoritative allocation of values.

THE PROSECUTOR'S OFFICE IN AN EXCHANGE SYSTEM

While observing the interrelated activities of the organizations in the legal process, one might ask, "Why do these agencies co-operate?" If the police refuse to transfer information to the prosecutor concerning the commission of a crime, what are the rewards or sanctions which might be brought against them? Is it possible that organizations maintain a form of "bureaucratic accounting" which, in a sense, keeps track of the resources allocated to an agency and the support returned? How are cues transmitted from one agency to another to influence decision-making? These are some of the questions which must be asked when deci-

"The Decision to Prosecute," George F. Cole. Law and Society Review, Vol. 4, No. 3, 1970. Reprinted by permission of the Law and Society Association.

sions are viewed as an output of an exchange system.

The major findings of this study are placed within the context of an exchange system. This serves the heuristic purpose of focusing attention upon the linkages found between actors in the decision-making process. In place of the traditional assumptions that the agency is supported solely by statutory authority, this view recognizes that an organization has many clients with which it interacts and upon whom it is dependent for certain resources. As interdependent subunits of a system, then, the organization and its clients are engaged in a set of exchanges across their boundaries. These will involve a transfer of resources between the organizations which will affect the mutual achievement of goals.

The legal system may be viewed as a set of interorganizational exchange relationships analogous to what Long (1962: 142) has called a community game. The participants in the legal system (game) share a common territorial field and collaborate for different and particular ends. They interact on a continuing basis as their responsibilities demand contact with other participants in the process. Thus, the need for the cooperation of other participants can have a bearing on the decision to prosecute. A decision not to prosecute a narcotics offender may be a move to pressure the United States Attorney's Office to cooperate on another case. It is obvious that bargaining occurs not only between the major actors in a case—the prosecutor and the defense attorney—but also between the clientele groups that are influential in structuring the actions of the prosecuting attorney.

Exchanges do not simply "sail" from one system to another, but take place in an institutionalized setting which may be compared to a market. In the market, decisions are made between individuals who occupy boundary-spanning roles, and who set the conditions under which the exchange will occur. In the legal system, this may merely mean that a representative of the parole board agrees to forward a recommendation to the prosecutor, or it could mean that there is extended bargaining between a deputy prosecutor and a defense attorney. In the study of the King County Prosecutor's Office, it was found that most decisions resulted from some type of exchange relationship. The deputies interacted almost constantly with the police and criminal lawyers, while the prosecutor was more closely linked to exchange relations with the courts, community leaders, and the county commissioners.

THE PROSECUTOR'S CLIENTELE

In an exchange system, power is largely dependent upon the ability of an organization to create clientele relationships which will support and enhance the needs of the agency. For, although interdependence is characteristic of the legal system, competition with other public agencies for support also exists. Since organizations operate in an economy of scarcity, the organization must exist in a favorable power position in relation to its clientele. Reciprocal and unique claims are made by the organization and its clients. Thus, rather than being oriented toward only one public, an organization is beholden to several publics, some visible and others seen clearly only from the pinnacle of leadership. As Gore (1964: 23) notes, when these claims are "firmly anchored inside the organization and the lines drawn taut, the tensions between conflicting claims form a net serving as the institutional base for the organization."

An indication of the stresses within the judicial system may be obtained by analyzing its outputs. It has been suggested that the

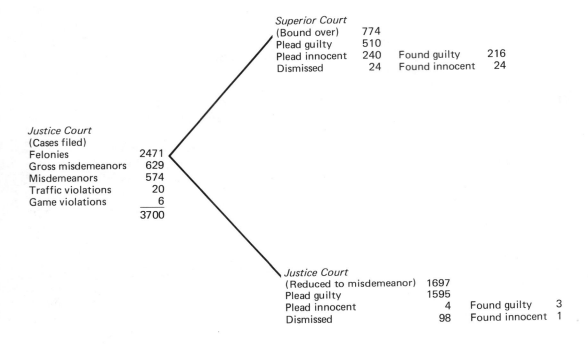

FIGURE 1. Disposition of felony cases—King County, 1964.

administration of justice is a selective process in which only those cases which do not create strains in the organization will ultimately reach the courtroom (Chambliss, 1969: 84). As noted in Figure 1, the system operates so that only a small number of cases arrive for trial, the rest being disposed of through reduced charges, *nolle pros.*, and guilty pleas. Not indicated are those cases removed by the police and prosecutor prior to the filing of charges. As the focal organization in an exchange system, the office or prosecuting attorney makes decisions which reflect the influence of its clientele. Because of the scarcity of resources, marketlike relationships, and the organizational needs of the system, prosecutorial decision-making emphasizes the accommodations which are made to the needs of participants in the process.

Police

Although the prosecuting attorney has discretionary power to determine the disposition of cases, this power is limited by the fact that usually he is dependent upon the police for inputs to the system of cases and evidence. The prosecutor does not have the investigative resources necessary to exercise the kind of affirmative control over the types of cases that are brought to him. In this relationship, the prosecutor is not without countervailing power. His main check on the police is his ability to return cases to them for further investigation and to refuse to approve arrest warrants.... As noted by many respondents, the police, in turn, are dependent upon the prosecutor to accept the output of their system; rejection of too many cases can have serious repercussions affecting the morale, discipline, and workload of the force.

A request for prosecution may be rejected for a number of reasons relating to questions of evidence. Not only must the prosecutor believe that the evidence will secure a conviction, but he must also be aware of community norms relating to the type of acts that should be prosecuted....

Factors other than those relating to evidence may require that the prosecutor refuse to accept a case from the police. First, the prosecuting attorney serves as a regulator of case loads not only for his own office, but for the rest of the legal system. Constitutional and statutory time limits prevent him and the courts from building a backlog of untried cases. In King County, when the system reached the "overload point," there was a tendency to be more selective in choosing the cases to be accepted. A second reason for rejecting prosecution requests may stem from the fact that the prosecutor is thinking of his public exposure in the courtroom. He does not want to take forward cases which will place him in an embarrassing position. Finally, the prosecutor may return cases to check the quality of police work.... Rather than spend the resources necessary to find additional evidence, the police may dispose of a case by sending it back to the prosecutor on a lesser charge, implement the "copping out" machinery leading to a guilty plea, drop the case, or in some instances send it to the city prosecutor for action in municipal court.

In most instances, a deputy prosecutor and the police officer assigned to the case occupy the boundary-spanning roles in this exchange relationship. Prosecutors reported that after repeated contacts they got to know the policemen whom they could trust....

Sometimes the police perform the ritual of "shopping around," seeking to find a deputy prosecutor who on the basis of past experience, is liable to be sympathetic to their view on a case. At one time, deputies were given complete authority to make the crucial decisions without coordinating their activities with other staff members. In this way the arresting officer would search the prosecutor's office to find a deputy he thought would be sympathetic to the police attitude....

An exchange relationship between a deputy prosecutor and a police officer may be influenced by the type of crime committed by the defendant. The prototype of a criminal is one who violates person and property. However, a large number of cases involve "crimes without victims." This term refers to those crimes generally involving violations of moral codes, where the general public is theoretically the complainant. In violations of laws against bookmaking, prostitution, and narcotics, neither actor in the transaction is interested in having an arrest made. Hence, vice control men must drum up their own business. Without a civilian complainant, victimless crimes give the police and prosecutor greater leeway in determining the charges to be filed.

.   .   .

Courts

The ways used by the court to dispose of cases is a vital influence in the system. The court's actions affect pressures upon the prison, the conviction rate of the prosecutor, and the work of probation agencies. The judge's decisions act as clues to other parts of the system, indicating the type of action likely to be taken in future cases.... Under such conditions, it would be expected that the prosecutor would respond to the judge's actions by reducing the inputs to the court either by not preferring charges or by increasing the pressure for guilty pleas through bargaining. The adjustments of other parts of the system could be expected to follow. For instance, the police might sense the lack of interest of the prosecutor in accepting charges, hence they will send only airtight cases to him for indictment.

The influence of the court on the decision to prosecute is very real. The sentencing history of each judge gives the prosecutor, as well as other law enforcement officials, an indication of the treatment a case may receive in the courtroom. The prosecutor's expectation as to whether the court will convict may limit his discretion over the decisions on whether to prosecute. . . . Since the prosecutor depends upon the plea-bargaining machinery to maintain the flow of cases from his office, the sentencing actions of judges must be predictable. If the defendant and his lawyer are to be influenced to accept a lesser charge or the promise of a lighter sentence in exchange for a plea of guilty, there must be some basis for belief that the judge will fulfill his part of the arrangement. Because judges are unable formally to announce their agreement with the details of the bargain, their past performance acts as a guide.

Within the limits imposed by law and the demands of the system, the prosecutor is able to regulate the flow of cases to the court. He may control the length of time between accusation and trial; hence he may hold cases until he has the evidence which will convict. Alternatively, he may seek repeated adjournment and continuances until the public's interest dies; problems such as witnesses becoming unavailable and similar difficulties make his request for dismissal of prosecution more justifiable. Further, he may determine the type of court to receive the case and the judge who will hear it. Many misdemeanors covered by state law are also violations of a city ordinance. It is a common practice for the prosecutor to send a misdemeanor case to the city prosecutor for processing in the municipal court when it is believed that a conviction may not be secured in justice court. As a deputy said, "If there is no case—send it over to the city court. Things are speedier, less formal, over there."

·   ·   ·

Defense Attorneys

In a legal system where bargaining is a primary method of decision-making, it is not surprising that criminal lawyers find it essential to maintain close personal ties with the prosecutor and his staff. Respondents were quite open in revealing their dependence upon this close relationship to successfully pursue their careers. The nature of the criminal lawyer's work is such that his saleable product or service appears to be influence rather than technical proficiency in the law. Respondents hold the belief that clients are attracted partially on the basis of the attorney's reputation as a fixer, or as a shrewd bargainer.

There is a tendency for ex-deputy prosecutors in King County to enter the practice of criminal law. Because of his inside knowledge of the prosecutor's office and friendships made with court officials, the former deputy feels that he has an advantage over other criminal law practitioners. All of the former deputies interviewed said that they took criminal cases. Of the eight criminal law specialists, seven previously served as deputy prosecutors in King County, while the other was once prosecuting attorney in a rural county.

Because of the financial problems of the criminal lawyer's practice, it is necessary that he handle cases on an assembly-line basis, hoping to make a living from a large number of small fees. Referring to a fellow lawyer, one attorney said, "You should see————. He goes up there to Carroll's office with a whole fist full of cases. He trades on some, bargains on others and never goes to court. It's amazing but it's the way he makes his living." There are incentives, therefore, to bargain with the prosecutor and other decision-makers. The primary aim of the attorney in such circumstances is to reach an accommodation so that the time-consuming formal proceedings need not be implemented.... One of the disturbing results of this arrangement is that instances were reported in which a bargain was reached between the attorney and deputy prosecutor on a "package deal." In this situation, an attorney's clients are treated as a group; the outcome of the bargaining is often an agreement whereby reduced charges will be achieved for some, in exchange for the unspoken assent by the lawyer that the prosecutor may proceed as he desires with the other cases....

The exchange relationship between the defense attorney and the prosecutor is based on their need for cooperation in the discharge of their responsibilities. Most criminal lawyers are interested primarily in the speedy solution of cases because of their precarious financial situation. Since they must protect their professional reputations with their colleagues, judicial personnel, and potential clientele, however, they are not completely free to bargain solely with this objective. As one attorney noted, "You can't afford to let it get out that you are selling out your cases."

The prosecutor is also interested in the speedy processing of cases. This can only be achieved if the formal processes are not implemented. Not only does the pressure of his caseload influence bargaining, but also the legal process with its potential for delay and appeal, creates a degree of uncertainty which is not present in an exchange relationship with an attorney with whom you have dealt for a number of years. As the Presiding Judge of the Seattle District Court said, "Lawyers are helpful to the system. They are able to pull things together, work out a deal, keep the system moving."

.   .   .

SUMMARY

By viewing the King County Office of Prosecuting Attorney as the focal organization in an exchange system, data from this exploratory study suggests the market-like relationships which exist between actors in the system. Since prosecution operates in an environment of scarce resources and since the decisions have potential political ramifications, a variety of officials influence the allocation of justice. The decision to prosecute is not made at one point, but rather the prosecuting attorney has a number of options which he may employ during various stages of the proceedings. But the prosecutor is able to exercise his discretionary powers only within the network of exchange relationships. The police, court congestion, organizational strains, and community pressures are among the factors which influence prosecutorial behavior.

REFERENCES

Chambliss, W.J. (1969) Crime and the Legal Process. New York: McGraw-Hill.

Gore, W.J. (1964) Administrative Decision Making. New York: John Wiley.

Long, N. (1962) The Polity. Chicago: Rand McNally.

Plea Bargaining Systems and Plea Bargaining Styles: Alternate Patterns of Case Resolution in Criminal Courts

Milton Heumann

INTRODUCTION

The study of local criminal justice has emerged in the past several years as a major concern for the student of public law. The fall of the "upper court myth" and the resultant realization of the importance of the "trial" court has spurred research into the dispositional processes of criminal courts. In the forefront of the results yielded by these efforts is a model of case disposition very different from the familiar Perry Mason courtroom interaction, a model predicated on negotiated dispositions rather than adversary combat, in short, a plea bargaining model.

· · ·

I will be primarily concerned with three sets of plea bargaining-related issues. First, I will examine the proposition that plea bargaining is a relatively new phenomenon necessitated by the increased volume of cases coming to the local criminal court. Second, I will present evidence suggesting variations in plea bargaining processes

Paper delivered at the 1974 annual meeting of the American Political Science Association, pp. 1–3, 5, 7–10, 13–18, 20–26, 33. Reprinted by permission of the author. Footnotes have been omitted.

across courts of different jurisdictions and within courts of equal jurisdiction. . . .

RESEARCH METHODS

Six courts in three cities in Connecticut were chosen for study. Each of the three cities is the site of a Circuit and Superior Court. The former have criminal jurisdiction over all misdemeanors and felonies punishable by up to five years imprisonment, while the Superior Courts have concurrent jurisdiction over any Circuit Court matters, and exclusive jurisdiction over felonies punishable by more than five years imprisonment.

From June 1973 to March 1974 in-depth interviews were conducted with seventy-one individuals working in these six courts. Almost every prosecutor (State's attorney in the Superior Courts) and public defender in each of the courts is included in this sample. Additionally, private attorneys with a reputation for handling criminal cases in the three cities were interviewed, as were those judges assigned to the courts during my stay in the particular locality.

· · ·

In addition to the interviews, quantitative data on case dispositions were collected from both published State reports and from the files of the public defenders in one of the Circuit and one of the Superior Courts. As is the case with the qualitative evidence, these data cover only Connecticut criminal cases....

THE TRIAL: A STRAW MAN

Plea bargaining can be defined as the process by which the defendant agrees to relinquish his right to go to trial in exchange for a reduction in charge and/or sentence. Case pressure imputably weighs heavily on the mind of the prosecutor and he willingly enters into such an agreement to save the state the time and expense of a trial. The figure most frequently bandied about as indicative of the pervasiveness of plea bargaining is something to the effect that roughly only 10% of all criminal cases go to trial.

... [I]n recent years recourse to trial has been the exception rather than the rule in Connecticut's Superior Courts. In not one of the [last] seven years [from 1966–1973]... [have] the trials [as a proportion of the] total cases disposed...exceeded 9%. The trial perceived by many as the touchstone of our legal system accounted for the final outcome of only 114 of the 2244 cases resolved in one fashion or another by the Superior Courts in 1972–73.

.   .   .

Thus far we have not encountered any novel ground—as indicated above the 10% trial figure is quite well advertised. But what is not commonly realized, though critical for an appreciation of the reality of plea bargaining, is that the relative lack of trials versus alternate modes of disposition is not a recent phenomenon.... The mean percentage trial/total disposition over [the] 75 year period [from 1880–1954] is 8.7%. From 1880 to 1910 the ratio was slightly above 10%;

from 1910 to 1954 it reached the 10% plateau only three times. Overall, the trial ratio does not differ to any great extent from the current figures. Historically it appears that the trial, as far back as 1880, did not serve as a particularly popular source of case dispositions.

The exaggerated ability of appellate courts to rectify trial court error was labeled an "upper court myth." The belief that most cases in the trial court were tried, and the overemphasis on trial procedures to the exclusion of guilty pleas, both recently outmoded ideas, should properly be viewed as forming a "lower court myth."...

The "discovery" of plea bargaining sounded the death knell for the "lower court myth." However, I think yet a third myth has arisen from the ashes of the "lower court myth"—a "plea bargaining myth." This is the assumption that case pressure is predominantly responsible for the low trial rate in the criminal courts. We are led to believe that crowded urban courts, obsessed with "moving the business," forsake the trial and in its stead plea bargain. This line of thought implies that if case pressure was lessened, trials would be the name of the game.

A partial test of this proposition is made possible by comparing trial rates in low volume Superior Courts with trial rates in the high volume courts. This test is at best "rough" because without staffing data no control over the number of prosecutors and judges working in the court is possible. Nevertheless these data should yield some clues concerning the ability and desire of local court officials to try cases.

Connecticut's nine Superior Courts were arrayed on the basis of the mean number of total cases disposed of annually between 1880 and 1954. The rank order based on these means can be found in Table 1. For purposes of further analysis, Tolland, Middlesex and Windham, the three courts with

TABLE 1

Rank Ordering of Connecticut Superior Courts by Mean Number Cases Disposed Annually, 1880–1954

Superior Court	Total Cases	Mean	Standard Deviation
Tolland	2468	34	21
Middlesex	4143	56	20
Windham	5362	73	25
Litchfield	6235	85	51
Waterbury*	6655	95	171
New London	8553	117	43
Fairfield	19,043	261	71
New Haven	20,326	278	104
Hartford	24,212	332	158

* Data missing for 1897 and 1900. The Waterbury Superior Court was established in 1893, thus the N is 70 for Waterbury and 73 for the others.

TABLE 2

Means of Annual Trial to Total Cases Ratio for Low and High Volume Superior Courts, 1880–1954

	Low Volume Courts			High Volume Courts		
	Tolland	Middlesex	Windham	Fairfield	New Haven	Hartford
Mean Trials/Cases	.16	.14	.11	.07	.12	.07
Standard Deviation	.12	.07	.07	.05	.06	.04

the lowest mean number cases per year were called "low volume courts"; Fairfield, New Haven and Hartford were similarly labelled "high volume courts." The ratio of trials/total dispositions for each of these six courts was calculated, and the mean of these ratios for the low and high volume groupings for each year was determined. The summary statistics over the 75 year period for each court are presented in Table 2. . . .

. . . [The findings] indicate that over this 75 year period the low volume courts did not try a substantial percentage of their cases,

and did not try substantially more cases than the high volume courts. Though in certain years and certain time periods (particularly 1894–1904) the predicted greater rate is found and is pronounced, I think it fair to conclude, especially from 1910 and on, that despite the large difference in actual case pressure which was used to dichotomize the groupings, trial rates between them varied minimally, and indeed often the low volume courts tried proportionately fewer cases.

.   .   .

I think it beneficial at this point to offer a recapitulation, clarification, and explanation of the data presented thus far. We have seen that trials are not now, nor have they been since 1880, the predominant method of case resolution in the local criminal court. This fact emerges from both the annual aggregate statistics for all the Superior Courts, and from breakdown by court. Furthermore, we have seen that variations in case pressure do not directly and appreciably affect trial rates—low volume courts historically have not tried significantly more cases, and recent decreases in volume have not led to markedly greater rates of trial.

Guilty pleas, and to a lesser extent, nolles [dismissals], have always been the best traveled routes to case disposition. Today we know, this is well documented by my observations and interviews, that these guilty pleas are the product of discussion and negotiation between the defense attorney and the state's attorney. We can attribute the low trial rate, and the high percentage of guilty pleas to plea bargaining. This is fine and well, except that by implication it suggests that plea bargaining has always played a role in the local court, and if this is true, it casts doubt upon the efficacy of proposals to eliminate so well entrenched a process.

One cannot speak with assurance about the procedures followed in the "old days" to obtain the high percentage of guilty pleas. However, several clues harvested from my interviews lend credence to the argument that plea bargaining is no "Johnny come lately." "Oldtimers," court personnel, and private attorneys who have been active in criminal courts since the 1930's—scoffed at the current clamor about plea bargaining. Though indicating that some of the steps followed in negotiating dispositions have changed, these "oldtimers" maintained that the core notion of arranging a deal with the state's attorney in return for a guilty plea was always central to the practice of criminal law.

This evidence is admittedly piecemeal, and subject to the problem of selective recall. But when juxtaposed with several other findings, I think the contention of these "oldtimers" is supported, and further insight into the reality of plea bargaining is gained. Almost every respondent accepted the three following propositions as being empirically correct: 1. Somewhere between 80–90% of the defendants in the Superior Court are factually, but not necessarily, legally guilty; 2. Of these, a sizable percentage have no substantial grounds to contest the state's case—i.e., they are factually and legally guilty, and their trials would be barren of any contentions likely to produce an acquittal; 3. If a defendant pleads guilty he is likely to be rewarded in terms of a reduction in charge and/or sentence. These perceptions do not necessarily add up to a negation of the legal tenet of presumption of innocence. Court personnel and defense attorneys simply recognize the factual culpability of many of the defendants, and the fruitlessness, in terms of case outcome, of a trial. From these perceptions flows the notion—and it cannot be emphasized enough that this third component in particular is not normatively subscribed to by all court personnel, but is accepted by them as the empirical reality—that if the obviously guilty defendant "cops a plea" he will receive some reward. . . .

Assuming that the criminal justice system has always processed a substantial number of defendants who were factually guilty and who did not stand a very good chance for acquittal at trial, the low rate of trials historically, and the reliance on the guilty plea, becomes more understandable. Regardless of whether or not actual discussions took place between prosecutors and defense attorneys as the oldtimers asserted, the plea of guilty itself probably earned the defendant—or was perceived as likely to earn the defendant—a more favorable disposition than if he insisted on trial. Pleading guilty was (and is) tantamount to engaging in "implicit plea bargaining." Today perhaps defense attorneys are more forceful in insuring that the reward is forthcoming, and perhaps their efforts in the "explicit plea bargaining" encounter yield even greater rewards, but the difference is one of degree and not of kind.

To state the argument in stark terms, plea bargaining appears to be as integral and inevitable in the local criminal court (whether high or low volume) as is something like the committee system of the Congress. Once concessions are made for the defendant who pleads guilty, or penalties exacted from the defendant who does not— even if these can be justified in terms other than saving the state time and money—the slippery slope from implicit to explicit plea bargaining is being traversed. Gradually, the defense attorney seeks assurances from the prosecutors that the expected implicit reward will be forthcoming, and as these discussions increase the full fledged plea bargining system emerges.

. . .

The "plea bargaining myth"—the belief that case pressure variations explain trial rates— implies that plea bargaining will vary almost directly with case volume. It should now be evident that guilty pleas will be proffered and accepted for reasons other than case volume, and that at a minimum, implicit plea bargaining will be the norm even in those courts that handle few cases annually.

Let me stress, though, that the argument that case pressure can be removed and plea bargaining remain does not mean that case pressure is without its effects on plea bargaining processes. It merely suggests that the relationship is far more complex than a simple dichotomization between trial and plea implies. For example, there is probably a critical ratio between volume and staff . . . i.e., when volume increases beyond a certain point and staff remains constant, changes in the plea bargaining process may become manifest. Final dispositions may not change much, but they become easier to obtain; or the prosecutor may nolle the marginal case which he might have pursued for a plea earlier. He may offer to reduce more charges and recommend lighter sentences, or he may simply push for more severe sentences after trial, and remain as firm as he ever was on his plea bargaining offers. Innumerable additional hypotheses along these lines can be posited, but I think these few make plain that not much is plain about the very involved relationship between volume and plea bargaining. . . .

PLEA BARGAINING SYSTEMS: NOTES TOWARD CLASSIFICATION

In developing the argument that plea bargaining is inextricably bound to the local criminal court, that it is the lowest common denominator crosscutting criminal courts, we ignored distinctions amongst plea bargaining systems and orientations. But once we move beyond this position—i.e., we accept as given the centrality of plea bargaining—differences amongst systems and actors blossom. Plea bargaining after all is not a homogeneous process with identical connotation and denotation for all criminal systems and the individuals involved in them. Indeed, I think one explanation for the confusion that surrounds plea bargaining is directly attributable to the failture to note these distinctions.

. . .

One obvious "break point" falls between the Circuit and Superior Courts. Though the

Circuit Court now has felony jurisdiction of up to five years, the overwhelming majority of its cases stem from misdemeanor offenses, such as breach of the peace, found intoxicated, violations of town ordinances, and disorderly conduct. As would be expected, the Circuit Courts' case volume is substantially higher than that of the Superior Court.

...[Study of] the disposition figures for non-motor vehicle criminal cases in Connecticut's eighteen Circuit Courts in 1972... [reveals] the almost complete absence of recourse to the jury trial in both the high and low volume courts, and indicate the extensive use of the nolle to dispose of charges levelled against the defendant....

There are many aspects of the plea bargaining process in both the Circuit and Superior Courts that could not be readily quantified in any event. The milieu surrounding the actual plea bargaining negotiations and the nature of the discussions themselves, differ greatly. Typically, in the Circuit Court, a line forms outside the prosecutor's office in the morning before court is convened. Defense attorneys shuffle into the prosecutor's office, and in a matter of two or three minutes dispose of the one or more cases "set down" that day. Generally, only a few words have to be exchanged before agreement is reached. The defense attorney mutters something about the defendant, the prosecutor reads the police report, and mutual concurrence on "what to do" generally, but not always, emerges.

. . . .

"Plea bargaining," then, for many Circuit Court cases is simply this rapid consensual agreement that the facts dictate certain dispostions—be it a reduced charge, a nolle, a nolle of a few counts for a plea to one charge, etc. Long ago the legal realists seemed to have put the mechanical jurisprudential school, and its slot machine theory of justice, to rest. It can now be reported that the slot machine is alive and well in Circuit Court.

. . . .

Plea bargaining in the Superior Court, on the other hand, is a less hurried and less sloppy process. Lengthier discussions take place in the office of one of the assistant state's attorneys. The facts of the case as well as the defendant's background and prior record (if any) are more thoroughly reviewed. Less room for post-plea discussion "hustling" is available. Witness the remarks of an attorney who practices in both the Circuit and Superior Court:

> IN THE SUPERIOR COURT YOU PLEA BARGAIN JUST LIKE YOU DO IN THE CIRCUIT COURT?
>
> No, no, all your cards are out on the table, it's not very much of a hustle, not a hustle at all...you don't prosecutor shop, there's a lot more at stake, it's totally different. It's like night and day.

The seriousness of the charges in the Superior Court case weigh against too heavy a reliance on pure gamesmanship. Delay and prosecutor shopping will only get you so far; the facts of the case will not disappear, and ultimately they will have to be confronted. Unlike the Circuit Court in which "time," i.e. a jail or prison sentence, is a rarity, "time" is what it is all about in the Superior Court. This is to say that the single most important question that state's attorneys and defense attorneys in the Superior Court confront is whether or not the defendant will have to "do time." If the answer is a mutual "no," but agreement exists on the defendant's guilt, the disposition of the case is a relatively simple matter; some combination of a suspended sentence and probation can be worked out with little difficulty. But "if you are talking time" negotiations become strained.

Defendants in the Superior Court generally have more than one charge outstanding in their files. Of the 88 defendants whose files I examined in one Superior Court public defender's office, only 12 were charged with a single count of a single offense, while the remaining 76 defendants had a total of 288 charges against them. The piling on of charges, when combined with mandatory five year minimum sentences for offenses such as Sale of Heroin, and Robbery With Violence, and with repeated offender statutes which double the exposure for the second offender in particular crimes, provide ample years for the state's attorney to "play with" in negotiations. In the Superior Court "charge bargaining" becomes far less important than "sentencing bargaining." Charges can be dropped without reducing the realistic range of years within which the defendant will be sentenced. For the most part, charge bargaining retains its significance only when a mandatory minimum sentence would be necessitated by a plea to a particular charge, or when the charge can be reduced from a felony to a misdemeanor. In almost all other situations, the state's attorney can appear to yield much in the way of charges without really giving much in the way of "time."

The agreement that emerges from the sentence bargaining can take several forms, all of which relate to what will, or will not, be said to the judge on sentencing day. The defense attorney and state's attorney may agree that the state's attorney will simply present the charges and read the facts but will not make any sentence "rec" (recommendation). This leaves the defense attorney free to make his "pitch" to the judge, and leave the final sentencing decision up to the judge. A second pattern allows the attorney to make any "rec" he desires, and the defense attorney can again respond with his pitch. This is commonly employed when the state's attorney "gives a lot" on charge but refuses to budge on sentence. The third form of agreement as to sentence is the "agreed

rec." This is by far the most controversial form of sentence bargaining, and the one that best distinguishes amongst Superior Courts. In two of the Superior Courts, the "agreed rec" means that the state's attorney will not ask for more than a specified in advance number of years; the defense attorney remains free to "pitch" to the judge for less. The expectation is that the judge will almost never go above the state's attorney recommendation, that he will most likely follow it, but that he may occasionally be swayed by the "pitch" and go below it. . . .

. . . It ought to now be evident that Circuit and Superior Court plea bargaining differ in several significant respects; actual physical location for the negotiations, extent of time accorded each case, "hustle factor," charge and sentence bargaining, etc. Similarly, variations exist within courts of equal jurisdiction, e.g., with regard to sentence recommendation patterns in the Superior Courts. No claim to an exhaustive or conclusive cataloguing of these differences is being made.

.   .   .

SOME FINAL COMMENTS

Plea bargaining is central to the process of allocating justice within the local criminal court. The very nature of the guilty plea itself leads inevitably to negotiated dispositions. Factually guilty defendants without much hope at trial will be disposed to plead guilty and avail themselves of the reward imputably accorded the contrite and cooperative defendant.

The centrality and importance of plea bargaining requires that we eschew the simplistic trial/plea bargaining dichotomization and work toward a more realistic appreciation of the dynamics and patterned differences that characterize plea bargaining systems and plea bargainers. . . .

The Effects of Heavy Caseloads

Malcolm M. Feeley

[The paper begins with an exploration of the arguments that are frequently made concerning the effects of heavy caseloads on the ways courts operate. These arguments suggest that heavy caseloads are responsible for the infrequency of trials, the great reliance on plea-bargaining, the tendency to shortcut the process by failure of lawyers to file motions, and the harsh and arbitrary treatment of defendants that inevitably results from mass production justice.]

One important feature of these arguments is that they all cut two ways. That is, each of them implies an opposite; in the absence of heavy caseloads, there will be more trials, less reliance on plea bargaining, an increase in motions, and different types of outcomes. Consequently this paper will examine the arguments by contrasting [the state of Connecticut's] high volume, heavy caseload Sixth Circuit with a neighboring court, the low volume, lighter caseload Eighth Circuit court. If the assertions about caseload are supported, there should be some differences

Paper delivered at the 1975 Annual Meeting of the American Political Science Association, pp. 4, 8–13, 15–18, 23, 28–30, 33–39, 41–42. Reprinted by permission of the author. Footnotes have been omitted.

in the ways cases are handled in the two settings. If on the other hand there are no substantial differences, one can begin to question the importance of caseload and begin to look elsewhere for explanations for the observed practices in criminal courts.

.   .   .

THE CASELOAD HYPOTHESES EXPLORED

The core of the heavy caseload-cursory disposition argument focuses on the degree of "adversariness" in the system. In its most general form this position argues that criminal cases should be resolved through combat between the two parties, with the state having to prove beyond a reasonable doubt to the judge or jury that the defendant did commit the particular offense with which he was charged. The defendant, on the other hand, is presumed to be innocent and should be able to invoke the available procedures to protect himself.

An examination of this position, however, poses serious problems for any researcher. At the outset it raises important conceptual questions—what precisely is an adversarial relationship? What is the minimum that the criminal process requires? To what extent must adversariness be characterized as a zero-sum game where one player's victory is another's loss? A mixed strategy game where both players can lose something but both can also gain?

Neither critics nor defenders of the general lack of trials or other combative features available in the criminal process have developed an explicit yardstick against which to judge actual practices. For the most part available standards are very general and discussions tend to proceed by assuming the obviousness of their claims. . . . A perusal of the various discussions of the problems of administering criminal justice leads to no clear consensus as to the precise nature of an "acceptable" or "typical" adversarial relationship. For instance, while some seem to suggest that anything less than a full-fledged jury trial is a departure from the ideal resolution of criminal charges, others adopting an implicit civil law analogy, seem to view the very inability to resolve cases by a negotiated settlement or through informal motion practices as unprofessional. My purpose here. . . is to identify at least several practices commonly associated with this process in order to determine how they may be affected by a variation in caseload.

Trials and Motions

Turning to the central concern of the adversary argument—that there is a relationship between heavy caseloads and lack of trials—the Connecticut data do not support the position. In fact, none of the cases in the samples of the two circuit courts was decided either by a jury or by a court trial. This pattern is not a result of a bias in sampling but represents the typical pattern in these two—and the other sixteen—circuit courts in Connecticut. A separate check of the annual reports of the state's Judicial Department

also indicated a paucity of trials in any of the circuits. . . . Thus not only is there a lack of trials in the busier and more rushed courts, there is also a corresponding lack of them in the smaller lower caseload circuits as well.

A trial, however, is only one of several possible indicators of an adversary relationship. Another more subtle indication is use of formal motions by the defense. Motions test the prosecutor's case against the defendant and require him to take seriously the defense effort. A defense attorney can use these as ways of forcing prosecutors to demonstrate the strength of their evidence and to confront the possibility of reducing the charges or abandoning prosecution altogether. Thus motions serve many of the same functions as trials, including the central one of making the prosecution "prove" its case.

There are a variety of motions available to the defense. Pleas in abatement, motions to dismiss, motions to suppress illegally seized evidence, probable cause hearings all attack the sufficiency of evidence and the grounds for arrest. Motions of discovery and bills of particulars both aid the defense in learning more about the charges and circumstances of the arrest. . . . A successful motion to have the court handle the charges under the state's youthful offender statute protects the defendant, if convicted, from having a public record of conviction. The frequency with which formal motions are filed then is another and perhaps more subtle measure of adversariness. Here too, then, one would have expected that the smaller caseload circuit would have produced a higher rate of motions. However, a comparison of the two circuits reveals no substantial differences between them. In the Eighth Circuit, most—90% of the cases—were resolved without the filing of any motions. In 9% more of the cases, one motion was filed and in only 1% of the cases were two or more filed. These figures are almost identical with the rates for the Sixth Circuit. In 92% of the cases no motions were filed, in another 7% one was filed and in only 1% of the cases were two or more filed. Thus by this indicator, as well, there is no significant difference between the degree of adversariness in the two circuits.

Plea Bargains

Plea bargaining occupies a central place in discussions of heavy caseloads. The standard argument holds that plea negotiations are a necessary evil reluctantly accepted by an overworked court, and by implication a reduction of caseload will result in less or perhaps no plea bargaining. However, such an argument is extremely difficult to either support or refute because it too is usually not stated with much precision and the logic of decision-making as it responds to the press of a heavy caseload is not clear. This lack of precision may stem from the ambiguity surrounding the central concept. Are *all* pleas of guilty *prima facie* evidence of plea bargaining? Are all nolles? Would critics of the very idea of plea bargaining expect to resolve *all* cases by trial? It is difficult to imagine such a position being taken although no doubt there may be some support for it. Thus the absence of trials need *not* be taken, by itself, as an indicator of plea bargaining—if bargaining implies actual give and take and acknowledged agreement to compromise by both parties before a final decision is arrived at.

.   .   .

One measure that has often been used to examine the magnitude of plea bargaining is the frequency with which the most serious charge(s) has been reduced. While defendants may plead guilty for a variety of reasons, pleas to *reduced* charges are much more likely to be the result of an explicit agreement between the defense and prosecution and represent a significant concession by both parties. They are then more likely to be a more meaningful indicator of plea bargaining than the rate of guilty pleas or the rate of cases with other types of charge reductions. Even more important are the cases in which original felony charges are disposed of by pleas of guilty to misdemeanors. From the defendant's perspective, escaping a felony record is extremely desirable. It keeps his record "clean." On the other hand prosecutors are reluctant to reduce a felony charge to misdemeanors since by doing so a relatively important and serious offense is reclassified for the record as just another routine misdemeanor. These types of reductions, then, are cases in which both the prosecution and the defendant have the most to gain and lose.

By the first measure, the percent of *total* charge reductions, the two circuits differ significantly. Thirty percent of all guilty pleas in the Sixth Circuit involve a plea to a lesser (or substituted) charge, while this is the case for only eleven percent of the guilty pleas in the low volume Eighth Circuit. The inference then is that at least in the lower volume circuit, there is less need or pressure to settle cases by resort to reduction of the charges.

Even more startling differences were found when only felony charges which eventually led to misdemeanor convictions were considered. Eighteen percent of the original class D felony charges in the Eighth Circuit were reduced to less serious charges, while in the Sixth Circuit the figure was seventy percent. Thus on this one crucial indicator it does appear that caseload is strongly related to at least charge reductions. The heavier caseload court appears much more willing to reduce charges than does the court with the lighter workload.

.   .   .

Pretrial Processing

One complaint about high volume systems is that...important early decisions must be made on the basis of incomplete and inadequate information...and thus...[they are] more likely [than low volume courts] to have..."restrictive" pretrial releasing policies.

Looking at release practices in the two circuits, however, this proposition is *not* borne out...[B]oth in terms of total numbers released and in numbers released without money bail, the high volume [court] fares slightly better than the low volume circuit. Over 89% of those in the former are released prior to trial, while only 86.9% of those in the low volume circuit are released. Furthermore, of those released, the high volume Sixth Circuit is more likely to release the accused on his own recognizance (52.4% to 47.2%).

Turning from the type of release conditions to the actual amount of money bond, the same pattern is seen. Overall the Eighth Circuit Court sets higher bonds than the Sixth. Not only is the high volume court slightly more willing to release arrestees, it

also tends to set lower bonds. 18.5% of those having money bond set in the Sixth Circuit have a bond of $50 or less, as opposed to only 2.7% for the Eighth Circuit....

One possible explanation for the more lenient release conditions in the Sixth Circuit is that the defendants are charged with less severe offenses. This, however, is not the case. When controls for seriousness of offense were introduced, still no significant differences appeared. Defendants in the high volume Sixth Circuit were still more likely to receive liberal release conditions.

Another important aspect of the pretrial process is the length of time an arrestee is held in pretrial custody. Conventional wisdom would expect the setting with the heavier caseload to have the longer delay in processing and releasing arrestees. Again, however, the data *do not* support the claim. Table 1 indicates that the heavy caseload Sixth Circuit has the larger percentage of arrestees released within three hours (60.4% to 49.7%), although the picture becomes mixed when the remainder of the table is considered. In both circuits around two-thirds of all arrestees are eventually released within seven hours, and only a handful are

TABLE 1
Time Spent in Pretrial Custody

	Circuit	
Time	*Sixth (high)*	*Eighth (low)*
0–3 hours	60.4%	49.7%
4–7 hours	5.7	21.3
8–12 hours	6.4	7.8
13–24 hours	21.4	17.0
Two or more days	6.1	3.6
	100.0%	100.0%
	(1436)	(141)

held beyond twenty-four. In sum, despite variations in workload there are no major pretrial releasing differences between the two settings. Both release in about the same way and at about the same rate.

.   .   .

Historical Support

The heavy caseload-cursory disposition argument contains a strong historical dimension as well. Some observers of contemporary courts speak of a "decline" of the adversary system due to the press of cases, while others speak of the crisis of criminal justice. However, while it is a rhetorical convenience to speak of greener pastures or better days of a bygone era when smaller caseloads and greater deliberation in criminal courts prevailed, it is not at all clear that this is an accurate comparison. Rather what is seen in the records and description of American Courts fifty and seventy-five years ago is a process easily recognized by contemporary students of criminal courts.

[What follows is a discussion and excerpts from: (1) a study published in 1922 describing the heavy caseload-cursory disposition situation in Cleveland; (2) another early study of Connecticut; and (3) one study of the criminal courts of Chicago. Also discussed are additional data from Connecticut and from New York City.]

.   .   .

In summary, ...historical findings... while sketchy and incomplete, all point in the same direction and reinforce the findings for the Sixth and Eighth Circuits. Obviously strict comparisions between the periods and courts is not possible due to a host of intervening and confounding conditions. The explosive changes in criminal procedure affect the comparisons in major and undeterminable ways, as do changes in the definitions and understanding of offenses and offenders. Nevertheless the similarities in the findings of these various courts and periods offer considerable support for the position that there has not been any particularly noticeable "decline" in or "twilight" of the adversary system, but rather that it has remained at a more or less constant level despite changes and variations in the magnitude of workload. Although some of the evidence dealt with felony cases, most of the evidence and discussions including the two circuit comparison, referred exclusively to misdemeanor and "minor" felonies, not all cases, particularly major felonies. Consequently while all conclusions and findings should be read and interpreted gingerly, the caseload argument appears strongest as it applies to minor cases in "lower" courts....
Lastly it should be emphasized that this caseload argument is also limited by the extremes found in the courts under study. Greater extremes in either direction may produce more noticeable differences. Keeping these caveats in mind it is of interest to ask why there has been such little actual change and why so many commentators have singled out spiralling caseloads to account for "recently" *observed* problems.

While there are some important differences between these two Connecticut circuit courts, there are few differences between them that tend to support the heavy caseload-cursory disposition position under primary consideration in this paper. Virtually all of this and the additional evidence challenges the ability of the heavy caseload theory to account for differences in the ways defendants are "processed" in lower courts. This conclusion of no effect, however, is by itself inadequate. A basic question still remains: are there alternative explanations which account for this seeming paradox? Why is there a belief in their importance in lower courts? And why are they less important than generally believed? There are, in fact, several arguments which when taken together provide a convincing explanation. They raise issues about the *ways* the problem is characterized and also point to some important features of the unique organization of lower courts.

WHY CASELOAD IS STRESSED

The Implications [for] Due Process

The thinking underlying the heavy caseload position is a pervasive but implicit assumption that is so ingrained in the thinking and ideology of American criminal justice that it frequently goes undetected and unexamined. This assumption holds that in the unimpeded course of events, each case brought into the criminal courts will "naturally" be resolved by means of heavy combat in the adversary arena. The idea of the adversary system—the basic instrument for protecting the innocent—is extended to mean that the sophisticated procedures and techniques for truth detection and rights preservation not only are available if desired, but will be desired and relied upon in every case. While this position is reinforced by popular presentations of the operation of criminal justice, historically there is no strong tradition or legal presumption that these devices are to be used in each and every case or in any proportion of them. Rather the *full-fledged* adversary process is only one of *several alternatives* available to the participants. Other more expeditious alternatives also enjoy a well institutionalized position in the criminal law. For instance, never has the right to plead guilty been seriously challenged, and while the United States Supreme Court has been somewhat squeamish about putting its formal stamp of approval on plea bargaining, through its traditional inaction and more lately through its explicit rulings,

plea bargaining has been gaining a legally acceptable and honorable position in the administration of criminal justice.

Thus a major assumption implicit in much of the literature examining the nature and function of lower criminal courts and commenting on the infrequency of trials rests on a premise that at best can be characterized as idealized myth. Despite this, much of the analysis of the criminal court system has been undertaken with an underlying premise that a full-fledged adversarial relationship is the most obvious and desirable form of proceeding. Thus the actual observed processes are frequently measured against an unexplored ideal of complete combat that has no firm basis in legal theory.

. . .

Non-reactive "Causes"

Whenever there is discontent there is a search for someone to blame. Social organizations are not immune from this, and indeed can function only because they are successful in assigning specific duties to designated individuals who can then be held accountable for their performance. Countering this, there is also a tendency for those with such responsibilities to develop techniques to protect themselves, devices which allow them to accept credit for successes but disavow responsibility for failures. In large complex organizations these practices can be refined to a high art. Specialization, minute division of labor, and the corresponding inability for any one person to see "the whole picture" make it difficult to trace the ultimate impact of a particular action, and hence facilitate the diffusion and transfer of responsibility.

Transferring responsibility is not, however, any easy task. Not surprisingly there is a tendency for those in whose arms the blame is cast to want to reject or pass on the unwanted burden. Also, blaming someone else creates the prospect that the allegation can be returned at some later date. It is a risky business at best. Not surprisingly then one solution to this dilemma is to find a more reliable culprit, a *non*-reactive agency on whom blame can be placed without fear of reciprocity. Perhaps the most common way to do this is to place blame not on any person but on a *process*. Pointing to factors beyond *anyone's* control is one way to avoid not only personal responsibility but also the possibility of retaliation and recrimination engendered by pointing to someone else. Such an explanation proves to be both safe and convenient. The culprit can neither defend itself nor query its accusers. Furthermore, it is difficult to contradict such assertions.

In the administration of criminal justice, three types of non-reactive factors have emerged as "the cause" of many problems confronting the system. Heavy caseloads, understaffing, and inadequate funding are all "enemies" which everyone can safely point to as causes for poor performance. They are culprits that neither speak back nor have any defenders....

So far this discussion has examined why heavy caseloads are *not* so important in accounting for the way cases are processed in lower criminal courts. If it is not the heavy caseload, however, then what does explain this ubiquitous practice of rapid and perfunctory processing of cases? There are two inter-related sets of factors that seem to account for it, factors which while affected by caseload are constantly present regardless of the magnitude of the caseload. Both sets of factors have to do with the nature of the organization of the court system. The first focuses on the peculiar and perhaps unique way the court's workload is distributed and the other is a consequence of the mutually advantageous practices that are inherent in a system of justice where the stakes are not very high in comparison to the costs of going through the system.

ALTERNATIVE EXPLANATIONS

The Organization of the Court's Business

The working hours in a lower court are scheduled in a distinctive if not unique way. Participants are interested in getting through the calendar as quickly as possible so that they can leave the courtroom for the day. If it is completed by noon, many of them can leave at that time. For others the incentive is not to go home but to get back to an office and other work. Prosecutors have to prepare the following day's cases. Defense attorneys have other clients to meet, cases to prepare, and records to file, and clerks have the day's work to record and file. Whatever the precise reasons for wanting to "move the day's business" in court, almost everyone, save perhaps the frequently bewildered defendant, seems anxious to go through the work as quickly as possible in order to get someplace else.

Concomitant with this desire to press through the work, is the general irritation at any of a variety of events that can disrupt the usually smooth and steady routine and extend the length of time court is in session. An attorney new to the court and unfamiliar with its workings is viewed as a minor irritant by the regulars. A defense attorney who raises more than the normal and perfunctory arguments in behalf of his client may be interrupted and prodded by the judge and urged to rush through his statement. At times a judge may indicate his displeasure at even having to listen to such additional arguments and will make a ruling before the attorney completes his argument.... This is a set of half-conscious norms about what one can and cannot do, and violation of them is met with disapproval.

[Disapproval] is not reserved wholly for uncooperative defense attorneys. There may be grumbling among defense attorneys and prosecutors when a judge new to a court conducts business at a much more leisurely pace than his predecessor. Usually, however, the judges will soon learn the norm of that courtroom and adjust to it. They may begin their rotation taking their time, carefully warning defendants of their rights, explaining procedures to them, and inquiring into any deals arranged with the prosecutor. But within a short time they too are like everyone else—running through the docket as quickly as possible.

A moment's reflection will lead to the conclusion that the common interest in the rapid processing of defendants goes far beyond simply the attempts of the various actors to keep their heads above the rising waters in an overburdened court. Stated more bluntly, regardless of caseload, there will always be *too many cases* for many of the participants in the system since most of them have a strong interest in being some place other than in court. Court personnel and others in the extended court organization have a distinctive if not unique work arrangement. They are neither required to be at their jobs from nine to five (in which case it could be argued they might as well spend the hours carefully handling the cases) nor do they get paid by the piece (other than private defense attorneys), in which case while there would be an incentive to move cases rapidly, there would also be an incentive to work longer hours. Rather, they are presented with a predetermined total daily workload, everyday, and when this task is completed, many of them can leave. While a court with a heavier load may adjourn for the day at 4:00 p.m. and take only brief recesses and the smaller court may adjourn at 12:30

p.m., the incentive for rapid processing remains. In each instance, the faster the work is done the sooner court can be adjourned and many people can go home or back to their offices. This simple feature of the way the court's business is organized—a predetermined workload scheduled on a daily basis—goes a long way in explaining why there will always be a strong incentive to move through cases at a rapid pace. While related to the total court workload in some ways, the connection is far from direct and immediate since there is a strong incentive for rapid processing regardless of caseload.

Mutual Advantages and Substantive Justice

Coupled with the peculiar nature of the daily organization of the court's workload is a much more fundamental feature of the court life, and one that provides a convincing explanation for the lack of trials and other time consuming and costly adversarial proceedings. It is the belief that disputes settled through negotiation and/or pleas of guilty provide mutually advantageous benefits for *all* the involved parties.

The savings in time and effort for the prosecutor and defense attorney are obvious. . . .

The normative stance that facilitates this "short circuiting" of the elaborate process is a consensus by nearly everyone involved in most every case that the defendant is, in fact, responsible for *some* wrongdoing which is connected with the charges. The question before the prosecutor and defense attorney then is not whether the defendant is innocent or guilty of the offenses charged, but rather "how should we dispose of this case?" and "what should we settle for?" "What is appropriate for this type of conduct?" The very phrasing of these questions presumes a *joint* enterprise rather than a warring set of parties, and presumes a consensus on the "verdict" on the actions which precipitated the arrest. Any stance other than this cooperative one is . . . almost inconceivable in a setting where there is such a pervasive belief in the defendant's guilt.

. . . [T]he emphasis is on an "equitable" disposition of the case. If the defendant is unfairly charged, or over-charged according to the prevailing norms of the courthouse, the defense counsel finds it more productive to "work with" the prosecutor to obtain an appropriate reduction in the charges or to quietly argue for a lenient sentence recommendation rather than to openly fight in court. Most defense attorneys defend this position as benefiting defendants both in the long run and in individual cases. By dispensing with the trappings of formal procedure, they argue, it allows them to provide efficient and equitable "substantive" justice.

. . .

There is still one more aspect of the process to be considered. Like both defense attorneys and prosecutors, defendants are also subject to decision making costs. . . . While it is clear that defendants rarely ever "manage" their cases or are even fully appraised of all the legal alternatives open to them, it is not at all clear that the defendants in circuit court are unwitting dupes who would much prefer to have their attorney go into full battle for them. Given the certainty of the small sanction, the defendant too has much to lose in extending his case and engaging in full fledged combat. Interviews with his attorney, corralling favorable witnesses, and repeated court appearances all take their toll on the defendant's resources as well as the prosecutor's and defense counsel's.

The defendant in a minor criminal case is much like a party in a civil suit; frequently the most economical course of action is to forego principle and settle in order to minimize the costs of pursuing a decision by means of a formal process, a process which entails expenses that can quickly come to outweigh the magnitude of the sentence itself. While the defendant who retains his own counsel must pay for this service, in most instances the costs of simply having to make repeated court appearances and visit the attorney during regular working hours in order to participate in the construction of the defense more than overshadows the magnitude of the eventual sentence. The loss of just one day's wages is likely to be greater than the typical fine imposed in circuit court.

Ironically the cost of *invoking* one's rights frequently is greater than the loss of the rights themselves. Given this one can see why so many defendants accept a guilty plea without a battle. This situation poses a major paradox for the administration of criminal law since this calculus applies equally well to those defendants who are or consider themselves to be innocent as well as to those who readily acknowledge their guilt.

This dilemma poses serious questions about the efficacy of the adversary process as an institution for protecting individual rights and assuring justice in lower criminal courts. When the costs of invoking the safeguards of the process are likely to be greater than the eventual criminal sentence there is little incentive to engage this process in an effort to vindicate oneself or to avoid or minimize the eventual sanction. Thus, the nearly standard response to problems of American criminal justice—to expand "due process" of the adversary system—may produce negligible results or worse yet may be counterproductive. Not only does expansion of the process give the illusion of improvement when none in fact may have taken place, it also contributes to a set of standards and controls so remote from the existing bureaucratic-cooperative system as to be inapplicable and meaningless in all but the occasional case. . . .

Is Plea Bargaining Inevitable?

Stephen J. Schulhofer

In most criminal cases, plea bargaining is necessary and inevitable—at any rate, that is the view of nearly all knowledgeable scholars and practitioners and much of the public at large. In this article, I suggest that this pervasively important assumption is erroneous. I shall argue that effective containment of plea bargaining is realistically possible for American criminal courts.... By plea bargaining I mean any process in which inducements are offered in exchange for a defendant's cooperation in not fully contesting the charges against him. Thus, I am asserting the feasibility of restricting or even eliminating not only formal, officially sanctioned plea bargaining, but also the wide variety of informal, sub rosa behavior patterns in which indirect inducements, unspoken commitments, and covert cooperation create the functional equivalent of explicit bargaining....

· · ·

THE PLEA BARGAINING DEBATE

Theoretical Perspectives: Case Pressure and Cooperation

Defenders of plea bargaining usually argue that bargaining is unavoidable for either of two reasons. First, a prohibition of plea bargaining, it is said, would generate enormous costs and monumental delays; plea bargaining is essential for handling massive criminal caseloads. Second, a prohibition of plea bargaining would be subverted by counsel and other participants in the system; thus, bargaining would continue and the courts would not collapse, but the resulting process would be less visible and would afford even fewer safeguards than the present one.

Illustrative of the first theme are the influential comments of Chief Justice Burger in a 1970 speech to the American Bar Association:

> The consequence of what might seem on its face a small percentage change in the rate of guilty pleas can be tremendous. A reduction from 90 per cent to 80 per cent in guilty pleas requires the assignment of twice the judicial manpower and facilities—judges, court reporters, bailiffs, clerks, jurors and courtrooms. A reduction to 70 per cent trebles this demand.

The assumed relationship between bargaining and judicial resources requires two qualifications. First, Chief Justice Burger was concerned not with bargaining but with the "guilty plea rate," and it is far from clear that an elimination of bargaining (in all its forms) would result in the elimination of all guilty pleas. Second, and perhaps more importantly, the analysis appears to assume that the existing stock of judicial resources is used exclusively for trials—that no "judges, court reporters, bailiffs, clerks, jurors and courtrooms" are needed to process the convictions currently obtained by plea. This is plainly something of an exaggeration. Yet nearly all discussion of the practical necessity for bargaining appears to assume that the time and effort expended in guilty plea dispositions are trivial compared to the time and effort required for trials.

The second line of argument asserts that we need not fear a collapse of the courts, but only because there can never be a genuinely effective prohibition of bargaining. For many observers, this conclusion follows from the caseload problems just discussed: lawyers and judges are forced to bargain (explicitly or covertly) because any other behavior would bring the judicial system to a halt. In this theory the inevitability of bargaining depends on the assumed need for bargaining, and the theory thus can be questioned to the extent that the "administrative need" can be shown to be illusory.

Some social scientists, including many who question the case pressure hypothesis, have advanced a different explanation for the inevitability of bargaining. For these scholars, plea bargaining is not the result of anything so transitory or (in theory) controllable as case pressure; rather, it is produced by much more complex factors that are deeply rooted in social dynamics and perhaps no more subject to change than is human nature itself. Thus, whether or not case pressure contributes to bargaining, these other factors ensure that bargaining will continue even if caseloads should slacken. This much stronger version of the inevitability hypothesis guides a now-substantial body of research organized around two separable, though not entirely distinct, theoretical perspectives—organizational analysis and socialization (or adaptation) analysis.

Building on studies of behavior in ordinary commercial enterprises and large public agencies, organizational theorists view the criminal process in terms of the structure of roles and relationships among workers in the courtroom setting. Because courtroom work groups display no formal hierarchical relationships, organizational theorists do not conceive of such groups as bureaucracies. Rather, the judge has a limited formal authority over attorneys and other participants, but all workers can influence one another. Although each worker has a specialized role, all share certain goals and have a mutual interest in avoiding conflict and maintaining group cohesion. The character of the work group is also influenced by outside groups—most immediately, the workers' "sponsoring organizations" (for example, the public defender's and district attorney's offices), but also police, the media, appellate courts, the public, and so on. As elaborated by James Eisenstein and Herbert Jacob, this perspective suggests four general goals that courtroom work groups seek to achieve: the internally generated goals of maintaining group cohesion and reducing uncertainty, and the externally inspired goals of doing justice and disposing of the caseload.

This analysis does not by itself imply the inevitability of bargaining. On the contrary, it posits the existence of one goal ("doing justice") that requries adherence to formal, adversary roles, and it draws explicit attention to factors that may affect the relative priorities of conflicting goals. In fact, Eisenstein and Jacob emphasize the way that different internal and external environments in the three cities they studied influenced the strength of particular goals and thus the behavior and output of particular courtroom work groups.

Organizational analysis of this sort provides a useful conceptual framework that—on its face—is sufficiently open textured to accommodate a great variety of messy empirical facts. Nevertheless, implicit and often explicit in the work of organizational theorists is a strong commitment to the importance of internal group dynamics and an assumption that the desire to minimize uncertainty and conflict is virtually inherent in human nature. These postulates suggest that, whatever changes may occur in caseload pressure (or, for that matter, in demands to "do justice"), the crucial internal considerations that drive the bargaining process will remain unaffected. Thus, cities may display marginally different bargaining rates, but this analysis anticipates no radical discontinuities in the extent of bargaining.

Adaptation analysis proceeds from much simpler premises. Although it treats courtrooms as work groups with internally generated norms and objectives, adaptation analysis views courtroom behavior primarily as the product of a socialization process. As developed by Milton Heumann, moreover, this approach attributes crucial importance to socialization through "learning" rather than through "teaching." Heumann acknowledges that a newcomer to the courts "may be taught that rewards and penalties are attached to certain actions." He stresses, however, that this "teaching" is not the paramount element in the process of socialization: "newcomers simply learn," he argues, that the "reality of the local criminal court differs from what [they] expected.... [M]uch of the variance in newcomer adaptation is a function of the newcomer's learning about his role and about the associated constraints that the 'realities' of the case characteristics impose upon him."

The "reality" Heumann has in mind is, above all, the hopelessness of defendants' cases. On the basis of extended interviews with defenders and other court personnel, he concludes that "[t]he most important thing the new defense attorney learns is that most of his clients are factually guilty"....

For Heumann, plea bargaining results neither from case pressure nor from group needs to avoid either conflict or, a fortiori, uncertainty. (Indeed, in Heumann's world, uncertainty does not appear to be much of a problem.) Rather, given "the defendant's factual culpability coupled with the absence of contestable legal and factual issues," counsel choose bargaining because there is simply no issue to take to trial.

Curiously, Heumann—a political scientist—does not appear to doubt either the intrinsic possibility of a "reality" such as the one his interview subjects described or the ability of individuals immersed in complex social relationships to provide accurate descriptions of their world. Although Heumann's conclusions therefore must be approached with great caution, they suggest questions that cannot simply be dismissed. What proportion of criminal cases filed (or adjudicated) are devoid of disputable issues of fact and law? To what extent do such cases prompt or impel bargaining? To what extent would effective barriers to bargaining influence the plea rate in such cases?...

I have thus far attempted to present the diverse hypotheses offered to explain the alleged inevitability of plea bargaining. Two bodies of empirical material lend further support to the contention that bargaining is unavoidable. One set of studies compares guilty plea rates during different periods of time within particular jurisdictions;

the other compares plea rates in different jurisdictions.

Comparative Studies: Changes over Time

A number of highly touted studies grow out of attempts to "abolish" plea bargaining in one jurisdiction or another. Some of these studies purport to prove the feasibility of a bargaining ban, but in nearly every case either the study or the abolition attempt itself has major shortcomings that undermine the experiment's relevance to that question. In several cases, for example, a ban on "bargaining" did not increase the trial rate, but the ban covered only one form of bargaining, and the researchers either knew that bargaining in other forms continued or never investigated this possibility. In a few cases, the trial rate did increase, but not unmanageably; in many of these cases, some varieties of bargaining could have continued, and in others, the ban failed to reach major segments of the criminal caseload.

The most serious study casting doubt on the inevitability of bargaining grew out of the prohibition instituted by Alaska's Attorney General in 1975. The 1975 ban covered all forms of prosecutorial bargaining; in 1977, the Alaska Supreme Court barred judges from bargaining over charges or sentences. Despite this comprehensive prohibition, the courts were not overwhelmed with trials. Researchers concluded, therefore, that "the incidence of plea bargaining *can* be substantially reduced without wrecking a criminal justice system." Unfortunately, even this relatively careful study did not actually support that conclusion: the "before-and-after" comparison was made prior to the 1977 ban on judicial bargaining, and some judges thus were offering explicit concessions during the study period. Moreover, some defense attorneys continued to recommend pleas be-

cause they feared that judges might penalize clients who insisted on trial, and analysis of sentencing data showed that in fact some groups of defendants who went to trial did receive much more severe sentences than did similarly situated defendants who pleaded guilty. The study would not in any event shed much light on the question whether a bargaining ban is feasible for a large urban jurisdiction, but it seems inconclusive even for Alaska.

In contrast to these uniformly unsuccessful attempts to demonstrate the feasibility of a plea bargaining ban, a number of studies have found clear evidence of covert tactical adaptations that substantially diminished or even nullified the effect of prohibition attempts in various jurisdictions. These studies do not suggest any particular explanation for the seemingly stubborn persistence of bargaining, but they do reinforce the notion that the process is indeed inevitable for one reason or another.

.   .   .

On the surface, plea bargaining and cooperation between prosecution and defense appear sharply at odds with American legal ideals. It was only natural that courts long sought ways to disregard the existence of these practices. When they could no longer do so, it might have seemed equally natural for courts, practitioners, and scholars to look very skeptically at alleged justifications for the deviation from tradition and to work tirelessly to bring practice back into conformity with prevailing ideals. That this did not happen is undoubtedly explained in part by problems of case pressure that are by no means imaginary; from the evidence available, some observers understandably viewed bargaining as inevitable and accordingly came to see "legitimization of bargaining through standards and judicial oversight" as an essential strategy for containing the damage to our aspirations. More puzzling is the fact that the legitimation of bargaining seems to have proceeded in the face of doubts about the extent of case pressure and the inevitability of cooperation; strong claims for the necessity of bargaining have even tended to suppress awareness of those doubts. Do plea bargaining and cooperation hold some more basic attraction, beyond their value as adaptations to the real problems of case pressure?

Though on one level plea bargaining has always seemed unnatural, at odds with our ideals, in a more fundamental sense the opposite is probably the case. Our ideals include, of course, the norms of the adversary system. But "[t]he essence of the adversary system is challenge[,]...a constant, searching, and creative questioning of official decisions and assertions of authority at all stages." Such a system cannot—should not—be a very pleasant one for officials seeking to exercise authority. We assume that an adversary system will nonetheless command the allegiance of society at large, but we also know that this assumption is based more on hope than on experience. Vigorous, unrelenting challenge to authority can only be viewed with ambivalence, if not hostility, by the communities for whom those in authority are attempting to act; the essentials of the adversary system have needed constitutional protection precisely for this reason.

Under these circumstances, it is the adversary system itself that may seem unattractive and even unnatural, not simply for members of a courtroom "work group," but for much of the community at large. In its constant probing and questioning, adversary behavior deliberately seeks to sow doubt—doubt about the facts, doubt about the law, doubt about the propriety and legitimacy of punishment, doubt about the probity and fairness of constituted authority at every level. These doubts must, in the nature of things, prove unfounded a good deal of the time. Thus, the impulse to disapprove conflict and to embrace cooperative modes of dispute resolution develops strength not only within the courtroom, but also on a much broader social and political front. Even the detached, scholarly observer can record, with all accuracy, that adversary behavior is irritating, inefficacious, and even, in important senses, unnecessary.

Is it not better for society to encourage opponents to negotiate in a spirit of shared interests and values? Is it not better if the defendant admits his guilt so that we need not doubt it ourselves? Is is not better if he accepts the punishment, or actually welcomes it as a "good deal"?

Even if one is prepared, as plea bargaining proponents are, to defend the particulars of the process that generates the defendant's acceptance of punishment, the essential point is that once defended and legitimated, the process no longer commands specific attention case by case. What remains—highly visible and directly experienced every day—is the fact that both sides see eye to eye, know "what the case is worth," and come to terms that all accept. Bargaining, from this perspective, is functional not only for the immediate participants, but also for an entire community that no longer needs to justify, on any substantive ground, its decisions to inflict suffering on individual citizens. The legitimation of bargaining in turn legitimates, at one stroke, every individual instance of criminal punishment.

In this move from adversariness, only one thing is lost—the vigorous probing and questioning that, in their very unpleasantness, have been thought to serve a crucial function in the preservation of freedom. One can, of course, question that view; many civilized nations have rejected it. But within the American constitutional tradition, the assumption remains.

. . .

If one accepts the importance of vigorous challenge within an overall scheme of limited government, then the attractions of cooperation and bargaining, though understandable, must be resisted. The questions facing the various bodies of cooperation theory may therefore be something like the following. First, if cooperation is not inevitable, does the case for legitimating it actually rest on an unspoken premise that cooperation is desirable? Second, if the case for cooperation is to be put in terms of desirability, from what societal perspective is that case to be made? Is the claim simply the plausible but unremarkable one that muted adversariness serves the interests of the community's prevailing social and political coalitions? Or can the claim address the more problematic but essential question whether the loss of vigorous adversary behavior in the long run threatens the foundations of legal control over organized governmental power? Finally, if a vigorous adversary system is worth preserving, under what conditions can the impulses toward cooperation be defeated—in the courtroom and, more importantly, in the wider political community?

CONCLUSION

From repeated pronouncements of the Supreme Court and a near-unanimity of scholarly opinion, we have learned that most felony cases are devoid of triable issues of fact or law; that a contested trial in such cases is therefore a needless waste of resources; that affording most defendants a contested trial is in any event wholly beyond the capacity of any American urban jurisdiction; and finally that even if we could somehow, heroically, make genuine trials available, opposing attorneys would nonetheless find ways to cooperate and would settle cases by negotiation anyway. It follows from all this that plea bargaining need not clash with due process values, that it is in any event inevitable, and that one had best accept this reality, make one's peace with it, and work to legitimate the plea bargaining process and to ameliorate its harshest effects.

. . .

Plea bargaining is not inevitable. In most American cities, judges and attorneys have *chosen* to process cases that way. The Supreme Court has chosen to tolerate, to legitimate, and finally to encourage the plea bargaining system. We can instead choose, if we wish, to afford criminal defendants a day in court. We can cease imposing a price, in months or years of incarceration, upon defendants who exercise that privilege, and can instead permit or even encourage defendants to ask for a hearing in which they may put the prosecution to its proof. We can make available a formal bench trial that permits the expeditious but fair and accurate resolution of criminal cases on the basis of public testimony, tested and challenged with the traditional tools of American adversary procedure. If we nevertheless continue to tolerate plea bargaining, that choice will not tell us that resources are too scarce or that *other* lawyers, those over there in court, are impatient with zealous advocacy and uncontrollably drawn to more comfortable modes of work. A choice to prefer plea bargaining to an inexpensive, feasible adversary trial will instead tell us a great deal about ourselves.

Managerial Judges

Judith Resnik

INTRODUCTION

Until recently, the American legal establishment embraced a classical view of the judicial role. Under this view, judges are not supposed to have an involvement or interest in the controversies they adjudicate. Disengagement and dispassion supposedly enable judges to decide cases fairly and impartially. The mythic emblems surrounding the goddess Justice illustrate this vision of the proper judicial attitude: Justice carries scales, reflecting the obligation to balance claims fairly; she possesses a sword, giving her great power to enforce decisions; and she wears a blindfold, protecting her from distractions.

Many federal judges have departed from their earlier attitudes; they have dropped the relatively disinterested pose to adopt a more active, "managerial" stance. In growing numbers, judges are not only adjudicating the merits of issues presented to them by litigants, but also are meeting with parties in chambers to encourage settlement of disputes and to supervise case preparation.

"Managerial Judges," Judith Resnick. *Harvard Law Review*, Vol. 96, No. 2, 1982. Copyright © 1982 Harvard Law Review Association.

Both before and after the trial, judges are playing a critical role in shaping litigation and influencing results.

Several commentators have identified one kind of lawsuit—the "public law litigation" or "structural reform" case—in which federal judges have assumed a new role. In these cases, judges actively supervise the implementation of a wide range of remedies designed to desegregate schools and to reform prisons and other institutions. Some commentators have questioned the legitimacy of judges' dominance in what is now generally acknowledged to be a "new model of civil litigation." Few, however, have scrutinized the managerial aspects of such postdecision judicial work. Even less attention has been paid to the role judges now play in the pretrial phases of both complex and routine cases.

I believe that the role of judges before adjudication is undergoing a change as substantial as has been recognized in the posttrial phase of public law cases. Today, federal district judges are assigned a case at the time of its filing and assume responsibility for shepherding the case to completion. Judges have described their new tasks as "case management"—hence my term "managerial judges." As managers, judges learn more about cases much earlier than they did in the past. They negotiate with parties about the course, timing, and scope of both pretrial and posttrial litigation. These managerial responsibilities give judges greater power. Yet the restraints that formerly circumscribed judicial authority are conspicuously absent. Managerial judges frequently work beyond the public view, off the record, with no obligation to provide written, reasoned opinions, and out of reach of appellate review.

.   .   .

MANAGERIAL JUDGING: A DESCRIPTION

The Models

I have constructed two hypothetical cases to illustrate what the new managerial role entails and how this role differs before and after trial. The contours of the first case are by now familiar; *Petite* v. *Governor* is a thinly fictionalized amalgam of several suits aimed at ameliorating conditions in institutions such as prisons and mental hospitals. The second case, *Paulson* v. *Danforth, Ltd.*, is a run-of-the-mill products liability case in its early stages of pretrial preparation. I elaborate and rely on the details of these hypothetical cases to demonstrate the ways in which managerial judges influence litigation. All of the details of the hypothetical cases parallel occurrences in real cases. The models I construct provide a graphic representation of the context in which management arises; they enable us to understand that, whatever is decided about its ultimate legitimacy, judicial management reflects the efforts of sincere individuals to respond to perceived needs.

***Petite* v. *Governor*.** *Petite* was filed in 1972 by William Petite on behalf of himself and all other inmates of Hadleyville, a maximum security state prison. Named as defendants were the warden and governor. In 1974, three months after a thirty-day trial, United States District Judge Denise Breaux found that the living conditions at Hadleyville violated the inmates' constitutional rights. Judge Breaux ordered the defendants to act "forthwith" to make incarceration in Hadleyville "constitutional." The order was affirmed in all respects on defendants' appeal; the Supreme Court denied certiorari.

In 1976, plaintiffs' counsel filed a motion for contempt. Counsel argued that defendants had done little to improve Hadleyville; conditions were worse than those found unconstitutional in 1974. Plaintiffs requested that the court revise its 1974 order to mandate specific changes and to set a timetable for their implementation.

Declining to hear argument on the motion, Judge Breaux called the parties' attorneys into her chambers and told them to resolve their differences. She rescheduled the contempt hearing for ten weeks later and ordered the parties to negotiate in the interim. Six weeks later, after plaintiffs complained that defendants would not negotiate in good faith, Judge Breaux agreed to join the discussions. She met weekly with the lawyers. At each meeting, she spoke separately with each side in an effort, which proved unsuccessful, to convince each to moderate its positions. At the opening of the third meeting, plaintiffs' counsel reported that an inmate had been stabbed to death by two cellmates. Plaintiffs requested immediate evacuation of 700 inmates so that each of those remaining could be confined in a separate cell. Judge Breaux scheduled a hearing on the request. After listening to testimony for ten days, she issued an order requiring that within thirty days the population be reduced by 300 inmates and the correctional staff be increased by twelve.

One month later, when plaintiffs reported—and defendants did not dispute—that the prison population had not been reduced, Judge Breaux held the governor in civil contempt and levied fines of $500 per day. Fifteen days later, the state sent 198 inmates to federal facilities. At a conference held in chambers, the state promised the judge that it would hire ten guards within the next six weeks. Judge Breaux then lifted the contempt order and directed the parties to hold weekly meetings to negotiate a revised judgment.

In 1977, unable to obtain agreement and dissatisfied with continued unsafe and unsanitary conditions at Hadleyville, Judge Breaux issued another interim order. She decreed that inmates be given three meals a day, that the first meal be served no earlier than 6:00 a.m. and the last no earlier than 4:30 p.m., that inmates be classified according to security risk and age, that any inmate accused of violent acts be immediately segregated, that four clean-up crews of at least six workers be hired to work five days per week, and that three plumbers be employed within ten days and remain employed until each cell had a working toilet and every ten men had a functioning shower. Defendants appealed. Again the appellate court affirmed. This time, the court of appeals noted its own distress with the slow pace of improvement at Hadleyville.

Since the case returned to her in 1976, Judge Breaux has spent forty-eight trial days hearing postdecision disputes and has issued ten orders. Although Judge Breaux has often expressed a desire to end her involvement, the case remains on her docket because of plaintiffs' continued reports of noncompliance with the court's orders.

Paulson v. Danforth, Ltd. On July 1, 1980, Sarah Paulson bought a "Zip," a car manufactured by the small British company Danforth, Ltd., from a dealer in Manhattan. She drove the car home to the state of Essex in the fall of 1980. On March 4, 1981, while driving at about fifty miles per hour on an interstate highway in Essex, Ms. Paulson lost control of the car and skidded into a side railing. The gas tank exploded immediately, and Ms. Paulson was badly burned. On January 4, 1982, Ms. Paulson's attorney, Robert Adams, filed *Paulson* v. *Danforth, Ltd.* in the United States District Court for the District of Essex. The complaint alleged that defective design had caused the gas tank to explode upon impact, and sought $750,000 in damages. The case was randomly assigned to Judge Edward Kinser.

Danforth's counsel in New York City received a copy of the complaint on January 15 and promptly telecopied it to Danforth's headquarters in London. Danforth retained Deborah Alford, an Essex City lawyer, on January 18. On February 4, Danforth filed a motion to dismiss the suit for lack of personal jurisdiction. Danforth claimed that, because its only business offices in the United States were in New York and California, it could not be sued in Essex. Ms. Paulson countered that Danforth was a commercial enterprise that voluntarily and deliberately did business with people coming from and going to Essex.

On June 10, Judge Kinser denied Danforth's motion to dismiss. On June 18, Danforth filed its answer denying liability. Thereafter, pursuant to rules 33 and 34 of the Federal Rules of Civil Procedure, Mr. Adams served a set of interrogatories and a notice to produce documents. Among the fifty interrogatories were the following:

> 13. From 1977 until 1982, did Danforth test the gas tank on the "Zip" to learn about the tank's durability and ability to withstand impact?
>
> 14. If the tests described in question 13

above were performed, list below the names of all personnel who had any responsibility for the tests.

Plaintiff also made several document requests, including this one:

> 8. Provide all data on the results of any tests performed on the "Zip" from January 1, 1977, through June 1, 1982.

Plaintiff served these discovery requests on Danforth's attorney on July 10, 1982. After the thirty days that the Federal Rules permit for response had passed, Mr. Adams reminded Ms. Alford of the discovery requests. She expressed reservations about the propriety of several questions. Aware of the local district court rule requiring counsel to negotiate discovery disputes "in good faith" before filing discovery motions, the lawyers discussed the questions for several minutes but could not resolve their differences.

Twenty days later, defendant moved for a protective order. Danforth asked Judge Kinser to rule that: (1) twenty-nine of the fifty interrogatories were vague, irrelevant, or overly burdensome, or requested privileged information, and therefore need not be answered; (2) Danforth need not produce crash test data for 1977–1979 and for 1981–1982, because such statistics were irrelevant; and (3) only plaintiff's attorney could see the information produced, because of its "commerical" nature. In opposition to the motion, Mr. Adams asserted the relevance of the information and the absence of any special reasons to protect the disclosure. Claiming that Danforth had no legal basis for a protective motion, Mr. Adams requested that his client be awarded the costs and attorney's fees incurred in opposing the motion.

After Judge Kinser read the papers on the pending discovery motion, he decided that he did not know enough about plaintiff's theories to decide the questions presented. He called the attorneys to his chambers and asked them to explain more about the case. After listening for several minutes to the lawyers' posturing, Judge Kinser asked whether all these legal battles were really necessary: was not settlement the least expensive, quickest, and fairest resolution of most disputes? When the attorneys insisted upon pursuing their arguments, the judge asked whether the lawyers were acting in their clients' best interests. Had they thought about how costly the litigation would be? Did the clients know how risky trials were? That the loser would have to pay the victor's court costs? That discovery could take years and that he, the judge, had control over the schedule?

Judge Kinser then asked Mr. Adams to leave the room so that the judge could confer privately with defendant's lawyer. Judge Kinser explained to Ms. Alford that he had learned a bit about plaintiff's case and that it looked "sound" to him. Did Danforth understand that a jury would surely be sympathetic to an injured plaintiff? What harm would there be in giving this injured victim some money? Had the parties talked numbers? Perhaps she could tell her client that $250,000 seemed "about right" to the judge. And perhaps she could mention that his court looked with disfavor upon uncompromising litigants.

Judge Kinser then called in plaintiff's counsel for a private meeting. Did Mr. Adams know how hard it was to prove a products liability claim? Had he thought about how long it might take to get to trial? What numbers would his client "go for"? The judge thought that $250,000 "sounded right" and that the case looked like one that "should settle."

Summoning both attorneys before him once more, Judge Kinser concluded the conference by announcing that he would defer ruling on the discovery motion until the parties had had time to negotiate further. He set a date to hold another conference in six weeks.

The New "Forms" of Litigation.   In cases like *Petite*, judges become enmeshed in extended relations with institutions. Many commentators have discussed the political and social ramifications of this involvement, but such ramifications are not the central concern of my analysis. *Petite's* purpose is to illustrate changes occurring within the lawsuit itself.

In public law cases like *Petite*, a new form of litigation is emerging—one that is no longer "bi-polar" or "retrospective." Judges are at the center; they are personally involved in the implementation of their decrees and in the prospective planning of posttrial relations among the parties. Judge Breaux's bargaining, frequent contact with the parties, and supervision of the minutiae of everyday life in prison contrasts sharply with our judicial customs. No longer a detached oracle, the judge has become a consort of the litigants. Moreover, judges like the fictional Breaux become openly involved in a power struggle: when defendants publicly defy or quietly evade court decrees, observers discover that judges are far less powerful than the goddess-symbol suggests.

On the other end of the litigation spectrum is *Paulson* v. *Danforth, Ltd.*—from its facts, an unexceptional tort case in the ordinary posture of pretrial preparation. Yet *Paulson*, like *Petite*, exemplifies the results of substantial change in the litigation process itself. Judge Kinser, like Judge Breaux, descended into the trenches to manage the case. Federal judges across the country are becoming engaged in similar pretrial managerial efforts. The new "forms" of litigation can be found in all types and phases of cases on the federal docket.

. . .

The emergence of managerial judging is not simply an artifact of discovery (which generates pretrial supervision) or public law litigation (which generates posttrial supervision). Judges have also become concerned with problems of their own—the perception that the courts are too slow, justice too expensive, and judges at least partly at fault. Since the early 1900's, judges have attempted to respond to criticism of their efficiency by experimenting with increasingly more managerial techniques. . . .

Aspects of Managerial Judging

The models demonstrate that federal judges today devote substantial amounts of time to case management. Only when informal discussions fail do judges take their places on the bench at formal trials and hearings. To illuminate this informal world, I have isolated several aspects of judge-litigant contact in case management.

Initiation.   I believe, without the benefit of much empirical work, that judges initiate judicial management during the pretrial phase. After trial, judicial intervention generally comes at the parties' request.

Why do judges initiate pretrial management? First, many are dissatisfied with the adversarial process and want to reduce attorneys' control over it. Judges who observe specific instances of attorney misbehavior and dilatory tactics may feel that the remedy is to supervise attorney conduct more closely. Second, judges may believe that their intervention speeds settlement and improves the litigation process. Third, as judicial management becomes a method of control, it creates incentives for its perpetuation. With the individual calendar system, the publication of each judge's case load, and comparative data on judges' performance, judges can learn which of their colleagues dispose of the most cases. When judges who dispose of many cases lecture other judges on how to reduce backlogs, peer pressure tends to generate more vigorous management.

In the posttrial context, different incentives are at work. By making decisions on the merits, judges "dispose of" cases. Given the large time investment required for postdecision case management, judges have every reason to avoid returning to "finished" cases. Accordingly, the instigators of posttrial management are usually the "winning" plaintiffs' attorneys, who seek help in implementing decrees. Occasionally, "losing" defense attorneys return hoping to have adverse court orders modified.

Once brought into the enforcement process, however, the judge often uses informal management techniques in an effort to save time and avoid the pressures of public controversy. In *Petite*, Judge Breaux first ordered the parties to negotiate, then joined the discussions herself after the parties' private conferences proved unsuccessful. Further, she instituted reporting requirements as a technique for enforcing compliance—in a sense, initiating contact with the parties.

Likelihood, Frequency, and Duration.
Although it is difficult to tally the overall resources devoted to judicial management tasks, some generalizations about pretrial and posttrial management are possible. . . .

In contrast, the occasions for posttrial management are few. Eighty-five to ninety percent of all federal civil suits end by settlement. Of those not settled, some uncalculated number are dismissed because of legal defects. In most of the remaining cases, the parties demand monetary rather than equitable relief. Postdecision collection problems sometimes arise when damages

are awarded. But judges can do little if the debtor is judgment proof, and in any event the judicial time required to order execution of a judgment is minimal. Thus, only a tiny fraction of all civil cases require significant postdecision judicial activity; generally such cases are like *Petite* v. *Governor*, cases in which equitable orders involving complex institutions have been made.

Unfortunately, little empirical work charts the frequency of judge-litigant contact either before or after decision. Without data, we can only guess how much time judges actually devote to management. But the very nature of the tasks involved suggests that both pretrial and posttrial intervention require large investments of judicial time and energy.

The duration of supervision, both before and after trial, may vary from a single meeting to a decade or more. Yet it is significant that pretrial supervision has a natural stopping point. In *Paulson*, Judge Kinser will relinquish his role as manager when the case is decided, either by settlement or by trial. In fact, the whole point of pretrial management is to end the dispute as rapidly as possible. After decision, on the other hand, judicial management has no clear-cut conclusion. In *Petite*, Judge Breaux may retain her role as manager indefinitely, and the questions whether and when the district court should terminate its jurisdiction may themselves be litigated.

Formality of Proceedings.
Managerial meetings both before and after decision are informal and contrast sharply with the highly stylized structure of courtroom interaction. When judges preside at hearings, they evoke the image of Justice: they wear robes and sit stony-faced behind elevated benches; they receive information but rarely impart it. Pretrial and posttrial conferences, on the other hand, are informal events. The parties

146 PLEA BARGAINING AND CIVIL SETTLEMENT IN TRIAL COURTS

talk with, rather than at, each other. The conferences often taken place in chambers. The participants sit around tables, and the judge wears business dress. But for the title of one of the participants—"judge"—these conferences could be confused with ordinary business meetings.

In public law cases, however, informal posttrial negotiations may fail. Posttrial disputes often lead to formal compliance and contempt hearings. Lawyers' in-chambers arguments are replaced by witnesses' in-court testimony; judicial proposals for compromise give way to formal orders; and the entire proceeding is placed in the public domain and often within reach of the appellate courts. In contrast, most pretrial conferences are not followed by formal adjudication, and judicial acts in the pretrial phase are rarely exposed to public scrutiny.

Scope of Information. Informal judge-litigant contact provides judges with information beyond that traditionally within their ken. Conference topics are more wide ranging and the judges' concerns are broader than either are when proceedings are conducted in court. The supposedly rigid structure of evidentiary rules, designed to insulate decision-makers from extraneous and impermissible information, is irrelevant in case management. Managerial judges are not silent auditors of retrospective events retold by first-person storytellers. Instead, judges remove their blindfolds and become part of the sagas themselves.

Consider again some details of the hypothetical *Paulson* case. Assume that Judge Kinser imposed a time limit for naming expert witnesses. Danforth objected: the company needed more time and information to assess the availability and desirability of various experts. Judge Kinser agreed to an extension. At a subsequent conference, Danforth asked for still more time on the ground

its first and second choices for experts were "unavailable" to testify on Danforth's behalf "because of prior commitments." Relying on his past experiences as a judge and a litigator, Judge Kinser translated "unavailable" into "unwilling." He gave Danforth another twenty days to find an expert but concluded (to himself) that the company's defense was weak; he therefore redoubled his efforts to pressure Danforth to settle. By being "in" at the planning stages, Judge Kinser made a premature and perhaps ill-founded evaluation of the strength of Danforth's defense.

Similarly, episodes in the *Petite* case demonstrate the effect of the large amounts of information available to a managerial judge. In *Petite*, Judge Breaux learned facts and opinions—information she might not have received in a more formal confrontation—that she could use to encourage settlement and bypass the adjudicatory process. At a meeting to discuss Hadleyville's broken toilets and clogged showers, defendants' attorney promised that the problems would be solved within the week. In a conference two weeks later, plaintiffs' attorney reported the continuing failures of the sanitation systems. The defense attorney was embarrassed and indicated that the governor was having "staff problems." Judge Breaux ordered that the warden attend the next conference.

At the following meeting, Judge Breaux saw what she believed to be animosity between the state's lawyer and the warden. After the meeting, she spoke in private with the attorney. She told him that she guessed the warden was "causing problems." Judge Breaux suggested that the governor might not wish to be held responsible for the health problems resulting from the lack of sanitation. She hoped the governor would see the choices before him: make the warden obey the court, replace the warden, or take the blame for the warden's misconduct.

In sum, in both the pretrial and posttrial contexts, managerial judges can acquire, test, and use knowledge in ways that judges adjudicating under the traditional model cannot.

Reach and Visibility.   Pretrial supervision affects fewer people than does posttrial management, and, as a result, tends to be less visible. The *Paulson* pretrial orders were felt primarily by the lawyers, who had to do the work, and by the litigants, who had to pay. Although pretrial orders occasionally affect third parties—such as Danforth's employees (who had to compile requested data) and Danforth's expert and lay witnesses (who had to appear for depositions)— such effects are generally transitory. Accordingly, pretrial judge-litigant contacts are relatively private events. Many judges conduct "pretrials" in their chambers; typically, neither court reporters nor the public attends.

Posttrial management frequently affects many nonparties. For example, Judge Breaux's order to increase the correctional staff at Hadleyville by twelve officers altered the seniority rights of the prison's unionized personnel and reduced the staff resources available to other state prisons; her order to transfer prisoners caused ripples in the federal prison system, which accepted some of the overflow. Such orders, of course, raise important political and constitutional issues. Judicially crafted remedial schemes may require large expenditures of public funds and involve judges in the detailed administration of institutions usually run by other branches of government.

Given the import of such events, posttrial judicial activity is likely to occur with stage lights. After judgment, the call for judicial assistance may herald a breakdown in the parties' negotiations—one side's "going pub-

lic" with allegations of the other's failure to obey a court order. Reform cases like *Petite* are especially likely to attract public attention. Contempt motions against government officials are newsworthy, and the public, concerned for its institutions and its pocketbook, takes note when judges' orders affect schools or prisons.

Discretion.   The two hypotheticals demonstrate the broad discretion of the trial judge who assumes a managerial role. Assume, for example, that Judge Kinser imposed a timetable for pretrial preparation and denied Danforth's motion for protection from Ms. Paulson's discovery requests. Danforth's attorney, Ms. Alford, was concerned: she thought that the time Judge Kinser permitted was egregiously short and that he had erred in denying the protective order. Ms. Alford asked Judge Kinser to "certify" an appeal on the ground that the discovery questions were so important that "immediate" review would "materially advance the ultimate termination of the litigation." The judge refused because he thought the discovery rulings raised no novel points of law. Ms. Alford could have requested a writ of mandamus commanding Judge Kinser to issue a protective order and to liberalize his pretrial schedule. But appellate courts rarely issue such writs to district courts. Moreover, Ms. Alford would have risked Judge Kinser's displeasure at being named the respondent in a mandamus petition. Danforth's remaining path to appeal—challenging a final judgment— would open only if Danforth lost at trial or by summary judgment. Absent a final decision, Judge Kinser would enjoy unreviewable discretion.

Litigants dissatisfied with Judge Breaux's postdecision rulings in *Petite* had far greater opportunities to secure appellate review. The underlying decision was tested on appeal, and the affirmance provided some guidance to Judge Breaux on the proper scope of relief. Further, many of Judge Breaux's post-decision orders gave injunctive relief and thus were appealable as a matter of right. Finally, even when Judge Breaux issued posttrial orders that were not appealable, public attention, described above, and institutional constraints, discussed below, confined her exercise of discretion.

Institutional Constraints. An array of institutional factors are far more likely to discipline judges' actions during posttrial management than during pretrial supervision. First, a large percentage of posttrial management occurs in public law cases, in which defendants are either federal or state officials. In these cases, federal judges are constrained by the obligation to respect the autonomy of coordinate branches of government and state executives.

Second, federal judges appreciate the limits of their posttrial enforcement powers. Decrees are enforced principally in a negative fashion—by threatening to hold the disobedient in contempt and to levy fines or impose jail terms. Judges understand that, however detailed their decrees, evasion is relatively easy; close monitoring for compliance is expensive and draining. To implement the terms of their decrees, judges need the cooperation not only of administrators and employees in defendant institutions, but also of state executives and the community.

Finally, the fact of decision must be considered. One might expect that, with the issuance of a decree, a judge would be emotionally and intellectually committed to the decree and would insist unrelentingly upon its enforcement. But overreaching and expressions of hostility toward noncomplying defendants are relatively rare. Earlier findings of defendants' culpability do not translate into unquestioned acceptance of

plaintiffs' subsequent requests for assistance.

There are many explanations for this reticence. The issues in public law cases are complex and often depressing. Third parties may impede implementation efforts, and fiscal constraints may limit defendants' flexibility to respond promptly to court decrees. Thus, even if personally sympathetic to plaintiffs' claims, and even if angered by defendants' disobedience, judges find it politic and appropriate to exercise restraint.

In contrast, few institutional constraints inhibit judges during the pretrial phase. First, many of the parties are private individuals or businesses rather than government officials. Second, even when governmental litigants are involved, the pressures of comity are far less when judges supervise pretrial litigation strategies than when they supervise the posttrial implementation of decrees reorienting government programs and facilities. Third, the effective power of judges is considerably greater at the pretrial stage than in postdecision enforcement. During pretrial supervision, judges make many decisions informally and often meet with parties ex parte, and appellate review is virtually unavailable. The judge has vast influence over the course and eventual outcome of the litigation. As a result, litigants have good reason to capitulate to judicial pressure rather than risk the hostility of a judge who, under the individual calendar system, has ongoing responsibility for the case. During pretrial management, judges are restrained only by personal beliefs about the proper role of judge-managers.

Some Preliminary Conclusions

Pretrial and posttrial management share certain characteristics. In both, judges interact informally with the litigating parties and receive information that would be considered inadmissible in traditional courtroom proceedings. Management at both ends of the lawsuit takes time and increases judges' responsibilities.

Nevertheless, the two management stages are dissimilar in many respects. Predecision management is initiated usually by the judges; postdecision supervision begins more often at a litigant's request. Pretrial management occurs much more frequently, but posttrial intervention tends to be more far reaching in its effects. Unlike pretrial management, posttrial activity occurs within a framework of appellate oversight, public visibility, and institutional constraints that inhibits overreaching.

Posttrial supervision thus represents a less striking departure from the American judicial tradition than does pretrial management. Because it is party initiated, visible, and reviewable, the judge's role in posttrial management is familiar. Moreover, many techniques of posttrial management, such as retaining jurisdiction and employing special masters, are not novel. In contrast, because pretrial management is judge initiated, invisible, and unreviewable, it breaks sharply from American norms of adjudication.

.   .   .

CHAPTER 4

Regulating Demands Made on Appellate Courts

Within American court systems another type of court exists above the trial level, commonly called appellate courts. In state judicial systems and in the federal system, any party not fully satisfied with the decision of a trial court, may, by right, file an appeal. An appeal typically is limited to a review of one or more specific aspects of a trial proceeding. The number of cases that are, in fact, appealed in any court system usually is only a portion of all of those that might possibly be appealed. For example, in the federal system in fiscal year 1970, the rate of civil appeal of appealable district court decisions was only about one in four.[1] By fiscal year 1986, less than one in ten civil cases decided by the district courts was appealed. What this means is that the role of appellate courts is limited to reviewing cases that are not necessarily representative of the range of cases heard by the trial courts, in either their content or the issues that they raise.

As one would expect, the cases that are appealed are likely to be more complex than those that are not, and they are cases that frequently raise broad general questions of legal policy. The cost of the process of appeal in terms of both time and money serves to regulate the number and types of cases appealed. Monetary costs include filing fees (which generally are not very substantial and may be waived for indigents), attorneys' fees, and the cost of transcription and reproduction of the trial proceedings. There may also be psychological costs of appeal that can be as important as the monetary and time costs. The delays associated with the process of appeal may impose substantial "uncertainty costs." In some cases the losing party may prefer the certain knowledge of defeat to the continued uncertainty that is part of the process of appeal. However, this is more likely to be true in civil cases than in criminal cases, where filing an appeal may be a strategic device to delay implementation of a prison sentence. Delay and uncertainty may, however, affect different types of litigants in different ways. Those for whom litigation is a routine matter may be better able to endure the costs of delay and uncertainty than those whose involvement in litigation is exceptional and those for whom the investment in each case is very great.

The style of dispute resolution found in appellate courts varies significantly from that typically found in trial courts. The former have a quite different and restricted cast of characters and a more limited interest in the dispute, and tend to be more formal and stylized in their procedures. Trial court proceedings typically bring together a diverse mixture of amateurs and professionals. In addition to judges and lawyers who are specifically trained in the law, participants with no legal training may play an important part. Litigants, witnesses, and jurors all act to democratize the trial court proceeding. Dispute processing in trial courts involves them in a process of clarifying events and interpreting norms.

As a dispute moves from the trial to the appellate level it is transformed, becoming almost exclusively a dispute about law or procedure. Issues of law or questions about the way in which the trial was conducted are argued in appellate courts. It is assumed that findings of fact produced by the trial proceedings are correct. Whereas the matters at issue in a trial are almost always subject to extensive oral argument, the time allotted for such argument before appellate courts is limited. The dispute is conducted largely through briefs, motions, and memoranda. What all this means is that disputing in appellate courts is a "lawyer's game". Only those trained in law are permitted to play; the amateur participants found in trial courts are eliminated.

In trial courts decisional responsibilty lies with a single judge or is shared by a judge and a jury. In appellate courts decision making is collegial and involves only judges. Disputing in appellate courts is far removed in time and substance from the events that gave rise to the original disagreement. The original parties, their dispute, and its specific resolution become less important than the legal context into which they are placed.

In the federal system and in many states there are two levels of appellate courts. The first level, intermediate appellate courts, stands between the trial level and the highest appellate or supreme court level. In theory, intermediate appellate courts are courts of review, whereas supreme courts may go beyond review and act as policy-making bodies. However, this distinction is very difficult to make because all types of appellate courts both review and make policy. Furthermore, it may be very difficult to determine whether, in any particular appeal, the decision reached involved either review or policy-making. Nevertheless, when appellate courts do review decisions of trial courts they serve in a supervisory or quality control capacity to ensure that the actions of trial courts are in conformity with the law. When they make policy they use the cases that are appealed to them as vehicles for developing the broad outlines of legal policy. Review tends to be concerned with the past, with ensuring that what was done at the trial level was fair. Policy-making is forward looking. Although courts are constrained to decide within the context of particular cases, when they make policy their decisions are intended to provide guidelines for future action. The issue of representativeness of the cases that are appealed is of less concern, for in policy-making what is at issue is not general supervision. In fact, appellate courts are frequently equipped with devices that allow them to screen out even those cases which are appealed to ensure that only the most important and controversial ones are given full attention. Appellate courts, like trial courts, are reactive but not defenseless.

In the first selection of this chapter, Lawrence Baum reviews the variety of techniques that appellate courts employ to avoid giving full consideration to cases that are appealed to them. Some of these techniques accrue to appellate courts as formal legal mechanisms of demand regulation. Others develop informally through the practices and decisions of the courts. One of the most important of the formal legal techniques is the *certiorari* power of the United States Supreme Court. The exercise of this power has been of continuing interest to political scientists who have approached it from a variety of methodological perspectives. The subsequent four selections consider Supreme Court agenda setting through its discretionary power to decide what cases to hear.

The article by Tanenhaus et al. presents pioneering research as to the variables associated with the granting or denying of certiorari. Tanenhaus and his colleagues offered a theory, *cue theory*, as a guide to their research which focused on the 1956–1958 terms of the Court. A retest of cue theory or at least the cues found by Tanenhaus et al. was conducted by Virginia Armstrong and Charles Johnson who examined two terms of the Warren Court and two terms of the Burger Court. D. Marie Provine conducted an extensive analysis of the granting or withholding of certiorari and drew upon voting data from the judicial conferences that were found in the papers of Justice Harold Burton. S. Sidney Ulmer offers a sophisticated statistical analysis of certiorari decision making that focuses on conflict as a major variable. The final article in this chapter is by William McLauchlan, who examines the question of how long it takes for the Supreme Court to process its cases and whether the time involved increased between 1971 and 1984.

NOTE

1. Jerry Goldman, "Federal District Courts and the Appellate Crisis," *Judicature* 57 (1973) 211.

The Judicial Gatekeeping Function: A General Analysis

Lawrence Baum

In recent years social scientists have shown an increasing interest in litigation as a political process. On the civil side of the law, scholars have examined such subjects as the decision to take disputes to court, the use of litigation to obtain policy change, and the role of the lawyer in litigation decisions. In the study of criminal litigation, extensive work has been done on the police decision to arrest, the prosecutor's decision to initiate prosecution, and the pretrial settlement of cases through plea-bargaining.

. . .

The setting of judicial agendas is a function which litigants share with judges themselves. Courts possess and utilize a variety of what may be called gatekeeping powers, powers with which they help to determine which demands they will address and how fully they will consider the demands they do address. These powers provide the basis for gatekeeping activities as diverse as the exercise of discretionary jurisdiction by the Supreme Court, the judicial manipulation of rules of jurisdiction, and the encouragement of pretrial settlement by trial courts.

. . .

Inattention to institutional gatekeeping activities has been particularly unfortunate in the study of the judiciary, for it has reinforced a long-standing view of the courts as virtually powerless to determine what demands they will address. With the exception of the Supreme Court, courts tend to be seen as agencies which must respond to agendas established by litigants, and even the Court's ability to help set its agenda sometimes is minimized. I believe that this conception of the courts' role is inaccurate and misleading. Courts possess significant powers to help determine what they will decide, and their use of these powers plays an important part in determining the outcomes of the judicial process. More specifically, two arguments on judicial gatekeeping may be put forward.

First, the holding of important gatekeeping powers is almost ubiquitous among courts, and the use of these powers substantially increases the difficulties faced by potential litigants in obtaining desired outcomes from the judicial system.

Reprinted by permission of the author from "The Judicial Gatekeeping Function: A General Analysis and a Study of the California Supreme Court," paper presented at the 1975 annual meeting of the American Political Science Association, pp. 1–11. Footnotes have been omitted.

Second, there is an important purposive element in the use of gatekeeping powers by at least some courts. These powers are employed as instruments to achieve policy goals. As a result, decisions in the gatekeeping process contribute to the same judicial ends as decisions "on the merits." This purposive use of gatekeeping powers increases their significance for litigants seeking certain policy outcomes, for policy-oriented gatekeeping creates systematic rather than random roadblocks to the achievement of favorable results.

GATEKEEPING POWERS: THEIR FORMS AND IMPORTANCE

As indicated . . ., gatekeeping powers may be defined as those with which courts help to determine which demands they will address and how fully they will consider those that they do address. This rather broad and ambiguous definition requires some explication. Litigants may be considered political actors who wish to obtain favorable responses to their demands. To achieve this end, they seek first to get these demands before judges and to have them considered fully and officially. Gatekeeping powers represent means by which courts help to determine litigants' success in achieving this intermediate goal. The decision whether or not to hear a case, the shunting of some cases to a category receiving limited consideration, the establishment of rules of access to the court, and the encouragement of litigation or of alternative paths of action all constitute types of gatekeeping. To understand the nature of judicial gatekeeping, it will be useful to examine briefly some major forms of judicial activity which may be classified as gatekeeping practices.

Discretionary Jurisdiction

Perhaps the most clearly delineated form of judicial gatekeeping is the exercise of discretionary jurisdiction. The Supreme Court's *certiorari* power has its counterpart in most of the states, where the highest appellate courts possess the power to refuse decision on the merits to some or all classes of appeals. In the 23 states with intermediate appellate courts, typically the supreme court is required to hear certain kinds of appeals but has discretionary jurisdiction over most appeals from the intermediate level. Several states without intermediate appellate courts give their supreme courts discretion in the hearing of some cases; most notably, Virginia and West Virginia allow no appeals as a matter of right. Procedures for decision on the acceptance of cases and the proportions of cases accepted both vary considerably. In each court, however, discretionary jurisdiction serves as a device by which a large number of appellants are denied formal consideration of their demands on the merits.

Summary Disposition

Siblings of discretionary jurisdiction, some of illegitimate birth, are the practices of summary dismissal of appeals and summary affirmance of lower-court decisions in cases which appellate courts legally must hear. These practices are widespread as means by which appellate judges dispose rapidly of appeals which they do not wish to accord full consideration. The federal courts of appeals have used statutory powers as bases for summary dismissal of *habeas corpus* cases involving state prisoners and of pauper appeals, and under court rules some have adopted procedures for summary disposition of other appeals. The Supreme Court summarily affirms and dismisses appeals under its mandatory jurisdiction in a procedure similar to its *certiorari* decisions. Some state supreme courts have adopted similar procedures. In Nebraska, for instance, the appellee may move for summary affirmance under court rule. Summary disposition differs in legal form from discretionary jurisdiction, but its impact on appellants is virtually the same.

Truncated Procedure

Cousins of the first two forms are the procedures increasingly used by appellate courts to classify certain cases as worthy of less than the court's full procedure for their consideration. In some state courts, a staff director classifies some appeals as easy to decide and assigns them to a staff member, who writes a memorandum on the case, proposes the court's decision, and writes a draft *per curiam* opinion for the court. These materials then go to the judges responsible for the case, who reach final decision without oral argument. Other kinds of truncated procedure, with and without extensive staff involvement, exist in both federal and state systems.

Like summary disposition, truncated procedure represents a kind of substitute for discretionary jurisdiction, but it constitutes a more ambiguous form of gatekeeping. It involves gatekeeping in two senses. First, most of the "easy" cases assigned to the group receiving limited consideration inevitably will be those in which the appellant's demand is perceived as having little merit, so that the assignment in itself serves as a signal to limit the seriousness with which that demand is considered. Second, the adoption of truncated procedure, particularly the avoidance of oral argument, limits the appellant's ability to overcome the presumption of lower-court correctness. In contrast with discretionary jurisdiction and summary disposition, however, the appellant retains a

chance for victory even if his case has been screened out of the mainstream.

.   .   .

Manipulation of Costs

Both trial and appellate courts can manipulate the financial costs of litigation, costs which may be crucial in a potential litigant's decision whether to go to court. Thus, the relaxation of rules of form for appeals by indigent appellants in the Supreme Court and other courts has eliminated a major financial barrier to the appeal of criminal convictions. An example of another kind is the imposition of financial penalties for appeals judged frivolous in the intermediate appellate courts of California, intended to discourage groundless appeals. Whether directed specifically at indigents or at the general population, the manipulation of financial costs inevitably has a differential impact on groups of different economic status. What serves as an important gatekeeping device in regard to some segments of the population may have no effect on others.

Manipulation of Courts' Right to Decide

A variety of characteristics of a case may deprive a court of the legal power to hear and to decide it, including lack of jurisdiction, mootness, and lack of adversariness. Many of the rules establishing restriction on courts' power to decide cases were created by courts themselves. Moreover, those "imposed" on the courts by constitutions and legislatures are subject to considerable leeway in their interpretation. As a result, these rules have served as judicial gatekeeping devices, manipulated in their general form and in individual cases to open or close access to litigants. The Supreme Court's use of such devices as rules of standing and the doctrine of political questions as gatekeep-

TABLE 1
Characteristics of Major Forms of Judicial Gatekeeping

| | | Impact | |
		Absolute	Limited
	Court-centered	Discretionary jurisdiction Summary disposition	Truncated procedure
Locus of decision-making	**Combined**	Manipulation of right to decide	
	Court-litigant	Manipulation of costs Encouraging civil settlement	Encouraging criminal settlement

ing procedures is part of the folklore of the judiciary. Thus, for instance, the requirement of adversariness is adhered to when the Court wishes to avoid decision, relaxed when the Court wishes to decide.

Manipulation of rules concerning a court's right to decide cases serves two rather separate gatekeeping functions. The rules in themselves constitute factors influencing potential litigants' decisions whether to go to court. In addition, their application in particular cases allows courts to determine whether particular litigants will obtain full consideration. The two functions together make this a significant form of gatekeeping.

These [five] forms of judicial gatekeeping, probably the most significant, provide a basis for some general conclusions about this form of judicial action. First, gatekeeping powers are used primarily to narrow access to judicial decision. Courts may relax or fortify barriers to litigants, and many gatekeeping powers are used for both purposes. But the emphasis of gatekeeping activity is one of making it more difficult for litigants to go to court and to obtain full consideration of their demands. This emphasis follows from the major purposes for the adoption of gatekeeping practices, the limitation of court workloads to improve court functioning and to ease judges' responsibilities.

Second, the possession of significant gatekeeping powers is not limited to a small number of fortunate courts. Relatively few courts possess highly formal, explicit gatekeeping powers like discretionary jurisdiction, but judges on other courts have made use of less explicit powers to achieve the same ends. Gatekeeping should be seen as a nearly universal function in the judicial system, an integral part of the judicial process at all levels.

Third, gatekeeping practices differ in some significant characteristics. One is the identity of the ultimate decision-maker in the gatekeeping process. In "court-centered" gatekeeping like the exercise of discretionary jurisdiction, the court determines whether or not each case will receive full consideration. In "court-litigant" gatekeeping, exemplified by encouragement of pretrial settlement, the court influences the *litigant's* decision whether to seek court decision.... [M]anipulation of the courts' right to decide cases involves both types of gatekeeping.

Another distinction among gatekeeping practices concerns the impact of the gatekeeping decision. In most forms of gatekeeping this action determines whether a case will be decided on the merits or dropped. In this sense the impact of gatekeeping is "absolute." Truncated appellate procedure...[is a] device of "limited" impact; even after a case is screened out a decision on the merits...remains to be made.

The gatekeeping devices which have been discussed may be characterized on these two dimensions in the way shown in Table 1.

... It is clear that judicial gatekeeping creates barriers to success for litigants. This fact is clearest in the case of discretionary jurisdiction, by which some courts turn back the vast majority of demands which are brought to them. But it is also true of very different forms of gatekeeping such as the manipulation of financial costs. Litigants face other barriers to success in the courts —including, of course, judges' decisions on the merits in those cases which get past the gatekeeping stage. The existence of gatekeeping powers simply adds to the difficulty of getting to court and securing favorable outcomes. The agenda-setting powers of courts are real and significant, and students of the litigation process must take these powers into account in examining the tasks faced by those who would use the courts for political or other action.

.   .   .

The Supreme Court's *Certiorari* Jurisdiction: Cue Theory

Joseph Tanenhaus
Marvin Schick
Matthew Muraskin
Daniel Rosen

...The theory that underlies our study ...[W]e call..."the cue theory of *certiorari*."...

[We] hypothesize that some method exists for separating the *certiorari* petitions requiring serious attention from those that are so frivolous as to be unworthy of careful study. We further hypothesized that a group of readily identifiable cues exists to serve this purpose. The presence of any one of these cues would warn a justice that a petition deserved scrutiny. If no cue were present, on the other hand, a justice could safely discard a petition without further expenditure of time and energy. Careful study by a justice of the petitions containing cues could then be made to determine which should be denied because of jurisdictional defects, inadequacies in the records, lack of ripeness, tactical inadvisability, etc., and which should be allotted some of the limited time available for oral argument, research, and the preparation of full opinions. Those remaining could

then be disposed of by denying *certiorari* or by granting it and summarily affirming or reversing the court below....

The data used in this study were drawn from the published records of the United States Supreme Court and the lower courts and administrative agencies in which the cases were litigated. No use was made of the *certiorari* documents themselves. A codebook was used in assembling the data for a systematic sample of applications for review for the 1947–1958 terms. Since both the codebook and sample were prepared for several purposes in addition to this study, something needs to be said in detail about each.

The sample was drawn as follows: Every fifth petition was coded for the ten terms 1947–1951, 1953–1955, and 1957–1958, and every petition for the two terms 1952 and 1956....

The cue theory of *certiorari* that maintains the justices of the Supreme Court employ cues as a means of separating those petitions worthy of scrutiny from those that may be discarded without further study. If the theory is valid, it should follow that:

Proposition I: Petitions that contain no cues will be denied.

Proposition II: Petitions that contain one or more cues will be studied carefully, and 25 to 43 per cent of them granted.

We estimate the percentage of petitions which contain cues and which are granted in the following manner. Previously cited statements by the members of the Court lead us to believe that 40 to 60 per cent of the appellate docket petitions have some merit, and therefore receive more or less careful attention. Since, furthermore, the Court grants the writ in 15 to 17 per cent of all appellate docket petitions, those granted should constitute from 25 per cent to 43 per cent of all meritorious *certioraris*.

It hardly needs to be said that we cannot expect to find the requirements of the cue theory completely fulfilled, if only because not all the hypothesized cues have been included in our analysis. But if we have accounted for most of the major cues, these requirements should be fairly well satisfied. At the very least, we should find a sizable and statistically significant correlation between the presence of one or more cues and the granting of *certiorari*. Before this relationship can be measured, however, it is necessary to determine whether each of the several possible cues about which we have collected data can properly be regarded as a cue. One method of doing this is to take cases involving none of the hypothesized cues and compare them in turn with those cases containing a given cue but no other. If a given cue is present, the likelihood of *certiorari* should be greater (to a statistically significant degree) than when none of the cues is involved. Whenever this turns out in fact to be the case, we shall accept it as satisfactory evidence that the hypothesized cue does exist. Because the large number of petitions involved causes rather small differences to produce large *Chi* squares, we have set the confidence level necessary to accept an hypothesis at 0.001.

The hypotheses concerning the several cues we wish to test may be stated as follows:

A. *Party as a Cue.* When the federal government seeks review, but no other cue is involved, the likelihood of *certiorari* is greater (to a statistically significant degree) than when other parties seek review and no other cue is involved.

B. *Dissension as a Cue.* When dissension has been indicated among the judges of the court immediately below, or between two or more courts and agencies in a given case, but no other cue is involved, the likelihood of *certiorari* is greater (to a statistically significant degree) than when no such dissension is present and no other cue is involved.

C. *Civil Liberties Issues as Cues.* When a civil liberties issue is present, but no other cue is involved, the likelihood of *certiorari* is greater (to a statistically significant degree) than when no civil liberties issue is present and no other cue is involved.

D. *Economic Issues as Cues.* When an economic issue is present, but no other cue is involved, the likelihood of review is greater (to a statistically significant degree) than when no economic issue is present and no other cue is involved.

We turn now to our reasons for selecting each of these hypotheses for testing, the procedures used in classifying the petitions, and the data we have developed.

HYPOTHESIS A: PARTY AS A CUE

This hypothesis finds some support in the literature. Frankfurter and Landis, in two of their early articles, observed that the Solicitor General speaks with special authority. They pointed out that during the 1929 and 1930 terms the federal government was extremely successful in having *certiorari* granted when it was appellant and denied when it was respondent. More recently Justice Harlan and the authors of a law review note made similar observations.

There are several reasons why the position of the federal government may be regarded as an important cue. For one thing, many of the persons who prepare petitions for *certiorari* are sorely lacking in the required expertise. This is decidedly not the case with the Solicitor General's staff and the other government attorneys who practice before the Court. They have the talent, the resources, and the experience fully to exploit the strong aspects of their own cases, and in reply briefs to expose the most glaring weaknesses of their opponents. We do not mean to imply that government attorneys are grossly unfair in seeking or opposing writs of *certiorari*. In fact, we place credence in the widely circulated gossip that when a clerk or justice wants to get to the nub of a complex case in a hurry he turns to the government's brief. Still, it is surely not invidious to suggest that government attorneys generally turn their assets to the government's advantage.

Another consequence of the government lawyers' expertise is its tendency to prevent them from deluging the Court with applications that they know the Court has no interest in reviewing.

Still another reason why the petitions for review submitted by the lawyers for the government tend to be meritorious is that only rarely are they under pressure to carry cases to the Court solely to satisfy a client who insists upon leaving no stone unturned in his search for vindication. Nor is the government lawyer tempted to pursue a case regardless of merit in the hope that he may gain the prestige of having argued once before the highest court in the land.

Finally, we suspect that the Court's defer-ence for the opinions of the executive branch tends to make it especially solicitous of the government's judgment that particular cases do or do not warrant review.

The data used to test Hypothesis *A* appear in Table 1. We have included in the group of cases "federal government favors review" not only those in which the United States and its agencies and officials were petitioners, but also others if they clearly indicated that review should be granted—e.g., official declarations that review would not be opposed, and cases in which the federal government intervened on the side of the appellant. Cases involving the District of Columbia and the territories were not included unless a federal judge was a party. Cases dismissed for technical reasons, such as the petitioner withdrawing the case or mootness, and cases for which data on the parties were inadequate have been excluded from the analysis altogether.

The data reveal that when the federal government favored review and no other cue was involved the writ was issued 47.1 per cent of the time. On the other hand, when all other parties sought review, and no other cue was involved, only 5.8 per cent of the petitions were granted. Since these differences are statistically significant at the .001 level of confidence, Hypothesis *A* is confirmed. We accept these data as satisfactory evidence that party is a cue.

HYPOTHESIS B: DISSENSION AS A CUE

Hypothesis *B* was formulated to determine whether dissension may be regarded as a cue. By dissension we mean disagreement among the judges in the court immediately below (one or more concurring opinions, dissenting votes, or dissenting opinions) or disagreement between two or more courts

TABLE 1
Party as a Cue

	Certiorari Granted		Certiorari Denied		Total	
	N	Percentage	N	Percentage	N	Percentage
Federal Government Favored *Certiorari*, Cue Involved	8	47.1	9	52.9	17	100.0
No Cues Involved	39	5.8	637	94.2	676	100.0
Total:	47	6.8	646	93.2	693	100.0

$$\phi = +0.25 \quad \chi^2 = 44.72 \quad P < 0.001$$

and agencies in a given case. We have employed the term dissension rather than conflict to avoid any possible confusion between the concept we are testing and conflict in circuits. We have not sought to test conflict in circuits, not because we do not regard it as an important cue, but because there was no systematic way to assemble the necessary data without going to the *certiorari* papers themselves. And this we were not in a position to do.

The justification for deciding to test dissension as a cue was suggested by Chief Justice Vinson when he said: "Our discretionary jurisdiction encompasses, for the most part, only the borderline cases—those in which there is a conflict among the lower courts or wide-spread uncertainty regarding problems of national importance." When lower court judges and quasi-judicial administrators disagree strongly enough officially to reveal their differences, petitions for *certiorari* concerned with these disagreements are, we think, bound to be studied closely by the members of the highest appellate tribunal in the land. This feeling was buttressed by an examination of the *certiorari* cases decided with full opinion during the 1947–1958 terms. At least 52 majority opinions during that period contained specific references to

dissension within the court immediately below.

Table 2 contains the data used to test Hypothesis *B*. All appellate docket applications for *certiorari* were included, except the handful decided on the technical grounds referred to just above.

The data disclose that 12.8 per cent of the petitions in which dissension, but no other cue, was present were granted. As earlier noted, *certiorari* was granted in only 5.8 per cent of the petitions without any cue at all. While the phi coefficient shows that the correlation between the presence of dissension and the grant of *certiorari* is rather weak, these differences are significant at the .001 level of confidence, and Hypothesis *B* is confirmed. We accept these data as satisfactory evidence that dissension is a cue.

HYPOTHESES C AND D: CIVIL LIBERTIES AND ECONOMIC ISSUES AS CUES

Hypotheses *C* and *D* were formulated to determine whether certain types of subject matter can be regarded as cues. They will be considered together.

The supposition that subject matter is a

TABLE 2
Dissension as a Cue

	Certiorari Granted		Certiorari Denied		Total	
	N	*Percentage*	*N*	*Percentage*	*N*	*Percentage*
Dissension Only Cue						
Present	37	12.8	253	87.2	290	100.0
No Cues Involved	39	5.8	637	94.2	676	100.0
Total:	76	7.9	890	92.1	966	100.0

$\phi = +0.12$ $\chi^2 = 13.69$ $P < 0.001$

major ingredient of what the Court refers to as "important" has been made so frequently that hypothesizing it as a cue needs no special justification. In fact, much data about subject matter appear in the literature. Petitions for *certiorari* granted and denied have been classified by subject matter by Frankfurter and his associates for the 1929–1938 terms, by Harper for the 1952 Term, and by the editors of the *Harvard Law Review* for all terms since 1955.

We settled upon two subject matter groups (with four subcategories each) as the most likely to attract the interest of the justices when scanning the mountainous piles of *certiorari* papers. In the civil liberties group we included petitions pertaining to (1) alien deportation, (2) racial discrimination, (3) military justice, and (4) miscellaneous civil liberties.[1] Our second group, economic issues, contain (5) labor, (6) regulation of economic life, (7) financial interest of the federal government, and (8) benefit and welfare legislation. Some of these categories are self-explanatory; others require a comment.

Miscellaneous civil liberties includes church-state relations, permits and licenses for the use of the streets and parks, postal and movie censorship, state and local censorship of reading matter, loyalty oaths, problems arising from the investigations of

legislative committees, disbarment proceedings, regulation of occupations and professions, picketing—free speech, and right to work litigation. The financial interest of the federal government includes excise, gift, income, and excess profit tax cases, and government contract disputes in time of peace and war. The benefit and welfare category refers to litigation concerned with civil service rights, wage statutes, the Federal Employers Liability Act, seamen and longshoremen welfare legislation, servicemen's benefits, workmen's compensation, social security legislation, tort claims, agricultural benefit regulations, and unemployment insurance. About 1 per cent of the applications for *certiorari* could not be classified with satisfactory precision because insufficient data were available. These cases have been omitted from the analysis.

Table 3 contains the data used to test the civil liberties issue hypothesis (Hypothesis *C*). These data show that about one petition in every three containing a civil liberties cue, but no other, was granted. The differences between the treatment of the petitions with civil liberties cues and petitions without any cues are significant at the 0.001 level of confidence. Hypothesis *C* is therefore confirmed, and we accept these data as satisfactory evidence that the presence of a civil liberties issue constitutes a cue.

TABLE 3
Civil Liberties Issue as a Cue

	Certiorari Granted		*Certiorari* Denied		Total	
	N	Percentage	N	Percentage	N	Percentage
Civil Liberties Issue						
Only Cue Present	57	32.9	116	67.1	173	100.0
No Cues Involved	39	5.8	637	94.2	676	100.0
Total:	96	11.3	753	88.7	849	100.0

$\phi = +0.35$ $\chi^2 = 101.46$ $P < 0.001$

TABLE 4
Economic Issue as a Cue

	Certiorari Granted		*Certiorari* Denied		Total	
	N	Percentage	N	Percentage	N	Percentage
Economic Issue						
Only Cue Present	59	8.5	637	91.5	696	100.0
No Cues Involved	39	5.8	637	94.2	676	100.0
Total:	98	7.1	1274	92.9	1372	100.0

$\phi = +0.05$ $\chi^2 = 4.11$ $0.05 < P < 0.001$

The data used to test Hypothesis *D* (economic issue as a cue) appear in Table 4. As the contents of this table make clear, the likelihood of review when only an economic issue is present is not much greater than when no cue at all is involved. The *Phi* coefficient shows the correlation between the presence of an economic issue and the grant of *certiorari* is only slightly positive. Nor can a *Chi* square of the magnitude attained be regarded as impressive for an *N* of nearly 1400 cases. Hypothesis *D* is not confirmed, and we cannot regard the presence of an economic issue as a cue.

Now that we have determined that party, dissension, and civil liberties issues are cues, we can return to the two propositions set forth.... We then pointed out that if the

cue theory were valid, it should follow that: (*Proposition I*) petitions which contain no cue will be denied, and (*Proposition II*) petitions which contain one or more cues will be studied carefully and 25 to 43 per cent of them granted. Data giving some indication of the extent to which these propositions are satisfied by the data in our sample...makes it quite evident that the requirements of *Proposition II* are satisfied. Of the petitions containing at least one cue, 27.5 per cent were granted. In addition, the petitions containing cues constituted 47.2 per cent of all appellate docket petitions. This falls within the estimate that 40 to 60 per cent of all appellate docket petitions contain some merit.

Proposition I is not fully supported, since

98 petitions containing no cues (7.1 per cent) were granted. But these 98 deviant cases do not in our judgment invalidate the cue theory, since all hypothesized cues have not been tested. Our judgment is reinforced by reading the opinions of the Court in those deviant cases decided with full opinion. In 19 instances the Court specifically pointed to a conflict in circuits, a cue we were unable to test. In one case, the Court pointed to dissents by intermediate appellate judges, and in another to the fact that the federal government did not oppose review. Still another case had civil liberties overtones which had been missed when the case was coded. More painstaking analysis would, we are convinced, still further reduce the number of deviant cases not readily accounted for by the cue theory.

We feel justified in concluding, therefore, that the cue theory of *certiorari* is valid.

[PREDICTIONS]

... [W]e had no theoretical or empirical bases for hypothesizing in advance of data processing about the interrelationships among the several cues and their usefulness as predictors of what the Court will do with sets of *certiorari* petitions containing given characteristics.

Insofar as the cue theory itself is concerned, the relative magnitude of the correlations between established cues and the grant or denial of *certiorari* (outcome) is of no particular consequence. All the cue theory requires is that the presence of a cue is enough to insure that a petition for *certiorari* will be studied with care. Hence, the presence of more than one cue, or for that matter the fact that one established cue may be more or less strongly correlated with outcome than another, will not alter the likelihood that a petition will be scrutinized.

However, these relationships do have enough intrinsic interest to warrant analysis.

In testing Hypotheses A, B, and C, ϕ coefficients were computed and included in the appropriate tables. The correlation between outcome and party was $+0.25$, outcome and dissension $+0.12$, and outcome and civil liberties $+0.35$. But these correlations are not very adequate measures of the relationship between the individual cues and the outcome because cases containing more than one cue were not taken into account. A more satisfactory method for determining the magnitude of the association between outcome and any given cue, when all other cues are held constant, is to compute the portion of the variance explained by each. The portion of the variance accounted for by a given cue is obtained by multiplying the coefficient of correlation between outcome and the cue by its standard partial regression (β) coefficient.

The β's were obtained by Doolittle's method and...[the findings] show, 7.4 per cent of the variance is explained by the party cue, 3.9 per cent by the civil liberties cue, and 2.4 per cent by the dissension cue. In our sample, therefore, party was relatively three times as important as dissension and almost twice as important as civil liberties in explaining outcome. Since the several contributions to the variance are additive, one may quickly determine the relative importance of the several cues in combination. For example, party alone was slightly more important than dissension and civil liberties combined, and all three cues taken together account for nearly twice as much of the variance (13.7 per cent) as party taken alone.

However, these data on the percentage of the variance explained by the three cues, independently and in combination, do not in themselves enable us to predict the likelihood of *certiorari* grants in sets of cases containing various assumed proportions of

TABLE 5
Predicted Percentages of *Certiorari* Petitions That Will Be Granted When All Cases in a Set Contain Indicated Cues

Cues			Predicted Percentage of Certioraris to Be Granted
Party	*Civil Liberties*	*Dissension*	
+	+	+	80
+	+	0	70
+	0	+	56
+	0	0	45
0	+	+	43
0	+	0	32
0	0	+	18
0	0	0	7

Legend

0 = Absence of a cue in all cases in set   + = Presence of a cue in all cases in set

cues. Such predictions are made possible by solving the regression equation $\chi_1 = B_2\chi_2 + B_3\chi_3 + B_4\chi_4 + A$, where outcome is the dependent variable (χ_1) and independent variables are party (χ_2), dissension (χ_3) and civil liberties issues (χ_4)....

Since our particular interest is to determine the predictive powers of the cues if every case in a set contains them in a given combination, we need to substitute 1.00 if we wish to include a cue and 0.00 if we wish to exclude it. For example, for a set in which every case contains all three cues, the following substitutions are made:

$$\chi_1 = (0.375)\ (1.00) + (0.18)\ (1.00) + (0.245)\ (1.00) + 0.076$$

Therefore, $\chi_1 = 0.804$, and 80 per cent of the petitions in the set will be granted. Similar substitutions provided the other results reported in Table 5.

We consider it important to reemphasize that the relationships discussed [here] ...unlike those [earlier]...were not hypothesized in advance of processing. As a result, we do not regard them as established, but only as useful bases for formulating hypotheses that need to be tested with fresh data....

NOTE

1. We decided at the outset not to include applications for review by criminal defendants in the civil liberties category even though the allegation of a deprivation of constitutional rights is usually involved. Our reason for the decision was our belief that such petitions tend to be so completely frivolous that the justices will ignore them unless some other cue is present.

Certiorari Decisions by the Warren & Burger Courts: Is Cue Theory Time Bound?

Virginia C. Armstrong
Charles A. Johnson

.   .   .

Tanenhaus and associates studied certiorari decisions of the Supreme Court from 1947 through 1958. The following analysis is based on decisions during four later terms—the 1967 and 1968 terms of the Warren Court and the 1976 and 1977 terms of the Burger Court. We selected these terms for several reasons. First, they were natural courts inasmuch as there were no changes in membership that might complicate the analysis. Second, since these courts are only a few years apart, they may be expected to have addressed similar issues, which would contribute to valid comparisons. Finally, use of these terms permits evaluation of the Tanenhaus cues in two ideologically different contexts—the liberal Warren Court and the conservative Burger Court.

.   .   .

The data base for our study includes all petitions granted and a sample of those denied. This sampling procedure has been used elsewhere and results in the maximum amount of information on the nature of the petitions granted certiorari. Our sample includes every fifth denial for the Warren Court (1967–1968) and every ninth denial for the Burger Court (1976–1977). This procedure has resulted in approximately equal-sized samples of denied petitions for these two courts. Since the combination of the universe of grants and a sample of denials would overrepresent the granted petitions, cases in the sample of denied petitions were weighted to construct the universe of petitions for all terms under study. The samples were weighted by multiplying the 1967–1968 sample of denials by five and the 1976–1977 sample by nine. Table 1 presents the frequencies of certiorari petitions granted during these terms, the size of the original sample and the reconstructed universe. The analysis below is based on the reconstructed universe.

Key variables analyzed in this study are the three cues found by Tanenhaus and associates to be significantly related to certiorari behavior—federal government as a petitioning agency, dissent below, and civil liberties issues. As far as possible, we have operationalized these cues as reported in Tanenhaus et. al.

.   .   .

Reprinted from Virginia C. Armstrong and Charles A. Johnson, "Certiorari Decisions By the Warren & Burger Courts: Is Cue Theory Time Bound?" *Polity* 15 (1982), pp. 143–150. Reprinted with permission of authors and publisher. Footnotes omitted.

TABLE 1
Appellate Docket for the 1967–1968 Warren Court and the 1976–1977 Burger Court

	Warren Court		Burger Court	
	Granted Petitions	*Denied Petitions*	*Granted Petitions*	*Denied Petitions*
Reconstructed universe	327	2695	318	4761
Original sample	327	539[a]	318	529[b]

[a] 20 percent sample of denials.
[b] 11 percent sample of denials.

TABLE 2
Certiorari with and without a Tanenhaus Cue
(Percent of Petitions which Were Granted and Denied)

Court and Action	*No Cue Present*	*Federal Government*	*Dissension Below*	*Civil Liberties*
Warren				
Certiorari granted	8	75	20	21
(N =)	(177)	(59)	(129)	(47)
Certiorari denied	92	25	80	79
(N =)	(2041)	(20)	(516)	(175)
Burger				
Certiorari granted	3	48	14	11
(N =)	(104)	(58)	(185)	(50)
Certiorari denied	97	52	86	89
(N =)	(3350)	(63)	(1137)	(403)

The results reported in Table 2 indicate that these cues remained important for the Warren Court in 1967–1968 and the Burger Court in 1976–1977. For certiorari petitions which contained none of the Tanenhaus cues, the acceptance rate was 8 percent and 3 percent in the Warren and Burger Courts, respectively. But if the petition contained at least one of the three cues, the probability increased from 8 percent to at least 20 percent for the Warren Court and from 3 percent to at least 11 percent for the Burger Court. As previous studies had found, petitions containing the federal government cue had the highest probability of acceptance.

Table 2 also reveals that the percentages of petitions granted with or without cues were generally lower for the Burger Court, although the differences were small. These differences may have resulted from the fact that almost twice as many petitions were filed with the Burger Court as with the Warren Court. While the number of requests increased, the number of those granted declined slightly. Assuming that the 300 or so petitions granted by both courts represented the upper limit of the court's case load, the percentage of petitions granted in any category had to be lower for the Burger Court because it received a larger number of requests.

Tanenhaus found that the presence of

TABLE 3
Percent of Certiorari Petitions with Increasing Numbers of Cues which were Granted and Denied by the Warren and Burger Courts

Court and Action	No Cue Present	One Cue Present	Two Cues Present	Three Cues Present
Warren				
Certiorari granted	8	14	49	100
(N =)	(177)	(93)	(67)	(3)
Certiorari denied	92	86	51	0
(N =)	(2041)	(572)	(69)	(0)
Burger				
Certiorari granted	3	10	27	100
(N =)	(104)	(136)	(69)	(7)
Certiorari denied	97	90	77	0
(N =)	(3350)	(1225)	(188)	(0)

more than one cue increased the probability of a petition's acceptance. The data reported in Table 3 reinforce this finding. In both courts, all of the handful of cases containing all three cues were granted certiorari. Again, while the percentages of successful petitions in the Burger Court are smaller, their absolute numbers indicate that the cues had just as great an impact on this Court as they had on the Warren Court.

CUES AND IDEOLOGICAL DIRECTION OF THE LOWER COURT DECISION

This analysis and that of Tanenhaus show that cue theory can have general application. But are there other factors which might also affect the Court's certiorari behavior? Recent research suggests that who won or lost in the lower court and the direction of the lower court decision may heavily influence the Supreme Court. For example, Baum argues that appellate courts (in his study, the California Supreme Court) are likely to grant an appeal from a lower court decision which is inconsistent with the views of the ideological majority on the superior court. This

strategy has been labeled the "error-correction strategy." Applying this idea to the Supreme Court, Songer suggests that the ideological direction of the lower court decision may be an error or policy "cue" and the Supreme Court may use the occasion to counter a decision of which it disapproves ideologically.

If the Supreme Court pursues the error-correction strategy, the cases accepted for review by different courts may share the same Tanenhaus cues, but have received very different treatments in the lower courts—especially their ideological direction or central issues. And these latter differences might affect the Supreme Court's reaction to the cases. . . .

. . . [T]he distribution of issues in the two sets of certiorari applications and the philosophical direction of the lower court decisions appealed to the two Supreme Courts did not differ substantially. But were their patterns of acceptance of these petitions different? Table 4 shows an interesting pattern in the percentage of liberal and conservative certiorari petitions with Tanenhaus cues granted by the two courts. The ideological direction of lower court decisions appeared to make little difference for the

TABLE 4
Percentages of Petitions with Tanenhaus Cues Granted Certiorari from Liberal and Conservative Lower Court Decisions in Civil Liberties and Economic Liberties[a]

Issue Area and Tanenhaus Cues	Warren Court		Burger Court	
	Liberal	Conservative	Liberal	Conservative
Civil liberties				
Federal government	100	0[b]	51	0[b]
Dissent below	27	22	36	5[c]
Civil liberties	17	22	27	5
Economic liberties				
Federal government	38	70	100	33
Dissent below	5	28	29	13
Civil liberties	0[b]	38	16	5

[a] Analysis includes certiorari petitions where direction of lower court decision was clear and Tanenhaus cues were present.
[b] No petitions filed for these categories.
[c] Differences in percentages significant at $p < .05$ level or less are boxed.

Warren Court in the civil liberties area. (It should be noted that in none of these cases did the federal government support the application.) In economic cases, the Warren Court granted certiorari more frequently to petitions which contained a Tanenhaus cue and involved a conservative lower court decision or "error."

These findings suggest that the Warren Court pursued the error-correction strategy with regard to economic issues but not when civil liberties were involved. As some scholars have suggested, civil liberties were of paramount concern to Chief Justice Warren, and he attempted to persuade the Court to handle civil liberties cases whenever possible.

For the Burger Court (which saw "error" in liberal lower court decisions), the pattern of approved certiorari petitions revealed in Table 5 is even more striking. In both civil liberties and economic cases, among the petitions containing a Tanenhaus cue, the Court consistently accepted more petitions involving liberal lower court decisions than those involving conservative lower court decisions. The one deviation from this pattern includes economic cases which contained civil liberties issues. While this comparison ran in the expected direction, the number of instances is small, and the percentage difference is only marginally significant ($p = .06$). The Burger Court would seem to have pursued the error-correction strategy in both areas.

CONCLUSION

...Analysis here suggests that the relationships discovered by Tanenhaus continue to exist in later terms of the Court. More importantly, the Tanenhaus cues were found to be influential in courts with differing ideological positions and different chief justices. From all appearances, the Tanenhaus cues are alive and well in the United States Supreme Court.

In addition, we have presented evidence to suggest that other factors may be interacting with the Tanenhaus cues to influence certiorari decision making. Specifically, it appears that the ideological direction of the lower court decisions influenced the courts in deciding whether to hear petitions which contained one or more Tanenhaus cues. The data indicated significantly greater probability that petitions would be granted if they contained a Tanenhaus cue and an "erroneous" lower court decision than if they contained a Tanenhaus cue but were ideologically "correct." The two courts' different reactions to "erroneous" and "correct" decisions occurred despite the fact that the two pools of certiorari petitions faced by them were similar in terms of issue distribution and the proportion containing "error."

.   .   .

Deciding What to Decide: How the Supreme Court Sets Its Agenda

D. Marie Provine

Since the passage of the 1925 Judiciary Act, the U.S. Supreme Court has enjoyed broad discretion to decide which cases it will resolve on their merits. As dockets have grown more crowded in recent decades, this discretion has become an increasingly significant feature of the Court's institutional power. Currently, for example, the justices refuse review to more than 90 per cent of the cases which come before them, which amounts to approximately 3,500 cases denied review per term. Clearly the criteria the justices use to set their agenda should be of considerable interest to students of the Supreme Court.

Research on the Court, however, remains fixed almost exclusively upon the cases to which the justices have granted review. One explanation for the paucity of research on case selection is lack of data. The Court issues no opinions and releases no votes in denying or granting review. Traditionally, the only exceptions to complete secrecy in case selection have been occasional published dissents from denials of review, sporadic

Reprinted from *Judicature* 64 (1981), pp. 320–321, 323–330, 332–333. Reprinted by permission of author. All footnotes and some tables omitted.

citations of reasons for granting review in opinions on the merits, general statements by justices and their law clerks on the case selection process, and the broadly-stated criteria of the Supreme Court Rules.

Scholars interested in analyzing case selection criteria with statistical tools had only the bare facts of grants and denials to work with until 1965, when the papers of Justice Harold H. Burton became available. Burton's papers, on file at the Library of Congress, include complete docket books recording the case selection votes of each justice for the 13 terms that Burton sat on the Court (1945–1957). . . .

The Burton data make it possible to analyze case selection and its relationship to the more familiar work of the Supreme Court on the merits. Such an analysis suggests that the justices' conceptions of the proper role of the Court have a major impact on their votes to select cases for review. Consensus about the Court's role appears to have channeled and limited the expression of individual policy preferences and political attitudes in review decisions during the Burton period. Even when the justices disagreed in assessing review-worthiness, role perceptions seemed to be significant to their decisions. . . .

THEORIES OF CASE SELECTION

.   .   .

Cue Theory

...In an often-cited article, Tanenhaus, Schick, Muraskin, and Rosen hypothesized that Supreme Court justices are concerned with reducing their workload.... The authors theorized that the justices cut down case-processing time by summarily eliminating much of the caseload from careful consideration. According to this hypothesis, they use a set of agreed-upon cues to differentiate cases that might be worthy of review from those they know they did not want to hear.

...Tanenhaus and his colleagues wrote before the release of the Burton papers, so they had only the pattern of grants and denials with which to work. Nevertheless, they established an ingenious test of their hypothesis that the Court uses cues to reduce its workload. Relying on the statements of Chief Justice Hughes and others that between 40 per cent and 60 per cent of the petitions filed were clearly without merit, the authors hypothesized that this percentage of the cases contained no cues and was not examined beyond the initial search for cues. The rest of the petitions, which did contain one or more cues, constituted the pool from which cases were selected....

The authors named three cues the Court used to select cases for careful scrutiny, and to eliminate summarily the remaining (cue-less) 40 to 60 per cent of the caseload:

· the presence of the United States as petitioner;
· the existence of a civil liberties issue;
· disagreement among the lower courts.

Testing Cue Theory

The accuracy of cue theory can be assessed by examining the fate of cue-containing cases during the Burton period, which matches almost exactly the 1947–1958 period Tanenhaus examined. Burton's papers permit a test of cue theory because his records reveal that a significant proportion of cases were eliminated with only cursory analysis, while the remainder were given more careful attention. The separation was accomplished by special listing, an administrative convenience devised by Chief Justice Hughes before Burton joined the Court.

The practice while Burton sat on the Court was for the chief justice and his staff to prepare a special list, or dead list, of cases deemed unworthy of conference time. The list circulated among the justices each week, and unless one of them put a special-listed case up for conference consideration, it was denied review automatically. Burton filed each week's special lists, and he kept a record of any changes justices requested. These records show that such alterations were rare.

Table 1 indicates the percentage of cue-containing cases that were put on the special list, and the number of votes attracted by those cases with and without cues that survived special listing. As this table shows, cases with cues were significantly more likely to get case selection votes than others on the Appellate Docket. Clearly the cues, especially the U.S. as petitioner, are related to the concerns the justices have in selecting cases for review on the merits. This is not surprising, since Tanenhaus settled upon the cues by examining the statements of Supreme Court justices and others about the types of cases of particular interest to the Court.

Were the authors simply suggesting that some types of cases have a better chance of getting votes for review than others, the Burton data would tend to substantiate the hypothesis. Cue theory, however, purports to

TABLE 1
Disposition of Cases Containing Tanenhaus Cues, 1947–57

Disposition of petitions	Tanenhaus Cues			All other appellate cases
	U.S. petn'r.	Dissen. below	Civ. libs. issue	
Special listed	1%	27%	16%	45%
In conference:				
Denied unan.	8%	23%	22%	21%
Denied nonu.	25%	25%	26%	18%
Gr'ntd nonu.	41%	16%	21%	12%
Gr'ntd unan.	25%	9%	15%	5%
Total cases:	554	131[*]	629	6323

[*] Includes data only for 1947 Term.

explain how the justices reduce the mass of petitions they receive to a more manageable number without actually considering the argument each petitioner makes for review on the merits. . . .

If the cues actually served this short-circuiting purpose, cases containing cues should not appear on the special lists. Yet as Table 1 shows, in all three categories, some cue-containing cases are special listed.

Not a Mechanical Process

This pattern of voting suggests that the case characteristics that Tanenhaus deemed cues may be significant to the justices in case selection decisions, but that the decision-making process is not as mechanical as the authors suggest. Of course, something differentiates special-listed cases from those discussed in conference. The memos Burton's clerks wrote for him on each case and the case selection voting patterns suggest that cases with jurisdictional defects, inadequate records, and no clearly presented issues were the most likely to be special listed.

No easily identifiable case characteristics are invariably associated with special listing, however. This suggests that neither the justices nor the clerks rely on a fixed set of cues to separate cases into those worthy of scrutiny and those to be discarded summarily. With the assistance law clerks provide in digesting cases and writing memos, there is little reason to expect Supreme Court justices need such an abbreviated preliminary screening procedure.

It is more likely that the justices reduce the time they spend in evaluating petitions by relying on the clerks' memos. The justices may then reach a decision by engaging in a weighing process in which a few characteristics of cases—including probably the Tanenhaus cues—encourage at least some of the justices to vote for review, while many other characteristics act like demerits, preventing review in the absence of strong reasons in favor. The special-listed cases are those which contain one or more demerits and no countervailing considerations in favor of review.

The pattern of voting in U.S.-brought cases supports this interpretation. Because of the Solicitor General's careful screening, these cases seldom contain characteristics strongly discouraging review, so the Court seldom puts them on the special lists. In fact, as Table 1 indicates, U.S. cases are sufficiently impressive that in the Burton period they usually received at least one justice's vote for review. The evidence does not suggest, however, that the justices initially separate U.S. cases from the rest in an attempt to save reading time.

The Attitudinal Hypothesis

Another approach for understanding how the Court selects cases for plenary review emphasizes judicial predispositions towards litigants and policies. Sidney Ulmer has actively promoted this perspective, using the Burton papers to test his attitudinal conception of the case selection process.

. . . Ulmer was able to show, for example, that for eight of the 11 justices whose votes he examined, a justice's vote to review helped to predict his vote on the merits. Votes to review were associated with votes to reverse on the merits, a pattern which Ulmer explained in terms of judicial attitudes. . . .

Recently Ulmer has gone further, arguing that the justices sometimes try to disguise the extent to which they are influenced by their attitudes towards litigants in case selection. According to this hypothesis, when a justice suspects he cannot win review on the merits, he suppresses his ever present desire to vote for the underdog or the upperdog. In so doing, the justices defer to, but do not assimilate, the norm of impartiality in judicial decisionmaking.

Ulmer's emphasis on judicial attitudes in his analysis of case selection raises a question familiar to students of judicial behavior: are broad, pre-existing attitudes toward litigants and the policy issues in which they are entangled the sole or primary determinant of the votes of judges? Or do judges internalize norms that significantly limit the expression of personal preferences in their decisions? This much-debated question is, of course,

central to traditional justifications for judicial power in a democracy. It is especially relevant in the context of case selection where, because of the secrecy of the process, external restraints on judicial judgment are absent. . . .

The procedure the Court uses to select cases for plenary review . . . ensures that each justice will be well-acquainted with the arguments for relief from the lower court judgment when he decides whether to vote for review. The parties incorporate their views of the proper resolution of the case into their briefs for and against review.

The Burton papers suggest that law clerks respond to these arguments and may even feel competent to pass on the merits at this stage in the proceedings: Burton's clerks typically suggested what they believed to be the correct outcome of the underlying dispute in their memos to the justice. The case selection process thus provides the justices with an easy opportunity to vote for review on the basis of their agreement or disagreement with the lower court result.

Ulmer's finding that votes to review and votes to reverse were correlated suggests that the justices *do* let their assessment of the merits of cases influence their review decisions. This finding does not necessarily mean, however, that the justices simply vote according to their attitudes towards certain types of litigants or policies at each stage of decision. The justices could just as well be responding to litigants in case selection, and later in votes on the merits, in light of general principles that determine the availability of judicial relief.

Ulmer's finding thus suggests two questions for further analysis: whether case selection and voting on the merits are, as a practical matter, indistinguishable; and, to the extent that they are, whether motivation can be persuasively explained in attitudinal terms.

AN OVERVIEW OF VOTING PATTERNS

If case selection is functionally equivalent to decisionmaking on the merits, most case selection decisions should be non-unanimous, as most decisions on the merits are. Also, individual decisions to grant review should correlate highly with votes to reverse the lower court on the merits, and votes to reverse should be rare when a justice did not vote for review. Finally, the frequency with which a justice votes for review should be directly related to the level of his overall dissatisfaction with lower court results.

If attitudes towards litigants explain why individual case selection votes correspond with votes in fully considered cases, then the justices generally presumed to be the most politically liberal and the most conservative should seldom vote to review the same case. On the Court as a whole, disagreement among the justices should be parallel at both stages of decision, and this pattern should be consistent with the liberal-conservative spectrum we see in on-the-merits voting.

With the Burton records, we can determine whether or not these patterns existed during a significant portion of the modern Court's history. Analysis of case selection votes can thus contribute to our understanding of the relative significance of role constraints and attitudes in judicial decisionmaking.

Contrary to what one would expect if judicial views of the merits alone determined review decisions, the prevailing pattern in case selection is unanimity. During the Burton period, 82 per cent of case selection decisions were unanimous: 79 per cent were unanimous denials of review, and three per cent were unanimous grants. Available evidence indicates that the level of unanimity in case selection has remained high since the Burton era. This numerical evidence alone suggests that case selection decisions are not functionally equivalent to decisions on the merits, and that some norm or norms guide the justices in deciding whether to vote for review.

Analysis of the types of cases decided unanimously during the Burton period suggests that the justices shared a conception of the work appropriate to the Court that overshadowed policy preferences and sympathies for certain litigants. Evidence of this is that the types of cases usually presumed to tap judicial attitudes most directly were the very types most often denied review unanimously: the petitions of prisoners and suits by business interests seeking relief from government regulation.

This pattern of unanimity in presumably ideologically-charged cases cannot be attributed to an unusual period of ideological uniformity on the Supreme Court. The Court's membership in this period included civil libertarians like Black and Douglas as well as nonlibertarians like Reed and Vinson. Yet all of them were in agreement that most of these cases should not be reviewed. In other words, all of the justices seem to have been convinced that certain types of cases were not important enough to review, even if they touched the private sympathies of individual justices.

A review of memos written by Justice Burton's law clerks suggests that this consensus has both procedural and subject matter aspects. As noted earlier, cases with defective records from below or other weaknesses unrelated to the substance of their claims tended to be denied review unanimously, usually by special listing. Likewise, certain subject matters almost never got votes for review. Contract disputes, common law issues, and real property litigation were prime candidates for unanimous exclusion. Sixty per cent of these cases were special listed.

The types of cases in which the justices

were most often unanimous in favor of review also suggests the importance of shared views about the proper business of the Court. During the Burton period, as Table 2 indicates, the justices tended to be unanimous in four types of cases which are related to basic areas of responsibility for the court of last resort in a federal system.

- · U.S. petitions and labor claims which are similar in frequently raising issues concerning the proper scope of federal law-making authority.
- · Civil rights and liberties petitions which usually claimed federal constitutional rights against asserted state and local authority.
- · Federalism cases, which require the Court to adjust competing jurisdictional claims among governmental and quasi-governmental authorities and which are clearly a central function for the court of last resort in a federal system.

When the justices of the Burton era disagreed in case selection, they differed considerably in the extent to which their votes to

TABLE 2
Unanimity in Favor of Review by Case Type, 1947–57

Case Type	N	% Granted Review Unanimously
U.S. petitioner	554	25%
Civil rights/ liberties claims	630	14%
Labor claims	593	15%
Federalism issues	578	11%
All criminal petitioners	8572	0%
All other cases not noted above	4311	2%

review paralleled their final votes on the merits, and they differed dramatically in the frequency with which they voted to review. These two measures of differences among the justices appear to be independent of each other.

The association between voting to review and to reverse already noted by Ulmer is evident in Table 3, which ranks the justices according to their tendency to vote for review and then vote to reverse on the merits. As the table shows, although the justices differed in the extent to which considerations favoring review and reversal paralleled each other, all of the justices were more likely to vote to reverse a case they voted to review than one they did not vote to review.

Were the justices considering simply the desired outcome of the dispute in case selection, however, the differences between the two columns in Table 3 would be much closer to 100 per cent. Nor can the failure of these differences to approximate 100 per cent plausibly be attributed to the effect of mistaken assessments of the merits at the case selection stage. The inadequacy of transposing the plenary decision to the case selection stage is particularly evident for the justices at the bottom of the table, for whom the relationship between case selection votes and votes for reversal is weakest.

It seems more likely that judicial beliefs concerning the proper work of the Supreme Court explain the imperfect correlations between votes to review and votes to reverse. A justice's failure to vote for reversal in every case he voted to review can be attributed to his belief that the subject was too important to pass over for reasons unrelated to the correctness of the outcome below. Likewise, a justice's vote to reverse a case he voted against reviewing can be attributed to the view that the case was wrongly decided below, but not important enough to review.

Considered in this light, departures from

TABLE 3
The Relationship Between Votes to Review and Votes to Reverse, 1947–57
(Nonunanimous cases)

Justice	Percent of Votes to Reverse in Cases He Voted to Review*	Percent of Votes to Reverse in Cases He Voted Against**	Difference between the Two Columns
Whittaker	93	43	50
Rutledge	85	37	48
Black	80	36	44
Minton	64	25	39
Warren	76	42	34
Vinson	61	31	29
Douglas	75	46	29
Jackson	62	34	28
Frankfurter	67	39	27
Brennan	79	52	27
Reed	58	31	27
Clark	62	35	27
Harlan	62	41	21
Murphy	74	57	17
Burton	56	39	17

* N=100 or more for all except Whittaker (27 votes to reverse in 29 cases favoring review).
** N=100 or more for all except Murphy, Rutledge, Brennan, and Whittaker where instances range from 20 to 50.

merits-consciousness in nonunanimous votes are consistent with the preponderance of unanimity in case selection: both depend on judicial conceptions of the proper role of the Court which limit the expression of individual sympathies and preferences in case selection votes.

The significance of role perceptions in case selection decisions is also evident when the Burton period justices are compared according to the frequency with which they voted for review.... [T]he justices differed greatly in the frequency with which they voted for review....

Certain justices during the Burton period consistently voted more often for review than their colleagues. The justices often divided into two groups on this issue, with 20 percentage points or more separating them....

This pattern raises the question of whether the review-prone justices voted most often for review because they were more dissatisfied with lower court outcomes than the rest of the Court. Such an explanation must assume that, for the more review-prone justices at least, votes to review are motivated primarily by disagreement with lower court outcomes.

Yet the ranking of the justices in Table 3, which estimates the relative tendency to vote to review in order to reverse, does not correlate with the ranking of the justices in their tendency to vote for review. The two justices who voted most often for review, for example, were not especially likely to equate case selection and plenary decisionmaking, while the two least review-prone justices were among the most likely to vote the merits in case selection.

In short, the tendency to vote often for review appears to be independent of the tendency to make disagreement with the lower court outcome the primary criterion of review-worthiness. Thus, while disagreement with lower court outcomes almost certainly influences the justices to vote for review, this variable cannot by itself account for differences in the tendency to vote for review.

It seems likely that differences in the frequency with which individual justices voted for review are related to differences in the disposition of the justices to exercise Supreme Court power. Clearly the structure of case selection requires the justices to consider the proper scope of Supreme Court activity in voting for or against review. The identity of the most review-prone and the most review-conservative justices during the Burton period also suggests the relevance of such a concern. . . .

CONCLUSION

This analysis suggests that Supreme Court justices during the Burton period shared a powerful conception of the role of their institution, which appears to have sharply limited the level of disagreement that could otherwise have been anticipated in case selection voting. Consensus on the norms of judicial behavior also appears to have discouraged these justices either from combining forces to achieve the results they preferred on the merits or from voting individually in a way that would indicate routine calculation of probable outcomes in the case selection process.

.   .   .

The evidence here . . . suggests that role conceptions can also be a source of disagreement in case selection. The considerable differences among the Burton period justices in their willingness to vote for review appear to be at least partly attributable to variation in conceptions of the Court's role.

The self-imposed limits of role conceptions, it is important to note, are essentially the only limits upon judicial discretion in case selection. Because of the secrecy of the process, case selection exceeds even plenary decisionmaking in the scope it provides for the exercise of unfettered judicial judgment. The Taft period justices campaigned hard for this broad authority, and until recently, Supreme Court justices were unanimous in their efforts to maximize their agenda-setting power.

Disagreement among the current justices has finally made Court-controlled case selection a public issue, however. The question for policymakers is whether the Court should be permitted to maintain complete control in setting its agenda, limited only by the conceptions the justices hold of the proper way to perform this function.

For students of judicial decisionmaking, the significance of role conceptions in case selection has additional implications. The explanatory power of the concept in this context suggests that role perceptions deserve more attention in analyses of Supreme Court decisionmaking on the merits. Differences in role conceptions have, of course, been the focus of some research, but the phenomenon of consensus among justices has received too little attention.

Preoccupation with voting differences among the justices gives a misleading impression of judicial motivation. Differences in judicial attitudes and role conceptions tend to receive lopsided attention, while the influence of shared norms derived from legal and professional socialization tends to be ignored. This makes it difficult to determine the extent to which judicial decisionmaking parallels political decisionmaking in other contexts. A more accurate picture will emerge only when political scientists acknowledge that the work of Supreme Court justices includes more than nonunanimous decisions on the merits.

The Supreme Court's Certiorari Decisions: Conflict as a Predictive Variable

S. Sidney Ulmer

...In theory, federal laws and the federal constitution are national in scope, granting and restricting rights and duties and allocating values equitably in all sections of the country. But a lower court decision in conflict with a Supreme Court precedent is good law until overruled, and intercircuit conflict among federal Courts of Appeals involves decisions that are binding in the circuits of origin until the Supreme Court speaks. Thus, uniformity of federal law is far from a certainty.

... [T]he uniformity of court rulings on federal questions is important to the functioning of our legal and political systems. The structure of our court system, however, assures that that the uniformity principle will be frequently violated. The Supreme Court can correct such violations via the use of its discretionary jurisdiction to review lower court decisions. Indeed the Court is expected to do so, and it does so on a number of occasions each term. Similarly, in each term

the Court allows a sizable number of conflicting lower court rulings to stand by declining to review them, which has led to various suggestions designed to alleviate the problem. Intelligent discussion in this whole area, however, tends to be hindered by lack of knowledge. We do not know, for example, how frequently the Supreme Court grants and denies plenary review of conflict cases, nor do we know how much weight the Court attaches to conflict as a reason for granting discretionary review, or whether such weights have varied across Courts.

Although one would be bold indeed to suggest that the precise amount of importance the Court attaches to conflict is discoverable, I believe it possible to go beyond the heavily caveated generalizations in the legal literature. The need to do so defines my research problem. I wish to know not just how many conflict cases are granted or denied certiorari, but whether such decisions are associated with the presence and absence of the conflict condition. Furthermore, I wish to know whether the associations discovered hold over time and whether they hold when isolated from other explanatory factors.

Reprinted from *American Political Science Review* 78 (1984), pp. 902–904, 906–911. Reprinted with permission of author and publisher. Footnotes, most references, and some tables omitted.

ORIENTING QUESTIONS

I examine the problem via three orienting questions:

Is the Supreme Court significantly more likely to grant plenary review of cases involving conflict with Supreme Court precedent than cases in which such conflict is absent?

Is the Supreme Court significantly more likely to grant plenary review of Courts of Appeals cases, the rulings in which are in conflict with other circuit court decisions, than Courts of Appeals cases in which conflict is absent?

Have the Vinson, Warren, and Burger Courts differed in the way they have handled cases involving conflict with Supreme Court precedents or conflicts in the circuits?

DATA SELECTION AND OPERATIONALIZATION PROCEDURES

The data encompass the 1947–1976 terms of the Court, that is, the last five terms of the Vinson Court, the 16 terms of the Warren Court, and the first eight terms of the Burger Court. In this 30-year period, a 10 to 20% random sample of the Court's paid docket was drawn. Owing to the relatively few instances in which the Court grants plenary review, however, random sampling of granted cases was repeated until 88 to 100% of such cases had been selected and coded.

Within these samples, all cases granted and denied certiorari were isolated and weighted to reflect the ratio of total certiorari grants and denials for each of our three Courts. The procedure was straightforward for the 1947–1969 terms because the number of grants and denials is available from published sources. Since the 1969 term, however, the Supreme Court has not compiled a breakdown of certiorari cases; that is, certiorari cases have not been separated in the statistics compiled by the Supreme Court Clerk from the cases brought on appeal. Consequently, the ratio used for the Burger Court was derived from a count of the certiorari cases in 1969, 1973, and 1976 terms. The ratio for these three terms was then used in analyzing the eight Burger terms. The weights actually utilized were: Vinson Court—3.76; Warren Court—6.26; and Burger Court—10.55. All analyses and tables use the weighted samples. The weighting procedures allowed me to control for variation in the raw sample categories.

The general hypothesis to be explored is that the decision to grant or deny certiorari—a purely discretionary act—is associated with the presence or absence of a civil liberty claim, an economic issue, the federal government as petitioning party, and conflict (intercircuit or with Supreme Court precedent). This model is dictated by the literature. Tanenhaus found that federal government as a petitioning party or the presence of a civil liberty claim increased the probability of certiorari being granted during the Court's 1947–1958 terms. Although generally rejecting cue theory, Teger and Kosinski (1980) replicated Tanenhaus's results for the 1975 term. They also resurrected and showed the significance of a cue rejected by Tanenhaus, the presence or absence of an economic issue. The economic issue, conceptualized as a policy cue, was also shown by Songer (1979) to be of some consequence for the Courts sitting in the 1935, 1941, 1967, and 1972 terms. In addition, in a recent article (Ulmer, 1983), conflict with Supreme Court precedent was shown to be significantly associated with the Court's review decisions. Thus, my hypothesis encompasses earlier findings. My primary interest, however, is in determining whether conflict has any explanatory power apart from that provided by the other factors mentioned above.

.   .   .

ANALYSIS OF PETITIONING PARTY CLAIMS

My first step was to identify all cases in which attorneys petitioning for certiorari claimed that the decision being questioned established a conflict with a Supreme Court precedent or an intercircuit conflict. On doing this, I discovered that petitioning attorneys are not reluctant to claim conflict. Indeed, in many instances, they claimed that the questioned decision below conflicted with six or more different precedents....

... [A] petitioning attorney was most likely to claim conflict with one or more Supreme Court precedents when petitioning the Warren Court and least likely to make such a claim when petitioning the Vinson Court. However, in all three Courts, conflict was claimed more than half the time.... In all three Courts, more than 10% of the certiorari applications claimed six or more conflicts. Although the percentage of claims in the Warren Court tracked the percentage of claims in the other two courts, the attorneys petitioning the Warren Court were much more likely to claim six or more conflicts than attorneys in the other two Courts.

... [P]etitioning attorneys also varied their claims of intercircuit conflict, being more likely to make the claim to the Warren Court and least likely to the Vinson Court. One may infer...that petitioning attorneys perceived the Warren Court as more sensitive to conflict than the Vinson and Burger Courts.... [C]laims of six or more conflicts were somewhat less when the claimed conflict was intercircuit than when Supreme Court precedents were involved, and although intercircuit conflict was claimed more than half the time in the Warren and Burger Courts, it was claimed less than half the time in the Vinson era.

To claim a conflict is not necessarily to establish that a conflict exists.... [A]ttorneys have good reasons to believe that the presence of conflict enhances the probability of discretionary review. Thus, it would not be surprising if petitioning attorneys padded or puffed their claims. At the least, they might be expected to follow the rule for claiming tax deductions—if in doubt, claim it! The ...[findings] suggest quite a bit of puffing of claims. To discount that possibility, I isolated all lower court decisions alleged to establish conflict, reading each in conjunction with the cases alleged to cause the conflicts. In each instance up to three cases were examined. The purpose of this procedure was to separate cases of genuine conflict from those in which conflict was a mere allegation of petitioning attorneys.

COMPARING CLAIMED CONFLICT WITH GENUINE CONFLICT

A comparison of genuine and alleged conflict...shows that the padding ratio ranges from 4 to 1 to 7 to 1 and that the puffing has been more prevalent in connection with Supreme Court precedents than with intercircuit conflict....

Feeney reports an average of 119 conflict cases in the 1971 and 1972 terms of the Supreme Court. I show an average of 113. Chief Justice Burger has suggested that 35 to 50 intercircuit conflict cases appear currently on the Court's argument docket each term. My sample shows an average across eight Burger Court terms of 32.7. My figures are obviously in the right ball park, and when one notes that Burger's estimate includes appellate cases whereas my count is limited to the certiorari docket, there is added reason to have some confidence in my calculations.

.   .   .

TABLE 1
Supreme Court Cases with and without Genuine Conflict and Court Decisions to Grant or Deny Certiorari

	Vinson Court		Warren Court		Burger Court	
	Conflict	No conflict	Conflict	No conflict	Conflict	No conflict
Certiorari						
granted	188	357	781	905	368	549
denied	53	2781	645	10,014	1013	10,348
Pearson *r*	.467		.433		.745	
Gamma	.930		.861		.745	

p < .001

TABLE 2
Cases Involving Intercircuit Conflict and Court Decisions to Grant or Deny Certiorari

	Vinson Court		Warren Court		Burger Court	
	Conflict	No conflict	Conflict	No conflict	Conflict	No conflict
Certiorari						
granted	130	273	521	741	262	500
denied	101	2033	469	7192	981	7057
Pearson *r*	.349		.390		.179	
Gamma	.810		.830		.580	

p < .001

ANALYSIS OF GENUINE CONFLICT

In Tables 1 and 2 the cases in which genuine conflict was present or absent have been cross-tabulated with the Court's certiorari decisions for each Court and for each type of conflict. In each of the six comparisons, the certiorari decisions are significantly correlated with conflict, but because significance levels are affected by marginals and large Ns, the Gs (Gammas) are more meaningful statistics. *G* is a proportional reduction in error (PRE) statistic which has a meaning beyond its own class (Kirkpatrick, 1974). It is an ordinal measure of association which tells us how well we can predict the rank order of measures on one variable from the rank order of another. A *G* of 1 indicates that prediction is perfect. A *G* of 0 means that predictive accuracy is only what one would expect from chance. In Table 1, for example, the *G* for the Vinson Court is .930, which means that if we expect one half of our predictions to be correct, the difference between the actually correct and expected correct predictions represents an improvement of 93%. This would be viewed as a high degree of association between conflict and decision.

In Table 1, there is a significant association between Court decision and conflict for all three courts, running from highest for the Vinson Court to lowest for the Burger Court. The three Courts denied from 88 to 93% of the applications when conflict was absent, but from 22 to 73% when conflict was present. The strength of the relationships is quite high in all three cases ranging from a G of .745 for the Burger Court to a G of .930 for the Vinson Court. We must conclude tentatively that the presence of a conflict with a Supreme Court precedent significantly enhances the probability that the Court will grant certiorari, but the measure of that enhancement is a declining variable. Whereas in the Vinson Court the presence of conflict made chance of review four times the probability of review without conflict, the ratio dropped to 2 to 1 in the Warren era and 1.3 to 1 in the Burger Court.

Table 1 arrays data for conflict with Supreme Court precedent, whereas Table 2 provides comparable data for courts of appeals cases and intercircuit conflict. Here, as in Table 1, there is a significant correlation between conflict and Court decision on certiorari applications. At the same time, several differences between the tables are apparent. First, the correlations are at a lower level across all three Courts. The same is true of measures on the strength of relationships. Nevertheless, prediction of certiorari decisions from information on the presence or absence of intercircuit conflict is dramatically more accurate than chance alone would lead one to expect, the Gammas indicating from 58 to 83% improvement in predictive accuracy. Unlike conflict with Supreme Court precedent, however, that which is intercircuit in nature appears to have been more important for the Warren Court than for the Vinson Court, with the Burger Court bringing up the rear as in Table 1.

Having established that conflict with Supreme Court precedent and intercircuit conflict are both indicators to the Supreme Court's decision on certiorari, one may wonder whether the correlations are spurious. Earlier research has shown that under certain conditions, the presence or absence of civil liberty or economic issues promotes the granting or denial of certiorari, as does federal government or another high status litigant as petitioning party (Ulmer, 1981). However, because conflict has not been isolated, measured, and systematically studied previously, I do not known whether it contributes to the explanatory power previously associated with alternate indicators or whether it contributes to explanation when those earlier variables are statistically controlled.

To answer these questions, I have conducted a series of discriminant function analyses with certiorari decision as the criterion and the other variables as predictors. The two-group discriminant function has been employed. The equation for the function may be stated as follows:

$$Z_i = c_1 X_{i1} + c_2 X_{i2} + \ldots c_n X_{in},$$

where Z_i is the discriminant function, X represents the predictor variable, and c the weight assigned by the discriminant analysis. The analysis assigns weights that will maximize the ratio of the variance resulting from group differences to variation resulting from differences within the group. An easily understood geometric representation of the method may be found in Ulmer (1974).

Basically, the method enables one to distinguish between two groups of cases on the same dimension. Here the two groups are those cases in which the Supreme Court granted certiorari and those cases in which it denied certiorari. The goal is to determine the extent to which a collection of discriminating variables will cluster cases granting

TABLE 3
Discriminant Analysis of Certiorari Decisions with Four Predictors, All Cases and Courts of Appeals Cases (Percentage of Variance Explained by Variable Alone)

	Vinson Court	*Warren Court*	*Burger Court*
All cases			
Federal government	5.4	4.1	19.1
Economic issue	.3	.5	.2
Civil liberty issue	.1	.1	—
Conflict with Supreme Court precedent	33.9	32.8	20.7
Courts of Appeals cases only			
Federal government	5.4	5.1	22.9
Economic issue	.4	.6	.2
Civil liberty issue	—	—	.1
Intercircuit conflict	20.7	27.0	9.5

certiorari at one end of the continuum and cases denying certiorari at the other. For example, if the grant cases were represented as $G1$ and the deny cases as $G2$, the ability of the weighted discriminating variables to assign cases correctly to the appropriate group would be equivalent to accounting for the variance in the dichotomy: $G1-G2$. If 100% of the variance were explained by the discriminating variables, then the sum of the weighted scores associated with the discriminating variables would be greater for any $G1$ case than for any $G2$ case, or vice versa, depending on scoring procedures for the discriminating variables. In the present instance, the aim is to ascertain the degree to which variation in the grant-deny patterns can be accounted for by four discriminating variables taken collectively, individually, and in various combinations.

A similarity between discriminant and regression analysis will be noted. However, where the dependent variable is dichotomous (or non-continuous), discriminant function analysis has been preferred (Kort, 1973). Because my criterion is the granting and denial of certiorari, discriminant function analysis is appropriate.

The most striking aspect of Table 3 is the data for the Burger Court. The levels of explained variance for each of the predictors taken singly are almost identical for the Vinson and Warren Courts. For these two Courts, conflict explains four to eight times as much of the variance in certiorari decision as federal government as petitioning party. For both, civil liberty and economic issues make trivial contributions. For both Courts, conflict with Supreme Court precedent is a better predictor than intercircuit conflict, although the disparity is less in the Warren Court.

The Burger Court, however, is a different story. Taken alone, the federal government as the petitioning party is about as effective a predictor as conflict with Supreme Court precedent, and in courts of appeals cases, it is twice as effective as intercircuit conflict. Thus, there is a distinct break in the patterns established by the Vinson and Warren Courts. The Burger Court also gives trivial weight to economic and civil liberty issues, indeed, even less weight than that assigned by the Vinson and Warren Court justices. Overall, it appears that conflict as a predictor of certiorari decision has been steadily declining in importance as one moves from the Vinson to the Burger Court.

TABLE 4
Discriminant Analysis of Certiorari Decisions with Four Predictors, All Cases and Courts of Appeals Cases Only

	Vinson Court		Warren Court		Burger Court	
	D.F. Coefficient	Sum of Explained Variance %	D.F. Coefficient	Sum of Explained Variance %	D.F. Coefficient	Sum of Explained Variance %
All cases						
Federal government	1.564		1.922		5.266	
Civil liberty issue	—	5.7	.051	4.7	.093	19.2
Economic issue	−.297		−.433		−.133	
Conflict with Supreme Court	4.166	36.9	3.308	34.8	2.404	33.8
Cases correctly classified (%)	86.6		87.1		87	
Courts of Appeals cases only						
Federal government	2.047		2.221		6.322	
Civil liberty issue	−.044	5.6	.1013	5.6	−.130	23.2
Economic issue	−.251		−.538		−.457	
Intercircuit conflict	3.338	23.8	3.217	29.3	1.531	29.3
Cases correctly classified (%)	84.6		86.2		83.3	

In Table 4, I array the results of applying discriminant function analyses to all variables collectively. The results confirm the suggestion that the Burger Court is either marching to a different drummer or that the band is playing a march unknown to the earlier Courts. The variance explained by the nonconflict variables in the Vinson and Warren Courts totaled from 4.7 to 5.7%. For the Burger Court, the range was from 19.2 to 23.2%, essentially all of which may be attributed to the federal government as petitioning party. When conflict with Supreme Court precedent is added, explained variance jumps approximately 30 percentage points in the Warren and Vinson Courts but only 14 percentage points in the Burger Court. For intercircuit conflict, explained variance increases from 18 to 23 percentage points for the first two Courts but only 6 percentage points in the Burger Court.

Conflict is clearly the most important predictor of Vinson and Warren Court decisions on certiorari. An examination of the discriminant function coefficients shows that conflict with Supreme Court precedent is 2 to 3 times as important as federal government as petitioning party. In the Burger Court, it is less than half as important. For the Burger Court, intercircuit conflict is only one-fourth as significant in explaining variance in decision as federal government as petitioning party. In the other two Courts, on the other hand, it is again 2 to 3 times as important. Thus, the Burger Court is something of an anomaly when compared to the earlier Courts.

.   .   .

CONCLUSIONS

To return to my three orienting questions, there is little doubt that the Supreme Court in its 1947–1976 terms has been significantly influenced in making certiorari decisions by factors of conflict. Moreover, when other factors are controlled or incorporated into the analysis, conflict is far and away the most significant predictor of certiorari decisions for two of our three Courts. For the Burger Court, conflict has been a significant indicator to certiorari decision, but a more important predictor is federal government as petitioning party....

Beginning with the work of Tanenhaus, those who construct models of certiorari decision making (including this author) have utilized such predictors as issue, petitioning party, socioeconomic status of petitioning and opposing parties, the ideological direction of the decision in the lower court, and the liberal or conservative makeup of the Court itself. None has included conflict as a variable in his or her models. The present study has shown, however, that conflict is highly germane to such models. It may now be suggested that in making up its plenary case agenda, the Court is significantly responsive to the legal-systemic variable—conflict—and less governed by case issue variables than one might have thought. From a theoretical standpoint, this may suggest a shift of focus to systemic factors if the predictive power of my theories or semi-theories is to be enhanced.

My results do not imply that idiosyncratic factors should now be ignored. Indeed, one might speculate that the disparities in my findings for the Warren, Vinson, and Burger Courts are the result of the varying importance different justices attach to conflict as a system problem or the extent to which they differentiate requests by the federal government for plenary review. Where conflict with Supreme Court precedent is concerned, however, I have shown that the predictive power of such conflict has steadily declined from the Vinson to the Warren to the Burger

Court, which suggests the possibility that other systemic variables are at work. The most likely culprit here is increasing caseload, but whatever the case, there is nothing here that argues for the exclusion of systemic or more traditional legal variables in an effort to improve our understanding of the Supreme Court's agenda-building processes.

A secondary finding is that the Supreme Court is not greatly influenced in granting and denying certiorari by the mere claims of conflicts by petitioning attorneys. Given that genuine conflict does exert such influence, I infer that the Court recognizes the self-interest of petitioning parties and simply discounts such claims overall. However, one must assume that the conflicts claimed by attorneys include both genuine and spurious conflicts. Thus, some separation must occur at the Supreme Court level. Given the time pressures on the justices who screen certiorari petitions, this need implies a large role for law clerks in distinguishing genuine conflict cases from those where the claim is too tenuous to warrant the Court's attention.

In an earlier article I reported that the Court was sensitive to claims of conflict with Supreme Court precedent when such claims were made by dissenting judges below (Ulmer, 1983). It is possible that such a cue, as well as others, is used by clerks and justices in picking genuine intercircuit conflict cases for review. Further research on other possible cues would seem warranted.

Finally, my analysis has shown that even in the Vinson and Warren eras, the Supreme Court allowed a large percentage of conflicting court rulings to stand. In the current era, the departures from the uniformity of law principle have become more frequent, as have the Supreme Court's failure to correct or eliminate such conflicts. In short, that problem has gotten worse.

REFERENCES

Feeney, F. Conflicts involving federal law: A review of cases presented to the Supreme Court. *Structure and internal procedures: Recommendations for change.* Washington, D.C.: Government Printing Office, 1975, pp. 93–94.

Kirkpatrick, S.A. *Quantitative analysis of political data.* Indianapolis: Bobbs-Merrill, 1974.

Kort, F. Regression analysis and discriminant analysis: An application of R.A. Fisher's theorem to data in political science. *American Political Science Review,* 1973, *67,* 555–559.

Songer, D.R. Concern for policy outputs as a cue for Supreme Court decisions on certiorari. *Journal of Politics,* 1979, *41,* 1185–1194.

Teger, S.H., & Kosinski, D. The cue theory of Supreme Court certiorari jurisdiction: A reconsideration. *Journal of Politics,* 1980, *42,* 834–846.

Ulmer, S.S. Conflict with Supreme Court precedents and the granting of plenary review. *Journal of Politics,* 1983, *45,* 474–478.

———. *Courts, law and judicial processes.* New York: Free Press, 1981, pp. 284–298.

———. Dimensionality and change in judicial behavior. In J.H. Herndon & J. Bernd (eds.) *Mathematical applications in political science VII.* Charlottesville: University Press of Virginia, 1974, pp. 40–67.

Managing the Supreme Court's Business, 1971–1983

William P. McLauchlan

The Supreme Court has been faced with increasing case filings for well over a century, and concern for the problems which that poses has been expressed by many observers and practitioners. This concern has focused largely on aggregate filings and what those might mean in terms of work for the Court. Yet, little empirical attention has been given to how long it takes the Court to process its cases, whether it grants or denies plenary review to the petitions. This study is a preliminary examination of how long it takes the Court to manage its case filings.

This report provides a picture of what the Court does with the cases brought to it, how long it takes the Court to handle its cases, and whether the time required to process its work has increased since the 1971 term. . . .

THE DATA

The data for this study are random samples of the paid cases filed with the Supreme Court for each Term of Court from the 1971

Reprinted from a paper delivered at the 1986 Annual Meeting of the American Political Science Association, pp. 1–4, 6–12, 14–18. Reprinted with permission of the author. Most notes, tables, and figures and all references omitted.

Term through the end of the 1983 Term (June, 1984). The population, from which the samples derive, does not constitute the entire pool of cases brought to the Supreme Court for consideration. In particular, *in forma pauperis* or unpaid cases from the Miscellaneous Docket are not sampled because the source of the data was U.S. Law Week, which does not document all of those unpaid cases that are presented to the Court. . . . Table 1 provides some general indication of the population and sample for each term of the Court.

. . .

[T]here has been little scholarly treatment of the *amount of time* the Supreme Court devotes to cases. As a result, the expectations which we might have about the Court's management of its business largely derive from common sense and our general understanding of the processes involved in treating the cases.

The decisional processes of the Supreme Court are fairly well understood even though much of the process is not public. The Court has two, almost completely discretionary, methods of appellate review. The Writ of Certiorari is discretionary and requires the losing party below to petition the Court for the Writ. Appeal, the other route, is sup-

TABLE 1
Tabulation of Population and Sample of Paid Cases Involved In This Study, 1971–1983 Terms

Term	Total* Filed	Granted* Review	Percent* Reviewed of Total	Sample Size	Granted Review	Percent of Sample Review
1983	2168	247	11.4	326	27	8.3
1982	2174	292	13.5	327	45	13.8
1981	2417	299	12.4	332	46	13.8
1980	2256	235	10.6	328	48	14.6
1979	1983	199	9.5	325	28	8.6
1978	1955	210	10.8	321	40	12.5
1977	1868	166	10.6	318	31	9.8
1976	1877	155	8.9	319	45	14.2
1975	1810	154	9.1	320	60	18.8
1974	1929	147	8.3	311	49	15.7
1973	1901	146	8.0	322	37	11.5
1972	1771	133	8.5	314	66	21.0
1971	1628	131	8.7	313	51	16.3
Total	25737	2514	9.8	4176	573	13.7

* SOURCE: Appropriate November issues of the *Harvard Law Review*.

posedly a matter of right, and it requires only a filing of the Jurisdictional Statement by the party losing below. However, the Court has manipulated the substantial federal question doctrine upon which Appeal is based so that the Court can avoid deciding Appeals on the merits in many instances.[1]

Once a Petition (or Jurisdictional Statement) is filed, the Court will decide if the Writ should be granted or there is a substantial federal question. This Screening Decision is usually negative, with the result that the Supreme Court's consideration of the case is finished and the lower court decision stands. If the Court grants the Writ or notes Probable Jurisdiction, the case has been selected for consideration and Oral Argument is scheduled. At some point after oral argument the Court renders a decision in the case, either a brief, summary Order or a Per Curiam opin-

ion, or it announces the decision with a full, signed opinion. The last stage in the process can be a Rehearing request, which was always denied in the cases in this sample. It is filed by a party, unsatisfied with the Court's decision in the case.

This brief outline of the general process indicates that there are several bench marks or stages in the Court's process.... Most cases are disposed of at the first, screening stage....

It is likely that the amount of time it takes the Court to process and dispose of filings will increase with increases in the total number of filings. Table 1 shows the total number of paid filings for each term, and it increased somewhat over the period, but not in linear fashion. In fact, the variation in processing time should depend on the number of filings rather than the Term of Court.

The hypothesis should be stated something like the following:

H₁: The amount of time required by the Supreme Court to dispose of its cases will vary with the total number of cases filed with the Court.

Another expectation about the processing time of the Court is that it will vary with the stage of the term. That means that as the Court becomes involved with oral argument and the preparation of written opinions over the course of the Term, the amount of time it takes to screen and dispose of its business should increase. Exactly how this may be reflected in the data remains to be seen. It could be that cases filed late in the Term will simply take longer to be screened (i.e., certiorari granted or denied or the appeal dismissed or probable jurisdiction noted). It could be that the screening decisions will not take longer later in the term, but the substantive work of the Court, namely the opinion preparation and announcement of decisions on the merits in the cases selected for plenary review, will be delayed because of the continued need to screen filings....

There are clearly "confounding" factors involved here, in the form of what kind of treatment the Court gives a case. A case placed on the plenary docket and decided on the merits with full opinion should take longer than one which is summarily reviewed. Both of these treatments, which are decisions, will take longer than a case in which review is denied altogether at the screening stage. A case which is carried over to the next term should take longer than one which is filed and disposed of within one term, regardless of how the case is processed. Thus, it is necessary to control for the kind of decisional treatment a case receives in outlining our expectations about change in processing time over the course of the term.

H₂: Controlling for Court treatment of filings, the Supreme Court will take increasingly longer to process or dispose of cases which are filed later in the term.

It is not at all clear that different kinds of cases will take longer to process than other types. It might be that cases raising certain kinds of questions, in which one or more of the justices has a particular interest, will be scrutinized more closely or take longer to process. Different justices may have much different areas of interest in this regard and those are generally not public knowledge. The result of this is that we cannot hypothesize about how long various kinds of cases may take....

THE CYCLE OF SUPREME COURT BUSINESS

.   .   .

... It appears as if the Court begins its Term each year with a tremendous effort at screening the pending filings, and conducting oral argument on those cases carried over, for decision. Then, the oral argument fluctuates somewhat over the rest of the Term. However, the production of decisions, which is quite labor intensive for individual justices results in a backlog of decisions which are released in the "rush to adjournment" in June. This set of patterns may be the logical result of the Court's inability to maintain a constant flow of screening decisions, oral arguments, and announcements of written decisions all at the same time.

Looking more closely at this cycle suggests just when the Court treats its cases.... Clearly those cases filed during July, August, and September are largely screened during October, although part of that October work involves cases filed late in the previous term—April, May, and June. As we move through the Term, the Court does not seem to get further "behind" *in screening cases*, (i.e., no more behind than about three months between filing and screening) until the latter part of the Term—usually the filings after March are not screened until the next term. The Cases filed in March are generally screened before July (and thus before the close of the Term) even though the Court is engaged in a good deal of oral argument and decision writing by that point in the Term.

. . .

The data show that decisions in cases usually follow within three to five months of the oral argument. There is some delay in the Court's decisional process—oral argument certainly does not immediately result in the announcement of decision. The Court reschedules oral argument on those cases which have been argued but are then carried over to the next term. The data. . . show that although the Court usually produces decisions within a few months of hearing oral arguments, that preparation time stretches out during the early months of the Term—October through about January—where a proportion of the decisions are handed down six to eight months after oral argument (near the end of the Term along with the other, later cases). Later in the Term, the time between oral argument and announcement of the decision decreases. This is probably a reflection of the Court's effort to render decisions before the end of the Term for cases heard at least before April. Once the case reaches the point of oral argument, the Court, depending on collegial dynamics and the development of written opinions, seeks to announce its decision within a few months.

Perhaps the most striking feature. . . is that the Court does seem to produce decisions relatively "on time," i.e., within the same Term, and, some within two or three months

of oral argument. No cases are argued in August and September, and very few have been argued in June or July, and those few are decided almost immediately, i.e., within a month. It is not clear what we should expect the Court's time line to be, and it has probably lengthened in the last decade. There is no indication here that the time between screening and oral argument has not lengthened, and that may be the period of time that absorbs most of the "shock" from increased filings.

Hypothesis 1, outlined above, can be explored by correlating the time required to process cases and the number of filings presented to the Court during a term. Using the data from the relevant columns of Table 1, and the median survival time, the correlation is $-.52$. This suggests no support for H1 since the correlation is negative and moderately large. The intuitive relationship is certainly *not* confirmed here, and it suggests that this measure of processing time is not related to the aggregate, paid filings.

Hypothesis 2, which relates when the case is filed in the term to when it is disposed, seems to be somewhat confirmed. The data. . . indicate the nature of the increasing delay over the course of the Term. However, there is no strong statistical connection between filing month and time of disposition. The Court keeps fairly current in screening its cases, even those filed late in the term. The Screening Decision is not the only relevant time frame involved here, although it is the only length of time we have for the vast majority of cases. . . .

SURVIVAL ANALYSIS OF SUPREME COURT FILINGS

Survival analysis is a technique developed largely to explore the effects of various medical treatments on patients by examining their post-treatment longevity. It can also be applied to court cases, and that technique provides useful information about the longevity of Court cases. The technique involves slightly different features in treating Court cases rather than terminally-ill patients. First, *all* the cases are disposed of (i.e., none are "censored"), so none of them "survive the treatment." Second, the "treatments" applied to cases cannot be controlled by the researcher. Those treatments can be anything from different filing months and different dispositions, to the presence of amicus or the involvement of particular lower courts. The dependent variable in this analysis is survival time. This examination will focus on the survival time of different categories of cases.

.   .   .

Survival analysis produces several different statistical indicators, the primary one used here is the cumulative proportion of cases surviving at the end of a uniform set of time periods. This results in a "decay" curve or a cumulative survival curve which begins at time zero (the beginning of the first period) with 100 percent of the cases surviving and ends with zero percent surviving at some point in time thereafter. The calculations treat a month, the interval of time between observations, as a homogeneous unit. A case terminated on the second day of the month is the equivalent of a case terminated on the 28th day. That is somewhat accurate, but it is sufficient for the analysis which will be presented here. . . .

The entire sample was disposed of in three years or less, and the vast majority of the cases took less than three months. The median survival time was 91 days, just over three, thirty-day months. In fact, the curve drops very sharply at the outset, until there is only about fifteen percent of the cases left. This means that nearly 85 percent of the cases stay in the system for relatively little

time. The Court screens these filings within about three months and usually decides not to decide them. The result is that they drop out of the system quickly. It is interesting to note that the final ten percent "persist" for some time, nearly a year. The last portion, which absorbs Court time and attention for well over a year, is small in absolute terms, six to eight percent, but they extend out for a long period of time. These are generally cases which the Court decides on the merits, but which require a good deal of decisional effort.

If the sample is divided into categories, depending on what happened to the cases— denied consideration, summarily decided, or decided with full opinion—the patterns of the survival curves change drastically. Figure 1 indicates the curves for those three dispositions. . . .

The bulk of the sample is contained in the first curve on the left, those cases screened out and not considered on the merits. . . . Nearly all of these cases are disposed of within five months, with a median survival time of 85.5 days. These cases have all left the system by about 21 months. That is a surprisingly long time for any case to take to be screened out. The fact that over five percent of these cases remain in the system for six months or more reflects (1) the delay from the summer recess, and (2) some "problem" cases which perhaps are discussed in Conference and may be rediscussed a second time before finally being rejected.

The Summary Decision curve is worth some attention because that is one way in which the Court can dispose of cases, *with a decision*, but with less work than a full opinion. It does not appear as if the Court has resorted to this method in a large portion of its cases but it certainly has a quicker decay pattern than those cases given full opinion treatment by the Court. The summary cases are all disposed of within 25

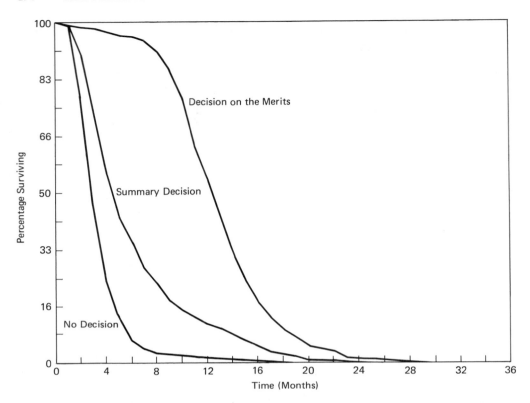

FIGURE 1. Cumulative Proportion Surviving (Decay Curve) for Supreme Court Filings by Method of Final Disposition. 1971–1983 Terms

months, actually just a few months longer than required for the last No Decision case to leave the system. The curve for Summary Dispositions does not drop as quickly as the No Decision cases. Comparing the median survival times of the No Decision and the Summary Decision curves shows about a two month difference (85.5 days compared with 133.64 days). However, one of the important points about the Summary Decision curve is that nearly ten percent of those cases remained to be disposed of at the twelve month mark. This proportion of cases takes the Court more than one term to treat.

The cases disposed of by a decision on the merits with a full opinion clearly constitute a substantial drain on the time and attention of the Court, even though these compose less than fifteen percent of the filings. The median survival time for these cases is just over twelve months (12.2). Almost twenty percent of these cases are still in the system after fifteen months, and the last ones drop from the system at the 34 month mark, nearly three years after they entered the system. Clearly these take a great deal of processing time, and certainly the Court's attention is intensively devoted to these cases.

One interesting difference between the two decision curves—Full Opinions and Summary Decisions—illustrates an important feature of these survival curves. The Summary Decision curve drops relatively sharply from the outset, until at about four months the

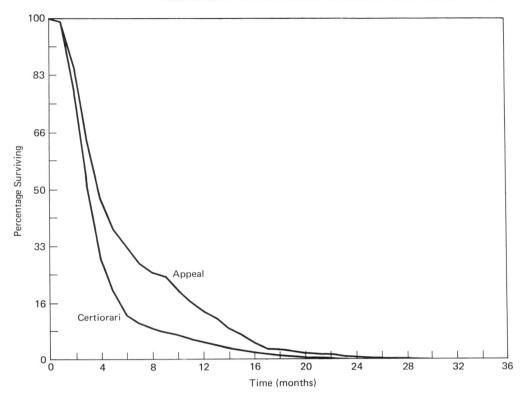

FIGURE 2. Cumulative Proportion Surviving (Decay Curve) for Supreme Court Filings by Method of Access. 1971–1983 Terms

slope of the line decreases markedly. The less the slope of the line, the fewer the cases disposed by the Court in that month. The slope of the Decision on the Merits line is quite small, nearly horizontal, during the first seven months of the life of those cases. This stage includes the screening decision for those cases, and perhaps even the oral argument. Since the final event in these cases does not occur during this early period, they remain in the system. The increased slope of the line from the seventh to the fifteen month indicates the period when the Court disposes of most of its full decision cases. (The median survival time of 12.2 months indicates half these cases remain to be disposed of after a full Term.)

Then the curve flattens out again. This involves the "problem" cases which require a great deal of time to form a majority and fashion an acceptable opinion. . . .

Earlier research has suggested that the method of access to the Court—primarily Certiorari or Appeal—results in different treatments by the Court. Figure 2 illustrates the survival curves for these two access methods. There is a statistically significant difference between them. The cases brought on Appeal take substantially longer, and there is particularly a larger segment of them remaining from the fourth through the sixteenth months. The slope of the curve for Appeal is less than for certiorari during this period, leaving a larger proportion of

Appeals to be disposed of because smaller portions have already been handled. The Court treats these cases to at least closer screening attention than Writs of Certiorari. This extra time also reflects the fact that a much higher proportion of Appeals are "decided" in some fashion than are Certiorari cases. That decisional treatment contributes to the lengthening of the time required to handle the bulk of Appeals, compared with Certiorari petitions.

. . .

There are other differences in the processing time for cases in the sample. . . . Cases in which an amicus curiae brief was filed *in support of granting certiorari* also survive significantly longer than those without such outside support. This may also be due to the fact that a much higher proportion of these cases are decided on the merits than if no such party is present, and that (a decision) does lengthen the survival time. The questions presented in such cases may be of interest to the Court. The presence of such a third party may call the Court's attention to the questions in the case, which may be considered significant policy issues by the Court. In this way, either more time is taken to screen the case, or the Court may feel the need to decide the case on the merits, thus the case survives longer.

The lower court from which filings come to the Supreme Court also affects the survival time of the cases. State court cases take less time than federal court cases. Although there does not appear to be a great difference in the curves, the difference is statistically significant. This might indicate that the Supreme Court considers federal cases more carefully—if time is an indicator of that—than state cases. It is clear that state court cases get less Court attention (in terms of time) than federal court cases. The bulk of cases come from the federal courts of appeals, and this "source" may signal the need for closer scrutiny to the Supreme Court.

One expectation mentioned above was that a filing would take longer to dispose of if it was filed later in the Term. As the Court becomes increasingly burdened with screening decisions, oral arguments, and the preparation of written opinions, it will probably take more time to dispose of cases. In fact, that appears to be the case in analyzing these data. The median survival time is longest for those cases filed in May through August, except that November filings have a relatively long median survival time as well. In terms of mean scores, May, June, and July filings take much the longer time to dispose of on average and March filings are the most quickly disposed of. . . .

CONCLUSIONS

It appears that the most significant time differences occur depending on the disposition that the Court gives to filings. Those cases decided on the merits remain in the system far the longest. Those not selected for a decision are disposed of in the least amount of time. The filings which are summarily treated yield a decision in a relatively small amount of time. That is, those cases are treated in slightly more time than is required for the no decision cases, but much less time than those cases decided on the merits with full opinions.

Other differences in processing time derive from these decisional differences. Cases which are appealed rather than brought on a Writ of Certiorari take substantially longer, because a higher proportion of Appeals are decided on the merits than Certiorari cases. This analysis also suggests that the presence of amicus curiae at the outset of a filing (supporting the petition for certiorari) lengthens the time required to dispose of those cases, probably because of the increased proportion of these cases decided on the merits. *In forma pauperis* respondents or appellees also greatly lengthen the Court's consideration of the cases, because of the higher proportion decided on the merits. These rudimentary characteristics of cases certainly affected treatment by the Court, and that in turn affects the processing time required for these.

It is interesting to note that even though the Court had more filings in the 1983 Term than in the 1971 Term, it did not take the Court much more time to handle the 1983 Term filings than the 1971 filings. Thus, some of the concern about the Court's workload may be misplaced, if we simply examine the processing time. It appears as though the Court is disposing of its filings promptly, requiring little more time than was the case a decade or more ago.

The Court does seem to get behind in screening its filings somewhat as the Term progresses. Filings after March are usually carried over to the next term, and that extends the processing time substantially. Carried-over cases do take substantially longer to dispose of, regardless of the method of disposition, than cases which are not carried over.... If the Court cannot screen a filing during the term in which it is filed, the time for disposing of that case will increase a great deal.

There is little correlation between aggregate filings and processing time, as measured by median survival time. In fact, there is a negative correlation between the two variables. Over the thirteen terms explored here, there also appears to be little *change* in processing time (median survival time). This suggests that if the burden of increased filings has grown over this period, it is not reflected in a substantial lengthening of the time it takes the Court to dispose of its cases.

This study focuses largely on the time required for the Supreme Court to process and dispose of the filings it receives. This has been instructive, but this work does not examine the *quality of the Court's work*. That is an important item, which we cannot address, because of the nature of the data which are available for analysis. Assessing the qualitative nature of the Court's work (and the work of individual justices) is quite essential to understanding the impact of case filings on the work of the Court and the performance of its duties. It is not accurate to consider only the time required to dispose of cases, since the quality of the Justices' efforts to screen petitions and prepare opinions may well suffer even if the time does not lengthen with more filings. However, in terms of the analysis presented here, the work product of the Court is generated in nearly the same amount of time as used to be the case.

In the future, closer attention to the actual time available to the justices would improve our understanding of the workload. Controlling for a "work week" of 40, 60, or even 80 hours might give us a better picture of how the Court treats filings and the length of time necessary to process them. Nothing here can address the issues relating to the quality of Court decisions. Perhaps the quality of what the justices do and how they feel about it has changed over the period, even if the time required to decide cases has not increased. We need a closer examination of these matters before it is possible to make final judgments about the Court's workload.

NOTE

1. For convenience in this paper, unless otherwise indicated, no distinction will be made between Certiorari and Appeal.... Supreme Court Rule 17 provides the only public indication of the basis upon which Certiorari can be sought....

CHAPTER 5

Public Opinion and the Courts

Whether an individual involved in a dispute will turn to the courts for help is to some extent a function of his or her attitudes and beliefs about the efficacy, fairness, and competence of judicial institutions. This means that one should have some understanding of such attitudes and beliefs to better comprehend which disputes reach the courts. It is possible to think about American attitudes toward courts in many ways. Do Americans approve of what courts do, of how they process cases and make decisions? Do they respect and trust judges? Do they think they will get a fair deal from courts?

Although most studies of support for the courts, including our selections, deal with the Supreme Court, some useful empirical research has been conducted that highlights the issues and questions important to an understanding of how the public thinks about courts at all levels of the judicial system. Such studies provide impressive evidence that courts are not particularly conspicuous in the minds of the American people. Public knowledge about courts, court personnel, and court decisions is slight.[1] This is no less true for the Supreme Court than it is for local trial courts. The theoretical significance of this lack of awareness is uncertain. However, there is some evidence that suggests an important and interesting paradox about public attitudes toward the courts. It appears that there is an inverse relationship between knowledge about courts and support for them; the more citizens know about courts the less happy many are with their operation and performance.[2] Although most surveys report general, if not intense, positive support for courts, they also indicate that support is eroded by information and that this erosion is especially dramatic for those whose information is gained through first hand experience as a litigant.

Two other variables seem important in shaping attitudes toward local courts. First, among people who believe courts to be too lenient in dealing with criminals, support for courts is greatly reduced. It appears that people typically blame the courts rather than the police or social conditions for the crime problem.[3] Second, there is a strong relationship between the way people expect to be treated by courts and their support for judicial institutions. Those who believe that some individuals or groups receive better treatment than others are almost uniformly more negative in their feelings about courts than are those who believe that the courts treat people equally.[4]

Where the Supreme Court is concerned, these findings, especially the inverse relationship between knowledge and support, are important. The Supreme Court, like the lower courts, seems to benefit from widespread ignorance of its decisions. Political scientists report that less than one-half of the respondents in each of two national surveys could think of any specific likes or dislikes about what the Supreme Court had done. Furthermore, the decisions that were most visible to the public tended to be those that were most controversial, dramatic, and unpopular. The public usually becomes aware of a Supreme Court decision only when there is a campaign of criticism against it. Nevertheless, although neither public knowledge nor public approval of specific decisions is very great, many people, including substantial numbers of those who disapprove of specific decisions, accord the Court high levels of support. Respect for the institution is not based on approval of its specific decisions.[5]

Rather, there appear to be two other bases for such respect. The first is the rather widespread diffusion of myths about the way in which the Supreme Court makes its decisions. Most people who are able to describe the operation of the Supreme Court describe it in mythic terms. There is strong adherence to the theory of "mechanical jurisprudence"—the theory that judicial decisions can be fully explained by reference to the facts of a case and to the relevant law, mechanically applied.[6] Those who have a mythic or highly idealized notion of what the Court does and of how it operates are more likely than others, whose perception is more accurate, to support the Court.[7]

Another frequent explanation for support of the Supreme Court posits an indirect flow of sentiment from the public to the Court. According to this argument the basis of support is citizens' attitudes toward what has been called the "governing coalition" at the federal level. If individuals identify with the party of the president, if they trust the federal government as a whole or the president in particular, they are likely also to support the Supreme Court. This explanation, along with several others, is discussed in the selection by Adamany and Grossman.

Most of the empirical research on public attitudes toward the courts is based upon a one time only sampling of opinion. The reading by Caldeira is one of the few to study those attitudes over time. Caldeira shows how attitudes toward the Supreme Court change and suggests that such change is a function of events over which the Court has no control, e.g., Watergate, as well as particular judicial decisions. Two other studies, one by Jack Dennis[8] and the other by Murphy and Tanenhaus,[9] have presented longitudinal data spanning the period of the late 1960s and early 1970s. Dennis found that in this period, support for the Supreme Court as well as for the entire national government suffered a significant decline. Murphy and Tanenhaus challenged the prevailing governing coalition hypothesis by suggesting that even after the Republicans gained the presidency, Democrats and liberals remained most supportive of the Supreme Court. The implication of this finding is that the governing coalition argument may only be applicable when the President and the majority of the Supreme Court are of the same political party or of the same general ideological bent.[10]

Perhaps as much as anything else the literature on public attitudes toward the courts provides a hint as to why the courts do not play a greatly expanded dispute-processing role. Courts are respected, yet they are also feared. Survey studies are also valuable simply because they reveal beliefs about the distribution of benefits resulting from court decisions. The selections in this chapter present a wide range of information and discussion about the nature of public support for American courts.

NOTES

1. See Darlene Walker *et al.*, "Contact and Support: An Empirical Assessment of Public Attitudes Toward the Police and Courts," *North Carolina Law Review* 51 (1972), 43; and Wesley Skogan, "Judicial Myth and Judicial Reality," *Washington University Law Quarterly* (1971), 309. In general see the discussion in Sheldon Goldman and Thomas P. Jahnige. *The Federal Courts as a Political System* 3rd ed. (New York: Harper & Row, 1985), pp. 107–118.

2. Jack Dennis, "Mass Public Support for the U.S. Supreme Court," paper presented at the 30th Annual Conference of the American Association of Public Opinion Research, 1975; and Kenneth Dolbeare, "The Public Views the Supreme Court," in *Law, Politics and the Federal Courts*, edited by Herbert Jacob (Boston: Little, Brown, 1967). See also Roger Handberg, "Public Opinion and the United States Supreme Court, 1935–1981," *International Social Science Review* 59 (1984), 3. But see, Thomas R. Marshall, "The Supreme Court as an Opinion Leader: Court Decisions and the Mass Public," *American Politics Quarterly* 15 (1987), 147.

3. See Monica Blumenthal *et al.*, *Justifying Violence* (Ann Arbor; Institute for Social Research, University of Michigan, 1972).

4. Austin Sarat, "Studying American Legal Culture: An Assessment of Survey Evidence," *Law and Society Review* 11 (1977), 427–488.

5. See Walter F. Murphy, Joseph Tanenhaus, and Daniel L. Kastner, *Public Evaluations of Constitutional Courts* (Beverly Hills: Sage Publications, 1973) and William J. Daniels, "The Supreme Court and its Publics," *Albany Law Review* 37 (1973), 632–661.

6. Skogan, *op. cit.*, note 1; and Richard Engstrom and Micheal Giles, "Expectations and Images: A Note on Diffuse Support for Legal Institutions," *Law and Society Review* 6 (1972), 631–636.

7. Gregory Casey, "The Supreme Court and Myth: An Empirical Investigation," *Law and Society Review* 8 (1974), 385.

8. Dennis, *op. cit*, note 2.

9. Joseph Tanenhaus and Walter F. Murphy, "Patterns of Public Support for the Supreme Court: A Panel Study," *Journal of Politics*, 43 (1981), 30.

10. See Gregory A. Caldeira, "Public Opinion and the U.S. Supreme Court: FDR's Court-Packing Plan," *American Political Science Review*, 81 (1987), 1139.

Support for the Supreme Court as a National Policymaker

David Adamany
Joel B. Grossman

The Supreme Court is a national policy-maker.... Under certain conditions, Supreme Court decisions nullifying policies made by lawmaking majorities do not endure. In most circumstances, however, the Supreme Court demonstrates remarkable resilience as a policy-maker. The reasons for that resilience are far from clear, but many commentators have attributed the Court's endurance as a national policymaker to its special status with the public. The validity of that assertion is a principal concern of this article....

This relative immunity from attack has caused scholars to ponder why the branch that possesses neither the sword nor the purse persists so successfully in making national policy. This search has often focused on the Supreme Court's asserted special standing with the American people. Legal Realists and political scientists in the 1930s argued that public reverence for the Constitution is rooted in psychological needs for stability and security in human affairs and in the powerful hold that constitutional symbolism has on the American mind. This

"Support for the Supreme Court as a National Policymaker," David Adamany and Joel B. Grossman. *Law and Policy Quarterly*, Vol. 5, No. 4, 1983. Reprinted with permission of publisher.

reverence is in turn transferred to the justices of the Supreme Court, as interpreters and protectors of the sacred Constitution (Frank, 1930: ch. 1; Arnold, 1962: 34; Corwin, 1936; Llewellyn, 1934; Lerner, 1937). Empirical support for this view emerged in an early, seminal socialization study (Easton and Dennis, 1969: 253–279). Children's images of the Court were discovered to be "of a special sort." Specifically, children regard the Court as more knowledgeable, more powerful, and less prone to mistakes than other political authorities; and they believe that it makes "important decisions."

These suggestions about the Supreme Court's special place in the public's heart or psyche, however, have not found support in subsequent, and probably more systematic, studies. Caldeira's (1977a) secondary analysis of open-ended interviews with a small sample of American children led him to conclude that the earlier results were "in large part methodological artifacts" (1977a: 864). Children, he concluded, have little knowledge of the Supreme Court or its constitutional role, and they do not find it particularly knowledgeable or important. This "lack or information or affect among both children and adults" compels the conclusion "that the Supreme Court does not have a tremendous store of legitimacy" (1977a: 868).

. . .

Indirect evidence also tends to show that the Court does not have a hold on the public mind that would protect it against reversal of its policies or restriction of its authority. Only about half the public can recall any Supreme Court decision; those with more detailed knowledge form a mere corporal's guard. . . . Generalized evaluations of the Court's "job performance" have tended to be more favorable than unfavorable, although favorable evaluations have declined through time and have often been offered by less than half of those surveyed (Kessel, 1966: 171; Dolbeare, 1967: 203; Murphy and Tanenhaus, 1968a: 374–375; Lehnen, 1976: 137; Tanenhaus and Murphy, 1981: 27–29).

Citizen judgments about specific Court decisions are much more hostile. Unfavorable reactions to major decisions in recent years outnumber favorable ones by a margin of at least two to one (Murphy and Tanenhaus, 1968a: 370; Murphy and Tanenhaus, 1968b: 35; Murphy et al., 1973: 46; Lehnen, 1976: 138; Tanenhaus and Murphy, 1981: 32). The public has repeatedly been asked to indicate its level of confidence in various governmental institutions. The Court ranks more favorably than Congress and/or the Presidency in only about half of these surveys . . . although confidence in the Court has risen somewhat in recent years.

If generous support for the Court is not found among the general public, it is plausible to suspect that the Court's apparent immunity to attack from the popular branches lies in special reverence or support among political elites. Murphy and Tanenhaus (1970) have shown that congressional administrative assistants, lawyers, and Princeton University students support the Court more strongly than do the public at large. Beiser (1972: 140), however, found

lawyers to be less supportive than the general public.

Support for the Court among these elites is, in any case, also very closely correlated with their approval of specific court decisions (Murphy and Tanenhaus, 1970: 27–28; Beiser, 1972: 142). One group of officials that supports the Supreme Court, even while disapproving specific decisions, is lower federal court judges. Among their state court brethren, however, general support for the institution and approval of its specific decisions tend to be highly correlated (Caldeira, 1977b: 219).

Ideology is a major factor in support for the Court both among elites and among those subgroups in the general public that are knowledgeable about the Court's work (Murphy et al., 1973: 45–51; Casey, 1976: 25–29). Indeed, ideology has emerged as the most important factor in explaining changes in support for the Court over time (Tanenhaus and Murphy, 1981). Ideological predispositions and reactions to specific judicial decisions are often found to be highly correlated.

Our investigation begins, therefore, from the baseline of previous studies that show only slight public support for the Supreme Court as a national policymaker. There is little evidence for the proposition that the Supreme Court has a special place either in the psyche or in the childhood socialization of Americans. There is also little evidence of widespread public support for the justices' specific decisions, and the Court does not appear to command sweeping generalized approval. Among elites and officials, support for the Court is highly correlated to approval of its specific decisions and compatibility with its ideological thrust. Such support is unlikely to protect the Court's most visible decisions, which often nullify policies with widespread support among elites.

Our purposes in this article are twofold. First, we press the investigation of support for the Supreme Court among politically important sectors of the public. Specifically, we are interested in whether or not special support for the Court is found among those whom Nexon (1971: 716–717) has called "occasional activists." ...We emphasize that our concern is whether there is disproportionate support for the Court among political activists. Whether activism *causes* support for the Court or whether support among activists is an artifact of other variables are also important questions, which we will address elsewhere.

Our second purpose is more global—to suggest a link between evidence about activist support for the Supreme Court and the larger question of why the Court and its policies display such remarkable endurance in the face of widespread public hostility toward many of its decisions. Activists' attitudes toward the Supreme Court appear to us to provide a small but revealing tile in a large mosaic. Even that bit of evidence, however, encourages us to discard some common explanations given for the Court's resilience, and it fits together with a gradually accumulating body of scholarship to make a larger picture of the Court's ability to survive as a policymaker. That picture, as we shall subsequently argue, portrays the Court's support base as narrower than is generally believed, but nonetheless strategically placed in a manner that usually protects the Court against restriction of its authority or reversal of its policies.

THE DATA

Our first line of inquiry relies on a statewide survey (N=581) conducted by the Wisconsin Survey Research Laboratory in November and December, 1976. It has been described fully elsewhere (Adamany and Shelly, 1980). In addition to standard questions about voting, political attitudes, and respondent characteristics, the instrument included a battery of questions about the Supreme Court.

Respondents were asked if they liked anything the Supreme Court had done, and were offered an opportunity to name a second decision of which they approved. They were then asked to name anything the Court had done that they disliked and a follow-up question invited the identification of a second disfavored Court action. From these questions, we have constructed a specific support variable. Respondents who named one or two Supreme Court decisions they liked were categorized as giving specific support; those listing only decisions they disliked were identified as negative on specific support. Those who both liked and disliked various Court decisions were treated as giving mixed support to the Court. The survey also asked respondents to evaluate the Supreme Court's overall performance as very good, good, fair, or poor. For cross-tabulation purposes, the first two categories were collapsed and treated together as a favorable performance rating while the latter two were treated as an unfavorable rating.

General support for twelve political institutions and processes was tapped by a standard question asking how much confidence a respondent had in each, using a seven-point scale. The respondents were grouped into those expressing any degree of confidence, those expressing any lack of confidence, and a middle group who positioned themselves at the midpoint of the scale.

Following other studies that tested comparative support for the three branches of the national government, the Wisconsin survey included an inquiry whether "in a disagreement over national policy between the Congress and the Supreme Court, the Congress should have the final authority to decide." A similar question matched the President and the Court. The seven-point response scale (from strongly agree to strongly disagree) was collapsed, so that all answers supporting the Court to any degree were treated as pro-Court responses, all supporting the Congress or Presidency to any degree were treated as anti-Court responses, and the midpoint (designated in the survey as agree-disagree) was treated as an uncertain or undecided response.

Finally, the survey asked respondents whether they had ever belonged to an American political party (by paying dues or holding a membership card), contributed any money to a political candidate or party, engaged in any campaign work (such as telephoning, mailing, door-to-door contacts, circulating nomination papers), or joined or actively supported a political cause or movement (apart from a party or candidate) by seeking to influence government policies through petitions, marches, referendum campaigns, demonstrations, and so forth. Fully 55.9% of respondents had *never* engaged in any of these modest political behaviors, and another 19.3% had participated in only one. We took as our group of "occasional activists" those who had engaged in two or more of these political behaviors; they constituted 24.8% (N=144) of the sample, a large enough subgroup for some cross tabulation.

PUBLIC SUPPORT FOR THE SUPREME COURT

Our survey results resemble those reported elsewhere: support for the Supreme Court is not high. A handful of respondents (7.6%) cited only specific Court decisions that they liked; nearly three times as many—20.7% named only specific decisions that they disliked. Both favored and disfavored decisions were mentioned by 9.5% of respondents, and 62.3% named no decision they

liked or disliked. On its overall performance, the Court got "very good" and "good" ratings from 42% of respondents, while 45.6% graded it only "fair" or "poor."

The mean confidence rating of the Court was 4.95 on a seven-point scale. However, the presidency (5.29), the local police (5.29), the military (5.20), and local government (4.96) garnered more confidence than did the Court, while national elections (4.92), state government (4.78), and Congress (4.77) were roughly in the same range. Only the federal government (4.55) as a generalized entity, the much despised bureaucracy (4.31), political parties (4.32), and organized interest groups (4.03) garnered mean confidence scores substantially below those of the Supreme Court.

In a disagreement over national policy, 39.3% of respondents preferred final resolution by the Court, while 45.1% favored congressional authority. On the other hand, the Court won support from 60.2% of respondents compared to 21.8% for the chief executive. We attribute this finding partly to the low esteem in which the presidency was held in the years immediately following Watergate. . . .

ACTIVIST SUPPORT FOR THE SUPREME COURT

A considerably different picture initially emerges when we examine support for the Court separately among activists and the politically inactive. Table 1 shows that to a statistically significant degree, activists offer greater support than inactives for the Court's specific decisions. Activists express slightly greater confidence in the Court than do inactives, and have a stronger preference than inactives to vest final decision-making authority in the justices when policy disputes arise between them and Congress or the

TABLE 1
Activists' and Inactives' Support for the Supreme Court, 1976

	Activists		Inactives		
	N	%	N	%	Chi Square
Specific Decision Support[a]					
Positive	23	28.4	18	14.1	
Mixed	22	27.2	30	23.4	p = < .02
Negative	36	44.4	80	62.5	
	81	100.0	128	100.0	
Overall Performance Rating[b]					
Positive	71	52.6	164	47.3	
Negative	64	47.4	183	52.7	p = N.S.
	135	100.0	347	100.0	
Confidence in Court[c]					
Much Confidence	99	68.8	232	59.9	
Mixed Confidence	20	13.9	107	27.6	p = < .01
Little Confidence	25	17.4	48	12.4	
	144	100.1	387	99.9	
Court vs. Congress[d]					
Pro-Court	67	47.5	136	36.3	
Undecided	17	12.1	64	17.1	p = < .06
Pro-Congress	57	40.4	175	46.7	
	141	100.0	375	100.1	
Court vs. President[e]					
Pro-Court	94	67.6	219	57.9	
Undecided	23	16.5	70	18.5	p = < .10
Pro-President	22	15.8	89	23.5	
	139	99.9	378	99.9	

[a] "Is there anything in particular that the United States Supreme Court has done that you have liked (disliked)? Is there anything else you particularly liked (disliked)?" See text for assignment of responses to categories of specific support.

[b] "In general, how good a job do you feel the U.S. Supreme Court has been doing lately? Very good—Good—Fair—Poor." See text for assignment of responses to categories of overall performance.

[c] "How much confidence do you have in the Supreme Court as an institution?" See text for assignment of responses on the seven-point survey scale to categories of confidence in the Supreme Court.

[d] "In a disagreement over national policy between the Congress and the Supreme Court, the Congress should have the final authority to decide." See text for assignment of responses on the seven-point survey scale to categories of support for Congress and the Supreme Court.

[e] "In a disagreement over national policy between the President and the Supreme Court, the Court should have the final authority to decide." See text for assignment of responses on the seven-point survey scale to categories of support for the President and the Supreme Court.

President. Activists also give the Supreme Court a slightly higher overall performance rating than do those who are politically active, but the difference is small and not statistically significant.

Before resting too heavily on these initial impressions, however, it is useful to examine the data more closely. Although more inclined than the general public to support specific Court decisions, activists nonetheless mainly oppose the Court's decisions—44% name only decisions they dislike, while 28% cite only decisions they support. Moreover, specific decision support is a weak reed on which to rest the Supreme Court's protection from attacks on its policies or its authority. Many of the Court's most significant policy decisions overturn policies made by elected officials who presumably reflect popular sentiment and especially the views of the politically active sectors of society. If the Court's safety from attack depends on specific decision support, then it can safely make policies only when those policies command majority support or when there is broad approval of a wide array of judicial decisions that would offset ire against an occasional unpopular ruling. However, these conditions do not conform to the evidence; some of the Court's most visible decisions in the modern era have been overwhelmingly disapproved by the activist public; and even the activists have knowledge of too few decisions to balance off disfavored rulings against an array of favored policies.

Difficulties also beset the findings that activists express greater confidence in the Supreme Court than do the politically inactive. Activists, as shown in Table 1, express both more and less confidence in the Court than do those who are politically inactive. A larger percentage of the inactive, on the other hand, express mixed confidence in the justices. Moreover, comparing the confidence of activists and inactives in the Supreme Court may not be useful in assessing the Court's ability to withstand attacks. A better assessment can be made by comparing activists' confidence in the Court with their confidence in the government institutions and political processes that are sources of assaults upon judicial authority and decisions. Our survey includes items eliciting confidence levels in eleven of these institutions and processes.

Activists expressed higher levels of confidence in the Court than they did in political parties (p = .000), interest groups (p = .000), federal administrative agencies (p = .000), the military (p = .056), and state governments (p = .02). A statistically significant difference was also observed between activists' confidence levels in the Supreme Court and Congress (p = .059), but here, unlike the previously mentioned cases, activists tended to be more polarized in their attitudes toward the Court than in their expressions of confidence in the Congress. More activists announced high confidence in the Court (68.8%) than gave a similarly high rating to Congress (61.7%). However, low confidence in the Court (17.4%) was also more pronounced among activists than was low confidence in Congress (13.5%). The legislature, by contrast, garnered a higher percentage of mixed or moderate confidence ratings (24.8%) than did the judiciary (13.9%). This pattern of comparative confidence ratings does not suggest greater activist support for the Court than for Congress in a clash between the two branches.

Activists did not express greater confidence in the Supreme Court than they did in the President, the police, the federal government (generally), local government, or national elections. Certainly the President, police, and local governments, as well as Congress, have been sources of opposition to some Supreme Court policies in recent decades. Yet the Court has endured their opposition despite the absence of greater activist confidence in the judiciary than in these other institutions.

These doubts about the evidence of greater activist support for and confidence in the Court do not, however, diminish the persuasiveness of the evidence that activists prefer judicial authority to congressional or presidential power. A clear plurality of activists in Table 1 favor judicial authority over congressional power; inactives favor congressional decision making by a similar plurality. Both activists and inactives prefer judicial policymaking to presidential authority, but support for the Court is significantly greater among activists than among inactives. While Watergate may, as previously suggested, explain the presidential authority, it does not explain why activists should hold that preference to a greater extent than do the politically inactive. One at least suspects that the relative preferences of activists and inactives for judicial and presidential power would remain constant, and thus significantly dissimilar, even as the taint of Watergate diminishes and public attitudes return to a more even balance between support for the judiciary and for the presidency.

IDEOLOGY AND SUPPORT FOR THE SUPREME COURT

Others have found that ideology is a major determinant of support for the Supreme Court (Murphy et al., 1973: 45–51; Casey, 1976: 25–29; Tanenhaus and Murphy, 1981). Yet, apparent support for the Court among political activists may turn on respondents' ideological predispositions. Some scholars have used a measure of ideology constructed from responses to specific questions about civil rights, civil liberties, and social welfare policies. Our survey does not contain similar items, but it does include self-ratings by respondents on a standard seven-point ideological scale (7 = extremely conservative, 4 = middle of the road, 1 = extremely liberal). When we cross tabulated ideology and support for the Court, we found little relationship. Among our full sample, liberals and moderates cited more decisions they liked and fewer they disliked than did conservatives (p = .018). On the other four measures of support used, ideology was not

significantly related to support for the Court.

However, when we held ideology constant and examined support for the Court among activists and inactives, we discovered that most of the special activist support for the Court simply disappeared. The data are provided in Table 2. Several of these cross tabulations, especially those involving attitudes toward specific judicial decisions, produce very small cells. Measures of significance must, therefore, be treated cautiously. Even these tabulations, however, are useful as impressionistic evidence.

Compared to politically inactive liberals, activists who described themselves as liberal gave significantly greater support to specific Supreme Court decisions, had greater confidence in the Court, and preferred judicial policymaking to decisions by Congress or the President. Politically moderate activists also expressed greater support for specific decisions than did moderate inactives. Specific decision support is, however, the only measure of support for the Court on which moderate activists were significantly more committed to the Court than were moderate inactives. There is not a single measure on which conservative activists gave significantly greater support to the Court than did conservative inactives.

.   .   .

It is, therefore, the combination of liberalism and activism, rather than either of these variables alone, that defines the Court's most committed constituency today. The extraordinary support for the Court among this single but strategically important subgroup of liberal activists may nonetheless direct us toward an explanation of the Court's resilience. Their ideological outlook may explain their disposition to support the Court, and their activism may be an important factor in protecting the Court against repeated attacks in the modern period.

TABLE 2
Support for the Supreme Court: Ideology and Activism[a]

	Liberals				Moderates				Conservatives			
	Activists		Inactives		Activists		Inactives		Activists		Inactives	
	N	%	N	%	N	%	N	%	N	%	N	%
Specific Decision Support												
Positive	8	32.0	2	9.1	10	41.7	9	15.8	5	15.6	7	14.3
Mixed	9	36.0	6	27.3	7	29.2	18	31.6	6	18.8	6	12.2
Negative	8	32.0	14	63.6	7	29.2	30	52.6	21	65.6	36	73.5
	25	100.0	22	100.0	24	100.1	57	100.0	32	100.0	49	100.0
	p = < .06				p = .03				p = N.S.			
Overall Performance Rating												
Positive	22	52.4	38	52.1	27	58.7	71	46.4	21	45.7	54	47.8
Negative	20	47.6	35	47.9	19	41.3	82	53.6	25	54.3	59	52.2
	42	100.0	73	100.0	46	100.0	153	100.0	46	100.0	113	100.0
	p = N.S.				p = N.S.				p = N.S.			
Confidence in Court												
Much Confidence	37	78.7	51	58.0	32	66.7	104	62.7	29	60.4	75	59.5
Mixed Confidence	4	8.5	26	29.5	9	18.8	45	27.1	7	14.6	31	24.6
Little Confidence	6	12.8	11	12.5	7	14.6	17	10.2	12	25.0	20	15.9
	47	100.0	88	100.0	48	100.1	166	100.0	48	100.0	126	100.0
	p = .02				p = N.S.				p = N.S.			
Court vs. Congress												
Pro-Court	26	57.8	28	32.2	20	42.6	53	32.1	21	43.8	54	45.8
Undecided	3	6.7	16	18.4	7	14.9	34	20.6	6	12.5	14	11.9
Pro-Congress	16	35.6	43	49.4	20	42.6	78	47.3	21	43.8	50	42.4
	45	100.1	87	100.0	47	100.1	165	100.0	48	100.1	118	100.1
	p = .01				p = N.S.				p = N.S.			
Court vs. President												
Pro-Court	36	80.0	53	60.9	32	66.7	88	54.0	26	56.5	74	60.2
Undecided	4	8.9	14	16.1	9	18.8	37	22.7	10	21.7	18	14.6
Pro-President	5	11.1	20	23.0	7	14.6	38	23.3	10	21.7	31	25.2
	45	100.0	87	100.0	48	100.1	163	100.0	46	99.9	123	100.0
	p = .08				p = N.S.				p = N.S.			

[a] Items in this table are described in the notes for Table 1. Construction of the scales is described in the text.

DIFFUSE PUBLIC VALUES AND NATIONAL VERSUS STATE POLICYMAKING

Theories explaining the remarkable endurance of the Supreme Court's authority and its resilience as a policymaker range from simple assertions about public support to elegant formulations combining assumptions about public values with insights about complex governmental arrangements. We have already pointed out the overwhelming evidence from other studies casting doubt on the straightforward explanations that the

Court has a special place in the American psyche, that the Court's decisions are approved by the public, and that the Court engenders special levels of confidence and support. Our survey does not address the first assertion, but—as suggested previously in the section on public support—it further heightens doubts about the latter two explanations for the Court's endurance as a policymaker. The section on activist support makes clear that these explanations are dubious even if trimmed to suggest only that the Court's base of support is limited to political activists....

An evaluation of public attitudes involves at least three inquiries: What judicial policies did the public know about? Did it approve or disapprove of these policies? Were its overall assessments of the Court favorable or unfavorable?

A series of surveys conducted by scholars over a 12 year period, from 1964 to 1976, used a similar methodology to tap opinion about Supreme Court policies. These polls asked respondents to name Court decisions they liked and disliked. While the number of decisions that could be named was limited by the number of probes in the survey instrument, the evidence is compelling that few respondents named more than one policy in either category. Hence, the number of probes, which differed slightly among the surveys, is not determinative of the results. In general, about 40% of respondents named at least one decision they favored or disfavored; the majority in each sample could not name a single decision.

Table 3 summarizes the judicial policies that were mentioned in each of the seven surveys. It is clear that in the 1960s, civil rights, criminal justice (mainly defendants' rights), and school prayers were the salient policies promulgated by the Supreme Court. Although reapportionment was of intense concern to politicians and scholars, it made

little impression on the public. In the 1970s, abortion and Watergate joined the agenda of Supreme Court policies that were visible to the public. In addition, the character of two of the earlier issues changed. More than half of the responses relating to civil rights were now about school busing, and the Court's capital punishment decisions accounted for nearly half of the responses about criminal justice.

Table 4 summarizes the direction of public opinion on the Court's visible decisions. The figure in each cell is the percentage of all comments unfavorable to the named judicial policy. Only the reapportionment and Watergate decisions were favorably evaluated. The former were mentioned by few respondents, and that issue quickly faded from visibility. The Watergate cases were cited more often, "but that issue is probably ephemeral and may have already ceased to enhance specific support" for the Court (Tanenhaus and Murphy, 1981: 33). The criminal justice and school prayer decisions were strongly disapproved across the entire 12-year period.

Responses to the Court's civil rights policies were about evenly divided in the 1960s, but they became strongly unfavorable in the 1970s, largely due to negative attitudes toward school busing. The abortion decisions were also mentioned unfavorably, although by less lopsided majorities than were other judicial policies....

Opinion about abortion has been gradually shifting toward support for the Court. In 1969, prior to the Supreme Court's decision, abortion during the first trimester of pregnancy was opposed by a margin of 50% to 40% (Gallup, 1969: 190). Subsequent surveys showed a growing majority favoring a woman's right to obtain an abortion, at least under certain circumstances (Gallup, 1973: 21–2; Gallup, 1974: 24; Gallup, 1978: 25–29). A constitutional amendment banning abortion, which would overturn the Court's

TABLE 3
The Visibility of Supreme Court Decisions: 1964 to 1976

	1964 SRC National[a] %	1966 SRC National[b] %	1964 SRC National Panel[c] %	1966 WSRL Wis.[d] %	1969 SERS National[e] %	1975 SRC National Panel[c] %	1976 WSRL Wis.[f] %
Civil Rights	38.1	24.7	26.6	45.8	21	28.6	22.0
(School Busing)	(—)*	(—)*	(—)*	(—)*	(—)*	(17.5)	(16.3)***
Criminal Justice	5.8	15.5	19.5	—**	44	19.6	22.0
(Death Penalty)	(—)*	(—)*	(—)*	(—)*	(—)*	(9.5)	(9.1)
School Prayers	30.6	23.4	21.8	17.4	15	10.8	4.3
Reapportionment	4.9	1.0	—**	—*	—**	—**	.3
Abortion	—*	—*	—*	—*	—*	8.7	16.9
Watergate	—*	—*	—*	—*	—*	6.1	10.6
Other	20.5	35.3	32.2	36.8	20	26.2	24.0
TOTAL	99.9	99.9	100.1	100.0	100	100.0	100.1
	(N = 915)	(N = 1075)	(N = 354)	(N = 236)	(N = 779)	(N = 378)	(N = 350)

* Cell is empty because major decisions in this area were not decided at the time of the survey.

** Cell is empty because the survey did not separately report responses to this specific judicial policy, presumably because the number of responses was too small.

*** The 1976 Wisconsin survey included references to school desegregation as well as to school busing in this category.

SOURCES:
[a] Survey Research Center, University of Michigan. Data presented in Murphy and Tanenhaus (1968a: 36).
[b] Survey Research Center, University of Michigan. Data retabulated by the authors from the presentation in Murphy et al. (1973: 46).
[c] Survey Research Center, University of Michigan. Respondents are those in a panel study of 1966 SRC respondents who could be identified and reinterviewed in 1975. Data reported in Tanenhaus and Murphy (1981: 32).
[d] Tabulations by the authors from Wisconsin Survey Research Laboratory (1966: 2-3).
[e] South East Regional Survey, University of North Carolina. Data reported in Lehnen (1976: 138).
[f] Tabulations by the authors from Wisconsin Survey Research Laboratory (1976: 15-19).

decisions, was strongly opposed, with both liberals and conservatives joining in that opposition (Gallup, 1976: 20; Opinion Roundup, 1981: 24).

Turning to aggregate evaluation, support for the Supreme Court's performance does not appear high. Table 4 shows that in six of the seven surveys between 1964 and 1976, unfavorable responses easily out-distanced favorable comments by a remarkably consistent margin of about 70% to 30%. (The 1966 Wisconsin survey, the sole exception, was skewed by an odd instrument that twice

invited respondents to name decisions they favored but gave only one opportunity to name a disfavored policy.) . . .

This review of survey data does not support a view that the Supreme Court's policies were consistent with diffuse or inchoate values widespread among Americans. The ephemeral Watergate cases and low-visibility reapportionment decisions did garner public support. At best, the abortion decisions gradually gained approval of a narrow majority, but then only in limited circumstances. Initially favorable opinion about the civil

TABLE 4
Unfavorable Public Evaluation of Supreme Court Decisions: 1964 to 1976[a]

	1964 SRC National %[b]	1966 SRC National %[b]	1966 SRC National Panel %[b]	1966 WSRL Wis. %[b]	1969 SERS National %[b]	1975 SRC National Panel %[b]	1976 WSRL Wis. %[b]
Civil Rights	51.9	48.9	50.0	8.3	45.7	70.4	61.0
(School Busing)	(—)[*]	(—)[*]	(—)[*]	(—)[*]	(—)[*]	(93.9)	(67.2)
Criminal Justice	88.7	86.8	85.5	—[*]	88.5	77.0	77.9
(Death Penalty)	(—)[*]	(—)[*]	(—)[*]	(—)[*]	(—)[*]	(75.0)	(56.2)[***]
School Prayers	90.4	91.3	90.0	82.9	95.0	95.1	73.3
Reapportionment	62.2	72.7	—[**]	—[**]	—[**]	—[**]	0.0
Abortion	—[*]	—[*]	—[*]	—[*]	—[*]	57.6	69.5
Watergate	—[*]	—[*]	—[*]	—[*]	—[*]	13.0	59.5
Other	73.4	66.5	67.5	48.3	78.2	60.6	66.7
TOTAL[c]	70.7 (N = 647)	71.2 (N = 765)	71.5 (N = 253)	36.0 (N = 85)	78.4 (N = 611)	67.2 (N = 254)	67.7 (N = 237)

[*] Cell is empty because major decisions in this area were not decided at the time of the survey.
[**] Cell is empty because the survey did not report separately responses to this specific judicial policy, presumably because the number of responses was too small.
[***] The 1976 Wisconsin survey occurred after the Supreme Court had rejected death penalty laws in 1972 and had then approved them—subject to stringent conditions—in 1976. It is unclear as to whether responses expressing disapproval of the Court's capital punishment policy refer to the 1972 or 1976 decision. See note 10 for further discussion of the coding and interpretative problems with this category.
[a] The sources of the data in each column in this table are detailed in the Table 3 notes.
[b] The figures in these columns are the percentages of total comments about each judicial policy that were unfavorable to that policy.
[c] The percentage figures in this row are the percentages of total positive and negative comments in each survey that were unfavorable to judicial policies. The numbers in the row are the total number of negative comments in each survey. The total number of all comments, both positive and negative, in each survey is reported in Table 3.

rights cases was badly eroded by hostile sentiment toward busing. There was overwhelming opposition to the Court in such highly salient areas as criminal justice and school prayers as well as on a scattering of lower visibility issues that were lumped together in the residual "other" category in our surveys. Overall evaluations of the Court were slightly tilted toward the Court in the 1960s but shifted heavily against it in the 1970s.

All of the Court's major interventions, . . . except the Watergate cases, were initially directed against state policies, and some of them—reapportionment, civil rights, abortion —have at some times appeared to appeal to majorities, however diffuse and badly organized. . . .

It is not persuasive to claim that the Court's resilience in the face of attack was because its policies were directed initially against "state" policies or were consonant with widespread but diffuse public values and opinions. They were "state" policies only in a technical and legal sense. In reality, they were the dominant noneconomic domestic issues of our time; they have been presidential campaign issues since 1964, and the subject of almost continuous efforts to reverse or curb the Supreme Court. Explanations of the Court's resiliency as a policymaker must recognize that many of its major interventions, although initially state directed, have become national issues. Nationally among the public, those interventions have been widely disapproved.

WHY THE COURT ENDURES

We believe that the explanation for the Court's endurance in the face of public hostility toward its decisions and repeated attempts to curb its policies and authority may lie in the complex interaction between ideological activists, ideological elites, the nation's institutional and structural arrangements, and the character of dominant political majorities in the United States. The explanation begins with the commonplace observation that decision-making authority in the national government is widely diffused because of the separation of powers, bicameralism, and complex procedural arrangements within the Congress—such as the filibuster and dispersion of authority among committees and subcommittees. Action by the President and Congress, therefore, generally requires determined and extraordinary majorities in the legislature as well as strong and persistent support among the key figures in the executive department. Given this diffusion of power, a substantial faction—especially if well placed and prepared to commit energy and resources to the task—can block most initiatives. This applies to curbing the Court or overruling its decisions (Murphy et al., 1973: 55) as well as to more conventional policy initiatives of the President and Congress.

In contrast to the complex and difficult path that lies before presidential and congressional initiatives including attacks upon

the Court, the decisions of the Supreme Court are made without prior clearance or approval of others.... Indeed, the Supreme Court has shown a capacity for independent action that has been surprising in light of the total subservience—indeed, the near demise—of judicial authority that New Deal commentators and justices often announced (Shapiro, 1979: 180). Thus, while overruling judicial policies is a complex process checked by decentralized authority, judicial policy initiation does not usually require formal collaboration of the other departments.

That does not suggest, however, that judicial policy initiatives are made without any constraints whatsoever. Dahl (1957: 293–294) has pointed out that the Supreme Court is part of the national lawmaking coalition and is likely on major issues to endorse and advance the major values of that coalition. Moreover, if its policies were to diverge from those on which the national lawmaking majority in the executive and legislative departments were in clear and strong agreement, reversal would be likely. Nonetheless, "within the somewhat narrow limits set by the basic policy goals of the dominant alliance, the Court *can* make national policy." In addition, there "are times when the [national lawmaking] coalition is unstable with respect to certain key policies" and at these times "the Court can intervene ...and may even succeed in establishing policy." The Court is most likely in these times to make policy when

> its action conforms to and reinforces a widespread set of explicit or implicit norms held by the political leadership; norms which are not strong enough or are not distributed in such a way as to insure the existence of an effective lawmaking majority but are, nonetheless, sufficiently powerful to prevent any successful attack on the legitimacy powers of the Court (Dahl, 1957: 293–294).

The national Democratic coalition since 1932 has largely been built on economic and social welfare policy.... Although there may be some increase in the attitudinal consistency of voters and activists on economic and noneconomic issues..., it is nonetheless clear that the Democratic coalition is divided on civil rights, civil liberties, and that collection of contemporary issues that has been recently dubbed "*the social issue*".... It is largely in these latter areas that the Court for the last decades has engaged in major policy initiatives (Shapiro, 1979: 179).

Support for these initiatives has been found among liberal activists. In general, liberal activists have been identified with the Democratic party, and especially its presidential wing (Kessel, 1980: 63–82). In our survey, 75.6% of the activists who described themselves as liberal also identified themselves as Democrats. Although our subsamples are small, some impression of the support for the Court's liberal decisions among Democratic activists is possible. We identified all comments supporting the Court's policies on abortion, defendants' rights, school prayers, civil rights (including school busing), and reapportionment as liberal positions, while opposition to these policies was treated as a conservative posture. Responses to these policies were 80% unfavorable among Democratic inactives and 88.9% hostile among Republican inactives. The comments of Democratic activists were 59.3% favorable to these liberal decisions of the Court, sharply contrasting with the responses of Republican activists, which were only 39.5% favorable.

. . .

What is the link between our finding that liberal "occasional activists" are the constituency within the public at large which supports the Court, and the evidence of the special role of liberal position-holders in the national government in protecting the Supreme Court against attack? First, our data tend to show that the Court's protectors in the national government are not responding to some widespread public reverence and support for the Court as an institution, as has sometimes been supposed. Second, our data add to the growing literature that shows that the public also has not supported many of the Court's most visible recent decisions; there is no widespread popular constituency for those seeking to sustain judicial policies against reversal.

Third, and the most important, however, our data suggest that the liberals in the national government do have a constituency for their efforts to protect the Court. That constituency is liberal political activists. By definition, activists are campaigners and suppliers of political resources. They disproportionately shape the constituency political environment of liberal elected officials, provide them campaign support, and contact them about issues. Liberal activists' support for the Supreme Court thus may reinforce the preexisting disposition of the liberal officeholders to oppose attacks on liberal judicial policies or on the jurisdiction of the courts. Moreover, activists are likely to be opinion leaders, and liberal activists thus may influence public opinion at large by explaining and defending the actions of liberal officeholders in specific battles to defend the Court.

Our findings that liberal political activists strongly support the Supreme Court thus provides an additional piece of the argument explaining the Court's endurance. This constituency encourages, reinforces, and supports the efforts of liberals in the national government, who have been strategically situated in the policymaking process as an important faction in the dominant party coalition, to resist reversals of the Supreme Court's liberal policies or restriction of its jurisdiction.

A similar explanation might well apply to the success of economic conservatives in sustaining the pre-1937 Court's decisions nullifying social welfare policies. Despite repeated adoption of social welfare policies by Democrats and progressive and moderate Republicans in Congress, and in the states, the Supreme Court's nullification of these initiatives was not overruled until a subsequent electoral realignment. Conservative activists within the dominant Republican coalition—especially in the executive branch and among the leadership in the Senate —were able to protect the Court from repeated demands for the restriction of its authority.

If these speculations are correct, the findings in this article and elsewhere of strong support for the modern Court among liberal elites, position-holders, and occasional activists may indeed suggest why, in most historical periods, the Court has survived attacks on its policies and its authority despite widespread public opposition to some of its most visible decisions. It is no longer tenable to continue to assert that the failure of attempts to curb the Court or overturn its policies lies in some widespread public or elite support either for the justices' decisions or for the Court as an institution.

Our explanation of the endurance of judicial authority and policy thus rests on factors for which there is some plausible, though not yet complete, supporting evidence. First, the modern Court's policies and authority have been favored by an ideological minority that was part of the dominant national party coalition. Second, that minority, because of its coalition membership, was represented in a substantial number of strategic positions in the highly diffuse lawmaking structure of the national government. Third, from those positions, it is generally possible to block or delay initiatives to overturn the Supreme Court's decisions or curb its authority. Final-

ly, the overturning of judicial policies that has sometimes occurred in the aftermath of realigning elections is not inconsistent with this explanation.... The ideological faction that has used its strategic location in government to protect judicial decisions is swept from power along with the majority party coalition of which it is part. The new majority party, brought to office by voter repudiation of the old coalition's policies, exercises the appointment power as well as policy making authority and court-curbing devices to sweep away the repudiated policies, including those made by justices of the old regime.

If the Reagan Administration is the beginning of a major political realignment, greater success in curbing the Supreme Court's power or repudiating its decisions—absent of any judicial retreat—would therefore be expected. There is some preliminary evidence that conservative domination of the executive branch and the Senate has displaced the Court's strategically placed liberal supporters and that court-curbing measures therefore now can be moved toward enactment....

Nonetheless, the 1982 congressional session demonstrated again the difficulty of enacting court-curbing legislation. Although a majority in the Senate apparently favored some curbs on the Supreme Court's abortion and school prayer policies, a liberal filibuster thwarted various court-curbing efforts.... The Senate did approve legislation prohibiting busing to desegregate schools..., but that policy languished in the liberal-dominated House Judiciary Committee.... The House approved an appropriations bill amendment prohibiting the Justice Department from seeking busing as a remedy in desegregation suits, but the appropriations measure itself finally failed to pass, partly because of objections to the anti-busing amendment.... Overall, then—despite support in the White House and majorities in the Senate and perhaps in the House—opponents of the Supreme Court's school busing, school prayer, and abortion decisions were unable to enact measures to curb the Court's authority or trim its policies in these areas.... Only the passage of time and events will finally confirm or deny the occurrence of a realignment and the final defeat of the Court's strategically placed liberal supporters in the national government and the country. The 1982 congressional elections, however, strengthened the liberal bloc in the House of Representatives at least temporarily, making any immediate overriding of the Court's policies unlikely.

The events of 1982, then, add weight to the argument that the Court's persistence as a policymaker is principally explained by the link between activist sectors of the population sympathetic to the Court's policies and elected officials whose strategic placement in the national policymaking process and employment of delaying tactics prevent curtailment of the Court's authority or policies. The temporary political victories may lead to long-term preservation of judicial policy when a subsequent election fails, as in 1982, either to confirm a realignment or to give the Court's opponents a decisive majority in the lawmaking branches.

REFERENCES

Adamany, D. and M. Shelley II (1980) "Encore! The forgetful voter." Public Opinion Q. 44 (Summer): 234–240.

Arnold, T. (1962) The Symbols of Government. New York: Harcourt, Brace, Jovanovich.

Beiser, E. (1972) "Lawyers judge the Warren Court." Law & Society Rev. 7 (Fall): 139–149.

Caldeira, G. (1977a) "Children's images of the Supreme Court: a preliminary mapping." Law & Society Rev. 11 (Summer): 851–871.

——— (1977b) "Judges judge the Supreme Court." Judicature 61 (November): 208–219.

Casey, G. (1976) "Popular perceptions of Supreme Court rulings." Amer. Politics Q. 4 (January): 3–45.

Corwin, E. (1936) "The Constitution as instrument and as symbol." Amer. Pol. Sci. Rev. 30 (December): 1071–1085.

Dahl, R. A. (1957) "Decision-making in a democracy: the Supreme Court as a national policy-maker." J. of Public Law 6 (Fall): 279–295.

Dolbeare, K. (1967) "The public views the Supreme Court," in H. Jacob (ed.) Law, Politics and the Federal Courts. Boston: Little, Brown.

Easton, D. and J. Dennis (1969) Children in the Political System: Origins of Political Legitimacy. New York: McGraw-Hill.

Frank, J. (1930) Law and the Modern Mind. New York: Brentano's.

Gallup, G. (1978) "Huge majority would grant right to abortion." Gallup Opinion Index 153 (April): 25–29.

——— (1976) "Anti-abortion constitutional amendment." Gallup Opinion Index 128 (March): 20.

——— (1974) "Abortion ruling." Gallup Opinion Index 106 (April): 24.

——— (1973) "Public evenly divided on issue of abortion during early stage of pregnancy." Gallup Opinion Index 92 (February): 21–23.

——— (1969) "Abortion." Gallup Opinion Index 54 (December): 19.

Handberg, R. and H. Hill (1980) "Court curbing, court reversals and judicial review; the Supreme Court versus Congress." Law & Scoiety Rev. 14 (Winter): 309–322.

Kessel, J. (1980) Presidential Campaign Politics: Coalition Strategies and Citizen

Response. Homewood, IL: Dorsey.

——— (1966) "Public perceptions of the Supreme Court." Midwest (Amer.) J. of Pol. Sci. 10 (May): 167–191.

Lehnen, R. and J. Reynolds (1978) "The impact of judicial activism on public opinion." Amer. J. of Pol. Sci. 22 (November): 896–904.

Lehnen, R. (1976) American Institutions, Political Opinion, and Public Policy. Hinsdale, IL: Dryden.

Lerner, M. (1937) "Constitution and court as symbols." Yale Law Journal 46 (December): 1290–1319.

Llewellyn, K. (1934) "The Constitution as an institution." Columbia Law Rev. 34 (January): 1–40.

Murphy, W. and J. Tanenhaus (1970) "The U.S. Supreme Court and its elite publics: a preliminary report." Delivered at the 1970 Congress of the International Political Science Association.

——— (1968a) "Public opinion and the United States Supreme Court." Law & Society Rev. 2 (May): 357–384.

——— (1968b) "Public opinion and Supreme Court: the Goldwater campaign." Public Opinion Q. 32 (Spring): 31–50.

——— and D. Kastner (1973) Public Evaluations of Constitutional Courts: Alternative Explanations. Beverly Hills, CA: Sage.

Nexon, D. (1971) "Asymmetry in the political system: occasional activists in the Republican and Democratic parties, 1957–1964." Amer. Pol. Sci. Rev. 65 (September): 716–730.

Opinion Roundup (1981) "Conservatism: a national review." Public Opinion 4 (February–March): 19–42.

Shapiro, M. (1979) "The Supreme Court: from Warren to Burger," in A. King (ed.) The New American Political System. Washington, DC: American Enterprise Institute.

Tanenhaus, J. and W. Murphy (1981) "Patterns of public support for the Supreme Court: a panel study." J. of Politics 43 (February): 24–39.

Neither the Purse nor the Sword: Dynamics of Public Confidence in the Supreme Court

Gregory A. Caldeira

. . . The lack of any formal connection to the electorate and its rather demonstrable vulnerability before the president and Congress mean that the United States Supreme Court must depend to an extraordinary extent on the confidence, or at least the acquiescence, of the public. Mr. Justice Frankfurter stated the quandary more eloquently: "The Court's authority—possessed of neither the purse nor the sword—ultimately rests on sustained public confidence in its moral sanction" (*Baker* v. *Carr* [1962]; see also *United States* v. *Lee* [1882]). Virtually all scholars agree that the Supreme Court plays a crucial role in the making of national policy (Casper, 1976; Dahl, 1957; Shapiro, 1979), but if the Court is the "least dangerous branch," how do the justices manage to hold sway much of the time even in the face of substantial "law-making majorities" (cf. Barnum, 1985)? To account for this anomaly, some "commentators have attributed the Court's endurance as a national policymaker to its special status with the public" (Adamany and Grossman, 1983, p. 406).

Reprinted from *American Political Science Review*, 80 (1986), 1209–1210, 1212–1214, 1219–1226. Reprinted with permission of author and publisher. All notes and most references omitted.

For the most part, lamentably, empirical researchers have painted a dreary and unencouraging portrait of public attitudes toward the Court. Citizens know surprisingly little about the Court and the workings of the judicial branch, manifest scant concern about its personnel and about most decisions, and offer support contingent upon agreement with specific public policies. . . . This brief set of generalizations, understandably enough, stems from data collected in cross-sections of the public. Yet, despite the widespread consensus these days about the importance and desirability of developing an understanding of the dynamics or temporal dimension of public opinion and other political phenomena, no one has undertaken a study of changes in public support for the Supreme Court across time. . . . Fortunately, since 1966 Louis Harris Associates and the National Opinion Research Center have queried members of the American public on a relatively regular basis about confidence in a number of institutions, including the Court. In this article, armed with a time series of observations from 1966 through 1984, I provide a description of the ebb and flow of public esteem for the Court and then develop and test several plausible propositions about the dynamics of support.

. . . .

MEASURING SUPPORT FOR THE SUPREME COURT

During the storm over Franklin D. Roosevelt's "Court-Packing Plan" in 1937 and in the aftermath of *Brown* v. *Board of Education*, pollsters invested a fair amount of expense and energy in monitoring public attitudes toward the Supreme Court repeatedly over an extended period of time—in the former case, throughout 1937; in the latter, from 1954 through the early 1960s.... Because the interest of elite and mass publics inevitably moved on to new topics, polling operations soon dropped questions on the Court. The wording of items on the Court shifted with the focus of controversy. Thus, even though we now have data on public opinion and the Court from 1935 to the present, we have only recently begun to accumulate a lengthy string of comparable observations....

In February of 1966, Louis Harris Associates, for the first time, asked a national sample of Americans, "As far as the people running the Supreme Court are concerned, would you say you have a great deal of confidence, only some confidence, or hardly any confidence at all in them?" Nearly a year later, Harris posed the question again and then dropped the matter entirely until August of 1971. In 1973 the National Opinion Research Center (NORC) began to ask the question on an annual basis in the General Social Survey, missing only one year in the last decade. Over the period from 1966 through 1984, NORC and Harris have asked the same question in 29 separate surveys. For students of the Court, these 29 points constitute a rich lode of data. To be sure, one wishes for a larger number; after all, research on public evaluations of the president often includes hundreds of observations. Accordingly, I have taken particular aim at the parsimonious selection of independent variables.

To measure support for the Court, I have opted for the percentage of each sample who responded with "great confidence" in the justices. Figure 1, which displays this number from 1966 through 1984, illustrates the ebb and flow of public support for the Supreme Court. To place public attitudes toward the Court in a broader context, I shall also call attention to materials on Congress and the executive branch (Harris, various years; National Opinion Research Corporation, various years).

Quite clearly, public confidence in the incumbents of the Court has taken a sharp secular decline from 1966 through 1984. More precisely, during this period support has on average dropped 2.2% each year ($Y = 35.5 - 2.2 \cdot Time$; $r^2 = .50$). Whereas about half of the public registered great confidence in the Court early in 1966, only one-third did so during 1984. Even if one considers 1967 as the base, support has dropped by a rather considerable amount. Public confidence in the Court hit rock bottom in 1971 and reached apogees in 1966 and 1974. Of course we have no way of knowing whether the degree of support recorded in 1966 typified public evaluations in the mid-1960s or whether it was entirely out of step. Confidence in the incumbents of the Court, unlike diffuse support..., has varied a great deal, as the jagged pattern attests. For the entire period, support has a mean of 32%, a standard deviation of 5.5, and a range of 27%. Much of the variation, to be sure, stems from the rapid decline in the late 1960s. If, for example, we restrict our attention to the 1970s and 1980s, confidence in the Court actually ranges from 23% to 40%, for a mean of 30.5 and a standard deviation of 4.0.

Yet confidence does not bob around randomly; change comes gradually. In the late 1960s and the early 1970s, the decline and then rebound of confidence in the Supreme Court marched in step with patterns for other

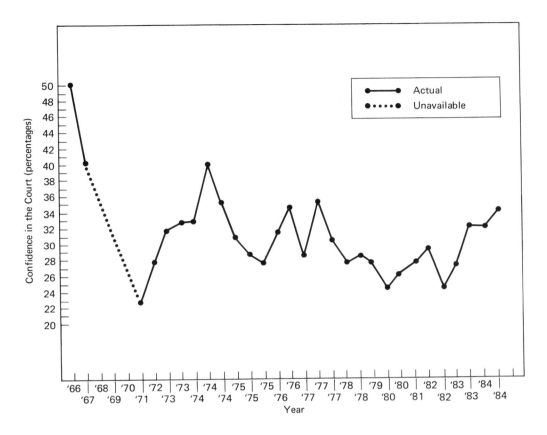

FIGURE 1. Patterns of Confidence in the Court: 1966–1984

political and social institutions. For the Court, "Watergate" translated into a major temporary gain of public support. Judges and courts, after all, had stood as bastions of the rule of law against the attempts by Nixon and associates to evade justice. Paradoxically, though Congress played a more central role in Watergate than did the Court, the public gave the incumbents of the national legislature much less credit. By 1978, confidence in the Court was again on the decline, perhaps reflecting a general discontent with institutions caused by economic instability. In the last four surveys, support for the Court, along with that for Congress and the president, has increased markedly, consonant with the many reports of an increase in optimism since the midpoint of the first Reagan administration. Finally, across the entire period, the public has bestowed greater confidence in the incumbents of the Court than in those of Congress and usually by quite a large margin.

EXPLANATIONS OF SUPPORT FOR THE COURT

Thus far I have established that support for the Court varies considerably over time;

of this there can be little doubt. Now, the more significant issue is, What, precisely, accounts for these perturbations in public confidence? It is conceivable, on the one hand, that support for the Court responds to changes in societal conditions: as the quality of life declines, so, too, does faith in the justices. On the other hand, perhaps members of the public react to events, politics, and judicial behavior. Large happenings on the political landscape could shape public perceptions of the high bench. The justices themselves, through their own actions, might increase or decrease esteem for the Court, or public feeling about the Court could simply follow sentiment toward other political institutions....

FINDINGS

Over the period from 1966 through 1984, ebbs and flows of confidence in the Court responded, to a surprisingly large extent, to the happenstances of political events (see Table 1). During and immediately after the consummation of Watergate and the resignation of President Nixon, support for the Supreme Court shot up more than 10 points. The Court benefitted from the president's woes, ...in part because of its association with defenses of the "Constitution" against what many in 1973 and 1974 perceived as frontal assaults on the underpinnings of the legal order. Similarly, before wholesale disillusionment and demoralization spread at the end of the Johnson administration, support for the justices ran a full 13% above the norm for the entire period under investigation ($\alpha_9 = 12.5$). Public attitudes toward the Court, as well as toward virtually every element of the American "Establishment," fell in the late 1960s from the lofty pedestals of the years of Eisenhower and Kennedy. The Court may have suffered somewhat more than others from loss of public esteem

because of perceived connections with problems of race, crime, and cultural disorder, but the justices shared the company of a distinguished group.

Confidence in the Court, unlike support for Congress and the president, reflects the palpitations of economic conditions in what I can most charitably describe as a muted fashion. Bad economic times do not, of course, translate into increases in public esteem for the justices, but they do not seem to hurt a great deal. Thus, for example, the rate of unemployment failed to muster a statistically significant coefficient even as it appeared to manifest the expected negative effect ($\alpha_2 = -0.55; p < 0.43$). Inflation presaged, as I hypothesized, deleterious consequences for public support for the Court; for each increase of 1% in the consumer index of prices, the proportion that recorded considerable esteem dropped more than half of 1% ($\alpha_1 = -0.51; p < .23$). This relationship, though far from secure, survived a passel of tests I contrived to detect spuriousness. How can we account for the differential effects of inflation and unemployment? For one, although most of us express concern over the plight of the jobless, the rate of unemployment directly affects only a fraction of the citizenry; even at the high tides of economic depression, only a few feel the pinch. To the contrary, because everyone purchases goods and services, inflation, particularly at high levels, presumably holds a greater potential for wreaking havoc with the overall public mood and feelings of confidence. It is commonplace that extended bouts of inflation call into doubt the performance of political and economic actors. That jobs and the stability of prices should on the whole make only a modest dent in confidence in the Court reflects, without doubt, the lack of any direct connection in the public mind between the justices and economic activities. In an odd way, then, the lack

TABLE 1
Confidence in the Supreme Court

Independent Variables	Estimates[a]		
	b	t ratio	Level of Significance
Intercept	45.44	4.58	.000
Political events/conditions			
Watergate	10.58	2.79	.012
Johnson administration	12.53	2.89	.010
Presidential popularity	0.11	1.85	.082
Social/economic conditions			
Rate of crime	−0.00	−0.01	.986
Rate of unemployment	−0.55	−0.79	.436
Inflation	−0.51	−1.24	.231
Judicial actions			
Salience of the Court	0.08	1.97	.065
Invalidation of federal laws	−2.35	−1.90	.074
Court's support for defendants' rights	−0.21	−1.98	.064
	$R^2 = .79$	$DF = 17$	$N = 27$

[a] After testing for the significance of the autoregressive terms in an initial run, I have excluded them from this equation.

of compelling relationships between confidence and economic conditions testifies to the rationality of the ebb and flow of public evaluations of the Supreme Court.

Surprisingly, despite record-shattering rates of change in the 1960s and 1970s, crime as recorded by the F.B.I. had no influence on the amount of confidence the public bestowed upon the Supreme Court. Indeed, of all of the variables, the rate of crime manifests the most diminutive regression coefficient and the least significant t ratio in the statistical sense. In the face of steep and very real increases in the rate of crime, the U.S. public apparently failed to hold the Court responsible for this social problem. The middle 1960s, a time of accelerating rates of crime, encompassed high levels of support for the Supreme Court; the late 1970s, a period of markedly less-pronounced movements upward in the incidence of criminal activities, produced relatively low evalua-

tions of the justices among the public. . . . Thus, if the local newspaper or television station dramatizes the threat of crime, members of the public manifest more anxiety about personal security. . . . In sum, from the results in Table 1 and earlier research, it seems likely that the media must focus on crime before people express much concern and place blame on the Court.

Proponents of the view that the citizenry associates the justices and the Supreme Court with the presidency can find considerable succor in the statistical results in Table 1. Presidential popularity does indeed exercise a statistically significant, albeit modest, influence on the amount of confidence the public accords the Court. For each 10% increase in popular approval of the president, *ceteris paribus*, public confidence in the Supreme Court increases by approximately 1% ($\alpha_3 = .114; p < .082$). Furthermore, in analyses not presented here, the relationship between presidential popularity and confidence in the Court grows ever stronger and more secure in successively more parsimonious versions of the model. These results, moreover, should encourage scholars who have hypothesized that the amount of public support for various institutions tends to move upward and downward together—to a considerable degree in lock step. Members of the public, in this conception, record happiness or displeasure with our institutions across the board. Some auxiliary statistical analyses provide further evidence of this phenomenon. For example, confidence in the Court and in Congress track closely during much of this period. Without more extensive data, however, I cannot make an informed choice between the two formulations outlined here. Let it suffice to say that, for whatever reason, presidential popularity and confidence in the Supreme Court most of the time move in the same direction.

Contrary to conventional wisdom, in the case of the Court, familiarity does not breed contempt—or so the results in Table 1 seem to suggest. Greater public visibility of the Court, in fact, translates into a higher degree of support among the public. For each increase of 12% in the amount of coverage of the Court in the *New York Times, ceteris paribus*, Harris and NORC have recorded on average an increase of 1% in confidence in the Supreme Court ($\alpha_5 = .077; p > .065$). . . . So the fundamental question remains, Why does public opinion behave in this fashion? It is, after all, difficult to believe that the Supreme Court reaps increased public esteem from publicity on the controversial decisions the justices must inevitably hand down each term. Quite to the contrary, I believe, we can account for the positive association between the salience of Court and public confidence in the justices if we concentrate on the institutional focus of much reporting in the newspapers. Apart

from the usual flow of stories on decisions, the *New York Times* and other newspapers on occasion write up individual justices or the Court as a whole, for the most part divorced from the content of the docket. Even so-called investigative stories on the Supreme Court or particular justices almost always present the institution in an extraordinarily positive light. The conjunctions between the ebb and flow of the *Times's* coverage of the Court and the series on public confidence provide some circumstantial evidence for these speculations. In the final analysis, I suspect the content of the stories on the Court matters a good deal more than the sheer number. That, of course, is an empirical issue and one someone can test with further data.

As expected, judicial activism, in the form of invalidations of federal statutes, cost the Supreme Court dearly in the court of public opinion. . . . For each federal statute the Court has struck down in the past 17 years, public confidence in the justices has declined about 2.4% ($\alpha_4 = -2.35; p < .07$). The losers of litigation, inside and outside the Court, have made such a claim for so long and so many times that the putatively negative consequences of judicial activism have risen to the status of a shibboleth. Nonetheless, the evidence presented here buttresses this ancient pearl of wisdom. To the extent that federal law at any point represents the strong preferences of a majority, the Supreme Court treads on thin ice in the act of invalidating large numbers of statutes. Over the years, as the Supreme Court invalidates federal laws, the justices amass a coalition of enemies, groups and individuals whose views of public policy have lost favor and who will naturally accord the high bench less confidence. Expressed consistently, judicial opposition to Congress may in and of itself lead to resentment and loss of trust among the public—not because of any great love of the national legislature but, rather, as a result of a perception that the Court has upset the balance of our constitutional system. Citizens may indeed view Congress as the "broken branch," but they also have a stake in the process by which national officials check one another. There is, of course, no way of knowing with these data why the public responds in a negative fashion to judicial negations of congressional statutes. Regardless of the precise mechanism, however, I have adduced strong evidence that judicial activism does exact a significant cost in the coin of public confidence.

Public support has, in fact, responded in a significant fashion to changes in the Court's solicitude for the rights of individuals accused of crime. As the Supreme Court has manifested proportionately greater sympathy for criminal defendants, the public has in turn registered a sharp drop in confidence in the justices. More specifically, for every increase of 10% in the share of cases decided in favor of the accused, public support has declined somewhat more than 2% ($\alpha_7 = -0.21$). Two percent does not sound like a devastating blow, but concrete applications provide a graphic illustration of the consequences of the Court's drift in public policy toward the accused: as an empirical matter, judicial support for criminal defendants varied from 12% to 83% during the period from 1966 to 1984, and a shift of 20% or more from year to year happened several times. It goes without saying that members of the public do not make subtle distinctions in their thinking about the direction of the criminal law, and in view of the soup-like quality of individual responses to law and legal institutions, I do not wish to argue that the citizenry forms sharply defined conceptions of the Court or its policies. However, these results suggest that the mass public as a whole responds in a systematic

fashion to shifts in the public policies the justices enunciate. Clearly, the public has little sympathy for either the esoterica of criminal procedure or the people who most often utilize these safeguards and apparently translates these attitudes into lack of confidence in the Court. Thus, like judicial activism, solicitude for the accused exacts significant costs to the Supreme Court among the citizenry.

CONCLUSION

Public support for the Supreme Court varies a great deal over time and eludes simple accounts, but in this article I have attempted to trace meaningful shifts in confidence and, more importantly, to frame and evaluate alternative explanations of the dynamics of esteem for the Court. These rival hypotheses include political events; the rates of crime, unemployment, and inflation; presidential popularity; judicial activism; salience of the Court among the public; and the justices' solicitude for the rights of the accused. Broadly speaking, I conclude that during the period from 1966 through 1984, crime and economic conditions played relatively small roles as determinants of public confidence and that political events and judicial actions registered striking impacts on changes in the public's view of the justices. More specifically, in descending order, the Johnson administration, Watergate, judicial support for the accused, the salience of the Court, invalidations of federal laws, and presidential popularity brought about statistically significant movements in public feelings toward the justices of the Supreme Court during this period.

What do these results mean? Citizens as individuals, evince little or no knowledge of or concern for the Court; to the extent that they express sensible opinions, they base judgments on the vaguest and crudest of ideological frameworks. Social scientists have demonstrated this over and over again, and yet, in the aggregate, shifts in public confidence in the Court march to the beat of a markedly policy-oriented drummer. Public evaluations of the Court do not float freely, in a seemingly aimless fashion, unconnected to the perturbations of the political and legal processes. Rather, in evaluating the justices, the public appears to respond to events on the political landscape and to actions taken by the Supreme Court. If, for example, the Court adopts a position against a law-making majority, the public accordingly exacts a cost in confidence—a rational calculus indeed. In broad outlines, then, the dynamics of aggregate support for the Court bear a remarkable resemblance to those for Congress and the presidency (Kernell, 1978; Parker, 1977). It is easy to forget that individuals' responses to the presidency and Congress hardly constitute a model of clarity or stability, for scholars of these institutions have spoiled us with crisp, neat political explanations of presidential popularity. Until now, however, scholars of the Court have worked solely with individual-level data and have, naturally enough, emphasized the poor quality of public evaluations of the justices. In this article, with aggregate data, I have portrayed the relationship between the public and the Court as somewhat more rational and calculated than have previous researchers. I do not, of course, wish to press my claim for rationality very far, but I do think that in the literature we have oversold our pessimistic view of public evaluations of the Court, just as students of elections for many years unfairly characterized voters as ignorant and apathetic. For the Supreme Court, as for Congress and the presidency, the movement of public—as opposed to individual—opinion comes much closer to meeting our conventional prescriptions.

REFERENCES

Adamany, David W., and Joel B. Grossman. 1983. Support for the Supreme Court as a National Policymaker, *Law & Policy Quarterly*, 5: 405–37.

Baker v. *Carr*. 1962. 369 U.S. 186, 267.

Barnum, David G. 1985. The Supreme Court and Public Opinion: Judicial Decision-Making in the Post-New Deal Period. *Journal of Politics*, 47: 652–66.

Casper, Jonathan D. 1976. The Supreme Court and National Policy Making. *American Political Science Review*, 70: 50–63.

Dahl, Robert A. 1957. Decision Making in a Democracy: The Supreme Court as a National Policy-Maker. *Journal of Public Law*, 6: 279–95.

Harris, Louis. Various Issues. *The Harris Survey*. New York.

Kernell, Samuel. 1978. Explaining Presidential Popularity. *American Political Science Review*, 72: 506–22.

National Opinion Research Center. Various Years. *The General Social Survey*. Chicago, IL.

Parker, Glenn R. 1977. Some Themes in Congressional Unpopularity. *American Journal of Political Science*, 21: 93–110.

Shapiro, Martin M. 1979. The Supreme court: From Warren to Burger. In Anthony King, ed., *The New American Political System*, pp. 179–211. Washington, D.C.: American Enterprise Institute for Public Policy Research.

United States v. *Lee*. 1882. 109 U.S. 196, 223.

PART TWO

Participants

CHAPTER 6

Litigants and Lawyers

Courts, as dispute-processing institutions, bring together a relatively distinct, if shifting, group of participants—legal specialists as well as people without such expertise. Furthermore, these participants bring to judicial proceedings diverse and divergent interests, values, and perspectives that exert important influences on the way in which disputes are processed.

Since the business of courts is to process disputes, the most obvious participants must be the disputants. Private citizens, private organizations, and government officials attempt to manage their own interpersonal relations and to regulate their own behavior and the behavior of others. They are the ones who initiate judicial proceedings. It is their inability to manage conflict successfully in private or informal ways that gives courts an agenda of dispute-processing business. However, not all citizens, organizations, or officials are equally able or willing to use courts. Problems of cost, efficiency, and appropriateness differentially affect potential consumers of court services. The result is that there are two distinct types of litigants.

Marc Galanter, in his now classic article, labels these two types of litigants "one-shotters" and "repeat-players." They are distinguished, as the labels suggest, by the relative frequency with which they are involved in litigation. As Galanter suggests, "Because of differences in their size, differences in the state of the law and differences in their resources, some of the actors in society have many occasions to utilize the courts...to make...claims; others do so only rarely."[1] Repeat-players are typically, according to Galanter, large units whose investment in or interest in a particular case is relatively small. Automobile insurance companies are a clear example of a type of repeat litigant that conforms with Galanter's description. Such companies are frequently involved in disputes with their policyholders or with those who have been injured by a policyholder. These disputes frequently end up in court. Because of the frequency of their participation in judicial proceedings, such companies have distinctive interests in litigation; for example, they have an interest in structuring judicial rules so as to provide advantages for themselves in subsequent cases.[2] Parties that have only a "one-shot" interest in litigation are typically more interested in the substantive result of their case than in the way in which the decision may in the future affect the disposition of other cases. The first selection in this chapter by Grossman et al., provides an interesting empirical test of aspects of Galanter's hypothesis.

The selections by O'Connor and Epstein and by Wasby demonstrate how a long-run interest in rules may lead private organizations to sponsor cases and invest resources in an attempt to influence the way in which courts deal with particular types of cases (although interest groups do not do this to the extent commonly assumed).[3] Not only do repeat-players have distinctive interests, but their frequent appearances in court enable them to develop expertise. Such expertise is reflected in the way in which they select cases for litigation as well as in the manner in which they carry on disputes that have been transformed into lawsuits. Their participation can be contrasted with that of the infrequent participant, whose interest in litigation is more substantive and whose expertise is minimal.

The fact that courts operate or are supposed to operate in accordance with standards and rules established by law means that participation in judicial proceedings is participation in a particular and special kind of process—a process of "discovering" and applying applicable rules. This process requires special knowledge, training, and expertise, all of which are provided by members of the legal profession. Lawyers stand between disputants and the judicial system. Disputants, before they can bring their problems to court, typically need to enlist the help of trained legal practitioners who advise disputants as to the state of legal rules and the ways in which those rules might apply to the issues in dispute. They do so by predicting how courts will interpret the law and find facts. Thus they screen out some types of disputes and, at the same time, promote the movement of other disputes into the judicial process.[4]

Lawyers are not, however, neutral technicians. They have their own interests and values, which affect the advice they give and their own performance in court. Lawyers are, to use Galanter's term, particular kinds of repeat-players. But not all lawyers are directly involved in litigation. Most lawyers in the United States are primarily givers of advice or technicians primarily responsible for carrying out certain routine transactions (such as writing wills). Relatively few lawyers regularly argue cases in court. Some of these litigating lawyers specialize in particular areas of law (such as criminal or divorce law); some represent only particular kinds of parties, and some limit themselves to representing particular parties within particular areas of law.

The most important distinction that can be made among types of litigating lawyers is the manner in which they perceive their clientele. This distinction has been discussed by political scientist Jonathan Casper.[5] Casper argues that some lawyers, admittedly a small although perhaps a growing number, see themselves primarily as representatives of the interests of the public as a whole. Individual cases are simply vehicles for achieving broad public objectives generally requiring significant changes in the law. This type of lawyer is interested in the issues of public policy raised by a case rather than in the case itself. Such lawyers typically take only cases that they believe involve issues of major importance.[6]

Another type of lawyer is identified as a representative of particular interests or organizations. For example, some private organizations establish their own in-house counsel whose function is to represent members of the organization in cases of importance to that organization.

The third type of lawyer, most commonly criminal defense lawyers, perceive their clientele as coextensive with the court in which they typically practice and their most important function as the maintenance of the efficiency and productivity of the court organization with which they deal. Since they generally practice before the same judges and prosecutors, it is in the professional interest of these lawyers to maintain good relations with those members of the court organization. This interest may, as the selection by Blumberg indicates, conflict with the interests of the individuals whom they nominally represent.[7]

The fourth and last type of litigating lawyers we call the "client advocate." It is described in the selection by Kenneth Mann. These lawyers approximate the stereotypic Perry Mason model. They see their role primarily as serving individuals. Client advocates are interested solely in the cases in which they are involved; they will do everything that they can to ensure favorable results for their clients. In the view of the client advocate the lawyer is merely a technician put in the service of a case, not a cause.

The different types of lawyers behave differently in advising disputants whether to litigate and in developing and employing strategies of litigation. The readings in this chapter analyze these differences and their consequences for disputants and for courts as dispute-processing institutions.

NOTES

1. Marc Galanter, "Why the 'Haves' Come Out Ahead: Speculations on the Limits of Legal Change," *Law and Society Review* 9 (1974), 95.
2. See Laurence Ross, *Settled Out of Court* (Chicago: Aldine, 1970).
3. See Clement Vose, *Constitutional Change* (Lexington: Lexington Books, 1972). Also Frank Sorauf, *The Wall of Separation* (Princeton: Princeton University Press, 1976) and Stephen Wasby, "Interest Group Litigation in an Age of Complexity," in *Interest Group Politics*, eds. Allan J. Cigler and Burdett A. Loomis (Washington: Congressional Quarterly, 1983).
4. See Douglas Rosenthal, *Lawyers and Clients: Who's in Charge?* (New York: Russell Sage Foundation, 1974). See also Austin Sarat and William Felstiner, "Law and Strategy in the Divorce Lawyer's Office," *Law and Society Review* 20 (1986), 93.
5. See Jonathan Casper, *Lawyers Before the Warren Court* (Urbana: University of Illinois Press, 1972).
6. Also see Philip Selznick, "Social Advocacy and the Legal Profession in the United States," *Juridicial Review* 1974 (1974), 113.
7. It is important to recognize that the largest number of lawyers in this category are employed by or work for government.

Dimensions of Institutional Participation: Who Uses the Courts, and How?

Joel B. Grossman
Austin Sarat
Herbert M. Kritzer
Stephen McDougal
Kristin Bumiller
Richard Miller

...Our central purpose is to examine the manner in which trial courts of general jurisdiction acquire their cases and process them. We are interested in....the "consumption" of court services, and in describing the range and particularities of differences among courts in patterns and styles of court usage.

There is no general theory of courts which provides the key to understanding differential court usage. There are, however, theories at all levels of generality which are relevant to our inquiry. For example, it is almost axiomatic among dispute-processing researchers that disputes involving closer, more intense, and, particularly, *continuing* relationships are less likely to be brought to court than are disputes between parties with only formal or fleeting ties to each other. Quite often the only relationship between the parties in a lawsuit is that arising out of the dispute itself; automobile accident cases are a prominent example.

Galanter has argued that litigation favors

"repeat players" over "one shotters," and his contention, bolstered by Wanner's data published almost simultaneously, has led to another common—but possibly erroneous—assumption that civil litigation is primarily (or at least prototypically) the forum where organizational creditors sue individual debtors. Our data cannot speak directly to the first theory, but they are at odds with the second.

A third cluster of middle-range theories holds that civil litigation has evolved into a forum which is concerned predominantly with the routine administration of legal documents rather than with the actual adjudication and resolution of disputes. There is no question that courts today are much less concerned with commercial disputes and conflicts over property, and much more concerned with family and domestic disputes and personal injury cases. These kinds of cases are settled characteristically out of court or, if uncontested, merely processed by the courts routinely. We do not have the longitudinal data needed to contest or to confirm the developmental aspects of this cluster of theories. But we can make a modest contribution to the normative issue

Reprinted from *Journal of Politics* 44 pp. 1, 86–114. © 1982 by the University of Texas Press. Footnotes omitted.

of whether the courts have strayed too far from their traditional adversarial mode.

Our emphasis in this paper is on macro-level variables, those more systemic than individual in nature, which speak to aggregate tendencies—the mores, values, and modes of participation. We see these kinds of variables, which are often grouped under the rubric of "political culture," as a *starting point* in understanding differential patterns of court usage from a political perspective. Our assumption was that such patterns would vary across the courts in our sample, and that the variance might be explained in whole or in part by the indicators commonly employed as surrogate measures of political culture.

Political culture is (in one of many competing definitions) a "pattern of orientation to political action in which each political system is embedded." Three political subcultures have been identified in the United States: traditionalistic, individualistic, and moralistic.

In the *traditionalistic* subculture, government is the means by which a hierarchical power structure is preserved. Politics—or at least political leadership—is a privilege for an established elite rather than a public right or duty. Participation is restrictive, conflict is discouraged or suppressed, and orderly processes are maintained. Generally speaking, the status quo is preserved. The role of government is limited; conflicts are resolved through private dispute settlement processes, often very informal ones. There is a great stake in establishing and maintaining personal relationships.

In the *individualistic* subculture, government is viewed as an extension of the marketplace. Its function is to assist in the smooth operation of the economic system. Politics is a low-status enterprise engaged in primarily by career politicians motivated by self-interest. Partisan politics is important, patronage valued, and civil service viewed with suspicion. The political role of citizens is to vote, but little else. Politics centers on parties and personalities rather than on issues or ideologies.

In the *moralistic* subculture, government is viewed more as a commonwealth. If the goal of government is enhancement of the public good, politics is its servant—a lofty and beneficial enterprise. Citizens are expected to participate fully, and public officials are chosen on the basis of merit rather than partisan service. Pursuit of the public interest is the engine which keeps the system going; elections focus on issues rather than on parties or personalities.

None of the political culture designations makes specific reference to participation in the legal process or use of the courts. It is therefore necessary for us to make certain assumptions. Participation in courts is a function of both the volume and type of dispute incidence, and the proportions of those disputes translated into lawsuits. The incidence of disputes is a function of the opportunity for conflicts to arise, a variety of individual and macro-level demographic variables (individual-disputing capability), and the local-disputing experience and culture. The dispute incidence is, in turn, the baseline measure from which we try to explain court participation, and we assume that the translation of disputes into lawsuits is affected by political culture variables. Our understanding of the translation of disputes into lawsuits is complicated, however, by the apparently inseparable effects of demographic variables on both dispute incidence and political culture. Notwithstanding this complexity of relationships, we are hypothesizing that political culture represents a cluster of intermediate-level variables which affect or produce a local culture of court usage.

Our inquiry is not limited to analyzing the

propensity to litigate. It extends to the *mode* of litigation, the ways in which courts are used in the resolution of disputes. We believe that the same political culture variables which might explain litigation propensity will also bear on aspects of litigation mode. For example, we are vitally interested in *who* litigates—which persons, organizations, and interests use the courts. Are the courts heavily involved in the resolution of personal disputes, or are they primarily oriented toward the business community? Is litigation dominated by elites and organizations? These are important questions. Our data can provide only partial answers, since we have limited our sample of cases to "middle-range" disputes in general jurisdiction trial courts. Many of the ordinary disputes of citizens might well end up in *a* court, but perhaps a lower-level tribunal such as a small claims court.

A second dimension of litigation mode is the source of litigation, and the motivations (goals) of those who bring disputes to court. What kinds of cases come to these courts? Apart from formal, legal designations, are they cases raising issues of personal rights, or are they primarily cases requiring adjustments for economic loss, or a balancing of interest?

Third, and finally, we are interested in the degree of adversariness which characterizes the litigation process, as measured by the rates (modes) of settlement of disputes and the contentiousness between the parties manifested in utilization of discovery procedures.

Characterizing these indicators of participation in litigation along political culture lines is not easy and the results, as the reader will soon observe, do not yield neat and easily explainable patterns. What we might expect to find, however, is that disputing incidence, the propensity to litigate, the domination of litigation by organizations and

business cases, and contentiousness would be highest in those locations with a moralistic (or modern) orientation. More litigation, and more contentious litigation, are to be expected among social or economic equals in an impersonal society where alternative informal social networks of dispute resolution may not be available.

Conversely, fewer, less contentious, less organization-dominated disputes are to be expected in the more traditionalistic cultures. Here, where litigation is resorted to less often and is, relatively speaking, much less "the norm," the use of courts would be more formal; more cases would be settled out of court. In such courts we also might expect to find that cases are more oriented toward resolution of "principled" disputes and less so toward the mere adjustment of interests....

[I]

The data and analysis presented in this paper are part of the Civil Litigation Research Project (CLRP). CLRP is a large-scale, federally funded investigation of the costs of civil litigation. Extensive data have been collected on samples of "middle-range disputes" which were settled bilaterally, disputes which were brought to various non-judicial dispute-processing institutions, and disputes which resulted in formal litigation. These data include information gathered by survey research techniques and from the official records of courts and other dispute-processing institutions.

Data utilized in *this* paper are drawn from four sources: a household telephone-screening survey of 5,000 individuals selected through random digit-dialing techniques; data from the records of 1,649 cases in state and federal courts; telephone interviews with litigants in these cases; and a survey of state and federal judges conducted for the U.S. Department of Justice contemporaneously with CLRP by an independent survey research firm. In each instance the data were collected in five federal judicial districts. To increase the generalizability of the overall study, we sought to insure that there was substantial variation among our five districts. Consequently, we selected two large urban districts, Central California (Los Angeles) and Eastern Pennsylvania (Philadelphia); two smaller urban districts, Eastern Wisconsin (Milwaukee) and New Mexico (Albuquerque); and one southern, predominantly rural district, South Carolina (Columbia). No five districts could constitute a true sample of the ninety-five federal judicial districts, but we did endeavor to create as much demographic variation as possible. No two districts, for example, were chosen from the same area of the country. We also sought variation in factors internal to the operation of the courts—caseloads, case-processing times, numbers of judges, organization of the state courts, presence or absence of compulsory arbitration in the state courts, and use of the federal rules of civil procedure (or their equivalent) in the state courts.

In each district samples totaling between 300–370 cases terminated in calendar 1978 were drawn from the federal court, the neighboring state court, and, in two districts, an outlying, "rural" state trial court. All told, twelve courts were sampled in the five districts. Our sample was limited, as already noted, to "middle-range disputes," a somewhat arbitrary categorization on our part designed to focus on the mainstream of adversarial litigation and, at the same time, exclude categories of cases which were so large as to preclude effective analysis within the parameters of the project, or so small that they would not fall within the jurisdictional minimums both of the federal courts and typical state courts of general jurisdiction.

Cases which were demonstrably non-adversarial (e.g. most "collections" cases in which no evidence of a response from the defendant was found in the files) were also excluded. Domestic relations cases were limited arbitrarily to about 20 percent of our state court samples; without this control such cases would have dominated those samples and obstructed comparisons between state and federal courts. Domestic relations cases, however, were excluded entirely from the data analyzed in this paper.

We already have described the three ideal types of political culture orientations as traditionalistic, individualistic, and moralistic. Attempts to operationalize them yield a modest consensus. South Carolina can be classified as traditionalistic and Wisconsin as moralistic. California, Pennsylvania, and New Mexico are more problematic. California and Pennsylvania seem to combine elements of both the moralistic and individualistic orientations, albeit in several different observed combinations. New Mexico, with strains of all three orientations, is the most difficult to classify. On the whole, it seems closer to South Carolina than to the other states in this regard. Placed on a continuum from least to most modern, our five states would be ordered as follows: South Carolina, New Mexico, Pennsylvania, California, Wisconsin.

Levels of Participation

Our initial and consistent expectation was that levels of participation in these courts would correspond to the ranking of the five states on the political culture spectrum. Wisconsin would have the highest level of participation, followed by California, Pennsylvania, New Mexico, and South Carolina. This did not hold on either of two types of measures. It had been our intention to

TABLE 1
Litigation Rates[a] in the Federal Courts, 1978 (per 100,000 Population)[b]

Court	Litigation Rate	Deviation from Mean
All Federal Courts	65.2	
Eastern Wisconsin (Milwaukee)	27.9	−37.3
Central California (Los Angeles)	45.3	−19.9
Eastern Pennsylvania (Philadelphia)	89.3	+24.1
South Carolina (Columbia)	86.4	+21.2
New Mexico (Albuquerque)	83.0	+17.8

[a] Number of civil cases filed. Source: Administrative Office of the U.S. Courts, Annual Report to the Director, 1978.
[b] Based on 1975 population figures.

calculate litigation rates for both state and federal courts in each district. However, we found that jurisdictional differences among the state courts made it impossible to calculate valid litigation rates. We are limited, therefore, to federal court data, with all the inherent limitations previously acknowledged.

Table 1, therefore, shows the litigation rates per 100,000 population for the five federal judicial districts in our sample, and compares them to the mean litigation rate for all federal courts in the same year. Only one district, Philadelphia, has a litigation rate which might have been predicted. Milwaukee and Los Angeles are unaccountably low, and Columbia and Albuquerque unexpectedly high. Without comparable rates for the state courts, however, these results do not, by themselves, disconfirm our expectations.

Litigation rates derived from aggregate court records—no matter how accurate and how complete—tell us little about dispute resolution in a society. . . .

A Household Screening Survey was designed to supplement our sample of court cases and cases (not discussed in this paper) from alternative dispute-processing institutions. A random sample of 5,148 households, approximately evenly distributed in our five districts, was contacted by telephone in January, 1980. Respondents were asked whether anyone in the household in the last three years had experienced one or more of a long list of "problems" read to them. If they answered affirmatively, additional information was requested about how that problem was handled. Respondents who reported "eligible" disputes—that is, disputes which corresponded in size, subject and scope to those middle-range disputes which constituted our court samples—were contacted again for detailed follow-up interviews. Eligible disputes were reported by 10.9 percent (562) of the households.

Table 2 presents two potential measures of comparative litigiousness. First, it shows the range of households in each district reporting at least one "eligible" dispute. Such disputes are reported by respondents in Los Angeles at a much higher rate than is reported elsewhere—about 20 percent higher than in Milwaukee or Philadelphia, and nearly 60 percent higher than in South Carolina. In no sense is this a measure of disputatiousness, but it does suggest a range of variation in dispute incidence which,

TABLE 2
Households Reporting "Eligible" Disputes. Percentage of Disputes Filed in Court

	Milwaukee	Los Angeles	Philadelphia	South Carolina	New Mexico
(Households) $N =$	998	1012	1020	1080	1036
Percent households reporting an eligible dispute[a]	10.6	13.1	10.7	8.1	11.4
Percent disputes filed in court[b]	15.1	17.3	19.3	10.2	16.9

[a] $\chi^2 = 14.96$, 4 d.f.
[b] Virtually all by plaintiff

except for the ranking of New Mexico, is consistent with our political culture classification.

The second measure suggests that not only the frequency of disputes, but the rate at which disputes are translated into lawsuits, vary across districts. Again, the proportions must be noted. *Most* disputes, in all districts, do not mature into lawsuits. Again, South Carolina, consistent with our expectation, is significantly lower than the other districts; just over 10 percent of its reported disputes are brought to court, compared to nearly twice that percentage in Philadelphia and substantially higher percentages in the other districts. The most interesting finding, perhaps, is in the comparison of the two scores for Philadelphia—a relatively low percentage of households reporting disputes, but the strongest reported tendency toward converting disputes into lawsuits.

Comparing these responses to the federal court litigation rates reported in Table 1, we observe some interesting if perplexing results. Philadelphia, New Mexico, and Milwaukee are consistent—the first two consistently highly litigious, the latter low. Los Angeles, with a low federal court litigation rate is almost as high as Philadelphia in percentage of disputes filed in court. And South Carolina, with a relatively high federal

litigation rate, is lowest by far in reported percentage of disputes filed in court. If accurate litigation rates for the state courts were available, one category of discrepancies might be resolved, since many of the cases reported "filed in court" in Los Angeles might well be directed toward the state courts. On the other hand, the anomalous results of the screener survey in South Carolina make us wonder what the very high federal court litigation rate consists of. It is easier, at least in theory, to "explain" high dispute-low litigation than it is to explain low dispute-high litigation.

The Disputants in Court

Who are the disputants who come to court? What kinds of disputes do they bring? Table 3 provides an initial answer. In four of the five state courts, the plaintiffs are individuals about 75 percent of the time, with organizations as plaintiffs from one third to one fifth as often; in New Mexico there is more balance between individual and organizational plaintiffs. Financial institutions comprise the largest single subcategory of organizational plaintiffs, ranging from nearly 5 percent in Philadelphia to 23 percent in New Mexico. Government agencies

TABLE 3
Nature of Plaintiffs and Defendants in Federal and State Courts
(in Percentages)

	Federal Courts					State Courts				
	Milw.	*L.A.*	*Phil.*	*So. Car.*	*N. Mex.*	*Milw.*	*L.A.*	*Phil.*	*So. Car.*	*N. Mex.*
Plaintiffs										
Individuals	42.1%	56.7%	60.3%	63.2%	63.7%	68.2%	75.0%	83.0%	72.0%	45.9%
Organizations	28.3	26.8	27.8	24.5	24.4	23.5	19.5	15.6	21.0	36.9
Government	17.8	11.5	6.0	9.7	6.4	1.5	2.3	1.4	2.1	10.2
Mixed*	4.6	4.5	4.6	1.3	4.7	3.8	3.1	—	.7	6.4
Other	7.2	.6	1.3	1.3	1.2	3.0	—	—	3.2	6.6
Defendants										
Individuals	13.2	8.3	17.9	27.1	16.9	19.7	52.3	48.3	51.7	48.4
Organizations	32.2	45.2	56.3	45.2	37.2	19.7	22.7	35.4	21.7	31.8
Government	18.4	20.4	7.3	16.8	22.1	2.3	2.3	2.7	7.7	3.8
Mixed*	23.0	26.1	18.5	11.0	22.1	53.0	22.7	13.7	17.5	14.6
Others	13.2	—	—	—	1.7	5.3	—	—	1.4	.6
N of Cases	152	157	151	155	172	132	128	147	143	157

* A residual category for cases with different types of plaintiffs and defendants—mostly individuals combined with financial institutions.

as plaintiffs account for virtually none of the business of these courts.

In the federal courts the picture, not unexpectedly, is different. Except in New Mexico there are substantially fewer individual plaintiffs than in the corresponding state court. There are somewhat more organizational plaintiffs, but the real increase (again except for New Mexico) lies in the greater proportion of cases brought by government.

Individuals are also the largest single category of defendants in the state courts, but organizations are more frequently represented. Governments appear slightly more frequently as defendants than plaintiffs, but the scarcity of government as either plaintiff or defendant suggests the essentially "private dispute" nature of state courts. There is a somewhat different mix of organizations in each state (not shown in Table 3). Insurance companies account for a substantial portion of the organizational defendants in Milwaukee, primarily because they may be listed as defendants in personal injury cases—a practice forbidden or not followed in other states. On the other hand, "services and trade groups" or businesses account for a substantial portion of the defendants in all the state courts but Milwaukee. In the federal courts the number of organizational defendants is somewhat higher than in the state courts; the number of cases in which government itself is the defendant is substantially higher.

We have also examined the configuration of the parties in each case in our sample, as shown in Table 4. In three of the state courts, the largest single category consists of disputes between individuals. This is probably also true for Milwaukee, since insurance claims in Wisconsin do not formally name the individual tortfeasor as a defendant; a substantial number of the "Individual-Mixed" category in Wisconsin are disputes between

individuals and would appear as "Individual-Individual" in the other state courts. The picture is quite different, of course, in the federal courts, where there are relatively few disputes between individuals, and substantially more between individuals and government. . . .

Orientation of the Participants

Another characterization of the mode of participation is the orientation and goals of the participants. What kinds of cases do they bring, and what kinds of remedies do they seek? Put another way, what is it that the civil courts can do for them? We have already provided a partial answer to the first question. Personal injury claims comprise the single largest category of civil actions in the state courts; commercial contract cases are a distant second. Public law cases are almost non-existent in our state court sample.

A second measure of litigant orientation is the types of remedies which they seek. Some litigants go to court for vindication of claims which *we* might designate as "rights oriented." These plaintiffs demand punitive monetary damages or seek court actions such as license revocations and confiscation of property. A second type of litigant may be characterized as "rule-conscious"; we have defined this orientation as seeking preventive court action in the form of injunctions, declaratory judgments, and similar judicial orders. Third, there are other plaintiffs whose main goal is restitution for monetary losses.

Our case-coded information on remedies sought by plaintiffs, reported in Table 5, indicates that in both the federal and state courts in South Carolina there is a significantly larger proportion of plaintiffs seeking "punitive" claims (the majority of which are punitive damages sought in conjunction with actual damages). In addition, both the South Carolina and New Mexico state courts, and

TABLE 4
Configuration of Parties, Selected Groups: * **State and Federal Courts**

Pltf-Def.	State Courts					Federal Courts				
	Milw.	L.A.	Phila.	So. Car.	N. Mex.	Milw.	L.A.	Phila.	So. Car.	N. Mex.
Ind-Ind	7.6	45.3	40.8	45.1	19.0	3.9	3.8	11.9	17.4	11.6
Ind-Org	14.4	12.5	27.2	13.9	17.1	10.5	19.7	31.8	25.8	19.8
Ind-Gov	1.5	2.3	2.7	5.6	2.5	13.8	20.4	6.0	15.5	20.9
Ind-Mix	40.9	14.8	12.2	6.9	7.0	9.2	12.7	10.6	4.5	10.5
Org-Ind	8.3	4.7	6.8	3.5	15.2	2.6	2.5	3.3	3.9	2.3
Org-Org	5.3	7.8	7.5	6.9	13.3	12.5	17.2	18.5	15.5	12.2
Org-Mix	8.3	7.0	1.4	8.3	7.0	7.9	7.0	5.3	4.5	8.1
Gov-Ind	1.5	.8	.7	.7	10.8	6.6	1.9	1.3	5.8	1.7
N of cases	132	128	147	144	158	152	157	151	155	172

* Reported are the most frequent categories out of 25 possible combinations of IND, ORG, GOV, MIXED, and OTHER.

all the federal courts, have a significant number of cases where the court is asked to enjoin potential "rule" violations. In contrast, three state courts, Milwaukee, Los Angeles, and Philadelphia, received almost entirely restitutional claims. Punitive damages were *awarded* in an even fewer number of cases; indeed the only state court in which an award of punitive damages was recorded was South Carolina.

The finding that South Carolina, our most rural district, has the highest number of "punitive" claims in both state and federal courts invites speculation that political culture has an important impact on the goals and orientations of the users of the courts in that state. The differences are greater in the state than in the federal courts but that may reflect the different mix of cases in those courts.

Participation in an Adversary Process

Participation is not one-sided. We are interested not just in which people come to court, and what kinds of disputes they bring, but also the modes of participation. Much attention in recent years has been lavished on the routinization of criminal-case processing and adjudication epitomized by plea bargaining. A great debate ranges over the causes and impact of plea bargaining, over the alleged decline of the adversary system, and the consequences of that decline. On the other hand, at least one scholar has argued that plea bargaining is not synonymous with the decline of adversariness, but is merely a less formal structure for its continued expression. Similarly, there is evidence that the agenda of civil courts is also becoming routinized and non-adversarial, but as in the case of plea bargaining in criminal cases, there is no uniformity of views on the subject. The implications of this debate are important

for research and understanding of civil justice. And they are particularly important for understanding the different modes of court usage.

There are several potential measures of the degree of adversarial participation in litigation. It is understood that litigation is part of a strategy of dispute settlement; few cases are filed with the hope and intention of actually having the dispute decided by a judge or jury. Filing of a case may indicate merely that serious but relatively routinized bargaining is about to begin. But there are degrees of adversariness that mark the rituals of negotiation and settlement and, we believe, differences in the culture of adversariness which mark the behavior of different courts. Some courts are likely to emphasize formal procedures; others, negotiation. Some judges are likely to play an active role in the settlement process; others regard such judicial activism as wholly improper. Some courts are likely to push cases to completion quickly and efficiently; others may leave control over the pace of litigation to the litigants.

Our data provide some indication of the variation in court settlement practices in both state and federal courts in our five districts. As shown in Table 6, there is some variation among the state courts ($\chi^2 = 78.03$, df = 8), virtually none among the federal courts ($\chi^2 = 17.21$, df = 8), and interesting differences between the state and federal courts. Quite clearly, most cases are settled by the parties, somewhat more frequently in the state than in the federal courts except for New Mexico. Reciprocally, cases are terminated more often by court judgments in the federal courts, again except in New Mexico. This suggests a less activist role by federal judges in promoting settlements but a more interventionist role in granting motions for judgment. Trials are more frequent in all the federal courts than in the corresponding

TABLE 5
Remedies Sought by Plaintiffs
(In Percentages)

	State Courts					Federal Courts				
Remedy*	Milw.	L.A.	Phil.	S. Car.	N. Mex.	Milw.	L.A.	Phil.	S. Car.	N. Mex.
Punitive	2.7%	3.6%	3.9%	29.0%	5.4%	6.3%	9.2%	8.7%	17.3%	9.1%
Restitutional	87.7	88.3	87.0	57.1	84.8	60.7	61.0	73.8	61.3	65.2
Preventative	5.7	6.0	1.8	9.2	8.5	26.1	26.0	12.5	16.1	19.9
Other	3.9	2.1	7.5	4.5	1.2	6.9	3.8	5.1	5.3	5.8
N of responses	367	418	285	238	446	555	534	393	341	592
N of cases	131	128	146	141	156	150	147	150	154	168
N of missing cases	1	0	1	2	1	2	10	1	1	4

* These percentages reflect multiple responses rather than cases.

TABLE 6
Modes of Disposition of Cases
(In Percentages)

	Federal Courts					State Courts				
Mode*	Milw.	L.A.	Phil.	S. Car.	N. Mex.	Milw.	L.A.	Phil.	S. Car.	N. Mex.
N =	142	153	151	155	169	125	125	145	141	150
Dismissals (Settlements)	69.7%	66.0%	78.8%	75.0%	69.8%	80.8%	82.4%	66.2%	75.2%	51.3%
Motions (Judgments)	24.6	28.8	17.9	19.1	18.9	16.8	14.4	33.1**	13.5	43.3
Trials	5.6	5.2	3.3	5.9	11.2	.8	3.2	.7	11.3	5.3

* These are collapsed categories. We consider dismissals to be a rough index of settlements, "motions" of judgments by the court.
** Includes court-ordered arbitration awards (25.5 percent of total).

state courts, except for South Carolina. The frequency of trials in the federal court in New Mexico and the state court in South Carolina is so much higher than in the other courts that a different set of expectations on the part of the participants probably exists.

. . .

[T]here are some differences in the adversarial culture in the five state courts, although not as many differences as we expected to find. There are even fewer differences among the counterpart federal courts. On the other hand, one can detect discernible differences between the state courts and the federal courts. The latter are somewhat less settlement oriented and, at least in the three most urban courts, have substantially more trials. . . .

[II]

The concept of political culture was employed to help explain variations in use of the civil courts. Our assumption was that there were mechanisms or ideas embedded in the political culture of a state or region which mediated between citizens and the courts and influenced their decisions to use or not to use the courts. Likewise, we hypothesized that some of the modes of court usage, while undoubtedly strongly reflective of legal factors, might also be responsive to political elements.

Quite clearly we can report no *overall* findings, no systematic pattern which links the use of courts to political culture, at least as we operationalized that concept. There were some *specific* findings for which a political culture explanation is credible. Patterns of court usage in South Carolina, while not perfectly responsive to political culture predictions, nonetheless were close to our expectations of a traditionalistic society. South Carolina was lowest in the percentages

of disputes reported to our screener survey, lowest in the percentage of disputes taken to court, highest in the rate of trials and relatively low in settlements and in judicial efforts to encourage settlements, relatively low in discovery use and contentiousness, and unique in its employment of punitive remedies in settling disputes. South Carolina's high rate of federal court litigation is inexplicable. Of the other courts, Philadelphia came close to approximating the pattern of an individualistic culture which might have been predicted for it. On the other hand, New Mexico proved to be completely enigmatic—not merely unpatterned but often downright contrary to any predictions we might have made about it.

Our major problem of analysis is that on most variables there was not as much difference among the courts as we had expected, with the exception of New Mexico which was often substantially different than the rest. This lack of differences was most surprising to us, especially since the sites were selected *because* they varied in obvious and important ways (or at least in ways that seemed obvious and important to us). . . .

It is distinctly possible that courts, and the propensity to use them, are not nearly so well integrated into the political culture as we have assumed. A political culture explanation assumes that courts are an integral part of political society, that variance consequently would be expected along political lines and could be explained as a function of political variables. But the data we have collected may be pointing in a different and unexpected direction. It may be that "courts are courts," and that what they (or at least the civil courts) share in common as participants in the American legal culture is more important than characteristics of the political environment in which they operate. Courts are not autonomous; they are part of a seamless web. Nevertheless, it may be that more weight should be given to "court" factors or even to random variations in the "local legal culture" or in the behavior of key individual actors....

Ultimately, it may be necessary to con- struct a scale of *legal* culture variables which is more sensitive to the operation of courts than either the political culture variable we have employed or the local legal culture alternative.

The Rise of Conservative Interest Group Litigation

Karen O'Connor
Lee Epstein

Scholars long have been aware that business and mainstream farm interests pursue their own generally conservative goals through litigation, just as unions and farm organizations try to advance parochial but liberal concerns (Bonnett, 1922; Truman, 1951; Cortner, 1968; Galanter, 1974). But for understandable reasons, most research has concentrated on broad-spectrum "liberal" litigating groups (Vose, 1959; Manwaring, 1962; Barker, 1967; Cortner, 1968; O'Connor, 1980).

These primarily ideological issue-oriented groups litigate in broad areas of constitutional law..., often engage in strategies to develop doctrine..., participate in as many cases within their domain as they can..., and are highly successful.... Arguably, scholars have been concerned too much with these highly visible efforts, but mundane pursuit of immediate self-interest in the legal field may not have the cumulative impact of strategic pursuit of long-term goals....

In any event, this has changed in recent years in a dramatic fashion. Conservatives have proven that they can play the game of litigation as well. This new climate has not yet been studied adequately. It raises questions about the currency of the conclusions of some researchers...who have found little conservative participation in the courts. Further, as we shall show, conservative organizations have developed different approaches to litigation and are not merely mirror images of liberal organizations.

To develop this evidence systematically we explore three questions:

1. To what extent do conservative groups litigate before the United States Supreme Court?
2. Do such conservative groups have a litigating style and do they develop strategies for doctrinal development?
3. Are particular areas of the law of special concern to broad-spectrum conservative litigating groups?

DEFINITIONS AND METHODS

Data for this study were obtained from the records of the United States Supreme Court. All of the 1,370 full opinion cases decided by the Burger Court (1969 to 1980 terms) were included. Each case was categorized into

Reprinted from *Journal of Politics* 45 (1983), 479–488. © 1983 by the Southern Political Science Association. By permission of the authors and the University of Texas Press.

one of five areas: (1) criminal; (2) economic liberalism; (3) civil liberties; (4) taxes; and (5) court authority.

The briefs of both the direct sponsors and of the amicus curiae (if any) were read to identify participating groups. These groups were classified either as liberal or as conservative based on the socio-political status of their clientele group as well as on their professed ideological stance. For example, liberal groups were those that regularly represented the interests of minorities, criminal defendants, or consumers. Groups that represented those who claimed civil liberties or civil rights abridgments also were included in this category. In contrast, conservative groups were those that, for example, represented the interests of employers and business. Groups that espoused socially conservative or law-and-order causes also were included in this category. Only groups that revealed a consistent ideological pattern were included. . . .

FINDINGS

Participation Rates

Either a liberal and/or a conservative interest group participated in 49.3 percent ($N = 676$) of the 1,370 cases decided by the Burger Court during its 1969 to 1980 terms. At least one liberal interest group participated either as a direct sponsor or as an amicus curiae in 40.3 percent ($N = 552$) of the cases, whereas at least one conservative group appeared in 19 percent ($N = 261$). Thus, over the twelve-year period, liberal interest groups participated to a significantly greater extent than did conservative interest groups. However, . . . the overall percentage rate obscures the increase in conservative interest group participation over time. Whereas liberal interest group participation reveals no

trend over time, conservative groups' appearances before the Court have increased. During the Court's 1969 term conservative interest groups participated in only 9 percent ($N = 7$) of the total cases. By the 1980 term their participation rate tripled and, in fact, conservative groups appeared in over 50 percent of the cases in which a liberal or a conservative interest group was present.

Low participation rates during the 1969 term substantiate political scientists' assumptions concerning conservative groups' use of the courts. By the 1980 term, however, conservative interest groups appeared before the Court on a regular basis. And while there still is some disparity between the participation rates of liberal and conservative groups, conservative interest groups no longer can be ignored as participants in the judicial process. Thus, these findings parallel those of other studies concluding that conservative interest group activity is increasing in other forums. For example, just as conservative groups have formed political action committees to finance the campaigns of their preferred candidates, and have conducted direct-mail fund solicitation, they have also used litigation to support their preferred cases.

Strategies

Examinations of disadvantaged interest groups' activities reveal that many of these groups adopt one of two tactics. Whereas groups like the National Association for the Advancement of Colored People Legal Defense and Education Fund (NAACP LDF) prefer to sponsor cases . . . , others including the American Civil Liberties Union (ACLU) rely heavily on amicus curiae briefs to lobby the Court. . . .

. . . [C]onservative and liberal groups generally adopt different forms of participation. Conservative interest groups' preference for participation as amicus curiae is clearly evident. Of the 261 cases in which they participated, conservative groups sponsored only 2 percent ($N = 7$). In contrast, liberal groups sponsored 39 percent ($N = 265$) of the 679 cases in which they appeared.

Conservative interest group reliance on participation as amicus curiae has several implications. First, although it is difficult to assess the relative merits of direct sponsorship versus amicus curiae participation, control over the course of litigation inherent in direct sponsorship generally is assumed to have a positive impact on the outcome of litigation.... Thus, conservative group use of amicus curiae briefs may have some adverse consequences, but these groups believe that the benefits of participation in already docketed cases far outweigh the risks....

Second, control may not be critical because conservative interest groups often have access to other political forums. For example, antiabortion groups, after their losses in 1973, were able to persuade several state legislatures to enact laws restricting abortion rights. Consequently, these and other conservative interest groups' stake in the outcome of litigation may not be as great as for those who rely more heavily on the judicial forum.

Third, amicus curiae briefs may be the only way that conservative interest groups can present their views to the Court. Governments often are parties to suits of interest to conservatives. Thus, the only tactic generally available to them is the amicus curiae....

Finally, Richard C. Cortner noted that although disadvantaged groups were important because they sponsored test cases, conservative groups did not "reveal any peculiar characteristics which (were) helpful in classifying them as particular kinds of participants in the judicial process" (1968, p. 288). *However, this is no longer the case.*

Today conservative interest groups can be characterized by their nearly exclusive participation as amicus curiae. These groups, in fact, view this form of participation as a strategy just as the NAACP LDF views direct sponsorship as the best strategy to pursue its goals.

Issue Concentration

Scholars who have examined liberal groups conclude that those groups litigate to expand constitutional guarantees. Areas such as race- and gender-based discrimination have attracted significant liberal interest group activity.

... [C]onservative and liberal groups have concentrated their litigation activities on different areas of the law. Conservative interest groups appeared most frequently in cases involving economic liberalism claims, whereas liberal groups participated most regularly in cases involving civil liberties. Liberal groups devoted 58.9 percent ($N = 325$) of their efforts to cases involving civil liberties whereas these claims represented 36 percent ($N = 94$) of conservative groups' activities. This relatively high conservative involvement in civil liberties can be attributed to increasing conservative participation in this area over time.... Within the civil liberties category, areas including abortion, obscenity, and employment discrimination have attracted considerable conservative interest group activity. And, in those areas, conservative interests have been primarily represented by single-issue groups including Americans United for Life, Citizens for Decency Through Law, and the Equal Employment Advisory Council, respectively.

Cases involving issues of economic liberalism represented only 13 percent ($N = 72$) of liberal groups' total participation. In contrast, this area of the law attracted 42.9 percent ($N = 112$) of conservative interest groups' involvement. The Chamber of Commerce and several business-oriented legal foundations regularly represented the conservative viewpoint.

Interestingly, criminal issues were of lesser importance both to conservative and to liberal groups. This area represented only 14.6 percent ($N = 38$) and 24.3 percent ($N = 134$) of conservative and liberal interest groups' respective caseloads. Of the thirty-eight cases with conservative interest group participation, Americans for Effective Law Enforcement participated in 72.8 percent ($N = 25$).

Thus, conservative and liberal groups clearly concentrated in different issue areas. Over the past twelve years, liberal groups have consistently focused their energies on civil liberties cases. In contrast, cases involving economic liberalism attracted the greatest attention of conservative interest groups. Their involvement in civil liberties issues, however, has increased since 1976.

CONCLUSION

In this analysis, we addressed several questions concerning conservative interest group participation in United States Supreme Court litigation. First, we found that conservative groups not only participated but that their involvement has increased over time. This increase may be due to several factors. With the addition of conservative Justices Rehnquist and Powell, conservative interest groups saw the Court as a more receptive forum than it had been during the Warren Court era. In fact, the EEAC and several conservative, business-oriented legal foundations were formed shortly after these justices were appointed to the Court. Additionally, conservative interest groups, learning from their liberal counterparts, saw litigation as a means of furthering their policy interests.

Also, during the 1970s and early 1980s, the increasing awareness and acceptance of conservativism in the United States have given added life to these groups. The Reagan Administration, in fact, numbers among its cabinet members a former head of a conservative legal foundation, James Watt.

It is clear that the judicial process now witnesses competitive articulation of points of view and to an increasing degree. The initial advantage gained by liberal groups when they invented such litigation is being narrowed. Conservative as well as liberal groups now aspire to be "private attorneys-general."

A second question addressed in this study was whether conservative groups developed strategies to lobby the Court. The data indicate that conservative interest groups rely heavily on participation as amicus curiae. Clement E. Vose has criticized reliance on amicus curiae activity as an indicator of interest group involvement in litigation (1981, p. 10). Development of easier access through class action suits and broader definition of standing and the rights to intervene render the amicus brief just one tool of many. This study, however, reveals that particularly when examining conservative groups, amicus curiae activity cannot be ignored. In fact, many of the groups claim that submission of amicus curiae briefs is their preferred strategy to lobby the Court.

Based on these findings, we conclude that both liberal and conservative groups view the Court as a political forum. Each sees the importance of lobbying the judiciary to achieve its goals. Writing in 1968, Cortner saw no pattern to conservative group litigation. Since 1968, however, the growth of conservative interest group litigation necessitates a reexamination of that conclusion and a recognition of the growing utilization of group participation as amicus curiae as a litigation strategy.

REFERENCES

Barker, Lucius (1967). "Third Parties in Litigation: A Systematic View of the Judicial Function." *The Journal of Politics* 29: 41–69.

Bonnett, Clarence (1922). *Employers' Associations in the United States: A Study of Typical Associations*. New York: MacMillan.

Cortner, Richard C. (1968). "Strategies and Tactics of Litigants in Constitutional Cases." *Journal of Public Law* 17: 287–307.

Galanter, Marc (1974). "Why the 'Haves' Come Out Ahead: Speculation on the Limits of Legal Change." *Law & Society Review* 9: 95–160.

Manwaring, David (1962). *Render unto Caesar: The Flag Salute Controversy*. Chicago: University of Chicago Press.

O'Connor, Karen (1980). *Women's Organizations' Use of the Courts*. Lexington, MA: Lexington Books.

Truman, David B. (1951). *The Governmental Process*. New York: Alfred A. Knopf.

Vose, Clement E. (1959). *Caucasians Only*. Berkeley: University of California Press.

——— (1981). "Interest Groups and Litigation." Paper presented at the 77th Annual Meeting of the American Political Science Association, New York City.

How Planned Is 'Planned Litigation''?

Stephen L. Wasby

. . .

This article explores the extent to which race relations litigation from the late 1960s through the early 1980s has been "planned" by organizations and lawyers associated with them. Examination of planned litigation for social change through race relations litigation is natural because race relations, along with other areas of civil rights and civil liberties, has historically been a principal area in which such litigation has occurred and because, in recent years, many more groups—including women's rights groups, Hispanics, and the handicapped—have engaged in such litigation. The subject of planned litigation for social change is also important because organizations, such as environmental groups and conservative public interest law firms, have also undertaken systematic litigation in pursuit of their interests....

. . .

Planned litigation can be undertaken to achieve a variety of goals. These include a result or outcome, the "constitutional goals" of precedent, and publicity, with the last

Reprinted from *American Bar Foundation Research Journal* Volume 1984 No. 1, pp. 84, 89–94, 100–101, 110–113, 115–117, 125, 127–128, 137–138. Reprinted with permission of author and publisher. Footnotes omitted.

likely to be emphasized when an organization's resources are limited. While seeking to create favorable precedent, litigators also seek to avoid bad precedent. This forces them to pay attention to "nonlandmark" cases, into which "some of the most difficult, creative work" has gone both "to get something for someone and to keep them from being bad precedent."

. . .

How Extensive Is Organizational Planning?

That an organization will do more than respond idiosyncratically to cases cannot be taken for granted. Even when organizations bring test cases—the quintessence of planned litigation—they may not have done so as a result of broad litigation planning. Instead they may have engaged in "an ad hoc search for targets of opportunity" or simply responded to "fortuitous events." ...

Even when an organization does attempt to plan litigation, its activities may not result from strategy. Although an organization may be capable of developing "offensive" strategies, "circumstances control." ...

Even when litigation in a particular area of the law has received focused organizational attention and the outlines of litigation have been planned, some aspects may not have been planned. Even planned lawsuits are often not thought through to the end before they are commenced. For example, because attention had to be given to defining "segregation" and to proving violations of the Constitution, less attention was given to appropriate remedies in school cases, despite the close relation between violation and remedy ("the violations charged will constrain the remedies available"). Such planning is difficult because local lawyers have not had experience elsewhere in developing remedies; they "know that segregation must end but cannot be familiar with the challenges its replacement will bring." . . .

. . .

An important element in the actual operation of "planned litigation" is the evolution of precedent or "common law accretion." For example, in the schools area after *Brown*, LDF followed an "incremental approach," "nudging the law along a bit at a time." This is a "case-by-case, building-block strategy," but not one in which each successive case is a step specified by a prior blueprint. The ultimate goal—for example, desegregation of public education—is not sought immediately: cases are brought and won, and then a goal that "seems crazy one year is reached as intermediate points are filled in." Thus, amid the complexity characterizing civil rights litigation, "there is the pursuit of the possible," with theory being deducted from individual cases. Development of even such an "incremental approach" is, however, "far more difficult" now than in the early 1950s"; where LDF "used to be able to decide what school cases to take, in the last 15 years there are many more actors."

Strategy sessions can be an important element of "planning" in planned litigation. Regular meetings of lawyers directly involved in a set of cases in a particular area of the law are not unusual, and meetings were held in

connection with the campaigns against racial restrictive covenants, school segregation, and capital punishment, and in the campaign to enforce Title VII. Larger conferences have also taken place, although not often; they were called particularly when there was a sense that new directions might have to be taken or new conditions confronted. Thus in 1981 LDF "sponsored a conference of its cooperating lawyers, education experts and academics to discuss emerging federal policies on equal rights in public education." This was stimulated by the need to deal with the Reagan administration's "new approach to enforcement of public school integration." Through such a meeting, LDF "sought to develop strategies to counteract the government's retreat from past support for desegregation."

Efforts to get lawyers together to plan strategy have, however, seldom produced "grand strategizing": they produced "petty strategizing if anything." When Jack Greenberg [Director-Counsel, NAACP Legal Defense Fund] brought six people together in a hotel room to plan, "not much came out of any of that" type of activity, because what results from "sitting around" is "too abstract" for use in actual situations and too divorced from "the grass roots" to be successful. Similarly, the existence of planned litigation does not mean that there has been "an organizational decision" or even coordination of large numbers of lawyers, although an "organizational base" may assist in getting the work done. Instead, such discussions, over months and even years, perhaps operating outside an organization's "bureaucratic structure," may "prepare" it so that it can take advantage of the window of opportunity and litigation can proceed "when the right type of case comes." . . .

Because LDF's planned litigation efforts have become the model for others' activities, reexamination of a ten-year-old statement by

LDF Director-Counsel Jack Greenberg is particularly instructive. Greenberg discounted the image of a planned litigation "campaign" as one of "military precision" because "time and again, cases take on lives of their own and mature along unexpected lines." His litany of potential difficulties was extensive: "Too much that occurs in court is not subject to control, such as the chance occurrences of any lawsuit, the defection of plaintiffs or capitulation of defendants, disagreement among counsel, the vagaries of legislation, unanticipated precedents, and the effects of public sentiment and political currents on constitutional adjudication." In addition, "litigation programs pose practical, political, and jurisprudential problems, large and small," and "one quickly learns that principles rarely can be established in single cases because they so often may be washed out for all manner of reasons."

PLANNING AS CHOICE

Organizational Choices of Areas of Law

An interest group's choice of particular areas of law in which to focus its litigation activities is a crucial part of its litigation planning. Indeed, the selection of issues "may...be no more than a synonym for the pursuit of a litigation strategy." In making their choices, litigators wishing to pursue strategy must choose areas of law in which a sufficient number of potential cases can be generated to provide a choice of those appropriate to pursue. This leads, as one lawyer put it, to a preference for choosing "a subject with broad interest and appeal through which branches and attorneys could get a feel for what they could do to implement law on the books."

Some areas in which organizations litigate, for example, LDF's attention to Title VII and capital punishment, are chosen with some care, with constraints imposed mostly by limited resources. In other areas, however, litigation evolves because many cases on a topic are brought to the organization....

.   .   .

There is also an interorganizational aspect of choices of areas of law in which to litigate—in which organizations have "to consider that other organizations were considering some issues": "If the ACLU is involved, the NAACP need not be." Because the ACLU was "ready to step into" criminal justice cases and public defender organizations were charged with protecting defendants' rights, the NAACP could refer cases to them. However, "notwithstanding, the NAACP needs to be involved to cover some of the issues," perhaps a function of its being a membership-based organization with some demands from members that have to be satisfied directly.

A major result of interorganizational interaction concerning areas of law in which to litigate is *division of labor*, in which one organization concentrates on an area of law and other organizations devote their efforts to other areas; this division can also be geographical, like, for example, the NAACP's concentration in recent years on northern school desegregation cases while LDF focused its school efforts primarily in the Southeast. In such "comparative advantage," some organizations concentrate on certain subjects while others, because of the former's efforts, focus their efforts elsewhere. For example, because other national groups already were investing efforts in the campaign against exclusionary zoning, LDF did not initially direct its resources to that cause.

.   .   .

Choices of Specific Cases to Be Litigated

There is a close relation between interest groups' choices of specific cases and their choices of areas of law in which to litigate. From a planning perspective, the latter, particularly if adequately communicated to lawyers in the field, will help channel certain types of cases and not others to organizational litigations. Conversely, the stream of cases will help an organization decide the areas of law in which to concentrate efforts. In working in a new area of law, an organization can "cast its net broadly and bring lots of cases." A certain proportion "turn out not to go very far," but appropriate issues can be identified from them. "By starting with a significant number of cases, we don't put all our eggs in one basket and find the basket has holes." As issues develop, the organization can "send out the word," indicating what cases it is looking for. Such case searching by LDF, whose lawyers at times "would see the need for intervention and would stimulate forces" leading to initiation of a case, suggests an active, planning element in the organization's activities. As this suggests, a nonmembership organization like LDF, particularly if many of its cooperating attorneys are effectively socialized to organizational priorities, is in a better position to attempt to engage in planned litigation than one with local units, like the NAACP's branches, that affect the basic pattern by which cases come to the organization.

Once cases are channeled to an organization, decisions must be made as to which ones to pursue. Lawyers associated with civil rights groups identify a variety of criteria used to select cases either from their initial stages, which facilitates choice and later control, or in which to intervene at later stages. Much of the latter selection of cases is "defensive"—to try to steer cases conflicting with an organization's overall strategy and to avoid or minimize "bad" precedent— and thus is an indication of limits on an organization's ability to choose freely and to plan litigation fully. However, lawyers involved in organizationally related race relations cases do not share a clear consensus on the criteria used for case selection. Moreover, a number of constraints affect attempts to apply criteria to case selection. Perhaps the most significant, and a constant, is the availability of resources, or the lack of them. Even when the major litigating organizations have "organizational names [that] carry an impressive ring," "the truth of the matter is vastly less impressive," a situation that "force[s] hard choices among possible cases."

.   .   .

Choice of Forum

Within certain legal constraints, litigators can choose to file cases in either federal or state courts. Such a choice is a function of several factors, which staff attorneys may "discuss in depth" with those initiating cases. Overall, however, there is a distinct preference for federal court, to which civil rights lawyers "gravitate naturally"—a "traditional tendency" reinforced by the Warren Court's attention to civil rights claims and assisted by its easing of federal standing requirements. Put simply, civil rights lawyers are "more comfortable" in federal court. One reason may be the attitude toward the federal courts communicated to lawyers during their law training. As a result of the Warren Court's rulings, observed a federal judge, several generations of lawyers were taught to "seek ye first the kingdom of the federal court." One can see the preference for the federal court by civil rights lawyers even in Mississippi in the 1960s, despite the conservatism of the federal judges there; even though many cases handled by the lawyers had to be handled in state court because of their subject matter, "a majority of the cases involving issues at the heart of the civil rights movement . . . were litigated in federal courts."

Litigators' choice of federal or state forum, which can affect the "pacing and sequence" of litigation, should nonetheless be treated as problematic, with the "choice between federal and state courts ultimately hing[ing] on the litigators' estimates of the probable decisions of the U.S. Supreme Court." Some cases are pursued in state courts for a variety of reasons. . . .

With less support from the Burger Court, liberals, including Justice Brennan, suggested use of state courts, and civil rights litigators have paid greater attention to state forums. "Depending on the state, state courts are viable—and perhaps more effective." Pragmatic lawyers know that there are some situations in which they should definitely consider state court. . . . Where state courts are "good," much litigation will be brought to them under the state constitution. However, attorneys are affected by their negative experiences in state courts, for example, with judges who "didn't want to hear the specifics" of a housing discrimination case or with serious docket problems that leave the "totally unsatisfactory" situation in which the lawyer doesn't get to see the judge and the judge doesn't write an opinion. These reinforce their feelings that "many state courts remain terrible," and that they often cannot obtain the "practical results" they seek "even in states with favorable policies."

.   .   .

Decision to Participate in Litigation as Amicus Curiae

Participation in a case as amicus curiae can be an important element of planned litigation. Indeed, some organizations, such as the ACLU in its earlier days, participated in cases only as amicus curiae at the appellate level. Amicus activity is also important for organizations lacking the resources to engage in more extensive participation in litigation.

When others have initiated cases, a litigating organization has the option of seeking to enter a case as amicus curiae; such choices are part of litigation strategy. No one forces an organization to be amicus: it can allow others to proceed with their cases and can plead scarcity of resources—"the constraints of a small staff and limited resources"—when requests for amicus participation are received. Yet when an organization engaging in planned litigation considers its strategic interests, the choice not to participate may be illusory. . . .

. . . [At] times interest groups' amicus participation is basically defensive and aimed to soften potentially negative precedents and limit defeats in cases others have brought. . . .

Many of the recurring factors playing a part in decisions to become amicus were cited by an LDF lawyer: "the importance of cases to minorities; the importance of the issue; the possibility of adverse precedent; the ability to limit negative precedent; [and] workload." The "importance of the issues to the litigating organization or to its clients"— sometimes stated in terms of whether the issues are "compatible with the [organization's] fundamental mandate"—is a factor cited over and over again. "Estimates of the quality of representation" connected with the case also played a part in decisions about amicus participation: "If the cause is worthwhile, but the advocate is inept," an organization might be *more* likely to file an amicus brief "to avoid bad law because the case would be decided." . . .

SOME DYNAMICS OF PLANNED LITIGATION

Choices of areas of law, cases, and forums establish broad parameters within which actual litigation occurs. In this section, we examine some aspects of the dynamics of litigation, from selection to conclusion, which affect outcomes and often lead to dispositions not originally planned. The importance of the internal dynamics of cases for the effectiveness of planned litigation can be seen in many situations.

. . .

Griggs v. *Duke Power Co.*, the Supreme Court's first pronouncement on the substantive issues in Title VII, provides a useful example. In that LDF case, "nothing during the pretrial discovery or the trial indicated its potential as a landmark case." The decision to proceed to the first appellate level was made only after the trial court's decision because the district judge, in addition to ruling that plaintiffs had failed to show that company transfer requirements led to disproportionate rejection of blacks, defined "professionlly developed" (for employment tests or requirements) in an unacceptable fashion and rejected the important theory that "present effects of past discrimination" must be dealt with. After plaintiffs had not fully succeeded in the Fourth Circuit, they had to decide whether to take *Griggs*, not "an ideal 'test case' for review by the Supreme Court," to the high court. Several factors had to be considered. One was the potential in other cases then being developed "to present more appealing records to raise the testing issues." Another was Fourth Circuit Judge Simon Sobeloff's "powerful" partial dissent supporting the plaintiff's position; that Sobeloff was "one of the most respected federal judges in civil rights litigation" was thought to give the dissent particular weight, particularly in the Supreme Court's eyes. Another was "whether the interests of the plaintiffs were compatible with the interests of all others who would benefit from a successful resolution of the issue" because a ruling would affect "millions of other blacks" who, like the four in the case, lacked a high school education (one of the company require-

ments). The interests of those affected also "had to be weighed against [LDF's] concern for an institutional programmatic development" of the law.

. . .

Not only do a single case's internal dynamics affect litigation, but the dynamics of developments in several related cases may also limit planning. At times, lawyers seeking the same goal and bringing other cases may pose more of an obstacle to implementation of strategy by getting their cases to the appellate courts, including the Supreme Court, first, before those engaged in planned litigation can do much about it.... This situation can develop even when lawyers involved in the various cases on their way to the Supreme Court have had earlier contact....

Source of Cases

Litigation organizations' sources of cases hold important implications for later dynamics of litigation. Some organizations have relatively structured processes for obtaining cases, but cases come to other groups in a more diffuse fashion, resulting in reduced ability to plan litigation. Headquarters or regional offices may even get "walk-in"—or "call-in"—cases from their immediate areas. In such situations, in the absence of guidance or control from the national level of organization, local pressures may dominate cooperating attorneys' decisions on the types of cases to which to give greatest attention. For national case priorities to be effective, they must be transmitted to cooperating attorneys and translated and incorporated into the cooperating attorneys' priorities. Dispersion of priorities is less likely when a national organization provides cooperating attorneys with the assistance they are more likely to need as cases become more complex.

. . .

Control and Momentum

An essential element of "planned litigation," ...is control over cases. Test cases, we are told, "should be managed from the outset because choices of forums, type of action, pleadings, appeal papers and the like affect the outcome." Such early involvement is "vital" for making a good record and for properly framing issues and preserving them for appeal. Similarly, control of cases is necessary "to assure that only the *best* cases—in the most advantageous order— reach the High Court." Yet despite these important reasons for control, lawyers do get involved in cases after their initiation, a situation likely to decrease control. This was true of the 1950s and 1960s public accommodations cases in the Supreme Court, where "legal strategy had to be improvised along the way." ...

If planned litigation is facilitated by control, a disadvantage is momentum or inertia—an *absence* of dynamics. When there is strategy, inertia hinders effective implementation of that strategy. Momentum or inertia—fixation on a strategic position— may hinder groups from responding to changes in their environment, the more so the more rigid the litigating position. For example, lawyers are said to have persisted in seeking racially balanced schools despite changes in judicial outlook, "reverses in the school desegregation campaign," and membership demands for more attention to quality education. Some of this inertia results from lawyers' personal values. "Attorneys are not necessarily neutral actors who are equally open to all litigative theories and strategies." Lawyers' values affect the type of law practice in which they engage; their orientations toward the law and toward clients; and the focus of their concerns—on client, group, or principle. It therefore should not be surprising that their orientations affect their deci-

sions to initiate litigation and, particularly important in planned litigation, decisions to proceed with cases already initiated, especially decisions to appeal.

Another part of inertia is momentum: "litigation begets litigation." There are several reasons for this. One is an important element in civil rights lawyers' ideologies, what has been called *the myth of rights*—the idea, reinforced by the Warren Court's expansion of rights, that litigation can produce statements of rights and their implementation. Despite some ambivalence, litigation is continued because lawyers, as well as many others, believe that rights exist, that courts can define rights, and that those rights can be enforced in the courts. Lawyers thus continue to turn to the courts to seek new precedent, even after they sustain defeats or when rights "won" in court are not implemented. This is quite likely when opponents' resistance strengthens attorneys' resolve, as it did in school cases where it led lawyers to press for not-easily-evaded quantitative measures of desegregation. In general, defeats do not easily change habits, even though they convey the "basic lesson" of "the difficulty of traditional litigation as a way of protecting...rights."

Further litigation may be necessary to translate initial victories into benefits for the intended beneficiaries; litigation is necessary to sustain initial precedents and to produce their implementation. For example, "victories that laid the legal groundwork for the [civil rights] movement were enforceable by further litigation." This creates problems for organizations wishing to invest resources in developing new precedent because attention to new precedent may mean neglect of follow-up suits. Moreover, the commitment to litigation may interfere with the most effective allocation of resources to produce achievement of those rights.

·   ·   ·

CONCLUSION

There is planning in civil rights litigation, but much is problematic about "planned" litigation. This is true even when such litigation is undertaken by the NAACP Legal Defense and Educational Fund, whose litigation "campaigns" serve as the model of planned litigation. Organizations litigating in the area of race relations do consciously choose some of the areas of law in which they focus litigation; involvement in other areas of law is less a matter of relatively unfettered choice than a function of reflexive action, with the flow of cases helping to determine an organization's focal areas. At times the choice of cases for litigation, affected by the areas of law in which an organization has chosen to litigate, proceeds deductively from predetermined criteria, but often it occurs inductively and reflexively on the basis of cases available, pressure, and circumstance. To facilitate planning and control organizational litigators prefer to initiate cases; but they will also enter them at later stages or as amicus, often in defensive action to minimize losses and to protect strategy. Civil rights lawyers have a clear preference for the federal courts when the choice of forum is theirs to make, but they may find that others have made the choice. However, the preference for the federal court also may act as a constraint on choice by effectively precluding full consideration of the state forum.

The dynamics of litigation are such that even "planned litigation" does not proceed in a straight line; in part because of the idiosyncracies of particular cases, lawyers attempting such litigation are often not in control of timing and other important elements of cases. Much is in opponents' hands or in the hands of potential allies operating independently of organizational strategy. Planning is also limited by the way in which cases come to an organization—through other lawyers, who may not be well socialized to organizational priorities—and by long-term organizational tendencies to undertake certain types of cases or to press certain arguments; such tendencies, which create momentum (or inertia), are in part a result of lawyers' ideologies and their belief in the *myth of rights*; the momentum may limit responsiveness and innovation. Supreme Court decisions, affecting all cases whether or not undertaken with an intent to go to that Court itself, are an important part of the dynamics of planned litigation. Both overall changes in the Court's direction and the specific decisions that force lawyers to respond, thus decreasing their control of cases, make planning difficult and serve to reinforce litigators' responsive posture.

Perhaps the most important generalization to be drawn from recent interest-group civil rights litigation concerning race relations is that much of it is responsive and reflexive, and not subject to organizational control except within important constraints, which significantly limit litigating organizations' choices. Those constraints, sometimes rather severe, are imposed by the organizational environment and the complexity of litigation. Nonetheless, organizations not without choice are able to develop litigation strategy and to focus resources on particular areas of law; they can steer the law in certain directions and, by their selection and pursuit of certain cases, make a difference in such focal areas. Thus the actions of those engaging in "planned litigation" are not without effects, but the organizational litigators definitely do not dominate the domain in which they seek to operate.

The Practice of Law as a Confidence Game: Organizational Cooptation of a Profession

Abraham S. Blumberg

. . .

...I wish to question the impact of three recent landmark decisions of the United States Supreme Court; each hailed as destined to effect profound changes in the future of criminal law administration and enforcement in America. The first of these, *Gideon* v. *Wainwright*, 372 U.S. 335 (1963) required states and localities henceforth to furnish counsel in the case of indigent persons charged with a felony. The Gideon ruling left several major issues unsettled, among them the vital question: What is the precise point in time at which a suspect is entitled to counsel? The answer came relatively quickly in *Escobedo* v. *Illinois*, 378 U.S. 478 (1964), which has aroused a storm of controversy. Danny Escobedo confessed to the murder of his brother-in-law after the police had refused to permit retained counsel to see him, although his lawyer was present in the station house and asked to confer with his client. In a 5–4 decision, the court asserted that counsel must be permitted when the process of police investigative effort shifts

"The Practice of Law as a Confidence Game: Organizational Cooptation of a Profession," Abraham S. Blumberg. Robert Kiddler, Editor. Law and Society Review, Vol. 1, 1967. Reprinted by permission of the Law and Society Association. Most footnotes have been omitted.

from merely investigatory to that of accusatory: "when its focus is on the accused and its purpose is to elicit a confession—our adversary system begins to operate, and, under the circumstances here, the accused must be permitted to consult with his lawyer."

As a consequence, Escobedo's confession was rendered inadmissible. The decision triggered a national debate among police, district attorneys, judges, lawyers, and other law enforcement officials, which continues unabated, as to the value and propriety of confessions in criminal cases. On June 13, 1966, the Supreme Court in a 5–4 decision underscored the principle enunciated in *Escobedo* in the case of *Miranda* v. *Arizona*. Police interrogation of any suspect in custody, without his consent, unless a defense attorney is present, is prohibited by the self-incrimination provision of the Fifth Amendment. Regardless of the relative merit of the various shades of opinion about the role of counsel in criminal cases, the issues generated thereby will be in part resolved as additional cases move toward decision in the Supreme Court in the near future. They are of peripheral interest and not of immediate concern in this paper. However, the *Gideon*, *Escobedo*, and *Miranda* cases pose interesting general questions. In all three decisions, the Supreme Court reiterates the traditional legal conception of a defense lawyer based on the ideological perception of a criminal case as an *adversary, combative* proceeding, in which counsel for the defense assiduously musters all the admittedly limited resources at his command to *defend* the accused. The fundamental question remains to be answered: Does the Supreme Court's conception of the role of counsel in a criminal case square with social reality?

The task of this paper is to furnish some preliminary evidence toward the illumination of that question. . . . This paper is based upon observations made by the writer during many years of legal practice in the criminal courts of a large metropolitan area. No claim is made as to its methodological rigor, although it does reflect a conscious and sustained effort for participant observation.

COURT STRUCTURE DEFINES ROLE OF DEFENSE LAWYER

The overwhelming majority of convictions in criminal cases (usually over 90 per cent) are not the product of a combative, trial-by-jury process at all, but instead merely involve the sentencing of the individual after a negotiated, bargained-for plea of guilty has been entered. Although more recently the over-zealous role of police and prosecutors in producing pretrial confessions and admissions has achieved a good deal of notoriety, scant attention has been paid to the organizational structure and personnel of the criminal court itself. Indeed, the extremely high conviction rate produced without the features of an adversary trial in our courts would tend to suggest that the "trial" becomes a perfunctory reiteration and validation of the pretrial interrogation and investigation.

The institutional setting of the court defines a role for the defense counsel in a criminal case radically different from the one traditionally depicted. . . . It is grounded in pragmatic values, bureaucratic priorities, and administrative instruments. These exalt maximum production and the particularistic career designs of organizational incumbents, whose occupational and career commitments tend to generate a set of priorities. These priorities exert a higher claim than the stated ideological goals of "due process of law," and are often inconsistent with them.

Organizational goals and discipline impose a set of demands and conditions of practice on the respective professions in the criminal court, to which they respond by abandoning their ideological and professional commitments to the accused client, in the service of these higher claims of the court organization. All court personnel, including the accused's own lawyer, tend to be coopted to become agent-mediators who help the accused redefine his situation and restructure his perceptions concomitant with a plea of guilty.

Of all the occupational roles in the court the only private individual who is officially recognized as having a special status and concomitant obligations is the lawyer. His legal status is that of "an officer of the court" and he is held to a standard of ethical performance and duty to his client as well as to the court. This obligation is thought to be far higher than that expected of ordinary individuals occupying the various occupational statuses in the court community. However, lawyers, whether privately retained or of the legal-aid, public defender variety, have close and continuing relations with the prosecuting office and the court itself through discreet relations with the judges via their law secretaries or "confidential" assistants. Indeed, lines of communication, influence and contact with those offices, as well as with the Office of the Clerk of the court, Probation Division, and with the press, are essential to present and prospective requirements of criminal law practice. Similarly, the subtle involvement of the press and other mass media in the court's organizational network is not readily discernible to the casual observer. Accused persons come and go in the court system schema, but the structure and its occupational incumbents remain to carry on their respective career, occupational and organizational enterprises. The individual stridencies, tensions, and conflicts a given accused person's case may present to all the participants are overcome, because the formal and informal relations of all the groups in the court setting require it. The probability of continued future relations and interaction must be preserved at all costs.

This is particularly true of the "lawyer regulars" i.e., those defense lawyers, who by virtue of their continuous appearances in behalf of defendants, tend to represent the bulk of a criminal court's non-indigent case workload, and those lawyers who are not "regulars," who appear almost casually in behalf of an occasional client. Some of the the "lawyer regulars" are highly visible as one moves about the major urban centers of the nation, their offices line the back streets of the courthouses, at times sharing space with bondsmen. Their political "visibility" in terms of local club house ties, reaching into the judge's chambers and prosecutor's office, are also deemed essential to successful practitioners. Previous research has indicated that the "lawyer regulars" make no effort to conceal their dependence upon police, bondsmen, jail personnel. Nor do they conceal the necessity for maintaining intimate relations with all levels of personnel in the court setting as a means of obtaining, maintaining, and building their practice. These informal relations are the *sine qua non* not only of retaining a practice, but also

in the negotiation of pleas and sentences.

The client, then, is a secondary figure in the court system as in certain other bureaucratic settings. He becomes a means to other ends of the organization's incumbents. He may present doubts, contingencies, and pressures which challenge existing informal arrangements or disrupt them; but these tend to be resolved in favor of the continuance of the organization and its relations as before. There is a greater community of interest among all the principal organizational structures and their incumbents than exists elsewhere in other settings. The accused's lawyer has far greater professional, economic, intellectual and other ties to the various elements of the court system than he does to his own client. In short, the court is a closed community.

. . . Rather than any view of the matter in terms of some variation of a "conspiracy" hypothesis, the simple explanation is one of an ongoing system handling delicate tensions, managing the trauma produced by law enforcement and administration, and requiring almost pathological distrust of "outsiders" bordering on group paranoia.

The hostile attitude toward "outsiders" is in large measure engendered by a defensiveness itself produced by the inherent deficiencies of assembly line justice, so characteristic of our major criminal courts. Intolerably large caseloads of defendants which must be disposed of in an organizational context of limited resources and personnel, potentially subject the participants in the court community to harsh scrutiny from appellate courts, and other public and private sources of condemnation. As a consequence, an almost irreconcilable conflict is posed in terms of intense pressures to process large numbers of cases on the one hand, and the stringent ideological and legal requirements of "due process of law," on the other hand. A rather tenuous resolution of the dilemma has emerged in the shape of a large variety of bureaucratically ordained and controlled "work crimes," short cuts, deviations, and outright rule violations adopted as court practice in order to meet production norms. Fearfully anticipating criticism on ethical as well as legal grounds, all the significant participants in the court's social structure are bound into an organized system of complicity. This consists of a work arrangement in which the patterned, covert, informal breaches, and evasions of "due process" are institutionalized, but are, nevertheless, denied to exist.

These institutionalized evasions will be found to occur to some degree, in all criminal courts. Their nature, scope and complexity are largely determined by the size of the court, and the character of the community in which it is located, e.g., whether it is a large, urban institution, or a relatively small rural county court. In addition, idiosyncratic, local conditions may contribute to a unique flavor in the character and quality of the criminal law's administration in a particular community. However, in most instances a variety of stratagems are employed—some subtle, some crude, in effectively disposing of what are often too large caseloads. A wide variety of coercive devices are employed against an accused-client, couched in a depersonalized, instrumental, bureaucratic version of due process of law, and which are in reality a perfunctory obeisance to the ideology of due process. These include some very explicit pressures which are exerted in some measure by all court personnel, including judges, to plead guilty and avoid trial. In many instances the sanction of a potentially harsh sentence is utilized as the visible alternative to pleading guilty, in the case of recalcitrants. Probation and psychiatric reports are "tailored" to organizational needs, or are at least responsive to the court organization's

requirements for the refurbishment of a defendant's social biography, consonant with his new status. A resourceful judge can, through his subtle domination of the proceedings, impose his will on the final outcome of a trial. Stenographers and clerks, in their function as record keepers, are on occasion pressed into service in support of a judicial need to "rewrite" the record of a courtroom event. Bail practices are usually employed for purposes other than simply assuring a defendant's presence on the date of a hearing in connection with his case. Too often, the discretionary power as to bail is part of the arsenal of weapons available to collapse the resistance of an accused person. The foregoing is a most cursory examination of some of the more prominent "short cuts" available to any court organization. There are numerous other procedural strategies constituting due process deviations, which tend to become the work style artifacts of a court's personnel. Thus, only court "regulars" who are "bound in" are really accepted; others are treated routinely and in almost a coldly correct manner.

The defense attorneys, therefore, whether of the legal-aid, public defender variety, or privately retained, although operating in terms of pressures specific to their respective role and organizational obligations, ultimately are concerned with strategies which tend to lead to a plea. It is the rational, impersonal elements involving economies of time, labor, expense and a superior commitment of the defense counsel to these rationalistic values of maximum production of court organization that prevail, in his relationship with a client. The lawyer "regulars" are frequently former staff members of the prosecutor's office and utilize the prestige, know-how and contacts of their former affiliation as part of their stock in trade. Close and continuing relations between the lawyer "regular" and his former colleagues in the prosecutor's officer generally overshadow the relationship between the regular and his client. The continuing colleagueship of supposedly adversary counsel rests on real professional and organizational needs of a *quid pro quo*, which goes beyond the limits of an accommodation or *modus vivendi* one might ordinarily expect under the circumstances of an otherwise seemingly adversary relationship. Indeed, the adversary features which are manifest are for the most part muted and exist even in their attenuated form largely for external consumption. The principals, lawyers and assistant district attorney, rely upon one another's cooperation for their continued professional existence, and so the bargaining between them tends usually to be "reasonable" rather than fierce.

FEE COLLECTION AND FIXING

The real key to understanding the role of defense counsel in a criminal case is to be found in the area of the fixing of the fee to be charged and its collection. The problem of fixing and collecting the fee tends to influence to a significant degree the criminal court process itself, and not just the relationship of the lawyer and his client. In essence, a lawyer-client "confidence game" is played. A true confidence game is unlike the case of the emperor's new clothes wherein that monarch's nakedness was a result of inordinate gullibility and credulity. In a genuine confidence game, the perpetrator manipulates the basic dishonesty of his partner, the victim or mark, toward his own (the confidence operator's) ends. Thus, "the victim of a con scheme must have some larceny in his heart."

Legal service lends itself particularly well to confidence games....

...Much legal work is intangible either because it is simply a few words of advice, some preventive action, a telephone call, negotiation of some kind, a form filled out and filed, a hurried conference with another attorney or an official of a government agency, a letter or opinion written, or a countless variety of seemingly innocuous, and even prosaic procedures and actions. These are the basic activities, apart from any possible court appearance, of almost all lawyers, at all levels of practice. Much of the activity is not in the nature of the exercise of the traditional, precise professional skills of the attorney such as library research and oral argument in connection with appellate briefs, court motions, trial work, drafting of opinions, memoranda, contracts, and other complex documents and agreements. Instead, much legal activity, whether it is at the lowest or highest "white shoe" law firm levels, is of the brokerage, agent, sales representative, lobbyist type of activity, in which the lawyer acts for someone else in pursuing the latter's interests and designs. The service is intangible.

The large scale law firm may not speak as openly of their "contacts," their "fixing" abilities, as does the lower level lawyer. They trade instead upon a facade of thick carpeting, walnut panelling, genteel low pressure, and superficialities of traditional legal professionalism. There are occasions when even the large firm is on the defensive in connection with the fees they charge because the services rendered or results obtained do not appear to merit the fee asked. Therefore, there is a recurrent problem in the legal profession in fixing the amount of fee, and in justifying the basis for the requested fee.

Although the fee at times amounts to what the traffic and the conscience of the lawyer will bear, one further observation must be made with regard to the size of the fee and its collection. The defendant in a criminal case and the material gain he may have acquired during the course of his illicit activities are soon parted. Not infrequently the ill gotten fruits of the various modes of larceny are sequestered by a defense lawyer in payment of his fee. Inexorably, the amount of the fee is a function of the dollar value of the crime committed, and is frequently set with meticulous precision at a sum which bears an uncanny relationship to that of the net proceeds of the particular offense involved. On occasion, defendants have been known to commit additional offenses while at liberty on bail, in order to secure the requisite funds with which to meet their obligations for payment of legal fees. Defense lawyers condition even the most obtuse clients to recognize that there is a firm interconnection between fee payment and the zealous exercise of professional expertise, secret knowledge, and organizational "connections" in their behalf. Lawyers, therefore, seek to keep their clients in a proper state of tension, and to arouse in them the precise edge of anxiety which is calculated to encourage prompt fee payment. Consequently, the client attitude in the relationship between defense counsel and an accused is in many instances a precarious admixture of hostility, mistrust, dependence, and sycophancy. By keeping his client's anxieties aroused to the proper pitch, and establishing a seemingly causal relationship between a requested fee and the accused's ultimate extrication from his onerous difficulties, the lawyer will have established the necessary preliminary groundwork to assure a minimum of haggling over the fee and its eventual payment.

In varying degrees, as a consequence, all law practice involves a manipulation of the client and a stage management of the lawyer-client relationship so that at least an *appearance* of help and service will be forthcoming. This is accomplished in a variety of ways, often exercised in combination with each other. At the outset, the lawyer-professional

employs with suitable variation a measure of sales-puff which may range from an air of unbounding selfconfidence, adequacy, and dominion over events, to that of complete arrogance. This will be supplemented by the affectation of a studied, faultless mode of personal attire. In the larger firms, the furnishings and office trappings will serve as the backdrop to help in impression management and client intimidation. In all firms, solo or large scale, an access to secret knowledge, and to the seats of power and influence is inferred, or presumed to a varying degree as the basic vendible commodity of the practitioners.

The lack of visible end product offers a special complication in the course of the professional life of the criminal court lawyer with respect to his fee and in his relations with his client. The plain fact is that an accused in a criminal case always "loses" even when he has been exonerated by an acquittal, discharge, or dismissal of his case. The hostility of an accused which follows as a consequence of his arrest, incarceration, possible loss of job, expense and other traumas connected with his case is directed, by means of displacement, toward his lawyer. It is in this sense that it may be said that a criminal lawyer never really "wins" a case. The really satisfied client is rare, since in the very nature of the situation even an accused's vindication leaves him with some degree of dissatisfaction and hostility. It is this state of affairs that makes for a lawyer-client relationship in the criminal court which tends to be a somewhat exaggerated version of the usual lawyer-client confidence game.

At the outset, because there are great risks of nonpayment of the fee, due to the impecuniousness of his clients, and the fact that a man who is sentenced to jail may be a singularly unappreciative client, the criminal lawyer collects his fee *in advance*. Often, because the lawyer and the accused both have questionable designs of their own upon each other, the confidence game can be played. The criminal lawyer must serve three major functions, or stated another way, he must solve three problems. First, he must arrange for his fee; second, he must prepare and then, if necessary, "cool out" his client in case of defeat (a highly likely contingency); third, he must satisfy the court organization that he has performed adequately in the process of negotiating the plea, so as to preclude the possibility of any sort of embarrassing incident which may serve to invite "outside" scrutiny.

In assuring the attainment of one of his primary objectives, his fee, the criminal lawyer will very often enter into negotiations with the accused's kin, including collateral relatives. In many instances, the accused himself is unable to pay any sort of fee or anything more than a token fee. It then becomes important to involve as many of the accused's kin as possible in the situation. This is especially so if the attorney hopes to collect a significant part of a proposed substantial fee. . . .

A fee for a felony case which ultimately results in a plea, rather than a trial, may ordinarily range anywhere from $500 to $1,500. Should the case go to trial, the fee will be proportionately larger, depending upon the length of the trial. But the larger the fee the lawyer wishes to exact, the more impressive his performance must be, in terms of his stage managed image as a personage of great influence and power in the court organization. Court personnel are keenly aware of the extent to which a lawyer's stock in trade involves the precarious stage management of an image which goes beyond the usual professional flamboyance, and for this reason alone the lawyer is "bound in" to the authority system of the court's organizational discipline.

Therefore, to some extent, court personnel will aid the lawyer in the creation and maintenance of that impression. There is a tacit commitment to the lawyer by the court organization, apart from formal etiquette, to aid him in this. Such augmentation of the lawyer's stage managed image as this affords, is the partial basis for the *quid pro quo* which exists between the lawyer and the court organization. It tends to serve as the continuing basis for the higher loyalty of the lawyer to the organization; his relationship with his client, in contrast, is transient, ephemeral and often superficial.

DEFENSE LAWYER AS DOUBLE AGENT

The lawyer has often been accused of stirring up unnecessary litigation, especially in the field of negligence. He is said to acquire a vested interest in a cause of action or claim which was initially his client's. The strong incentive of possible fee motivates the lawyer to promote litigation which would otherwise never have developed. However, the criminal lawyer develops a vested interest of an entirely different nature in his client's case: to limit its scope and duration rather than do battle. Only in this way can a case be "profitable." Thus, he enlists the aid of relatives not only to assure payment of his fee, but he will also rely on these persons to help him in his agent-mediator role of convincing the accused to plead guilty, and ultimately to help in "cooling out" the accused if necessary.

It is at this point that an accused-defendant may experience his first sense of "betrayal." While he had perhaps perceived the police and prosecutor to be adversaries, or possibly even the judge, the accused is wholly unprepared for his counsel's role performance as an agent-mediator. In the same vein, it is even less likely to occur to an accused that members of his own family or other kin may become agents, albeit at the behest and urging of other agents or mediators, acting on the principle that they are in reality helping an accused negotiate the best possible plea arrangement under the circumstances. Usually, it will be the lawyer who will activate next of kin in this role, his ostensible motive being to arrange for his fee. But soon latent and unstated motives will assert themselves, with entreaties by counsel to the accused's next of kin, to appeal to the accused to "help himself" by pleading. *Gemeinschaft* sentiments are to this extent exploited by a defense lawyer (or even at times by a district attorney) to achieve specific secular ends, that is, of concluding a particular matter with all possible dispatch.

The fee is often collected in stages, each installment usually payable prior to a necessary court appearance required during the course of an accused's career journey. At each stage, in his interviews and communications with the accused, or in addition, with members of his family, if they are helping with the fee payment, the lawyer employs an air of professional confidence and "inside-dopesterism" in order to assuage anxieties on all sides. He makes the necessary bland assurances, and in effect manipulates his client, who is usually willing to do and say the things, true or not, which will help his attorney extricate him. Since the dimensions of what he is essentially selling, organizational influence and expertise, are not technically and precisely measurable, the lawyer can make extravagant claims of influence and secret knowledge with immunity. Thus, lawyers frequently claim to have inside knowledge in connection with information in the hands of the D.A., police, probation officials or to have access to these functionaries. Factually, they often do, and need only to ex-

aggerate the nature of their relationships with them to obtain the desired effective impression upon the client. But, as in the genuine confidence game, the victim who has participated is loathe to do anything which will upset the lesser plea which his lawyer has "conned" him into accepting.

In effect, in his role as double agent, the criminal lawyer performs an extremely vital and delicate mission for the court organization and the accused. Both principals are anxious to terminate the litigation with a minimum of expense and damage to each other. There is no other personage or role incumbent in the total court structure more strategically located, who by training and in terms of his own requirements, is more ideally suited to do so than the lawyer. In recognition of this, judges will cooperate with attorneys in many important ways. For example, they will adjourn the case of an accused in jail awaiting plea or sentence if the attorney requests such action. While explicitly this may be done for some innocuous and seemingly valid reason, the tacit purpose is that pressure is being applied by the attorney for the collection of his fee, which he knows will probably not be forthcoming if the case is concluded. Judges are aware of this tactic on the part of lawyers, who, by requesting an adjournment, keep an accused incarcerated awhile longer as a not too subtle method of dunning a client for payment. However, the judges will go along with this, on the ground that important ends are being served. Often, the only end served is to protect a lawyer's fee.

The judge will help an accused's lawyer in still another way. He will lend the official aura of his office and courtroom so that a lawyer can stage manage an impression of an "all out" performance for the accused in justification of his fee. The judge and other court personnel will serve as a backdrop for a scene charged with dramatic fire, in which the accused's lawyer makes a stirring appeal in his behalf. With a show of restrained passion, the lawyer will intone the virtues of the accused and recite the social deprivations which have reduced him to his present state. The speech varies somewhat, depending on whether the accused has been convicted after trial or has pleaded guilty. In the main, however, the incongruity, superficiality, and ritualistic character of the total performance is underscored by a visibly impassive, almost bored reaction on the part of the judge and other members of the court retinue.

Afterward, there is a hearty exchange of pleasantries between the lawyer and district attorney, wholly out of context in terms of the supposed adversary nature of the preceding events. The fiery passion in defense of his client is gone, and the lawyers for both sides resume their offstage relations, chatting amiably and perhaps including the judge in their restrained banter. No other aspect of their visible conduct so effectively serves to put even a casual observer on notice, that these individuals have claims upon each other. These seemingly innocuous actions are indicative of continuing organizational and informal relations, which, in their intricacy and depth, range far beyond any priorities or claims a particular defendant may have.

Criminal law practice is a unique form of private law practice since it really only appears to be private practice. Actually it is bureaucratic practice, because of the legal practitioner's enmeshment in the authority, discipline, and perspectives of the court organization. Private practice, supposedly, in a professional sense, involves the maintenance of an organized, disciplined body of knowledge and learning; the individual practitioners are imbued with a spirit of autonomy and service, the earning of a livelihood being incidental. In the sense that the lawyer in the criminal court serves as a double agent, serving higher organizational rather than professional ends, he may be deemed to be engaged in bureaucratic rather than private practice. To some extent the lawyer-client "confidence game," in addition to its other functions, serves to conceal this fact.

THE CLIENT'S PERCEPTION

The "cop-out" ceremony, in which the court process culminates, is not only invaluable for redefining the accused's perspectives of himself, but also in reiterating publicly in a formally structured ritual the accused person's guilt for the benefit of significant "others" who are observing. The accused not only is made to assert publicly his guilt of a specific crime, but also a complete recital of its details. He is further made to indicate that he is entering his plea of guilt freely, willingly, and voluntarily, and that he is not doing so because of any promises or in consideration of any commitments that may have been made to him by anyone. This last is intended as a blanket statement to shield the participants from any possible charges of "coercion" or undue influence that may have been exerted in violation of due process requirements. Its function is to preclude any later review by an appellate court on these grounds, and also to obviate any second thoughts an accused may develop in connection with his plea.

However, for the accused, the conception of self as a guilty person is in large measure a temporary role adaptation. His career socialization as an accused, if it is successful, eventuates in his acceptance and redefinition of himself as a guilty person. However, the transformation is ephemeral, in that he will, in private, quickly reassert his innocence. Of importance is that he accept his defeat, publicly proclaim it, and find some measure of pacification in it. Almost

TABLE 1
Defendant Responses as to Guilt or Innocence after Pleading Guilty
N = 724; Years—1962, 1963, 1964

Nature of Response		N of Defendants
Innocent (Manipulated)	"The lawyer or judge, police or D.A. 'conned me'"	86
Innocent (Pragmatic)	"Wanted to get it over with" "You can't beat the system" "They have you over a barrel when you have a record"	147
Innocent (Advice of counsel)	"Followed my lawyer's advice"	92
Innocent (Defiant)	"Framed"—Betrayed by "Complainant," "Police," "Squealers," "Lawyer," "Friends," "Wife," "Girlfriend"	33
Innocent (Adverse social data)	Blames probation officer or psychiatrist for "Bad Report," in cases where there was prepleading investigation	15
Guilty	"But I should have gotten a better deal" Blames lawyer, D.A., Police, Judge	74
Guilty	Won't say anything further	21
Fatalistic (Doesn't press his "Innocence," won't admit "Guilt")	"I did it for convenience" "My lawyer told me it was only thing I could do" "I did it because it was the best way out"	248
No response		8
Total		724

immediately after his plea, a defendant will generally be interviewed by a representative of the probation division in connection with a presentence report which is to be prepared. The very first question to be asked of him by the probation officer is: "Are you guilty of the crime to which you pleaded?" This is by way of double affirmation of the defendant's guilt. Should the defendant now begin to make bold assertions of his innocence, despite his plea of guilty, he will be asked to withdraw his plea and stand trial on the original charges. Such a threatened possibility is, in most instances, sufficient to cause an accused to let the plea stand and to request the probation officer to overlook his exclamations of innocence. The table that follows is a breakdown of the categorized responses of a random sample of male defendants in Metropolitan Court[1] during 1962, 1963, and 1964 in connection with their statements during presentence probation interviews following their plea of guilty.

It would be well to observe at the outset, that of the 724 defendants who pleaded guilty before trial, only 43 (5.94 per cent) of the total group had confessed prior to their indictment [see Table 1]. Thus, the ultimate judicial process was predicated upon evidence independent of any confession of the accused.

As the data indicate, only a relatively small number (95) out of the total number of defendants actually will even admit their guilt, following the "cop-out" ceremony. However, even though they have affirmed their guilt, many of these defendants felt that they should have been able to negotiate a more favorable plea. The largest aggregate of defendants (373) were those who reasserted their "innocence" following their public profession of guilt during the "cop-out" ceremony. These defendants employed differential degrees of fervor, solemnity and credibility, ranging from really mild, wavering assertions of innocence which were embroidered with a variety of stock explanations and rationalizations, to those of an adamant, "framed" nature. Thus, the "Innocent" group, for the most part, were largely concerned with underscoring for their probation interviewer their essential "goodness" and "worthiness," despite their formal plea of guilty. Assertion of his innocence at the post plea stage, resurrects a more respectable and acceptable self concept for the accused defendant who has pleaded guilty. A recital of the structural exigencies which precipitated his plea of guilt, serves to embellish a newly proffered claim of innocence, which many defendants mistakenly feel will stand them in good stead at the time of sentence, or ultimately with probation or parole authorities.

Relatively few (33) maintained their innocence in terms of having been "framed"by some person or agent-mediator, although a larger number (86) indicated that they had been manipulated or "conned" by an agent-mediator to plead guilty, but as indicated, their assertions of innocence were relatively mild.

A rather substantial group (147) preferred to stress the pragmatic aspects of their plea of guilty. They would only perfunctorily assert their innocence and would in general refer to some adverse aspect of their situation which they believed tended to negatively affect their bargaining leverage, including in some instances a prior criminal record.

One group of defendants (92), while maintaining their innocence, simply employed some variation of a theme of following "the advice of counsel" as a covering response, to explain their guilty plea in the light of their new affirmation of innocence.

The largest single group of defendants (248) were basically fatalistic. They often verbalized weak suggestions of their innocence in rather halting terms, wholly without convictions. By the same token, they would not admit guilt readily and were generally evasive as to guilt or innocence, preferring to stress aspects of their stoic submission in their decision to plead. This sizable group of defendants appeared to perceive the total court process as being caught up in a monstrous organizational apparatus, in which the defendant role expectancies were not clearly defined. Reluctant to offend anyone in authority, fearful that clear cut statements on their part as to their guilt or innocence would be negatively construed, they adopted a stance of passivity, resignation and acceptance. Interestingly, they would in most instances invoke their lawyer as being the one who crystallized the available alternatives for them, and who was therefore the critical element in their decision-making process.

In order to determine which agent-mediator was most influential in altering the accused's perspectives as to his decision to plead or go to trial (regardless of the proposed basis of the plea), the same sample of defendants were asked to indicate the person who first suggested to them that they plead guilty. They were also asked to indicate which of the persons or officials who made such suggestion, was most influential in affecting their final decision to plead.

The following table indicates the breakdown of the responses to the two questions:

It is popularly assumed that the police, through forced confessions, and the district

TABLE 2
Role of Agent-Mediators in Defendant's Guilty Plea

Person or Official	First Suggested Plea of Guilty	Influenced the Accused Most in His Final Decision to Plead
Judge	4	26
District Attorney	67	116
Defense counsel	407	411
Probation officer	14	3
Psychiatrist	8	1
Wife	34	120
Friends and kin	21	14
Police	14	4
Fellow inmates	119	14
Others	28	5
No response	8	10
Total	724	724

attorney, employing still other pressures, are most instrumental in the inducement of an accused to plead guilty. As Table 2 indicates, it is actually the defendant's own counsel who is most effective in this role. Further, this phenomenon tends to reinforce the extremely rational nature of criminal law administration, for an organization could not rely upon the sort of idiosyncratic measures employed by the police to induce confessions and maintain its efficiency, high production and overall rational-legal character. The defense counsel becomes the ideal agent-mediator since, as "officer of the court" and confidant of the accused and his kin, he lives astride both worlds and can serve the ends of the two as well as his own.

While an accused's wife, for example, may be influential in making him more amenable to a plea, her agent-mediator role has, nevertheless, usually been sparked and initiated by defense counsel. Further, although a number of first suggestions of a plea came from an accused's fellow jail inmates, he tended to rely largely on his counsel as an

ultimate source of influence in his final decision. The defense counsel, being a crucial figure in the total organizational scheme in constituting a new set of perspectives for the accused, the same sample of defendants were asked to indicate at which stage of their contact with counsel was the suggestion of a plea made. There are three basic kinds of defense counsel available in Metropolitan Court: Legal-aid, privately retained counsel, and counsel assigned by the court (but may eventually be privately retained by the accused).

. . .

The overwhelming majority of accused persons, regardless of type of counsel, related a specific incident which indicated an urging or suggestion, either during the course of the first or second contact, that they plead guilty to a lesser charge if this could be arranged. Of all the agent-mediators, it is the lawyer who is most effective in manipulating an accused's perspectives, notwithstanding pressures that may have been previously applied by police, district attorney, judge or any of the agent-mediators that may have been activated by them. Legal-aid and assigned counsel would apparently be more likely to suggest a possible plea at the point of initial interview as response to pressures of time. In the case of the assigned counsel, the strong possibility that there is no fee involved, may be an added impetus to such a suggestion at the first contact.

In addition, there is some further evidence. . . of the perfunctory, ministerial character of the system in Metropolitan Court and similar criminal courts. There is little real effort to individualize, and the lawyer's role as agent-mediator may be seen as unique in that he is in effect a double agent. Although, as "officer of the court" he mediates between the court organization and the defendant, his roles with respect to each are rent by conflicts of interest. Too often these must be resolved in favor of the organization which provides him with the means for his professional existence. Consequently, in order to reduce the strains and conflicts imposed in what is ultimately an over-demanding role obligation for him, the lawyer engages in the lawyer-client "confidence game" so as to structure more favorably an otherwise onerous role system.

CONCLUSION

Recent decisions of the Supreme Court, in the area of criminal law administration and defendant's rights, fail to take into account three crucial aspects of social structure which may tend to render the more libertarian rules as nugatory. The decisions overlook (1) the nature of courts as formal organization; (2) the relationship that the lawyer-regular *actually* has with the court organization; and (3) the character of the lawyer-client relationship in the criminal court (the routine relationships, not those unusual ones that are described in "heroic" terms in novels, movies, and TV).

Courts, like many other modern large-scale organizations possess a monstrous appetite for the cooptation of entire professional groups as well as individuals. Almost all those who come within the ambit of organizational authority, find that their definitions, perceptions and values have been refurbished, largely in terms favorable to the particular organization and its goals. As a result, recent Supreme Court decisions may have a long range effect which is radically different from that intended or anticipated. The more libertarian rules will tend to produce the rather ironic end result of augmenting the *existing* organizational arrangements, enriching court organizations with more personnel and elaborate structure, which in turn will maximize organizational goals of "efficiency" and production. Thus, many defendants will find that courts will possess an even more sophisticated apparatus for processing them toward a guilty plea!

NOTE

1. The name is of course fictitious. However, the actual court which served as the universe from which the data were drawn is one of the largest criminal courts in the United States, dealing with felonies only. Female defendants in the years 1950 through 1964 constituted from 7–10% of the totals for each year.

Defending White-Collar Crime

Kenneth Mann

. . .

At its very foundation, an essential objective of the defense function in the Anglo-American system of criminal justice is to prevent imposition of criminal sanctions against a person accused of crime. But this objective has been masked in recent years by the overwhelming predominance of street crime in the criminal courts. Defense attorneys handling street crime are usually restricted to helping their clients arrange a plea of guilty, and they bargain over facts already known to the government when they enter the case. Not only does the defense attorney typically assume that his client is guilty, but he usually assumes when he takes the case that the government has sufficient evidence to convict his client. Plea bargaining has become the norm, and, most observers agree, this has led to a system of assembly-line justice where compromise is the rule. Legal rights are not fully exploited in the interest of protecting the defendant. Norms

Reprinted from Kenneth Mann, *Defending White-Collar Crime: A Portrait of Attorneys at Work* (New Haven: Yale University Press, 1985), pp. 4–15. Footnotes and notes omitted.

of efficiency outweigh norms of due process. The defense function is weakened and distorted because attorneys do not have the opportunity to do more than negotiate a compromise.

..., I present a picture of a very different system of criminal defense work. It is a picture highlighted by the increasing investigation and prosecution of white-collar crime and by a group of attorneys who have become specialists in white-collar crime defense. It brings to light in a new way fundamental qualities of the defense function: its commitment to helping the guilty go free, its adversarial character, its tendency to operate on the margin of ethical, moral, and legal standards, and its reliance on the manipulation of people and organizations.

The white-collar crime defense attorney, like his counterpart handling street crime, typically assumes that his client is guilty. Certainly that assumption held in every case I describe in this book. But unlike the street-crime defense attorney—and this is a critical difference—the white-collar defense attorney does not assume that the government has the evidence to convict his client. Instead, he starts with the assumption that, though his client is guilty, he may be able to keep the government from knowing this or from concluding that it has a strong enough case to prove it. Though in the end he may have to advise his client to plead guilty and bargain, he often starts his case with the expectation of avoiding compromise.

The white-collar crime defense attorney is zealous in his advocacy of his client's interest, often rejecting government overtures to negotiate and compromise. In contrast to the attorney handling street crime, his time is not a scarce resource, and each case is individually cultivated with great care. In white-collar cases, the defense attorney is usually called in by the client to conduct a defense before the government investigation is completed and in some cases even before it begins. The defense attorney employs his own investigators, who are experts in accounting and finance, a well as a staff of legal researchers. He learns thoroughly the details of the case, usually having a greater ability to do this than the government investigator and prosecutor. This attorney, in distinct contrast to the attorney handling street crime, has a number of opportunities to argue the innocence of his client before the government makes a decision to issue an indictment. A plea agreement may be an important element in the final disposition of the white-collar case, but the compromise that leads to a plea agreement is the result of a carefully managed process of adversary interaction in which cooperation with the government plays little or no part. And in many cases the guilty plea is followed by a second period of intensive advocacy—at the time of sentencing—where compromise and negotiation again remain conspicuously absent. But above all, and this is the central theme of the white-collar crime defense function, the defense attorney works to keep potential evidence out of government reach by controlling access to information.

THE INFORMATION CONTROL DEFENSE AND THE SUBSTANTIVE DEFENSE

The defense attorney's adversaries are the government agents who decide whether a criminal charge should be made—government investigators and, eventually, prosecutors. To prevent issuance of an indictment, the attorney must keep these persons from concluding that the client has done something that warrants criminal prosecution. The central strategy question for the attorney is how to accomplish this end, and this applies in all cases, irrespective of whether the attorney's client has in fact committed a crime, or whether it is a white-collar or a street crime.

This question might seem to lead to a straightforward answer. If an attorney does in the white-collar case what is done in the street-crime case, he takes the evidence presented against his client, and other evidence known to him that is exculpatory of the client, and makes the appropriate legal argument. This evidence, so the attorney argues, fails to show adequately, that is, beyond a reasonable doubt, that the client committed a crime. The defense attorney's task is to draw on conventional sources of law—statutory and case law—to show his adversary that the client's behavior falls on the "not guilty" side of that line created by the substantive standard of criminal responsibility. This task is conventional legal argument and takes place at all stages of the criminal process. I will call this defense strategy substantive defense.

In making a substantive defense, the defense attorneys studied had a distinctive role because they were handling white-collar cases. Rather than waiting until trial or until the immediate pretrial period when plea negotiations usually take place, these defense attorneys had an opportunity to make a substantive defense before a charge was made. While attorneys in other types of cases also make opportunities for adversary argument before charging, in white-collar cases there is typically a series of institutionalized settings for conducting precharge adversarial proceedings on questions of substantive criminal responsibility. Substantive legal argument before the charge decision is a routinized pattern of defense advocacy in white-collar cases.

The substantive defense is not, however, the initial defense strategy for a competent attorney. The defense attorney's first objective is to prevent the government from obtaining evidence that could be inculpatory of his client and used by the investigator or prosecutor to justify issuance of a formal criminal charge. Instead of preparing legal argument, the defense attorney first devotes himself to keeping evidence out of any prospective adversary forum in which legal argument about the client's criminal responsibility might take place. This action is crucial to prevent issuance of a criminal charge. I call this task information control and the defense strategy built on these actions an information control defense.

Information control entails keeping documents away from and preventing clients and witnesses from talking to government investigators, prosecutors, and judges. It will become evident as I describe defense attorneys handling actual cases of white-collar crime that information control is not the conventional advocacy task of substantive argument in which the defense attorney analyzes a set of facts and argues that a crime is not proved. It occurs before the substantive defense and is in some ways a more important defense. If successful, it keeps the raw material of legal argument out of the hands of the government, it obviates argument about the substantive legal implications of facts about crime, and it keeps the government ignorant of evidence it needs in deciding whether to make a formal charge against a person suspected of committing a crime. And, even if a formal charge is made, it keeps facts about a crime out of the arena of plea negotiations and out of the courtroom if a trial takes place. For these reasons, information control lies at the very heart of the defense function, preventing the imposition of a criminal sanction on an accused person who has committed a crime, as well as on the rare one who has not. . . .

Information control as a defense strategy is not exclusive to white-collar cases. In many kinds of criminal cases, defense attorneys move to exclude illegally seized evidence, an adversarial control device, and they engage in pretrial coaching of witnesses, a managerial control device. What is distinctive in white-collar cases is the centrality of information control strategies to defense work: they are fundamental modus operandi constituting a basic defense plan, rather than merely tactics in a broader strategy.

While adversarial information control is well recognized—particularly the law of search and seizure—characteristics of managerial information control are not well identified in the literature on law. In the past decade and earlier, attorneys and scholars raised issues bearing on the propriety of information control in the intensely debated question of whether a defense attorney can put a defendant on the witness stand when he suspects that false testimony will be given. But the broader range of information control strategies that will be examined here has not been brought together and considered as a systematic method of action. In large part, this is a result of the difficulty of obtaining research access to the setting in which managerial information control occurs: the attorney-client relationship. But it is also a result of the fact that managerial information control is in the criminal process distinctive to cases of white-collar crime, and white-collar crime has not drawn until recently a substantial research concern.... In cases of white-collar crime, particularly when attorneys are brought into the case early, there are many opportunities for information control, and experienced attorneys have developed special skills for exploiting them.

STAGES OF THE CRIMINAL PROCESS

Defense attorneys handling white-collar cases rarely try cases. Occasionally a trial occupies an attorney for an extended period of time, but this is regarded as an exceptional event in most of the offices I studied. In this important respect, the work of the white-collar crime specialist is similar to that of the defense attorney handling street crime. But there are many differences between the practices of these two attorneys. These will emerge in looking at the typical, patterned ways that white-collar and street-crime cases go through the criminal process.

Precharge

In the street-crime practice, defense attorneys are brought into cases by clients after a charge has been made. Before the charging decision, there is little or nothing that the defense attorney can do to control information or argue that the facts available do not prove a crime. This period is therefore generally unimportant for bringing defense resources to bear on the question of the guilt of the client for the crime that is likely to be charged. To the extent that defense attorneys do intervene actively before a charging decision, their work is concentrated on arrest, arraignment and bail processes. Some impact on the fundamental question of guilt may be had here, but substantive argument

and information control will rarely reach the high intensity achieved by attorneys in white-collar cases.

The white-collar crime defense attorney more often gets into his case at this stage. Clients typically recruit their attorneys before an official charge is made and are sometimes able to do this simultaneously with or even before the beginning of a long investigative period leading up to the consideration of charges by an investigative agency or prosecutor. It is during the period before the government makes its charging decision that white-collar defense attorneys spend by far the largest portion of their work hours. They discuss their cases with their clients, evaluate documents held by clients, interview third parties, take affidavits from third parties, examine documents held by third parties, meet with investigators to argue their case, and return to clients, third parties, and documents to refine their knowledge of the case and their strategy.

The two main defense strategies—information control and substantive legal argument—are already being used at this period and with more intensity than at any subsequent point in the criminal process. The defense attorney is using all available resources at this stage because his primary objective is to prevent the government from discovering the guilt of the client or from coming to the conclusion that it can prove the guilt of the client. In the white-collar crime defense practice, issuance of a criminal charge is already a significant failure for the defense attorney and is for the client often the most severe sanction that can be meted out, even if at the end of the process a short prison term is given by the sentencing judge.

The centrality of this period to white-collar practice is indicated also by the attorney's desire to enter into plea negotiations at this time if he is forced to give up the preferred strategy of demonstrating the client's innocence. Before charging, the defense's bargaining position is stronger: the government has made less of an institutional commitment to the case, the investigation is at an earlier stage, and the defendant can earn credits for early cooperation. The defense attorney who gets in early wants to take advantage of this potentially better bargaining position. Whether and when to enter into plea negotiations (discussed separately below) is the major strategic choice for a defense attorney during the precharge period of the criminal defense in white-collar cases.

Pretrial

The street-crime defense attorney concentrates his work in the pretrial stage of the criminal process, that is, from the time his client has been charged up to the formal disposition made by guilty plea. In the vast majority of cases processed in lower criminal courts in the United States, this stage is short and the services provided by the attorney to the client are minimal, often negligible. The negotiated deal is the almost exclusive method of disposition. Milton Heumann aptly describes this defense process:

> Typically...a line forms outside the prosecutor's office the morning before the court is convened. Defense attorneys shuffle into the prosecutor's office and, in a matter of two or three minutes, dispose of the one or more cases "set down" that day. Generally, only a few words have to be exchanged before agreement is reached. The defense attorney mutters something about the defendant, the prosecutor reads the police report, and concurrence on "what to do" generally, but not always, emerges.
>
> [In court]...the defense attorney embellishes the defendant's perfunctory plea of guilty with a brief statement about how repentant the defendant is, and/or how trivial

an offense this actually was, and/or what a wonderful person the defendant really is. As the defense attorney drones on, the judge joins the prosecutor in directing his attention to matters other than the words being spoken in the court.

... [T]he street-crime defense attorney devotes most of his time to his cases during the pretrial period. That period may be longer or shorter or more or less adversarial depending on the resources of the client and the amount of time available to the attorney. But only in a very small number of cases does the attorney decide to argue that his client is innocent, which means going to trial. In presenting an overall analytic picture of the criminal process, Malcolm Feeley assigns most of what is significant that occurs to a defendant in a lower criminal court into what he calls the pretrial period. Chronologically, some of this—arrest, bail, and arraignment—occurs in what I have called the precharge period, but the processes for determining outcome—plea bargaining, adjudication, and sentencing—occur after charging and without trial. The pretrial period is the most significant phase in the defense and prosecution of street crime, not at all because a trial is planned for, but because this is where the prosecutor and defense attorney apply whatever resources they have in coming to a resolution about outcome.

The pretrial period may also be important for the white-collar defense attorney, but only where there has been some prior defense failure. This occurs when the defendant fails to recruit an attorney before the government charges or when the attorney fails in an attempt to prevent charging and fails to make a plea bargain before the charge is issued. Though it may seem inappropriate, white-collar defense attorneys tend to regard the case that extends past the precharge stage as a failure. This expresses the defense attorney's perception that a large proportion of guilty clients in white-collar cases are not charged, because they work their way out of the system before the government collects sufficient evidence.

Where the white-collar case moves past the precharge stage into pretrial, strong forces push the defense attorney to have his client plead guilty. But this is not due to the defense attorney's heavy caseload or lack of client resources, factors that make plea bargaining attractive in cases of street crime. It results from the perceived low possibility of winning after indictment, particularly when the defense attorney has already argued his main defense with the investigator or prosecutor in the precharge period.

Trial

The third stage of the criminal process presents very similar problems for the white-collar and street-crime defense attorneys. The defense attorney handling the white-collar case may find it easier to meet his client, and the client may be better at grasping legal principles he needs to know to testify, if he so chooses. But these factors are likely to be insignificant in the overall case. Both attorneys face the well-known problem of keeping witnesses willing to testify and keeping themselves apprised of potential changes in the content of witnesses' testimony. And both attorneys face the problem of picking a jury that will not be biased against either the client's class and place in life or the particular crime he is charged with committing.

One distinguishing feature—so some attorneys contend—is that the white-collar case gives the defense attorney more room to create doubt in the jurors' minds, due to the high level of ambiguity in many white-collar statutes, such as fraud statutes, compared to street-crime statutes, such as assault. These attorneys argue that the average juror has a less well-formed idea of what fraud is than of what assault is, and that this difference makes it easier to raise doubt about the prosecution's case.

This observation about statutes appears true, but a major problem in determining how it affects the trial stage is that white-collar cases are more often subjected to intensive adversarial argument prior to trial. It follows that the case that gets to trial is more likely to be a strong case (from the perspective of the prosecution). The weak cases that get to trial are more likely to be the street-crime cases because investigators and prosecutors are tested by defense attorneys less often and less resolutely. Thus, an alternative view of how ambiguity in statutes affects the criminal process would assert that it creates opportunities for legal argument but that in white-collar crime this effect is vitiated by the time a case gets to trial. Then, the defense attorney has fewer opportunities to create doubt.

It is thus difficult to determine whether there is any difference between white-collar and street-crime cases at trial, other than the amount of resources put into the cases by the defendants. What emerges as persuasive is that there are fewer differences between white-collar and street-crime cases at the trial stage than at other stages of the criminal process.

Sentencing

Much of the sentencing process in cases of street crime takes place in the pretrial stage, during and as a result of plea bargaining. The defendant wants to extricate himself from the criminal process as soon as possible, but not at the cost of a prison sentence or other heavy sanction. The defense attorney aims at getting the client out of the system quickly, a goal that coincides with his own need to handle a large number of cases efficiently, while negotiating to obtain the lowest possible sentence. In most lower criminal courts the range of expected sentences for typical street crimes is familiar to defense attorneys and prosecutors. The bargaining process is then focused on reaching agreement about how to present the case to the judge in order to achieve an agreed-upon sentence. Though the judge is probably not bound by this presentation, the sentence decision is usually predictable within a small margin of error. By the time the formal sentencing stage arrives, the defense attorney expects to have a fairly limited role. The attorney makes a routine plea for leniency and routine recitations of the defendant's good and repentant characteristics. . . .

In the white-collar case, the sentencing hearing is the most important stage in the process, after precharge. The plea bargain reached by the defense attorney at an earlier stage will have been constructed, as in the case of street crime, with the intent of reducing the seriousness of the sanction. But in white-collar cases the role of the defense attorney in setting sentence continues to be important after the completion of the plea bargain. Defense attorneys use the sentencing stage as an opportunity to repeat one of the major tasks of earlier stages: substantive legal argument.

Traditional models of the criminal process place legal argument about substantive responsibility in the stages before sentencing. Distinctive to white-collar cases is the persistence of ambiguity about the true nature of the crime committed and the true extent of the defendant's blameworthiness. The persistence of ambiguity, coupled with the high level of client resources in white-collar cases, extends the salience of substantive legal argument beyond the formal determination of guilt into the formal sentencing stage.

The interaction of this factor with the absence of adequate decisional guidelines in a discretionary system of judicial sentencing has given defense attorneys a central role in determining type and length of sentence in white-collar cases.

.   .   .

PLEA BARGAINING AND THE MAJOR STRATEGIC DECISION

Striking a plea bargain for clients is no less important in cases of white-collar crime than it is in street crime. The statutory charges in a charging instrument, the number of counts alleged, the description of the crime, and the sentencing plea made by the government can all be influenced by a plea bargain. Whether the defense attorney enters into serious negotiations before or after charging, what has occurred before those negotiations may determine the nature of the deal that can be struck with the prosecution. There are important differences in the way that plea negotiations are prepared in cases of white-collar crime and street-crime.

In a street-crime case, the defense attorney has limited opportunities to control the facts that reach the government and determine its readiness to make a deal. The defense attorney will have to find substantive weaknesses in the government's case and play on the government's need to resolve cases quickly and efficiently. In addition to making conventional legal arguments about what the available evidence proves, the defense attorney emphasizes the amount of resources that the government will need to take the case to trial.

Because the white-collar crime defense attorney gets into his case earlier, he prepares for plea bargaining by attempting to limit the government's access to facts inculpatory of his client. The strength of his position at the bargaining table vis-à-vis the government is often the result of steps he takes early in an investigation to protect documents from discovery and to influence the content of witnesses' statements. When negotiations are begun, the defense attorney will already have done a substantial amount of fieldwork.

The decision to start plea negotiations is a critical point in white-collar cases. An attorney who starts negotiations is communicating to the government that the client he represents is guilty of something and that the attorney thinks that the government will be able to prove it. When the attorney is conducting an information control defense aimed at preventing the criminal charge, he will not want to communicate this message to the government. The converse is true. The attorney wants to communicate a message of not guilty as long as there remains some possibility of preventing the government from coming to the conclusion that it has a chargeable case. If the defense attorney forgoes negotiations, he increases the possibility of persuading the government not to indict in the marginal case.

The decision not to enter into negotiations in order to maintain the facade of innocence is a difficult one because there are countervailing reasons to negotiate early. If at the end of an investigation the government is likely to decide that it has a strong enough case to charge, the defense attorney has an advantage if he negotiates early. The government will be more ready to grant concessions before it completes its investigation. At an early point in the investigation the government may falsely assume that necessary evidence is inaccessible. If the attorney gets to the investigator or prosecutor when the going is tough, he will be able to obtain a good plea bargain with substantial advantages for his client. The longer the defense attorney waits to start negotiations, the

harder it will be to find flexibility in the government's position.

Not only is the government likely to have a stronger case as the investigation advances, but its readiness to compromise in the interest of efficiency becomes progressively weaker. Investigators and prosecutors often work on cases for many months, during which they develop a substantial personal commitment to seeing the results of their investigation bear fruit. When this happens, there is a tendency to be overcommitted to prosecution, rather than, as in the street-crime case, overcommitted to disposing of cases through a plea bargain. Street-crime defense attorneys depend on backlog pressure to facilitate a deal. White-collar defense attorneys lose this advantage, particularly when they wait too long to negotiate.

Because of the importance of the decision to negotiate, one of the main tasks of the defense attorney at the precharge stage is to evaluate the probability of the government's finding enough evidence to charge. To accomplish this goal, the defense attorney must obtain access to the potential pool of information about his client's crime. First, he wants to know, ... what might be discovered if the government were to be completely successful in its investigation. "What is the objective seriousness of the crime committed by my client?" asks the attorney. "What penalties might the client be exposed to if the government were to discover all the evidence?" Second, and here there is no exception, the attorney wants to know what information has already been found by the government and what information is likely to be found given its present location.

Essential to defense planning is knowing whether the government will be able to prove a crime against the client and, if so, whether it knows the true extent of the crime. Without this information, the attorney cannot properly determine his own position. The defense claim of innocence or limited culpability must be correlated to what the government knows and is likely to learn during the course of its investigation. The attorney conducts his own defense investigation to learn the facts and evaluate what the government knows.

On completion of the defense investigation, the attorney must make the major strategic decision of the precharge stage and what may turn out to be the most important decision in the entire defense: either to go ahead with the information control strategy —essentially a strategy of noncooperation— or to negotiate with the prosecution. As the defense attorney receives new information about what the government is likely to discover, he will have to reconsider this decision throughout the precharge period.

.   .   .

CHAPTER 7

Judges: Selection and Backgrounds

On September 1, 1976, shortly after 9:30 A.M. the Subcommittee on Nominations of the Senate Judiciary Committee convened a public hearing on three federal judicial nominations. The first two nominations typically went smoothly, quickly, and predictably. However, the third nomination, that of United States District Judge Harry Wellford, did not. President Ford had submitted to the Senate the nomination of Judge Wellford from Memphis, Tennessee, to fill a vacancy on the United States Court of Appeals for the Sixth Circuit. Wellford, a former state chairman of the Republican Party in Tennessee and one-time campaign manager for then-Senator Howard Baker, had received his federal district judgeship in 1971 with Baker's backing. Now Baker and his Republican senatorial colleague, William Brock, wanted Wellford to fill a Sixth Circuit vacancy that had previously been filled by a Tennessean. The elevation of Wellford would create a vacancy on the district bench that Baker and Brock would have a strong hand in filling. The only hitch was that Judge Wellford was bitterly opposed by civil rights and poverty groups in Memphis.

Civil rights groups accused Judge Wellford of being extremely conservative politically and highly insensitive to the rights of blacks and of poor people in general. Some civil rights lawyers also seriously questioned the judge's competence by pointing to his high reversal rate (about three times the overall reversal rate in the circuit) and to instances where he allegedly garbled questions of federal jurisdiction, procedure, and statutory and constitutional law.[1] This was emphasized at the Senate hearing as several witnesses made their case against Wellford. But the judge had supporters who testified on his behalf and they included leaders of the Memphis Bar Association and the Chief Judge of the United States Court of Appeals for the Sixth Circuit, a fellow Tennessean, Judge Harry Phillips. Furthermore, it was noted at the hearing that Judge Wellford received a rating of "Qualified" from the American Bar Association's Standing Committee on Federal Judiciary.

The Wellford nomination was particularly troublesome for the liberal members of the Senate Judiciary Committee. Coming out of the hearing, a young lawyer on Senator Kennedy's staff whose task it was to evaluate the situation for the senator remarked to Sheldon Goldman that "There's got to be a better way to pick judges."

This observation, although it reflects the frustration of the moment, is a reaction that is frequently found among many lawyers and some students of the judiciary. Interestingly, it is not confined to federal judicial selection but extends as well to the different methods used by the states to choose their judiciaries—and we will briefly examine these methods in this chapter. What informs the critical appraisals of selection methods is the recognition that the judicial position is at the heart of the court system and that what continues to characterize courts as special forms of conflict-management institutions is, in particular, the unique role of the judge as a conflict manager acting within more or less well-defined boundaries of legality, legitimacy, and notions of due process and "guaranteed" rights. Judged by these standards, Judge Wellford apparently failed in the eyes of a substantial portion of his judicial constitutency. That he nonetheless received the nomination points up the problems that the federal selection process can pose for the judicial system. The legitimacy of a court is surely in jeopardy when a major portion of a judge's constituency questions the judge's fairness or competency. The Wellford nomination also highlights the political nature of the selection process that must be appreciated to understand the problem-solving abilities, potential, and limitations of the particular kinds of people who become judges. It is significant to note, however, that the controversy over Wellford's qualifications, coming as it did during the 1976 presidential election campaign, gave the Democrats on the Senate Judiciary Committee an incentive to stall the nomination on the chance that the Democrats would win the election. The members of a new administration would be able to name one of their own instead of a former Republican politician. Consequently, the Senate Judiciary Committee took no action at all on the nomination and it died with Gerald Ford's electoral defeat (and incidentally the electoral defeat of Republican Senator Brock). The vacancy was eventually filled in 1977 by a Carter-appointed Democrat, Gilbert Merritt, a considerably more liberal and younger man than Wellford and a person with good ties to the black community. Merritt also had been active in party politics and, among other activities, served as Treasurer of the state Democratic Party.

Merritt's nomination in part resulted from the new procedure instituted by President Carter for screening potential appeals court nominees. On February 14, 1977, the President issued an Executive Order creating at least one judicial selection panel for each judicial circuit. Each panel consisted of eleven members chosen by the President and they were charged with submitting within sixty days five names from which the President would select a nominee. One objective of the circuit court commission was to open up the recruitment process to women, minorities, and well-qualified persons without political connections. This raised some serious controversy over the appropriateness of the concept of affirmative action for the judiciary (see the selection by Sheldon Goldman) and whether the emphasis on affirmative action was lowering the quality of the federal bench (see the selection by Elliot Slotnick that systematically seeks to answer this question). As it turned out in this particular instance, Mr. Merritt, a white male Democratic Party activist, was on the list submitted by the Sixth Circuit panel to fill the vacancy. However, among those on that panel who passed on Merritt's qualifications was the well-known black political leader Coleman Young, Mayor of Detroit.

But this is not the end of the story. In 1980, Jimmy Carter was defeated for reelection and Ronald Reagan was elected president. He brought with him a Republican Senate, which meant that Reagan loyalist Republican Senator Strom Thurmond became chairman of the Senate Judiciary Committee. President Reagan abolished the Carter circuit court selection commissions. For the duration of the Reagan presidency the Administration took the initiative in recruiting and selecting candidates for federal judgeships (see the selection by Sheldon Goldman for evidence of the extent to which Reagan and his Attorney General during the second term, Edwin Meese III, sought to remake the judiciary) although Republican senators, particularly those sharing the Administration's conservative orientation, exerted more influence than their more moderate colleagues. Senator Howard Baker, who in 1981 became the Senate Majority Leader, once again recommended his former political ally Judge Wellford for elevation to a vacancy on the Sixth Circuit and on July 27, 1982, the Reagan Administration sent the nomination to the Senate. Extensive hearings were held on August 4 and 11 in which civil rights groups argued that Judge Wellford's "insensitivity to the legal rights of black people has continued."[2] But this time around, the American Bar Association gave Wellford a "Well Qualified" rating and among those testifying in favor of Wellford was a black colleague on the district court, Carter appointee Odelle Horton. Wellford was confirmed by the Senate.

Selection of Supreme Court justices, although somewhat different from selection of lower court judges, is nonetheless a political process as was dramatically demonstrated to the nation with the failed nominations of Judges Robert Bork and Douglas Ginsburg to the Supreme Court seat created by Justice Lewis Powell's retirement in 1987. The reading by Henry Abraham offers an overview of some of the backgrounds of Supreme Court justices and their selection to the nation's highest court.

State judicial selection methods, like federal judicial selection, involve similar negotiation processes and kinds of considerations. But the participants and the weight given to the various considerations vary according to the method used. There are five principal methods in use by the states. Two are electoral methods (partisan and nonpartisan elections); one is the functional equivalent of federal selection (gubernatorial selection); another is the method vigorously pushed by bar groups and the method to which a number of states have shifted ("merit" selection); and the last and least frequently used method is a holdover from colonial days (legislative selection).

Table 1 lists states by the method in formal use to select most or all members of the judiciary. As we can see, twenty-three states use electoral methods. In partisan elections, individuals run for judicial office for a fixed term under a party label. Candidates may conduct a partisan campaign and be endorsed by party leaders and other candidates running for other offices. Nonpartisan elections are those in which judicial candidates must run without a party designation and in which there are typically some restrictions as to the kind of campaign that may be waged. In practice both electoral methods are similar in that judicial elections tend to be noncompetitive, low-visibility, low-turnout elections.[3] Furthermore, it has been repeatedly found that a majority of the judges in states that use electoral methods first came to the bench as gubernatorial interim appointees, that is, they were appointed by the governor to fill vacancies that occurred between elections.[4] Once on the bench they had the inside track for reelection.

Gubernatorial selection with the advice and consent of another political body (such as the state senate or governor's council) is the method used by six states. This method bears many similarities to federal judicial selection. Legislative selection by the full legislature is used by only three states, and it should be noted that in these states the governor plays some part in the process.

Merit selection has captured the fancy of the organized bar and is the method advocated by judicial reformers. The American Bar Association and the American Judicature Society have long pushed for adoption of the merit plan. Its origins date back to the 1920s,[5] but the first major success of its advocates occurred in the state of Missouri in 1940. Subsequently the merit

TABLE 1
Principal Methods of Judicial Selection in the States

Partisan Election	Nonpartisan Election	Legislative Election	Gubernatorial Appointment	Merit Plan
Alabama[a]	Georgia[a]	Rhode Island[b,c]	California[b]	Alaska
Arkansas	Idaho[a]	South Carolina[a]	Delaware	Arizona[a]
Illinois[a]	Kentucky	Virginia	Maine[a]	Colorado[a]
Mississippi[a]	Louisiana[a]		Massachusetts	Connecticut[a]
New Mexico	Michigan[a]		New Hampshire	Florida[c]
North Carolina[c]	Minnesota		New Jersey[a]	Hawaii
Pennsylvania[a]	Montana			Indiana[b]
Tennessee[a,c]	Nevada			Iowa
Texas[a]	North Dakota			Kansas
West Virginia	Ohio[a]			Maryland
	Oregon[a]			Missouri[a]
	Washington			Nebraska
	Wisconsin			New York[a,b,c]
				Oklahoma[a,c]
				South Dakota[a,b,c]
				Utah
				Vermont
				Wyoming[a]

[a] Minor court judges chosen by other methods.
[b] Appellate judges only. Other judges selected by different methods.
[c] Most but not all major judicial positions selected this way.

SOURCE:
The Book of the States 1986–1987 (Lexington, Ky.: The Council of State Governments, 1986), pp. 161–163; *Sourcebook of Criminal Justice Statistics 1985* (Washington, D.C.: Bureau of Justice Statistics, 1986), pp. 76–79; Marvin Comisky and Philip C. Patterson, *The Judiciary-Selection, Compensation, Ethics, and Discipline* (New York: Quorum, 1987); and *Judicature*.

plan has also been known as the Missouri Plan. Essentially, its sponsors seek to remove partisan considerations from judicial selection and to replace them with strictly legal qualifications as determined primarily by the bar and the bench. States that have legally adopted merit selection have a judicial nominating commission composed of members of the organized bar (selected by the bar itself), the judiciary, and lay public (chosen by the governor). For each judicial vacancy the nominating commission has the job of screening potential candidates, selecting a small group of people (usually three) qualified for the position, and presenting their names to the governor. The governor is legally required to make the final selection from this list of qualified people. Today eighteen states have legally required merit selection. (Most of them have adopted it since 1960; the most recent adoption occurring in Connecticut in 1986.) Some other states require that merit selection be used to fill vacancies that arise between elections. In several states and in some cities there is an informal merit-type process that is followed voluntarily by the governor or mayor; however, these officials are under no legal obligation to follow the commission's recommendations and occasionally they do not.

There seems to be accumulating evidence that although party politics affects merit plans less than other plans, partisan considerations still affect the thinking of many members of the commissions and many governors.[6] It also appears that bar association ties, mores, and "politicking" influence merit plans more than they do other selection methods. There is no clear evidence, however, that merit selection produces better-qualified judges or results in patterns of judicial policy-making that are distinct from those of judges selected by the more partisan methods.[7]

It is thought that tenure provisions may affect the way judges manage conflicts. The United States Constitution provides for life tenure for federal judges and guarantees that their salary will not be diminished. The basis of these provisions is the belief that job security is essential for an independent judiciary insulated from partisan pressures and considerations of popular approval. On the other hand, fixed terms of judicial office that require the incumbent to be reappointed or reelected are thought to add an important democratic element to an essentially nondemocratic institution. Presumably the knowledge that a judge in a limited-tenure system will be held accountable at some point in time for past judicial performance will induce the judge not to become too far removed from the social, political, and economic consequences of judicial decisions. The judge may thus be induced not to become trapped within a closed system of legal thought divorced from reality.

In practice, however, judges, regardless of formal method of tenure, tend to serve on the bench at their pleasure. Reelection or reappointment in most instances is routine. Merit plan tenure consists of retention elections (essentially plebiscites) in which the electorate answers the ultimate question, shall Judge X remain in office? A vote of no confidence means the judge is out of a job. In practice, here too, merit tenure has not, in most instances, resulted in serious scrutiny of judicial performance. Thus, in the overwhelming majority of retention elections the incumbent wins a vote of confidence. One spectacular departure from this pattern occurred in California in 1986 and is discussed by John Wold and John Culver. What this augurs for the courts is a matter of concern for those who value an independent judiciary.

What are the social, economic, political, and professional backgrounds of the people chosen for the bench? Lower federal court judges historically have tended to come from the middle or upper classes and have tended to have a history of party identification, if not activism.[8] These characteristics are also highlighted at the Supreme Court level as suggested by the Abraham reading.[9] The composite portrait of the recent lower-court appointees by Presidents Carter and Reagan is similar in some respects to the collective portrait of Supreme Court appointees and is also somewhat similar to the portrait of lower-court judges suggested by the historical evidence. Interestingly, there are some differences in the background characteristics of the appointees of the two most recent administrations as shown in Table 2. Carter appointees were more likely than Reagan appointees to be engaged in a modest law practice at the time of appointment. The Reagan Administration, unlike previous Republican and even Democratic administrations, appointed an unprecedented large proportion of Catholics. Of President Reagan's four successful Supreme Court appointments two went to Catholics. Both groups of appointees had engaged in partisan activity to some extent and tended to have prosecutorial and/or judicial experience. Women and blacks were seriously underrepresented in administrations before Carter but were appointed in unprecedented

TABLE 2
Selected Background Characteristics of Carter and Reagan Appointees to the Federal District and Appeals Courts (Percent)

Characteristic	Carter Appointees		Reagan Appointees*	
	District	*Appeals*	*District*	*Appeals*
Major Occupation				
Politics/Government	4.4	5.4	14.0	6.8
Judiciary	44.6	46.4	37.1	54.0
Large Law Firm**	14.0	10.8	14.8	12.2
Moderate Size Firm***	19.8	16.1	20.8	10.8
Solo or Small Law Firm	13.9	5.4	10.2	1.4
Professor of Law	3.0	14.3	2.3	13.5
Other	0.5	1.8	0.8	1.4
Proportion who are Millionaires	4.0	10.3	22.4	17.6
Type of Experience				
Judicial	54.5	53.6	47.4	59.5
Prosecutorial	38.6	32.1	45.4	29.7
Neither judicial nor prosecutorial experience	28.2	37.5	26.1	35.1
Party Affiliation				
Democratic	92.6	82.1	4.5	0.0
Republican	4.4	7.1	93.6	97.3
Other	0.0	0.0	0.0	1.4
Independent	2.9	10.7	1.9	1.4
Partisan Activism				
Prominent Partisan Activism	60.9	73.2	57.6	66.2
Religion				
Protestant	60.4	60.7	59.8	55.4
Catholic	27.7	23.2	31.8	31.1
Jewish	11.9	16.1	8.3	13.5
Ethnicity or Race				
White	78.7	78.6	92.8	97.3
Black	13.9	16.1	1.5	1.4
Hispanic	6.9	3.6	4.9	1.4
Asian	0.5	1.8	0.8	0.0
Gender				
Male	85.6	80.4	91.7	94.6
Female	14.4	19.6	8.3	5.4
Average Age at Nomination	49.7	51.9	48.8	50.0
Total Number of Appointees	202	56	264*	74*

* Confirmed by the U.S. Senate as of March 30, 1988
** Over 25 partners/associates
*** Between 5 and 24 partners/associates

numbers and proportions by President Carter. President Reagan did not match Carter's record but appointed more women than any other president with the exception of Carter and, of course, named the first woman (Sandra Day O'Connor) to the Supreme Court. President Carter named a record number (and proportion) of blacks but Reagan largely overlooked blacks. Of course, Democratic President Carter appointed primarily Democrats, and Republican President Reagan appointed primarily Republicans.

The selection by Henry Glick and Craig Emmert offers a study of the backgrounds of state supreme court justices. Previous work by Bradley Canon had found that the Catholic and Jewish state supreme court justices were likely to be Democrats and that most judges had prosecutorial and/or lower-court judicial experience.[10]

Ultimately we must confront the question, why should we care about how judges are selected and what their backgrounds happen to be? The answer is complex and can be derived from a number of premises. At the outset we can look back to the example that opened this chapter, the controversial Wellford appointment to the Court of Appeals for the Sixth Circuit. If the essential job of a judge is to try, at least for the short run, to solve the problems that inevitably arise when there are conflicting social, economic, and political interests, and if the judge's objective is to manage conflict within the framework of legality and thus to maintain the stability of the political system, then it is crucial that the person who occupies the position of judge possess the qualities, *and be perceived as possessing the qualities*, necessary to manage conflict fairly and competently. But if a substantial proportion of the judge's constituency believes otherwise, the very legitimacy of the judiciary is thrown into doubt. Analysis of judges' backgrounds and of the ways in which the selection process may stress certain types of backgrounds over others tells us something about the kinds of people who come to the bench and hints at their potential abilities and limitations in the art of conflict management.

Furthermore, as Wellford's federal district court nomination in 1971 and subsequent elevation more than a decade later to the appeals court suggested, judicial appointments provide rewards and benefits to particular individuals and, at the symbolic level, to particular groups. Analysis of selection processes and backgrounds can give us some indication of the representativeness and accessibility of the political system. Finally, it is widely believed and amply documented in numerous judicial biographies that particular configurations of backgrounds and experiences shape the judicial philosophies and subsequent decision-making propensities of future judges (see the discussion in Part Three, Chapter Ten). Yet it should be noted that empirical analyses of backgrounds and selection methods do not indicate that markedly diverging backgrounds emerge when one selection method is employed rather than another.[11] What is more, the evidence, although limited, suggests that, at least in terms of aggregate analysis, no one selection method produces markedly different decisional results (in terms of who wins) than another selection method. These findings suggest that however backgrounds and selection processes may affect the way judges and courts go about their business, the influence is subtle. The findings also suggest that the backgrounds of the members of the American judiciary, as well as the basic selection methods, have much in common and that the distinctions that are frequently made, albeit of some importance and interest, should not obscure the facts that collectively, the judges belong to the Establishment, and that wide areas of consensus exist as to how problems are to be solved and what alternatives are acceptable in the management of conflict.[12]

NOTES

1. Statement of William E. Caldwell, Lawyers' Committee for Civil Rights Under Law, before the Senate Committee on the Judiciary, September 1, 1976, *Hearings on the Nomination of Harry Wellford to Fill a Vacancy on the United States Court of Appeals for the Sixth Circuit* (unpublished hearing on file at the National Archives).

2. *Hearings, Senate Judiciary Committee, 97th Congress, Second Session*, August 11, 1982, p. 151.

3. In general, see Phillip L. Dubois, *From Ballot to Bench: Judicial Elections and the Quest for Accountability* (Austin: University of Texas Press, 1980).

4. See James Herndon, "Appointment as a Means of Initial Accession to State Courts of Last Resort," *North Dakota Law Review* 38 (1962), 60–73.

5. See Alan Ashman and James J. Alfini, *The Key to Judicial Merit Selection: The Nominating Process* (Chicago: The American Judicature Society, 1974); Burton M. Atkins, "Merit Selection of State Judges," *Florida Bar Journal* 50 (April 1976), 203–211; and Richard Watson and Rondal Downing, *The Politics of the Bench and the Bar* (New York: Wiley, 1969).

6. See Watson and Downing, *op. cit.*; and James J. Alfini, "Partisan Pressures on the Nonpartisan Plan," *Judicature* 58 (December 1974), 216–221.

7. See Bradley C. Canon, "The Impact of Formal Selection Processes on the Characteristics of Judges—Reconsidered," *Law and Society Review* 6 (1972), 579–593; Burton M. Atkins and Henry R. Glick, "Formal Judicial Recruitment and State Supreme Court Decisions," *American Politics Quarterly* 2 (1974), 427–449; Henry R. Glick and Craig F. Emmert, "Selection Systems and Judicial Characteristics: The Recruitment of State Supreme Court Judges," *Judicature* 70 (1987), 228–235.

8. Kermit L. Hall, *The Politics of Justice: Lower Federal Judicial Selection and the Second Party System, 1829–61* (Lincoln, Nebraska: University of Nebraska Press, 1979).

9. Also see John R. Schmidhauser, *Judges and Justices: The Federal Appellate Judiciary* (Boston: Little, Brown, 1979).

10. Bradley C. Canon, "Characteristics and Career Patterns of State Supreme Court Justices," *State Government* 45 (1972), 34–41.

11. See the discussion in Glick and Emmert, *op. cit.*

12. Compare the findings in Thomas G. Walker and Deborah J. Barrow, "The Diversification of the Federal Bench: Policy and Process Ramifications," *Journal of Politics* 47 (1985), 596–617.

Why Supreme Court Justices Get There: Qualifications and Rationalizations

Henry J. Abraham

In view of what is minimally required of a Supreme Court nominee, it is hardly astonishing that many of them have come to the bench with no previous judicial experience. Among the 102 Justices who had served on the Court by mid-1984, only 22 had had ten or more years of experience on any tribunal—federal or state—and 42 had had no judicial experience at all. Yet...many of the most illustrious members of the Court were judicially inexperienced. Among them were 8 of the 15 Chief Justices: John Marshall, Roger B. Taney, Salmon P. Chase, Morrison R. Waite, Melville W. Fuller, Charles Evans Hughes, Harlan F. Stone, and Earl Warren; and such outstanding Associate Justices as Joseph Story, Samuel F. Miller, Joseph P. Bradley, Louis D. Brandeis, Felix Frankfurter, Robert H. Jackson, and Lewis F. Powell, Jr.

In a learned essay calling for selection Supreme Court Justices "wholly on the basis of functional fitness," Justice Frankfurter keenly argued that judicial experience, poli-

tical affiliation, and geographic, racial, and religious considerations should not play a significant role in the selection of jurists. He contended that a Supreme Court jurist should be at once philosopher, historian, and prophet—to which Justice Brennan, in a conversation with this writer, proposed to add "and a person of inordinate patience."
. . .

Yet the matter of judicial experience, although periodically ignored or downgraded by some Presidents, rarely lies dormant long—indeed, it has been present in almost exactly one half of all Presidential nominations to the Supreme Court to date. To Franklin D. Roosevelt judicial experience was of little importance; to Dwight Eisenhower it was crucial: after his initial appointment of Earl Warren as Chief Justice, Eisenhower insisted that future nominees have judicial background, no matter how limited. Of the nine men who served on the Court as a result of F.D.R.'s appointments (or promotion to Chief Justice in the instance of Harlan F. Stone), six had had no judicial experience when they ascended the bench: Chief Justice Stone and Associate Justices Stanley F. Reed, Felix Frankfurter, William O. Douglas, James F. Byrnes, and Robert H. Jackson. Of the three with experience, Wiley B. Rutledge had served on the Court of

Appeals for the District of Columbia for four years and Hugo L. Black and Frank Murphy on state tribunals for one and one-half and seven years, respectively. Harry Truman had a mixed record: of his four appointees, Harold H. Burton and Tom C. Clark had no judicial experience at all, but Fred M. Vinson and Sherman Minton had seen five and eight years, respectively, of service on lower federal courts. The four men Eisenhower appointed following Warren—Associate Justices John M. Harlan II, William J. Brennan, Jr., Charles E. Whittaker, and Potter Stewart—all had had judicial experience, although the total number of such years for the four was but fifteen. Neither Associate Justices Byron R. White nor Arthur J. Goldberg, appointed by John Kennedy, nor Abe Fortas, appointed by Lyndon Johnson, had served below the Supreme Court, although L.B.J.'s last successful appointee, Thurgood Marshall, had been a federal appellate judge for three and one-half years. Of President Nixon's four selections, Chief Justice Warren E. Burger and Associate Justice Harry A. Blackmun had served on lower federal tribunals for thirteen and eleven years, respectively, but Associate Justices Lewis F. Powell, Jr., and William H. Rehnquist had served on no court. Although their service on tribunals below was quite brief, both Justices Stevens and O'Connor, appointed by Presidents Ford and Reagan, respectively, had judicial experience. Thirteen appointees with no judicial background were sent to the Court by the eight most recent Presidents; but with the exception of one or two, all possessed at least some qualifying attributes: broad experience in the public sector, strong personality and strength of character, capacity for hard work, political *savoir faire*, a modicum of intellectualism. . . .

A glance at the personnel of the 1980–1981 Court will perhaps serve to underscore that judicial experience is not necessarily vital to a Supreme Court jurist. Of the nine men. . .who commenced that term of Court, only six could point to judicial experience on lower courts, and in four instances it was for but a period averaging five years.

Yet *all* of the members of that Court had come to the high tribunal with considerable experience in *public* life, frequently of an administrative-executive nature. In order of seniority of service on the bench: Justice William J. Brennan, Jr., an army colonel in World War II, had practiced law for fifteen years and had served for seven years on three state courts in New Jersey, including the State Supreme Court, before he was appointed in 1956. Justice Potter Stewart, who saw three years of service overseas during World War II, had practiced law for more than a decade, had been a member of the City Council of Cincinnati, and had served on the U.S. Court of Appeals for the Sixth Circuit for four years when he was appointed in 1958. Justice Byron R. White, Rhodes scholar and All-American football star, had been Chief Justice Vinson's law clerk, had practiced law for fourteen years, and was Deputy Attorney General of the United States when John Kennedy sent him to the Court in 1962 at age forty-four. Justice Thurgood Marshall—the first black to reach the highest court and a nationally known civil rights leader—had practiced law for three decades, much of it constitutional law at the bar of the Supreme Court, and had served for three and three-quarter years on the U.S. Court of Appeals for the Second Circuit. When he was appointed in 1967 to the Supreme Court, he held the position of U.S. Solicitor General. Chief Justice Warren E. Burger, appointed in 1969, had practiced law for twenty-three years, had been politically active in his native Minnesota, and for three years had held the post of Assistant Attorney General, heading the Civil Division, before becoming a federal jurist in 1956. With thirteen years on the U.S. Court of Appeals for the District of Columbia, he had had the most extensive judicial background. Justice Harry A. Blackmun, appointed to the Court in 1970, had a record similar to that of his fellow Minnesotan Burger, having practiced law in a Minneapolis firm for sixteen years, and had served as General Counsel for the Mayo Clinic and Rochester, Minnesota, for seven years when in 1959 he was named to the U.S. Court of Appeals for the Eighth Circuit. Justice Lewis F. Powell, Jr., appointed to the Court late in 1971, had a long and distinguished record as a legal practitioner and civic leader in Virginia— including the chairmanship of the Richmond public school board in the late 1950s and, later, the Virginia State Board of Education— and he had been President of the A.B.A. Justice William H. Rehnquist had clerked for Justice Robert H. Jackson, had practiced law and been active in Arizona politics for many years, and was serving as Assistant Attorney General of the United States, in charge of the office of Legal Counsel, at the time of his elevation to the Court in December 1971. And John Paul Stevens, the sole Ford appointee, had clerked for Justice Wiley B. Rutledge, and had practiced private law, specializing in antitrust litigation, when he was sent to the U.S. Court of Appeals for the Seventh Circuit, five years antecedent to coming to the Supreme Court in 1975.

... [A]lmost all Supreme Court jurists have had extensive *legal* experience. Moreover, all of the 102 who actually served on the Court, with the sole exception of Justice George Shiras, Jr. (1892–1903), had engaged in at least some public service at various levels of government or had actively participated in political enterprises....

Table 1 indicates the occupations (at the time of appointment) of those (using the full figure of 105 [appointments] here) who have served on the Supreme Court.

TABLE 1

Occupations* of Supreme Court Designees at Time of Appointment†

Federal Officeholder in Executive Branch	22
Judge of State Court	22
Judge of Inferior Federal Court	21
Private Practice of Law	18
U.S. Senator	8
U.S. Representative	4
State Governor	3
Professor of Law	3
Associate Justice of U.S. Supreme Court‡	2
Justice of the Permanent Court of International Justice	1

* Many of the appointees had held a variety of federal or state offices, or even both, prior to their selection.

† In general the appointments from state office are clustered at the beginning of the Court's existence; those from federal office are more recent.

‡ Justice E.D. White and H.F. Stone, who were *promoted* to the Chief Justiceship in 1910 and 1941, respectively, while sitting as Associate Justices.

Discounting rare individual exceptions, the caliber of the Supreme Court has been universally high. No other part of the American government can readily match its general record of competence and achievement. Yet there is nothing particularly astonishing about the essentially upper-middle-class "establishment" components that by and large have tended to characterize the members of the Court. A fusing of the background characteristics of the 102 individuals who have sat on the Court thus produces the following profile:

NATIVE-BORN (there have been but six exceptions, the last two being the England-born George Sutherland and Austrian-born Felix Frankfurter); WHITE (the first nonwhite, Thurgood Marshall, was appointed in 1967); MAN (there was no woman on the Court until President Reagan's appointment of Sandra Day O'Connor in 1981); GENERALLY PROTES-

TANT (six Roman Catholic and five Jewish Justices); FIFTY TO FIFTY-FIVE years of age at the time of appointment; FIRST-BORN (fifty-six); ANGLO-SAXON ETHNIC STOCK (all except fifteen); UPPER-MIDDLE TO HIGH SOCIAL STATUS: REARED IN A NONRURAL BUT NOT NECESSARILY URBAN ENVIRONMENT; MEMBER OF A CIVIC-MINDED, POLITICALLY ACTIVE, ECONOMICALLY COMFORTABLE FAMILY; B.A. AND LL.B. OR J.D. DEGREES (usually, although not always, from prestigious institutions); SERVICE IN PUBLIC OFFICE; from POPULOUS STATES.

Present-day egalitarian trends may well operate to alter that profile somewhat: assuredly, a "woman's seat" and a "black seat" are political certainties, conceivably in multiples. Yet a dramatic alteration of the other major components of the depicted profile is not likely. With the indicated exceptions, the described composite is not only more or less self-operating, but most members of the American body politic would not welcome any drastic change in it. Notwithstanding the frequent attacks on the Supreme Court as an institution, its personnel has generally been held in high esteem by the average citizen.

The religious factor is based on the notion of a "Roman Catholic seat" and a "Jewish seat" on the Supreme Court. A development of dubious communal wisdom, the concept of religious-group representation has become one of the facts of American political and judicial life (see Table 2)—although it has been less of an emotional problem in the courts than in the makeup of election slates in minority-conscious cities, such as New York, for example, and it has become far less of a problem *cum* consideration than race or gender.

Six men have occupied the "Roman Catholic seat" to date: Chief Justice Roger B. Taney (Jackson, 1836); and Associate Justices Edward D. White (Cleveland, 1894—he was promoted to Chief Justice by Taft, 1910), Joseph McKenna (McKinley, 1898), Pierce

TABLE 2
Acknowledged Religion of the 102 Individual Justices of the Supreme Court (at time of appointment)

Episcopalian	27
Unspecified Protestant	25
Presbyterian	17
Roman Catholic	6
Unitarian	6
Baptist	5
Jewish	5
Methodist	4
Congregationalist	3
Disciples of Christ	2
Lutheran	1
Quaker	1
	——
	102

Butler (Harding, 1922), Frank Murphy (F.D. Roosevelt, 1940), and William J. Brennan, Jr. (Eisenhower, 1956). With the exception of the seven years between Justice Frank Murphy's death in 1949 (when President Truman deliberately ignored the unwritten rule of the "reserved" seat and nominated Protestant Tom C. Clark to the vacancy created by Murphy's death) and the nomination of Justice William J. Brennan, Jr., in 1956, a Roman Catholic has been on the Supreme Court continually since White's appointment. In characteristically forthright manner, Truman (a good Baptist) had commented publicly when he broke the unwritten "religion seat" code: "I do not believe religions have anything to do with the Supreme Bench. If an individual has the qualifications, I do not care if he is a Protestant, Catholic or Jew."

The "Jewish seat" was established in 1916 with the appointment of Louis D. Brandeis. That tradition was broken when in 1969 President Nixon successively nominated three Protestants (Haynsworth, Carswell, and Blackmun) to succeed Fortas. In 1971 Nixon had two opportunities to appoint a Jewish Justice, but he again nominated two more Protestants—William H. Rehnquist and Lewis F. Powell, Jr. Questioned on the continued "oversight" at one of his infrequent news conferences, Nixon gave the appropriately logical response: that merit rather than religion should and must govern—a laudable aim provided it is indeed invoked. The five occupants of "the Jewish seat" to date have been: Louis D. Brandeis (Wilson, 1916), Benjamin N. Cardozo (Hoover, 1932), Felix Frankfurter (F. D. Roosevelt, 1939), Arthur J. Goldberg (Kennedy, 1962), and Abe Fortas (L.B. Johnson, 1965).

In June 1967 Lyndon B. Johnson designated Thurgood Marshall, the first black ever to be nominated to the Supreme Court. The President, leaving no doubt that the nominee's race was probably the major factor in his decision, told the country: "I believe it is the right thing to do, the right time to do it, the right man and the right place." There is no doubt that there now exists a "black seat" on the bench that is, in effect, far more secure than a "Catholic seat" or a "Jewish seat." That is unquestionably also true of a "woman's seat," to all intents and purposes established with President Reagan's dramatic appointment of Judge Sandra Day O'Connor of Arizona in September 1981 as the first woman Justice of the Supreme Court of the United States.

Political and ideological compatibility often go hand in hand in influencing Presidential choices for the Supreme Court. Among the points a President is almost certain to consider are the following: (1) whether his choice will render him more popular among influential interest groups; (2) whether the nominee has been a loyal member of the President's party; (3) whether the nominee favors Presidential programs and policies; (4) whether the nominee is acceptable (or at least not "personally ob-noxious") to the home-state Senators; (5) whether the nominee's judicial record, if any, meets the Presidential criteria of constitutional construction; (6) whether the President is indebted to the nominee for past political services; and (7) whether he feels "good" or "comfortable" about his choice.

It is an unwritten law of the judicial nominating process that the President will not normally select an individual from the ranks of the political opposition. To lessen charges of Court politicizing, however, this rule is purposely relaxed now and then—but only within "political reason"—which seems to have meant roughly to the tune of six percent of all appointments to district and appellate tribunals and an on-its-face-surprising fifteen percent to the Supreme Court. In at least thirteen instances, the appointee to the Supreme Court, including two to the post of Chief Justice, came from a political party other than that of the President: Whig President John Tyler appointed a Democrat, Samuel Nelson, and Republican Presidents Abraham Lincoln, Benjamin Harrison, William Howard Taft, Warren G. Harding, Herbert Hoover, Dwight D. Eisenhower, and Richard M. Nixon appointed nine Democrats—Taft alone three! The nine Justices and their nominators were Stephen J. Field (Lincoln); Howell E. Jackson (Benjamin Harrison); Horace H. Lurton, Edward D. White (promoted to Chief Justice), and Joseph R. Lamar (Taft); Pierce Butler (Harding); William J. Brennan, Jr. (Eisenhower); and Lewis F. Powell, Jr. (Nixon). And Democratic Presidents Woodrow Wilson, Franklin D. Roosevelt, and Harry S. Truman appointed three Republicans: Louis D. Brandeis (Wilson), Harlan F. Stone (promoted to Chief Justice by F.D.R.), and Harold H. Burton (Truman). To this list some would add F.D.R.'s selection of Felix Frankfurter, who labeled himself an Independent.

There will always be some crossing of

party lines, particularly at the lower court levels, to maintain at least the appearance of judicial nonpartisanship and to placate the opposition, but the practice may be safely viewed as the exception rather than the rule. . . . Many a President has been told by his political advisers to stay on his side of the fence, where surely there are just as many qualified and deserving lawyers as on the other side. "Think Republican," Republican National Chairman Rogers C.B. Morton urged President Nixon at the latter's first opportunity to fill seats on the Supreme Court. . . . If the percentage of "other party" *Supreme Court* appointees has been markedly higher than that of the lower federal courts, it is because the President recognizes that what matters more than anything else, certainly more than a nominee's *nominal* political adherence, is the ideological compatibility of the candidate—what Theodore Roosevelt referred to as the nominee's "real politics."

Whatever the merits of the other criteria attending Presidential motivations in appointments may be, what must be of overriding concern to any nominator is his perception of the candidate's *real* politics. The Chief Executive's crucial predictive judgment concerns itself with the nominee's likely future voting pattern on the bench, based on his or her past stance and commitment on matters of public policy insofar as they are reliably discernible. All Presidents have tried, thus, to pack the bench to a greater or lesser extent. They will indubitably continue to do so!

In the public eye Court-packing has been most closely associated with Franklin D. Roosevelt. Having had not a single opportunity to fill a Court vacancy in his first term (1933–1937) and seeing his domestic programs consistently battered by the Court, the frustrated President attempted to get his way all at once. His Court-packing bill, however, died a deserved death in the Senate.

It is not surprising that Court-packing and the name of President F.D. Roosevelt have become synonymous. Yet even such popular heroes as Jefferson, Jackson, and Lincoln followed similar courses of action in the face of what they considered "judicial intransigence and defiance." Their approach was not so radical as Roosevelt's, but they very likely would have been sympathetic to his efforts. George Washington, although broadly regarded as far removed from "politics," insisted that his nominees to the Court meet a veritable smorgasbord of specific qualifications. In fact, every President who has made nominations to the Supreme Court has been guilty of Court-packing in some measure. It is entirely understandable that a President will choose individuals he hopes will share his own philosophy of government and politics, at least to the extent of giving him a sympathetic hearing. . . .

Thus, concern with a nominee's *real* politics is a fundamental issue—and examples abound. It prompted Republican Taft to give half of his six appointments to kindred souls who were Democrats; Republican Nixon to appoint Democrat Powell; Democrat Roosevelt to promote Republican Stone; and Democrat Truman to appoint Republican Burton. Yet there is no guarantee that what a President perceives as *real* politics will not fade into a mirage. Hence Charles Warren, eminent chronicler of the Court, observed entirely realistically that "nothing is more striking in the history of the Court than the manner in which the hopes of those who expected a judge to follow the political views of the President appointing him are disappointed." Few have felt the truth of that statement more keenly than Teddy Roosevelt did with Oliver Wendell Holmes, Jr., whose early "anti-administration" opinions in antitrust cases (notably in *Northern Securities* v. *United States*) were entirely unexpected. A bare 5:4 majority in that case did uphold the government's order under the Sherman Antitrust Act dissolving the Northern Securities Company, a brainchild of E.H. Harriman and J.J. Hill—the rich and powerful owners of competing railroads who had organized the company to secure a terminal line into Chicago. Roosevelt had won that important litigation, but he was furious about his recent appointee's "anti-antitrust" vote in the case and stormed: "I could carve out of a banana a Judge with more backbone than that!" Holmes reportedly merely smiled when told the President's remark, made a *sotto voce* reference to "shallow intellects," and noted his intention to "call the shots as I see them in terms of the legal and constitutional setting." Later, during T.R.'s second term of office (1905–1909), Holmes expressed his sentiments to a labor leader at a White House dinner with characteristic directness: "What you want is favor, not justice. But when I am on my job, I don't give a damn what you or Mr. Roosevelt want."

James Madison was similarly chagrined with his appointment of Justice Joseph Story, having refused to heed his political mentor, Thomas Jefferson. The Sage of Monticello had warned him that Story was an inveterate Tory who would become a rabid supporter of Chief Justice Marshall—and he was right: Story not only instantly joined Marshall's approach to constitutional adjudication and interpretation, he even out-Marshalled Marshall in his nationalism! Perhaps even more chagrin was felt by Woodrow Wilson when the first of his three Supreme Court appointees, his Attorney General, James C. McReynolds, proved himself quickly to be the antithesis of almost everything for which his nominator stood and in which he believed.

More recently, Harry Truman observed that "packing the Supreme Court simply can't be done...I've tried and it won't work.... Whenever you put a man on the Supreme Court he ceases to be your friend. I'm sure of that." Future Presidents may well be advised to heed the admonition of Zechariah Chafee, Jr., Harvard's famed expert on the judicial process, who contended that to forecast the behavior of a future jurist it is wiser to consider the books in his library than the list of clients in his office.

There is indeed a considerable element of unpredictability in the judicial appointing process. To the often-heard "Does a person become any different when he puts on a gown?" Justice Frankfurter's sharp retort was always, "If he is any good, he does!" At least to some extent, F.F. assuredly did! In the tellingly colorful prose of Alexander M. Bickel, "You shoot an arrow into a far-distant future when you appoint a Justice and not the man himself can tell you what he will think about some of problems that he will face." And late in 1969, reflecting upon his sixteen years as Chief Justice of the United States, Earl Warren pointed out that he, for one, did not "see how a man could be on the Court and not change his views substantially over a period of years...for change you must if you are to do your duty on the Supreme Court." It is a duty that in many ways represents the most hallowed in the governmental process of the United States.

.   .   .

Should There Be Affirmative Action for the Judiciary?

Sheldon Goldman

The Carter Administration jolted the legal community with its outspoken and widely-publicized affirmative action policy of placing women and ethnic minorities on the federal bench. Many of the arguments raised against the implementation of affirmative action programs elsewhere were heard with regard to the judiciary along with arguments attuned to the special status of the federal bench. . . .

. . . , [S]ix major objections were raised against an affirmative action approach to federal judicial selection. Each, I believe, can be persuasively answered. I . . . discuss these objections briefly and the rejoinders I find convincing.

1. The dangers of classifying people. Affirmative action inevitably leads government agencies to define race, critics argue, and it leads government officials to make judgments about racial characteristics. Is an individual with one black grandparent or great-grandparent (say, Homer Plessy) to be classified as black? What about someone with one black parent who was raised by white foster parents? Is an American-born individual with an American father and

From *Judicature* 62 (1979), pp. 489–494. Reprinted with permission of the author. Footnotes omitted.

Mexican mother Hispanic? The argument, essentially, is that it is dangerous for government to make any racial classifications. Such activities stir memories of the racial laws of Nazi Germany and run counter to the value Americans have traditionally placed on treating individuals on the basis of their personal qualities and not their racial attributes.

Response: While many (including myself) are uncomfortable with government concern with race/ethnicity, I believe there is a crucial and fundamental distinction between America's official racial consciousness for purposes of affirmative action and the racial classifications of totalitarian regimes. America's purpose is to aid definable classes of persons who have historically suffered from official discrimination. Racial classifications in Nazi Germany were, of course, for horrible purposes and in more contemporary totalitarian societies ethnic designations on identity cards and other records form the basis for official discrimination.

The federal judiciary has been and still is an overwhelmingly white, male institution, for many reasons. America's long-standing racism and sexism, for example, have historically limited opportunities in the judiciary for women, blacks and Hispanics. It does not seen unreasonable to make special efforts to recruit from these groupings of Americans for federal judgeships. Deliberate considerations of race and sex should not be given negative connotations so long as the government demonstrates positive, anti-racist, anti-sexist motives and purposes.

2. The threat of reverse discrimination. The real result of affirmative action, opponents argue, is reverse discrimination. Government selects a group or groups of persons for favored treatment, thereby putting all others at a disadvantage. This is reminiscent of George Orwell's *Animal Farm* where all animals are equal but some are more equal than others. On an individual basis this produces reverse discrimination; individuals are ruled out of consideration *because* they are the "wrong" race or sex. Furthermore, when it comes to judicial selection, those women, blacks and Hispanics who are favored for judgeships are frequently from the same social class and similar backgrounds as competing white males and their careers have not necessarily suffered from discrimination. Why then should they have an advantage?

Response: I cannot be persuaded that affirmative action is reverse discrimination— at least when the objective is *not* to give minorities a majority hold. I have not seen evidence that any affirmative action program of any kind in the United States has seriously threatened the majority status of white males in government, industry, the professions or academia. Certainly the type of affirmative action that the Carter Administration... promoted for the judiciary in no way threatened the overwhelming majority status of white males.

Although the Administration's efforts...to place women, blacks, and Hispanics on the federal bench [were] spectacular when compared with the record of previous administrations, taken alone the results of the Carter Administration's affirmative action policy [were] actually very modest. About 12 per cent of the Carter nominees [were] black and about the some proportion [were] women. In terms of the entire federal bench, the proportions of blacks and women are exceedingly small and for Hispanics almost non-existent.

At the individual level, the charge of reverse discrimination potentially can be more troublesome, as it was in the *Bakke* case. But we do not have to be concerned with this since judicial selection traditionally has involved numerous variables. The addition of racial/ethnic and sexual considerations is in no way inconsistent with the host of other considerations that have been involved in judicial selection, including geography, party affiliation, party activity, sponsorship by senators and other key politicians, professional connections, ideological or policy outlook, and so on. Race/ethnicity and sex are today politically relevant variables and they have been added to other political type variables in a selection process that historically has been political.

3. The error of focusing on group affiliation. No matter how worthy an objective it may be, critics say, affirmative action is inconsistent with the professed goal of merit selection which many judicial reformers and the Carter Administration itself espouse[d]. How can one accept the principle that only the best qualified should be given judgeships and then decree that women, blacks, and Hispanics are to be given special preference? Merit selection emphasizes individual qualities; affirmative action stresses group affiliation.

Response: It does a disservice to women, blacks, and Hispanics to suggest that they do not ordinarily possess as strong a set of professional credentials as white males do, but I will not dwell on this obvious rejoinder. What I find persuasive is the fact that, based on my own extensive research and that of others, we never had, we do not now have, and we probably never will have a judicial selection method based solely on professional merits. The professional credentials of candidates do play a part in judicial selection, but rarely have they been the determining factor. . . .

Ironically, affirmative action may provide a more potent push towards merit selection than anything else that has ever been done. By searching for well qualified women, blacks, and Hispanics, the [Carter] Administration and Democratic senators . . . downplay[ed] party activity and political connections. This [broke] with the past judges-as-patronage syndrome that historically characterized much of judicial selection.

Let me add for the record that the [Carter] Administration's so-called merit selection of appeals judges was not merit selection in fact. . . . [M]ostly Democrats (including large numbers of Carter loyalists) . . . chose mostly other Democrats for placement on the lists given the President. Other Democrats then lobb[ied] the Democratic President as to which Democrats to choose.

However, the selection process . . . became more open in large part due to institution of merit commissions and the affirmative action push. It is highly unrealistic to expect a civil service type merit approach to judicial selection ever to be established. Even assuming that an effective merit selection process could be instituted, I would have to be persuaded that the sorts of people chosen were better suited for the bench than the sorts of people chosen through our traditional political processes.

4. The need for government neutrally, not favoritism. Affirmative action is a remedy to right a proven constitutional wrong, critics emphasize. Even if it could be proven that racism and sexism served to exclude blacks, women and Hispanics from the judiciary, that would not justify affirmative action in choosing the highest officials of the federal government. It would only justify efforts to ensure that these groups were no longer deliberately excluded.

Blacks prevented from voting were eventually protected by federal legislation and action to enable them to exercise the franchise, but they were not given the right to elect so many black congressmen or black state representatives. Women given the right to vote in 1920 were not given the right to have a specific number of women in high elective or appointive office. Isn't it sufficient that the judicial selection process be non-discriminatory? Isn't affirmative action inappropriate here?

Response: The racial and sexual make-up of the judiciary, past and present, speaks for itself. It is clear that all-pervasive societal attitudes toward women, blacks, Hispanics, and indeed other groups such as Asian-Americans and American Indians severely limited their opportunities in the law and that they were, in fact, routinely and systematically excluded from federal judgeships. Justice Department officials and senators were not necessarily themselves racist or sexist. It is simply that within the framework of political reality and racist and sexist belief systems in the larger society, appointments of women, blacks, and some other ethnic groups were impossible.

But leaving aside the difficult questions of proof, and, indeed, whether constitutional wrongs were committed in the past, it can be argued that government can serve as a teacher by setting a good example and structuring situations in which learning and personal growth can occur. Clearly, the widespread racist and sexist attitudes of the past and the discrimination so widely practiced were moral, if not constitutional, wrongs. We should seize this opportunity to correct them.

By seeking out and appointing to federal judgeships a visible number of qualified women and minorities, government [was] teaching the nation that racial and sexual stereotypes are invalid. Government [was] also teaching young women, young blacks and young Hispanics that it no longer recognizes as political reality the racial and sexual biases of the past, and that individual accomplishment and achievement are more important than race and sex.

Yes, it is ironic that affirmative action which recognizes race and sex is necessary in order to hasten the time when race and sex will be irrelevant, and when racism and sexism are virtually non-existent....

5.   The problem of quotas. Affirmative action in practice results in a quota system, opponents contend, and quotas are dysfunctional for the workings of American institutions. Quotas based on group affiliation and not individual merit can work grave hardship on well-qualified individuals who are in excess of their group's quota, and, in general, quotas tend to promote mediocrity. Quotas can exclude superior qualified persons who have the wrong sex, race, religion, or ethnic affiliation; they can include not only the marginally qualified, but even unqualified persons. Affirmative action is the first step on the road to the balkanization of America, and the courts—our prized palladiums of justice—should be the last place where this concept is imposed.

Response: Affirmative action programs have existed for [over] a decade, and I am not persuaded that the parade of horrors suggested above has even begun to come about. I see no movement within the United States for each ethnic or religious grouping to claim a quota of public or private jobs. Most Americans accept individual merit as the proper basis for school admissions and employment opportunities.

Although the distinction may be fuzzy, I do see a difference between affirmative action and a quota system. Affirmative action does not have a rigid numerical goal; it retains flexibility yet is a good faith effort to widen the recruitment net, indeed to vigorously recruit, and pay particular attention to women and disadvantaged racial/ethnic groups. Affirmative action also means selecting the individual from the previously discriminated-against group when all else is approximately equal.

[There were no quotas] in connection with the Carter Administration's...judicial selection. [U]se of a quota system [is]... unnecessarily rigid and singularly inappropriate for the judiciary, but this is not at issue. The Carter Administration itself [made]

...strenuous efforts to recruit, or have selection commissions and senators recruit, qualified women, blacks, and Hispanic candidates. The Administration [was]... quite concerned with the qualifications of minority and women candidates.

If the politics of federal judicial selection today make it unlikely that incompetent white males will go on the bench, the politics of affirmative action requires that only competent minorities and women be appointed. The surest way to sabotage affirmative action is to link it with incompetency. The Carter Administration's record of minority and women appointments [was]...excellent... [and yielded] well-qualified judges.

6.   An inappropriate program for the judiciary. No matter what the merits of affirmative action may be for other spheres of American life, critics insist, it is highly inappropriate for the judicial branch. Even though merit may not actually be the sole criterion for judicial selection, it is recognized as ideally the basis for choosing judges, and leading professional groups have been working to make progress towards that goal. But if a criterion other than individual merit gains legitimacy, it becomes all the more difficult to assign to oblivion the "extraneous" political considerations that have traditionally "polluted" the process. And it becomes more difficult to win support for a partisan-free merit selection process.

Part of the justification for merit selection is that a federal judge must be highly skilled since the federal courts are the fastest legal tracks in town. We need the best people for the job; would we select a surgeon to perform a highly complex and delicate operation on any basis other than the best person available? Why should we do less with the judiciary? We need the best people on the bench regardless of race, sex or national origin. . . .

Response: This is a slippery argument to counter. To be sure, there must be highly competent judges to service the trial and appellate courts of the nation. Official recognition of race and sex does appear at first blush to detract from the goal of a non-discriminatory process for obtaining the best qualified persons to serve. But a closer look at the job of federal judges should make it clear that our judges have always been involved in the major political controversies of the day. As Tocqueville so perceptively observed over 140 years ago, "Scarcely any political question arises in the United States that is not resolved, sooner or later, into a judicial question."

Today, racial and sexual discrimination are major legal issues before the courts. A judge who is a member of a racial minority or a woman cannot help but bring to the bench a certain sensitivity—indeed, certain qualities of the heart and mind—that may be particularly helpful in dealing with these issues. This is not to say that white judges are necessarily insensitive to issues of racial discrimination or that male judges cannot cope with issues of sexual discrimination. But the presence on the bench in visible numbers of well qualified judges drawn from the minorities and women cannot help but add a new dimension of justice to our courts in most instances.

These judges cannot help but educate their colleagues by the example they set, by the creation of precedents, and by informal as well as formal interchange. They are likely the "best" people to fill certain of the vacancies and new judgeships.

Yes, we ought to aspire to obtaining the "best" people for our judiciary—but the "best" bench may be one composed of persons of all races and both sexes with diverse backgrounds and experiences. . . . It is difficult to define—much less find—the "best." Despite occasional mistakes, the current selection process with its political sensitivity has served the nation well. But affirmative action of the sort advocated and . . . practiced by the Carter Administration should strengthen the federal bench. And perhaps most significantly, it may be that by searching for the best possible women and minority candidates a precedent will be established for emphasizing the individual professional merits of all candidates for judgeships, regardless of race and sex.

Judicial Selection: Lowering the Bench or Raising It Higher?

Elliot E. Slotnick

...The purpose of this article is to examine affirmative action and judicial recruitment during the Carter Administration.... [W]hat implications did affirmative action have for nomination outcomes? Did affirmative action "dilute" the quality of the federal bench (as critics of the Carter effort claimed) or, alternatively, did threshold requirements for the appointment of "non-traditional" (that is, non-white or female) judges actually exceed, on some dimensions, the apparent criteria for white male appointees? In order to examine these and other questions, data on all judicial nominees whose names were sent to the Senate Judiciary Committee for a confirmation hearing during the 96th Congress will be analyzed.

. . .

Our examination of affirmative action and judicial recruitment during the Carter Administration reveals a policy program which was the subject of much debate, controversy, and disagreement. Supporters, opponents

Reprinted from Elliot E. Slotnick, "Lowering the Bench or Raising it Higher?: Affirmative Action and Judicial Selection During the Carter Administration," *Yale Law & Policy Review* 1 (1983), pp. 271, 280–282, 284–287, 290–291, 293–298. Reprinted with permission of author and publisher. Footnotes and tables omitted.

and analysts of the Carter effort failed to agree on the impact and implications of this effort. One thing, however, does remain clear. Recruitment outcomes during the Carter Administration resulted in a more "representative" bench than had ever existed if the concept of representation is assessed by the sheer number and percentage of appointees who were *not* white males. Of Carter's 262 district and appeals court appointees 40 were women, 38 were black, and 16 were Hispanics (7 of the black and 1 of the Hispanic nominees were women). This constituted a greater number of non-traditional appointees that had been designated over the course of the nation's entire history and, clearly, was an obvious departure from the selection behavior of recent Presidents....

AFFIRMATIVE ACTION AND THE CHARACTERISTICS OF JUDGESHIP NOMINEES

...[M]any assertions and much rhetoric have characterized the debate over affirmative action. Little, if any, empirical research, however, has explored the consequences of recruitment outreach for the quality of the American bench. Clearly, "quality" is an elusive concept—particularly when society remains ambivalent about what constitutes a "good" judge. Nevertheless, it is possible to compare and contrast non-traditional nominees with their white male counterparts in terms of certain background characteristics, some of which are thought to be related to judicial performance. How do women, and Hispanic nominees differ from the traditional white males nominated at the same time? Can the judgment reasonably be made that non-traditional nominees were "inferior" candidates? On the other hand, is there any evidence which suggests that higher threshold qualifications were imposed before non-traditional candidates could successfully emerge from the recruitment process? . . . Our analysis will compare white male and non-traditional nominees on several dimensions including their demographic profiles, educational achievement, level of politicization, legal career patterns, and litigation records. The analysis is exploratory in nature. Since advocates and opponents of affirmative action programs differ so fundamentally on what their consequences will be, no effort has been made to develop formal hypotheses about the differences between white male and all other nominees.

Demographic Backgrounds

Presumably, the most graphic consequences of affirmative action in judicial recruitment would be evident in the demographic and socio-economic profiles of nominees. At the most obvious level, nominations during the Carter years revealed a proliferation of what we have labelled "non-traditional" judgeship candidates—that is, nominees who were *not* white males. The larger question remains, however, of whether increased representation of minorities on the bench actually resulted in a more "representative" judiciary

in substantively meaningful ways. Our data on several demographic and socio-economic variables do suggest a variety of differences between white male and non-traditional nominees which go well beyond simple considerations of race and gender.

The strongest demographic and socio-economic differences between white male and other nominees emerged in age and income. . . . [N]on-white and women nominees were significantly younger and were found disproportionately in lower income brackets than their white male counterparts. A clear majority of non-traditional nominees (62.1%) were under the age of 50 as compared to 38.7% of the white males. Twice as great a percentage of white male nominees were over the age of 60 at the time of their nomination. In addition to and, perhaps, reflecting these age differences, non-traditional nominees tended to have substantially lower incomes. Fully 25.0% of the white males averaged more than $100,000 per year income during the five year interval prior to their appointment, while the corresponding figure was only 8.8% for non-traditional designates. A clear majority (60.2%) of the non-traditional nominees earned less than $60,000 per annum prior to their judgeship nomination while the corresponding figure was substantially lower (43.5%) for white males. Importantly, such income differences reflect more than simply the aggregate age (and, presumably, career stage) differences among nominees. Rather, . . .they appear to reflect different career patterns and professional experiences characterizing the two classes of appointees.

Other demographic and socio-economic differences among the nominees are also of some, although less dramatic, note. For one, non-traditional nominees were considerably more likely to be born outside of the state or circuit in which their appointment was made (38.2%) than were their white male counterparts (24.3%).... This finding, however, was largely the result of gender based differences in birthplace..., with 51.7% of all female nominees born outside of the state or circuit of their appointment. The data support the view that local roots could facilitate access to the federal bench. While the argument could be made that extended search efforts were necessary to locate suitable women nominees and often resulted in candidacies of non-local lineage, such an assertion fails to explain the absence of differences in the birthplaces of whites and non-whites where a similar search is presumably needed. More to the point, we may speculate that the legal careers of the successful women nominees evidenced greater geographic mobility than that of the white males since the women's careers may have been more closely linked to the geographic mobility of their spouses. Presumably, the males could more easily pursue career opportunities closer to home and, therefore, would have access to the less difficult path to a judgeship.

In sum, the socioeconomic and demographic data reveal that the differences between white male judicial nominees of the Carter Administration and non-traditional candidates went well beyond the obvious race and sex differences. Non-white men and women nominees added greatly to the representation on the bench of younger segments and of those with relatively lower incomes....

Educational Backgrounds

Since advocates and opponents of affirmative action differ markedly in their assertions about the consequences of such programs for meritorious advancement, one would expect them to have different expectations concerning how white male and non-traditional judicial nominees would fare on

possible measures of their qualifications. Presumably one dimension of "quality" in judges is their educational training and attainments. Critics of affirmative action contend that those advanced through such programs received inferior educations which would result in inferior judicial performance. Advocates of affirmative action, however, assert that non-traditional candidates are the equals of white males in their professional training. Indeed, they argue that the non-traditional candidate generally required better educational credentials than white males in their professional training to cross the threshold of recruitment discrimination. Our analysis focused on several variables to compare the educational backgrounds of white male and non-traditional candidates. These included information about the college and law school the nominees attended, where they went to law school (in or out of the state or circuit of their appointment), and whether or not they received law school honors during their professional training.

In the aggregate there were no statistically significant differences between white male and non-traditional nominees in *any* of these measures of educational background and achievement. In examining the educational backgrounds of nominees, however, the argument could reasonably be made that our non-traditional nominee status is too broad in its inclusion of all non-white and female candidates and that important differences among the groups are subsumed in the categorization. In keeping with this view it could be argued that the historical pattern of disadvantagedness and institutionalized discrimination against blacks in American educational institutions would be evidenced in lower levels of educational attainment and fewer graduates of elite law schools for non-white candidates. The argument, however, might run somewhat differently for women; the successful few might disproportionately emerge from a relatively advantaged status. Thus, women, more so than non-whites, could be expected to attend the more prestigious law schools and further, might be expected to earn a relatively greater percentage of law school honors than non-white nominees.

To explore these possibilities, additional analysis was performed comparing white and non-white nominees and male and female nominees on our educational measures. The secondary analysis resulted in some findings which did not emerge from the broad comparison of white male with *all* non-traditional judgeship candidates. Thus, . . . white nominees were more likely than non-whites to have earned law school honors and attended elite law schools—tending to bolster the arguments of affirmative action's critics. On the other hand, the data also supported the "threshold" theory for non-traditional appointees when applied to women candidates on the same dimension.

. . . Historically, the federal bench has not only been disproportionately white, but disproportionately male as well. From this perspective, in the aggregate, it is clear that affirmative action in judicial selection during the Carter administration did *not* dilute the quality of the federal judiciary (or, for that matter, raise it higher) when the educational backgrounds of non-traditional nominees are juxtaposed with those of white males. We do not mean to suggest that the "quality" of a judge is wholly reflected in his or her educational background. However, educational background and achievement are frequently issues in debates over the consequences of affirmative action for the quality of the federal bench.

Politicization

A third set of variables that we examined focused on several available measures of a nominee's politicization or political activity in an effort to assess whether white males differed from all other judgeship candidates on these indicators. While our measures of political involvement are somewhat imperfect, they should collectively create a portrait of the level of political activity of Carter nominees. The variables utilized included measures of whether the nominees had made any speeches during the past five years that they characterized as "significant," whether they had ever held (through appointment or election) a public office, whether they had ever played a significant role in a political campaign, and whether they had ever been a candidate for a non-judicial elective office. . . . [The findings reveal that] there is little difference between white male nominees and non-traditional candidates on the relatively diffuse measures of self-ascribed significant speeches (of unspecified, open content), and the holding of public office (honorific or otherwise). When we move to more blatantly political activity involving campaign work and political candidacies the differences between the white male and non-traditional candidates emerge more strongly.

These patterns are not surprising. Both conventional wisdom and academic research have demonstrated the tendency for federal judges to emerge from among attorneys who "knew" a senator—sometimes as a campaign worker and sometimes as a fellow candidate. Political activism, however, has less often been associated with racial minorities and women. Consequently, it has not been as frequently associated with their elevation to the bench. Nevertheless, it should be noted that the differences between white males and non-traditional nominees on politicization measures are largely the result of gender associated differences. . . . [W]omen and men differed significantly on *each* of our four politicization measures.

Whites and non-whites differed significantly on none.

Curiously, the gender differences were not all in the expected direction. Thus, women were *more* likely to perceive themselves as having made significant speeches than men. Therefore, this variable may not be tied solely or predominantly to political activity *per se* but may include a broad range of speechmaking in other areas such as charitable, social, or cultural concerns. On the other politicization measures however, the gender based differences strikingly demonstrated relatively lower levels of political activity and involvement by women appointees than men.

While the Carter Administration's affirmative action program in judicial recruitment did not depoliticize the federal bench, it did result in the appointment of greater numbers of judges lacking active political backgrounds. Analysts have long disagreed about the virtues of having politically active individuals serving in judicial positions but, thankfully, that is a debate which need not be entered into here. From the perspective of assessing the consequences of affirmative action in judicial recruitment it suffices to note that the pattern of lower politicization characterizing non-traditional nominees emerges as yet another component of the increased representativeness such appointees have brought to the federal bench.

Legal Careers

The most compelling questions surrounding affirmative action and recruitment to the federal bench, as seen, concern the implications of such programs for the qualifications and likely performance of those chosen to serve. Indeed, the pluralist premises behind affirmative action envision an enrichment of perspectives in judicial decision-making as a consequence of increased representation.

On the other hand, critics of affirmative action counter that such an "enrichment" is merely a euphemism for the lowering of standards and qualifications for those gaining entree to judgeships.

As we have seen, defining "quality" in a judicial nominee is an elusive endeavor. Nevertheless, it has proven instructive to juxtapose white male and non-traditional nominees on dimensions including their demographic, educational, and politicization profiles. Most central to our empirical analysis, however, remains the question of how affirmative action has altered, if at all, possible paths to federal judgeships. In the final analysis, has affirmative action made a significant difference in the types of attorneys raised to the bench when attention is focused on the professional qualifications and legal careers of the newly appointed?

Numerous indicators were used to examine the legal careers from which judgeship nominees emerged. Among them were the following:

1. Prior Judicial Experience
2. Prior Prosecutorial Experience
3. Legal Aid or Public Defender Experience
4. Clerking Experience with State Supreme Court Justice, U.S. District Judge, U.S. Supreme Court Justice
5. Last Job Prior to Nomination
6. Highest Court Before which Nominee has been Admitted to Practice (State Court, U.S. District Court, U.S. Court of Appeals, U.S. Supreme Court)
7. Years at Bar
8. Professional Publication Record
9. ABA Rating
10. Litigation Experience

Each candidate was also required to provide detailed case studies of the ten most significant legal matters that they had personally handled during their careers. Operating on the assumption that those case studies offered important evidence of how nominees perceived their own careers, each case was coded on a number of variables for each nominee. Summary variables were also created for each nominee based on aggregating the data obtained from the ten case studies. Included were measures of the percentage of the case studies arising in the federal judiciary, involving civil law, and reaching appellate courts. Finally, each case study was also coded according to its subject matter and an attempt was made to operationalize the concept of a "non-traditional" legal practice based on the summary aggregation of the case studies for each nominee.

. . . [O]ur two classes of nominees differed significantly on some measures of professional experience prior to being nominated to the federal bench, while they were indistinguishable from each other on several others. Thus, the likelihood of having served as a prosecutor or a law clerk did not appear to differ for white male and other candidates. Dramatic differences emerged, however, when the prior judicial experience and public defender/legal aid backgrounds of candidates were considered, with non-traditional candidates more likely to enjoy both such credentials in their backgrounds. Indeed, less than half of the white male nominees as compared to approximately two thirds of the non-traditional candidates had served as judges before their federal appointment. Equally noteworthy, more than twice as many non-traditional nominees (48.6%) had served in a public defender-legal aid capacity than had the white males (23.7%). Further, consideration of the last job held by nominees prior to their appointment demonstrated that non-traditional nominees were predominantely drawn from the ranks of sitting judges (59.5%). The corresponding figure for white males was only 39.4%. In a similar vein, nearly half (49.6%) of the white males chosen ascended to the bench from private practice with the corresponding figure for non-traditional nominees a substantially less robust 25.7%. When it is added that nearly twice as many non-traditional nominees (9.5%) held law school professorships immediately prior to their appointment than white males (5.1%) affirmative action can be seen to have led to greater diversification of career experiences on the federal bench. Given the nature of these aggregate career experiences one would be hard pressed to assert that non-traditional candidates have diluted the quality of the federal bench. Indeed, it is data such as these which have led spokespersons for the expansion of the representativeness of the federal bench to conclude that non-traditional candidates need to surpass a threshold for appointment consideration placed at a higher plane than that used to gauge white male candidacies.

Additional insights are gained when it is noted that some of the differences found in professional background are most associated with the patterns revealed by an identifiable segment of the broad non-traditional nominee category. For example, the tendency for non-traditional nominees to have had judicial and public defender/legal aid experience was more highly associated with racial as opposed to gender differences among nominees. On the other hand, while white male and all other nominees demonstrated no differences regarding their prosecutorial or law clerking experiences, women were approximately half as likely to have served as prosecutors than men, . . . and non-whites were only about one third as likely to have gained clerking experience as white nominees. . . .

Other professionally oriented measures revealed additional differences between white male and non-traditional nominees. For one, the white males evidenced considerably more years of legal experience than other nominees. . . . Indeed, only 19% of the white male nominees had under 20 years of legal experience while nearly half (46%) of the non-traditional nominees fell into this category. On the other side of the experiential coin 57.6% of the white males had more than 25 years to their credit in the legal profession while the figure dropped dramatically to 27% for non-traditional nominees. Similarly, white male candidates tend to have been admitted to practice before a "higher" level court than non-whites and women. . . . Thus, 57.8% of the white male nominees have been admitted to practice before the U.S. Supreme Court, and 81.5% have been admitted to the federal bar at least as high as the circuit court level. The corresponding figures for non-traditional candidates are 45.9% and 68.9% respectively.

It should be noted, however, that admission to practice before prestigious courts, such as the U.S. Supreme Court, is often largely honorific—requiring only a sponsor and the payment of a fee. Perhaps the data does reflect however, the tendency of the non-traditional nominees not to share equally in the accoutrements of status as defined by the established bar. On yet another possible measure of professional prominence and prestige, however, candidates' publication records, there are *no* aggregate differences between white male and all other appointees.

Examining the litigation experience of the Carter nominees also reveals a mixed pattern of similarities and differences between white males and all other designates. No significant differences appeared between white male and non-traditional nominees in the frequency of their court appearances; the relative percentages of their federal and state litigation; and their propensity to choose appellate versus trial and civil versus criminal cases as the most important legal matters personally handled. It does appear, however, that non-traditional nominees, particularly non-whites, were more heavily involved, in the aggregate, in criminal litigation than their white male counterparts. . . . Similarly, there was a greater likelihood for the non-traditional candidates to be classified as being engaged in a non-traditional legal practice on the basis of coding the subject matter of the ten volunteered case studies . . . . Thus, a solid majority (55.7%) of the non-traditional nominees (57.9% of the non-whites) were classified in this fashion as compared to 40.2% of the white males (and 41.5% of all whites). The greater likelihood for non-traditional candidates to engage in non-traditional legal practices offers additional evidence of the greater diversity and representativeness brought to the federal bench by the workings of affirmative action in the judicial recruitment process.

The most dramatic differences between white male and other nominees on a measure putatively related to professional concerns emerged on the American Bar Association's ratings of judgeship candidates. It must be noted, however, that this relationship remains somewhat puzzling, troubling, and largely inexplicable in the context of the data examined throughout this article . . . . [U]nder one quarter (24.7%) of non-traditional candidates received the two highest ABA designations while a substantial majority of white males (68.4%) enjoyed this distinction. Nearly four times as many white males (9.6%) were designated "exceptionally well qualified" when juxtaposed with non-whites and females (2.6%). The data are suggestive of a number of possibilities. For one, it is possible that the ABA ratings reflect a bias in favor of some of the measures of professional prestige which we have been viewing (that is, years experience, income, etc.). Conversely, the ABA focus may work to disadvantage those who have pursued less traditional paths in their legal careers in terms of the clients they represent and the types of cases in which they are involved. Another possibility is simply that the multiple measures utilized here may not tap the same elements that lead to the ABA rankings. Nevertheless, in view of the realities of the data viewed there is little evidence, in the aggregate, that non-traditional nominees have been less qualified to serve on the federal bench than their white male counterparts. Certainly, given the extreme differences in ABA ratings received by white male and non-traditional candidates (which appear equally strong when all whites are compared to non-whites, and all men to all women), the continued charges of conservatism (and sometimes racism and sexism) levelled at the ABA's Standing Committee on Federal Judiciary, and the importance of the Committee in the judicial recruitment process, wise counsel suggests the need for further analysis of the Committee, its operation, and the correlates of its candidate evaluations.

SOME CONCLUDING THOUGHTS

Much debate has occurred in American society focusing on the legitimacy, wisdom, and consequences of affirmative action programs. Particular emphasis has been placed on the issue of whether added attentiveness to the demands of one group, by definition, constitutes invidious discrimination against another as well as on relationship between affirmative action and merit. Our focus has been on the latter of these concerns.

For the most part, public dialogue on affirmative action has taken place at a highly rhetorical and polemical level with little attempt to generate or utilize empirical evidence. Within the context of judicial selections during the tenure of the 96th Congress, this article has attempted to set out a data base which might be useful in evaluating one specific affirmative action program while also serving to help inform ongoing debates on affirmative action.

Our research has revealed that non-traditional judgeship candidates, who emerged in large numbers as a consequence of the Carter Administration's affirmative action efforts, differed greatly from the traditionally recruited white males in ways that went well beyond the obvious racial and gender lines. Clearly, affirmative action did *not* lead to the appointment of non-whites and females who were the mirror images of the white males they would sit beside on the bench. Rather, along with great diversity within their ranks, enhanced gender and racial representation on the bench added substantially to pluralism in the federal judiciary with increased representation of, among others, the young, the relatively less affluent, the less politically active, the attorney with non-traditional and, especially, criminal law practices, and the attorney with public defender/legal aid backgrounds.

It is not an easy task to measure "quality" among judicial nominees and, indeed, it is highly unlikely that a consensus could ever be fashioned around the question of what goes into the making of a "good" judge. We have however, examined white male and all other Carter nominees on a host of variables, some of which are bound to be an integral part of *any* analyst's measure of quality and *all* of which would undoubtedly find their way into some analyst's metric. On some such measures, white male nominees appeared to come out "ahead" of their non-traditional counterparts. Often, these variables were related to general societal norms attached to professional prestige, stature, and success. Thus, white male nominees were significantly older, wealthier, more experienced, more likely to practice before higher level courts, and more likely to have gained a higher ABA rating than non-traditional designates. On most of our measures, however, non-traditional nominees appeared equally qualified or, indeed, fared somewhat "better" than the white males. Most prominent among these, perhaps, was the greater propensity for the non-traditional candidate to have gained judicial experience prior to his or her current federal appointment.

. . . [G]iven the data we have presented it is certainly difficult, if not impossible, to convincingly argue that the quality of the federal bench has been diluted by affirmative action. Indeed, on measures ranging from educational training to several aspects of legal backgrounds, litigating behavior, and publication records of the nominees it is impossible to draw meaningful distinctions between white male and non-traditional

nominees that could lead to assessments of differential quality. Furthermore, there is some evidence which supports the threshold theory discussed throughout the paper. That is, perhaps some criteria for the advancement of non-whites and women are placed at a relatively *higher* level of attainment before such individuals are given serious consideration. This appears to be the case when the questions of prior judicial experience and the most recent employment of judgeship nominees were considered. Indeed, the data viewed including, in particular, the ABA ratings of judicial nominees suggest that the primary issue implicated by the judicial selection process during the Carter years was not, necessarily, merit *versus* affirmative action. Rather, it appears, the central issue may have been the question of whose definition of merit would prevail? That is, would selection outcomes reflect the traditional standards of the established legal (and governmental) community or, alternatively, would new interests active in the selection process be successful in imposing their standards of merit to a greater extent than ever before on recruitment outcomes?

Reagan and Meese Remake the Judiciary

Sheldon Goldman

Ronald Reagan with the help of Attorney General Edwin Meese III is responsible for a major change in the makeup of the federal judiciary that will likely be a major legacy of the Reagan presidency. The most important change has the potential to fundamentally alter the civil liberties and civil rights Americans enjoy under the federal Constitution. This trend began during Reagan's first term with William French Smith as Attorney General but has accelerated during the second term with Meese at the helm of the Justice Department.

The Reagan Administration is reshaping the federal courts by appointing men and women committed to a judicial philosophy of restraint in the interpretation of the Constitution, deference to the other branches of government, and sympathy for state powers under the American system of federalism.

This means in practice that the Administration has declared war on judicial activism which it sees as having brought about, for example, rulings establishing a woman's right to have an abortion, affirmative action in education and at the workplace, busing

Adapted from "Reaganizing the Judiciary," *Judicature*, 68 (1985), 324–339. Reprinted with permission of the author. Tables and footnotes omitted.

for the purpose of desegregating the public schools, the elimination of prayer in the public schools, the rights of criminal defendants including the exclusionary rule and the Miranda warnings, and the right to privacy including sexual privacy.

Meese is an aggressive and outspoken Attorney General whose style contrasts sharply with that of Smith. Meese took the lead in initiating a public debate about the role of judges in interpreting the Constitution which in turn prompted vigorous public responses from, among others, Supreme Court Justices William Brennan and John Paul Stevens and the ranking Democrat on the Senate Judiciary Committee and now its Chairman, Joseph Biden.

Meese actively defended several controversial nominations including that of Daniel Manion to an appeals court position which in 1986 resulted in a bitter and close vote in the Senate after the President himself was brought into the battle to win votes.

The first half of Reagan's second term was also marked by the appointment of a new chief justice and associate justice, and the appointment of 95 federal district judges and 32 appeals court judges to lifetime positions on courts of general jurisdiction. The Reagan Administration during its first six years named 290 judges out of a total of 741 such positions. This is close to 40 percent of the federal bench. By the end of his second term President Reagan will likely pass the 50 percent mark.

To understand how the Reagan judicial legacy is taking shape we need to answer a number of questions including: What changes in the selection process have occurred under Meese? Who are the second term appointees and how do they compare to those from the first term and those of Reagan's immediate predecessors? How successful in terms of court rulings has the Administration been in placing on the bench those sharing the Administration's judicial philosophy? What can we expect during the remainder of the second term with the Senate being controlled by Democrats, the uncertainties of how the Iran/Contra affair will unfold, and the emerging race for the presidency in 1988?

SELECTION UNDER MEESE

Meese has put his special imprint on the selection process by making certain organizational changes which reflect his intense concern with choosing judges. The Assistant Attorney General heading the Office of Legal Policy which is the center of judicial selection activity now reports directly to the Attorney General rather than the Deputy Attorney General. Meese also appointed a special assistant to handle selection. Like the first term, however, a number of Justice Department lawyers participate in the selection process including recommending names and interviewing candidates. In fact, the Reagan Administration has utilized personal interviews of prospective judicial nominees to an unprecedented extent.

Those involved in selection are concerned with an individual's overall judicial philosophy not how the candidate will necessarily decide a particular issue. Of course, Justice officials have an interest in an individual's track record if the candidate has judicial experience or has scholarly writings or delivered public speeches.

Although previous Administrations engaged in extensive negotiations with senators of the President's party when it came to district court positions, the Justice Department under Meese had made an even stronger stand than under Smith and the previous four administrations for the appointment of judges sharing the Administration's judicial philosophy.

The President's Committee on Federal Judicial Selection continues its innovative role in the judicial selection process but unlike the first term, when the head of the committee, then presidential counselor Fred Fielding (who resigned in 1986), was a dominant figure, Meese is now the key person.

DISTRICT COURT APPOINTMENTS

A comparison of certain backgrounds of the 95 Reagan appointments to the federal district courts during the second term with the 129 Reagan first term appointments and the appointees of Reagan's predecessors Carter, Ford, Nixon, and Johnson reveals:

· A smaller proportion (about one third) of second term than first term appointees were members of the judiciary at the time of their federal judicial appointments and close to 20 percent were government lawyers or held other governmental positions. Unlike the pattern in the first term and that during the Carter Administration, the U.S. Attorney's office proved to be a direct stepping stone to the federal bench for close to 13 percent of the appointees. This is consistent with the record of administrations before Carter.

· Over 70 percent of the second term appointees had either judicial or prosecutorial experience. In fact, the proportion of district court appointees with *neither* judicial nor prosecutorial experience fell to a modern record— about 23 percent, down from close to 29 percent for the first term appointees. Judicial experience enables Justice Department officials the opportunity to examine a track record to determine the professional ability as well as the judicial philosophy of a potential appointee.

· The first term record of the Reagan Administration was second only to that of the Carter Administration in the history of the nation in appointments made to women and hispanics, but the worst since the Eisenhower Administration in terms of appointments to blacks. The second term record for women and hispanics shows a continuation of these trends. In proportional terms, the Reagan second term record of black appointments is approximately the same as that of the Nixon Administration but markedly lower than that established by the Carter Administration.

· The ratings of the ABA Standing Committee on Federal Judiciary for the second term reveal a lower proportion than the first term appointees given the highest rating of *Exceptionally Well Qualified*, but a higher proportion of the next highest rating, that of *Well Qualified*. The proportion of those rated *Well Qualified* exceeded those of the previous four administrations.

· Of the 44 second term district judges given the lowest *Qualified* rating, fully one-fourth had split ratings with a minority of the ABA Standing Committee voting *Not Qualified*. The proportion of the entire group of appointees with such split ratings was over 11 percent. During the first term, in contrast, only about 2 percent (or 3 appointees) had split ratings. But no Reagan appointee has ever received an ABA majority rating of *Not Qualified*. The Carter Administration had over 12 percent of its appointees (25 in number) given split ratings or a *Not Qualified* rating.

· An analysis of the second term Reagan appointees with split ratings reveals that seven of the eleven given that rating were under the age of 40. Half of those under 40 had split ratings as compared to only 5 percent of those age 40 and above. None of the lawyers from large law firms were given split ratings. One fourth of the female appointees but only ten percent of the male appointees were given split ratings.

· In terms of party affiliation, the group of second term appointees had proportionately fewer Republicans (just under 90 percent) than the Nixon but not the Ford administrations. The proportion of Democrats more than doubled over the first term appointees. By reaching out to a limited extent to Democrats and Independents, the first term image of narrow partisanship was blunted.

· Compared to the first term appointees, proportionately fewer Catholics and more Jews were appointed. The proportion of Catholic appointees (about 25 percent) was still a modern record for Republican administrations and so was the proportion of Jewish appointees (over 10 percent). This suggests that more Catholics and Jews were part of the pool of Republicans from which potential judges were chosen. This also suggests the absence of subtle or subconscious religious discrimination in the judicial selection process.

· The average age of the second term appointees was 48.2 years, down from 49.6 years for the first term appointees. The second term appointees were the youngest group of appointees in at least the past half century.

· The proportion of those under 40 has more than doubled since the first term to about 15 percent. The proportion under the age of 45 was 40 percent (compared to 26 percent in the first term and about 20 percent for the Carter appointees). The conclusion is inescapable that the Administration is giving preference to younger candidates for judgeships with the hope that their likely extended tenure on the bench will prolong the Reagan judicial legacy.

· The net worth of the second term appointees was approximately the same as that for the first term appointees. Over one in five appointees were millionaires. This becomes all the more significant in light of recent efforts to raise the salary of federal judges. It would appear that individuals who can financially afford it are willing to serve on the federal bench. But if we do not want financial considerations to provide obstacles to recruiting the best legal talent and if we do not want the federal bench to become dominated by the wealthy, then it is necessary to substantially raise judicial salaries over their current levels.

APPEALS COURT APPOINTMENTS

The Reagan Administration has energetically sought to place on both the district and appeals courts those sharing the Administration's ideological/philosophical perspective. Appeals court appointments, however, have traditionally offered Justice officials more opportunity than district court appointments to appoint those preferred by their administrations. When we turn to the 32 second term appointees to the appeals courts and compare them to the 31 first term appointees and to the 56 Carter, 12 Ford, 45 Nixon and 40 Johnson appointments we find the following:

· Only about 40 percent of the second term appointees were members of the bench at the time of their appointment to the appeals courts. The second term Reagan appointees had the least judicial experience of all four previous administrations and of the Reagan first term appointees. The Reagan Justice Department under Meese relied less on judicial track records than during the first term and more on Meese's personal knowledge of the appointees' orientation.

· The number and proportion of those who were law professors at the time of appointment remained at the same relatively high level (over 15 percent) as that for the first term appointees. Their appointments were expected to provide new or additional conservative intellectual leadership on their circuits. It is significant that when President Reagan elevated William Rehnquist to the chief justiceship, he filled the associate justice vacancy with former law professor Antonin Scalia, a first term appeals court appointee.

- The proportion of second term appointees with neither judicial nor prosecutorial experience (over half) was twice as high as the first term appointees and was dramatically higher than the proportions for the Carter, Ford, Nixon, and Johnson appointments. The Justice Department under Meese was less concerned with the more traditional professional credentials of prior judicial and prosecutorial experience and more concerned with the judicial philosophy of its appointees. This reflects a recognition by Meese that the appeals courts are second only to the United States Supreme Court and that it is crucial that appointees share the Administration's orientation.
- In terms of the appointment of women to the appeals courts, the second term is a major improvement over that for the first term. Only the Carter Administration had a superior record. The Reagan Administration has appointed more women (25) to the three major levels of the federal bench than any other Republican Administration. The same cannot be said for the appointment of blacks. The second term appeals court appointees were all white.
- The second term appointees had the lowest proportion of all four previous administrations of those with high ABA ratings. There was also a dramatic increase over the first term appointees in the proportion given the lowest *Qualified* rating. None of the other four administrations had such a high proportion (over 50 percent) with that rating. Furthermore, over half of those with the *Qualified* rating in fact received a split *Qualified/Not Qualified* rating.

- Of the five appointees who were law professors at the time of appointment, four were given a split rating of *Qualified/Not Qualified*. Of the three women appointees, two were given the split rating. All five appointees under the age of 40 were given the split rating. However, none who were members of the judiciary at the time of their appointments were given a split rating.
- Like the first term appointees, no Democrat received an appointment. Not since Warren Harding have no members of the opposition political party been chosen for the appeals courts. The Reagan Administration's appeals court appointments have a hard edge of partisanship associated with them that is not as evident with the district court appointments.
- Thirteen of the 32 appointees, or about 40 percent, were Roman Catholic. This is a modern record for any Administration, Democratic or Republican. The proportion of Jewish appointees (close to 20 percent) is a record for Republican administrations. It is possible that anti-abortion Roman Catholics were actively recruited. While this explanation is plausible there is no objective evidence to support it independent of religion.
- The average age at nomination of the second term appeals court appointments was 48.3 years, lower than that for the first term appointees and the youngest since the appeals courts were established in 1891. The proportion of second term appeals court appointees under the age of 40 was close to 16 percent. For the first term it was about 6 percent and for the Carter appointees it was about 5 percent. The

proportion of second term appointees under the age of 45 was over one third (34.4 percent) whereas the proportion was less than half of that (16 percent) for the first term appointees and about 18 percent for the Carter appointees. These figures again point up that under Meese there is an active effort to recruit younger people who can be expected to remain a long time on the bench prolonging the Reagan legacy. The net worth figures for the second term appeals court appointees show that there were proportionately fewer millionaires than for the first term appointees. There is the distinct possibility that some of the younger appointees without a substantial net worth might not make the judiciary their life's work so that when financial demands of their families so require, they might resign from judicial office to take advantage of perhaps three times the earnings that await them in private practice. Therefore, it is in the Administration's interest to take the leadership in substantially increasing judicial salaries. By not having done so, the Administration is working at cross-purposes and may be sabotaging its design for an enduring judicial legacy.

JUDICIAL PERFORMANCE

The success of the Administration in placing those sharing its judicial philosophy requires an analysis of the judicial decisions of its appointees. There have been several recent studies by political scientists that have been concerned with this.

One major study by Jon Gottschall, a professor at the State University of New York at Plattsburgh, examined the Reagan appointments to the courts of appeals and concluded that the Reagan appointees voted considerably more conservative than did the Carter appointees and those of previous Democratic presidents (notably Kennedy and Johnson). This was particularly true for civil rights and civil liberties issues. But Gottschall also found that the Reagan appointees were similar in their voting behavior to the appointees of previous Republican presidents (Nixon and Ford). He also found that the differences were a matter of degree, so that, for example, the Reagan appointees' average support of the civil rights or civil liberties claims was 31.5 percent, the Nixon/Ford appointees' average support was 34 percent, the Kennedy/Johnson judges' average support was 46 percent, and the Carter appointees' average was 53.

Another statistical analysis was conducted by C.K. Rowland, Robert A. Carp, and Donald Songer (professors at the University of Kansas, University of Houston, and the University of South Carolina, respectively), which focused on both district and appeals courts and criminal justice policy. The researchers looked at the Nixon, Carter, and Reagan appointees in cases decided between 1981 and 1984. Here, too, the Reagan appointees decided cases in a more conservative fashion than did the Carter appointees, and, unexpectedly, even the Nixon appointees.

For the courts of appeals the researchers found that in nonunanimous decisions, the Carter appointees were "almost five times more likely than the Reagan appointees to support the criminal litigant." A study by Thomas Hensley and Joyce Baugh (both at Kent State University) of the nonunanimous criminal justice policy decisions of the appeals courts decided in 1982 also found that the Carter appointees were more liberal than the Reagan appointees and that the Reagan appointees were even more conservative than the Nixon and Ford appointees.

Ronald Stidham (of Lamar University) and Robert A. Carp conducted a study of the decisions of federal district judges and concluded that the Reagan appointees gave the *least* support and the Carter appointees the *most* support for the claims of disadvantaged minorities and other civil rights and civil liberties claims, with the appointees of other presidents falling in between the two extremes.

The key, however, to the turnaround in constitutional law lies with the Supreme Court. As of April 1988, the Administration has made four confirmed appointments and two unsuccessful nominations for a fourth seat that was filled by Judge Anthony Kennedy. While it is too early to evaluate definitively Justice Scalia's record on the high Court, he seems to be following a generally conservative course. Justice O'Connor and Chief Justice Rehnquist have clearly promoted the judicial philosophy favored by the Administration. In raw statistical terms, Justice O'Connor was either the second or third most conservative justice on the Burger Court and Justice Rehnquist was the most conservative.

On balance and with few exceptions, the Reagan Administration during the first half of the second term appears to have been successful in recruiting qualified individuals who share the Administration's judicial philosophy.

A LOOK TO THE FUTURE

A reasonable prediction about future appointees during the remainder of the second term is that we can expect most of them to be white male Republicans, many of whom are at the upper end of the socioeconomic spectrum. I think it probable that the second term trend to appoint more relatively younger judges will continue. We can also anticipate a continuation of the good record of women appointments (although not at the level achieved by the Carter Administration).

The second term record of the appointment of black Americans surpassed the first term record but still has not equalled that of the Nixon Administration in absolute numbers. As the 1988 election year unfolds, it is possible that some Republican senators up for reelection in states where the black electorate can provide the margin of victory or defeat, aware of the 1986 results where some Republican senators in such states lost by small margins, will promote the candidacies of qualified blacks for district judgeships. Were this to occur, the Justice Department should be accommodating.

It is possible that the Reagan Administration will have an additional vacancy to fill on the Supreme Court before the second term ends. But the filling of any vacany may be more difficult the closer it occurs to the 1988 presidential election.

Historically, it has been difficult for a lame duck president in his last year, particularly with the Senate in control by the opposition party, to successfully make an appointment. Another unknowable is what will occur as a result of the Special Prosecutor's investigation of the Iran/Contra affair. One or more indictments of former or current Administration officials and their trials in a presidential election year could seriously undermine the President's authority and prestige. If the Democrats believe they have a good chance at winning the presidency, it might be impossible for President Reagan under those circumstances to successfully make a Supreme Court appointment in 1988.

As for lower court appointments, if the Administration sends highly qualified noncontroversial conservatives to the Senate it is not likely that the liberals will oppose the nominations simply on grounds of ideology. Liberal Democrats by using ideology as the basis for opposition would provide a precedent for Republicans to actively oppose liberal Democratic nominees sent by a future Democratic president.

Were the Administration to send to the Senate controversial nominees about whom there was serious question about legal competence, judicial temperament, or commitment to the principle of equal protection under the law, even were the Administration satisfied that such concerns were groundless, would be draining and costly politically. The bottom line, however, is that most Democratic senators concede to the President the right to name qualified individuals to the courts who share the President's judicial philosophy.

The Iran/Contra affair, serious difficulties with the economy, the stock market crash of 1987, and the narrow senatorial victories that gave the Democrats control of the Senate, call into question whether the cycle of Republican domination of presidential politics will be at least temporarily halted in 1988. Although it might be stretching the historical analogy, we can nevertheless observe that Franklin Roosevelt also faced similar problems towards the end of his second term. He suffered setbacks in the 1938 senatorial elections, the country was still experiencing economic difficulties, he was preoccupied by foreign affairs (although there were no prosecutorial investigations under way), and he still had yet to name enough justices to the Supreme Court to assure the permanent triumph of his policies. Nevertheless, the Democrats went on to win the White House again in 1940.

Although Ronald Reagan will not be on the ballot in 1988, his Administration's accomplishments will be judged by the American people. The voters, among other concerns, will see a judiciary that if not dominated numerically by Reagan appointees will come close. It will see a Supreme Court with a Reagan appointed chief justice and probably three Reagan-appointed associate justices. It will be generally aware of the Reagan social agenda and to what extent that has been achieved by the Reagan appointments to the federal courts. And voters, among other questions, will in effect be asked if they wish that agenda to be pursued by another Republican administration's appointments to the federal courts. The future of the Constitution and the rights of Americans under it as well as the Reagan Administration's vision of American federalism rests upon the electorate's answer.

Characteristics of State Supreme Court Judges

Henry R. Glick
Craig F. Emmert

．　．　．

A gap in our knowledge of state courts is the lack of a comprehensive examination of the characteristics of state supreme court judges in all 50 states. The most recent national study of state supreme courts was published in the early 1970s and was based on information gathered over several years in the 1960s.

．　．　．

We have obtained data on the background characteristics of state supreme court judges who were serving in 1980–81. Data sources include various biographical directories and questionnaires mailed to political science professors in each state, the judges themselves, and court administrators. The questionnaires supplemented information gleaned from published sources. Approximately 180 questionnaires were sent, of which 75 per cent were completed and returned. Overall, our data collection efforts were very successful: we have complete biographies of more than 85 per cent of the judges and certain data on all state supreme court judges.

Reprinted from Henry R. Glick and Craig F. Emmert, "Stability and Change: Characteristics of State Supreme Court Judges," *Judicature* 70 (1987), pp. 107–112. Reprinted with permission of authors and publisher. Footnotes omitted.

．　．　．

In this article, we will survey the characteristics of judges serving on all of the state supreme courts. Because we are also interested in determining if judges' characteristics have changed, we will compare them with judges serving on the courts during the 1960s. We also shall compare the recent group of state judges with those recruited to the federal courts of appeals during the Carter years. We have included federal judges for two reasons. First, it is useful to have similar data on state and federal judges together so that an overview of the characteristics of American judges is available. Second, we believe many legal writers and others assume that the federal courts are "more important," and that federal judges are more qualified for office than their state colleagues. Consequently, a close comparison may be enlightening. We have chosen the circuit court level because we believe it is the most comparable federal position, and we chose the Carter administration because the emphasis on judicial qualifications probably reached its peak during these years; also, affirmative action was stressed only during President Carter's tenure.

We present selected judicial background characteristics for 1980–81 supreme court

TABLE 1
Characteristics of State Supreme Court Judges, 1960s and 1980–81

	1961–68 N = 441	1980–81 N = 300
Race and sex		
Female	NDA	3.1%
Non-white	NDA	0.6
Religious affiliation		
High status Protestant*	38.8%	29.9
Low status Protestant	41.5	30.3
Catholic	16.1	23.9
Jewish	3.6	11.6
Other	NDA	4.2
Localism		
In-state birth	74.6	78.1
In-state undergraduate school	73.9	69.5
In-state law school	64.6	69.0
Possesses bachelor's degree	57.8	80.0
Democratic party affiliation	57.4	67.0
Gov't career experience		
Prosecutor	51.5	21.5
Legislator	19.3	20.2
Previous judicial	57.8	62.9
Other	NDA	39.2
Average no. years practiced law	NDA	14.5

Data for the 1960s is based on a recalculation of data reported in Canon, *The Impact of Formal Selection Process on the Characteristics of Judges—Reconsidered*, 6 LAW AND SOC. REV. 575, 579–93 (1972).
Missing data is excluded from the calculations in this table and Table 2.

* High status Protestant denominations include Episcopalian, Congregationalist, Presbyterian and Unitarian. These are conventional categories and were used by Canon.
NDA = No data available.

judges and compare them to similar characteristics for state judges in the 1960s (Table 1) and federal appeals court judges appointed in the late 1970s (Table 2). Certain comparable data is not available for all three sets of judges; therefore, we have separated the comparisons into two tables. We have included social information about groups of people who are selected for the courts and information on their political and legal experience indicating career characteristics important for obtaining judicial positions.

SEX, RACE, AND RELIGION

First, it is notable that state supreme courts still are controlled overwhelmingly by white males. Ten women and two blacks served on the supreme courts in 1980–81. Although there are very few women and non-whites on the courts, there were only three women in the 1960s. The increase today is important, but clearly the representation of women and non-whites on state supreme courts still is basically token representation. In contrast,

TABLE 2
Characteristics of State Supreme Court Judges and Federal Appeals Court Judges

	State supreme court judges 1980–81 N = 300	Federal appeals court judges (Carter appointees)* N = 56
Race and sex		
Female	3.1%	19.6%
Black	0.6	16.1
Religious affiliation		
Protestant	60.2	60.7
Catholic	23.9	23.2
Jewish	11.6	16.1
Other	4.2	NDA
Government career experience		
Prosecutor	21.5	32.1
Previous judicial	62.9	53.6
Type of undergraduate school		
State	55.2	30.4
Private	34.0	50.0
Prestigious	10.8	19.6
Type of law school		
State	66.0	39.3
Private	12.6	19.6
Prestigious	16.2	41.1
Proprietary	5.2	0.0
Type of law practice		
Solo	26.1	1.8
2–4 partners	54.0	3.6
Larger firm	19.9	26.9
Average age upon reaching court	53.0	51.9

* Figures are reported in Goldman, *Reaganizing the judiciary: the first term appointments*, 68 JUDICATURE 313, 324–25 (1985). NDA = No data available.

as Table 2 shows, the federal system opened to a considerable degree under the Carter administration. However, the openness of the federal system under Carter's three immediate predecessors was more in line with that of the state judiciaries: only one woman and two blacks were brought into the federal appellate courts during all of their tenures combined. Reagan [in his first term] has appointed one woman and one black.

An ideal model of judicial selection based on merit imposes no obstacles based on inherent, in-born characteristics, but clearly judicial selection at the highest state levels still substantially excludes large portions of the population. The results of affirmative action under Carter should allay fears that selection of women and non-whites means that unqualified individuals will be chosen for the courts. Carter's recruitment system was the most open among all presidents, yet a high percentage of his appointees had previous judicial experience and the educational credentials of his appointees generally were considered to be outstanding. There should be no reason why officials, especially in large, urban states, where women and minorities increasingly attend law school and have frequent and varied opportunities for legal and political careers, should not be able to locate highly qualified women and non-whites for the state supreme court.

Although the state recruitment process has opened only a little to women and racial minorities, it has opened much more to religious minorities. As Table 1 indicates, the proportions of Catholic and Jewish judges have substantially increased, while the proportions of both high and low status Protestants have correspondingly decreased. It appears that the rules of access have changed so that members of religious minorities no longer are widely excluded from consideration for high judicial office.

The proportions of Catholic, Jewish, and Protestant state and federal judges were quite similar around 1980 (Table 2) and the state and federal systems appear relatively equal in their openness to members of religious minorities....

LOCALISM

Although state judicial selection has become somewhat more open by selecting a larger percentage of religious minorities, the states continue their strong attachment to recruiting local people for the state supreme courts. Table 1 shows that more than two-thirds of the judges in the 1960s and in 1980–81 were born in-state and attended in-state undergraduate and law schools. Local ties, then, remain very useful to prospective state supreme court judges.

The strong tie between judicial recruitment and in-state backgrounds also is found in judges' prior governmental experience. Table 1 includes the percentages of judges who

have had prosecutorial, legislative, judicial or other governmental experience before ascending to the state supreme courts. (We shall refer to variations in their prior careers shortly.) Nearly all of this experience for the 1980–81 judges is *state* experience: only 13 per cent of the judges had any form of prior federal experience, whereas 93 per cent had some form of prior state experience. Only 7 per cent reached the state supreme court without some form of previous involvement in state government.

EDUCATION

As indicated above, the location where state judges obtained their educations has not changed very much since the 1960s. More than two-thirds continue to attend in-state schools. However, the percentage of judges possessing a bachelor's degree has increased from 58 to 80 per cent (Table 1). In previous decades obtaining a bachelor's degree was a "luxury" because many states and law schools did not require a bachelor's degree as a prerequisite for law training or practice. More recently, however, requirements for a baccalaureate degree have become common; therefore, more judges will have a degree and this percentage would be expected to increase in coming years. Although possessing a bachelor's degree is desirable as a broad, preliminary, non-professional education, we cannot conclude that the legal educations of judges have changed very much in recent years, because most judges continue to attend in-state schools.

It is difficult to classify judges' educations in terms of overall quality. A superior education often is construed to mean attendance at private and, in particular, prestigious Ivy League undergraduate and law schools. In these terms, the federal courts of appeals judges appointed during the Carter administration clearly have superior educations to those of the state judges (Table 2). Carter appointed more appellate court judges with prestigious law school educations than Reagan or previous presidents since Lyndon Johnson, but the educations of the state supreme court judges generally fall below the levels of previous administrations as well. The undergraduate educations of Carter's appointees are similar to those of other administrations. The educations of state supreme court and federal *district* judges during the Carter years are nearly identical. However, the percentage of Carter-appointed federal district judges who had attended private or Ivy League undergraduate and law schools was five to ten points lower than in previous administrations dating from that of Johnson. Therefore, overall, there is a difference in the quality of the educations of state and federal judges.

We cannot compare the educations of the current group of state supreme court judges with those chosen during the 1960s because specific data on types of education was not reported. However, because the percentage of the 1980–81 judges who attended in-state schools is similar to the percentage who attended state *public* schools, we speculate that judge's educations probably have not changed very much in 15 to 20 years. From the reform point of view, if a private or prestige degree is considered an important part of quality judicial recruitment, the state courts probably have not improved greatly.

POLITICAL AND LEGAL CAREERS

The political and legal careers of the 1980–81 judges have much in common with their state predecessors, although there are some important changes. Table 1 indicates that

the Democrats have increased their edge in judgeships over the years; this trend generally parallels the fortunes of the Democratic Party in the 50 states. Democrats consistently controlled more governorships and state legislatures than Republicans in the 1960s and 1970s, and their influence extended to the courts. Democratic power was especially high in the mid-1970s. The increase in Catholic and Jewish judges may be due partly to this high point in Democratic power, but because the Democrats typically have exceeded Republican control in the states by considerable margins, the substantial recent increase in religious minorities on the courts probably is due mainly to a gradual and general opening of the courts to previous outsiders.

The percentage of judges who have served as state legislators is about the same as in the earlier period, and there is only a slight increase in the percentage of judges who have held other judicial posts prior to elevation to the state supreme courts. Considering the success achieved by judicial reformers in promoting merit selection and sensitizing political elites generally to judicial qualifications, it is noteworthy that the level of prior judicial experience is only slightly higher than in the 1960s. Combined with the similar educations of judges in both periods, it does not appear that the credentials of state judges have changed appreciably in nearly two decades.

A major change that has occurred since the 1960s is the substantial decrease in the percentage of state supreme court judges who have been prosecuting attorneys. In the 1960s, slightly over half of the judges had been prosecutors and a prosecutorial position was considered a major stepping stone to the courts. In recent years, however, serving as prosecutor is no longer the major career path to the state supreme court.

It is unclear why serving as a prosecutor

no longer appears in the backgrounds of most judges, but we can speculate that the decline may reflect a general shift away from obtaining political visibility and experience in partisan, elective political positions. (The judges with legislative experience are accounted for overwhelmingly by the three states where legislatures continue to elect judges.) We have examined the frequency of elective and appointive positions for the 1980–81 judges and discovered that nearly one-third of them have held only appointive governmental posts. Slightly more than one-third have held only elective posts while another quarter have held both elective and appointive positions. The few remaining have held no prior offices. We have no precise data on elective and appointive positions from earlier years with which to compare, but there is good reason to believe that in the 1960s, most judges held elective positions before their recruitment to the courts. Canon reports that 85 per cent of the judges in the 1960s had held positions either as prosecutor, state legislator or state judge. Because non-elective merit systems were much less common in the 1960s, more state judgeships were elective posts. Therefore, it probably is safe to conclude that the combination of these three positions produced many more elective posts in the backgrounds of the 1960s judges than in those in 1980–81. At a minimum, it is clear that there has been a substantial drop in the percentage of judges who have served as elected prosecutors.

A comparison of the state and federal judges also provides several surprising differences in career patterns (Table 2). More federal than state judges have served as prosecutors. But state judges have a slight edge in prior judicial experience. State judges in the 1960s also exceeded the federal level of judicial experience. However, the percentage of federal appeals court judges appointed by Carter with prior judicial experience was below that of previous administrations, although the state judges still compare favorably with earlier federal appointees. Only the small group of appeals court judges appointed by President Ford had significantly higher levels of prior judicial experience. (The percentage of state judges with prior judicial experience was markedly higher than that of federal district judges both during and before the Carter years.) The lead that the state judges have in prior judicial experience is especially significant, given the explicit attention that the Carter administration gave to recruiting judges with solid legal and judicial credentials. If we measure qualifications for office partly by the presence of prior judicial experience, then the state judges compare admirably. This is true even though the prior judicial experience of state judges has not increased very much in nearly two decades.

We have no comparable data on the specific prior judicial posts held by the federal judges. It is likely that some of them have been federal district or state supreme court judges or judges on major urban trial courts and that their judicial experience is perhaps more varied and substantial than that available to most state supreme court judges. Nevertheless, the state judges appear very respectable in terms of legal and judicial qualifications, because many of them have prior judicial experience and the percentage is similar to that of most federal appellate appointees in most years and exceeds that of federal district judges.

The legal careers of the state and federal judges (Table 2) suggest that more federal judges than state have had high-powered legal careers, presumably involving them in "big business" and "big government" practices. About one-quarter of the Carter appointees were recruited from large law firms, while only a small percentage were recruited from small partnerships or solo practices.

The reverse is true for state judges. Only a fifth were members of large law firms before sitting on the state supreme court. Most were members of small firms or were lone practitioners. (These figures are not perfectly comparable, because the percentages for the federal judges are for occupation immediately preceding judicial appointment, while those for the state judges include any previous type of law practice.)

The 1980–81 state judges had practiced law an average of 14 years before sitting on the state supreme court (Table 1). The range included a few who had only one year of prior law practice experience, to 15 who had practiced law for 30 years or more before being elevated to the supreme court. Only 15 per cent of the state judges had fewer than five years of law practice before becoming state supreme court judges. Comparable data on the length of law practice is not available for the 1960s state judges nor for the federal district judges. Nevertheless, in terms of prior legal experience, most of the state judges appear to satisfy demands that they have substantial prior legal experience before being selected for a state's highest court.

CONCLUSION

The state supreme court judges in 1980–81 are similar to their 1960s counterparts in many respects. They are still state people with extensive local ties. Political careers continue to be stepping-stones to judicial office, although significantly fewer judges have prosecutorial and (probably) elective political experience. Previous judicial experience has increased, though by a relatively small amount, given the extensive efforts of judicial reformers. But the judicial experience of state judges exceeds that of federal court judges and, overall, the legal and judicial experience and educations of the state judges compare favorably. An important

change is the increase of Catholic and Jewish judges on the courts. In 1980, both the state and federal recruitment systems were equally open to members of religious minorities, but only the federal system had been opened in a meaningful way to women and racial minorities.

The decline in prosecutorial and probably other elective political experience is significant; it may indicate a shift away from elective politics as part of the career paths of state judges. However, there is no evidence that the legal and judicial credentials of the judges have changed or improved over the years, for they have similar educations and levels of judicial experience. We have not, therefore, witnessed a shift from highly visible public careers to more prestigious prior legal and judicial careers; the judges only seem to have reduced their public visibility. We believe that the lower level of public visibility also is reflected in the general absence of judges' party affiliations in published sources. Non-reporting does not mean, however, that judges have no party affiliations. As a result of our mail questionnaires we were able to identify the party affiliations of more than 95 per cent of the judges. Only 3.5 per cent claimed to be independents; all others were identified as Democrats or Republicans. Recall also that although prior elective posts have declined in judicial profiles, 93 per cent of the judges have had some form of prior and mostly state governmental experience. Consequently, we believe it would be incorrect to conclude that state supreme court judges have substantially reduced their governmental or political involvement and affiliations, but only that they have been in less visible roles.

It is interesting to speculate on the effects that changes in judges' backgrounds may have on judicial decisionmaking. As we have seen, Democrats and religious minorities have made gains in the past 15 to 20 years, and we expect women and non-whites to increase their representation in the future.

The effects of these changes are uncertain, but we present several possibilities. First, compared with their predecessors, these judges may increase the tendency to liberal decisionmaking on courts where Democrats and religious minorities have made the greatest gains. This hypothesis must be moderated, however, because public issues and judicial attitudes change over time. It is very likely, for instance, that all courts produce more "liberal" decisions today, especially in the area of individual rights, than they did in the 1960s. But, in the near future, with "conservative" leadership from the U.S. Supreme Court, conservative judges in traditional states may act to restrain departures in civil rights and civil liberties policies. In addition, we would expect minority judges to be more liberal than their brethren on particular courts. It is also likely that the level of disagreement on certain supreme courts will increase because of greater disparities in the backgrounds of the judges. Levels of dissent have increased in many states, some probably due to a greater mix of judicial characteristics. More research on decisionmaking needs to be done, however, before we can confirm these hypotheses.

.   .   .

The Defeat of the California Justices

John T. Wold
John H. Culver

In our pre-election article on the background to the controversy over Chief Justice Rose Bird of the California Supreme Court, we noted the comments of Bill Roberts, a veteran campaign manager and head of a prominent anti-Bird organization: "The only question is can we make it so the other two are gone, too. There's nothing that's going to save her. She is going to be slam dunked out of business."[1] Roberts' remarks were accurate, though hardly startling, since it had long been apparent to most observers that Bird had no realistic chance of surviving the November, 1986, retention election. The question Roberts posed as to the fate of the "other two" was also settled by the voters on election day. For the first time since retention elections were adopted for the state's appellate justices in 1934, the public not only rejected a chief justice, but defeated two other justices, Cruz Reynoso and Joseph Grodin, as well. In renouncing the three jurists, the voters in one stroke removed from

the high court three of the four remaining appointees of former Governor Edmund G. (Jerry) Brown, Jr.

. . .

THE CAMPAIGN

In an unusual set of circumstances, six of the seven justices on the California supreme court were on the retention ballot in 1986. Allen Broussard, the only remaining appointee of Jerry Brown on the court, was the only justice not required to face reelection. There was no controversy regarding the retention of two other justices, Malcolm Lucas and Edward Panelli, both of whom were appointed to the bench by Brown's successor as governor, George Deukmejian.

Justice Stanley Mosk was also on the ballot. A former state attorney general, Mosk had been appointed to the court by Governor Edmund G. (Pat) Brown, Sr., in 1964 and was the senior member of the court. (We shall refer to the two Browns by their nicknames, in order to avoid confusing Brown, Sr., with his son, who also served two terms as governor of California.) Mosk had been targeted for defeat by the organized opposition in early 1986, but had been deleted as a

Reprinted from John T. Wold and John H. Culver, "The Defeat of the California Justices: the Campaign, the Electorate, and the Issue of Judicial Accountability," *Juticature* 70 (1987), pp. 348–355. Reprinted with permission of authors. Most footnotes and all tables and figures omitted.

target later that year when the two major anti-Bird groups, Californians to Defeat Rose Bird, and Crime Victims for Court Reform, joined ranks under the Crime Victims banner. Mosk was a highly respected justice who had authored many significant decisions during his 22 years on the court. Although Mosk had voted to overturn death sentences in the past, he had also voted to uphold the sentences in 14 of the 15 capital cases decided between December 1985 and October 1986. According to Mosk, his death penalty decisions had not "changed significantly" over the years, but rather "the bugs and flaws in the 1978 death penalty law" had gradually been eliminated by the court, thereby making it easier to affirm capital sentences.

In late August 1986, Governor Deukmejian publicly indicated that he would vote to retain Mosk. At the same news conference, he also announced that he would oppose Justices Grodin and Reynoso, in addition to Bird, because their votes and opinions on death penalty cases "indicate a lack of impartiality and objectivity."

Opposition to Bird, Reynoso and Grodin came from a variety of sources. Governor Deukmejian, other Republican incumbents and challengers, Crime Victims for Court Reform, and a coalition of state and local prosecutors (the Prosecutors' Working Group), all actively campaigned against the three. Most law enforcement organizations also opposed them.

Only a few Democrats publicly supported the justices. Others, such as Mayor Tom Bradley of Los Angeles and Senator Alan Cranston, refused to state their positions concerning Bird. Because they took a neutral stance, they were portrayed by Republicans as in effect supporting her.

Until mid-summer, Bird's own Committee to Conserve the Courts did not mount any effort on her behalf. Moreover, it was never made clear whether the Committee to Conserve the Courts was to speak for just Bird, or for Reynoso and Grodin, or for all six of the justices on the ballot. Bird contracted with a Santa Monica political consulting firm in 1985 to manage the campaign, but she disagreed with the firm's strategy and severed ties with the organization several months later. She then engaged John Law, a Washington political consultant, but that relationship ended several months later as well. In both instances, the terminations resulted from Bird's refusal to consider running negative campaign ads and her reluctance to engage in large-scale fundraising.

To credit the Committee to Conserve the Courts with a campaign strategy is to be charitable. Two television ads were run, which Bird wrote and appeared in, stressing the traditional independence of the judiciary. In one ad, Bird spoke of a "court system with the courage to protect our form of government," i.e., a government in which freedoms of speech, religion and press were upheld, in contrast to their suppression in the Soviet Union and South Africa. In the second, she addressed the cultural, racial and religious diversity of California: "Our diversity of ideas and viewpoints makes us stronger. In California, we have a Supreme Court that reflects that diversity. That's a California tradition to be proud of." Both ads showed Bird, wearing a dark blue dress rather than her judicial robes, seated in her Los Angeles chambers with an open book in front of her and law books filling the shelves behind her.

According to Bill Zimmerman, the first consultant Bird retained, her emphasis upon judicial independence ran directly counter to the approach he felt would be the most effective, such as emphasizing the court's environmental record or focusing upon her detractors as corporate special interests. Essentially, Bird's opponents charged her with being soft on criminal matters, especially the death penalty, and Bird's response focused on judicial independence rather than a defense of the court's overall record in criminal cases. In a post-election essay, Zimmerman succinctly articulated the problems with her "remarkably inept" campaign: "she had no campaign manager, no political consultant, no advertising agency, no pollster, no steering committee and no fundraising coordinator.... And although polling indicated that judicial independence was the one message that would *not* work, she adopted it as the sole basis of her campaign."

Former Governor Pat Brown tried to breathe new life into the pro-Bird effort by establishing the Independent Citizens' Committee to Keep Politics Out of the Courts. The elder Brown and Shirley Hufstedler, former U.S. Secretary of Education, served as co-chairs. This committee drew some support, primarily from Democratic activists in labor, ethnic, environmental and women's organizations. The organizations supported retention of all six justices on the ballot. In one of the letters sent to prospective financial contributors, Brown and Hufstedler linked the effort to unseat Bird to "the Moral Majority and the rest of the radical right." (In literature sent out by Californians to Defeat Rose Bird, references had been made to the fact that Bird was supported by Tom Hayden and Jane Fonda—e.g., "Do you want a Supreme Court that will be dominated by the extremist left-wing philosophy of Jerry Brown, Tom Hayden and Jane Fonda?...") With specific references to several conservative California lawmakers, the letter added, "If these home-grown California fanatics are successful in defeating Rose Bird and other targeted Supreme Court Justices in November, it will send an unmistakable message to every judge in every county in California who has ever drawn the line between Church and State or tried to protect and enhance our civil rights: either do what the radical right says,

or we'll be coming after you." Aside from showing the flag for Bird, the Committee did not generate much publicity in the state's media, at least in part because the group was formed only four months before the election.

The state's major newspapers split in their endorsements of the justices. The *Los Angeles Times*, *San Jose Mercury*, and *Sacramento Bee* endorsed all six justices. The *San Diego Tribune* opposed Bird and Reynoso, while the *San Francisco Chronicle* and *San Francisco Examiner* recommended the ouster of Bird, Reynoso and Grodin.

The voters in any event had firmly linked Reynoso and Grodin with Bird by election day. Bird received a positive vote of only 34 per cent, Reynoso tallied 40 per cent, and Grodin 43 per cent. Voters in only two counties (Alameda and San Francisco) supported all three justices; Reynoso carried a third (Marin), which Grodin also won along with two others (Santa Clara and Santa Cruz). All of these counties are in the San Francisco Bay area. The pattern of voting for the justices in these counties mirrored the statewide vote in terms of Grodin's receiving the most votes to confirm, Reynoso's occupying the middle ground, and Bird's finishing last.

FUNDRAISING AND DECISIONMAKING

Even by California standards, the amount of money raised and spent by the pro- and anti-Bird factions was phenomenally high— an estimated seven and one-half million dollars. The amount may prove to be closer to eight million dollars when all financial disclosure forms relating to the campaign are filed with the California secretary of state. Analysis of these data will reveal the extent to which interest groups financed the contest. Throughout the campaign, some Bird supporters charged that special interests had contributed large amounts to the anti-Bird groups. In response, Crime Victims for Court Reform claimed that the majority of its contributions were from private citizens in amounts of $100 or less. Quarterly campaign statements revealed that sizable contributions to anti-Bird organizations were from oil and gas, agribusiness, auto dealers, and real estate interests, while contributions in support of the chief justice included the California Trial Lawyers Association, which contributed more than $200,000, and four Los Angeles personal-injury firms, which added another $217,000 to her cause. Collectively, Bird, Reynoso and Grodin spent about two million dollars, in contrast to the five and one-half million expended by their opponents. The other three justices spent nothing beyond the filing fee.

As Schotland has noted, changes in partisan electoral politics have had an impact upon the judiciary. Judicial contests that were once "personal, quiet, and inexpensive, have now become noisier, nastier and costlier."[2] Whether multimillion dollar campaigns will be waged subsequently against California justices remains to be seen. However, it is not unreasonable to forecast less expensive but nevertheless well-organized challenges against individual justices in the future.

Justices who frequently hand down controversial decisions may invariably be faced with challenges to their retention. They could respond by mounting a campaign against the challengers, as Chief Justice Bird did. Another approach would be to ignore the potential opposition. Such was the response of Justice Mosk when targeted for defeat by anti-Bird groups in early 1986. He chose not to react, perhaps concluding that after 22 years on the court, and as a former attorney general, his legal qualifications were beyond reproach.

A third possible response would be for justices to alter their positions on controversial issues when faced with hostile public opinion. To do so, of course, would be to compromise to some degree the concept of an independent judiciary. The point may be illustrated by citing the comments of former Justice Otto Kaus. Kaus, a Jerry Brown appointee to the high court, has revealed that his then-upcoming appearance on the November, 1982, ballot might have influenced his decision regarding the constitutionality of the Victim's Bill of Rights, a popular initiative passed by the voters in June of the same year. Kaus voted with the 4–3 majority to uphold the initiative. As he said in 1986, "I decided the case [the initiative] the way I saw it. But to this day, I don't know to what extent I was subliminally motivated by the thing you could not forget— that it might do you some good politically to vote one way or the other."[3]

The defeat of the three California justices may well prove to be a historical aberration, but few justices in the future should be able to ignore the 1986 results altogether when contemplating their own chances for retention. More frequently than in the past, jurists will probably calculate, if only privately, the potential reactions to their decisions of affected interest groups and the public at large.

SOME HISTORICAL COMPARISONS

The ability to cashier judges has been a prerogative rarely exercised by the electorate in retention elections. Nation-wide, few jurists have been rejected at the polls. According to Carbon, from 1934 to 1980, only 33 judges were not retained; and from 1972 to 1978, of 1,499 judges on retention ballots in 20 states, a minuscule 1.6 per cent were not retained (n=24).[4] The votes typically have not only retained sitting jurists, but have done so by wide margins.

Compared with historical patterns, the California election of 1986 was an obvious aberration. Among the anomalies was the defeat of several members of a multimember court. Never before had the voters of any state rejected more than a single judge of an appellate tribunal in any particular election. California voters not only rejected three justices, but defeated all three decisively....

Another anomaly was the apparent absence of "voter fatigue" or "voter roll-off," i.e., the tendency of many voters to leave unmarked the portion of their ballots dealing with the judiciary. Scholars have attributed "voter fatigue" to the customary low salience of judicial elections. In fact, exit polling revealed that, far from being uninterested in the judicial section of the ballot, voters in California had actually been drawn to the voting booth on November 4, 1986, by the opportunity to vote on Bird's confirmation. Voting on Bird was second only to voting in the gubernatorial race among reasons given for casting ballots on election day. The difference between the number of ballots cast in the governor's race and for or against the retention of Bird, Reynoso and Grodin was only 9.5 per cent. Interestingly, many voters who marked their ballots on the three targeted justices actually refrained from voting on the other three jurists on the ballot. The difference between the number of ballots cast in the governor's race and the average number on the retention of Mosk, Panelli and Lucas was 18 per cent.

Prior studies have also indicated that judicial campaigns and elections are typically low-visibility affairs. In contrast, the issue of Bird's retention was a prominent, if not the *most* prominent, issue of the entire 1986 California campaign. One needed only to be exposed to televised campaign spots to appreciate the extent to which candidates for partisan state offices vied with one another as to the degree of their opposition to Bird.

Bird was also not the unknown quantity that appellate jurists in most states have been. In fact, her professional qualifications, personality, and record as a justice had been long-term issues in California. Much of the controversy surrounding Bird dated back virtually to the time of her elevation to the high court.

Conventional wisdom likewise suggests that an officeholder's incumbency benefits him or her at election time.... Bird, Reynoso and Grodin nonetheless proved to be exceptions.... Despite a tenure on the supreme court of more than nine, four, and four years, respectively, all three were overwhelmingly defeated by the California voters.

.   .   .

STANDARDS OF ACCOUNTABILITY

What standards might the individual voter employ in "judging judges" in retention elections? The possible positions may be arrayed along a continuum...from those maximizing judicial independence to those maximizing judicial accountability....

Most supportive of independence would be a standard under which the voter viewed himself as constrained to retain all judges except those who have committed impeachable offenses. If employed by a majority of the electorate, such an approach effectively would extend to state jurists the same type of tenure historically enjoyed by federal judges.

A standard somewhat less supportive of judicial independence would be one under which the voter also believed it legitimate to remove "behavioral misfits": judges who are, e.g., alcoholic, abusive, or mentally ill. This standard would in effect duplicate other formal mechanisms available in all states.

Under a third standard the voter would, in addition, consider it acceptable to remove jurists on the basis of a criterion of "professional merit," i.e., in terms of the quality of a judge's written opinions. . . .

None of the foregoing approaches would permit an individual to vote against a judge because of the jurist's vote in particular cases. In contrast, the voter's adoption of the next position on the continuum would allow him to cast a ballot against a judge simply because the voter disagreed with the judge's decisions. That is, under the next approach, the voter would consider it legitimate to evaluate the *substance* of a judge's decisions, not merely his or her personal behavior or the process used in arriving at decisions. This approach would include voting based upon ideological consideration, e.g., upon the perceived "liberalism" or "conservatism" of a jurist's decisions.

Most restrictive within this standard would be a requirement that the judge had engaged in an "excessive" number of what the voter perceived as "incorrect" or offensive decisions in more than one area of the law. Less restrictive requirements would permit the voter to cast a negative vote on the basis of decreasing numbers of decisions. The approaches would thus range from a single line of decisions, to several particular decisions, and ultimately to a single unpopular decision.

Near the end-point of our continuum is a position based upon partisan considerations. This standard would permit the voter to cast a negative ballot for such reasons as the party affiliation of either a particular judge or the governor who had appointed the jurist.

.   .   .

THE VOTERS' STANDARDS

Upon what standards did California voters base their ouster of Justices Bird, Reynoso, and Grodin? To attempt to answer this question, we examined relevant data collected by the California (Field) Poll between 1972 and 1986. Our examination led us to conclude that a majority of the California electorate employed an exclusively *decisional* standard of accountability in 1986. The voters appeared to have been particularly exercised by two lines of decisions handed down by the state court. Of apparent primary concern was the three jurists' perceived opposition to the death penalty; of secondary concern, the justices' perceived leniency toward criminal defendants generally.

.   .   .

. . . There is little evidence . . . that voters were willing to oust judges for "nonjudicial" factors such as the judge's gender, religious affiliation, racial or ethnic background, or other "personal" characteristics. The California vote suggests that, although a majority of the electorate spurned standards that stress judicial independence, they also were not motivated, at least in the 1986 election, by extreme concepts of judicial accountability or by concepts extraneous to judicial performance.

IMPLICATIONS

What do our findings imply with respect to future judicial retention elections? One implication is that, although voter indifference to judicial elections may be the historical norm, such indifference can be dispelled by a pattern of highly publicized judicial decisions. In other words, lines of decisions that arouse voter attention *and* hostility can become influential factors in retention elections. Likewise, despite historical patterns throughout the nation, judicial retention campaigns *can* become highly visible phenomena.

Another implication is that voters may not uninterruptedly permit interpretation of the law to be solely the province of the courts. In the 1986 election a majority of California voters apparently believed it legitimate to reject jurists on the basis of lines of judicial decisions that did not comport with what voters thought the law *should* be.

Last, and probably not surprisingly, the California results suggest that voters in state retention elections do not necessarily view themselves as bound by standards similar to those protecting federal judges. A state judge's *decisions*, and not merely his or her adherence to accepted norms concerning personal and professional behavior, may be considered by the public a legitimate basis for voting the jurist out of office.

.   .   .

Do the election results of 1986 augur a long-term assault by California voters upon the basic independence of their high court? It is impossible at this early juncture to foretell. On the one hand, the 1986 election may prove to have been a historical aberration, reflecting a profound public concern with specific lines of decisions handed down by the justices over several years. Even if jurists were to be defeated upon a similar decisional basis in the future, their removal might not seriously infringe upon judicial independence. On the other hand, the California voters may prove willing in the future to defeat justices upon grounds much more tenuous than those that apparently motivated the electorate in 1986. Likewise, last year's results may also prove to have had a chilling effect upon the willingness of California judges to hand down potentially unpopular decisions, even when jurists deem such decisions to be legally "correct." Should either of the latter eventualities occur, judicial accountability will have been enhanced, but at a considerable, and possibly unacceptable price in terms of judicial independence.

NOTES

1. Culver and Wold, *Rose Bird and the Politics of Judicial Accountability in California*, 70 JUDICATURE 81, 87 (1986).
2. Schotland, *Elective Judges' Campaign Financing: Are State Judges' Robes the Emperor's Clothes of American Democracy?*, 2 J. OF L. & POL. 76 (Spring 1985).
3. LOS ANGELES TIMES, Sept. 28, 1986, at I:3.
4. Carbon, *Judicial retention elections: are they serving their intended purpose?*, 64 JUDICATURE 221–223 (1980). See, also, Jenkins, *Retention elections: who wins when no one loses?*, 61 JUDICATURE 70 (1977); Griffin and Horan, *Patterns of voting behavior in judicial retention elections for supreme court justices in Wyoming*, 67 JUDICATURE 68 (1983); Hall and Aspin, *What twenty years of judicial retention elections have told us*, 70 JUDICATURE 340 (1987).

CHAPTER 8

Juries

The Sixth and Seventh Amendments to the United States Constitution guarantee the right to a trial by jury in all serious criminal cases processed by the federal courts and in certain types of civil suits. These constitutional guarantees provide for the participation in the processing of disputes by judicial institutions of a group of citizens drawn from the community in which they live—a group given the responsibility for finding facts and determining fault, blame, guilt, or innocence. Giving ordinary citizens an institutionalized role in the judicial process has always been understood as a device for democratizing the law.[1] The jury, reflecting a democratic suspicion of public authority, has traditionally been regarded as a means of checking and preventing the abuse of power by judges. The presence of a jury ensures, at least in theory, that the purposes of the state will be subjected to the common-sense judgment of citizens having no official public position.[2]

Juries are employed exclusively in trial courts. Dispute processing in trial courts centers on two generic types of issues: issues of law and issues of fact. Issues of law arise as the parties to a dispute seek to identify and interpret norms that will legitimize their behavior. A trial is, to some extent, a contest of interpretation and legal reasoning. The judge, with special training and expertise in matters of law, has the authority and responsibility to determine which interpretations of law are proper and acceptable. But a trial is more than an argument over applicable norms; it also provides the occasion for a reconstruction, description, and interpretation of events.[3] The purpose of a trial is to answer the question of who did what to whom, as well as the question of whether such conduct is legal. It is the special province of juries to listen to and decide among competing and conflicting versions of events. The jury is to use its collective judgment to referee an adversary contest in which the truth is expected to emerge from the presentation of differing versions of the same occurrence. In the division of labor in a trial court, the jury is the authority on facts; the judge is the authority on law.

Although this distinction is generally accurate, there is a blurring of it in contemporary American courts. Judges have the power to determine what evidence can properly be presented to the jury, and they have the power in certain circumstances to direct a verdict or to set aside the verdict of a jury if they believe it not to be one that reasonable people would have returned if they had understood the evidence presented to them and the law as interpreted to them by the judge. On the other hand, American practice allows for "jury nullification," that is, juries are permitted to refuse to convict if they believe that the law at issue in a case is unfair or arbitrary. Despite these practices the major role of the jury remains one of determining facts.

Several important issues surround the participation of jurors in the processing of disputes by American courts.[4] The first is whether juries are effective checks on government power. There is, in fact, no way of determining whether the institution of jury trials ensures that public officials will be more restrained in using their power than they would otherwise be. We cannot know how many more political prosecutions would be initiated were it not for the realization on the part of public officials that such prosecutions are subject to the scrutiny of a group of private citizens. The famous Chicago Jury Project, an excerpt from which is found in this chapter, attempted to determine the effectiveness of the jury in checking official power by examining the percentage of cases in which the judges and juries involved in the same cases agreed as to the appropriate verdict. The authors, Kalven and Zeisel, found a high degree of agreement between judge and jury—approximately 75 percent. Furthermore, in almost all criminal cases in which judge and jury disagreed, Kalven and Zeisel found the jury to be more lenient. Whether the leniency of the jury can be construed as limiting the exercise of official power is open to question; it does, however, indicate that the participation of laymen in the making of decisions does make a difference in the results of court processing of disputes.

A second issue frequently discussed in the academic literature on juries is whether they typically are or need to be representative of the community. The legitimacy of the jury as a democratic influence in the trial court is largely a function of its representativeness. The assumption is sometimes made, although it is frequently subject to challenge, that a jury that is representative of the community it serves is one that provides judgment by peers. Several studies, however, have revealed that American juries are not always representative,[5] mainly because the sources from which lists of potential jurors are drawn—typically voter registration lists or telephone directories—do not include people from all segments of the community. The representativeness of such lists is important not only because of the need to maintain the legitimacy of the jury but also because different kinds of people bring different attitudes and values to their service on a jury. If particular groups of people are underrepresented, then their attitudes and values are systematically underrepresented, and different types of decisions are reached than would be reached by more fully representative juries. It is of interest to note that in 1986 the Supreme Court forbade prosecutors from using peremptory challenges to keep blacks from serving on juries.[6] Racial discrimination may not be used by government to underrepresent black people on juries.

A third issue is the question of juror competence.[7] This subject is discussed in the selection by Hastie, Penrod, and Pennington. Critics of the jury system suggest that the disputes that typically reach courts are so complex that the average citizen is not capable of understanding them or the issues raised by them. Defenders argue that jurors are as able as judges to comprehend the factual issues presented in most lawsuits. They cite the high level of agreement between judges and juries reported in the Chicago Jury Project as support for their contention. Furthermore, although there is evidence that jurors are influenced by such "irrelevant" factors as the order and manner in which evidence is presented, there is no evidence that jurors are any more susceptible to such influences than judges or other legal experts.

Finally, the participation of citizens in the American judicial process may be important not only because it affects the way in which the state exercises its power and the way in which disputes are processed but also because it affects the individuals who participate. Service on a jury may be an important experience in participatory democracy as well as an important experience in exercising the responsibilities of judgment. Alexis de Tocqueville, writing in the early 1800s, described jury service as follows:

> [Jury service]...imbues all classes with a respect for the thing judged and with the notion of right.... It teaches men to practice equity; every man learns to judge his neighbor as he would himself be judged.... The jury teaches every man not to recoil before the responsibility of his own actions.... By obliging men to turn their attention to other affairs than their own, it rubs off that private selfishness which is the rust of society.[8]

However, in American trial courts today the jury is seldom used, since most criminal and civil cases are decided without trial. Of the small percentage of cases that go to trial, many are tried by the judge alone without the use of a jury. Ultimately the importance of the jury may lie in the anticipation of both sides to a dispute of what a jury might do if the case were to go before a jury. And in a broader sense the value of the jury may lie in its democratic symbolism.

NOTES

1. Alexis de Tocqueville, *Democracy in America*, Vol. 1 (New York: Vintage Books, 1954), Chap. 16.
2. Occasionally events have called into question the utility of the grand jury as a device for checking government power. The function of the grand jury is to make a judgment as to whether there is sufficient evidence to justify putting an individual on trial. Like the petit or trial jury, it is composed of citizens chosen from the state and district in which the alleged offense was committed. However, the argument has been advanced that the grand jury is little more than a tool of the prosecutor. See Richard Harris, *Freedom Spent* (Boston: Little, Brown, 1976). Also see Marvin E. Frankel and Gary P. Naftalis, *The Grand Jury* (New York: Hill and Wang, 1977); Robert A.Carp, "The Behavior of Grand Juries: Acquiescence or Justice?," *Social Science Quarterly* 55 (1975), 853.
3. Lance Bennett and Martha Feldman, *Reconstructing Reality in the Courtroom* (New Brunswick: Rutgers University Press, 1981).
4. On the general role of jurors and the function of juries, see Rita James Simon, ed., *The Jury System in America* (Beverly Hills: Sage, 1975).
5. See Howard Erlanger, "Jury Research in America," *Law and Society Review* 4 (1970), 345; Hayward R. Alker, Jr., Carl Hosticka, and Michael Mitchell, "Jury Selection as a Biased Social Process," *Law and Society Review* 11 (1976), 9; Edward N. Beiser, "Are Juries Representative?" *Judicature* 57 (1973), 194; and C.K. Rowland, W.A. Macauley, and Robert A. Carp, "The Effects of Selection System on Jury Composition," *Law & Policy Quarterly* 4 (1982), 235.
6. *Batson* v. *Kentucky*, 106 S. Ct. 1712 (1986).
7. Broadly encompassed under this concern is the question of whether jury verdicts ought to be unanimous. Supreme Court decisions, particularly *Apodaca* v. *Oregon*, 406 U.S. 404 (1972), have established the principle that the fairness or validity of jury verdicts may be unrelated to the question of unanimity.
8. Tocqueville, *op.cit.*, note 1, p. 295.

The American Jury: Some General Observations

Harry Kalven, Jr.
Hans Zeisel

. . .

In the large, the mind of the jury in criminal cases might perhaps be said to exhibit four dominant traits. First, there is the niceness of its calculus of equities; it will treat provocation as justifying defensive moves by the victim but only to the extent of the one-punch battery; it may even treat injury to the victim as punishment for the actor, but only where the relationship is close and the conduct is inadvertent. Second, there is the jury's broad tendency to see little difference between tort and crime and thus to see the victim rather than the state as the other party to the case, with the consequence that the public controversy is appraised largely as though it were a private quarrel. Third, there is a comparably broad tendency to merge at several points considerations of penalty with those of guilt. Finally, . . .there is a quality of formal symmetry about the jury's responses. In what we have called the simple rape cases the jury seems to say, whatever kind of offense the defendant had committed, it just was not rape; conversely, in the cases of sexual approach to children, it says that

whatever the defendant did, even though far short of rape, it was some kind of offense. Thus while the jury is often moved to leniency by adding a distinction the law does not make, it is at times moved to be more severe than the judge because it wishes to override a distinction the law does make.

. . .

Although a substantial part of the jury's work is the finding of facts, this, as has long been suspected, is not its total function in the real world. As a fact-finder it is not in any interesting way different from the judge, although it will not always reach the same conclusion. When only pure fact-finding is involved the jury tends to give more weight than the judge to the norm that there should be no conviction without proof beyond a reasonable doubt. And there is every indication that the jury follows the evidence and understands the case.

The more interesting and controversial aspects of the jury's performance emerge in cases in which it does more than find facts; where, depending on how one looks at it, the jury can be said to do equity, to legislate interstitially, to implement its own norms, or to exhibit bias.

All this is fairly familiar. The distinctive bite of this study resides in the following supplementary propositions about the jury as legislator.

First, we can estimate with some precision how frequently the jury engages in more than fact-finding. . . . [A]bout three quarters of the time it agrees with the judge; and that most, but not all of the time it agrees with him, it is not importing values of its own into the case. But roughly two thirds of the disagreements with the judge are marked by some jury response to values.

Second, the jury imports its values into the law not so much by open revolt in the teeth of the law and the facts, although in a minority of cases it does do this. . . . The jury, in the guise of resolving doubts about the issues of fact, gives reign to its sense of values. It will not often be doing this consciously; as the equities of the case press, the jury may, as one judge put it, "hunt for doubts." Its war with the law is thus both modest and subtle. The upshot is that when the jury reaches a different conclusion from the judge on the same evidence, it does so not because it is a sloppy or inaccurate finder of facts, but because it gives recognition to values which fall outside the official rules.

Third, we suspect there is little or no intrinsic directionality in the jury's response. It is not fundamentally defendant-prone, rather it is non-rule minded; it will move where the equities are. And where the equities are at any given time will depend on both the state of the law and the climate of public opinion.

Fourth, the extent to which the jury will disagree with the judge will depend on the selection of cases that come before the jury. Since, under current waiver rule and practice, the defendant in effect has the final say on whether there is to be a jury trial or a bench trial, the cases coming before the jury will be skewed and include a disproportionate number in which there are factors that

appeal to the jury. The selection will be affected also by pleas of guilty and, to a lesser degree, by decisions of the prosecutor not to prosecute, and even in some instances by decisions of the police not to arrest. Thus, the commonplace impression that the criminal jury is defendant-prone may be largely an artifact of the dynamics by which the cases are sorted out for jury trial.

Fifth, we have said, the jury's reaction will in part depend on the lay of public sentiment on any given point. The extensive agreement between judge and jury indicates that there is in our society at this time widespread consensus on the values embodied in the law. As a result, a jury drawn at random from the public, does not often have representatives of a dissenting view.

On some points there is sufficient dissent so that the random drawing will at times place on the jury representatives of a view contrary to the existing law. Indeed on some matters the public will even be ambivalent, with factions that deviate from the law in opposite directions.

Thus, it makes a good deal of difference in this decision-making who the personnel are. The consequence of the fact that no two juries are alike is that statements about trends in jury decision-making are probabilistic at best. We cannot assert that all juries will always feel that a man who has suffered personal disasters since committing the crime has been punished enough. We can only say that this idea is prevalent enough so that it has some chance of moving the jury away from the judge in any given instance in which it is present.

Sixth, the explanation of how a disagreement is generated requires one more fundamental point. The thesis is that to a substantial degree the jury verdict is determined by the posture of the vote at the start of the deliberation process not by the impact of this process as rational persuasion. The jury tends to decide in the end whichever way the initial majority lies. The result is that a sentiment need be spread only so widely among the public as to produce enough representatives on the jury to yield the initial majority. . . .

Seventh, and as a corollary, the deliberation process although rich in human interest and color appears not to be at the heart of jury decision-making. Rather, deliberation is the route by which small group pressures produce consensus out of the initial majority.

.   .   .

As we attempt to step back and gain some distance from the detail of the study, it may be useful to put two quite general and interrelated questions: Why do judge and jury ever disagree, and why do they not disagree more often?

Judge and jury have experienced the same case and received the same rules of law to apply to it; why do these two deciders ever disagree? We seek for the moment an explanation more general than that [previously] offered. . . in terms of specific factors of evidence, sentiment, and defendant. Why do they not react the same way to the stimuli? Why does the judge not move over to the jury view, or the jury stay with the judge?

The answer must turn on the intrinsic differences between the two institutions. The judge very often perceives the stimulus that moves the jury, but does not yield to it. Indeed it is interesting how often the judge describes with sensitivity a factor which he then excludes from his own considerations. Somehow the combination of official role,

tradition, discipline, and repeated experience with the task make of the judge one kind of decider. The perennial amateur, layman jury cannot be so quickly domesticated to official role and tradition; it remains accessible to stimuli which the judge will exclude.

The better question is the second. Since the jury does at times recognize and use its de facto freedom, why does it not deviate from the judge more often? Why is it not more of a wildcat operation? In many ways our single most basic finding is that the jury, despite its autonomy, spins so close to the legal baseline.

. . .As just noted, the official law has done pretty well in adjusting to the equities, and there is therefore no great gap between the official values and the popular. Again, the group nature of the jury decision will moderate and brake eccentric views. Lastly, the jury is not simply a corner gang picked from the street; it has been invested with a public task, brought under the influence of a judge, and put to work in solemn surroundings. Perhaps one reason why the jury exercises its very real power so sparingly is because it is officially told it has none.

The jury thus represents a uniquely subtle distribution of official power, an unusual arrangement of checks and balances. It represents also an impressive way of building discretion, equity, and flexibility into a legal system. Not the least of the advantages is that the jury, relieved of the burdens of creating precedent, can bend the law without breaking it.

.   .   .

Inside the Jury

Reid Hastie
Steven D. Penrod
Nancy Pennington

...At an abstract level, the Supreme Court has defined the function of the jury as to create an effective deliberation process. We translated this general function into five empirically measurable characteristics of effective jury performance: representing a cross-section of the community, expressing a variety of viewpoints, performing accurate and thorough factfinding, remembering and properly applying the judge's instructions on the law, and rendering accurate or proper verdicts. The present study addresses each of these aspects of jury performance except for composition and representation. However, the individual differences found in deliberation behavior are relevant to jury composition and thus to any consideration of which classes or types of individuals ought to be included on (at least not excluded from) juries.

Decision rule affects each of the remaining characteristics of effective deliberation. Decision rule affects the counterbalancing of viewpoints during deliberation, because dissenting viewpoints, or views favored by

relatively small numbers of jurors within a jury, are at a relative disadvantage in nonunanimous juries as compared to unanimous juries. Members of very small dissenting factions participate at lower rates in majority rule juries and are less satisfied with the jury verdict when compared to small-faction members in unanimous juries.

Decision rule also affects the thoroughness of the jury's consideration of evidence and the law during deliberation, although measures of accuracy on facts and the law per se are not affected by decision rule. Nonunanimous juries discuss both evidence and law during deliberation far less thoroughly than do unanimous rule juries. However, there is no indication that juries are biased in favor of either prosecution or defense as a function of decision rule.

The effect of decision rule on verdict accuracy is not dramatic. However, because even subtle signs of a decision rule effect on verdicts are important to a policy maker, it is significant that in the study the first degree murder verdict was rendered only by nonunanimous juries. We argued that a first degree murder verdict could be treated as an error because it required a truly exceptional interpretation of the evidence presented at trial. The relationship obtained between first degree murder verdicts and nonunanimous

336

rule juries should be viewed with caution because of the sampling variability in the study, which produced an uneven distribution of large first degree murder factions across juries. However, an examination of juries with equivalent starting points supports the conclusion that juries in majority decision rule conditions as compared to the unanimous rule are more likely to reach improper, first degree murder verdicts for the stimulus case. For example, five of the unanimous rule juries started deliberation with four or more jurors favoring first degree murder verdicts, but none of these juries rendered such verdicts. Under majority rules, eleven juries started with four or more jurors favoring first degree murder, and four of these juries rendered that verdict. Furthermore, the moderating influence of the longer, more thorough deliberations under the unanimous rule might have damped the sampling effects that occurred in the study and that can also occur in actual juries. A systematic pattern of errors on the law, not the evidence, is also associated with first degree murder verdicts. Again, the evidence suggests that longer, more thorough deliberation might eradicate these errors, as in the unanimous rule juries.

Two other findings on the thoroughness of deliberation, and by implication on the jury's accuracy on the evidence and the law, favor the unanimous decision rule. First, in unanimous juries, a substantial number of important events occur during deliberation after the largest faction has reached a size of eight members. For example, a large proportion of discussion occurs during the interval between the largest faction reaching ten and the verdict being rendered. This discussion usually includes several error corrections and references to the standard of proof. Typically this is also the interval during which requests for additional instructions from the trial judge occur. Second, in juries

under the unanimous decision rule, majority factions with eight members, a sufficient number to render a verdict under the eight-out-of-twelve rule, do not always prevail in the final jury verdict; these juries also hang and reverse themselves. In effect, the jury decision task is not completed even when the majority faction is quite large.

Decision rules also affect conditions at the end of deliberation. Majority rule juries finish more quickly than unanimous rule juries. Typically in majority rule juries there are small factions of holdouts, jurors who do not subscribe to the majority-rendered verdict. These holdouts express negative views of the quality of deliberation, and jurors from both majority and holdout factions have lower respect for their fellow jurors' open-mindedness and persuasiveness under the nonunanimous decision rules. These findings favor the unanimous rule.

Other findings emphasize the positive characteristics of majority rule juries. Deliberation time is shorter on the average in majority rule juries. The distribution of final verdicts does not shift dramatically from decision rule to decision rule. Deadlocked juries are also less likely to result under majority rules, and deliberation is more direct, unequivocal, and fierce.

It is up to policy makers and perhaps the voting public to assign appropriate weight to these empirical results. In our view, the unanimous rule appears preferable to majority rules because of the importance of deliberation thoroughness, expression of individual viewpoints, and protection against sampling variability effects of initial verdict preference. Furthermore, because respect for the institution of the jury is a critical condition for public acceptance of jury decisions, the lower postdeliberation evaluations of the quality of their decision by jurors in nonunanimous juries and the larger number of holdouts who reject the jury's verdict under these rules greatly diminish the usefulness of the majority rule jury as a mechanism for resolving legal disputes.

Other factors affect the quality of the jury's performance of deliberative functions. One is the counterbalancing of biases. This counterbalancing has two aspects: inclusion of a variety of viewpoints on the jury panel and expression of all viewpoints during deliberation. The issue of inclusion of viewpoints lies outside of the present study because it depends on the composition of the jury pool and the particular impanelment and selection procedures implemented at trial. But the study's focus on the contents of deliberation yields findings about the expression of views. Members of small factions express themselves less fully under majority decision rules as compared to unanimous rules. Juries that deliberate with an evidence-driven style, starting deliberation with a discussion of evidence rather than law and deferring formal voting until later in deliberation, also tend to discuss more fully and equitably. However, this latter trend is not statistically significant and deserves further study.

In their task of factfinding, juries perform efficiently and accurately. The reconstruction of the testimony and the construction of plausible narrative schemes to order, complete, and condense the trial evidence occur with thoroughness and precision. These accomplishments in jury deliberation are especially impressive when compared to the performance of even the most competent individual jurors. The view of the evidence produced by deliberation processes is invariably more complete and more accurate than the typical individual juror's rendition of the same material. This conclusion is supported by postdeliberation measurement of jurors' memory for trial evidence. Not only do erroneous statements about evidence occur roughly half as frequently as errors on the law, but evidence errors are also more

likely to be corrected during deliberation.

Because jury performance of the fact-finding task is so remarkably competent, few innovations are needed to improve performance. An evidence-driven deliberation style produces more thorough and impartial assessment and integration of the evidence. Thus, an instruction to the jury to begin deliberation with a review of the evidence and to avoid early or frequent vote-taking might facilitate performance.

.   .   .

As for accuracy on the law, jury decision processes do not falter when confronted by abstract legal concepts, such as the beyond reasonable doubt standard, reasonable inference, and the presumption of innocence. Perhaps juries should balk at these conceptual hurdles, but on the whole they manage with an impressive display of common sense. By their actions, jurors acknowledge the impossibility of perfect conceptual clarity and accept crude, but serviceable, approximations.

The major conceptual obstacles to reaching a proper verdict arise from jurors' inability to keep the verdict categories and their elements in order. These conceptual errors do not occur because the judge's instructions are jumbled or overly complex. In fact, the contents of the instructions in the stimulus case are unusually succinct, clear, and crisp. Nonetheless, comprehension, memory, and application of the law are major problems for juries.

To avoid these failures of jury decision making, improvements are needed in the manner in which the trial judge communicates the law to the jury. Many, if not all, of these verdict errors can be avoided if the jury accurately comprehends and retains the judge's substantive instructions concerning the crime categories. Providing the jury with a written transcript, written summary, or audiotaped recording of the final charge can effectively remedy these confusions. The repetition or elaboration of specific instructions by the judge will help when the jury appears to be blocked or requests further instructions. Of course, the judge must exercise care to avoid a misleading or biasing emphasis and must not encourage the jury to depend on the Court rather than its own resources for solutions to the factfinding task. Yet concise, responsive additional instructions can facilitate error correction and productive discussion by the jury.

.   .   .

Three phenomena are associated with variations in the jury decision rule, which are important targets for future conceptual and empirical analysis. First, the decision rule does not simply cut off deliberation at the point at which the required quorum to render a verdict is reached. Rather, various types of events are distributed proportionally across deliberation. However, the social mechanism that adjusts discussion to reflect a typical pattern of content, regardless of duration, is a mystery. Second, the largest faction grows more quickly during deliberation under majority rules as compared to the unanimous rule. At least four factors may account for these differences in growth. Jurors may take their task less seriously in the nonunanimous decision rules as contrasted with the unanimous decision rules. Jurors may want to avoid membership in the holdout faction in verdict-rendering nonunanimous juries and so defect from factions that are likely to lose in the race to render a verdict. Jurors may also be motivated to shift to join the largest faction and put the jury over the top of the quorum requirement. Finally, the suppression of discussion by small faction members in nonunanimous juries may produce an imbalance in participation rates that gives larger factions an advantage in information pressure to persuade other jurors to join their faction. The third phenomenon is the differential participation rates for members of small factions in unanimous and majority decision rule juries. This phenomenon may be accounted for by motivational factors affecting the small faction members' probability of speaking or the large faction members' probability of cutting off argument by the small faction members.

One view of the individual in jury deliberation is provided by jurors' perceptions of each other. An egocentric bias characterizes jurors such that each juror sees himself or herself as exceptionally persuasive and exceptionally open-minded. This bias generalizes, so that other members of the juror's own faction are seen as more persuasive and more open-minded than members of opposing factions. Since this finding holds across all jurors, regardless of faction membership, it seems to be a general bias of social perception that transcends the specifics of a particular view of the case.

Comparison of individual and group memory for information from the testimony and from the judge's instructions replicates the common finding that groups outperform individuals on such memory tests. The group memory advantage over the typical or even the exceptional individual is one of the major determinants of the superiority of the jury as a legal decision mechanism.

.   .   .

In summary, although differences in the frequency of verdicts rendered by juries under the three decision rules are not large, the final verdict patterns are important. First, only majority rule juries return first degree murder verdicts. Some of these verdicts occur because of predeliberation sampling variability in the assignment of jurors to experimental conditions. However, there is convincing evidence that a part of this result is due to decision rule influence on performance. Even quantitatively small effects such as those observed are of great significance in the context of the legal commitment to a trial process that is not biased against the defendant. Second, hung juries are less likely under majority decision rules, and majority rule juries reach verdicts more quickly than unanimous juries. Furthermore, deliberation quality with respect to thoroughness or seriousness is diminished, minority or small faction viewpoints are suppressed, and overall juror satisfaction is lowered in majority rule as compared to unanimous juries. The proper decision rule is thus the unanimous rule.

The major obstacle to proper jury decision making is also the difficulty of correctly comprehending, remembering, and applying the trial judge's substantive instructions on the law. Procedures or devices should be adopted to aid the trial judge in communicating the law to the jury. Two specific procedures are written transcripts or summaries of the instructions and audio-taped recordings to go into the jury room.

.   .   .

Legal institutions are conservative. They exhibit great resistance to new findings and new procedures. Resistance is greatest when new concepts challenge traditional assumptions or methods. Modern behavioral science creates many such threats to fundamental assumptions. New conceptions of motivation and preference replace the concept of free will; new empirical methods for determining truth challenge traditional rational analysis and trial procedures; and new trial tactics extend the adversarial competition to jury selection and beyond. However, the conservativism of legal institutions is sensible. The foundations of behavioral science are uneven. For example, scientists know much more than the man-in-the-street or the philosopher-in-an-armchair about attention, perception, memory, and decision making, but they know little more than nonscientists

about human motivation or altered states of consciousness. Uncritical acceptance of social science findings and theories is a mistake. Even when a scientific result is clearly established, the question of generalization to new conditions must be addressed.

Behavioral science is starting to exert a small influence on some judicial decisions and policies. Acknowledgment by some jurists that empirical data may sharpen and advance legal arguments and even resolve disputes is relatively recent. The use of research findings and methods to guide policy decisions is increasing. The employment of social scientists to assist attorneys in their preparation for trial is new and increasingly popular. One avenue for the introduction of scientific results into the literature of legal precedents is the presentation of evidence by expert witnesses. Such witnesses from the field of psychology include clinicians who testify when a case involves insanity or other questions of mental condition, experts who comment on other witnesses' ability to observe, remember, or accurately report on events, and experts who present research results that are relevant to a practice challenged on constitutional grounds.

In many instances the adversarial system shields the legal process of determining truth from the influence of equivocal or weak scientific procedures, such as clinical analysis of insanity or polygraphic lie detection. However, the acceptance of unequivocal, valid scientific results is also frustratingly slow. Although the institutional safeguards, such as adversarial testing in court, should not be removed, legal scholars, practitioners, and policy makers should be more open to the findings of behavioral science. Just as with the laws of society, those who ignore the laws of science will be controlled by those who understand them.

PART THREE

Judicial Decision Making

CHAPTER 9

Facts and Environmental Variables as Bases for Decisions

In Part Three we turn our attention to the way in which disputes, once translated into lawsuits, are dealt with by judges. We are concerned with how judges decide cases and why they make particular decisions. The decision making behavior of judges is of critical importance in any inquiry into the nature of dispute processing by courts. Such dispute processing should proceed, at least in theory, in a principled and impartial manner. Judicial decision making may be distinguished from the decision making of other public officials because it is expected to be guided strictly by clearly articulated rules and to proceed with reference solely to the facts in dispute. In Part Three the extent to which American judges, in fact, live up to this expectation is described and analyzed.

The traditional model of dispute resolution by trial courts suggests that the judge applies the relevant law to the relevant facts that have been established by the jury or the judge during the trial. The outcome of the case is thus considered to follow, routinely and indeed mechanically, determination of facts and law. The model, of course, assumes that legally relevant facts as well as the applicable law can be established as a result of the trial. However, we have already seen that the traditional model's assumption that trials are the ordinary vehicle for dispute resolution is simply not true. In terms of the total business of trial courts, the fact-finding role of judges and juries is minimal.

We shall also be observing in subsequent chapters that the determination and application of "the law" is far from the straightforward technical process the traditional model suggests it is, particularly when disputes raise new questions of public policy. Our task initially is to examine the traditional model's assumptions about "facts" and the place they have in judicial decision making in those cases that involve the full scope of the judicial process.

First, the traditional model of dispute resolution assumes that the facts of the case *can* be established by the judicial process. There is the underlying assumption that the adversary system, whereby opposing counsel present their respective sides of the dispute and have the opportunity to closely scrutinize each other's evidence and witnesses, facilitates the emergence of the truth. The beliefs that facts can be discovered and that the adversary system aids in their discovery are cornerstones of the traditional model.

Second, there is the assumption in the traditional model that only certain kinds of facts are legally relevant and can potentially be established and taken into account in decision making.

This means, for example, that ordinarily the race or gender of the criminal defendant, or his or her socioeconomic status, or the type of lawyer defending the accused are not legally relevant but are rather legally irrelevant and should have no bearing on the resolution of the dispute. Judges and jurors who take such "irrelevant" facts into consideration are thought to violate basic legal norms. This second assumption, in effect, suggests a distinction between (1) the facts of the dispute, that is what happened (most of which is legally relevant); (2) the facts about the personal attributes of the disputants, that is, their race, gender, age, class, and so on (most of which is legally irrelevant); and (3) the facts concerning the processing of the litigation itself, such as the type of lawyer involved—for example, privately retained or court appointed—and whether a plea bargain has been made (also generally not legally relevant).

A third traditional assumption is that judges give the same weight to the same legally relevant facts and that the result is individual decisional consistency as well as uniformity in decision making among different judges. Sentencing disparity among judges, where similar facts in similar cases produce different results, is considered to be an indication of judicial pathology. This underscores a related assumption that there is predictability and hence continuity in the law. There is the expectation that judges apply the same law to similar factual situations, thereby producing similar decisional results. Lawyers expect to be able to tell their clients what "the law" is and what it requires. Individuals, organizations, and governments expect to be able to know in advance the legal consequences of their actions. The concept of settled law is simply the expectation that any competent judge in a court of law will behave predictably given certain facts and the law as it is widely understood.

There is a fourth assumption that the facts of the case are important only at the trial court level. Once established by the trial court the facts are not supposed to be questioned at all by appellate courts. The traditional model considers trial courts as triers of fact and appellate courts as being concerned only with questions of law.

How do these assumptions concerning "facts" as the bases for decisions stand up against studies of decisional behavior? The answer is brief: not very well.

Observers of trial courts such as Jerome Frank (who himself had a distinguished career on the United States Court of Appeals for the Second Circuit), raised fundamental questions about the nature of fact finding by means of the judicial process.[1] Frank developed the school of thought popularly dubbed "fact skepticism," that cast doubt on the ability of the adversary system to determine the truth. Frank argued that it is difficult to objectively determine "facts." For Frank, the fact-finding enterprise is so subjective that it is impossible to predict in advance how a dispute is going to be resolved in court.

Many researchers who focus attention on the relationship of facts to judicial behavior ignore the subjectivity of the fact-finding process. They assume that most facts *can* be objectively determined. But the fact-oriented researchers do not make the distinction between legally relevant and legally irrelevant facts made by the traditional model. Rather they consider as fair game *all* facts—those pertaining to the dispute and disputants as well as those concerning the processing of the litigation, as argued in the reading by Fred Kort. Studies of both trial courts and appellate courts have suggested that the race of the defendant, although usually legally irrelevant, may affect case outcomes.[2] This assumed tremendous importance in a captital punishment case in Georgia where the statistical evidence was overwhelming that blacks convicted of killing whites were more likely to be sentenced to death than whites convicted of killing blacks or whites or blacks convicted of killing blacks. The U.S. Supreme

Court, however, rejected the argument that this overwhelming statistical evidence of the relevance of a legally irrelevant fact in the imposition of the death penalty constituted cruel and unusual punishment in violation of the Constitution.[3]

Some have argued that the nature of the crime and the socioeconomic status of the criminal may be tied to decisional behavior in that white-collar crime and criminals may be treated less severely than blue-collar crime and criminals.[4] Other legally irrelevant facts that have been linked with judicial behavior include whether a plea bargain was negotiated,[5] and whether the lawyer was privately retained or assigned by the Court or whether defendants had no lawyer.[6]

The third assumption that judges give approximately the same weight to the same facts, has been seriously undermined by a variety of research findings. At the trial court level a study conducted by researchers for the Federal Judicial Center explored the question of whether different judges would make similar sentencing decisions when confronted with the same facts. They found, however, wide sentencing disparity.[7] However, the traditionalist assumption that individual judges are consistent in the weight they give certain facts *is* supported by fact-pattern studies of appellate courts. The study included in this chapter by Jeffrey Segal is one such study. Obviously, if individual judges on a collegial court were inconsistent in the weights they gave the facts from one case to the next, fact-pattern analysis, as discussed in the Kort reading and shown by Segal would result in the disproving of the fact-pattern analysis hypothesis that particular configurations of both legally relevant and legally irrelevant facts are associated with particular case outcomes.

Finally, the traditionalist assumption that the facts of the dispute are not questioned by the appellate courts is apparently undermined by the successful application of the fact-pattern approach. Of course, witnesses and physical evidence are not presented before appellate courts. Yet appellate judges on occasion differ with trial judges over the weight and interpretation given certain facts.

Although the traditional model's assumptions about the relationship of facts to judicial decisions can be effectively challenged, it is interesting to note that both the traditional model and its challengers place great importance on the facts. With the exception of fact skeptics such as Jerome Frank, there seems to be widespread agreement that facts can be objectively determined and that predictable patterns of judicial behavior can be expected. Where there is disagreement, it is over what facts are to be considered, whether appellate courts consider them, why judges weigh and weight them the way they do, and how the "law" is applied to the facts.

We have already suggested that the traditional model's treatment of "facts" is inadequate. The other side of the coin is the traditional model's treatment of "law." Here we find prominent challenges going back to the legal realists of the 1920s and 1930s. Legal realists argued that the legal rules and principles cited by judges, particularly appellate court judges, as the bases for their decisions are largely a smoke screen for the furtherance of their own views on social and economic policy. The realists argued that this occurs because inherent in judicial decision making is a large amount of discretion in choosing which precedents or principles to follow. These realists emphasized judicial discretion and played down law and the nature of judicial institutions. Yet, as John Brigham argues, there is a language of law and a constitutional discourse that sets the parameters within which the exercise of judicial discretion occurs as to the applicable law. This may be considered the legal environment within which courts and judges operate. There are other environmental variables that also deserve to be considered when exploring the nature of judicial decision making.

Environmental influences are peculiar to the geographic area in which courts are located. American courts have well-defined geographic jurisdictions. What this means is that they can only process disputes occurring in the area they serve or between a resident of that area and a resident of another area. Courts thus may be said to have relatively definable and distinct constituencies and clienteles. It may seem strange to use the term judicial *constituencies*, since that word is most often used to describe legislatures and other representative institutions. Judges, on the other hand, are expected to supply an impartial evaluation of conduct and behavior—an evaluation that is generally supposed not to consider the wishes of the parties to a dispute or of those living within the geographic jurisdiction of the court.

Nevertheless, there are audiences for most disputes that come to courts—audiences that are more or less clearly defined and more or less attentive. In order to guard against the pressures these audiences might generate, American courts have been insulated through the idea that judges must be independent in order to be impartial. Judicial independence implies institutions that are formally separate from and not subservient to any other branch of government. Furthermore, judicial independence may be associated with particular types of judicial selection and with long and secure tenure for judges. Essentially, independence exists when judges feel that they need not take account of the wishes of the audiences to a dispute or those of their geographic constituents.

The establishment of particular geographic loci for courts and of norms of judicial independence results in a paradox for judges. They are expected to act without reference to environmental influences, yet the localism of the organization of the American judiciary operates to enhance such influences. How might environmental pressures influence judicial decision making? First, environmental factors, such as the relative wealth or poverty of an area, influence the kinds of disputes that come to court and impose limits on what judges can require in their decisions. Second, environmental influences affect judicial decision making through the process of judicial selection, which works to ensure that lawyers with strong local connections become judges in courts serving the local area. What this means is that judges typically share the attitudes and values peculiar to the culture of the area they serve. To the extent that those cultures vary, the way the judges perceive and decide disputes may also vary.[8]

A third explanation of environmental influences on judges involves the judge's sense of what will be acceptable to his or her "significant others," that is, to those people whom the judge respects and looks to for approval. Among the most important of these people are the local lawyers comprising the local bar. Judges may exercise their discretion in such a way as to try to win the respect of local lawyers and other politically significant people and groups. This is, according to the article by Beverly Cook, especially true of trial court judges in the exercise of their sentencing powers, and it is especially true in visible, controversial cases. Cook, elsewhere, has demonstrated the linkage of changing public opinion on the Vietnam War from 1967 to 1975 to changing sentencing patterns of selective service law violators. As public opinion turned against the war, sentences by judges became more lenient.[9] This linkage of environmental variables to behavior was also demonstrated in a study by James Gibson of the sentencing behavior of trial court judges in Iowa. Gibson found that judges' sentencing behavior could be explained in part by their perception of local opinion; that is, judges appeared to increase or decrease the severity of the criminal sentences they imposed in accord with their own impression of how the public viewed the seriousness of the crime in question.[10] In subsequent chapters we will consider a number of variables that have been thought by legal realists and others to be related to decision making. We will consider in turn backgrounds of judges and judicial attitudes and values, the judicial role, and the small-group influence on collegial court decision making. The extent to which these variables are shown to be associated with decision making is the extent to which the traditional model's assumptions about the place and uses of law are inadequate.[11]

NOTES

1. Jerome Frank, *Courts on Trial: Myth and Reality in American Justice* (Princeton, New Jersey: Princeton University Press, 1973). The book was originally published in 1949.

2. See, for example, Fred Kort, "Content Analysis of Judicial Opinions and Rules of Law," in Glendon Schubert, ed., *Judicial Decision-Making* (New York: Free Press, 1963), pp. 133–197; S. Sidney Ulmer, "The Discriminant Function and a Theoretical Context for Its Use in Estimating the Votes of Judges," in Joel Grossman and Joseph Tanenhaus, eds., *Frontiers of Judicial Research* (New York: Wiley, 1969), pp. 335–369; Marvin E. Wolfgang and Marc Riedel, "Race, Judicial Discretion, and the Death Penalty," *The Annals of the American Academy of Political and Social Science*, 407 (1973), 119–133; James L. Gibson, "Race as a Determinant of Criminal Sentences: A Methodological Critique and a Case Study," *Law and Society Review*, 12 (1978), 455–478; Cassia Spohn, John Gruhl, and Susan Welch, "The Effect of Race on Sentencing—A Re-Examination of an Unsettled Question," *Law and Society Review*, 16 (1981), 71–88; Charles R. Pruitt and James Q. Wilson, "A Longitudinal Study of the Effect of Race on Sentencing," *Law and Society Review*, 17 (1983), 613–635; Samuel L. Myers, Jr., "Race and Punishment: Directions for Economic Research," *The American Economic Review*, 74 (1984), 288–292; Joan Petersilia, *Racial Disparities in the Criminal Justice System* (Santa Monica, Calif.: Rand Corp., 1983); Raymond Paternoster, "Prosecutorial Discretion in Requesting the Death Penalty," *Law and Society Review*, 18 (1984), 437–478; Michael L. Radlet and Glenn L. Pierce, "Race and Prosecutorial Discretion," *Law and Society Review*, 19 (1985), 587–621.

3. *McCleskey* v. *Kemp*, 107 S. Ct. 1756 (1987). The study presented to the Court was conducted by Professors David C. Baldus, George Woodworth, and Charles Pulanski.

4. See, for example, *Federal Offenders in United States District Courts, 1971* (Washington, D.C.: Administrative Office of the U.S. Courts, 1973), pp. 149, 157. Also see, Marvin E. Frankel, *Criminal Sentences: Law Without Order* (New York: Hill & Wang, 1973), pp. 23–24; John Hagan and Ilene Nagel Bernstein, "The Sentence Bargaining of Upperworld and Underworld Crime in Ten Federal District Courts," *Law and Society Review*, 13 (1979), 467–478.

5. See, for example, *Federal Offenders, 1971*, pp. 14–15; David Brereton and Jonathan D. Casper, "Does it Pay to Plead Guilty? Differential Sentencing and the Functioning of Criminal Courts," *Law and Society Review*, 16 (1981), 45–70. The attributes and attitudes of prosecutors and defense attorneys appear to be important for plea-bargained sentencing. See Peter F. Nardulli, James Eisenstein, and Roy B. Flemming, "Unraveling

the Complexities of Decision Making in Face-to-Face Groups: A Contextual Analysis of Plea Bargained Sentences," *American Political Science Review*, 78 (1984) 912–928.

6. *Federal Offenders, 1971*, pp. 8–9. Also see Stuart S. Nagel, "Effects of Alternative Types of Counsel on Criminal Procedure Treatment," *Indiana Law Journal*, 48 (1973), 404–426. But see David Willison, "The Effects of Counsel on the Severity of Criminal Sentences: A Statistical Assessment," *Justice System Journal*, 9 (1984), 87–101.

7. Anthony Partridge and William B. Eldridge, *A Report to the Judges of the Second Circuit* (Washington, D.C.: Federal Judicial Center, 1974). Also see the findings and discussion in Shari S. Diamond and Hans Zeisel, "Sentencing Councils: A Study of Sentence Disparity and its Reduction," *University of Chicago Law Review*, 43 (1975), 109–149.

8. See Martin A. Levin, *Urban Politics and the Criminal Courts* (Chicago: University of Chicago Press, 1977).

9. Beverly B. Cook, "Public Opinion and Federal Judicial Policy," *American Journal of Political Science*, 21 (1977), 567–600. Also see, in general, Herbert M. Kritzer, "Political Correlates of the Behavior of Federal District Judges: A 'Best Case' Analysis," *Journal of Politics*, 40 (1978), 25–58.

10. James L. Gibson, "Environmental Constraints on the Behavior of Judges: A Representational Model of Judicial Decision Making," *Law and Society Review*, 14 (1980), 343–370. But cf. George W. Pruet, Jr. and Henry R. Glick, "Social Environment, Public Opinion, and Judicial Policymaking," *American Politics Quarterly*, 14 (1986), 5–33.

11. There are other variables that may be relevant for decision making. For example, some scholars have suggested that the personality of the judge should be treated as a decision-making variable. See Harold Lasswell, *Power and Personality* (New York: Norton, 1948), pp. 59–88; Willard Gaylin, *Partial Justice: A Study of Bias in Sentencing* (New York: Random House, 1974); and Harry N. Hirsch, *The Enigma of Felix Frankfurter* (New York: Basic Books, 1981).

Quantitative Analysis of Fact-Patterns in Cases and Their Impact on Judicial Decisions

Fred Kort

Studying the dependence of court decisions on facts can be clearly associated with traditional conceptions of the judicial process. There are, however, salient problems in the relationship between facts and decisions which cannot be solved by conventional methods. Such problems must be attacked by mathematical and statistical methods which have been extensively employed in the behavioral sciences. These methods are not limited to research on social backgrounds of judges, their values, and their individual positions as members of appellate courts. It has recently been suggested that the process of decision-making on the basis of relevant facts involves an attitude of the judge toward his responsibility which may be examined in the same manner as other judicial attitudes. If this view is accepted, the study of the dependence of decisions on facts could rely on methods that are also appropriate for the study of other aspects of judicial behavior. But even if traditional conceptions of the relationship of court decisions to facts

are preferred, mathematical and statistical methods provide insights which otherwise cannot be obtained.

The use of mathematical and statistical methods yields such insights in areas of law where comprehensive sets of facts have been specified by appellate courts as relevant and controlling for reaching decisions. In such areas of law, it has been stated by courts that some combinations of the facts would lead to decisions in favor of one party to the dispute and that other combinations would result in decisions for the opposing party. Beyond the association of *some* combinations of facts with decisions which already have been reached, it is not known, however, what decisions can be expected on the basis of *other* combinations of the specified facts. For example, in the involuntary confession cases under the due process clause of the fourteenth amendment, the Supreme Court has clearly stated that each decision depends on the particular circumstances surrounding the interrogation of each petitioner. Workmen's compensation cases provide another example: reviewing courts have indicated that an award or denial of compensation must be decided on the basis of such facts as the nature of the injury, the circumstances under which the accident occurred and became known, and the health record of the claimant prior to the injury. In both of these areas of adjudication recurring relationships between certain fact configurations and decisional patterns can be identified. A more difficult question is to predict the decisions that other combinations of these facts would justify.

In recent years several studies have attempted to predict decisions by using mathematical and statistical techniques. But a serious problem confronts the scholar in this area: he must identify which facts appellate courts accept as controlling from lower court records and appellate briefs. The problem thus presents two aspects: (1) the acceptance or rejection of facts by appellate courts from lower court records and appellate briefs, and (2) the dependence of the decisions of appellate courts on facts that have been accepted as controlling.

THE ACCEPTANCE OR REJECTION OF FACTS THAT CONTROL JUDICIAL DECISIONS FROM LOWER COURT RECORDS AND APPELLATE BRIEFS

Many legal realists argue that the acceptance or rejection of facts by appellate courts cannot be reduced to regular patterns. If the contrary can be shown, however, the prediction of the acceptance or rejection of facts, and ultimately the prediction of decisions, will become possible. As an initial hypothesis, it can be stated that the acceptance of a fact by an appellate court depends upon identifiable conditions surrounding the presentation of the fact in the briefs and record below. These conditions can be stated as follows: the appellate court will accept the fact *if and only if* it appears at one or more of the stages which the lower court records and

appellate briefs represent, *or* is not denied at one or more of these stages, *or* one or a combination of other facts also is accepted by the appellate court. A specific application of this compound statement may be exemplified by the involuntary confession cases decided by the Supreme Court. The alleged fact that the defendant had not been advised of his right to remain silent is accepted by the Supreme Court *if and only if* (a) the fact appears in a dissenting opinion of the lower appellate court *and* in the respondent's briefs to the Supreme Court *and* is not denied in the allegations of the respondent in the transcript of the record *and* in the opinion of the lower court, *or* (b) it appears in the allegations of the respondent in the transcript of the record *and* in a dissenting opinion of the lower court *and* in the brief of the petitioner to the Supreme Court *and* is not denied in the respondent's brief, *or* (c) it appears in the petitioner's brief to the Supreme Court *and* is not denied in the opinion of the lower court *and* in a dissenting opinion, *and* the alleged fact that the petitioner was not advised of his right to counsel also is accepted by the Supreme Court. [This example, of course, applies to involuntary confession cases decided before the 1966 ruling in *Miranda* v. *Arizona*.]

The complexity of this statement directs attention to the need for a more concise formulation. Such a formulation can be obtained by using the algebraic notation devised by the nineteenth century British mathematician George Boole—Boolean algebra—first applied to the analysis of judicial decisions by Reed C. Lawlor. The notation also can be regarded as a form of symbolic logic. The purpose of the concise formulation is not merely the convenience of relative brevity, but the important objective of reducing the compound statement to a form which permits further analysis.

The compound statement which specifies the conditions under which a fact is accepted by an appellate court—the acceptance rule—can vary considerably for different facts. Initially it is not known which combination of appearances, nonappearances, or denials of a fact, as well as the acceptance of other facts, provides the acceptance rule for the fact. For example, in both the involuntary confession cases and the Connecticut workmen's compensation cases over one billion such combinations are possible for each relevant fact. Although not every possible combination needs to be examined to determine which compound statement can be correctly inferred for each fact from the applicable case, the number of combinations which must be examined makes human inspection prohibitive. However, the systematic search for the applicable compound statement can be performed by a digital computer—in fact, it was in this way that results for the Connecticut workmen's compensation cases and for the involuntary confession cases were obtained.

· · ·

[Another] method employs a system of equations. Each case is represented by an equation, in which an index denoting the acceptance or rejection of a fact by an appellate court is set equal to the combination of appearances, nonappearances, and denials of the fact at the preceding stages. The weights of the fact at the various stages—in the sense of how persuasive its appearance at the respective stages is toward its acceptance by the appellate court—are the *unknowns* in the equations. As the equations are solved, the weights are determined. To be sure, the complex procedures which are required for the solution of the equations again necessitate the use of a computer, especially because there is a separate system of equations for each fact. By using the weights in a case not previously encountered, one can predict for each fact

an acceptance or rejection that would be consistent with the established pattern of past cases. . . .

THE DEPENDENCE OF APPELLATE COURT DECISIONS ON FACTS THAT HAVE BEEN ACCEPTED AS CONTROLLING

The methods which can be used for analyzing the acceptance or rejection of facts by appellate courts also can be employed in examining the dependence of the decisions of these courts on the facts that they have accepted as controlling. The initial approach is essentially the same. Starting from the hypothesis that a decision in favor of the aggrieved party requires the occurrence of specified conditions regarding the facts accepted by the appellate court, the following compound statement can be formulated. The decision is in favor of the aggrieved party *if and only if* facts in one of several specified combinations have been accepted by the appellate court. In its specific applications this compound statement can assume forms amounting to several billions. But, through the use of a computer, it becomes possible to provide a basis for predicting decisions by deriving the correct compound statement from past cases.

The alternative method of a system of equations also has to be considered here. Again, each case is represented by an equation. In this instance, an index which denotes the decision (in favor or against the party seeking redress) is set equal to the combination of facts that have been accepted by the appellate court. The weights of the accepted facts—in the sense of how persuasive they are toward a decision in favor of the aggrieved party—are the *unknowns* in the equations. It may be impossible, for want of sufficient available data, to solve these equations. This problem can be attacked, however, by restating the facts in terms of *factors*, and by employing *factor analysis*. In the involuntary confession cases, for example, some of the facts which have been accepted as controlling by the Supreme Court include a delay in the formal presentation of charges, the incommunicado detention of the defendant, and the failure to advise the defendant of his right to remain silent or his right to counsel. These facts can be restated in terms of a factor described as "a tactic to keep the defendant in isolation and uninformed about the proceeding against him." This would be an example of the intuitive meaning of restating facts in terms of factors. It should be noted, however, that applicable factors actually are found by relying *exclusively* on the mathematical technique which factor analysis employs. It also should be noted that—in addition to solving the problem encountered in the original equations— factor analysis fully explores the mutual dependence or independence of the facts. For this reason, it always is advisable to attempt to restate the facts in terms of factors. For the same reason, it also would be irrelevant to say that factor analysis does not increase the predictability of the decisions.

On the basis of the restatement of the accepted facts in terms of factors, the original equations now can be restated as new equations, with indices denoting the decisions set equal to the various combinations of factors in the cases. The weights of the factors—again in the sense of how persuasive they are toward a decision in favor or against the aggrieved party—are the *unknowns* in the equations. The weights of the factors are found by solving the equations. As new cases arise, the applicable facts can be reduced to the factors which have been identified, and the decisions can be predicted.

Of primary interest to the present discussion is the combination of the methods for analyzing the acceptance of facts and the methods for exploring the dependence of decisions on facts. Such a combination of methods makes it possible to predict first the acceptance or rejection of facts by appellate courts from lower court records and appellate briefs, and then the decisions of the appellate courts on the basis of the accepted facts. . . .

PURPOSES, LIMITATIONS, AND IMPLICATIONS OF THE PROPOSED METHODS

The purposes of the proposed methods must be understood not only in terms of their effective combination for prediction, but also in terms of their potentials for analyzing separately the two aspects of the problem under discussion. With regard to the acceptance and rejection of facts by appellate courts, the methods offer insights into matters about which there has been considerable speculation. Since the emergence of "fact-skepticism" in the framework of legal realism, there has been a widespread belief that courts pay relatively little attention to facts. The application of the proposed methods has refuted such a belief in at least some areas of law.

With regard to the dependence of decisions on facts, the proposed methods provide a precise and exhaustive distinction between combinations of facts that lead to decisions in favor of one party to the dispute and combinations of facts that lead to decisions in favor of the opposing party. Thus, the methods offer information about the content and the application of rules of law which verbal statements of these rules do not provide. The given examples show that courts employ rules which state that the decisions shall be made on the basis of combinations of facts. The verbal statements of these rules specify which facts shall be regarded as relevant but do not specify which combinations of these facts call for a decision in favor of the party seeking redress and which do not. This is the information which the proposed methods can provide.

It already has been seen that prediction is another purpose of the proposed methods. Prediction is possible only if it can be assumed that the patterns of consistency in past cases—with regard to the acceptance of facts as well as with regard to the decisions—will continue in the future. The proposed methods are not designed to predict doctrinal changes and the adoption of new rules of law. Furthermore, prediction does not apply to a case in which a fact *not previously encountered* appears, although a series of such cases provides a basis for the prediction of subsequent decisions. Thus the methods can demonstrate their validity, provided that their limitations are clearly recognized and understood, and that claims never made on their behalf are not carelessly attributed to them.

It should be noted that, in examining past cases by means of the proposed methods, no assumption is made regarding the existence or nonexistence of consistent patterns in the acceptance of facts or in decisions based on facts. Whether or not consistency does exist in a given area of adjudication is determined by the use of the methods. If consistent patterns cannot be identified, it must be concluded that judicial action in the given area of law cannot be understood in terms of the dependence of decisions on facts. If, on the other hand, consistent patterns are found, an important implication of the proposed methods is apparent. Should it be possible to predict only later cases from earlier cases, the underlying pattern of consistency could be explained in terms of stare decisis. But if earlier cases could be predicted from later ones, adherence to precedent would have to be explained in terms of an independent—although convergent—recognition and acceptance of similar standards of justice by different judges at different times. Thus not only the existence of consistent patterns but also the basis for their consistency can be evaluated.

Where patterns of consistency in the acceptance of facts and in corresponding decisions appear to be absent, other explanations of judicial action obviously must be given. Such explanations could be obtained from studies concerned with other aspects of the judicial process, such as the characteristics and changes in the attitudes and values of judges, their social backgrounds, and their individual positions as members of appellate courts. The possibility of effective coordination of these various endeavors remains an open question. Gustav Bergmann called attention to the fact that free-falling bodies, the inclined plane, and the pendulum originally were explained in terms of three separate empirical laws. Later, these three phenomena were regarded as special cases of a set of general laws—the laws of mechanics—and a scientific theory replaced the empirical laws. It is not inconceivable that similar developments will eventually lead to a scientific theory of the judicial process.

Supreme Court Justices as Human Decision Makers: An Individual–Level Analysis of the Search and Seizure Cases

Jeffrey A. Segal

On July 5, 1984, the United States Supreme Court decided in *United States* v. *Leon* that the exclusionary rule of the Fourth Amendment should not be used to bar evidence obtained by officers relying on a warrant ultimately found to be invalid. This good faith exception was clearly one of the major Burger Court decisions on search and seizure. Justice Brennan felt strongly enough to declare that with this decision "the Court's victory over the Fourth Amendment is complete."

Brennan's assessment is probably not (yet) correct. While the Burger Court has limited the scope of both the exclusionary rule and probable cause, it has been unwilling to overturn the exclusionary rule. Further, it has upheld the sanctity of one's home from warrantless invasions and generally refused to sanction searches without probable cause.... Despite the efforts of Justices Rehnquist and Burger, both of whom, for example, would eliminate the

exclusionary rule, the Court can go no further than its center justices are willing to take it.

The purpose of this article is to determine if we can better understand the search and seizure decisions of the justices at the center of the Court through a fact model of their decision making....

The data are all search and seizure cases decided through June 1981 by Justices Stewart, White, Powell and Stevens. The facts are those modeled in my aggregate analysis of the Court's decision making (Segal, 1984), and are presented in Table 1. The parameters are estimated by probit (McKelvey and Zavoina, 1975). Though one might wish to expand such a study to all of the Burger Court justices, two methodological problems intervene when considering the more extreme Brethren. First, there is little variance to explain. For Rehnquist, Blackmun, Brennan and Marshall, simply knowing that a case involves search and seizure would lead to correct predictions of votes between 78% and 90% of the time. Further, such extreme decision making inevitably means that there will be facts that are perfectly correlated with a justice's decisions. For example, Rehnquist, Burger, and Blackmun all voted conservatively in every case in which a warrant had been obtained. Under such circumstances, the probit model becomes inestim-

TABLE 1
Specification of Basic Search and Seizure Model

I.	Place of Search		
	1. House:	1 = yes; 0 = no	
	2. Business:	1 = yes; 0 = no	
	3. Car:	1 = yes; 0 = no	
	4. Person:	1 = yes; 0 = no	

When variables 1–4 all take on the value 0, the search took place in an area over which the accused had no property interest.

II.	Extent of Intrusion		
	5. Search:	1 = full search; 0 = lesser intrusion	
		(e.g., stop and frisk)	
III.	Prior Justification		
	6. Warrant:	1 = yes; 0 = no	
	7. Probable Cause:	percent of lower court judges finding probable cause	
IV.	Arrest		
	8. Incident Lawful:	percent of lower court judges finding search incident to a lawful arrest	
	9. After Lawful:	percent of lower court judges finding search after a lawful arrest	
	10. Unlawful:	percent of lower court judges finding search after an unlawful arrest	
V.	Exceptions:		
	11. Exceptions:	The number of the following facts present in any case	
		(a) hot pursuit:	1 = yes; 0 = no
		(b) search at fixed or functional border:	1 = yes; 0 = no
		(c) search statutorily allowed by Congress:	1 = yes; 0 = no
		(d) evidence not used for criminal trial:	1 = yes; 0 = no
		(e) evidence in plain view:	1 = yes; 0 = no
		(f) permission granted for search by owner or accused:	1 = yes; 0 = no
VI.	Party to Suit		
	12. United States:	1 = yes; 0 = no	

able. Similar problems exist for Brennan and Marshall. While this limits what we might be able to learn, it is the center justices who determine the outcome of the cases, and thus it is they who are most interesting.

JUSTICES AND DECISION MAKING

Although there have been attempts to model Supreme Court justices as utility maximizing, . . . it has been noted by others, such as Simon (1976), that humans are not capable of maximizing. Rather, says Simon, the decision maker is boundedly rational. "The capacity of the human mind for formulating and solving complex problems is very small compared with the size of the problem whose solution is required for objectively rational behavior in the real world—or even for a reasonable approximation of such objective rationality" (1957, p. 198).

Such a decision maker focuses "on a few incoming variables while eliminating entirely any serious calculation of probable outcomes" (Steinbruner, 1974, p. 66). Recognition of the limits of human decision making has been one of the predominant trends in the social cognition literature over the past ten years. . . .

The use of heuristics and cues to cut down on comprehensive decision making may have particular relevance to Supreme Court decisions....

Previous studies present some clues as to how such a simplified process might operate. Tanenhaus, et al. have shown that a small number of "cues" present in briefs influence the Supreme Court's certiorari decisions. Ulmer (1969) suggests that various "signs" derived from lower court records affected Justice Frankfurter's civil liberty decisions. It is suggested herein that the justices monitor a relatively small number of facts from the case, and that the presence or absence of these facts strongly predisposes the justice in his decision on the reasonableness of a search and seizure. These few facts should explain a significant amount of the variation within the decisions of each justice.

Alternatively, one could adopt a rational or comprehensive model of decision making, view each case as idiosyncratic and consider the innumerable factors claimed to affect search and seizure law. Amsterdam (1974) cites over 100 Fourth Amendment rules and talks of his compression of the law. LaFave (1978) divides his treatise into 11 chapters and 85 sections. Each section contains from four to eight subsections. Thus, there are about 500 different factors affecting search and seizure decisions.

It is not claimed that the use of cues and heuristics is proper, only that they are necessary. And while the major alternative theory defines itself as "rational choice," there is nothing irrational about bounded rationality. Simplified decision making strategies "produce vastly more correct or partially correct inferences than erroneous ones, and they do so with great speed and little effort" (Nisbett and Ross, 1980, p. 18). In line with these cognitive assumptions, the decisions of the centrist justices will be examined.

The justices constituting the center of the Court on search and seizure for a majority of the Burger Court were Stevens, Stewart, White, and Powell. This is best seen by ...inspection of the cumulative scaling of the nonunanimous decisions of the 1975–80 natural Court.... [T]he cases fit well-recognized standards of scalability....

Of the 37 cases scaled...one of the four justices entered fifth 36 times. White provided the minimum winning vote 24 times, with Stevens following at five and one-half, Powell at four, and Stewart at three and one-half. Additionally, it can be noted that the four center justices cast a majority of their votes for the winning side in 29 of the 37 cases. In the remaining seven cases their votes were split. As expected, there was not a single case in which the Court voted against a majority of the center.

RESULTS

Justice White

As Justice White is clearly the median justice, the analysis will begin with him.... The 12 variables used do explain a significant amount of the variance in White's decision (p < .01). The estimated R^2, .36, though, is not as high as one would want to be able to support confidently the notion of a completely simplified decision-making process for Supreme Court justices. Nevertheless, these 12 variables do explain enough of the variance to make one skeptical of the notion that each case is unique and requires a highly complex decision-making function.

The parameter estimates tell us the following. Like the results found for the Court as a whole (Segal, 1984), Justice White provides more protection to houses (−.99), businesses (−1.54), cars (−1.44), and one's person (−1.09) than he does to places over which one does not have a property interest. Unlike the results for the Court as a whole though, we do not find the clear ordering of one's house and business receiving more protection than one's car or person.... Overall, White voted to uphold 15 out of 21 car searches, which is virtually the same percentage as the 20 of 29 house searches he upheld. The Court, close to White, upheld 14 of the 21 car searches, but contrary to the Justice, validated only 11 of the 29 house searches.

Measures of the prior justification for the search (i.e., the existence of a warrant and the proportion of lower court judges finding probable cause) were not of much use to Justice White.... White voted to uphold 60% of the searches in which the lower court found probable cause, versus 65% when it did not. He found searches reasonable in 67% of the cases that had warrants, versus 62% when no warrant was obtained. This does not mean that White finds either warrants or probable cause superfluous. He did find valid 78% of the searches in which a valid warrant was obtained. The problem is finding clearly independent indicators of these facts.

. . .

... [I]t can be noted that White pays careful attention to other exceptions to the probable-cause and warrant requirements as well. White voted to uphold searches in 57% of the cases in which no exceptions existed, 75% of the cases in which one exception existed, and in all six of the cases in which two or three exceptions existed. The parameter estimate, .88, is quite strong and is statistically significant at $p < .01$.

Finally, the variable U.S. was added to determine whether White treats searches involving the United States more leniently than cases involving the various states. Although overall White upheld only 52% of state searches and 76% of federal searches, this is not enough to claim favoritism toward the national government; the facts of the case

must first be controlled, and that is precisely what has been done here. We see that the strong bivariate relationship remains after controlling for the nature of the search. The estimate, .58, is large enough to have a substantial effect on White's decision making. A state search having a 52% chance of being upheld by White would have a probability of .74 of being upheld if it were a federal search. The estimate is significant at $p < .05$.

Justice Stewart

The late Justice Stewart was not at one with the Warren Court's criminal justice revolution. He did not join the majority opinion in *Mapp* v. *Ohio* and dissented in *Miranda* v. *Arizona*. Nevertheless, he wrote the opinion of the Court in *Katz* v. *United States*, which revolutionized the Court's thinking about what constitutes an unreasonable search (LaFave, 1978, p. 228), and *Chimel* v. *California*, which drastically curtailed the right to search after but not incident to a lawful arrest. As Burger Court justices replaced Warren Court holdovers, the views of the Court came more closely to resemble his own.

The results of the model estimation for Justice Stewart are... significant at $p < .01$, and 73% of the cases are predicted correctly. On the other hand, the estimated R^2, .34, is no better than that of Justice White. Like White, Stewart gives significantly greater protection to those places in which one has a property interest, without granting more protection to homes (−.73) and places of business (−1.32) than to cars (−1.25). It was Stewart, in fact, who wrote the judgment of the Court in *Coolidge* v. *New Hampshire*, limiting the automobile exception to the warrant requirement to those situations in which there were exigent circumstances. This arguably overruled White's opinion in *Chambers* v. *Maroney*.

The relaxed right to frisk established in *Terry* v. *Ohio* shows that if the Burger Court has not been as conservative as its critics have suggested, neither was the Warren Court as liberal as its critics have charged. Stewart joined the 8–1 decision permitting frisks and other lesser intrusions without either a warrant or probable cause. Stewart has consistently supported such a position, upholding only 55% of full searches but 77% lesser intrusions. An additional limit to the warrant requirement has been the right to search incident to arrest. The broad scope of this power, originally enunciated in *United States* v. *Rabinowitz* (1950), was sharply limited in Stewart's *Chimel* v. *California* opinion to the person of the arrestee and the area within his or her immediate control. The results show Stewart giving tremendous protection to searches incident to lawful arrests (1.38), but absolutely no additional protection to searches after but not incident to such an arrest (.00). This is in stark contrast to Justice White, a dissenter in the *Chimel* case, who found no constitutional differences between the two types of cases.

As noted above, the probable-cause and warrant requirements cannot be easily operationalized in a nontautological manner. Though the existence of a warrant does not make a search more reasonable to Justice Stewart, it should be noted that he did uphold 80% of the cases in which the Supreme Court found the warrant to be valid. A lower court finding of probable cause was similarly unrelated to the reasonableness of the search. Strongly related to the reasonableness of searches were the exceptions to the warrant requirement, such as searches in plain view. The estimate obtained was .51. Finally, as did Justice White, Stewart showed far greater leniency to searches conducted by the United States (.53) than searches committed by local authorities.

Justice Powell

Estimation of the full model was not possible for Justice Powell, as he voted conservatively in every case that the lower court found to be incident to a lawful arrest. To escape the statistical problems that appear when such patterns occur, a slightly revised model was estimated by eliminating the three different arrest variables and utilizing one variable, arrest, which simply measures whether or not the search was preceded by an arrest. . . .

The limited model explained 44% of the estimated variation and predicted 79% of the cases correctly. The model was significant at $p < .05$. As do White and Stewart, Powell gives significantly more protection to places where one has a property interest than places where one does not: the estimates for House, Business, Car and Person are all negative. Powell gives the most protection to houses (-1.83), upholding only half of the searches conducted there. Seventy percent of the business searches were upheld, as were 71% of the searches of one's person. While 80% of the car searches were upheld, controlling for other factors shows Powell to give such intrusions about the same weight as business searches $(-1.48$ and -1.51, respectively).

Great leeway is given when searches are preceded by arrests (1.14). All five searches incident to lawful arrests were upheld, as were five of six searches after lawful arrests. Even when the lower court found the arrests to be illegal, Powell found propriety in the searches, upholding five of six. Arrests are obviously an important cue in his decisions. The other exceptions to the warrant requirement were similarly significant. The estimate, 1.16, is quite large and is significant at $p < .01$. Powell, unlike Stewart and White, does not give greater protection to searches committed by the U.S. than he does to searches committed by states. This is not surprising, as Powell has not accepted the view that incorporated provisions of the Bill of Rights apply to the states in every detail. Although he does not here appear to give the states more leeway than the federal government, he does not follow the trend of the other centrists and the Court as a whole (Segal, 1984) by giving the states less leeway.

Justice Stevens

The estimates for Justice Stevens are made from only 43 cases, and thus must be interpreted with great care. The summary statistics show an estimated R^2 of .68 and 77% of the cases predicted correctly; nevertheless only two of the variables, Person and Incident Lawful Arrest, are significant in the expected direction. Searches of one's home, for instance, though upheld by Stevens in only one of five cases, did not occur frequently enough to result in a significant estimate. On the other hand, Stevens upheld six of seven car searches. Again, the estimate is not significant.

Stevens seems to allow broad leeway to search incident to lawful arrests, having upheld all three of such searches, but heard only one case involving a search after a lawful arrest, so no generalizations can be made. None of the other exceptions to the warrant requirement occurred often enough to draw reliable conclusions. The same holds true for warrants themselves.

.   .   .

CONCLUSIONS

.   .   .

The model presented in this study rejects the notion that overburdened Supreme Court justices can attend to hundreds or thousands of pieces of information in a given case. Rather, the justices inevitably rely on cues to guide their decisions. Arrests make searches more reasonable; violations of one's home make searches less reasonable. A handful of such cues were used to explain the decision making of the center justices in search and seizure. For all four justices, a significant proportion of the variation was explained. While much variation remains unexplained, we certainly can doubt the proposition that each case is idiosyncratic and the decision dependent upon hundreds of different variables. Fifty years ago the legal realists taught us that judges were human in terms of ideological behavior (Rumble, 1968). That humanity should be extended to their cognitive abilities as well.

REFERENCES

Amsterdam, Anthony G. 1974. Perspectives on the Fourth Amendment. *Minnesota Law Review*, 58:349–447.

LaFave, Wayne. 1978. *Search and Seizure*, Vols. 1–3. St. Paul, MN: West

McKelvey, Richard, and William Zavoina. 1975. A Statistical Model for the Analysis of Ordinal Level Dependent Variables. *Journal of Mathematical Sociology*, 4:103–120.

Nisbett, Richard, and Lee Ross. 1980. *Human Inference: Strategies and Shortcomings of Social Judgment*. New Jersey: Prentice-Hall.

Rumble, Wilfred E. 1968. *American Legal Realism*. Ithaca, NY: Cornell University Press.

Segal, Jeffrey A. 1984. Predicting Supreme Court Cases Probabilistically: The Search and Seizure Cases, 1962–1981. *American Political Science Review*, 78:891–900.

Simon, Herbert. 1957. *Models of Man*. New York: John Wiley.

———. 1976. *Administrative Behavior*. Third ed. New York: Free Press.

Steinbruner, John D. 1974. *The Cybernetic Theory of Decision*. Princeton, NJ: Princeton University Press.

Ulmer, S. Sidney. 1969. The Discriminant Function and a Theoretical Context for its Use in Estimating the Votes of Judges. In Joel Grossman and Joseph Tanenhaus, ed., *Frontiers of Judicial Research*. New York: John Wiley.

Constitutional Language

John Brigham

. . .

In explaining decisions on appeal to the Constitution, the Justices of the Supreme Court employ a unique body of concepts derived from experience with the Constitution. The use of these concepts is also evident in legal briefs, oral arguments, and law review commentary, to cite only the public sources. The tradition constitutes a unique language, at least insofar as understanding it requires considerable experience.... As a result of the orientation of past research to either norms or behavior, the manner in which linguistic experience functions in constitutional interpretation has not been adequately demonstrated. The approach developed here resists the choice between one or the other. I have attempted to show that the theory evident in ordinary language philosophy, and to a lesser extent in linguistics, suggests a new approach to the study of judicial action in that it reconsid-

ers some basic premises about symbolic processes.

One source of insight for this study is the idea that native speakers of English do not say things like "red is industrious," "colorless green ideas sleep furiously," or "bring Thursday." A basic premise of this study is that the same kind of constraint operates on the Justices of the Supreme Court when they decide a constitutional issue. That is, they are not likely to hold that "equal protection prohibits unreasonable searches," since this formulation is beyond the sensible options from which they must choose.

Because law operates as an authoritative-formal language for most citizens and as a professional-formal language for lawyers, this study of the judicial decision as "ordinary" language concentrates on the Supreme Court. Although these other spheres, since they employ systems of related symbols, can be better understood by attention to properties of language, the Justices of the Supreme Court are in a unique position. Their interpretation of the Constitution is not governed by the same system of authority that operates on ordinary citizens. Indeed, they use the constitutional tradition much as the ordinary citizen uses language....

On the basis of its grammar and unique practices, constitutional law may be described as a language and not simply as use of English in a particular setting. The grammatical relations that exist in the Constitution delineate a professional language which, at least at the highest appellate level, has the qualities of a "natural" rather than formal language. Practices exist in constitutional law whose sense is determined by the relations delineated in the Constitution and the spheres of activity on which it depends, law and politics.... Grammar, as discussed here, ...addresses conceptual structures unique to the Constitution and develops their significance for judicial decision. The grammar of constitutional language reveals social practices fundamental to the formulation of judicial opinions.

The language of constitutional law is a legal language. The special significance of the political relations in the Constitution shows the difference between the language of the Constitution and that of law generally. However, the difference between the language of the Constitution and legal language in general is less important to this investigation than the difference between ordinary English and this particular legal language. The ways in which the language of constitutional law differs from ordinary English are emphasized [here]....

Constitutional language involves grammatical relations which influence the way in which a particular constitutional question may be understood. Examples of the grammar of constitutional law which distinguish it from other spheres of language are evident in (1) legal practices such as the case or controversy requirement, the appellate process, the issue of retroactivity, and the legal guarantees of the Bill of Rights and (2) practices in the Constitution of a basically political nature such as "judicial review," the "commerce power," "search and seizure," and "privacy."

GRAMMAR AND LANGUAGE

...In examining linguistic theory...the important consideration for how we come to acquire a language is learning not merely the definitions of words but also their role in the lives of those who use them. This important insight of ordinary language philosophy distinguishes the description of language proposed by this school from positivist or empiricist theories. The existence of such grammatical relations in constitutional law is the key to the claim that this body of tradition can be treated as a language. It is possible to know an ordinary English approximation of such constitutional concepts as "interstate commerce" or "equal protection" without knowing the constitutional tradition. Without knowing that tradition, however, it would be impossible to begin to use these concepts in an appeal to the Justices of the Supreme Court. As has been demonstrated with regard to linguistic theory, knowledge of the meaning of a word depends on knowing its use. Although we can get clues to the use of a word from a dictionary, perhaps to fill in gaps in our training, we cannot get the use from a dictionary.... Descriptions of legal vocabulary and of legal forms no more get at what is central to language than ostensive definition of diagrammed sentences tell what a language is.

Similarly, checking a precedent through the reference to the numerous resources available to the lawyer or Justice must be considered the last stage of the process of formulating an opinion. This task, which is often left up to the clerks in the Supreme Court, is a process that follows rather than precedes the conceptualization of a particular issue as falling in a certain tradition of use. Whether in consideration of a petition for *certiorari* or in the formulation of an opinion of the Court, the resort to reference material can only fill in the gaps. It can only refine the final judicial product and is not appropriately considered the basis for the decision. It is in order to support this contention that constitutional language is seen as based in the unique conceptual factors rather than in the vocabulary. If the process were merely one of looking up precedent, then of course, there would be no difference in the decision-making capacities and propensities of a layman and a judge trained in the law. The fact that all Justices of the Supreme Court have been trained in the law has meant that the decisions they render are different from those that would be rendered by lay magistrates.

On the basis of the significance of grammar, the student of judicial decision can begin to examine the important distinction between the rules which delineate conventional procedures and the established linguistic practices which are fundamental to these procedures. There is an important difference between a statement that a claim in law has a poor chance of being ruled on favorably and a statement that a claim makes no sense at all, i.e., that it is unintelligible. The difference exists because some aspects of practices or concepts can be designated by rules, while the role of these practices or concepts in our lives, i.e., the kind of practices which they are, depends on grammar....

The difference between the practices in the Constitution and related concepts in ordinary English is not always obvious. Constitutional practices are designated by English words. They look like English. Yet, many practices which have become institutionalized in constitutional law are very different from related activities not so institutionalized. "Due process" is a constitutional concept that can stand apart from ordinary interpretations of what the words mean. Indeed, in this case, the ordinary words give very little indication of constitutional mean-

ing or significance. The constitutional concept of "due process" is different enough so that the language which is appropriate to describe it includes a significant conceptual overlay that gives it a unique meaning. The meaning here is not simply that which might have been meant by the authors of the Fourteenth Amendment, but includes the wealth of material on the meaning of the concept that has developed in the subsequent 100 years of interpretation and use of the concept. Constitutional "due process" is in this sense a practice apart from the ordinary English words that comprise it.

Constitutional law contains unique practices which suggest the validity of considering it as a language. Many of the practices that distinguish constitutional law from human activity in general derive from the legal sphere.... The fundamental aspects of constitutional law are legal; in addition, we learn a number of other more political practices when we learn the nature of the Constitution.

THE CONSTITUTION AS A LANGUAGE

Theories of language based on verification principles, like the theories of the early Wittgenstein, argue either that propositions can be ill-formed and thus violate logical rules of the language, or that they can be shown to be false by appeal to the world. The theories of language considered here emphasize that an important factor in language is the grammar of that language, i.e., what it makes sense to say. Grammar, as the foundation for the appropriate use of words, determines sense in language. The notion of sense or intelligibility has a bearing on the use of concepts in ways established by the grammar of a language. When use is inappropriate to the grammar of a language, the nature of the inappropriateness may be something other than that such use can be shown to be empirically false or illogical.

In working out the limits of the sensible, the source of an analysis is the conventions by means of which we think and talk. Waismann discusses intelligibility in grammar in terms of the conventions that prevent us from being able to make sense out of the phrase "red is industrious." He argues that grammatical conventions have taught us that color words such as "red" are not the sorts of things that can be "industrious." With some effort, one could develop a context in which meaning might be accorded to this utterance. Such a context would not, however, be what we conventionally understand by the word "red."

Since constitutional law is a language because it has a unique grammar, certain statements do not make sense in the context of constitutional law. This view of constitutional law as language suggests the "legal" constraints on judicial interpretation. Some things come to be understood as appropriate to say when the language of constitutional law is learned. The determination of what is appropriate in this sense need rely neither on logic nor on an appeal to the world. What is appropriate is to a great extent a function of the grammar of constitutional law.

The appellate interpretation of the meaning of "equality," or what can properly be considered to fall within the scope of that concept, demonstrates that the grammar which shows the role of the concept in language is fundamental to raising an intelligible claim as well as to making a judgment. This is true even though such judgments may significantly alter the rules which determine the applicability of the concept in particular cases. . . .

The aspect of language examined here is the language user's ability to make an infinite number of new sentences from the grammatical patterns previously described as fundamental to language use. An association is proposed between a decision as to how to "go on" in a new situation with language and the decision of the Supreme Court as to what it is appropriate to say about a particular constitutional issue. Judicial decision is described as a linguistic act. That is, on the Supreme Court when a Justice confronts a new issue, as whether the provision for a jury is satisfied by a body of six persons, the process of decision is analogous to the ordinary situation when an individual is presented with an opportunity to say something that he or she has never said before. The intent here is to suggest the utility of language analysis for understanding the nature of legal politics by demonstrating the similarities between linguistic interpretation and interpretation of the Constitution by the Supreme Court.

LINGUISTIC PRACTICE AND THE NATURE OF INTERPRETATION

The decision of a Justice, when interpreting a constitutional provision, parallels the situation in ordinary language when the speaker decides how to formulate an appropriate sentence in a novel context. Traditionally, theories of language have implied that rules exist by which language can be judged. Modern linguistic theory explains the use of language, especially the stringing together of words, by reference to the capacity of the speaker to make intelligible statements. Explanation of this process of interpretation has distinguished modern theories from the empiricist theory of language. Attention to this issue makes modern conceptions of ordinary language important for depicting what the Justices go through when they analyze a case.

The language of law is not purely legal; it emerges from ordinary discourse. Ordinary language is essential for discussion of legal concepts. It has an on-going significance in their development. The special quality of legal language lies not in its terms but rather in the development of particular legal practices. Learning the language of constitutional law entails grasping the nature of these practices. In establishing a correlation between language and law, the aspects of judicial decision are demonstrable without dependence on the conception of formal rule-following in terms of precedent. This thesis suggests that what distinguishes judicial interpretation from other kinds of political activity is a particular linguistic capacity.

In "going on in the same way" in novel situations, language presents certain guides for the appropriate decisions, but only as a result of practice, not because of a set of rules. It is more accurate to describe judicial decision on the Supreme Court as consisting of making judgments as a result of practice rather than in accordance with a rule. In ordinary language, the speaker's choice as to how to "go on" must conform to appropriate practice. Following the guidelines of the linguistic model, questions of "going on" in a language can be settled only by reference to convention. No logical necessity or empirical referent is governing.

In his *Philosophical Investigations*, Wittgenstein describes some dimensions of "going on" as he understands them. Knowing the principles that allow one to proceed intelligibly does not mean that some formula has occurred to the speaker. At least, when we are able to use language we cannot usually say that the capacity is one to be explained as the revelation of some formula. No such occurrence can be described as happening behind or side by side with the act of "going on." When we traditionally think of the operation of precedent in the law, it is more like such a formula than like the linguistic or conceptual competence that more accurately describes the basis of a Justice's ability to see a new situation that fits

into the patterns and trends of the law. . . .

According to this view, no single prescriptive rule or formula serves as a guide, but rather the whole body of experience through which we have learned how to use the language. Wittgenstein points out that there is nothing behind our ability to proceed that is more certain than this body of experience. He cautions against thinking of formulating sentences as a mental process because such a conception suggests a calculation on the basis of prescriptive rules. He proposes that we emphasize *when* it is appropriate to go on in a certain way rather than *why*.

When Justice Blackmun used the concept of privacy in the 1973 abortion decision, he explained that the Court has recognized the right and that it was "broad enough to encompass a woman's decision whether or not to terminate her pregnancy." According to the discussion of "going on," we can say of Blackmun's decision that the circumstances which reveal the use of the privacy concept provided him with a conceptual capacity. By those circumstances, he could view state regulation of abortion as at least a potential intrusion on the right. The situation is, of course, different from ordinary speech, given the assistance afforded the Justice by such things as lawyer's briefs and oral argument. Yet, we can still say that the circumstances of prior use (which are employed in the opinion as justifications) rather than a formula or mental picture enable the Justice to decide.

In these investigations, Wittgenstein attacks a view of linguistic activity which suggests that in our imagination we perform an operation which is like fitting something to a definite shape. Such a view perpetuates the idea of an "essence" of meaning, since it suggests that the activity of "going on" is like doing a second thing that is identical with the first. Wittgenstein proposes, on the other hand, that "going on in the same way" must be appropriate to the body of convention that surrounds the activity: "...when he suddenly knew how to go on, when he understood the principle, ...it is *the* circumstances under which he had such an experience that justify him in saying in such a case that he understands, that he knows how to go on." The body of conventions in operation are proposed as a description of going on rather than the traditional reliance on mental processes which is inconsistent with the use theory of meaning....

In the case of privacy in the Constitution, like other instances of judicial decision by Justices of the Supreme Court, past experience is closer to custom than to the idea of a rule. Regular use or even, as in this case, simply some instance of accepted use provides the conceptual possibility for symbolic action. It does not compel. In the case of privacy, Blackmun had the opportunity to use or not to use the concept in the particular case. He did not have the opportunity to use privacy in unintelligible ways or to introduce some new concept picked up in foreign travels. Knowledge of constitutional law affects the initial judgment as to whether a claim is worth hearing. It sets the parameters for the decision and provides a basis for elaborating an opinion. In law, as in ordinary language, events can only be understood if they relate to some body of symbolic communication. Prior knowledge indicates how they are to be interpreted.

In the context of behavioral research, to assert that a limited body of claims is intelligible raises compelling questions about the impact of tradition on judicial action. Legal battles are fought at a margin of clarity which presumes an understanding of constitutional language. With regard to "state action," for instance, Justices have at times "stretched" the concept in order to make a claim, but the requirement does operate as a conceptual constraint and hence as a limit

to action. The concept can "be used as the basis for not extending rights, more easily than it can be used to further those rights." Such constraints operate not because they are rules but because they are conventions supplying meaning through use.

Barry Stroud, a philosopher working in the Wittgensteinian tradition, offers a description of "going on" in language that conveys the effect of grammar. He argues that the sense of appropriate utterances that operates is not "like rails that stretch to infinity and compel us to go on in one and only one way." But neither is it the case that there is no compulsion. The guides, the indication of what it is appropriate to do, are those of experience.... This vivid metaphor is immediately applicable to the Supreme Court. It has the continuity that is evident in judicial decision without losing the creative, human dimension. It calls attention not to moving down the track, but to laying down the tracks. This is the very nature of how constitutional formulations emerge and of the development of new concepts by incorporation into a particular setting....

The capacity to proceed in the linguistic sense just described is evident in the unique judicial responsibility for deciding both what to decide and how to decide. In the decision as to what cases to look at carefully, the Supreme Court sifts through over 4,000 claims. For the most part, these claims have already been filtered by lawyers in accordance with previous indications of judicial interest. Yet, as Justice Douglas has said, the claims "are often fantastic, surpassing credulity." When a Justice finds a claim credible, that decision is a necessary condition for its being accepted. If it does not fit into the framework of constitutional language, that is, if the Justice cannot see the instance being described as a case of even a potentially valid constitutional claim, the claim, of course, has no chance of success.

In the case of *Gideon* v. *Wainwright* (1963), for instance, the Justices found Gideon's claim for representation by a lawyer to be one of potential merit. Although the claim he made, that he was constitutionally guaranteed a lawyer, was not technically true when he made it, it may be said to have made sense to the Justices. On a subsequent conviction (with representation) for the same offense, however, Gideon's claim that his second trial violated the double jeopardy provisions of the Constitution did not make any sense and was not reviewed by the Court. . . .

Knowledge of constitutional language involves an ability which influences the activity of lawyers and judges. Where attitudes and social background are used alone to measure the judicial decision, legal interpretation is placed in conflict with political factors; the result is that one or another factor is taken to characterize the process. When the linguistic model is used, whether or not political considerations have a bearing on the decision does not detract from the fact that judges possess a skill which is fundamental to interpretive behavior.

Legal training imparts the tradition and conceptual foundations on which the legal process operates. Modern linguistic theory provides a way of assessing the impact of this training on the behavior of judges by proposing a less rigid measure of law than the traditional reliance on precedent and *stare decisis*. The uniqueness of legal language sets those who know how to use it, and whose activity provides a forum for such use, apart from other political actors. Many who are not lawyers or judges know something of the legal language, and many with legal training do not practice only as attorneys. Knowing the language of law can be a useful tool in a variety of endeavors because it involves an expertise of social significance.

.   .   .

CONSTITUTIONAL SENSE

As with ordinary language, the analysis of "ill-formed" or nonsensical statements serves to explicate the nature of constitutional intelligibility. The following observations are based on statements using concepts that have been dealt with in American courts in a constitutional setting. There are innumerable matters that do not make sense in constitutional law because they raise issues or rely on concepts that are not available in American constitutional language (e.g., mixed tribunals, divine right, alienation, or surplus value). Their use is a matter related to a larger issue of ideological constraints. However, at this point, in introducing the study of symbols in law, the traditional notion of sense arising from a linguistic context deserves limited treatment. The data to which these statements are subjected are therefore the decisions of the Supreme Court. In addition to showing some of the limits imposed by the constitutional tradition, the analysis shows how different classes of concepts function. Structure, as investigated here, involves abstract covering rights such as equal protection, explicit rights against the powers of government like the limits on search and seizure, the specific provisions of constitutional authority such as the power to regulate commerce, and satellite concepts like "illicit articles" emerging from the conflict over other provisions in the document. Their sense is derived from judicial interpretation. It goes beneath particular holdings, treating the opinions as revealing the structure in constitutional law. Following a convention in linguistics, statements that are ill-formed are marked with an asterisk(*).

The statement

*(1) Equal protection prohibits unreasonable searches

does not make constitutional sense. It is not the sort of claim that would be raised by an accomplished lawyer for consideration by the Supreme Court, although in *in forma pauperis* petitions the Court may be confronted with such claims. The tradition of constitutional interpretation compels the Justices to consider such claims nonsense. Sense in this context depends on an understanding of the Constitution, just as sense in ordinary language depends on the capacity to use language as a form of communication. The ordinary meaning of "equal protection" does not itself preclude (1). Indeed, if it were not for the structure of the Constitution and the existence of certain other rights, the statement might make some sense. (But that is like saying if it were not for the Constitution, the statement would make sense.) It is because other rights, those of search and seizure and due process, are traditionally the appropriate grounds for prohibiting unreasonable searches that the statement is ill-formed.

In another statement

(2)   Unreasonable searches restrict the regulation of interstate commerce

the concepts are brought together in a way that makes sense. Their sense is not dependent here on the state of congressional regulation. Whether Congress has passed regulatory measures that involve the regulation of interstate commerce, or whether the Court has held the Constitution to apply to such statutes, does affect the truth of the claim. The sense of (2) is dependent on the constitutional tradition. Unlike (1), there is no more appropriate concept or structural element in the Constitution that would preclude such an application. The Fourth Amendment right, in its application to the federal government, may at some point cover an exercise of this power in the realm of commerce. There is no reason, in the tradi-

tion of use, why the Fourth Amendment might not be applied in this way. The openness of the categories to this connection depends on the fact that federal power is limited by fundamental constitutional rights.

One of the traditional limits on the use of equal protection is its application to state rather than private action. This is a unique aspect of constitutional language, as anyone who has tried to convey it to students of the Constitution is aware. As a result of this tradition, it would not make sense to claim that

*(3)   My neighbor's refusal to invite me to his party on account of my sex violates my constitutional right to equal protection of the laws.

This is the sort of claim to a basic right that an ordinary citizen might well wish to make. Certainly similar, though less clearly ill-formed, statements like those that might surround instances of racial discrimination in rental housing intuitively suggest a constitutional ground. But an equal protection claim to the Constitution is appropriate only if the state is implicated. Although the reach of state implication has broadened considerably in the last two decades, it is not close to statement (3)—not if the party is an ordinary social gathering in a private home.

On the other hand, although it may be bewildering to those not conversant with constitutional development, the following statement makes sense in constitutional terms:

(4)   The refusal of a private club, which holds a liquor license, to serve me on account of my sex violates my right to equal protection.

The tradition of interpretation bearing on (4) indicates that it makes sense, whether or not the particular holdings at any given time make it an accurate description of the law. The creativity of the Warren Court in this area, as in commerce and search and seizure, widened the sphere of possible interpretation, but the underlying logic predates and indeed supports this development. The Justices performed their wizardry with the tools available and in light of the constraints of the Constitution.

As . . . in the case of privacy, claims that may once have made no sense can become intelligible. Thus,

(5) The right to privacy prohibits states from making all abortions illegal

would have made no sense in 1873, but 100 years later, it was authoritatively announced from the high bench. The law moves in this way when an activity not normally covered can be conceived to be within the bounds of intelligibility with regard to a claim.

This move is evident in the claim made by Clarence Earl Gideon . . . ,

(6) The Supreme Court guarantees me a right to counsel.

It was not only a sensible claim, but it came to be true following the success of Gideon's appeal. The preceding discussion proposes that before it was true, it was reasonable to extrapolate to the claim from established understanding of the concepts. Unlike (1), which is unintelligible, (6) would have been wrong prior to 1963, but it was intelligible and hence the basis of a petition accepted by the Court. An unintelligible claim in this area of law might involve a request from a state to have the Supreme Court appoint counsel for its response to a criminal appeal such as that filed by Gideon. An even more interesting prospect, however, is the range of intelligibility evident in the right to counsel cases. *Betts* v. *Brady* had established that the right to counsel existed where special circum-

stances warranted it. *Gideon* v. *Wainwright* expanded the law to include all felony prosecutions. *Argersinger* v. *Hamlin* developed the right still further to included all prosecutions where there was a threat of imprisonment. The underlying logic is, of course, that ordinary citizens would not be able to successfully handle the legal technicalities of a trial. The system requires that a defendant have trained counsel available to guide him through the legal maze. Not only does the very logic of these cases support the notion that there is a distinct legal sphere that even a wise man cannot penetrate without proper training, but also the evolution of these holdings suggests the nature of the evolution of intelligibility in the law. It is doubtful that the sensibilities evident in 1972 in *Argersinger* would have had grounds for expression in 1942 when *Betts* was decided. It may be further suggested that the notion of fairness and equal protection that underlie the evolution from *Betts* to *Argersinger* would still not be able to support a claim that one has a right to the best lawyer that money can buy—although the provisions of such necessities as expenses for attorney's fees or funds to pay for the subsistence of witnesses are not beyond the vision of the Justices. Here it is perhaps not the structure of the Constitution that stands as a limitation but the underlying ideological limitation of a market economy that still tolerates vast inequities in wealth. The limitations on constitutional sense are not only in the Constitution, but the description of constitutional limitations of this sort is a step toward demonstrating the ideological ones. . . .

While the preceding examples rely on the words of the document, the investigation may be expanded by looking at concepts developed in working with the basic provisions and rights. A class of concepts bearing on constitutional adjudication has been referred to as "satellite concepts." These concepts represent interpretations of the written Constitution in light of the conflicts that have arisen over it. Although the underlying structural relations bear on the development of these concepts, the contribution of this notion in the present context is the identification of a class of concepts which develop out of constitutional conflict. "Moral pestilence" delineates a concept that has evolved as covered by the congressional right to regulate commerce. "Moral pestilence" as a concept facilitated the constitutional justification of the Mann Act.

The satellite categories are interpretive tools which also depend on relations with other concepts for their meaning. Hence, the statement

(7) Congress may not regulate illicit articles unless they are part of interstate commerce

makes sense given the understanding that such articles are within the scope of the commerce power. On the other hand, the statement

*(8) Congress may regulate illicit articles unless they are part of interstate commerce

does not make sense. Since the concept expresses a limited dimension of a power granted to Congress, it has no meaning except in the exercise of that power. In this case, interstate commerce is a realm into which Congress can enter with qualifications, and illicit articles are some of the things that allow such entry. It is not simply false to suggest that illicit articles cannot be regulated when they are part of interstate commerce. Rather, since the concept was introduced as a factor in that sphere, such a

statement makes no sense. Similarly, the following statement

*(9) The extent of congressional involvement with state problems is dependent on its regulation of illicit articles

is ill-formed because it misstates the function of the satellite category which articulates a congressional power in a restricted sphere. Its dependence on interstate commerce is missing here in a more expansive claim than the sense of the Constitution can carry.

Particular concepts can thus be said to have a meaning acquired through use and to depend on the tradition of constitutional interpretation for appropriate application. In examining this tradition, it has been helpful to indicate different ways that concepts relate to a conceptual structure. Whether these ways are the most significant is a matter for further study. They are mentioned here as an outgrowth of the effort to show the existence of structures governing intelligible constitutional discourse. . . .

A model of the judicial decision based on language rather than on rules or attitudes best portrays how students of politics may characterize the place of law in this situation. Rather than as rules, which are most significant for the ordinary citizen or the lower courts, conceptual structures constitute the greatest limitation on judicial action and thus distinguish the legal from the political sphere. Rather than as attitudes, which delineate the political inclinations that constitute choice among possible forms of action, conceptual structures operate as characteristics of the symbolic activity that we know as law. . . .

Sentencing Behavior of Federal Judges: Draft Cases—1972

Beverly Blair Cook

Judicial decision-making is of interest to the political scientist and the lawyer, and of significance to the public, where the judge exercises choice: at the appellate level in making new law and at the trial level in making discretionary decisions. In areas of discretion such as the management of the trial and the selection of the sentence, the trial judge utilizes his own experiences, preferences, and common sense. Where law and precedent provide weak guidelines rather than mandates, the chief factors associated with the judge's choice may be discovered in his personal history and in his political and social environment. This study seeks such explanations for judicial discretionary behavior by examining the choice of sentences for 1,852 draft offenders by 304 federal district judges in 1972. . . .

Judges exercise wide discretion over decisions on penalties. Within the limits prescribed by law, a judge can suspend sentence at one extreme, or give a combination of prison, fine, and supervised probation at the other. . . . In the absence of appellate precedent or supervision, what accounts for the wide variance in sentences? . . .

"Sentencing Behavior of Federal Judges: Draft Cases—1972," Beverly Blair Cook. University of Cincinnati Law Review, Vol. 42, 1973. Reprinted with permission of author and publisher.

THE SENTENCE AS DEPENDENT VARIABLE

"Dependent variable" is the term used for the behavior to be explained: in this study the 1972 set of draft sentences. In order to employ certain statistical tests in accord with their underlying assumption, the dependent variable should be continuous rather than dichotomous. Judicial dispositions (sentences in criminal cases and awards in civil cases) are obviously more compatible with the requirement of such tests than are judicial opinions on constitutional or statutory issues. A particular sentence may be described in terms of the number of months of probation or prison, or the amount of the fine. A set of sentences may be described in terms of percentage of probation or prison terms, or average length of sentence. . . .

The set of draft sentences treated as the dependent variable in this study are those decided in the forty-eight continental states in 1972 by federal trial judges sitting in their own districts. District judges serving as visiting judges heard 95 cases. Since some propositions in the research required the judge to act within his local environment, these cases were excluded from the analysis. During 1972 seven appellate judges on assignment decided draft cases in district

TABLE 1
Disparities of Draft Sentences, 1972

Severity Index	Number of Cases	Percent of Cases	Percent of Judges	Number of Judges
Under 10	326	18%	10%	29
10–19	938	50%	51%	156
20–29	203	11%	20%	61
30–39	164	9%	7%	22
40–49	140	8%	6%	18
50–59	66	3%	3%	10
60–69	1	—	—	1
70–79	0	—	—	1
80–89	0	—	—	0
99	14	1%	2%	6

courts. Their sentences also were eliminated from the set, leaving 1,852 cases.

Data on the cases was supplied by the Administrative Office of the United States Courts. The Administrative Office collects data from the clerk of each district court on criminal case forms and transfers the data to tape for computer analysis. . . .

A severity index of draft sentences ranging from 1 to 99 is the specific dependent variable employed in this study. The index is based on the weighting scale first developed by the Administrative Office in 1964. The weighting of each kind of sentence, whether fine, probation, prison, or other, allows the formation of a single scale. The draft severity index was created by the multiplication of the Administrative Office weights by four and the assignment to the highest statutory sentence for a draft offense, five years in prison, the value of 99. . . . The translation of a sentence into an index can be followed in this example: a draft sentence of three years in prison and a $500 fine with one year of probation upon release involves the addition of the weights of 48 and 3 and 12 to form an index of 63.

The analyses in this study use case indices and judge indices as dependent variables

(i.e., measures of the sentencing events to be explained). Each judge has a severity index which is the average of all his case indices for the year. The range of the case and judge indices is shown in Table 1. The table indicates that ten percent of the judges have routinely issued a nominal sentence which appears to be a rejection of the legislative and bureaucratic draft policy. Six of the trial judges followed a settled policy of five-year prison terms and two judges a pattern of four-year terms, both likely indicators of strong support for the selective service system and its affective penumbra of patriotism and national security consciousness.

A majority of the judges limit their sentences to probation only. Approximately the same percentage of judges and cases are in the index category of 10–19, which gives only lip-service to the draft policy. One-third of the judges employed a range of sentences between the moderate majority and the extremely punitive minority. Evidently these judges were individualizing punishment of the offender according to some pattern. The "correlates" of factors associated with these various sentence choices will be the topic of the next section.

INDEPENDENT VARIABLES: PROPOSED EXPLANATIONS FOR SENTENCING BEHAVIOR

"Independent variable" is the term used for a factor which is believed to vary with the event the social scientist seeks to understand. It can be an explanatory factor for the dependent variable, here, the severity of draft sentences. . . .

Precedent and Public Opinion

.   .   .

Precedent is of little predictive value in an area of broad judicial discretion such as sentencing, where by definition the judge must exercise his own judgment. Such areas of judicial discretion invite investigation with the concepts and indicators of the social sciences. Where appellate courts have defined abuse of discretion in a particular area, their guidelines could serve to improve the utility of the predictive equation by limiting its parameters. For example, one might predict that the range of future draft sentences in the Sixth and Eighth Circuits would not include the maximum five-year prison term.

In the absence of precedent to explain decision-making, a systemic support variable, new to judicial behavior but familiar in studies of voting behavior, fills the explanatory vacuum. Public opinion correlates to a high degree with the changing pattern of draft sentences over time and with the regional variation in draft sentences in a single year. . . . Opinion may explain from 60 to 85 percent of sentencing choices. . . .

Case Attributes

In several statistical studies the attributes of the case have been treated as cues which trigger the response of the judge. Race, class, sex, and nationality are some of the ascrip-tive, and therefore nominal, characteristics of defendants which have been employed as predictors of sentences. The criminal record of the defendant is another factor often proposed as an explanation for apparent sentence disparity. There have been strong differences of opinion, based on data selection and the controls used in analysis, over the validity of studies using such independent variables.

Certain characteristics of draft defendants—age, sex, nationality, and criminal record—are held constant, but race is a distinguishing feature. Of the defendants identified by race in [Walter] Markham's five-year set of offenders, 19 percent were non-white. The black defendants received an average prison sentence 1.38 months longer than the white defendants, although the difference was not statistically significant. However, the difference in the average percentage of non-whites (75.8 percent) and whites (71.6 percent) imprisoned by district could not be explained by chance.[1] Moreover, the variation in imprisonment by race did not disappear even when Markham held constant the probation report, the defendant's criminal record, and the type of counsel.[2] Seventy white offenders, or three percent of those found guilty, received a lighter sentence than statistically expected. Ten black offenders, or three percent of those sent to prison, could have expected milder sentences. Consequently, race cannot be discounted as part of the explanation for sentence severity, but evidently its contribution to sentence variation is limited.

.   .   .

Of the draft defendants sentenced in 1972, 57 percent had pled guilty, 35 percent were convicted by a judge, and 8 percent were convicted by a jury. In light of this distribution it is possible that some of the variance in 1972 sentences is attributable to the judges' patterns of sentencing according to plea and type of trial. . . . [D]efendants who pled guilty and thereby waived their "day in court" on the factual and legal issues received an average severity index sentence almost nine points lower than those who went to trial. Those who pled not guilty and were tried before the court received an average index sentence over 4.5 points lower than defendants who did not waive the jury. The difference of the means and of the distribution of the sentences in each category is statistically significant. . . .

Environment

Social, economic, demographic and political variables of the environment within which the court operates have seldom been used as predictors of criminal case output, although they have been utilized extensively in studies of legislative output. Students of judicial behavior have tended to treat judges as if they worked in a subsystem with impermeable boundaries, isolated from any outside pressures, affected only by their internalized norms and the review power of the appellate judges. Although the interrelatedness of the judicial and political subsystems, with their entrenchment in a social milieu, have often been discussed in a theoretical context, research designs have seldom incorporated such environmental variables. Environmental factors have been treated in an impressionistic way in conventional studies dealing with periods of executive or congressional attack on the Supreme Court and apparent changes in the direction of common law development. Only a few attempts have been made to study the effect of environmental variables on trial courts.

Economic-Social Variables

.   .   .

In the study of the 1972 cases reported here, two economic-social variables are in-

troduced: Poor, operationalized by the percentage of families with less than $5000 per year income in the city where the case was decided; and Crime, operationalized by the 1971 FBI crime index for that city. In every analysis the same relationship appeared: the more poor families in the city, the more severe the sentence; the more crime in the city, the more mild the sentence. The correlations, however, were very low, and the two variables combined contributed only one percent to the explanation of severity.

Evidently, the environmental variables are more useful in a comparison of district performance. . .than individual judicial performance. These variables may belong in a causal chain, their vitality not obvious without a subset analysis. The sentence severity of judges with Republican party affiliation showed a strong correlation with the environmental variables. The explanatory power increased to two percent. Subset analysis revealed that Democratic judges' severity varied only slightly with Crime, and the environmental variables had no explanatory power. Judges serving in metropolitan areas (over 500,000 population) were examined separately and the severity of their sentences varied significantly only in relation to the poverty of the city. It should be noted, however, that their populations included more blacks and more criminals than the cities with a lower Poor factor. The Poor variable added four percent to the explanation of the sentencing severity of metropolitan judges. It is possible that poor draft offenders are treated like ordinary criminals, particularly by Republican judges in metropolitan areas.

Demographic Variables.   The two demographic variables of concern in this study are the size of the population and the size of the black population. Markham discovered that the size of the district population correlated positively and significantly with the percentage of offenders sentenced to prison, but not with the length of the prison term nor the disparity of sentences within the district.[3] With a single severity index, the present study tends to support the opposite conclusion. The severity indices of the judges themselves differed according to the population of the city in which they decided the case, with the judges in the smallest cities giving the most severe sentences.

.   .   .

In this study a variable, Black, was operationalized by the percentage of the black population of the city where the case was decided. Since federal judges, particularly in the more decentralized Southern districts, often sit at different court locations within the district, this indicator measures more precisely the immediate demographic setting of the deliberating magistrate. On a regression analysis of all 1,852 cases, the Black variable did not correlate at all with severity of sentences. The results . . . suggest that the racial variable comes into play only in cases with black defendants and perhaps with particular judges.

.   .   .

Political.   The thesis that judges respond to the political culture is part of our conventional wisdom, but selected features of the political system have not been measured and related to judicial output. . . .

In this 1972 study two political variables are introduced: one, an indicator of political party dominance; and another, an indicator of pressure group strength. The party indicator is based on the party affiliation and percentage of voters for the United States senatorial candidate who received a plurality in the city where the case was decided. The preappointment party affiliation of each judge is compared with that of the winning local candidate to generate four subsets for analysis: Republican judges in congruent and incongruent partisan milieus; and Democratic judges in congruent and incongruent partisan milieus. The percentage of voter support is used as a variable to test the impact of the intensity of local partisanship upon the judge's sentencing.

Table 2 shows that judges vary their sentences to some extent in relation to the political dominance in their environment. About one-third of the Democratic judges sit in a Republican environment and two-thirds of the Republican judges sit in a Democratic environment. The severity of the sentences given by Democratic judges is two points higher in Republican territory. Apparently, the Democratic judge responds to the poll power of the Republican party with more severe sentences. The Republican judges, however, do not temper their severity to suit the Democratic milieu and the correlation between severity and the size of the vote for

TABLE 2
Severity of Draft Sentences by Political Environment, 1972

	Democratic Judges (165)		Republican Judges (128)	
	Democratic Environment	*Republican Environment*	*Republican Environment*	*Democratic Environment*
Percent of Judges	65%	35%	31%	69%
Mean Severity Index	19.6	21.7	19.9	23.4

the opposite party shows that they are not influenced by the strength of the opposition. The judges were not affected by the relative strength of their own parties among the voters.

The second political culture variable, AmLeg, was intended to measure the strength of political pressure groups. The American Legion, a pressure group with an intense commitment to national security was chosen as an indicator for the variable. The supportive attitude of the American Legion toward the selective service system is exemplified by the fact that more than 70 percent of the local draft board members came from the Legion. The indicator was operationalized by the percentage of veterans in the state who belonged to the Legion. A positive correlation between the AmLeg variable and the severity index was expected based on the hypothesis that local judges would adjust their behavior to the preferences of the most relevant organized interest in the policy area of the case.

The correlates showed that the size of American Legion membership in the state did not vary significantly with the severity indices of most judges. There was no correlation for the universe of cases.... Only Democratic judges serving in a Republican environment revealed a significant relationship between severe sentences and state Legion size. On the whole, the judges appeared unaffected by pressure group preferences. The Legion evidently provides policy cues only to judges without other sources of input, e.g., from their political party, court cohort group, service experiences, or local reference groups.

Court Structure

. . .

The present study employed a number of structural variables—three were nominal and two ordinal.[4] . . .

Circuit Organization. The federal judicial system is organized by circuits, which include a number of districts. Some of these circuits are more compact and identifiable with geographical regions than others. Internal relations among the district judges and with their circuit judges are much closer within the circuit boundaries.... The Fifth Circuit, in the South, has the highest severity index and the Sixth Circuit, in the East-Central region, the lowest. The variables which are related to severity differ in each circuit. In the Sixth Circuit, the heavier the judge's caseload, the more severe the sentence; but in the Seventh Circuit a light caseload correlates with severity.

Case Distribution

. . .

The number of draft cases disposed in 1972 ranged from one to 62 per judge. Only one case was handled by 72, or 24 percent of the judges, and two cases each by 50, or 16 percent of the judges. Approximately one hundred active judges had no draft cases. At the other extreme, six judges decided more than forty draft cases in that single year....

The significant difference between the mean severity indices of judges with light and heavy caseloads suggests that the judges for whom a draft case is a unique event during the year are more severe....

For the universe of cases there was a significant correlation between severity and percentage of the draft caseload handled by the judge. The judge who handled the largest proportion or even monopolized the selective service docket was severe....

Judicial Leadership. Within the court organization only a small proportion of judges accept national level responsibilities. Those who do might be expected to identify with the nation-state and accept the role of protector of the political system more fervently than other judges. In their special capacity as judicial leaders they would be likely to sentence draft offenders severely even after the majority of judges had begun to reduce their penalties. In fact, the 56 judicial leaders have an average severity index two points higher than the universe of judges.

Characteristics of the Judge

. . .

Judicial Attributes. The ascribed judicial attribute employed in this research is age. Age is expected to correlate positively with any question regarding the status quo. It is hypothesized that the older judge, with patriotic notions of earlier generations and memories of two great wars, is likely to give more severe sentences. . . .

The older judges as a group have a mean severity index over three points higher than the younger judges. . . .

The "achieved" judicial attributes employed in this study involve prior personal experiences in military service and public office experience in the legal process. . . .

The Service index is based first, on the participation of the judge in World War I or II, Korea or Vietnam, or in the regular service between wars; second, his highest rank; and third, the number of medals he received. Eight of these 304 judges served in World War I and nine served during two wars. One general and a number of Army colonels and Navy captains are represented. A high Service index was expected to correlate with high severity.

The Service index correlations produced an unexpected result. . . . Judges with a high Service index were less severe than the judges who had no service at all by 3.3 index points. The direction of correlation on the high service judges was negative, and on the

no service judges positive. Memberships in veterans organizations varied with severity among the high service judges, but not at a significant level. Membership in such groups had no relation to the sentencing severity of low service judges.

Evidently the judges who served in the armed forces were less reliant upon reference groups for cues as to the proper stance toward the draft issue. The high service judge made up his own mind on the basis of personal experience. Moreover, he had no motivation to prove his devotion to national security by giving severe sentences since he already had earned his credentials. It is possible that his more lenient sentences are compensation for his known association with the military. The same argument seems persuasive when applied to the high severity index of no service judges: are they displaying their own patriotism by requiring obedience and service from others?

Reference Groups. Four kinds of reference group variables—family, civic, "policy specific" and political party—are tested to discern whether they affect sentencing. The family reference group is composed of the sons in the judge's family. They are perceived as agents of communication between the judge and the new generation with its liberal attitudes toward war and draft resistance. Moreover, paternal affection for a draft age son was predicted to carry over to other young men who appeared before the judge as draft offenders. Consequently, the hypothesis was that the judge's acquaintance with a contemporary viewpoint, plus his emotional attachment to his sons, would lead to a lenient sentencing policy.

The son index was constructed by assigning five points for each son, plus five points if the son were of draftable age (18 to 26) between 1962 and 1972. The variable performed exactly opposite to the prediction.

The more sons, and sons of draftable age, the more severe the judge. Perhaps the judge's sons were in service and he was only demanding a similar sacrifice of other young men, but without data this remains pure speculation. . . .

The civic reference group variables were used to separate the judges into the "parochials," the "nationals," and the "altruists." Parochial judges belonged only to local groups, such as fraternal clubs (Lions, Elks, Eagles, Woodmen); social clubs (country, city and yacht); and booster clubs (Chamber of Commerce, Rotary, Kiwanis, Civitan). They had attended state law schools and participated in local partisan and business activities. National judges, in addition to local activities, also participated in national political and legal organizations, took their law degrees outside the state where their district is located, or served in the national government in Washington, D.C. The altruistic judges were either parochial or national but, in addition, belonged to reference groups devoted to charitable, health, or cultural pursuits, such as hospital, museum, or law school boards of trustees.

The hypothesis was that parochial judges would reflect the "law and order" concerns of their local associates, that national judges would reflect a concern with national security, and that altruistic judges would sympathize with personal moral commitments of draft resisters. Therefore, it was expected that the severity indices of the parochial judges would be higher than nationals, and nationals higher than altruists. The [results] . . . show that these predictions were verified. Further, the regression analysis revealed a signficant relationship between the intensity of the judge's participation in altruistic activities and the mildness of his sentences. Active judges, senior judges, metropolitan judges, judicial leaders, and judges with small caseloads all had a significant correlation between a high altruist index and a low severity index. . . .

. . . The party affiliation of political decision makers has been established as a powerful but not sufficient explanation of public choice. Earlier studies have indicated that judges who belonged to the Democratic party tended to be more sympathetic to the underdog and the civil rights claimant. This would suggest that Democratic federal judges act less severely than Republican judges toward draft offenders.

Since party is not an ordinal variable, it was used to dichotomize the cases and judges for subset comparisons. The mean severity index of all cases decided by Democratic judges was only 1.3 points lower than that of Republican judges. The variance in distribution of the indices within each party was significant, however, suggesting that party affiliation does have some bearing on the draft sentence decision.

As individuals, the Democratic judges had a mean severity index 1.2 points lower than Republican judges. . . . At the lower range, 63 percent of the Democratic judges and 58 percent of the Republican judges had indices below 20; and at the higher range, 18 percent of the Democratic judges and 22 percent of the Republican judges had indices of 30 or higher. The leniency of the Democratic judges is evident only at the tails of the curve.

Explanatory Power of the Variables

A number of variables together, environmental, structural, and personal (but not public opinion or case attributes), in a regression analysis explain only five percent of the variation in the universe of 1,852 draft cases. However, the variables were much more useful in understanding the sentence choices of subsets of judges. For instance, a group of variables could explain 14 percent of the variation in cases decided by older judges, 15 percent of Seventh Circuit cases, 24 percent of the judicial leader decisions, 34 percent of senior judges' decisions, 35 percent of small town cases, and 36 percent of Sixth Circuit cases.

If the model is correct in claiming that precedent and public opinion can explain 60 to 85 percent of the sentence choice variance, and if case attributes (type of defendant, trial, etc.) can explain 5 to 10 percent, then the regression analysis using the other three kinds of variables does not need to explain more than 35 percent of the variation at most.

.   .   .

CONCLUSION

The differences between the judges who gave very light sentences (suspended or short probation) and those who gave very harsh sentences (four to five years in prison) may be instructive. Table 3 confirms the earlier discoveries that mild judges are altruists who have served in the military and belong to civil liberties organizations, while stern judges are parochials or nationals and work in a community with a large Legionnaire membership. The Seventh and Tenth circuits have average to harsh judges, while the Second, Fourth, Fifth and Ninth Circuits have average

TABLE 3
Characteristics of Severe and Mild Judges, 1972

	Mild Judges (29)	Severe Judges (8)
"Altruist"	100%	25%
Democrat	62%	50%
Military Service	45%	12.5%
Libertarian	17%	0%
Strong Legion Environment	3%	25%

to mild judges. Both harsh and mild judges are found in the Third, Sixth and Eighth Circuits.

From the entire analysis it is possible to extract models of the severe draft judge and the mild draft judge. These models may be particularly interesting in comparison with local folklore about individual judges. . . .

Model of the Severe Judge

He sits in the South, in the Fifth Circuit, in a poor small town. He is a Republican in a Democratic area, 67 years old with several sons. He has just taken senior status but the regular seat is vacant so he sits alone in his division and handles only one or two draft cases per year. He never served in the armed forces, and his associations are exclusively with his local fraternal, business, and country clubs. He once gave a lecture at a seminar for new judges.

Model of the Mild Judge

He sits in the East, in a metropolitan area with a high crime rate. He is a Democrat in a Democratic area, 60 years old, with no sons in his family. He sits on a multijudge court and handles a large but equal share of the draft caseload. He served in World War II as a major and has a nominal membership in the American Legion. His organizational affiliations are with the ACLU and the symphony association. He has not been tapped for work on any national judicial committees.

Some Useful Generalizations

These stereotypes may not be useful in predicting the future decisions of a particular judge, but they do suggest some clear findings which emerge from the analyses undertaken in this study.

1. Sentencing behavior varies with the strength of the relevant pressure

group in the environment only when the judge lacks other cues to appropriate choices.

2. Judges who handle three or more cases per year on a multijudge court are less severe than judges who handle few cases of that type and serve alone.

3. Older judges and judicial leaders (cross correlation .304) are significantly more severe than younger nonleaders, but senior judges perform much like active judges.

4. Judges whose only reference groups are local are more severe than judges with national associations.

5. Judges give milder sentences in proportion to the number of their altruistic associations.

6. Democratic judges give milder sentences than Republican judges, but party affilitation is not the major factor in severity.

7. Democratic judges give harsher sentences in a Republican environment than in a Democratic environment.

8. Trial judges who belong to "policy specific" groups decide in the direction of the group commitment.

9. Trial judges are not biased by personal allegiances, i.e., by paternal affection or by military service.

. . .

NOTES

1. W. Markham, "Draft Offenders in the Federal Courts: A Search for the Social Correlates of Justice" at 145, 1971 (unpublished Ph. D. thesis in University of Pennsylvania Library).

2. Markham, *supra* at 146, 148, 155.

3. Markham, at 179–180.

4. A nominal scale is one in which the categories function as labels. In an ordinal scale the categories are labeled and ordered. A typical nominal scale would be religion, e.g., Protestant, Catholic or Jewish. An ordinal scale might be illustrated by social class: upper, middle, and lower, or an interval scale by age: 1–99.

CHAPTER 10

Backgrounds, Attitudes, Values, and Decisions

Why do judges decide cases the way they do? Thus far we have examined how particular facts may affect the outcomes of particular cases and how environmental influences affect the way judges and courts function. We have seen that the traditional model of dispute processing is inconsistent with the research findings. Continuing our testing of the traditional model and our examination of alternative perspectives, we now consider the personal attributes, backgrounds, attitudes, and values of judges.

How does a judge's socioeconomic, political, and ethnic-religious background influence judicial decision making, if at all? Assuming that it does and that a judge's background is known, how well does it explain judicial behavior? These questions have puzzled more than one generation of scholars and have stimulated much research effort, some of it producing conflicting results. Judicial biographies typically have traced what appear to be the formative background influences and experiences that have shaped the future judge's personality and philosophy. The intriguing research question has been whether there are regularities in the link between certain background characteristics and judicial decision making or whether each judge is idiosyncratic and to be understood in terms of a unique configuration of backgrounds and life experiences.

If regularities of behavior were linked to certain attributes or background characteristics, then a sociological model of decision making could be established, and it, in turn, would have broad implications for the judicial selection process. If it were conclusively demonstrated that there are distinctive decisional tendencies for judges with certain attributes or background characteristics (for example, age, gender, race, political party affiliation and activism, religion, education, group memberships, types of law practice), then a number of arguments could be made about the sorts of people who should be selected for judgeships. Those with certain demographic and personal attributes could argue that some of their kind are entitled to "representation" on the bench not only to assure justice for these people but also to counter the biases or insensitivities of others already on the bench. Supporters of merit selection of judges could argue that merit selection results in the selection of the best legal minds and that such people can transcend their backgrounds and behave more in line with the traditional model of judicial behavior. Merit plan supporters could also argue that in the long run, selection on the basis of merit, assuming that there are no demographic or attribute biases in selection and that there is an equal distribution of skill and intelligence among those with different attributes, should result in a mix of backgrounds that would emerge on the bench. Party officials could argue that because party affiliation is linked with judicial behavior, it can reasonably and legitimately be considered in the selection process; and so on.

One of the first and most widely cited background-behavior studies was a study of state supreme court judges conducted by Stuart Nagel. Nagel found that political party affiliation was associated with decisional propensities. Democratic judges were more liberal than Republican judges and more often found for the criminal defendant in criminal cases, for the employee or union in labor-management cases, for the economic underdog in a wide variety of economic cases, and for the injured in personal injury cases.[1] In another article he presented findings that suggested that religion was also somewhat related to decisional propensities. Catholic judges tended to be more liberal than Protestants.[2] Other researchers soon undertook similar studies, and a considerable literature developed.[3]

The first of the initially raised questions concerned the influence on decision making of a judge's background. Kenneth Vines pursued this question with reference to the decisional behavior of Southern judges during the era of the civil rights revolution. Vines' study[4] persuasively portrayed the interlocking web of social-political-economic backgrounds that molded those who became segregationist judges as opposed to those who became integrationists on the bench. Giles and Walker, as seen in the reading, conducted a follow-up study at a later point in time and, using somewhat different methods, found that indeed times had changed and that their findings differed from those of the earlier period studied by Vines. These two studies suggest both the promise and the difficulties of backgrounds research. At certain points in time, backgrounds can be shown to be associated with certain behavioral patterns. But at later points in time, those same backgrounds may represent different socialization and cultural experiences and result in different behavioral syndromes. This is clearly shown with the backgrounds of Supreme Court justices in the article by S. Sidney Ulmer.

Party affiliation and particularly appointing president have been shown to be most strongly related to the decision making of lower federal court judges.[5] In the article by Jon Gottschall this is demonstrated by the voting behavior of courts of appeals judges.[6] The article by C. K. Rowland, Donald R. Songer, and Robert A. Carp focuses on criminal justice policy by both federal district and appeals judges and highlights the impact of the Reagan appointees.

In general, caution is needed when assessing the background-behavior studies of aggregates of judges because taken literally, the sociological model of decision making does not make sense. It is inaccurate to assert that someone behaves in a certain way *because* that person is black, female, Catholic, Democrat, old, Harvard educated, in solo law practice, and so forth. Rather what is being argued is that because one has certain attributes means that one will have had certain socializing experiences. These experiences will have stimulated the development of certain attitudes and values and even conceptions of the judicial role. But in reality most of the background or attribute variables tested using aggregates of judges are not necessarily associated with the same or similar experiences; hence background or attribute variables are not easily linked to just one set of attitudes and values.[7] A major exception is party affiliation and appointing president, but these variables are likely reasonably accurate surrogates for attitudes and values. There are statistical associations between other attributes and certain types of behavior; however, the background-behavior model has not been conclusively proven, and for the reasons just suggested it is unlikely that it can be. However, it should be kept in mind that a judge cannot be divorced from his or her life experiences and that detailed knowledge of backgrounds may be crucial for our understanding of the development of attitudes and values and ultimately the judicial behavior of individual judges.

Unlike attribute and background variables, the attitudes and values of judges are not external to the judge and cannot ordinarily be identified by the researcher independent of the judge's decisional behavior. By focusing on attitudes and values we again test the traditional model of judicial decision making. If a significant part of judicial behavior can be shown to be linked with political attitudes and values, we must then consider judges to be political actors and courts to be political institutions. Judicial selection and the evaluation of judicial policy-making must then take into account the reality of the decisional process. The judicial process, although distinctive in many important ways, must be seen as closely linked to the political system.

To understand contemporary judicial behavior research focusing on attitudes and values, one must appreciate its intellectual origins in the political behavioralism and legal realism movements of the 1920s and 1930s. Within the political science discipline, behavioralism provided a radically new perspective on the study of politics and consequently a major new research agenda for the field. Behavioralism shifted the focus of political science from legalistic institutional description and normative prescription to the analysis of empirical reality—what really happens in political life—and the search for underlying regularities or patterns in the behavior of political actors and participants, thus facilitating an understanding of why and how people behave politically. This meant a concern with the development of methods and procedures that would allow systematic analyses and objective interpretation of political phenomena.

Among students of courts and law, a parallel movement arose—legal realism—whose adherents were profoundly skeptical of the legal rules and principles that appellate court judges (especially Supreme Court justices) were offering as the bases for their decision making. Political science professor C. Herman Pritchett linked political behavioralism to legal realism, although he rejected the extremist position of some of the rule skeptics—that law was merely the political preferences of judges.[8] Pritchett appreciated the fact that courts of law are unique institutions and that judges occupy a very special position within them. He took the view that in some cases we can reasonably infer that judges had sufficient discretion (given certain ambiguities in the factual situation, statute, constitutional provision, and precedents) so that disputes could be resolved in markedly different ways. With regard to a collegial court like the U.S. Supreme Court, Pritchett argued that it is the nonunanimously decided cases that should be studied, for here the judges are in open disagreement and there is no doubt that there are alternative paths to dispute resolution. Pritchett theorized that by studying the votes of the justices in nonunanimously decided cases, it is possible to discover whether there are underlying patterns of voting behavior and if so, what those patterns represent. The article by Pritchett is one of the landmark judicial behavior studies.

Pritchett's methodology involved the calculation of agreement scores (the proportion of all nonunanimously decided cases in which each pair of judges voted together) and the determination of voting blocs (of like-voting judges). By examining the opinions as well as the votes of the justices, Pritchett was able to identify liberal and conservative blocs on the Court. Although there have been methodological refinements since Pritchett did his studies, bloc

TABLE 1
Bloc Voting in Nonunanimously Decided Civil Liberties Cases: 1980–1986 Terms of the United States Supreme Court

Term	Bloc	Type
1980	Brennan-Marshall	Liberal
	Burger-White-Blackmun-Rehnquist-Powell-Stewart-Stevens	Conservative
1981	Brennan-Marshall	Liberal
	Stevens-Blackmun	Moderate
	Burger-Rehnquist-Powell-White-O'Connor	Conservative
1982	Brennan-Marshall-Stevens-Blackmun	Liberal
	Burger-Powell-White-Rehnquist-O'Connor	Conservative
1983	Brennan-Marshall-Stevens	Liberal
	Burger-Powell-White-Rehnquist-O'Connor-Blackmun	Conservative
1984	Brennan-Marshall-Stevens	Liberal
	Burger-White-Rehnquist-Powell-O'Connor-Blackmun	Conservative
1985	Brennan-Marshall-Stevens-Blackmun	Liberal
	Burger-Rehnquist-O'Connor-White-Powell	Conservative
1986	Brennan-Marshall-Stevens-Blackmun	Liberal
	Rehnquist-Scalia-White-O'Connor-Powell	Conservative

analysis remains a tool for the identification of voting alignments on collegial courts. Table 1 shows the bloc voting of the last six terms of the Burger Court and the first term of the Rehnquist Court. The blocs are derived from an analysis of voting patterns in all nonunanimously decided civil liberties cases. Table 2 presents the proportion of justices' votes in all civil liberties cases (both nonunanimously and unanimously decided) in favor of the civil liberties claim. The findings in Table 2 are the basis for the classification of the blocs in Table 1.

For a considerable number of years, Pritchett stood virtually alone in political science as a practitioner of systematic empirical analysis of judicial behavior. Eventually in the mid-1950s, as political behavioralism was conquering the other subfields within political science, renewed interest in judicial behavior emerged. A leading figure at that time and through the present was and is Professor Glendon Schubert. Schubert took the initiative in developing the methodological apparatus that today is largely at the foundation of the study of judicial attitudes. One of the earliest and major demonstrations of the new methodology used to map the basic attitudes and values underlying Supreme Court decision making is Schubert's article on the 1960 term of the Supreme Court. Although Schubert has since made some complex and sophisticated refinements in his methods,[9] his essential approach is presented in this article.

One of the principal building blocks of the Schubert methodology that has subsequently been used by many others as well to study collegial court behavior is Guttman (or cumulative) scaling. Devised by social psychologist Louis Guttman, cumulative scaling tests whether a series of questions and responses tap a single dimension underlying those questions. Questions and responses are placed in a certain order according to the direction of the total number of responses and the minimization of "inconsistent" responses. If a pattern of response emerges that meets certain criteria, such as reproducibility and scalability, then the questions and responses scale. It is recognized that with attitudinal questioning there may be

TABLE 2
Proportion of All Votes in Civil Liberties Cases (Nonunanimous and Unanimous Decisions) in Favor of Civil Liberties Claims: 1980–1986 Terms of the United States Supreme Court

Justice	Term						
	1980	1981	1982	1983	1984	1985	1986
				(Percentage of votes)			
Brennan	74	81	76	81	84	78	95
Marshall	78	84	85	79	81	86	95
Stevens	51	53	68	58	63	62	72
Blackmun	40	56	58	40	49	66	70
Stewart	33	—	—	—	—	—	—
White	42	37	33	29	34	32	25
Powell	31	28	28	28	40	33	36
O'Connor	—	29	25	24	34	30	28
Burger	23	15	26	22	29	21	—
Scalia	—	—	—	—	—	—	27
Rehnquist	14	16	15	19	22	14	14
Court	34	40	36	30	45	37	43

an inconsistent (in terms of the scale pattern) response. Inconsistent responses can occur because the respondent has misunderstood the question, or because the question has been incorrectly communicated to that individual, or because the individual is responding to that question on another dimension. Obviously only a limited proportion of inconsistent responses can be tolerated before an array of questions and responses no longer scale, hence the necessity for such criteria as reproducibility and scalability. If a set of questions and responses is found to scale, then certain statements can be made about the questions and the respondents (such as, the questions are linked to an underlying attitudinal dimension; one can "predict" the response of a respondent simply by knowing the respondent's scale position; one can "predict" the response of a respondent who did not respond to a question on the scale).

When scaling is applied to the U.S. Supreme Court, the cases are treated as questions and the votes of the justices are treated as responses. The number of respondents at any one time never exceeds nine. Schubert and others have hypothesized that cases raising various issues of civil liberties have in common an underlying civil liberties attitudinal dimension to which the justices may be responding. A similar hypothesis for issues involving economic liberalism has repeatedly been formulated and used. C (civil liberties) and E (economic liberalism) scales for various terms of the Supreme Court have been found, and the accumulated weight of the evidence strongly suggests that the attitudes and values of the justices are directly linked to their votes.[10]

But the existence of inconsistent or nonscalar responses in these and other scales troubled some scholars. Harold Spaeth and David Peterson, in particular, argued that more refined scales representing more than one or two basic dimensions provide a more accurate description of Supreme Court behavior.[11]

There was clearly a difference of opinion among students of judicial behavior. Leading judicial behavioralists such as Schubert and S. Sidney Ulmer have argued that those engaged in the scientific enterprise look for the most parsimonious explanation of the phenomena under investigation. If much of judicial behavior can be "explained" by a small number of attitudinal dimensions, then that is a better and more satisfying explanation than that provided by a larger number of dimensions. These contradictory positions were resolved in a later work by Spaeth and David Rohde,[11] in which attitude and value theory were applied and a large number of scales were utilized, but most of them were then found to be clustered into one of three groupings. These clusters were considered to represent certain values: Freedom, Equality, and New Dealism (economics). The Freedom cluster is akin to the older civil liberties scale except that it does not include disputes that center around equal protection of the law, racial and sexual discrimination, and poverty law. These issues are related to the Equality value dimension. New Dealism is similar to the old economic liberalism scale. Thus it would seem that although a more thorough understanding of judicial behavior requires knowledge of the numerous attitudes of justices concerning different issues and different types of litigants, as few as three (or perhaps even two) major value clusters can be found that explain much of that behavior.[12]

We have been employing the terms "attitude" and "value" without explicitly defining them. It is reasonable to ask whether these terms are synonymous. (If so, is it not redundant to use both?) In much of the literature they are used interchangeably, although the implication is that the term "value" is more comprehensive, encompassing clusters of "attitudes." Harold Spaeth and David Rohde were concerned with a more precise definition of attitudes and values and they utilized the attitudinal theory of Milton Rokeach.[13] Spaeth and Rohde suggested that basic to an attitude is a "belief," which is "any simple proposition, conscious or unconscious, inferred from what a person says or does, capable of being preceded by the phrase 'I believe that....'"[14] An attitude, then, "is nothing more than a set of interrelated beliefs about at least one object and the situation in which it is encountered."[15] A value is "an interrelated set of attitudes."[16] Spaeth and Rohde argued that a further distinction can be made between attitudes towards objects, or the litigants (AO) and attitudes towards situations, or the legal issues of the cases (AS), and that judicial behavior is considered a "function of the interaction of AO and AS."[17] Their theory of judicial decision making is fleshed out by the construction of numerous attitude scales to determine which attitude scales are highly correlated. These interrelated attitudes are then categorized as values.

One final point. It is appropriate to briefly confront one persisting criticism of the attitudinal studies of judicial behavior: the allegation that behavioralists use attitudes to explain votes but that those attitudes are derived from the very same votes they purport to explain. Thus critics accuse the attitudinalists of circular reasoning and argue that, absent any independent measure of attitudes and values, one cannot offer an attitudinal explanation of voting phenomena. It is of interest to note that in one study David Danelski did employ an independent measure of values[18] based on a content analysis of off-the-bench speeches and that his findings were similar to those of scholars who only examined votes. But even more to the point, it is fair to observe that the continued finding of patterns of voting (by Supreme Court justices, and lower court judges) that can be interpreted as representing attitudes and values puts the overwhelming weight of evidence on the side of the attitudinalists. However, it would be more prudent for behavioralists to claim that judges behave *as if* they held certain attitudes and values. It is impossible to demonstrate conclusively that judges hold particular attitudes and values, for they are not things or events to be observed. But the voting patterns can certainly imply the existence of such attitudes and values, and it is the more modest *as if* qualification that is perhaps the most persuasive response to the critics.

NOTES

1. Stuart S. Nagel, "Political Party Affiliation and Judges' Decisions," *American Political Science Review*, 55 (1961), 843–850.
2. Stuart S. Nagel, "Ethnic Affiliations and Judicial Propensities," *Journal of Politics*, 24 (1962), 92–110.
3. See the citations in Sheldon Goldman, "Voting Behavior on the U.S. Courts of Appeals Revisited," *American Political Science Review*, 69 (1975), 491–506. Also see C. Neal Tate, "Personal Attribute Models of the Voting Behavior of U.S. Supreme Court Justices," *American Political Science Review*, 75 (1981), 355–367.
4. Kenneth N. Vines, "Federal District Judges and Race Relations Cases in the South," *Journal of Politics*, 26 (1964), 338–357.
5. See Robert A. Carp and C.K. Rowland, *Policymaking and Politics in the Federal District Courts* (Knoxville: The University of Tennessee Press, 1983).
6. Also see Sue Davis, "President Carter's Selection Reforms and Judicial Policy making: A Voting Analysis of the United States Courts of Appeals," *American Politics Quarterly*. 14 (1986), 328–344 and Thomas Hensley and Joyce Baugh, "Impact of the 1978 Omnibus Judgeships Act," in Stuart Nagel, ed., *Research in Law and Policy Studies* (Greenwich, Conn.: JAI Press, 1987), p. 112ff.
7. Being a member of a racial minority, however, may be, in some ways, an exception to this statement. See Susan Welch, Michael Combs, and John Gruhl, "Do Black Judges Make a Difference?" *American Journal of Political Science*, 32 (1988), 126–136.
8. Robert C. Welsh, "C. Herman Pritchett and Public Law: Toward an Understanding of the Political Role of the Supreme Court," paper presented at the annual meeting of the American Political Science Association, 1976, pp. 11–27.
9. See Glendon Schubert, *The Judicial Mind* (Evanston, Ill.: Northwestern University Press, 1965) and *The Judicial Mind Revisited* (New York: Oxford University Press, 1974).
10. Note that there is some evidence that even unanimously decided cases by the Supreme Court are linked with attitudes and values particularly when the unanimous decision differs from that of a lower court. See, Saul Brenner and Theodore S. Arrington, "Unanimous Decision Making on the U.S. Supreme Court: Case Stimuli and Judicial Attitudes," *Political Behavior*, 9 (1987), 75–86. There is also some evidence that unanimously decided federal appeals court decisions that reverse district courts are linked to attitudes and values. See, for example, Sheldon Goldman, "Voting Behavior on the United States Courts of Appeals, 1961–1964," *American Political Science Review*, 60 (1966), 374–384; Sheldon Goldman, "Backgrounds, Attitudes and the Voting Behavior of Judges," *Journal of Politics*, 31 (1969), 214–223; Burton M. Atkins and Justin J. Green, "Consensus on the United States Courts of Appeals: Illusion or Reality?" *American Journal of Political Science*, 20 (1976), 735–748; Donald R. Songer, "Consensual and

Nonconsensual Decisions in Unanimous Opinions of the United States Courts of Appeals," *American Journal of Political Science*, 26 (1982), 225–239.

11. Harold J. Spaeth and David J. Peterson, "The Analysis and Interpretation of Dimensionality: The Case of Civil Liberties Decision Making," *Midwest Journal of Political Science*, 15 (1971), 415–441.

12. David W. Rohde and Harold J. Spaeth, *Supreme Court Decision Making* (San Francisco: Freeman, 1976).

13. Note that with respect to New Dealism or economic liberalism, there is some evidence that this dimension has more recently undergone restructuring so that federalism rather than economic liberalism or conservatism seems to best explain voting behavior in the economic cases decided by the Supreme Court. See Craig R. Ducat and Robert L. Dudley, "Dimensions Underlying Economic Policymaking in the Early and Later Burger Courts," *Journal of Politics*, 49 (1987), 521–539.

14. Milton Rokeach, *Beliefs, Attitudes and Values* (San Francisco: Jossey-Bass, 1968).

15. Rohde and Spaeth, *op. cit.*, p. 76.

16. *Ibid.*

17. *Ibid.*, p. 77.

18. *Ibid.*

19. David J. Danelski, "Values as Variables in Judicial Decision-Making: Notes Toward a Theory," *Vanderbilt Law Review*, 19 (1966), 721–740.

Judicial Policy-Making and Southern School Segregation

Micheal W. Giles
Thomas G. Walker

...In this study we will examine the policy-making behavior of Southern federal judges in school segregation controversies in 1970. The desegregation of public schools provides an excellent subject for study because this category includes the most frequently heard and publicly sensitive of the race relations disputes. In 1954, Southern school systems were totally segregated by law, but by 1970 some level of desegregation was evident in every school system in the region.

As the judiciary learned from painful experience the school segregation question was not one which could often be resolved by a single hearing or judicial decree. In most instances once a school district's desegregation efforts were challenged in court as being inadequate it marked only the beginning of long and continuous litigation lasting in some districts for more than a decade. In such circumstances the district judge having jurisdiction over the case maintained constant surveillance over the district to insure adequate compliance with constitutional standards.

The basic unit of analysis in the present

"Judicial Policy-Making and Southern Social Segregation," Micheal W. Giles and Thomas G. Walker. Reprinted by permission from the *Journal of Politics*, Vol. 37 (1975), 917–936. Most footnotes have been omitted.

study was the combination of a school district and its supervising judge. In order to gather the necessary data to conduct the designed research, we began with the approximately 400 Southern school districts listed by the U.S. Department of Health, Education and Welfare as being in compliance with court ordered desegregation in 1970.[1] Officials in each of these school districts were contacted and asked to supply information regarding the legal status of desegregation disputes in their districts in 1970. A total of 288 school districts responded and of these 151 provided complete information including verification that they were operating under active court supervision in 1970 and the name of the district judge involved.

The basic unit of analysis, therefore, became the 151 school district/supervising federal judge combinations. Of the 95 United States district judges serving the South in 1970, 42 (44 percent) were supervising at least one school district in the sample.

DEPENDENT VARIABLE

To measure the level of enforcement of desegregation an index of school segregation was computed for each of the 151 school districts. This index was adopted from Taeuber's index of residential segregation.[2] The index measures the amount of departure of each school in a school district from the racial balance for the entire district. The index varies from zero, signifying that each school in the district mirrors the racial balance of the district as a whole, to 1.00, indicating that a school district is totally segregated with no racial heterogeneity in any of its schools. The value that the index attains between these extremes may be interpreted as the percentage of Black and/or White students who must be transferred in order to obtain district wide racial balance.[3] The information necessary to compute the index for each of the 151 districts was drawn from racial/ethnic surveys of the public schools conducted in 1970 by the U.S. Department of Health, Education and Welfare.

The dependent variable, then, represents the degree of segregation remaining in the sampled Southern school districts in 1970. Because each of these districts was operating under court issued desegregation orders, the dependent variable also represents the amount of deviation from perfect racial balance which the supervising judge has allowed. This can be interpreted as the district judge's policy decision in implementing the *Brown* mandate at the local level. Operationalized in this manner, judicial policy-making is studied not in terms of the words the judge uses in his opinions but on the basis of the actual level of desegregation he enforces on the litigated school district.

The dependent variable improves upon previous research in two ways. First, it provides an exact measurement of desegregation levels within the litigated school districts. This procedure is superior to a simple "pro/con" measurement of a judge's decisions as employed in several previous studies. Second, the dependent variable is restricted to a single type of desegregation controversy, i.e., public schools. This allows a more accurate analysis than occurs when all race relations cases are grouped together (e.g., public accommodations, employment, juries, voting rights, etc.). These improvements, however, do not absolutely insure comparability across judges and judicial districts. Obviously there may be systematic differences in the conditions within the schools, as well as variation in local resistance to desegregation efforts; and these are factors which necessarily will be taken into account by the supervising judge. In order to compensate for this variation, the impact of school district and environmental variables will be included in the analysis presented below.

For the 151 sampled school districts the mean index of segregation was .3227, with a standard deviation of .2145. Individual school district segregation levels ranged from a low index score of .0111 to a high of .8640.

INDEPENDENT VARIABLES

In order to explain the desegregation policies imposed by district judges in the sampled school districts we tested the impact of twelve independent variables which have been suggested as possible determinants of judicial behavior in this area of litigation. These independent variables can be classified into four categories: social background variables, environmental variables, community linkage variables and school district variables.

Social Background Variables. . . . [S]ocial background experiences which indicate a judge's degree of association with the traditional Southern culture may be related to how vigorously he enforces desegregation policy. In order to test this proposition we selected six judicial social background variables for analysis: birthplace, location of higher education, religious affiliation, political party identification, local political office held, and state political office held.... Judges who were expected to be less favorable toward massive desegregation were those who were born and educated in the South, were closely tied to (frequently racist) state and local politics, were aligned with the Democratic Party, and held membership in a fundamentalist Protestant faith. Judges without such ties to the traditional Southern culture were hypothesized to be more sympathetic to the desegregation policy established in *Brown*. Relatively complete social background information was collected from standard biographical sources for all of the 42 judges in the sample.

For purposes of analysis birthplace was coded "0" for judges born outside the South and "1" for those born within the region.[4] Judges receiving neither college nor law school training in the South were given a "0" on the education variable, while those attending *either* college or law school in the Southern region received a "1", and those who attended *both* a Southern college and law school were coded "2". Fundamentalist Protestant religion, Democratic Party affiliation, local and state political offices held were similarly scored with the judge receiving a "1" if the variable was present and a "0" if it was not.

Environmental Variables. In order to consider the impact of community opinion on desegregation policy, some measure needed to be devised to tap the local cultural ethos within a judge's jurisdiction. Given the importance in the literature placed on this variable, a study of Southern desegregation

would be incomplete without including it. For this reason we examined the impact of two environmental variables. The first of these was the proportion of Blacks among the general population in the judge's district or division.[5] The literature has consistently indicated that the percentage Black within a population is related to the racial climate. The presumed linkage between percent Black and resistance to desegregation is through the social, economic or political threat perceived by Whites who reside in greater concentrations of Blacks. The greater the percent Black, the greater the perceived threat and the greater the resistance to school desegregation.... The second environmental variable was the percentage of total 1968 presidential election votes within the judicial district or division which were cast for George Wallace. The degree of support for the Wallace candidacy would appear to give a good indication of public attitudes toward desegregation. As Wallace support increases so too should a lack of community sympathy for court imposed desegregation.

Community Linkage Variables. If we assume a generally negative community climate toward court ordered integration in the South, it does not necessarily follow that all district judges will be similarly affected by this public sentiment. Some judges tend to be more vulnerable to public opinion than others. While there may be several plausible reasons for the differential impact of local sentiment, a particularly important one may be the strength of the judge's linkage to the community. For purposes of analysis we isolated two possible indicators of a judge's relationship with the community. First, a judge's linkage to local attitudes may be reflected in the number of associational memberships he holds within the community. Based upon information provided in standard biographical sources, each judge was given an organizational score equal to the number of civic and fraternal groups in which he listed membership (i.e., Elks, Lions, Chamber of Commerce, country clubs, etc.). There was a wide range of scores on this variable with several judges listing no organizational memberships and three listing ten or more. As the number of associational ties increases we would expect the district judge to pay more attention to community pressure. The second community linkage variable involved the location of the judge's court vis-à-vis the school district being desegregated. A judge's regular jurisdiction, be it an entire district or a division, generally encompasses several cities and counties and, therefore, several school districts. A judge, however, will usually hold his court in a single location within the judicial district, although he may occasionally hear cases throughout his jurisdiction. Judges are likely to live and develop associations in the area immediately surrounding the established locations of their courts. Therefore, we might expect that a judge would be more reluctant to impose activist desegregation policies on school districts which envelop the judge's court than if the schools are located in an outlying area. The pressure of the local community would appear more immediate and pertinent to the judge if it originated from his "home" area than if it came from a more remote portion of his jurisdiction. In order to test this variable, each school district/judge combination was coded "0" if the judge's court was not held within the litigated school district, and "1" if the locus of the court fell within the school district.

School   District   Variables. ....Two school system variables were used in the present study. The first was the percentage of students in the school district who were Black.

The influence of this variable theoretically is similar to that of percent Black among the general population. As the concentration of Blacks increases in the schools so, too, may White fear of the consequences of integration....

The second school district variable examined was the size of the educational system (measured in terms of total district enrollment).... School district size is primarily a technical variable. The logistics of desegregation in a small district are simply less complex than in a large one. For this reason we would expect judges to tolerate somewhat higher levels of segregation in larger districts than in smaller ones.

FINDINGS

In order to evaluate the explanatory power of our independent variables, we first tested the association of each with the levels of segregation which existed in the 151 school systems and then analyzed the combined impact of these variables.

Zero-Order Relationships

For the most part, our analysis of social background characteristics contributed little to an increased understanding of judicially imposed desegregation policy. The expectation that those judges most closely tied to the South would allow the highest levels of school segregation received little support. The relationships between two of the social background variables (birthplace and party identification) and level of school segregation are in the predicted direction, but fail to reach statistical significance. The level of segregation in school districts under the surveillance of judges born outside the South is only slightly lower than that allowed in districts supervised by judges of Southern origin. The utility of the birthplace variable, however, is severely restricted by its lack of variation. Only four of the 42 judges were born outside the South. Similarly, the correlation between party identification and school segregation is in the expected direction with Democrats approving higher levels of segregation than non-Democrats, but the relationship is quite weak. The analysis of three social background variables yielded unanticipated results. Although not statistically significant, holding a state or local political office and membership in a low status Protestant faith are negatively correlated with segregation. What makes this result particularly important is that Vines previously found the political office and religious affiliation variables to have a significant *positive* relationship with segregationist decisions.

Among the background variables only the location of a judge's education is related to school segregation in the predicted direction and at a statistically significant level. The mean level of segregation allowed by the policies of judges who received non-South college *and* law school education is .233; for judges attending non-Southern schools for *either* college *or* law school the segregation level rises to .304; and the segregation index increases to .345 for judges obtaining *all* of their advanced education from institutions within the region. From these data we may conclude that the years spent by judges in non-Southern educational institutions expose them to national norms of race relations and mollify social attitudes acquired during the course of a Southern upbringing. This, of course, does not mean that Southern schools indoctrinate their students with racist attitudes; rather it indicates that Southern judges who attend only schools within the region receive less exposure to non-Southern views toward race.

The environmental variables fare little better than the social background characteristics in predicting desegregation policies. Black concentration within the judicial district or division is positively associated with segregation levels, but the relationship may easily be attributable to chance. The community's support for the 1968 Wallace candidacy, surprisingly, is negatively associated with the amount of school segregation tolerated by federal judges, albeit the association fails to reach conventional levels of statistical significance.

The lack of predictive ability provided by the environmental variables does not necessarily preclude the possibility that the analysis of community linkage may yield productive results. The first community linkage variable analyzed, the number of local organizational memberships held by the supervising judge, exhibited no relationship whatever to the level of segregation permitted. The court location variable, however, provided altogether different results. As hypothesized, a judge's policy will allow significantly higher levels of segregation if the court is located within the school district under supervision than it will if the school system is geographically divorced from the location of the court. This demonstrates that federal judges tend to be more vigilant in enforcing national desegregation standards in remote areas than when similar issues arise within the judge's immediate work/residence locale. This finding might lead one to speculate that while a judge may not generally be affected by hostile community pressures, such factors are relevant when a judge must desegregate his own community. This, however, is not the case. When we examined only those school district/judge combinations in which the court was located within the school system, the percent Black, Wallace vote and organization membership variables remained non-significant.

There are three possible explanations for

TABLE 1
Zero-Order Correlations (r) of Social Background, Environmental, Community Linkage, and School District Variables to Segregation in 1970

Social Background Variables	
Birthplace	.022
Education	.160[a]
Religion	−.028
Political Party	.086
Local Political Office	−.026
State Political Office	−.032
Environmental Variables	
Percent Black	.095
Percent Wallace Vote	−.096
Community Linkage Variables	
Organizational Memberships	−.018
Court Location	.448[b]
School District Variables	
Percent Black Enrollment	.125
School District Size (in hundreds)	.537[b]

[a] $p < .05$
[b] $p < .01$

the significance of the court location variable. First, the court location variable may link the judge to environmental forces not included in the present study. Second, a judge's personal attitudes against massive social change may be greatly activated when he is desegregating his own community, whereas he is able to maintain greater detachment in litigation involving communities in which he has little personal stake. Finally, when faced with desegregating his own community a judge may be more concerned with public reaction than when dealing with an outlying area. Consequently, he may perceive a hostile environment— which may or may not exist.

School district variables provided additional insight into the desegregation policy process. While the percentage of Black enrollment in the school district was positively associated with segregation, the relationship failed to attain statistically meaningful levels. However, the size of the school

district was substantially associated with the level of desegregation enforced by the supervising judge. As the size of the school district increases so too does the existing level of racial segregation within that education system.

The Combined Model

While the zero-order relationships tell us a great deal about possible determinants of court ordered desegregation policy, they do not provide a complete account of the explanatory power of the variables under analysis. First, zero-order relationships do not demonstrate the combined impact of the independent variables on Southern school segregation. And second, zero-order relationships fail to give adequate warning of the possible effects of inter-correlation among the independent variables. For example, two independent variables used in the present analysis, court location and school district

TABLE 2
Partial Regression Coefficients and Standardized Betas for Selected Variables with Segregation in 1970

	b	Standardized Beta	F
School district size (in hundreds)	.00048	.42000	26.861[b]
Percent Black enrollment	.00251	.25914	14.923[b]
Court location	.13949	.23861	8.936[b]
Education	.04946	.15490	5.273[a]
(constant)	.05518		

[a] $p < .05$ R = .624 R^2 = .389
[b] $p < .01$

size, are significantly correlated ($r = .575$). This should not be surprising because of the fact that most district courts are located in urban centers with large school systems. Therefore, the previously discussed relationship between court location and school segregation levels may simply be an artifact of the size of the school districts in which the courts are located. In order to deal with the question of spuriousness and assess the combined explanatory power of the independent variables, the data were examined using multiple regression. The results are presented in Table 2.

With one exception the results of this analysis are consistent with the zero-order correlations presented in Table 1. Percent Black enrollment is not statistically significant in Table 1 but does make a significant contribution to the multiple regression. This inconsistency arises from the fact that Black enrollment and school district size are negatively correlated and, therefore, the size variable suppresses the zero-order correlation between Black enrollment and segregation. Apart from Black enrollment, none of the independent variables which had nonsignificant zero-order correlations with segregation make a significant contribution to the regression equation.

The combined efforts of school district size, Black enrollment, court location, and judicial education explain 39 percent of the variance in Southern school segregation. An examination of the standardized betas shows school district size to have the largest independent effect of any of these four variables. But even with the effects of size accounted for, court location remains significantly related to segregation levels. Indeed, court location, a previously unexplored variable, appears to have independent effect comparable to percent Black enrollment, a variable that has received considerable attention. Southern education, while making a significant contribution to the regression equation, is the least helpful of the four independent variables in explaining the desegregation policies of federal judges.

Although explained variance is the most common means for interpreting regression, the "dummy" variable structure of the court location variable permits another interpretation. The regression coefficient for court location is the difference between the mean segregation index scores for the dichotomized observations on this variable, adjusted for the effects of school district size, Black enrollment, and judicial education. Thus, when the school district encompasses the location of the district court, the level of segregation averages 14 index points higher than when the court is not held within the school district boundaries. This means that in these school districts an average of 14 percent more of the Black and/or White students would need to be transferred to achieve racial balance than in those school districts geographically separated from the supervising judge.[6] Similarly, the adjusted average difference between judges who received college and law school training in the South and those who received both outside the region is ten index points.[7] These are not trivial differences from either a practical or statistical standpoint.

CONCLUSION

...A number of conclusions may be drawn from the data analyzed in the present study, especially when considered in light of previous research. First, the influence of judicial social background characteristics, which were found to be significantly related to district court race relations decisions by Vines, was minimal on the desegregation policies examined here. This may well be due to the fact that by 1970 a new generation of federal judges was staffing the Southern courts. Of the judges in our sample, a full two-thirds took office after the period studied by Vines.... Apart from the education variable, none of the social background factors were found to be significantly related to school desegregation levels.

Second, the environmental factors examined in the present study demonstrated no substantial relationship with school district segregation. This again is in conflict with studies conducted during the years immediately following *Brown* which generally linked the district's racial climate and public attitudes to race relations decisions of local federal judges.

Third, the community linkage variables yielded mixed results. The number of organizational ties which the judge had with his community showed no relationship to the degree of school desegregation imposed. Once again much of the literature on Southern school integration efforts would predict otherwise. The linkage variable which does have a demonstrated impact is court location. Judges tend to allow substantially more segregation in their own communities than when implementing desegregation policy in other areas. What makes this variable particularly intriguing is that its influence occurs independent of environmental factors or the number of community associational memberships held by the judge. The differential application of law indeed appears to be worthy of more extensive analysis than we are able to provide here.

Finally, the school district variables yielded the greatest amount of explained variance. Both the Black concentration within the schools and the size of the school district were significantly related to the level of segregation allowed by district court orders. The Black enrollment variable may suggest the continuing impact of public resistance to desegregation. On the other hand, the combined importance of Black enrollment and school district size may well signify a substantial change from the original round of Southern desegregation efforts. Emphasis appears to have shifted from intense battles over the principle of integration to a judicial analysis of conditions within the schools. The prominence of these variables indicates that desegregation may be in the process of becoming a more technical procedure. The primary question (both legally and behaviorally) may now focus on how much desegregation can be practically ordered by the judge given extant school district characteristics, rather than whether integration should occur at all. This interpretation is consistent with the tone of Supreme Court desegregation precedents handed down in the late 1960s and early 1970s. The evolution of the desegregation process may be following the same pattern as exhibited in the reapportionment cases—that is, an intensely political question gradually eroding into technical applications of Supreme Court established national legal policy. The history of desegregation, however, has been a much more lengthy and painful one.

NOTES

1. To receive federal education funds H.E.W. requires under Title VI of the Civil Rights Act of 1964 that a school district either comply with H.E.W. desegregation guidelines or have a desegregation plan accepted by a U.S. district court. In 1970, approximately 400 Southern school districts indicated their compliance with Title VI by means of court ordered desegregation. In some districts the order to desegregate was issued in 1969 or before. Thus, many of the 400 districts listed would not be under active supervision by a federal district judge in 1970.

2. Karl E. Taeuber and Alma F. Taeuber, *Negroes in Cities* (Chicago: Aldine, 1965), 195–245....

3. For example, if the index value for a district was .60 this would indicate that either 60 percent of the Black students or 60 percent of the White students or some combination thereof would have to change schools in order to achieve racial balance.

4. In using dichotomized or ordinal variables in correlation and regression analysis we are following the lead of Ulmer, Tanenhaus, and others....

5. The basic unit of the federal court system is the judicial district which is comprised of one or more counties. In some instances a judicial district will be subdivided into divisions. Where a judge serves a district the environmental variable data are aggregated across all counties constituting the district. Similarly, if a judge serves a division of a district, the environmental variable data are aggregated across the counties comprising the division.

6. The unadjusted mean segregation index for those school districts having the district court located within their boundaries is .543; whereas, those school districts separated from the court retaining jurisdiction have an unadjusted mean of .281. Clearly a good deal of this raw difference is attributable to size differences between the two groups of school districts.

7. This figure is derived by multiplying the regression coefficient for education (.04946) by the "2" code for those judges receiving all of their advanced education in the South. The education variable most properly should be broken down into two "dummy" variables—one measuring the difference between its "0" and "1" categories and one to measure the difference between its "1" and "2" categories. The present procedure is simpler, but does not give misleading results. The difference between the unadjusted means of categories "0" and "2" is .112. Since education has low correlations with school district size, Black enrollment, and court location, it is not surprising that the adjusted differences differ little from the unadjusted.

Are Social Background Models Time-Bound?

S. Sidney Ulmer

...The fundamental proposition underlying the social background models employed in the judicial area is that past social experience, broadly defined, significantly influences the decisions that judges will make when confronted with socio-legal conflicts in their courts. Although tests of this proposition with federal and state judges through the years have produced mixed results, a number of studies have reported interesting findings.... The most ambitious of these studies (Tate, 1981) has reported recently that from 70% to 90% of variance in the voting of Supreme Court justices in a 30-year period was accounted for by seven variables: political party identification, the appointing president, prestige of prelaw education, appointment from elective office, the region of appointment, extensiveness of judicial experience, and type of prosecutorial experience. Yet, as impressive as these studies may be, skeptics have not been lacking.... Some critics have reported negative results with social background models. Others have articulated theoretical weaknesses in the model. None, however, have explored what I consider to be a major shortcoming in past applications: the failure to control for the possibility that such models are time-bound.

In a good play, one act is as good as any other. Similarly, other things being equal, if the past experiences of judges explain their decisional behavior, these explanations should hold in any and all segments of the time span examined. The relationship between social backgrounds and the decisions of judges should not depend on the particular composition of courts, nor on any other variables for which time is a surrogate. If that is not the case, what has been offered as theoretical results may be merely descriptive of particular courts at particular points in time. In such an event, the ability of social background theory to account for judicial behavior would be undermined. A proper assessment of such models, therefore, requires attention to time as a possibly confounding factor. In the remainder of this paper, the question posed in the title is explored by (1) constructing a social background model that explains a significant percentage of the variation in justice voting, (2) examining the model to see if it is time-bound, and (3) assessing the implications of the results.

"Are Social Background Models Time-Bound?" S. Sidney Ulmer. American Political Science Review, Vol. 80, 1986. Reprinted by permission of author and publisher.

RESEARCH DESIGN

Let us begin with the assumption that governmental authority is an attitudinal object, with justices differing as to whether such authority should be maintained when in conflict with individual liberty, and at what cost.... Our first question is whether the support given governmental authority by Supreme Court justices has varied appreciably across justices in the Court's terms from 1903 to 1968. Table 1 provides an affirmative answer to that question. Four versions of a social background model are hypothesized to account for the observed variation.

Predictor Variables

To assess the constancy of the model, analyses are carried out for two different time periods: 1903–1935 and 1936–1968. In effect, we compare two equal time periods, each of which is longer than that examined by Tate (1981). The analysis is pursued via several predictor variables.

The first predictive factor is whether the justice is an only or first-born child. In the last 20 years the scholarly community has produced over 400 articles and dissertations on birth order (Weber, 1984). In general, this work suggests that social and personality development is in part a function of birth order, mediated of course by the experiences one has with other family members as a consequence of being the oldest, middle, youngest, or only child. Such experiences are thought by some to influence the choice of marriage partner and vocation, and to have something to do with level of achievement.

Weber has applied birth order analysis to 102 Supreme Court justices. He reports that first-borns "tend to imbibe parental norms to a greater extent than later children, are conscientious, *anxious to please authority*, am-

bitious, and high achievers.... They... either prefer and/or have a high tolerance for tightly structured situations" (Weber, 1984, p. 561, italics mine). Although controversially, it has been contended that first-borns, since they tend to be conservative and authoritarian, do not empathize with underdogs.

According to Weber, first-born Supreme Court justices, 56 in number, significantly exceed the expected number of 38—the approximate percentage of first-borns in the general population. Using Tate's ranking of 25 justices on support for civil liberties, he also reports that no significant correlation was found between birth order and support for civil liberty claims. However, I have calculated the mean rank for first-borns and compared it to the mean rank for those who were middle- or last-born. The respective means were found to be 15.33 for first-borns and 10.84 for non–first-borns. Consequently, we surmise that first-born Supreme Court justices will significantly favor government (authority) over underdog and criminal litigants in the Court's cases matching the government against such litigants.

The second factor to be considered is whether a justice's father was at any time a state or federal judicial officer, a legislator, or an executive officer—elected or appointed. This choice is based upon the assumption that government service promotes a favorable attitude toward government and its needs. It is consistent with Tate's (1981) finding that justices who had been prosecutors were more conservative than nonprosecutor judges, and with my earlier finding that federal administrative experience was positively related to support for government in criminal cases (Ulmer, 1973). Our expectation is that Supreme Court justices whose fathers had governmental experience imbibe progovernment sentiments, and thus significantly favor the government in

TABLE 1
Supreme Court Justices' Support for the Government in Government vs. Criminal Cases, 1903–1968 Terms, by Court, Individual Justice, and Level of Government

Justice	State and Local Government				Federal Government			
	Court Support (%)	Justice Support (%)	Above or Below Court	N	Court Support (%)	Justice Support (%)	Above or Below Court	N
White, E.	92.9	91.4	−	70	73.2	69.0	−	71
McKenna	92.9	92.9	—	85	69.3	67.0	−	88
Holmes	90.4	92.5	+	135	67.1	63.3	−	161
Day	93.3	92.0	−	75	75.7	71.4	−	70
Van Devanter	89.0	86.6	−	127	63.7	62.5	−	179
McReynolds	81.8	83.3	+	132	59.7	58.0	−	186
Hughes	75.6	75.6	—	74	63.5	62.7	−	118
Brandeis	87.0	86.0	−	115	59.7	56.8	−	176
Taft	89.1	89.1	—	55	58.1	58.0	−	62
Sutherland	86.2	84.0	−	94	61.2	58.9	−	139
Butler	83.3	81.2	−	96	59.7	55.5	−	144
Stone	65.0	68.5	+	143	55.8	60.1	+	206
Roberts	58.3	67.7	+	96	53.6	53.5	−	153
Black	32.3	26.6	−	401	47.0	32.3	−	421
Reed	45.2	58.9	+	146	54.2	66.5	+	212
Frankfurter	43.7	47.2	+	199	50.0	46.7	−	312
Douglas	31.8	11.4	−	393	45.9	27.4	−	405
Murphy	41.6	23.5	−	89	47.5	26.7	−	101
Jackson, R.	50.5	60.9	+	105	52.7	48.8	−	129
Rutledge	44.4	22.2	−	63	54.1	40.5	−	74
Burton	50.5	67.8	+	109	52.1	67.8	+	165
Vinson	57.6	66.6	+	66	57.3	70.6	+	75
Clark	32.2	49.1	+	236	46.6	65.4	+	249
Harlan II	25.0	51.1	+	268	41.2	61.9	+	226
Warren	24.4	14.7	−	272	43.0	27.7	−	249
Whittaker	38.2	50.9	+	55	47.4	57.8	+	95
Stewart	22.6	37.1	+	234	41.1	54.7	+	168
White, B.	20.9	41.8	+	191	37.2	54.6	+	86
Fortas	22.3	17.3	−	121	35.1	40.3	+	57
Brennan	24.7	15.8	−	259	41.0	28.7	−	212
Sanford	—	—	—	—	55.6	51.8	−	54
Minton	—	—	—	—	62.8	75.6	+	78
Goldberg	16.9	12.3	−	65	—	—	—	—
Marshall	19.4	17.9	−	67	—	—	—	—

NOTE:
Cases involving litigants characterized as black, alien, subversive, or labor union members are excluded from the data.

cases in which it is matched with underdog and criminal litigants.

The third and last predictor is the political party affiliation of the justices. One may note earlier findings that, in limited settings, Democratic judges have significantly favored the claims of the injured and the unemployed (Nagel, 1961, 1962; Ulmer, 1962) and of the defendant in criminal cases (Nagel, 1961). Democratic judges have also been found to be more likely than Republican judges to find a constitutional violation in criminal cases (Nagel, 1961) and to be more liberal than Republican judges (Goldman, 1975; Goldman and Jahnige, 1985). At the Supreme Court level, Tate has shown that party is a significant predictor of the justices' votes in civil liberty cases, which means, among other things, that Republicans favor government in such cases while Democratic justices tend to favor underdog and criminal litigants.

Such findings, of course, do not tell us whether party shapes attitudes or attitudes are shaped by party choices, or whether other experiences in life determine attitudes and party choice. We surmise that, unlike some experiential variables, party choice is a function of multiple experiences, and thus a surrogate for the aggregate of attitudes these multifarious experiences produce. It may not be strictly logical, therefore, to argue that party "causes" or influences judicial votes. It is logical to view the variable as a surrogate for background factors that, for the present, remain unidentified. Our general expectation is that when government is matched against underdog and criminal litigants, Republican justices will favor government significantly more often than Independent justices, and Independents more often than Democrats.

These predictors are employed with four versions of the same model, each of which incorporates the same dependent variable—support for government. Table 2 summarizes

and distinguishes the four versions of the model (hereinafter referred to as Models 1, 2, 3, and 4). In each case, we suggest that the three predictors will account for a significant portion of the variation in the support the justices give state/local or federal governments, as appropriate.

Dependent Variable

To construct a measure of the dependent variable, we first determine the support each justice gave to government during his entire career by taking support for government as a percentage (A) of all cases falling in the prescribed category. A similar percentage (B) is taken for each Court (the majority vote) in the same time period. The ratio of these percentages (A/B) is then calculated for use as the criterion in an ordinary least squares regression (OLS) analysis.

For each of the models summarized in Table 2 the first question is whether the three independent variables are effective predictors of the criterion appropriate for each model. An ordinary least squares analysis is then applied to each of the four models for the Court's terms from 1903 to 1968, using only those justices who participated in at least 50 cases on the dimension being analyzed.

FINDINGS

The results for Models 1, 2, and 4 may be quickly summarized. These models explain an insignificant and miniscule proportion of the variance in the justices' voting behavior. Thus, the expectations expressed for these models are not realized.

For Model 3, the picture is somewhat different. Several regression analyses have been run for this model. . . .

In Table 3 [i]t will be noted that the OLS regression for the Court's 1903–1935 terms

TABLE 2
Four Models for Predicting Variation in Support for Government from Backgrounds of Selected Supreme Court Justices, 1903–1968 Terms

Model	Predictors	Criterion
1. Cases matching state or local government against underdogs	Father a state officer; party of justice; justice a first-born	Support for state or local government
2. Cases matching federal government against underdogs	Father a federal officer; party of justice; justice a first-born	Support for federal government
3. Cases matching state or local government against non-underdog criminals[a]	Same as 1	Support for state or local government
4. Cases matching federal government against non-underdog criminals[a]	Same as 2	Support for federal government

[a] Cases involving criminals characterized as black, alien, subversive, or labor union members are excluded.

TABLE 3
OLS Regressions of Father as State Officer, Justice as First-Born, and Party of Justice on Support for Government, 1903–1935 and 1936–1968 Terms

Variable	Regression Coefficients	Standard Error	Significance
1903–1935			
Father as state officer [FAST]	−2.25	5.10	n.s
Justice as first-born [FB]	2.16	2.75	n.s
Party of justice [PARTY]	1.34	1.50	n.s
Constant = 97.57			
R^2 = .184			
1936–1968			
Father as state officer [FAST]	287.72	58.33	p < .001
Justice as first-born [FB]	−8.29	25.90	n.s.
Party of justice [PARTY]	17.67	13.95	n.s.
Constant = 99.22			
R^2 = .723			

accounted for 35.9% of the variance when time was ignored, but 72.9% when time was incorporated in the analysis. In Table 3 the regression is run first for the period 1903–35, and compared with the results of a regression analysis run on the 1936–68 terms. The significant disparity between variance accounted for in the first period (18.4%) and

that accounted for in the second (72.3%) underscores the impact of time period when the effect of *FAST, FB,* and *PARTY* on voting ratios is determined. One can only infer that in the initial 66-year analysis of support for government, the impact of social background factors on the justice's voting decisions was time-bound.

SUMMARY AND DISCUSSION

This paper asks whether social background models for explaining the votes of Supreme Court justices are time-bound. Adopting a research design that made it unlikely that social background would explain variation in justice voting across a 66-year period, a three-predictor model was identified that accounted for a statistically significant percentage of the variance: 35.9%.

Incorporating a time dimension in the analysis, however, we found a statistically significant difference in the impact of the three predictors in the Court's 1903–1935 terms when compared to its 1936–1968 terms. Indeed, when regression analyses were run separately for these two periods, the model accounted for 72.3% of the variance in the second period, but only 18.4% in the first. The result for the 1936–1968 terms compares favorably with the most successful use of social background models in studying justice voting. Such a result would be eminently publishable by past standards. The result for the first period, on the other hand, would not likely be considered worth reporting to the discipline. The conclusion to be drawn, in any event, is that the social background model examined in this paper is not time-neutral.

Although our results do not speak directly to past applications of social background models, our analyses suggest the possibility that all past applications in the judicial area have been time-bound—that is, they work only for particular sets of judges at particular points in time.

If this fact were established, it would tend to undermine a major tenet of social background theory, namely, that social background is a relatively unattenuated program for future behavior. At least it would seem essential that future users of the model explore nonbackground variables that possibly condition the impact of social attributes on subsequent behavior—variables for which time is possibly a surrogate.

None of our findings establishes necessarily that social background models in general are time-bound, although they do suggest that such a question must now be raised about any such model that claims to explain Supreme Court decisions. The reasons are two. First, we have investigated particular sets of cases in particular time periods. Our results may not hold for other cases or other time spans. Second, and more important, the failure of our models or others to predict voting behavior does not establish that social background has nothing to do with shaping attitudes toward objects. Certainly it does not establish that attitudes toward objects are irrelevant to voting behavior, for we are left with the possibility that, while social backgrounds do shape attitudes, and attitudes influence behavior, held attitudes will not always be reflected in behavior that would be consistent with them. Just as a racist, if appropriately circumscribed by law, peer pressure, likelihood of censure or sanction by relevant others, etc., may withhold racist behavior, a Supreme Court justice whose political loyalties would normally induce him to support the president who appointed him may not do so given significant countervailing pressures. This point is illustrated, perhaps, by Chief Justice Burger's vote in *United States* v. *Nixon* (1974), and that of Oliver Wendell Holmes in the *Northern Securities Case* (1904).

All this suggests the need for new research addressed to (*a*) the direct relationship between social attributes and attitudes, and (*b*) the conditions under which established attitudes will lead to specific behavior among judges. The second of these can only be addressed satisfactorily after the first has been established. To reach solid inference about the first for Supreme Court justices is admittedly a difficult challenge.

I would distinguish attribution of attitudinal objects from inferences about such objects derived by such reliable procedures as interviews and survey instruments. The latter investigatory tools are simply not available for assessing attitudes in the Supreme Court. A possible strategy here would be to investigate the validity of social background linkages to attitudes by focusing on lower court judges who will give interviews and, possibly, even respond to questionnaires. Establishing the validity of the general model in that rather direct fashion would presumably then lend greater credence to more indirect efforts to account for the behavior of Supreme Court justices by examining their social backgrounds.

REFERENCES

Goldman, Sheldon. 1975. Voting Behavior on the United States Courts of Appeals Revisited. *American Political Science Review*, 69:491–506.

Goldman, Sheldon, and Thomas P. Jahnige. 1985. *The Federal Courts as a Political System*. New York: Harper and Row.

Nagel, Stuart. 1961. Political Party Affiliation and Judges' Decisions. *American Political Science Review*. 55:844–50.

Nagel, Stuart. 1962. Ethnic Affiliations and Judicial Propensities. *Journal of Politics*, 24:94–110.

Northern Securities Inc. v. *United States*, 193 U.S. 197 (1904).

Tate, Neal. 1981. Personal Attribute Models of the Voting Behavior of United States Supreme Court Justices: Liberalism in Civil Liberty and Economic Decisions, 1946–1978. *American Political Science Review*, 75:355–67.

Ulmer, S. Sidney. 1962. The Political Party Variable in the Michigan Supreme Court. *Journal of Politics*, 11:352–62.

Ulmer, S. Sidney. 1973. Social Background as an Indicator to the Votes of Supreme Court Justices in Criminal Cases: 1947–1956 Terms. *American Journal of Political Science*, 19:622–30.

United States v. *Nixon et al.*, 418 U.S. 683 (1974).

Weber, Paul J. 1984. The Birth Order Oddity in Supreme Court Appointments. *Presidential Studies Quarterly*, 14:561–68.

Reagan's Appointments to the U.S. Courts of Appeals

Jon Gottschall

. . . The relevance of political partisanship to voting behavior in the courts of appeals has been illustrated by numerous studies. In the current study, the votes of appointees of six administrations are aggregated into four separate politically related groupings; Reagan appointees, Carter appointees, the combined Nixon/Ford appointees, and the combined Kennedy/Johnson appointees. These groups are ranked according to their relative tendency to vote in favor of: defendants and prisoners in cases involving defendants' or prisoners' rights; females or members of racial minorities in cases of alleged sexual or racial discrimination; claimants of First Amendment protection in cases involving alleged infringements on First Amendment rights; labor unions in labor-management disputes; claimants of welfare or disability benefits in cases where those benefits have been denied or terminated; and the personally injured or the estates of wrongful death victims in personal injury and wrongful death suits.

Reprinted from Jon Gottschall, "Reagan's Appointments to the U.S. Courts of Appeals: the Continuation of a Judicial Revolution." *Judicature* 70 (1986), pp. 50–54. Reprinted with permission of the author. Footnotes and most tables omitted.

Individual judges and their judge groupings have been assigned a liberal vote in cases where they joined a panel or *en banc* majority which decided in favor of one of the classes of litigants described above, or when they dissented in whole or part from a majority decision adverse to the claims of one of the specified groups. Panel or *en banc* decisions of the courts of appeals have been characterized as liberal when they reverse, in whole or part, decisions of lower courts or administrative agencies adverse to the claims of the specified groups or when they have affirmed lower court and administrative rulings favorable to the claims of the specified groups. A rough ideological portrait of each of the four judge groupings has thus been obtained.

There are a number of limitations to methods such as these when they are applied to any court, but particular caution must be exercised with regard to the courts of appeals. To begin with, this study will be confined to cases decided within a one and a half year period from July 1, 1983 to December 31, 1984. Therefore it is at best a glimpse of decisional tendencies in a limited number of issue areas over a limited period of time. Although judicial attitudes have been shown to be relatively enduring, it must be recognized that judges new to the courts of appeals, such as Reagan's recent appointees, may be in a state of professional and/or ideological evolution. In this sense, this study is not intended to be a last word on the Reagan appointees but rather an opening glimpse. In fact, the study may tell us as much about earlier administrations' appointees who have been the subjects of previous study as it does about the Reagan appointees.

Still another problem regarding voting studies of the courts of appeals (and, to a greater extent, the federal district courts) is that judges must often be compared on the basis of votes cast in factually and legally disparate cases in different geographical regions. These additional variables, absent in studies of United States Supreme Court decisions, complicate analysis. Whenever possible, direct comparisons of judges participating in identical panel or *en banc* decisions have been used but the problem of comparability of cases cannot be completely resolved at the lower federal court level, and this introduces another note of caution to interpretation of the results.

. . . [T]he study included 3,752 cases. Sixty per cent (2,399 cases) involved prisoners or defendants rights, whereas the remaining 1,353 cases are divided more evenly among the other six categories. Rates of dissent ranged from a low of 10 per cent in the defendants' and prisoners' rights cases to a high of 32 per cent in First Amendment cases. Rates of dissent in the other five issue categories ranged between 13 per cent and 17 per cent. Overall, the average rate of dissent in the seven issue categories was 17 per cent, which appears to be a higher rate of dissent than has been found in earlier studies of courts of appeals decisionmaking. Although this higher rate of dissent may reflect increased partisanship in the judicial selection process, it may also reflect a bias in

the decision to study politically controversial issues.

The Non-unanimous Cases

In the cases in which the judges do disagree, however, those appointed by Democratic Administrations are more than twice as likely to have voted "liberally" than those appointed by Republican administrations in all categories of cases except personal injury and wrongful death cases, where the results are more mixed. . . . [I]n non-unanimously decided civil rights and liberties cases, appointees of the Carter and the Kennedy/Johnson administrations cast, respectively, 63 per cent and 61 per cent of their votes for the liberal result, whereas the Reagan and the Nixon/Ford appointees both cast only 26 per cent of their votes in favor of what has been defined as the liberal outcome.

When non-unanimous cases involving the legal claims of those involved in disputes about the distribution of economic rewards and benefits are examined, very similar patterns emerge: Appointees of the Reagan and the Nixon/Ford administrations cast 33 per cent and 30 per cent of their votes respectively in favor of the liberal outcome, whereas appointees of the Carter and the Johnson/Kennedy administrations cast 69 per cent and 65 per cent of their respective votes for the liberal outcome. Clearly, when courts of appeals judges do divide on these issues, as well as on civil rights and liberties issues, they appear to do so along party and ideological lines.

Direct Comparisons of Reagan and Carter Appointees

In order to further test the hypothesis that Reagan appointees are more conservative than Carter appointees and to eliminate the possibility that these results are derived from spurious comparisons of votes in dissimilar cases, Carter and Reagan appointees were compared only on the basis of 1,037 instances in which they voted together in the same cases.... Carter and Reagan appointees agreed in 74 per cent of those cases in which they jointly participated and disagreed in 26 per cent of them. In those instances in which they disagreed while participating in the same case, Carter appointees voted for what has been defined as the liberal outcome 95 per cent of the time, as compared to 5 per cent for the Reagan appointees. Thus, in this admittedly small sample of 262 instances of direct disagreement, Carter appointees are clearly the more liberal group.

Direct Comparisons between the Reagan and the Nixon/Ford Appointees

The ideological differences between the Reagan and the Carter appointees come as no surprise. That Reagan appointees vote much like those of the Nixon and Ford administrations tends to contradict the conventional notion that Reagan is appointing radically more conservative judges. Yet direct comparisons between Reagan and Nixon/Ford appointees again suggest that there is little ideological difference between appointees of these three most recent Republican administrations.... Reagan appointees agree with those of the Nixon/Ford administrations in 93 per cent of the civil rights and liberties cases and in 92 per cent of the economic distribution cases in which they jointly participated. Moreover, in those few instances in which they disagreed while participating in the same decision, Reagan appointees supported the liberal outcome in 51 per cent as compared to 49 per cent for the Nixon/Ford appointees. These results, which are based on 961 instances of joint participation, again suggest that the probable

conservatism of at least the first term Reagan appointees to the courts of appeals has been exaggerated by the media and by some academic commentators.

The Influence of Reagan's More Centralized Selection Procedures on the Ideological Homogeneity of the Reagan Appointees

According to the conventional wisdom, Reagan appointees were expected to be not only more conservative than previous appointees but also more *uniformly* conservative. The establishment of a highly centralized Federal Judicial Selection Committee was expected to reduce the rate of ideological error in judicial selection.... Reagan appointees do appear to be a more ideologically homogeneous group than are the Carter appointees, at least in voting on civil rights and liberties issues. Reagan's appointees agreed among themselves in 91 per cent of those civil rights cases in which they jointly participated as compared to only a 79 per cent rate of agreement among the Carter appointees. In fact, Carter appointees agreed among themselves only slightly more often than they agreed with the Reagan appointees.... Nixon's and Ford's appointees, however, were even more ideologically homogeneous than were the Reagan appointees, agreeing in 94 per cent of the civil rights and liberties cases in which they jointly participated.

Apparently the disparity in ideological cohesiveness between Carter appointees and those of the Reagan administration is attributable less to the centralizing influence of Reagan's innovations in judicial selection than to the decentralizing effects of Carter's use of regional nominating commission panels and affirmative action criteria in judicial selection. As yet, there appears to be little discernible difference between those

TABLE 1
Comparison of Judge Groups in Unanimously and Non-unanimously Decided Civil Rights and Economic Distribution Cases

Issues	Kennedy/ Johnson per cent liberal	Nixon/ Ford per cent liberal	Carter per cent liberal	Reagan per cent liberal
Criminal justice	44%	36%	55%	34%
	(437)	(806)	(1394)	(172)
Race discrimination	51	36	46	31
	(92)	(143)	(263)	(100)
Sex discrimination	43	35	63	30
	(44)	(93)	(145)	(53)
First Amendment	45	34	53	31.5
	(60)	(10)	(139)	(97)
Civil rights & liberties cases (average score)	46	34	53	31.5
Labor	67	52	69	47
	(129)	(210)	(315)	(156)
Welfare	67	59	63	56
	(150)	(119)	(243)	(183)
Personal injury	55	48	48	47
	(78)	(157)	(281)	(123)
Economic distribution cases (average score)	63	53	60	50

Number of votes cast are shown in parentheses.

Reagan appointees selected by the Federal Judicial Selection Committee and Nixon/ Ford appointees selected by more traditional methods.

REAGAN APPOINTEES' IMPACT

By most indications, ideological differences among appointees to the courts of appeals which are obvious in non-unanimous decisions account for only a small proportion of the variance in case outcomes. Songer estimates that in only perhaps one case in six is judicial ideology a significant factor in case outcome. Goldman has also observed that only a small amount of variance in case

outcomes can be explained by partisan considerations such as party affiliation. Thus it should be expected that when the far more numerous unanimously decided cases are combined with the smaller percentage of those decided non-unanimously, the ideological differences between appointees of different administrations, which are so apparent in the non-unanimously decided cases, will be obscured or may disappear altogether. This was not, however, the case in this particular study.

As can be seen in Table 1, when voting results in both unanimously and non-unanimously decided cases were combined, appointees of the Carter and the combined Kennedy/Johnson administrations still exceeded the liberalism scores of the appointees of the Reagan and the combined Ford/Nixon administrations in every civil rights and liberties issue category and in two of the three issue categories involving the distribution of economic benefits. Although the differences observed in the welfare category are small, only in personal injury and wrongful death suits in the economic issue category do the judges fail to divide along administration and party lines on case outcomes. Generally speaking, when the entire case universe was analyzed, the margin of difference between appointees of Democratic and of Republic administrations was 20 per cent in civil rights and liberties cases and 10 per cent in economic distribution cases.

When the impact of individual administrations is observed, Carter appointees cast the highest percentage of liberal votes in civil rights and liberties cases (53 per cent), followed respectively by the Johnson/Kennedy appointees (46 per cent), the Nixon/Ford appointees (34 per cent) and the Reagan appointees (31.5 per cent). Although the Reagan appointees voted least liberally of the four judge groups, the margin of difference between the Reagan and Nixon/Ford appointees was only 2.5 per cent.

When the cases involving distribution of economic benefits are analyzed, similar results are obtained: appointees of the Kennedy/Johnson and the Carter administrations vote more liberally (53 per cent and 60 per cent respectively) than appointees of the Nixon/Ford and the Reagan administrations (53 per cent and 50 per cent respectively), although the margin of difference between appointees of the Democratic and of the Republican administrations of approximately 10 per cent is less than in the civil rights and liberties cases (20 per cent). Moreover, a margin of only 3 per cent separates the Kennedy/Johnson appointees from the Carter

appointees, just as a similarly slight margin separates the Reagan appointees from the Nixon/Ford appointees.

The impact of the Reagan appointees on case outcomes in the courts of appeals is a conservative one, although probably not at this time decisively more conservative than that of appointees of the Nixon and Ford administrations. Thus the Reagan appointees represent not so much the beginnings of a judicial revolution as the continuation of a pattern of Republican conservatism on civil rights and liberties issues which may have begun in 1968 with Nixon's pledge to appoint "strict constructionists" to federal judicial posts—a revolution which was decisively interrupted by the Watergate debacle and the subsequent election and judicial appointments of President Carter. Viewed in this way, the anticipated transition to a conservative judicial majority on the courts of appeals is an accomplished fact and does not await Reagan's second term appointments, as some commentators have suggested.

SUMMARY AND CONCLUSIONS

This study of first-term Reagan appointees should be regarded as an opening glimpse rather than as the last word on their ideological predilections. Because of the limited number of issues considered, the small size of the case sample, and also perhaps because Reagan appointees were observed in the infancy of their courts of appeals careers, the results of this study must be regarded as tentative and subject to revision. Nevertheless, several conclusions can be reached with varying degrees of certainty.

When voting on four civil rights and three economic issues which were thought likely to divide judges of different ideological predispositions, Reagan's appointees are not clearly or dramatically more conservative than Nixon's or Ford's appointees, although they *are* clearly more conservative than appointees of the Carter, Kennedy and Johnson administrations.

Moreover, despite the dramatic influx of supposedly more politicized appointees of the Carter and Reagan administrations and an apparent increase in the frequency of dissent, consensus still prevails for the most part in voting on the courts of appeals. Although Carter appointees almost invariably voted more liberally than Reagan appointees in those cases in which appointees of the two administrations disagreed, those disagreements occurred in only 26 per cent of the cases in which they jointly participated, while appointees of three different Republican administrations disagreed in fewer than 10 per cent of such cases.

In addition, there is some evidence that Reagan administration appointees were more ideologically homogeneous than were the Carter appointees. However, Reagan appointees were not more ideologically cohesive than were the Nixon and Ford appointees. These findings suggest that the difference in ideological homogeneity between Reagan and Carter appointees is attributable less to the centralization of the judicial selection process in the Reagan White House than to the systematic decen-tralization of the judicial selection process in Carter's regionally based federal Judicial Nominating Commission panels, which sought through affirmative action to variegate the racial and sexual attributes of its appointees.

Finally, at least among the cases selected for analysis, prominent civil rights and liberties issues may now serve as a more potent source of partisan cleavage on the courts of appeals than do issues involving the distribution of economic rewards and benefits. Although this finding is also highly tentative, it may reflect changes in the basis of partisan identification in the United States from New Deal economic issues to the more symbolic and political life style issues of the seventies and eighties.

These findings suggest a continuity amidst change. . . . To the limited extent that Reagan's appointees do represent a transition to a more conservative judiciary which mirrors a more nationally conservative electorate, this transition appears to have begun not with the Reagan appointees but with the Nixon and Ford appointees who preceded them. Viewed from this perspective, Reagan's appointees represent both the continuation of a judicial revolution and also the continuation of a contemporary Republican tradition.

Presidential Effects on Criminal Justice Policy in the Lower Federal Courts: The Reagan Judges

C.K. Rowland
Donald R. Songer
Robert A. Carp

·   ·   ·

In many ways the political roots of the Reagan appointment process can be traced to the 1980 Republican platform's promise to "secure the appointment of women and men...whose judicial philosophy is characterized by the highest regard for protecting the rights of law-abiding citizens." The 1984 Republican Platform reaffirmed the judicial appointment philosophy spelled out in 1980 and commended Reagan's "fine record" of appointing federal judges, "committed to the rights of law-abiding citizens."... [In] October, 1986 Reagan warned that if the Democrats won control of the Senate it would undermine his attempt to appoint tough federal judges: "We don't need a bunch of sociology majors on the bench. What we need are strong judges...judges who do not hesitate to put criminals where they belong, behind bars," (N.Y. Times, Oct. 9, 1986).

As his predecessors discovered, Reagan learned that a president's ideological appointment goals cannot be achieved without support from senators in general and home-state senators in particular. In this

"Presidential Effects on Criminal Justice in the Lower Federal Courts: The Reagan Judges," Claude K. Rowland, Donald R. Songer, and Robert A. Carp. Law and Society Review, 22 (1988), pp. 191–200. Reprinted by permission of Law and Society Association.

regard, until 1987 he benefited from a politically sympathetic Senate Judiciary Committee. Of particular importance is the commitment by home-state senators and Reagan supporters in several of the largest states to recruit judicial candidates who meet the platform's appointment criteria. In California, for example, Republican Sen. Wilson has established two nominating commissions in each of the state's four federal judicial districts; one is a "merit commission", the other a "political commission" to insure that those potential appointees found to be meritorious also have the appropriate conservative political and judicial philosophy. Moreover, Sen. Wilson has abolished the long-standing agreement whereby the out-party senator(s) were allowed to choose every fourth appointee in the state. Today Senator Cranston's staff learns the identity of nominees "when and if we are contacted by the FBI as part of its security check."

Reagan's home-state ideological support extends to many states without Republican representation in the Senate. In many of these states the senior Republican Congressman coordinates the selection of judicial candidates and forwards three to five names from which the White House can choose a legally and politically acceptable nominee. In Illinois, for example, this role is performed by Rep. Michel, the conservative House Minority leader whose presidential support score for 1985 was an exceptionally high 85 per cent.

In states whose Republican representatives have been less supportive of the President, the tendency has been to circumvent elected officials by appointing informal selection committees whose membership includes representatives of the Reagan/Bush campaign organization. In Massachusetts, where Representative Conte's support score (36) was lower than those of many Democrats and barely half the 1984 Republican average (67), a selection panel is chaired by the chairman of the state's 1984 Reagan/ Bush committee and includes as an ex-officio member Roger Moore, general counsel for the Republican National Committee.

In combination, the Reagan administration's politicized appointment process and the history of appointment effects on criminal-justice judgments lead us to anticipate a Reagan bench that is substantially less supportive of criminal litigants than are Carter or Nixon appointees seated at the same time. We now test this expectation.

APPOINTMENT EFFECTS OF REAGAN

Support for criminal litigants is defined as acquittals, decisions granting the trial or pre-trial motions of criminal defendants, and decisions granting state or federal habeas corpus relief. Each presidential cohort is assigned a criminal support score equal to the percentage of its decisions that support criminal defendants. We compute criminal support scores from random samples of 1500 district court opinions published in the *Federal Supplement* and 1500 appellate opinions published in the *Federal Reporter* between 1981–1984; however, to control for potential temporal effects and increase the number and comparability of Reagan appointees' opinions, we have stratified the sample to overrepresent 1983 and 1984 opinions.

Table 1 compares the criminal support scores of Carter, Reagan and Nixon appointees on the district courts. These findings are of the sort predicted by previous research; moreover, the degree of polarization between Carter and Reagan appointees is unprecedented. In the aggregate Carter appointees are almost twice as supportive of criminal defendants as are Reagan appointees.... The odds ratio (2.81) indicates that the relative odds of supporting the defendant are greater than two to one. The Nixon appointees, while less supportive than Carter appointees, are significantly more supportive of criminal litigants than are Reagan appointees. At first blush their moderate position might seem the result of the moderating influence of age or experience. However, studies of federal trial judges and Supreme Court Justices reveal virtually no

TABLE 1
Support for Criminal Litigants by Presidential Appointment Cohorts; the Federal District Courts: 1981–84.

	Appointing President		
	Nixon	*Reagan*	*Carter*
Support	32 (N = 499)	24 (N = 217)	47 (N = 784)
	$\alpha = 1.49$	$\alpha = 2.81$	
	p < .05	p < .01	

maturation effects on civil liberalism. Thus, the most plausible explanation for the moderation of the Nixon cohort is that, despite Nixon's commitment to "law and order" appointments, his discretion was constrained by a Democratic majority in the Senate and by moderate home-state Republican recruiters (Rowland, Carp and Stidham, 1984).

The ambiguous nature of many appellate case stimuli leads us to expect even greater presidential effects at this level and maximum presidential effects for dissenting decisions within that arena. Table 2 indicates that this expectation is fulfilled. Although both cohorts are reluctant to support criminal appeals, for the entire sample of appellate judgments the Carter appointees are almost twice as likely as Reagan appointees to support the criminal litigant. . . .

As anticipated, the magnitude of presidential effects increases dramatically as dissension increases. Even for nonconsensual

cases in which the entire panel votes to reverse the trial judge, the Carter cohort's support score (72) remains approximately 90 percent greater than the Reagan cohort's (37). But, as indicated by the non-unanimous category, when judges who hear the same case disagree, the polarization between Reagan and Carter appointees is dramatic, suggesting that when appointees respond differently to the same stimuli, these differences parallel differences in the administrations' ideological appointment criteria.

As with their district court counterparts, Nixon's appellate appointees occupy a moderate position roughly equidistant from the polarized Carter and Reagan cohorts. The Nixon cohort's consistent moderation suggests that presidential compromises with the Democratic Senate and its Judiciary Committee had a moderating influence on Nixon's appointment strategies. However, this apparent moderation should not divert attention

TABLE 2
Comparison of Support Scores Among Carter Appointees, Reagan Appointees, and Nixon Survivors on Courts of Appeal: 1981–1984.

CASES		Appointing President		
		Nixon	Reagan	Carter
All	Support	26 (N = 518)	17 (N = 213)	32 (N = 769)
			$\alpha = 1.72$ $p < .05$	$\alpha = 2.30$ $p < .01$
Unanimous[1]	Support	11 (N = 286)	10 (N = 157)	15 (N = 537)
			$\alpha = 1.10$ $p = NS$	$\alpha = 1.59$ $p = NS$
Non-Consensual[2]	Support	54 (N = 151)	37 (N = 56)	72 (N = 232)
			$\alpha = 2.00$ $p = NS$	$\alpha = 4.38$ $p < .05$
Non-Unanimous[3]	Support	35 (N = 136)	14 (N = 21)	67 (N = 102)
			$\alpha = 3.31$ $p = <.05$	$\alpha = 12.47$ $p < .001$

[1] Unanimous affirmation of trial court.
[2] Unanimous reversal of trial court.
[3] Split decision by 3-judge appellate panel.

from the fact that, for nonunanimous decisions, his cohort's support score is more than double that of the Reagan cohort and barely half that of the Carter cohort. Thus, even though Nixon's appointment discretion was constrained, his appointment cohort remains statistically and substantively distinct.

DISCUSSION

The polarization between Reagan and Carter appointees indicates that appointment effects on the lower courts are increasing and that they are maximized when the president's appointment discretion and his appointees' judicial discretion are maximized. Moreover, our findings suggest that the contemporary polarization is a product of the Carter cohort's high level of support for criminal defendants as well as the Reagan appointees' low level of support. Thus, while the data constitute evidence that, yes, the Reagan Administration's explicit, platform-based appointment criteria are reflected in its appointees' allocation of criminal justice values, they also suggest that implicit ideological criteria affected the allocation of values by the Carter appointees more strongly than would be predicted by most descriptions of the Carter appointment process. At the risk of oversimplification, it is difficult to avoid the observation that the differences in support resemble differences one would expect if Presidents Carter and Reagan were Judges Carter and Reagan.

Some implications of this research for future study are fairly obvious; for example, a comparison of Reagan effects before and after the 1987 shift to a Democratic Senate majority and the associated changes on the Senate Judiciary Committee would help clarify the interaction between presidential and senatorial effects on judgment and jurisprudence. But the more important questions, such as why appointment effects persist in a common-law system, will remain unanswered until they are accommodated by new theoretical developments.

If future research is to do more than chronicle incremental changes in the link between politicized appointment and judicial allocation of values we should heed the calls of Jacob (1983) and others (Gibson, 1983; Boyum and Mather, 1983) and develop a theoretical framework that accommodates multiple levels of the dispute resolution process and synthesizes the disparate threads of current scholarship. Such a framework would, at a minimum, adapt from social and cognitive psychology the conceptual distinction between judgment and other forms of decision making and recognize cognitive constraints on the exercise of judgment (by judges and disputants) in response to ambiguous case stimuli (Hammond, McClelland and Mumpower, 1980; Segal, 1986). Such an adaptation will require careful operationalization of key concepts (e.g. ambiguity, judgment) and encourage methods, such as fact pattern analysis (Ulmer, 1969), not associated with contemporary judicial research. The effort will be time consuming and arduous. The result, however, may significantly advance our understanding of judicial judgment and, therefore, our ability to understand the larger dispute resolution process and the influences of appointment politics on that process.

REFERENCES

Boyum, Keith and Lynn Mather, eds. (1983) *Empirical Theories About Courts*. New York: Longman, Inc.

Gibson, James L. (1983) "From Simplicity to Complexity: The Development of Theory in the Study of Judicial Behavior," 5 *Political Behavior* 7.

Hammond, Kenneth, Gary McClelland, and Jeryl Mumpower (1980) *Human Judgment and Decision-Making: Theories, Methods and Procedures*. New York: Praeger.

Jacob, Herbert (1983) "Presidential Address: Trial Courts in the United States: The Travails of Explanation," 17 *Law and Society Review* 407.

Rowland, C.K., Robert A. Carp, and Ronald A. Stidham (1984) "Judges' Policy Choices and the Value Basis of Judicial Appointments: A Comparison of Support for Criminal Defendants Among Nixon, Johnson, and Kennedy Appointees to the Federal District Courts," 46 *Journal of Politics* 886.

Segal, Jeffrey (1986) "Supreme Court Justices as Human Decision Makers: An Individual-Level Analysis of the Search and Seizure Cases," 48 *Journal of Politics* 938.

Ulmer, S. Sidney (1969) "The Discriminant Function and a Theoretical Context for its Use in Estimating the Votes of Judges," in J. Grossman and J. Tanenhaus, eds. *Frontiers of Judicial Research*. New York: Wiley.

Voting Behavior on the
United States Supreme Court

C. Herman Pritchett

"We are under a Constitution," said Charles Evans Hughes when he was governor of New York, "but the Constitution is what the judges say it is...." Several theories of jurisprudence have arisen which attempt to take into account this personal element in the judicial interpretation and making of law. The so-called "realistic" school has argued that law is simply the behavior of the judge, that law is secreted by judges as pearls are secreted by oysters.[1] A less extreme position was taken by the late Justice Holmes, who said: "What I mean by law is nothing more or less than the prediction of what a court will do." While these views go rather far in eliminating any idea of law as a "normative, conceptual system of rules," no one doubts that many judicial determinations are made on some basis other than the application of settled rules to the facts, or that Justices of the United States Supreme Court, in deciding controversial cases involving important issues of public policy, are influenced by biases and philosophies of government, by

Reprinted by permission of author and publisher from C. Herman Pritchett, "Divisions of Opinion Among Justices of the U.S. Supreme Court, 1939–1941," *American Political Science Review* 35 (1941), 890–898. Most footnotes have been omitted.

"inarticulate major premises," which to a large degree predetermine the position they will take on a given question. Private attitudes, in other words, become public law.

More precisely, it is the private attitudes of the majority of the Court which become public law. As an inexact science, issues at law are settled by counting the noses of jurors and justices. About 150 times every term the judges of the Supreme Court announce to the world in a formal written opinion the result of their balloting on the questions raised by a legal controversy before the Court. Happily, in the great majority of these ballots the decision is unanimous. In such cases, presumably the facts and the law are so clear that no opportunity is allowed for the autobiographies of the justices to lead them to opposing conclusions. It is always possible that the members of the Court may be agreeing for different reasons, but no hint of that fact is given unless concurring opinions are written.

In a substantial number of cases, however, the nine members of the Court are not able to see eye to eye on the issues involved. Working with an identical set of facts, and with roughly comparable training in the law, they come to different conclusions. If our thesis is correct, these divisions of opinion grow out of the conscious or unconscious preferences and prejudices of the Justices, and an examination of these disagreements should afford an interesting approach to the problem of judicial motivation. These cases in which dissent is expressed are particularly deserving of study because they furnish data which are not simply the verbalizations of Justices, to be handled by the typical process of interpretation, analysis, comparison, search for inconsistencies, and general legal exegesis. Instead, they contribute the tangible data of a series of yes and no votes on a variety of issues. Analysis of this voting behavior should be of value in explaining Supreme Court action, in revealing basic relationships among the justices, and, in short, in "predicting" the law.

It may be suggested that the nature of the division of opinion on the Supreme Court at any given time is a matter of common knowledge among those who follow Supreme Court thinking. In the hope, however, that a more precise analysis might have some value, the divisions of opinion in Supreme Court decisions during the past two

years (the October terms, 1939 and 1940) have been analyzed. This period was one in which the membership of the Court was fairly stable. The only changes in its composition came when Butler died soon after the beginning of the 1939 Term (without having participated in any cases) and was replaced by Murphy, and when McReynolds resigned during the 1940 Term.

During this two-year period, dissent was registered to more than one-fourth of the decisions rendered by the Court. In the 1939 Term, the rate was 30 per cent (42 dissents in a total of 140 decisions), and for the 1940 Term it dropped slightly to 28 per cent (47 dissents out of 169 decisions). There were thus 89 decisions during the period in which one or more of the Justices dissented, at least in part, from the conclusion reached by the majority. Table 1 shows the extent of each justice's participation in these dissents. The judge most persistent in disagreement was McReynolds, who took a minority stand in 22 per cent of the decisions in which he participated. Justices Roberts and Hughes were next in order, with records of 18 per

TABLE 1
Participation of Supreme Court Justices in Dissenting Opinions, 1939 and 1940 Terms

Justice	Number of Dissents			Opinions Participated In	Per Cent Dissents
	1939	1940	Total		
McReynolds*	32	9	41	184	22
Roberts	23	31	54	300	18
Hughes	14	24	38	305	12
Black	4	15	19	306	6
Douglas	4	15	19	303	6
Stone	4	7	11	303	4
Reed	1	8	9	302	3
Murphy**	1	6	7	215	3
Frankfurter	2	2	4	309	1

* Resigned February 1, 1941.
** Began service February 5, 1940.

TABLE 2
Agreements among Supreme Court Justices in Dissenting Opinions, 1939 and 1940 Terms

Justice	McReynolds	Roberts	Hughes	Stone	Reed	Frankfurter	Murphy	Black	Douglas
McReynolds	(13)	26	20	4	2				
Roberts	26	(10)	33	5	3			2	2
Hughes	20	33	—	10	3				
Stone	4	5	10	(1)	1				
Reed	2	3	3	1	(1)			4	4
Frankfurter						—	1	4	4
Murphy						1	—	7	7
Black		2			4	4	7	—	19
Douglas		2			4	4	7	19	—

cent and 12 per cent respectively. On the other hand, Frankfurter found himself on the losing side in only four of the 309 decisions rendered by the Court, a fact which calls attention to the central position which he appears to occupy on the Court. It should also be noted that he was the only justice whose dissents did not increase in number from 1939 to 1940 (with the exception of McReynolds, who did not serve out the 1940 Term). Justices Reed, Murphy, and Stone are also shown by the data to be consistently members of the Court's majority.

Of these 89 dissents, 25 were one-man affairs. McReynolds dissented alone in 13 cases, Roberts in 10, and Reed and Stone once each. In the other 64 dissents, the concurrence of two, three, or four Justices in deviation from the majority view raises interesting problems of judicial interrelationships. Was there a regular pattern of dissent? Did certain Justices tend to agree with each other in expressing dissent? Table 2 attempts to answer such questions by showing the number of times each justice joined each other Justice in a dissenting opinion. A well-defined pattern of relationships was found to exist on the Court, and the names have been arranged in the table so as to bring out this relationship most

clearly. Figures on the one-man dissents have been included in parentheses.

The table appears to reveal a marked division of the Justices into two wings or groups. The first is composed of McReynolds, Roberts, Hughes and Stone; the other includes Murphy, Frankfurter, Black, and Douglas. With the exception of two cases, no Justice in one of these groups ever joined in a dissenting opinion with a Justice from the other group. While every one of the eight Justices on occasion dissented in company with other members of his own bloc, in only two out of 89 dissents was there fraternization with the enemy. Both of these exceptional cases saw Roberts crossing the line to vote with Black and Douglas.[2] Justice Reed presents a special problem, since he was found in company with justices from both groups. His nine dissents included four with judges from each wing, and one lone dissent. He thus appeared to have one foot in each camp.

To the extent that Table 2 appears to show the existence of two self-contained blocs of opinion on the Court, it obviously misrepresents the situation. The pattern of relationships which begins to emerge from the table needs to be made clearer by presenting more complete data which will show all

TABLE 3
Agreements among Supreme Court Justices in Controversial Cases, 1939 and 1940 Terms (In Percentages)

Justice	McReynolds	Roberts	Hughes	Stone	Reed	Frankfurter	Murphy	Black	Douglas
McReynolds	—	64	64	41	35	31	38	24	24
Roberts	64	—	75	51	45	45	39	37	36
Hughes	64	75	—	78	63	64	53	49	49
Stone	41	51	78	—	81	84	75	69	68
Reed	35	45	63	81	—	86	80	79	79
Frankfurter	31	45	64	84	86	—	91	85	84
Murphy	38	39	53	75	80	91	—	89	89
Black	24	37	49	69	79	85	89	—	100
Douglas	24	36	49	68	79	84	89	100	—

judicial agreements, whether on the majority or minority side. Table 2 reveals that Frankfurter and Hughes were never in dissent together, but it does not tell us how often they agreed with each other when other justices were in dissent. Table 3, consequently, is arranged to show the extent of agreement between each pair of Justices in the 89 controversial cases (or rather, in so many of them as were participated in by that pair). The number of agreements is expressed in percentages of total cases participated in by each pair.

The table reveals some interesting facts. Justices Black and Douglas are shown never to have been on opposite sides of a decision during the entire period. On the other hand, McReynolds disagreed with them in three-fourths of all the decisions in which there was division of opinion. Chief Justice Hughes was closer to Stone than to any other Justice, Stone found himself most often in agreement with Frankfurter, and Frankfurter's views coincided most often with those of Murphy. The most important fact about this complex of individual relationships, however, is that it conforms to a basic underlying pattern. Examination of the table shows that the Justices ranked as they are, every member of the Court is placed next to or between

the Justice or Justices with whom he is most completely identified in agreement, and farthest away from those with whom he has least in common. The only important exceptions to this rule are found in the McReynolds-Murphy and the Stone-Frankfurter relationships.

The division of opinion thus takes the form of Figure 1, which locates the Justices along a continuum from one extreme to the other according to the direction and intensity of their deviation from the normal majority position of the Court, represented by the zero point on the scale. Frankfurter is closest to this point, since he dissented from only one per cent of the Court's decisions. Reed is given a position on both sides of the zero point, since his dissents were divided between the two wings. The scale makes apparent the existence of a fairly cohesive six-judge majority, most of the dissents being entered by the right-wing minority of McReynolds, Roberts, and Hughes.

This use of the term "right-wing" assumes that the division of opinion on the Court results from differences of opinion as to desirable public policy. It assumes that the above scale reflects relative "liberalism" and "conservatism" as those terms are understood by the man in the street. This assump-

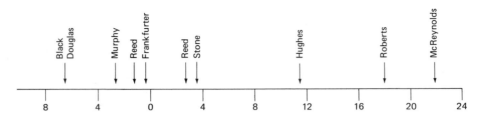

FIGURE 1. **Deviations expressed in percentages.**

tion should be checked by an examination of the issues actually involved in the cases where dissents were filed. Did all of these cases present issues of public policy on which liberals and conservatives might well be expected to differ, or did a number of them involve "purely legal" questions? A proper answer on this point would require the setting up of elaborate criteria for distinguishing between these two kinds of issues, and application of the criteria in a detailed analysis of each case. Such an analysis has been attempted here to only a limited degree, and covering only the dissents of the 1939 Term.

A case which requires a decision as to the extent of governmental powers, or presents an issue between the government and an individual, is obviously one in which the result may be affected by the judges' views on public policy. Our present stereotypes picture the conservative as anti-government (in the sense of opposing new or more effective forms of governmental control over individuals or corporations), and the liberal or New Dealer as pro-government. An examination of the 1939 Term's 42 dissents shows that in at least 36 an issue was presented which required the Justices to vote for or against the government, to uphold or deny a government contention, to approve or disapprove an exercise of governmental authority. The voting record of the Justices in these 36 cases shows that in 27 the dis-

senters were right-wingers taking an anti-government position; in three more cases, the dissenters were left-wing Justices voting for the government. Thus in 30 of the cases judicial action ran true to form.

Of the six remaining cases in this group, four saw the situation exactly reversed, with the government's support coming from the right wing. The explanation is simple, however. All four were civil liberties cases (involving free speech, the right to picket, and freedom from wire-tapping), and in all four McReynolds was the lone dissenter voting to uphold government restrictions on individuals. His action was in line with the traditional conservative position on the Court. It will be recalled that in 1931 the famous free press case of *Near* v. *Minnesota* brought out a perfect conservative dissenting lineup of Butler, Van Devanter, McReynolds, and Sutherland. By the 1939 Term, only one of this old guard remained to take a stand against civil liberties.

In the remaining two of these 36 dissents, the vote is completely inexplicable in terms of the scale positions of the Justices. One dissent was that of Justice Stone in the well-known flag salute case,[3] in which he alone maintained a strict civil liberties position in the face of the justification for the compulsory salute which the rest of the Court found compelling. The other exception came in a case presenting the thorny question of taxability of trust income, and saw

Reed alone voting for the government's contention.[4] Apart from these cases, however, the judicial reaction to a "government" issue was so consistent that it must be considered a definite factor in the Court's divisions of opinion.

Examining the 42 dissents of the 1939 Term from another point of view, we find 18 cases in which the Court was required to make a decision for or against "business." The issue was presented in many forms—the validity of a business tax, an alleged violation of the antitrust laws, the constitutionality of a federal or state regulatory scheme. But wherever the issue was present, the reaction pattern was consistent, support for business coming always from the conservative end of the Court. Specifically, there were 15 dissents by right-wingers taking the side of business, and three by liberals voting against a majority decision favorable to business. Again, in five cases during the 1939 Term the Court was dealing with a "labor" issue, and here also the reaction was uniform. There were four conservative dissents to decisions favoring labor, and one dissent by Douglas and Black from a majority decision slightly weakening the effect of a N.L.R.B. order.

The 1939 dissents included seven cases in which state or local action was attacked as violating provisions of the federal Constitution; for example, state and local taxes were resisted as burdening interstate commerce or contrary to due process or infringing a privilege of national citizenship. Here the consistent policy of the Justices at the Black-Douglas end of the Court was to uphold state action, in line with the traditional liberal belief that state legislative powers should be left as unrestricted by federal constitutional limitations as possible. It may also be noted that an issue involving the extent of judicial review was raised in some form in four cases; the left-wing wanted to narrow review, and the right-wing opposed

any narrowing. Public operation of a power system was an issue in one case; McReynolds opposed it.[5] The rights of a debtor under the Frazier-Lemke Act were involved in another case; a liberal minority voted in his favor.[6]

One or more of the seven issues just considered was present in every one of the cases where opinion was divided during the 1939 Term. In other words, none of these cases appears to present a "purely legal" question, for in each instance the observer can find a facet of the case which might offer an opportunity for the decision to be influenced by judicial views as to desirable public policy. It is not contended, of course, that the decisions were motivated wholly by the personal views of the Justices, but the data clearly indicate that these views had a considerable effect in the process of making up the judicial mind.

It would be interesting to discuss the records of several of the individual Justices in the light of the information which this analysis has supplied. The case of the Court's new Chief Justice is particularly worthy of notice. The participation of Justice Stone in right-wing dissents may seem strange, in view of his reputation as one of the soundest and ablest liberals on the Court. Two explanations suggest themselves. One is that he has deviated slightly to the right in his views with the passage of time. The other is that he has maintained very nearly his original position, but that the Court has with recent appointments moved so substantially leftward that views which put Stone to the left of the Court ten years ago now occasionally leave him exposed in dissent on the right. Whatever the cause, the process appears to be accelerating, for Stone's dissents with the conservative group numbered three in the 1939 Term and six in the 1940 Term.

The general result of this study has been to emphasize the influence of personal attitudes in the making of judicial decisions and the interpretation of law. To prevent over-emphasis on this point, it would be well to recall that even in a Court representing as wide a range of views as has been found during the last two terms, 71 per cent of the cases were decided by unanimous vote. Where there were divisions of opinion, however, they appear to be for the most part explicable in terms of the opinions of the respective judges on public policy. This conclusion hardly comes as a surprise. For few are likely to deny that Justices of the Supreme Court have always, to paraphrase Justice Frankfurter, "read the laws of Congress through the distorting lenses" ground by their own experience. On the other hand, there are many who agree that the Supreme Court's vision is better today than it has been for many years past.

NOTES

1. This figure and the quotations following are taken from Francis D. Wormuth, "The Dilemma of Jurisprudence," *A.P.S.R.* 35 (1941), 44.

2. The cases are *Neuberger* v. *Commissioner of Internal Revenue*, 61 S.C. 97 (1940); and *Union Pacific R. Co.* v. *U.S.*, 61 S.C. 1064 (1941).

3. *Minersville School District* v. *Gobitis*, 310 U.S. 586 (1940).

4. *Helvering* v. *Fuller*, 310 U.S. 69 (1940).

5. *U.S.* v. *San Francisco*, 310 U.S. 16 (1940).

6. *Union Joint Stock Land Bank* v. *Byerly*, 310 U.S. 1 (1940).

A Psychological Analysis
of the Warren Court

Glendon Schubert

Much recent research in the decision-making of the United States Supreme Court has been characterized by a pronounced emphasis upon the invocation of sociopsychological theory and statistical methods of data processing in lieu of exclusive reliance upon the legal-historical theory and methods typical of most research in this field of study. Symbolic of this development is the increasing tendency of political scientists to consider constitutional law as an aspect of political behavior as well as a branch of law, and correspondingly, to study the subject matter as judicial behavior. Naturally, this recent work has evinced a preoccupation with unidimensional analysis, since it is less complicated to work with one variable than with many, and the experience so gained no doubt is a prerequisite to multivariate study. Nevertheless, students who remain committed to the more traditional workways in constitutional law are quite right in insisting, as they do, that most Supreme Court cases raise what at least appear prima facie to be

Reprinted by permission of the author and publisher from "The 1960 Term of the Supreme Court: A Psychological Analysis," *American Political Science Review* 56 (1962), 90–107. Most footnotes and tables have been omitted.

many issues for decision, and that their more subjective and impressionistic mode of analysis retains the great virtue of not oversimplifying the rich complexity of many Supreme Court cases to the extent that inescapably seems to be required by the newer theories and methods. Clearly, further advances in the behavioral study of Supreme Court decision-making depend upon the development of multidimensional models of Court action, which will make possible the observation and measurement of interrelationships among the significant major variables that in combination provide the basis for an adequate explanation of the manifest differences in the voting and opinion behavior of the justices.

The purpose of this article is to describe one such multidimensional model of the Court, and...to demonstrate that the psychological approach...leads to more significant, more comprehensible, and more valid insights into the political behavior of the Supreme Court than seem to be provided by the case-by-case approach.... The specific hypothesis to be tested is that most of the *variance* in the voting behavior of the justices can be accounted for by the differences in their individual attitudes toward a small number of fundamental issues of public policy. These public policy issues constitute the variables of this study.

A BRIEF DESCRIPTION OF THE MODEL

...In accordance with modern psychometric theory which generalizes the basic stimulus-response point relationship, Supreme Court cases are treated as raw psychological data which embody the choices of the individual justices among a variety of stimuli. Each case before the Court for decision is conceptualized as being represented by a stimulus (j) point, which is located somewhere in a psychological space of the relevant dimensions, depending upon the number and intensity of issues that it raises. The combination of the attitudes of each justice toward these same issues also may be represented by an ideal (i) point, located in the same psychological space. In each decision of the Court, what is observed is the relationship between the i-point of each justice and the j-point for the case. The relationship that is measured is one of dominance; that is, whether the position of the i-point in the dimensions that define the space equals or exceeds, or is less than, the position of the j-point in these dimensions. Technically, an individual-compensatory composition model is assumed: for an i-point to dominate a j-point, it is not essential that the individual equal or exceed the stimulus on *all* of the relevant dimensions, since an individual may (in appropriate instances) be able to compensate for his deficiency on one (or more) dimensions by an excess on other dimensions....

Next let us consider the conjoint relationship between the i-points of all nine justices, assuming full participation in the decision, and a particular j-point. Obviously, how the case will be decided will depend upon whether a majority or a minority of the i-points dominate the j-point. If a majority of i-points dominate, then the value or values raised by the case will be upheld or supported by the decision "of the Court"; and if, to the contrary, the j-point dominates a majority of the i-points, then the value or values raised by the case will be rejected—"the Court" will refuse to support them. To take a concrete example, let us assume the general value "civil liberty," and the specific question whether "the Fourteenth Amendment requires" the Supreme Court to reverse a state court conviction of a criminal defendant, based in part upon evidence procured as the result of an unreasonable search or seizure. According to the theory proposed, it would be assumed that the i-points of no more than three justices dominated the j-point representing this issue at the time of the decision in *Wolf* v. *Colorado*, and that no more than four did so throughout the following decade. As a consequence of Stewart's appointment and of Black's explicitly avowed shift in attitude toward this issue, a majority of i-points did dominate when the issue arose once again for disposition in *Mapp* v. *Ohio*, a decision announced on the closing decision day of the 1960 Term; and consequently, *Wolf* v. *Colorado* was overruled. Actually, the voting division in *Mapp* v. *Ohio* was 6–3, with Clark both supplying the extra favorable vote and writing the opinion of the Court; Clark's position should have occasioned no surprise, however, because it was in precise accord with the intention that he had announced seven years earlier when concurring in *Irvine* v. *California*. Clark considered himself bound by the *Wolf* precedent unless and until a majority could be formed that would agree to overrule that decision—an event that was forestalled for several more years, apparently, by Black's idiosyncratic blind spot for the Fourth Amendment.

We can now consider an operational definition of the Court's decision-making. In one dimension, the voting division of the Court is precisely determined by the intersection of the j- point with a line along which are arrayed the i-points of the justices. (This definition, it should be noted, is the one which applies for cumulative [or Guttman] scaling of Supreme Court cases.) In two dimensions, a decision is determined by the line orthogonal to the j-point vector; all justices whose i-points fall on the orthogonal line, or beyond it (in the positive direction of the variable) will vote in support of the value, and the remaining justices whose i-points lie on the negative side of the line will vote to reject it; while unanimous decisions occur, of course, when all i-points lie on, or on the positive side of, the orthogonal line, or else when all i-points lie on the negative side of this line. In three dimensions, the decision is determined by the plane which intersects the space orthogonally to the j-point vector; and more generally, in r-dimensions by a hyperplane of $r-1$ dimensionality which intersects the r-dimensional space in a similar manner.

Thus, we conceive of both i-points representing the composite attitudes of individual justices, and j-points, representing the composite issues raised by individual cases, as sets of vectors terminating in points, each with a unique position in the same psychological space. Hereinafter we shall assume that this space is three-dimensional. . . . Cases in a set which raises questions of differing degrees of valuation about the same variable (e.g., sympathy for the constitutional claims of the right to counsel in state criminal trials) are located at various points in the space, but in an approximately linear relationship to each other; thus, each such point may be conceived of as lying upon or near a scale axis, representing the subvariable, which transects the space. Through the centroid of a set of scale axes, representing a set

of civil liberties subvariables, would pass an axis representing a broadly defined heterogeneous major variable (such as 'all civil liberties" issues for a given term); and this scale axis would follow the trace of the mean of the projections from all of the relevant j-points. But the i-points also project upon any scale axis; and therefore, a one-dimensional solution for the Court's decision-making function may be achieved by measuring the relationship between the projections from j-points and from i-points upon a scale axis representing any variable that is of interest. This, in effect, is precisely what is happening, in theory, when an analyst constructs a cumulative scale of a set of decisions that are postulated as pertaining to a single dominant variable, and positions the scale as an axis in the space. It is apparent that if the model is adapted for analysis invoking this particular definition of the decision-making function, as we shall do in the discussion which follows, the Court's decision-making is still being measured in unidimensional terms. But the model itself is multidimensional. . . .

In order to utilize the model that has been described, what we require are procedures to locate both i-points and j-points in three-dimensional space, and to measure the dominance relationship for any dyad, with each dyad consisting of a j-point and an i-point. Factor analysis affords a readily available technique for locating the set of i-points for a given set of decisions, such as a term of the Court, in a fixed spatial configuration. But the raw data come in a form that preclude the use of factor analysis, at least in the same manner, in order to locate the j-points. The reason for this is that, in a typical recent term, the Court divides in about a hundred decisions on the merits. Consequently it is possible to make a relatively large number of observations—about one hundred—of the location of a relatively small number of i-points—never more than nine. But more than nine observations of the location of any specific j-point are never possible, because there are never more than nine votes recorded in a single case. One hundred observations are ample to locate the i-points, by factor analytic techniques, with considerable precision; but nine observations are far too few to permit the same thing to be done for j-points. . . .

[F]actor analysis is essentially a statistical method for breaking down a correlation matrix into its principal component elements; and it can never be more reliable than the matrix upon which it works. No single Supreme Court decision contains enough votes to allow the computation of reliable correlation coefficients. If we had a hundred justices participating in the decision of each of, say, a dozen cases in the typical term, factor analysis could serve very well to locate a configuration of j-points, but it would then be incapable of locating the i-points. If there were a hundred justices participating in the decision of a hundred or more cases in each term, factor analysis could be used to locate both types of points with what ought to be good precision. . . .

Although it is not possible to locate j-points in the space as precisely as i-points, at least by factor analysis, it is possible to locate *sets* of j-points in the same space with the i-points. This is done by cumulative scaling of sets of cases. Each cumulative scale measures the one-dimensional alignment of the attitudes of the justices toward a single variable. If most of the Court's decisions can be associated with a set of cumulative scales, and if the set of scales can be passed through the space as axes in such a way that the projections from the i-points on the scale axes are consistent with the alignments of the justices on the cumulative scales, then it will be assumed that the scale axes are indeed the counterparts of

their analogue cumulative scales; and that the variance in the voting behavior of the justices is adequately accounted for by the manifest differences in the attitudes of the justices toward the cumulative scale variables. . . .

THE UNIVERSE OF RAW DATA

The sample of decisions to be analyzed consists of all cases in which the Supreme Court divided on the merits during the period of the 1960 Term, which extended from October 10, 1960, through June 19, 1961. Both formal and per curiam decisions accordingly are included, but unanimous and jurisdictional decisions were excluded. . . . [A]lmost three-fourths of the Court's formal decisions were reached over the disagreement of one or more justices, while this was true of less than one-fourth of the per curiam decisions. . . .

For purposes of this study, each *case*, to which the Court had assigned a unique docket number and for which the Court had made a disposition on the merits, was a unit for voting analysis. As a unit of content, the docketed case offers the advantages of being specifically and uniquely identifiable, and of providing what with very rare exceptions is an unambiguous basis for voting attribution which can readily be replicated by other analysts. . . .

For each case, one set of nine votes was counted. In each of eleven cases, one justice did not participate in the decision on the merits; and in one other, two justices did not. There were also two Federal Employers' Liability Act evidentiary cases and one Jones Act case in which Frankfurter, according to his custom, persisted in jurisdictional dissent at the time when his colleagues voted on the merits; these three jurisdictional dissents were classified as nonparticipations, for purposes of the present analysis. Eight votes could not be specified, in one case in which the Court divided equally, without opinion. After these nonparticipations and unspecifiable votes were deducted, a total of 867 votes remained; they constituted the basis for the factor analysis and the cumulative scaling.

THE FACTOR ANALYSIS

Computation of the Correlation Matrix

The initial task in any factor analysis is the construction of a correlation matrix. In the present study, the correlation matrix was based upon a set of fourfold tables which, in turn, were constructed directly from the 867 votes just described. These votes were tabulated to show the totals of agreement and disagreement with the majority, in the decision of each case, for every pair of justices. For any such pair, each case holds five possibilities: (1) both may agree in the majority; (2) both may agree in dissent; (3) the first member of the pair may vote with the majority, while the second dissents; (4) the second member of the pair may vote with the majority, while the first dissents; or (5) either or both members may fail to participate, in which event there is no score for the pair for that case. In the tabulation of votes for the factor analysis, no attention is paid to the substantive variables to which the decisions relate; the sole criterion for the attribution of votes in each case is agreement or disagreement with the majority.

It is most convenient to arrange the summary tabulation of agreement-disagreement, for each judicial dyad, in the form of a fourfold table. . . .

In order to measure precisely the relationship among the four cells of a fourfold table, phi correlation coefficients are computed.[1] . . .

Since there are nine justices on the Court, there are fourfold tables and correlation coefficients for each of the thirty-six dyads. . . .

The Factor Loadings

The initial product of a factor analysis is a set of derived correlations (or "loadings," as they customarily are called) which purport to measure the extent to which each element, of whatever has been associated in the correlation matrix, is related to the components or dimensions into which the basic correlation matrix has been broken down. In the present study, the elements are the justices, and the factor loadings purport to express the correlation of each justice with the basic underlying dimensions of the phi matrix. Although it is technically possible to extract as many factors as there are elements intercorrelated in the phi matrix—nine, in the instant case—only six factors actually were computed, and of these, only three will be used . . . [because] the residual matrix, representing the amount of variance unaccounted for by the first three factors, was very small, and less, indeed, than the estimated error variance. . . .

The usual procedure in factor analysis is to rotate the orthogonal factor axes, which are the direct product of a complete centroid routine, to oblique positions that are presumed to correspond to some criterion related to empirical reality, and thus to make possible a more meaningful psychological interpretation than would usually be possible if the orthogonal axes were retained.[2] The orthogonal axes have not been rotated in the present study, but for the reason that, contrary to the usual procedure, no reliance is placed upon the association of substantive meaning with the factors. Substantive mean-

TABLE 1
Factor Loadings for Judicial Ideal-Points, 1960 Term

Justices	Factors		
	I	*II*	*III*
D	.754	.283	.170
Bl	.769	−.259	−.130
Wa	.699	−.456	.089
Br	.578	−.298	.291
S	−.289	.126	.363
Wh	−.571	.065	−.108
H	−.714	−.373	.226
F	−.736	−.338	.270
C	−.519	−.245	−.309

NOTE:
The justices are coded as follows: D (Douglas), Bl (Black), Wa (Warren), Br (Brennan), S (Stewart), C (Clark), Wh (Whittaker), F (Frankfurter), H (Harlan).

ing is associated, instead, with the scale axes which are passed through the space defined by the orthogonal factor axes; and thus the scale axes—which are oblique—perform the same function, for purposes of interpretation, that is usually accomplished by rotation of the orthogonal axes. The orthogonal axes are used, therefore, only as a set of reference axes to define the three-dimensional space in which the *i*-points of the justices and the *j*-points of the cases are located. And the factor loadings, shown in Table 1, function as Cartesian coordinates which locate the *i*-points of the justices in the factor space.

Factor loadings can vary, in principle, from +1 to −1; in practice, their variance is bounded by the extremity of the correlation coefficients upon which they are based. It will be observed that, on the average, the highest loadings (both positive and negative) are on the first factor, and that the mean magnitude of the third factor loadings is smallest. This is inherent in the centroid routine, which assumes that the first factor, to which the largest portion of the variance is

attributed, is the most important factor, and so on. The loadings on the first factor range from a high of approximately +.77, for Black, to a low of −.74, for Frankfurter. . . . Mere inspection of the factor matrix of Table 1 suggests that the multidimensional relationships among the justices are going to be somewhat different, and certainly more complex, than the simple bifurcation of a single dimension which will account for much, but not enough, of the variance in the voting behavior of the justices. For a fuller understanding than a single dimension—even when it is overwhelmingly the most important one—can afford, we must turn to an examination of relationships made possible by work with the three-dimensional factor space.

THE CUMULATIVE SCALES

Cumulative scaling is a research operation completely independent of the factor analysis, and so may be undertaken before, at the same time, or after the factor analysis is completed. In cumulative (or Guttman) scaling, the same universe of raw data is used as for the factor analysis. But instead of tabulating votes by dyads and in terms of agreement with the majority, for scaling purposes votes are tabulated by cases, and are classified as being either in support of, or in opposition to, certain defined scale variables. The variables employed here were identified on the basis of experimental work in previous terms of the Warren Court. . . .

Consistent votes in support of the scale variable are denoted by the symbol x, and inconsistent positive votes by x̲. A blank space indicates a consistent negative vote, and the symbol − is used to signify an inconsistent negative vote. An asterisk signifies nonparticipation. Scale scores are simple functions of scale positions, and a justice's scale position is defined as being fixed by his last consistent positive vote. Where one or more nonparticipations separate a justice's consistent positive and negative votes, his scale position is assumed to be at the midpoint of the nonparticipation or nonparticipations, since it cannot be determined how he might have voted. A justice's scale score is computed by the formula:

$$s = \frac{2p}{n} - 1,$$

where s is his score, p his scale position, and n equals the number of cases in the scale. Scale scores, like correlation coefficients and factor loadings, can range in value from $+1$ to -1, with the significant difference in practice that scale scores frequently attain these extreme values, reflecting the extremity of attitude of several of the justices. . . .

The C Scale

Figure 1 is a cumulative scale of the fifty-one civil liberties cases that the Court decided by divided votes on the merits during the 1960 Term. In content, the C variable was defined broadly to include all cases in which the primary issue involved a conflict between personal rights and claims to liberty, and governmental authority. The number of cases included in the scale—over half of the total—was somewhat larger than in other recent terms; but the ranking of justices on the scale was very similar to that of the 1959 Term, and precisely the same as in 1958, which was Stewart's first term on the Court.

The scale accords with common knowledge that Douglas, Black, Warren, and Brennan are more sympathetic to civil liberties claims than the other members of the present Court. But there are definite gradations among the attitudes of these four "libertarian" justices toward the civil liberties claims of this term, and the scale distance separating Douglas and Brennan is just as great as the scale distance separating Whittaker and Clark. The mean rate of support for civil liberties claims of the four justices with high positive scale scores (the liberals on this issue) is 85 percent; the mean rate of opposition for the four justices with high negative scale scores (the conservatives on this issue) is 86 percent. This differentiation of the Warren Court into a set of liberal justices and a much more conservative group agrees with Pritchett's findings[3] for the Vinson Court, except that Frankfurter now appears as a conservative rather than as an exponent of "libertarian restraint."

It is certainly noteworthy that Douglas, over a wide range of specific issues, supported civil liberties claims in all except two out of fifty-one cases. His two inconsistent (and C −) votes both came in cases that raised technical questions of procedure relating to the statutory rights of federal criminal defendants, in cases where another variable (J −: Supreme Court deference to lower courts) also was present. Douglas was the

FIGURE 1 Judicial Attitudes Toward Civil Liberties, 1960 Term

| | 1960 Term, C Scale Justices | | | | | | | | | |
Cases	D	Bl	Wa	Br	S	Wh	F	H	C	Totals
5/762	×									1−8
6/308	×									1−8
6/420	×									1−8
6/582	×									1−8
4778:200	×	×								2−7
5/265	×	×						*		2−6
4/507	—	×	×							2−7
4/611	—	×	×							2−7
5/458	×	—	×							2−7
4/388	×	×	×							3−6
3370:685	×	×	×							3−6
4839:122	×	×	×							3−6
5/381	×	—	×	×						3−6
4/372	×	×	×	×						4−5
4/426	×	×	×	×						4−5
5/43	×	×	×	×						4−5
5/301:70	×	×	×	×						4−5
5/301:179	×	×	×	×						4−5
5/399	×	×	×	×						4−5
5/431	×	×	×	×						4−5
6/36	×	×	×	×						4−5
6/82	×	×	×	×						4−5
6/117	×	×	×	×						4−5
4581:1	×	×	×	×						4−5
4623:12	×	×	×	×						4−5
4719:486	×	×	×	×						4−5
6/617	×	—	—	×	×					3−6
6/599	×	—	—	×	×		⊠			4−5
4/587	×	×	×	—	×					4−5
4/479:14	×	×	×	×	×					5−4
4/479:83	×	×	×	×	×					5−4
5/85	×	×	×	×	×					5−4
5/551	×	×	×	×	×					5−4
6/1	×	×	×	×	×					5−4
4694:233	×	×	×	×	×					5−4
4842:161	×	×	×	×	×		⊠			6−3
5/715	×	×	×	×	×				⊠	6−3
4798:236	×	×	×	×	×				⊠	6−3

FIGURE 1 Judicial Attitudes Toward Civil Liberties, 1960 Term (Continued)

	1960 Term, C Scale Justices									
Cases	D	Bl	Wa	Br	S	Wh	F	H	C	Totals
4/631	×	×	×	×	×	×				6–3
5/312	×	×	×	×	×	×				6–3
6/213	×	×	×	×	×	×				6–3
6/418	×	×	×	×	*	×				5–3
4703:238	×	×	×	×	—	×				5–4
4754:4	×	×	×	×	×	×			×	7–2
4577:669	×	×	×	×	—	×			×	6–3
4/350	×	×	×	×	—	—	×	×		6–3
5/534	×	×	×	×	—	×	×	×		7–2
4/454	×	×	×	×	×	—	×	×		7–2
4687:181	×	×	×	×	×	—	×	×		7–2
5/610	×	×	×	×	×	×	×	×		8–1
5/167	×	×	×	×	×	×	—	×	×	8–1
										221–236
Totals										
Pros	49	43	43	38	20	10	7	6	5	221
Cons	2	8	8	13	30	41	44	44	46	236
Scale positions	51	47	45	39	25	13	6	6	1	
Scale scores	1.00	.84	.76	.53	−.02	−.49	−.76	−.76	−.96	

$$R = 1 - \frac{22}{403} = .945 \qquad S = 1 - \frac{23}{79} = .709$$

NOTE:

In Figure 1 . . . cases are cited in either of two ways. Those decided prior to June 1961 are cited to the official *United States Reports*: the digit preceding the slash bar is the third digit of the volume number, and should be read as though preceded, in each case, by the digits 36; the number following the slash bar is the page cite; and if more than one case begins on the same page, a docket number follows the page cite, separated from it by a colon. Official citations are not available, at the time this is written, for cases decided during the final three weeks of the term; such cases are cited to Volume 29 of *United States Law Week, Supreme Court Section*, with a four-digit page number followed by the docket number.

Two coefficients appear at the bottom of each scale; they purport to measure the degree of consistency in the set of votes being scaled. R is Guttman's coefficient of reproducibility; .900 or better is conventionally accepted as evidence to support the hypothesis that a single dominant variable has motivated the voting behavior of the justices in the set of cases comprising the sample. S is Menzel's coefficient of scalability; it provides a more rigid standard than R, because S (unlike R) does not capitalize upon the spurious contribution to consistency that arises from the inclusion in the scale of either cases or justices with extreme marginal distributions. Menzel has suggested that the appropriate level of acceptance for S is "somewhere between .60 and .65"; the scale presented in Figure 1 . . . [is] well above the suggested minimal levels of acceptability for both R and S. . . .

only justice to dissent alone against C − decisions of the Court; and his four solitary C + dissents identify him as the justice most sympathetic to civil liberties claims. At the opposite extreme was Clark, who found only five civil liberties claims, out of the total of fifty-one, sufficiently persuasive to gain his vote. Moreover, four of Clark's five C + votes were inconsistencies, suggesting that in these cases he may have been motivated by his attitudes toward other variables than C; there is, of course, little empirical basis for assuming that all justices perceive all issues raised by cases in the same way, or that any justice's voting behavior will be perfectly consistent. The Guttman model assumes that if in a particular scale most respondents are highly consistent most of the time, it is reasonable to infer that they are predominantly motivated by their differential attachments to a common value. And it is in precise accord with the assumptions of the "individual-compensatory composition model," mentioned earlier, that a justice may, in some decisions, compensate for his lack of sympathy for, say, civil liberties by his strong attachment to other appropriate values that he may perceive to be present in the decisions. This theory seems to provide a plausible explanation for Clark's inconsistencies. His most inconsistent votes, for instance, came in two cases, *Burton* v. *Wilmington Parking Authority* and *Mapp* v. *Ohio*, where he joined C+ majorities against the dissents of Harlan, Frankfurter, and Whittaker. The first case involved racial discrimination in a restaurant in a publicly owned building; and the second was the decision, already mentioned, which overruled *Wolf* v. *Colorado*. In both cases, Clark's strong attachment to stare decisis appeared to overcome his basically C − attitude sufficiently to cause him to support the majority, although such a consideration obviously did not forestall the more activist conservatives from voting as dictated

by their convictions about libertarian claims.

The key decision-maker in C cases during the 1960 Term, however, was Stewart, whose propensity to function as the swing man in an otherwise well-balanced Court was sufficiently obvious to attract journalistic comment. Although Stewart tied with Clark for inconsistency with four such votes, he nevertheless voted consistently over 90 percent of the time, and his scale score of −.02 indicates the close balance of his voting on civil liberties issues. Stewart was in the majority far more often than any of his colleagues, dissenting in only seven of the fifty cases in which he participated; and in nineteen 5−4 decisions, Stewart's vote was determinative. Slightly less than half (43 percent) of the cases on the scale were decided C +, but the failure of the cases to break evenly cannot be attributed to Stewart. The division between C plus and minus decisions would have corresponded precisely to Stewart's scale position, except for the inconsistent negative votes of Black, Warren, and Brennan, in the bottom three C − cases near the middle of the scale. Brennan's inconsistency is of no particular interest; it occurred in a routine case of statutory interpretation involving the imposition of multiple sentences upon a federal criminal defendant. But the Black and Warren inconsistencies appeared in two of the "Sunday Closing Law Cases," *Gallagher* v. *Crown Kosher Super Market* and *Braunfeld* v. *Brown*, both decided on May 29, 1961. Many dispassionate observers will agree that the Black and Warren votes in these cases to uphold the constitutionality of the Massachusetts and Pennsylvania "blue laws," which upheld the principle of majority transgression of both the religious and the economic claims of the defendants, were clearly illiberal; and the fact that such votes appear as inconsistencies in the C scale should enhance confidence in the proposition that the C scale provides an adequate general measure of the civil libertarian sympathies of the justices....

[Schubert also presents findings for the Economic Liberalism Scale or E Scale and the Fiscal Claims or F Scale.]

SCALE AXES IN THE FACTOR SPACE

The next step is to position the scale axes, which are considered to be the psychological analogues of the cumulative scales, in the space defined by the factorial reference axes. It will be recalled that the configuration of i-points for the justices is uniquely determined by the set of factor loadings given in Table 1. The problem now is to determine whether it is possible to pass a set of axes through the factor space in such a manner that the rankings of the projections, from the i-points onto the axes, are equivalent, in a statistically acceptable sense, to the rankings of the justices on the scale axes. What is required mathematically in order to accomplish this are sets of weights which will determine the position of the axes in the space, and the points on each axis where the projections from the i-points fall. Given such data, it will then be possible to compare the rankings of the justices, on the cumulative scales, with the rankings of the projections from their i-points on the counterpart scale axes....

A TEST OF THE BASIC HYPOTHESIS

The principal hypothesis underlying this study is that differences in the attitudes of the justices toward the basic issues raised by the cases that the Court decides account for the differences in their voting. In short, Supreme Court justices vote as they do because of their attitudes toward the public policy issues that come before them. We are now in a position to make a statistical test of this hypothesis.

The i-points of the justices are separated in the factor space because of variance in the extent of majority participation of individual justices; but the factor analysis routine knows absolutely nothing about the subject matter of the values to which the decisions relate. The relative degrees of support by the justices of the key substantive issues can be determined by cumulative scaling; but cumulative scaling is a unidimensional measurement device, and each such scale is based upon a different universe of content, and is quite independent *methodologically* (as distinguished from psychologically) from every other scale. Moreover, the cumulative scale data are inadequate to permit the recovery of the configuration of the i-points in multidimensional space. We shall assume, therefore, that if the cumulative scales can be reconstituted as a set of scale axes whose position is consistent with the configuration of i-points in the factor space, then the attitudinal differences of the justices on the cumulative scales account for the variance in the voting behavior of the justices, which is represented by the spatial separation of their ideal-points in the multidimensional factor space. If the correspondence between the set of cumulative scales and their scale axis analogues can be established in accordance with accepted procedures of statistical proof, then we shall have proved, in a mathematical sense, that the justices of the Supreme Court vary in their voting behavior according to the differences in their attitudes toward the scale variables.

Table 2 presents a comparison of the cumulative scale scores, and the distances along the counterpart scale axes at which the i-points project...together with the corres-

TABLE 2
Correlation of Judicial Ranks on Scales and Scale Axes

C			E			F		
Axis	Ranks	Scale	Axis	Ranks	Scale	Axis	Ranks	Scale
.791	1 D 1	1.00	.308	4* D 1	1.00	.341	2* Bl 1	1.00
.614	2 Bl 2	.84	.752	1 Bl 2	.92	.474	1* Wa 2	.86
.609	3 Wa 3	.76	.749	2 Wa 3½	.44	.272	3 C 4	.71
.599	4 Br 4	.53	.498	3 Br 3½	.44	.263	4 Br 4	.71
−.104	5 S 5	−.02	−.116	5 C 5	.28	.205	6* F 4	.71
−.553	6 Wh 6	−.49	−.357	6 H 6	−.16	.251	5* H 6	.57
−.610	7 F 7½	−.76	−.406	7 S 7	−.40	−.232	8* S 7	.36
−.612	8 H 7½	−.76	−.409	8 F 8	−.68	−.081	7* Wh 8	.14
−.627	9 C 9	−.96	−.411	9 Wh 9	−1.00	−.256	9 D 9	−.89
Rank correlation coefficient (tau)	.986			.901			.870	
Significance level, 1-tailed (p)	<.000025			.00012			.00043	

* Inconsistent rankings.

ponding sets of rankings, for all justices on each of the three major variables. . . . [I]t has been determined experimentally that the error variance in the factor analysis routine is usually around 10 percent; while the error variance in the cumulative scales is only slightly less; and there are other sources of error variance implicit in the general method. Therefore, it seems reasonable to employ the nonparametric rank correlation test for the purpose of making the comparison. In spite of the seeming precision of coefficients carried to the third decimal place, it would be fatuous to pretend that the measurement employed in this study can hope to be more than a rough approximation of empirical reality.

As Table 2 indicates, there are no inconsistencies in the two sets of rankings for C. The correlation coefficient is less than +1.00 because of the tie in the scale scores of Frankfurter and Harlan, which increased very slightly the probability of perfect agreement

with another set of rankings. The correspondence between the two sets of rankings for E also is perfect, except for Douglas, whose loading on the scale axis is much too low to correspond well with his maximal scale score. . . .

. . . [T]he correlation between all three sets of rankings is very high. . . . From a statistical point of view, it should be noted that the probabilities shown in Table 2 relate to the probability of producing, by chance alone, the indicated congruence between any *one* scale and the point configuration. The prospect of chance replication of as good a fit for all three scales simultaneously, with the same fixed point configuration, is of course very much more remote; indeed, the joint probability, which is the product of the three discrete probabilities, is a truly astronomical number. . . approximately one chance in a trillion. It seems warranted, under these circumstances, to accept the hypothesis that the variance in the voting behavior of the justices during the 1960 Term can be adequately accounted for by the differences in their attitudes toward the fundamental issues of civil liberty, economic liberalism, and governmental fiscal authority.

THE PSYCHOLOGICAL DISTANCE SEPARATING THE JUSTICES

Taking the judicial ideal-points in the factor space as reasonably adequate symbolizations of the respective attitude syndromes of the individual justices, we can use them to examine one final question. Discussion about the justices frequently revolves around such questions as which ones tend to share the "same point of view," and which ones are "furthest apart" in their thinking. The factor space provides a convenient basis for objective measurement of the psychological distance which separates each justice from each of the others.

Since the measurement of these psychological distances is purely mathematical, we shall carry it out in five-dimensional space. . . .

[Schubert discusses the formula which we omit here.]

The result of [the] computations . . . [shows that] Harlan and Frankfurter are by far the closest two justices, in terms of their attitudes toward the policy issues that the Court decided in the 1960 Term; they are separated by a distance of only .14 in the five-dimensional factor space. Contrary to what even many close observers of the work of the Court seem to believe, however, it is Warren and Brennan—not Douglas and Black—who are next most similar in attitude, at a distance of .42 . . . . [T]he greatest difference in attitude is that between Douglas and Black, on the one hand, and Frankfurter and Harlan, on the other. . . . Moreover,

Douglas, Black, Warren, and Brennan all agree that Frankfurter and Harlan are the justices whose point of view is most different from their own; and, conversely, Harlan, Frankfurter, Whittaker, Clark, and Stewart all agree that Douglas and Black are the justices most distant psychologically from themselves.

If we seek an "average" justice whose point of view best typifies that of the Court as a whole, he is clearly Stewart. . . . The variation of Stewart's separation from his colleagues also is confined to the smallest range. Such a finding is perfectly consistent, of course, with the findings of scale analysis. . . . In similar accord with expectations is the finding that the most atypical justice was Douglas who . . . entertained the most generally extreme views of any of the justices. . . .

SUMMARY

The objective of this paper has been to demonstrate the utility, for a more accurate insight into the basic factors that underlie disagreement among Supreme Court justices, of a more rigorous psychological approach than has been characteristic of most discussion of their attitudes. The attention of scholars always has focused upon the values articulated in the opinions of the justices, and particularly in majority opinions; but much less attention has been given to the possibility that an examination of the voting behavior of the justices might provide a better and more reliable approach to the understanding of their attitudes than the study of opinions. Research during the last two decades has turned increasingly to the analysis of judicial voting records, in addition to opinion language; and reliance understandably has been placed, during what might well be termed the pioneering stages of the development of a science of judicial behavior, upon unidimensional models. These necessarily are limited in their capacity to represent adequately the complex interplay of attitudes in the mind of any human being. The time has now come when it may be appropriate for students of judicial behavior to consider the advantages to be gained by utilization of multidimensional models of the behavior of Supreme Court justices.

One such model, exemplified here, is suggested by recent (and ongoing) research in psychometrics. It proceeds on the premise that a justice reacts in his voting behavior to the stimuli presented by cases before the Court in accordance with his attitudes toward the issues raised for decision. This article has presented what is believed to be persuasive evidence that this is precisely what the justices were doing when they voted in the decisions of the 1960 Term.

NOTES

1. The phi coefficient is an approximation of the Pearsonian r correlation coefficient, and is appropriate to use when, as here, the two distributions to be correlated reflect a genuine dichotomy. . . .

2. Perhaps it should be noted, for the benefit of readers not familiar with the method, that orthogonal axes are statistically independent, while oblique axes are correlated with each other; therefore, making a factor interpretation based directly upon a system of orthogonal axes implies an assumption that there is no relationship among the factors, which must be conceived to be independent of each other. Applied to the present data, this would involve the assumption that there was no relationship, at least in the minds of the justices, among the major issues of public policy toward which they responded in their voting.

3. *Civil Liberties and the Vinson Court* (Chicago: University of Chicago Press, 1954), p. 227.

CHAPTER 11

Aspects of the Judicial Role

The concept of role has been developed by social psychologists. Role is related to the official position occupied by an individual. An individual's role concept consists of his or her views concerning the range of behavior that is compatible with the common understanding of how that role is to be performed.

Role theory has been adapted to the study of judicial decision making. There are some aspects of the judicial role about which there is a great deal of consensus among judges. For example, it is expected that: (1) judges will appear to be, and in fact will be impartial with respect to the disputants; (2) judges will acknowledge precedent and legally justify their decision; (3) judges will adhere to the obvious requirements and intent of the relevant (and presumably constitutional) statute.[1] However, there are other important facets of the judicial role about which there is considerably less agreement among judges. Our attention is focused in this chapter on one such facet, the proper scope of judicial decision making. Here, just as with judicial attitudes, the judge's view of the scope of the decision making role is considered a behavioral variable.

A judge's concept of the decision-making role is manifested by his or her judicial philosophy as explicitly stated by the judge in personal interviews, questionnaires completed by the judge, written opinions, or other writings, or as inferred from behavior. However, students of judicial behavior who have employed the role perspective have for the most part investigated concepts of decision-making role by conducting personal interviews with judges. The ways the role concept has been used in judicial research are discussed in the reading by James L. Gibson, who also offers his own research strategy.

Role is considered an important variable because it is believed that an individual's role concept is tied to the exercise of discretion and that the judge's concept of role can inhibit the full flowering of political attitudes and values. Indeed, the special position of *judge*, with its role constraints, makes *judicial* decision making different from legislative, bureaucratic, or executive decision making. The role of the judge is thought to be an important, even crucial variable in making courts unique conflict-managing institutions and judges the unique conflict managers they are.

The concept of role seems to be implicit in much of the attitudinal research. After all, the focus on certain kinds of decisions (nonunanimous and some unanimous) suggests that it is these cases that permit choices to be made within the framework of the judicial role (however it may be conceptualized by respective judges). For the attitudinalist, then, role is a given, differences in role perceptions are not explored, and the explanation of judicial behavior is in terms of *judicial* attitudes and values. For example, suppose that one judge has a self-limiting role concept and that another judge has a more expansive and creative concept of role. Both may swear to friends and colleagues alike that they are political liberals, but if the former usually is found on the negative side of civil liberties disputes while the latter primarily opts for the positive side of those same disputes, the former will emerge as a judicial conservative while the latter will be classified as a judicial liberal. Students of the judicial role have taken the position that while it is important to discover voting patterns in terms of attitudes and values, in order to get a better understanding of judicial behavior it is also important to discover how judges perceive their role.

Judicial role analyses have been most highly developed by students of state courts. Nonunanimous decisions on the state supreme courts are relatively infrequent. Whereas dissent rates on the United States Supreme Court have, in recent decades, typically been over 60 percent of the decisions on the merits, most state supreme courts have dissent rates that are less than 25 percent.[2] This means that the relatively sophisticated methodology developed to study the United States Supreme Court cannot for the most part be utilized for the analysis of judicial behavior on state supreme courts.

Two leading scholars of state court judicial behavior, Henry Glick and Kenneth Vines, pursued their interest in role analysis and, on the basis of the personal interviews they conducted with state supreme court judges, developed three basic role models according to which those judges could be classified:[3] the law maker, the law interpreter, and the pragmatist. These models are discussed in the selection by J. Woodford Howard, Jr., although he uses somewhat different classifications. Howard's "innovator" is Glick's and Vines's "law maker"; Howard's "realist" is Glick's and Vines's "pragmatist." The law interpreter role model is used in both studies. Howard's study is based on interviews with judges of federal courts of appeals for three circuits. Howard, however, went one step further than Glick and Vines and tied role concepts to judicial voting behavior.[4]

The selection by David O'Brien focuses on the United States Supreme Court but does not utilize the role models employed by Howard or Glick and Vines or considered by Gibson. Rather, O'Brien is concerned with the political charge made against the Supreme Court institutionally and the justices (and lower federal court judges) collectively that an expansive role concept (the "imperial judiciary") dominates their decision making. By examining the evidence objectively and dispassionately, O'Brien deflates the claims that federal judges in recent decades have expanded their role in an unprecedented fashion and have become "law makers" or "innovators" such as the nation has never seen. O'Brien's analysis places the broader issue of the role of the courts and the Supreme Court in particular in a larger perspective, a task much needed in an era when the Supreme Court and lower federal courts have been the focus of intense political debate.

NOTES

1. For a discussion of these and other aspects of the judicial role about which there appear to be a broad-based consensus, see Sheldon Goldman and Thomas P. Jahnige, *The Federal*

Courts as a Political System, 3rd ed. (New York: Harper & Row, 1985), pp. 162–169.

2. See Henry R. Glick and George W. Pruet, Jr., "Dissent in State Supreme Courts: Patterns and Correlates of Conflict," in Sheldon Goldman and Charles M. Lamb (eds.), *Judicial Conflict and Consensus: Behavioral Studies of American Appellate Courts* (Lexington, Kentucky: The University Press of Kentucky, 1986), pp. 199–214.

3. Henry R. Glick and Kenneth N. Vines, "Law-making in the State Judiciary: A Comparative Study of the Judicial Role in Four States," *Polity* 2 (1969), pp. 142–159.

4. Also see J. Woodford Howard, Jr., *Courts of Appeals in the Federal Judicial System* (Princeton N.J.: Princeton University Press, 1981).

The Role Concept in Judicial Research

James L. Gibson

Over the last two decades substantial research effort has been directed to applying role theory to the process of decision-making within judicial institutions. Role-theoretic approaches have been applied to both appellate and trial courts...and, although the principal focus has been upon judges, to actors other than judges.... Role concepts have been used as independent, dependent, and intervening variables, within a variety of settings, and with different substantive concerns. Few other theories have generated as much empirical research, nor have made as sweeping claims of applicability and generalizability.

Yet role theory to date has generated few empirical payoffs—the potential of the approach has not been realized. Most seriously, very little research has been successful in linking role concepts to actual decisional behavior. In part this stems from the preoccupation with typology building, although few of the efforts to test role-behavior hypotheses have been successful. As a heuristic device, role theory may have some utility: As a theory of decision-making,

Reprinted from *Law & Policy Quarterly* 3 (1981), pp. 291–308. All notes, and most references and tables omitted.

its utility has only rarely been demonstrated.

Why have role variables been such weak predictors? First, the dominant conceptualization of the manner in which role orientations influence behavior is inadequate. A direct, covariation relationship between role attributes and behavior is usually hypothesized. For instance, a typical hypothesis is that "activism" (a role orientation) is related to "liberal" decisions. Yet there is no theoretical structure supporting such a hypothesis—activism may be in favor of conservative values (e.g., the Hughes Court) or liberal values (e.g., the Warren Court). Thus, the relationship needs to be reconceptualized, and more appropriate statistical models need to be developed....

The second reason why role attributes have not been good predictors of behavior stems from the inadequate conceptualization and measurement of the role orientation construct. So much diversity exists in the way in which role orientations have been conceptualized and measured that it is not surprising that this area of research is rich in measurement problems, with inadequate consideration of the problems of validity, reliability, measurement error, and dimensionality. Without proper conceptualization and valid measurement, prediction and explanation of role behavior is nearly impossible. . . .

MAJOR ROLE CONCEPTS

To role theorists the most salient characteristic of decision-making within institutions is the constraint imposed on decision makers by the institutional context. These constraints on choices limit, but do not eliminate, discretion in the interest of advancing organizational objectives. Few institutions exist that do not attempt to circumscribe the alternatives available to the decision maker. Thus, role theory posits that individuals acting within institutions act differently than they act in noninstitutional settings; the context of their behavior influences how they behave. But precisely what elements of the context constrain behavior and how do the constraints operate?

Institutions can be defined in part by positions. That is, within every institution a number of formally defined positions exist. Within a judicial system the positions include those of "judge," "prosecutor," "defense attorney," and the like. Each of these is assigned particular responsibilities, and prescriptions and proscriptions (e.g., Code of Judicial Ethics) are attached to the position. Within role theory the position is known as a "role" and the particular person occupying the role is known as the "role incumbent" or "role occupant." Thus, the first set of constraints on behavior stems from the formal definition of the role itself.

Beyond this, however, the individuals with whom the role incumbents interact (known as "role alters") develop expectations of how the role incumbent should behave. Judges, for instance, are expected by others to act impartially; in the views of the role alters, a necessary component of the role of judge is impartial behavior. These expectations, which are normative, are referred to as "role expectations," and emanate from those who interact with the role occupant. By supplementing the formal requirements of the position, role expectations also constrain institutional behavior.

Individuals occupying institutional positions also develop beliefs about what constitutes proper behavior on their part. This belief is a "role orientation" and may stem from role expectations. More likely, role orientations represent a synthesis of perceptions of expectations and the occupants' own values. Role behavior is constrained by these role orientations.

According to role theory, role behavior is to some extent a function of the role orientation of the role occupant. Most research therefore focuses upon role orientations as the key determinant of behavior. Although differing greatly in operational approaches, researchers define role orientations as varying in the degree to which the judge feels bound to adhere to precedents, constitutions, and statutes in making decisions. "Adherence" includes "following" precedents, "strict construction" of constitutions, and deference to "legislative intent." In essence, the role orientation construct represents a unidimensional continuum of legitimate discretion in decision making—the degree to which legitimate opportunities for decisional creativity exist.

MEASURES OF ROLE ORIENTATIONS

Four approaches to measuring role orientations characterize this research: (1) inferences from the decisional behavior of judges; (2) typologies based on open-ended questions; (3) self-reports of the influence of certain stimuli on decisions; and (4) multi-item scales. Each of these approaches has several liabilities which severely limit its utility.

Inferential Approaches

The inferential approach is a direct extension of attitudinal research on appellate courts. Because interviews with judges were thought to be difficult to secure, the researchers had to make inferences from the observed decisional behavior of judges to their role orientations.... [S]tatistical examination of the process by which judges make decisions is used to infer the existence of particular role orientations.

In the absence of interview data this approach is necessary, and indeed, a conceptual approach that emphasizes *how* decisions are made is extremely useful (see below). However, several limitations are imposed on the analysis when *independent* measures of role orientations and behavior are not available. In particular, the *degree* to which role orientations are related to behavior cannot be specified. Indeed, the hypothesis that role attributes and behavior are unrelated cannot be tested. Nor can the relative impact of role orientations and other possible determinants of behavior be estimated. Finally, it is not possible to test sophisticated models (e.g., interactive, curvilinear, and similar relationships) of the process through which role orientations influence behavior. This approach, though necessary under some conditions, is suboptimal—a much more direct measurement strategy is needed.

Open-Ended Typologies

Research in the 1960s demonstrated that some judges can indeed be interviewed. The earliest interview measures of role orientations adopted open-ended measures that essentially asked judges to characterize the nature of their decisional process....

Perhaps the most enduring set of categories of judges' role orientations emerging from this research is the "law making" versus "law interpretation" distinction. As opposite ends of a continuum measuring decisional role orientations, these categories purport to identify "activist" and "restraintist" judges. However, a number of conceptual and methodological problems exist, making it unclear just what the lawmaker-law interpreter typology measures. Consider statements by a judge Vines considers to be prototypic of law interpreters:

> I think that it is terrible that judges interpret the laws or the Constitution in accordance with what they think it should be instead of interpreting the language of the Constitution or the statute.... The United States Supreme Court and other state courts, too, have set themselves up as some sort of super-Congress, and they interpret the Constitution to mean what they think it should say. That's a violation of the separation of powers [Vines, 1969: 475].

It is clear that this judge believes that interpreting the "language of the Constitution or the statute" is not only desirable but possible. In this respect he is at odds with legal realists who believe that precedents and statutes and even constitutions are ambiguous, conflicting and generally capable of providing only post hoc rationalization and legitimation of decisions. On the other hand, the lawmaker asserts:

> Inevitably, a judge makes law as does a legislative body. No matter how you decide a case, you're making law.... That whole idea about whether a judge makes law or whether he found what the law always was by looking somewhere up in the blue is not true. Judges always made law and always will.... In interpretation you're trying to give answers to problems that were not considered by the legislature, and you try to guess what the legislature would have thought had they thought about this problem. But you get away from this quickly. What do you do

when you get a question like this? You can't send it back to the legislature for a decision.... The question comes up, and you decide it [Vines, 1969: 475–476].

This judge is *not* necessarily making a normative statement about the desirability of law interpretation but instead is arguing, as a realist would, the empirical position that judges *cannot* make decisions on the basis of precedents, statutes and constitutions. In fact, it is possible that disagreement between "lawmakers" and "law interpreters" is largely over the *empirical* question of the degree to which precedents, statutes and constitutions allow logically deducible decisions, rather than over the normative question of what a judge ought to do. Because role orientations represent normative positions it is imperative that the analyst maintain the distinction between "is" and "ought."

In addition to the conceptual problem, measurement deficiencies exist. First, the question generates little variance among judges.... Most studies have revealed that a majority of judges are "law interpreters," but it is extremely unlikely that judges are as homogeneous as the responses to this question make them appear. Instead there is probably substantial variation in the beliefs of "interpreters" about what constitutes the proper bounds of "interpretation," variation which is critically important to understanding the decisions of the judges.

Because the format of this question is open-ended, serious threats to reliability also exist. Even though coding open-ended responses is a perilous task, intercoder reliability coefficients are rarely reported (and are somewhat disconcerting when they *are* reported: e.g., Howard, 1977: 926). This approach also makes comparison across studies difficult, especially since there is no evidence that different researchers use a standardized set of coding instructions.

(Note that the most rigorous coding procedure—Howard's—resulted in the largest percentage of "mixed" orientations.) Finally, the question results only in a trichotomy (and one that may not even be an ordinal measure), ignoring gradations within each category. While there are some advantages to open-ended questions at exploratory stages of research, the potential for judges to give self-serving, traditional and largely symbolic responses is quite high.

Self-Reports Decision-Making

A second major interview-based approach to judges' role orientations comes out of Becker's (1966) research on Hawaiian judges. Becker's measure reads: "How influential do you believe the following factors to be in your deciding case?" and includes in the list of factors: "highly respected advocate (as a lawyer)," "my view of justice in the case," "what the public needs, as the times may demand," "precedent, when clear and directly relevant," "common sense," "highly respected advocate (as a member of the community)," "what the public demands" and "other." It is similar to the lawmaker-law interpreter typology in that its main concern is with the role of precedent in judges' decisions. Becker reports that 43% of the judges who rated "precedent, when clear and directly relevant" at the highest point on the scale ("extremely influential") decided a simulated case "objectively" (i.e., consistent with a "clear and directly relevant precedent"). Presumably, the objective decision was contrary to the preferences of the judges. Of the judges rating "precedent" as less than extremely influential, only 13% decided "objectively". There is also some relationship between the judges' responses to "my view of justice" and "common sense" and a propensity to decide objectively.

This question suffers from the same short-comings of the openended measure of role orientations, but also has unique difficulties. First, there is very little variance in the responses to the question. Over 90% of the judges in Becker's study rated "precedent" as "extremely" or "very" influential, and the remaining two judges rated it as "influential." The variance of the responses to this item is smaller than the variance for any of the other items. Becker's analysis is based in part on dichotomizing the judges into two groups: those who rated precedent as "extremely influential" and those who rated precedent as "very influential" or as just "influential." This seems a rather artificial division point, one which is dictated by the lack of variance in the responses rather than by a theoretical concern. Again, it seems possible that a great amount of within-group variance still exists.

Perhaps a more significant problem with the measure lies in its lack of conceptualization. What does it mean to say that a judge is strongly oriented toward precedent? Is this a measure of activism-restraintism? If strong precedent orientation is one end of the continuum, what is the other end? Does a weak precedent orientation necessarily mean that judges rely on their own values in making decisions? What about the numerous instances of judicial decision-making in which precedent has little if any relevance (e.g., sentencing, bail, questions of fact, certiorari decisions, and so on)? Indeed, further examination of the responses of the Hawaiian judges indicates that responses to "precedent" are most strongly correlated with responses to what the public demands ($r = -.38$; computed from the data presented in Becker, 1966: 679). However, Becker essentially argues a "subjective-objective" dimension to this role orientation, with the dimension presumably bounded by precedent and subjective criteria such as common sense and the judge's own view of justice. But the correlations of the precedent responses with these two criteria are .12 and $-.04$, respectively. . . .

One further problem arises with the Becker measure of role orientations. The question requires judges to determine how influential several decisional criteria *actually are* in their decision calculus. As such the question is empirical and nonnormative. The proper form of the question, if it is to be used as a measure of role orientations, should express valuation of each of the criteria—the question should ask how influential the criteria *should* be. Much, however, of what is known about judges' role orientations is based on this question.

Scales

The last of the approaches to measuring judges' role orientations is that of multi-item inventories. Scales of this type have a number of advantages: the response sets are closed-ended; the use of multiple indicators reduces the impact of measurement error; and continuous ordinal or interval level scale scores can be generated. However, just as with the other approaches, the conceptualization of the orientation idea is crucial. Operationalization and scaling techniques are also somewhat more complex.

. . .

. . . [A] new conceptualization and a new operationalization of role orientations is in order. There is no doubt that precedent is a quite important element of judicial role orientations and any new measure must be sensitive to this. However, researchers must be very careful in measuring role orientations with precedent questions: the highly abstract notion of "following precedent" may have virtually no impact on how judges feel about making decisions. Few judges, even activists, are likely to publicly disavow precedent; as legal realists have asserted for years, the abstract commitment to precedent may be compatible with any of the variety of styles of dealing with precedents in making decisions. The more important question is the degree to which judges believe it legitimate to manipulate precedent to achieve the decision results they prefer. Any reconceptualization should be sensitive to this fact.

A RECONCEPTUALIZATION OF ROLE ORIENTATIONS

The position of judge is incredibly complex. Consequently, judges' beliefs about the limits of proper behavior are also complex. Simplistic typologies of role orientations, such as the lawmaker-law interpreter distinction and orientation toward precedent, are unlikely to be of much utility for understanding judges' role orientations or behavior. Instead, it is necessary to reconceptualize role orientations, as well as the process that relates them to role behavior. If such a reconceptualization is possible, perhaps role theory can live up to its advance billing.

Judges' role orientations are their beliefs about the kind of behavior that is proper for a judge. In the case of decisional role orientations, the beliefs concern proper decision behavior. "Proper" does not, however, refer as much to the policy content of the behavior as it does to the *process* of decision-making and, in particular, to the kinds of stimuli that influence decisions. A decisional role orientation identifies for the judge the criteria that are legitimate for proper decision-making. Some judges may believe it proper to be influenced by a particular stimulus while other judges regard it as improper. More generally, judges vary in the breadth of stimuli they deem legitimate.

Such a conceptualization of role orientations is compatible with the traditional norms for judging. A central expectation of judicial and legal traditions concerns the decision-making criteria employed by judges. For instance, equality before the law is not an empirical statement; it does not assert that individual litigants are in fact equal. Rather, the phrase is an exhortation to ignore the variables (stimuli), such as power, on which litigants are unequal and render decisions only on variables that provide for equality. For instance, it is generally regarded as illegitimate to discriminate on the basis of social class in sentencing decisions. This means that it is illegitimate to allow the social class of the defendant to influence the decision: class should be weighted at zero. Similarly, such concepts as the presumption of innocence in criminal cases are expectations that court officials will not allow empirical stimuli relating to the factual guilt of the defendant to influence their pretrial decisions (e.g., bail). The presumption of innocence is a norm which defines some criteria of decision-making as proper and others as improper....

Thus, the basic function of decisional role orientations is to specify which variables can legitimately be allowed to influence decision-making, and in the case of conflict, what priorities to assign to different decision-making criteria. Role orientations are conceptualized as normative weights attached by each judge to different decisional stimuli. A stimulus viewed as illegitimate therefore would receive a weight of zero. Like cue theory...and fact pattern analysis... decision-making is viewed as a process of combining bits of information to form a choice. Unlike these approaches, however, role theory posits that the primary basis for assigning weights is normative.

While this conceptualization is more general and theoretical, it is not entirely incompatible with the lawmaking-law interpretation and precedent approaches. Lawmakers, it might be hypothesized, rely on more and different criteria for decision making than law interpreters. They might consider social injustice as a legitimate criterion upon which decision can be based. Law interpreters probably view social injustice as a less legitimate, and possibly as even illegitimate, basis for decision-making. The law interpreter would surely assign greater weight to precedents, statutes and constitutions. Generally, lawmakers would rely on extralegal decisional criteria while law interpreters would rely on strictly legal criteria as much as possible. But although this notion of role orientations is compatible with the lawmaking-interpreting and precedent approaches, it has the advantage of being more general (incorporating all criteria, not just precedents, statutes and constitutions), and also provides a more theoretical basis for expecting role orientations to influence role behavior. . . .

OPERATIONALIZING ROLE ORIENTATIONS

One approach to measuring role orientations might be to ask judges to rate a large number of decisional stimuli in terms of the degree of legitimate influence on decisions. In some contexts this approach may be useful. However, less lengthy scales can be developed by taking advantage of the highly salient and symbolic positions of precedent and ideology in the American legal system. Because these decisional criteria are so fundamental to the legal process, beliefs about their proper role in decision-making can serve as a useful summary measure of role orientations. The data in Table 1 report the responses of a group of California and Iowa judges to a set of items designed to measure role orientations from this perspective.

Several aspects of these data are worthy of discussion. First, the responses of the two groups of judges are generally similar. Only the last item generated substantially different response patterns—overall the statements seem to be tapping the same dimension. This conclusion is reinforced by the results of a nonmetric multidimensional scaling of the items: The configurations generated for the two groups of judges are remarkably similar. . . . Although the response frequencies may be subject to minor intergroup variation the pattern of responses, as represented in the scaling results, is quite similar. . . .

Very considerable variation across items also exists. The "easiest" item to accept is number 1: Significant majorities of both groups agree that good judges follow precedents. Yet what does the response to this item mean? A quite significant proportion of these judges believe that "precedents" should not and do not limit the degree to which a judge's own views influence their decisions. One half of the total group believes it possible to find a precedent compatible with the judges' own view of justice, while one-third openly assert the legitimacy of such a decisional strategy. Thus, questions that reference "precedent" in a very general way tend to produce a "restraintist" consensus. This consensus, however, is illusory and therefore it is essential to use multiple indicators.

The concept measured by these six items is a general orientation toward a style of decision-making. Judges at one end of the scale perceive it legitimate to use considerable discretion in making decisions whereas judges at the opposite end of the dimension reject discretion in favor of deference to precedents, constitutions, and so on. The first group of judges are probably more "results" oriented than the "process" oriented group and therefore may be termed "lawmakers" or "activists." This general, normative orientation toward discretion is an extremely important part of the judicial role. . . .

TABLE 1
Scale for Measuring Precedent Role Orientations—Iowa and California Trial Judges

Item	Response (in percentages)[a]			
	Agree Strongly	Agree	Disagree	Disagree Strongly
1. A good judge is one who sticks as closely to precedents as possible.				
California	40.5	37.8	16.2	2.7
Iowa	23.1	65.4	7.7	0
2. Judges should be allowed great discretion in decision making to insure that their decisions are "just."				
California	18.9	48.6	27.0	5.4
Iowa	34.6	46.2	15.4	0
3. It is wrong for a judge to allow his personal philosophy to influence his decisions				
California	21.6	29.7	40.5	8.1
Iowa	23.1	46.2	23.1	3.8
4. Precedents are rarely conclusive: usually a judge can find a precedent which supports his own point of view.				
California	13.5	43.2	37.8	5.4
Iowa	3.8	34.6	43.3	11.5
5. Precedents and statutes are only a few of the factors which should influence judges' decisions.				
California	5.4	35.1	40.5	18.9
Iowa	11.5	69.2	19.2	0
6. It is just as legitimate to make a decision and then find the precedent as it is to find the precedent and then make the decision.				
California	5.4	35.1	43.2	16.2
Iowa	7.7	15.4	50.0	15.4

[a] The Ns are: California, 37; Iowa, 26.

In summary, this scale has several advantages over previous instruments: (1) its format is closed-ended; (2) it is a multiple item measure, with considerable variation on the items; (3) it is unidimensional; and (4) the measure has generated reasonably stable response patterns across two different groups of judges.

CONCLUSIONS

The purpose of this article has been to investigate the utility of the measures used in one area of research on decision-making in the legal process. After identifying a number of conceptual and operational problems with extant uses of the concept "role orientation," a new measure has been proposed. The measure is based on a conceptualization of role orientations as beliefs about the legitimacy of relying on various criteria in making decisions. The dimension identified may be thought of as an "activist-restraintist" dimension, although not in the traditional sense in which it has been applied to the Supreme Court. Instead, the continuum represents the degree of willingness to move beyond (for any purpose) strictly legal criteria in making decisions; that is, the degree of perceived (legitimate) constraint on decisions imposed by legal factors. While the empirical measure reported in this article focuses heavily on "precedent" as the major legal constraint, this is only because of its symbolic importance. Many other constraints exist and a number of types of decisions within the judicial process have nothing to do with precedent. However, due to its central and highly symbolic position within common law thought, and given the empirical results, it is clear that the belief being tapped by the items is a more general orientation toward discretionary versus "legal" decision-making, and indeed it

has been demonstrated that the measure strongly predicts the *sentencing* behavior of *trial* court judges (see Gibson, 1978). Such an approach to role orientations is sufficiently general that it is likely to be useful within a variety of judicial contexts....

REFERENCES

Becker, T.L. (1966) "A survey study of Hawaiian judges: the effect on decisions of judicial role variations," *Amer. Pol. Sci. Rev.* 60 (September): 677–686.

Gibson, J.L. (1978) "Judges' role orientation, attitudes and decisions: an interactive model." *Amer. Pol. Sci. Rev.* 72 (September): 911–924.

Howard, J.W., Jr. (1977) "Role perceptions and behavior in three U.S. Courts of Appeals." *J. of Politics* 6 (November): 916–938.

Vines, K.N. (1969) "The judicial role in the American states: an exploration," pp. 461–485 in J. Grossman and J. Tanenhaus (eds.) Frontiers of Judicial Research. New York: John Wiley.

Role Perceptions and Behavior in Three U.S. Courts of Appeals

J. Woodford Howard, Jr.

The concept of "judicial role" refers to normative expectations shared by judges and related actors regarding how a given judicial office should be performed. Scholars have long debated whether judges' perceptions of these norms influence judicial decisions. . . .

The purpose of this paper is to explore the relationships among judicial role perceptions and voting behavior in three leading intermediate tribunals—United States Courts of Appeals for the Second, Fifth, and District of Columbia Circuits—against a backdrop of the political orientations of their members. . . .

The data concerning political values and role perceptions are derived from off-the-record interviews conducted by the author with 35 active and senior circuit judges of the three tribunals during 1969–71. The voting data are derived from analysis of all decisions by the three tribunals after hearing or submission during FY 1965–67 (N = 4,941), roughly 40% of total cases so decided by U.S. circuit courts in this period. Thirty judges, slightly less than a third of total federal circuit judges, participated in both the interviews and decisions. . . .

"Role Perceptions and Behavior in Three U.S. Courts of Appeals," J. Woodford Howard, Jr. Reprinted from the Journal of Politics, Vol. 39, No. 4, November 1977. Copyright by the Southern Political Science Association. By permission of author and the University of Texas Press. Most footnotes have been omitted.

ROLE PERCEPTIONS

These judges shared a strong consensus, heavily influenced by official and professional prescriptions, that their central mission is to adjudicate appeals as agents of the national government. Little disagreement also existed about their duty to enforce the laws of Congress, Supreme Court, and their circuits. Considerable tension emerged, nonetheless, over the proper scope of judicial lawmaking in an estimated tenth of their cases having innovative potential. The appropriate limits of judicial creativity, to one judge "the stinking question," was clearly a highly salient issue, especially in the Fifth and D.C. Circuits.

Whereas studies of state legislatures and Congress indicate that role conflicts among legislators center on the purposes of representation, accumulating studies of judges suggest that the sharpest role conflicts in American appellate courts concern judges' functions as legislators. However, it is important to note that these federal circuit judges, unlike some members of state supreme courts, differed over issues of degree rather than of kind. Virtually all of them agreed that, while bold policy ventures such as *Brown* v. *Board of Education* should be left to the high court or Congress, *stare decisis* is "not an unbreakable rule." Within these extremes, their responses to questions concerning the

TABLE 1
Attitudes toward Judicial Lawmaking

Circuit	Innovator N	Realist N	Interpreter N	Other N	Total N
Second	0	8	1	1	10
Fifth	2	9	6	0	17
D.C.	3	3	2	0	8
Sums	5	20	9	1	35

propriety of judicial innovation fell into three broad groupings along a continuum which for convenience are summarized in Table 1 as ideal types.[1]

Innovator

Five judges left the impression that they felt obliged to make law " whenever the opportunity occurs." Creative opportunities were usually described as legal vacuums created by unclear precedents, unanticipated situations, and political stalemates. In aiding the Supreme Court, Innovators also emphasized their filtering or "gatekeeping" functions less than their lawmaking. As one senior circuit judge declared:

> The Supreme Court cannot be expected to be supermen. The Courts of Appeals should take a definite lead in innovating in the law—even at the risk of being overruled. Of course, we've got to be cautious, but we shouldn't leave it to the Supreme Court.... Courts of Appeals are a laboratory to try out ideas on a regional basis.

The most unqualified expression of this view came from a jurist who considered the best part of the job to be "launching new ideas." Did this mean that circuit courts participate in policy formation? "Certainly," he said. "And the greatest abuse of power is failure to exercise it."

Interpreter

At the opposite pole were nine judges who emphasized that judicial lawmaking should be held to a minimum. Two judges, harboring a "phobia" against "the modern trend of judicial legislation," bitterly denounced jurists who "can't wait for the people's representatives; they must seize power for themselves." "Activism," a term the interviewer avoided, was a favorite pejorative, which one judge defined as follows:

> It means 15% concentration on personal justice, about 20% on sociological values, 20% on psychiatry, 15% on economics and on through the social sciences. An activist is a kind of Leonardo, a master of many crafts. Nonactivists believe courts are confined to the law of cases. I am a nonactivist, which means of course that I am a reactionary. I believe courts should confine themselves to legal problems. You know where that places me on the animal farm, among progressive sheep and reactionary goats.

Only one judge, a Southern newcomer, unqualifiedly endorsed the view that judges should merely interpret the law, a traditional conception of judicial duty still prominent on several state supreme courts and trial courts. Recognizing that lacunae inevitably occur in statutes and case law, these judges objected most to courts reaching out "beyond the case" to legislate. Almost a paradigm of modern "strict constructionism" was this soliloquy from a Nixon appointee:

> I certainly do have views on that. There is a lawmaking power in every judge, whether he likes it or not. It is inescapable. You can't just leave the law blank because Congress did. To that extent the judges fill in the gaps to determine the rights of parties and get on to decisions. You can't be a pink funk and do nothing!
>
> However [with emphasis], the judge should avoid this process whenever possible. He should leave innovation within the confines of the particular case and leave wholesale innovation to the legislature, where Madison said it should be left.... Some judges just go way out of line beyond the case.... It's a grand forum, you know. The opinions get printed. Lawyers have to read them. Some judges just can't resist temptation. I call it diarrhea of the pen.

Realist

Almost two-thirds of these circuit judges, including the majority of the Fifth Circuit and all but one member of the Second Circuit, took middle positions, recognizing more demands for judicial creativity than Interpreters and more restraints than Innovators. Like Innovators, Realists saw no conflict with *stare decisis* when precedent is ambiguous or "when Congress abdicates." Like Interpreters, Realists cautioned against anticipating the Justices and emphasized "the professional way" of initiating legal change. What distinguished Realists from the other judges was their common tendency, when acknowledging legislative responsibilities, to differentiate carefully various types of judicial lawmaking and appropriate occasions for innovation. For example, several judges saw more room for creativity in civil rights than in commercial law, which requires planning

and stable rules, and attributed the conservatism of the Second Circuit to its heavy commercial docket. A few judges, following Karl Llewellyn, stressed the innovative potential of "shaping the rules to the facts." Others, shading close to Interpreters, believed that judicial policy-making should be restricted to the Judicial Conference and the Supreme Court's power to define procedural rules.

. . .

This summary scarcely captures the subtlety with which these jurists pondered the dilemmas of lawmaking by intermediate courts in a federal republic. But it helps to delimit the problems of relating roles and behavior in circuit courts. On the one hand, these judges plainly shared what Chief Justice Burger has called a "basic divergence between two schools of thought among professors, lawyers and judges as to the proper role of judges," a divergence ranging from emphasis on precedent and the status quo to innovation and policy-making. On the other hand, they differed over issues of degree within a relatively narrow range of creative opportunities. Despite a robust commitment to rendering justice in individual cases, and recognition that Supreme Court reversal is rare in practice, nearly all of them manifested strong precedent orientations. Most agreed further that, lacking docket control, their opportunity to fashion new legal rules seldom exceeds a tenth of their cases. Though they may disagree as to what cases properly constitute the fertile tenth, these judges felt obliged to lead as well as to follow. Hence, their conflicts over judicial lawmaking are inadequately captured by such popular dichotomies as "activism" versus "restraint," or the so-called "objective" role of adherence to precedent versus subjective preference....

Because circuit judges are called upon to reconcile values of continuity and change in adjudication, usually in advance of the Justices and with little assurance that their mistakes will be corrected, tension is inherent in their positions. Strain among expectations *within* a role perhaps characterizes their situation better than does the concept of conflict *between* roles. In any event, ambiguity of appropriate limits on lawmaking by intermediate courts softens the control of received interpretations and elevates the significance of situational factors in decision-making. *Stare decisis* is thus an "open norm," to use Richard Lempert's term, which cannot specify precise forms of action in all cases.[2] When norms are open to further specification, individuals or groups can establish socially approved rules of conduct of greater particularity. That is why these jurists often illustrated their disputes over lawmaking with specific issues, e.g., problems of criminal responsibility in the D.C. Circuit or race relations in the Fifth Circuit, in which policy conflicts were sharp and the law in flux. When judges are free to choose, personalities, predilections, and group relations perforce fill the void. Open or ambiguous roles inevitably enlarge the personal discretion of judges.

POLITICAL ORIENTATIONS

What then guides a circuit judge's conception of judicial duty when rules and roles are unclear? Of the welter of factors that may bear on this issue—psychological, social, institutional—we shall focus on political and professional values. Both are central to popular theories of the judicial process. According to political interpretations, judicial decisions are heavily influenced by the political philosophies that judges bring to the bench. In legal theory, contrarily, professional norms control political and other personal preferences. The trouble with these formulations is that political orientations and role conceptions are not mutually exclusive. In plumbing the sources of role conceptions among these circuit judges, for instance, we find intriguing associations among the judges' political orientations before ascending the bench and their attitudes toward judicial lawmaking. . . . [T]he dotted squares in Table 2 show that role conceptions, unlike party or participation variables, ran in the same direction as self-estimated political orientations. Four of the five Innovators identified themselves as having been political liberals before becoming federal judges; only one of nine Interpreters did so. A single Innovator called himself a former political conservative, perhaps as a joke. Otherwise, the large majority were men in the middle, self-styled moderates before becoming jurists, who likewise straddled the conflict over lawmaking.

The fuzziness of both political and role categories, not to mention the small number of judges involved, warns against pushing attitudinal associations very far. The data do not prove that philosophies of the judicial function are berobed political ideologies. Yet, on the whole, these jurists tended to favor conceptions of judicial role in accord with their prior political convictions. Hardly surprising given the realities of their recruitment, this connection is an important link among personal values and the judicial process. Because the socialization of American judges is largely informal and anticipatory, in contrast to jurists in France, federal circuit judges are expected to learn their roles largely via experiences prior to appointment. Their perceptions of judicial duty are likely to interact with their prior political beliefs, because both sets of values develop from the same antecedent experiences.

Political values thus pervade the world of circuit judges as well as other political elites. Their philosophies of politics and the judi-

TABLE 2
Political Backgrounds of Circuit Judges and Attitudes toward Judicial Lawmaking

Political Background Characteristic	Attitudes toward Judicial Lawmaking			
	Innovator N (5)	Realist N (20)	Interpreter N (9)	Total N (35)*
Political Party Affiliation				
Democrat	4	13	4	22*
Republican	1	6	4	11
Other	0	1	1	2
Political Participation				
Voter only	0	3	2	5
Party worker	0	2	3	5
Party official	3	6	1	10
Candidate**	2	9	3	15*
Political Values before Appointment				
Conservative	1	0	3	4
Moderate	0	11	4	16*
Moderate-liberal	1	0	1	2
Liberal	3	5	0	8
Other	0	4	1	5

* Includes one unscorable response.
** Includes 1 Innovator and 2 Realists who were candidates for party posts only.

cial function, notwithstanding official efforts to separate the two, *are* entwined in resolving and rationalizing the normative ambiguities of their work.

VALUES AND VOTES

The proof of the pudding is whether...role conceptions affect adjudication....

The reader should keep in mind the many pitfalls confronting efforts to answer this question. Theoretically, a person's...role perceptions are but single aspects of a vast cognitive network, which may be rooted in the irrational. Even discounting disparities between what people say and think, a direct relationship is seldom to be expected among an individual's social roles, role perceptions, and conduct.

Methodological problems compound the difficulty of establishing links. The most formidable are subjectivity in classifications, a multiplicity of competing variables (e.g., collegial decision-making or personality) intervening between general attitudes and specific choices, and the lack of transitivity among aggregated votes. Panel techniques were used to reduce the subjectivity of inferred role perceptions, but disagreement among the author and two assistants regarding 6 of 35 judges on both margins of the Realist category indicate that standardization of terms remains a serious problem in judicial role analysis.... Equally problematic is the assumption that votes accurately mirror individual attitudes on collegial courts, where "give and take" is also expected. More troublesome is violating the assumption of transitivity (i.e., that all judges participated in the same cases) for purposes of aggregation in rotating courts. Even though this study rests on a sample of over 5,000 votes, relaxation of transitivity standards proved necessary because panel rotation and low dissent rates on these courts yielded frequencies too small for conventional analysis of variance of different subjects and individuals. Finally, the difficulty of isolating the cases that comprise the creative opportunities of circuit judges precluded testing of judicial role perceptions in exclusively lawmaking situations.

...Still, for exploratory purposes it is useful to establish whether general... professional predispositions are related to aggregate voting behavior.... For this purpose the judges'...attitudes toward judicial lawmaking were compared with the policy outcomes of their votes in selected subjects.

Few concepts in the American political lexicon are more elusive than "liberal" and "conservative." While these jurists readily classified their prior political values on a liberal-conservative continuum, they often affirmed common observations that neither label describes a unitary ideology but rather a cluster of attitudes toward different policy referents. To capture some of this complexity, broad policy subjects are differentiated in Table 3 which compares the...role perceptions of these jurists with the outcome of their votes during FY 1965–67....

...Assuming that role conceptions were in fact related to political values evident in circuit decisions, as popularly assumed during the era of the Warren Court and implied by the overlapping attitudes in Table 2, Innovators should have been more likely than Interpreters to favor workers and claimants in injuries cases, public rights in patent and copyright cases, and the government in NLRB and tax cases. Innovators more than other judges also would be

expected to favor individuals in civil rights, prisoner petitions, and criminal cases.

The distribution of votes in Table 3 offers moderate support for the proposition that Innovators generally were more libertarian in voting behavior than were Realists and Interpreters. The evidence bolsters confidence especially in the distinction between Innovators and Interpreters and in the association of Innovators on the Courts of Appeals with "libertarian activism."... [D]ifferences among Innovators and the other judges were statistically significant when role perceptions were compared with mean percentages of liberal voting per judge.... [T]he direction of voting between the two groups of judges followed the liberal-conservative continuum in every field save the ideologically elusive subject of income tax. Furthermore, the strongest overlap among role conceptions and voting behavior occurred precisely in subjects, e.g., civil rights and criminal justice, with which the judges illustrated their disputes over lawmaking. In criminal appeals Innovators favored defendants more than did Interpreters by a 2 to 1 margin. The odds that this occurred by chance were less than 1-in-1,000.

Granted, judges and cases are not fungible. Given the size of the voting universe and the low levels of dissensus in these courts, even these modest relationships are among the most positive associations yet uncovered between judicial role perceptions and aggregate voting behavior....

CONCLUSIONS

A classic question in the theory of judicial decision is whether judging is "political behavior" or "judicial role behavior." The short answer from this study is a qualified neither. The basic findings are that fairly uniform political orientations and role

TABLE 3
Attitudes toward Judicial Lawmaking and Votes in Selected Subjects FY 1965–1967

	Attitudes toward Judicial Lawmaking								
	Innovator (5)		Realist (19)		Interpreter (6)		Total (30)		
Subject	Votes %	(N)	Votes %	(N)	Votes %	(N)	Votes %	(N)	
Employee Injury pro-employee	63.5	(52)	57.8	(211)	58.5	(118)	58.8	(381)	$X^2 = 0.56, p > .70$ $\gamma = .038$
Other Personal Injury pro-claimant	54.2	(72)	44.2	(265)	45.2	(104)	46.0	(441)	$X^2 = 2.32, p > .30$ $\gamma = .085$
Patent & Copyright anti-claimant	61.5	(39)	65.9	(129)	54.3	(35)	63.1	(203)	$X^2 = 1.64, p > .30$ $\gamma = .078$
Labor-Management defer to agency	64.5	(110)	61.7	(311)	55.5	(108)	61.1	(529)	$X^2 = 2.0, p > .30$ $\gamma = .108$
Income Tax pro-government	69.1	(94)	73.9	(307)	69.8	(106)	72.2	(507)	$X^2 = 1.2, p > .50$ $\gamma = (-).004$
Civil Rights pro-individual	65.4	(81)	57.1	(238)	48.4	(95)	56.8	(414)	$X^2 = 5.19, p > .05$ $\gamma = .200$
Prisoner Petitions pro-individual	34.1	(226)	25.3	(688)	23.3	(231)	26.6	(1,145)	$X^2 = 8.29, p < .02$ $\gamma = .153$
Criminal pro-individual	35.6	(368)	22.0	(1,132)	17.1	(374)	23.7	(1,874)	$X^2 = 39.6, p < .001$ $\gamma = .282$
		(1,042)		(3,281)		(1,171)		(5,494)	
Sums	47.3		39.7		37.0		40.6		

df 2
γ = Goodman-Kruskal gamma

perceptions prevailed on three major Courts of Appeals, though substantial tension flourished among circuit judges over their lawmaking roles. The judges' role perceptions and their past political orientations were related at perceptual levels, suggesting interaction among political and professional attitudes in their socialization. . . . In general, different role perceptions, though untested in exclusively lawmaking situations, were moderately associated with liberal-conservative voting behavior. . . . Especially was this so of Innovators who, on circuit courts as on the Supreme Court during this period, gravitated toward "libertarian activism" in civil rights and criminal justice. . . .

These conclusions . . . have several implications for students of the judiciary. First, judicial role perceptions in the three courts appear neither so weak as to be subsumed under personal preferences nor so strong as to be considered "the most significant single factor in the whole decisional process." Federal circuit judges enjoy more discretion to make policy than presumed in deterministic theories of judicial decision, whatever the postulated control.

Second, these mixed results should not cast a plague on political or professional theories of judicial decision-making, but point up the need to refine both by developing finer measures of political and professional ideologies and by differentiating conditions under which they may be expected to affect judicial behavior in different courts. Contrasting role perceptions among the judges of these circuits and state supreme courts, for example, shake the notion that a uniform role structure controls American judges, irrespective of jurisdiction, organizational level, or political environment. Capturing such differences will aggravate dilemmas of measurement; but the evidence suggests that the effects of political and professional values vary substantially with institutions, issues, and situations. . . . Role-playing is also likely when issues are perceived in terms of victory or defeat for an organization against rivals. The self-consciousness of the Fifth Circuit in civil rights and the Second Circuit in patents offer examples. Discretion and role strain, in turn, coalesce with policy disputes on legal frontiers, where ambiguity breeds subjectivity.

Lastly, the cohesion among these circuit judges concerning the constraints of precedent and national office, which limit creative opportunities, warns against exaggerating this leeway into license. Shared normative beliefs help to institutionalize the federal judiciary. Role conflict, according to participants, is absent from the overwhelming majority of circuit cases. Ordinarily, the mutual expectations of *stare decisis,* . . . enable circuit judges to control the premises of decision of subordinates who exercise discretion in particular cases. Common policy values among judges, neglected as a source of cohesion in legal theory, likewise contribute to the integration of federal courts.

Even so, some circuit judges now consider the Supreme Court's supervision of tribunals below to be "patently inadequate." The practical problem, however, is not whether the Justices can effectively monitor all federal appeals in a law explosion, but rather the creative tenth in which judicial roles and policy directions are relatively open. This study suggests that professional discipline *is* an imperfect surrogate for institutional controls in cases of greatest policy-making potential. The irony is that pragmatic and middle-of-the-road policy values, dominant among federal circuit judges by virtue of professional socialization and political recruitment, make it unlikely that circuit courts as institutions will stray far from the reservation.

NOTES

1. Role perceptions were inferred from the judges' responses to open-ended and structured questions, including the following query concerning innovation: "Some people think circuit judges should be legal innovators, thus illuminating issues for the Supreme Court; others argue that circuit judges should merely apply the law, leaving legal innovations to legislatures and the Supreme Court. What do you think?" No problems of intersubjectivity of meaning arose on this score in the interviews. . . .

2. "Norm-Making in Social Exchange: A Contract Law Model," *Law and Society Review* 7 (1972), 1–32.

"The Imperial Judiciary"

David M. O'Brien

Critics of "the imperial judiciary" typically focus on particular instances in which judges have undertaken the supervision of public institutions. Regardless of the merits of the normative debate that surrounds such judicial intervention, empirical generalizations about "the imperial judiciary" made from the small, disproportionate number of such cases are misleading. From an historical and political perspective, changes in the business and role of contemporary courts are due less to judicial usurpation and entrepreneurship than to broader trends associated with "our litigious society," the rise of interest-group liberalism and the administrative state.

COURTS AND CRITICS—"OLD WINE, NEW BOTTLES"?

In the past decade, legal scholars, historians and social scientists have charged that "an imperial judiciary" threatens to dominate

Reprinted from David M. O'Brien, "'The Imperial Judiciary': Of Paper Tigers and Socio-Legal Indicators," *Journal of Law & Politics* 2 (1985), pp. 1–16, 17–21, 29–30, 44–46, 49, 53, 56. All footnotes, tables and diagrams omitted.

American politics. Some years earlier the "imperial presidency" seemingly presaged and then receded with the constitutional crisis identified with Watergate. These critics would, however, have us resist the impulse to reject current charges as either a new cycle in social criticism, or the rejuvenation of a long tradition of attacks on the judiciary as an anti-democratic institution.

A tradition of judicial criticism, paralleling that of judicial independence, has maintained itself throughout the bicentenary of the republic. Such contempt of courts found expression in debates running from those between early Federalists and Anti-Federalists, to those of later Federalists and Jeffersonian Republicans, and of abolitionists and "states rights" advocates both before and after the Supreme Court's "self-inflicted wound" in *Dred Scott* and the Civil War that followed. In the late 19th century, controversy over courts was fueled by laissez faire capitalists and Reform Darwinists, and eventually culminated in President Franklin Roosevelt's proposed "Court-packing plan" and the Court's "switch-in-time-that-saved-nine" in 1937. The contemporary controversy, stemming from 1937 and from the Court's assumption of the guardianship of civil liberties and civil rights, perhaps remains symbolized by the constitutional revolutions forged in the areas of school desegregation, reapportionment and criminal procedure.

In other words, whereas for James Madison and others during the Founding period the Court was at best an auxiliary precaution, by 1937 it had become the primary check on governmental activity. Whereupon it retreated and then reasserted itself "as a surrogate for revolution," in the words of Alpheus Mason, as "a major creative force in American life." Since World War II, as Judge Irving Kaufman puts it, "the judiciary has been an accelerator of governmental activity rather than a brake."

The contemporary debate, like those in the past, seems to turn on whose ox is gored. But the debate, like the gored ox, gives rise not to simply normative arguments, for it purportedly responds to an event—an empirical development and unprecedented, unparalleled transfer of power in government. Consider Nathan Glazer's characterization in his influential article, "Towards An Imperial Judiciary?":

> The Courts have changed their role in American life. American courts, the most powerful in the world—they were that already when Tocqueville wrote and when Bryce wrote—are now more powerful than ever before...[C]ourts, through interpretation of the Constitution and the laws, now reach into the lives of the people, against the will of the people, deeper than they ever have in American history.

Like other commentators, Glazer indicts the Supreme Court, as well as the lower federal courts, for *expansionism*—that is, for intervening in a growing number of areas—and for assuming the role of a *super legislature*. At the same time, he criticizes courts for *mandating affirmative governmental action* to correct socio-economic and political inequities and questions *judicial competence* to effect such changes. The latter three concerns have engendered considerable empirical study and debate. Since these concerns have been addressed elsewhere, they are addressed only indirectly here when examining the claim of judicial expansionism.

AN IMPERIAL OR IMPERIALIST JUDICIARY?

Before examining the charge of judicial expansionism, it bears emphasizing that the indictment of "an imperial judiciary" is so provocative because of the play on the word "imperial". Critics are not so much concerned with changes in the judicial role caused by the rise of "big government," or what political scientists term "the administrative state." Instead, the brunt of their criticism is implied in the connotation of "an *imperial* judiciary": a judiciary which conspires to rule despotically and arbitrarily for its own interests.

The charge of "an imperial judiciary," however, may be understood in either a weak or a strong sense. In the weak sense, changes in the role and function of the judiciary are attributed largely to the development of the administrative state and broader changes in American politics. Conversely, in the stronger sense judges usurp and exercise power in an entrepreneurial fashion. Critics of "the imperial judiciary" make not merely the latter, stronger claim, but one which they cannot fully document, and which appears undermined by more fundamental socio-economic and political changes.

Judicial Expansionism

Critics of judicial expansionism typically focus on and generalize from extraordinary examples of judicial intervention in public administration. In so doing they rarely distinguish between different kinds of judicial intervention, or consider the import of the broader political context in which judicial power is structured, allocated and exercised.

Federal district court judges, for instance, have in some cases assumed the task of overseeing the operation of public schools, mental health institutions, and prisons. In the widely publicized case involving the Boston school district, Judge Arthur Garrity, Jr., in the span of ten years of litigation, not only ordered the busing of some 24,000 pupils to achieve school desegregation, but ordered and supervised the renovation of the South Boston high school to accommodate the influx of black students. Similarly, Judge Frank Johnson's decree ordering extensive remedial changes in Alabama's mental health hospital increased that state's annual expenditures "from $14 million before the suit was filed in 1971 to $58 million in 1973 after the decree was rendered." Such intervention disrupts and changes the organizational life of public institutions, and requires trial judges to assume a more active, managerial posture.

While some federal district court judges have commandeered the operation of public institutions, federal courts of appeals have had equally important effects on public administration and policy in reviewing administrative appeals and challenges to the formulation and implementation of regulatory standards. For example, Pennsylvania lost $91 million in federal highway funds after a panel of the Third Circuit Court of Appeals ruled that the state had failed to establish a vehicle emissions testing program. That program was required under a consent decree signed by the Environmental Protection Agency and the Delaware Valley Citizens' Council for Clean Air, but state agencies were barred from spending the necessary money because of an act passed,

over the governor's veto, by the state legislature. In the last 20 years, federal courts of appeals—and, in particular, the Court of Appeals for the District of Columbia—have emerged as the senior partners in regulatory politics, subjecting the process of administrative rulemaking and final agency decisions to a "hard look" substantive review. The traditional judicial deference accorded administrative expertise has given way to a more activist, policy-oriented judicial posture, particularly in the areas of health, safety and environmental regulation....

Federal appellate courts' assumption of a more activist-participatory role in regulatory politics not only deprives them of their traditional justification for exercising judicial review, but also leads to substantive review of administrative decisions and regulatory policies in areas in which judges have no special expertise.

In addition, the Supreme Court, as well as other state and federal courts, has been criticized for ruling on some of the most fundamental and personal decisions that confront an individual. In the emerging area of "rights of life," for example, the courts have considered the permissibility of terminating a pregnancy, the issue of surrogate parenthood, and other matters such as whether a parent, spouse or other individual may withdraw life-support machinery from one who is terminally ill. These kinds of cases raise moral and religious issues for which judges may again claim no particular expertise or competence. Courts face similarly vexing issues of a complex science-policy nature, such as the patentability of organic life-forms and the product liability of manufacturers of synthetic-organic chemicals.

The judiciary has intervened—sometimes extensively, if not also excessively—in public administration, rendering decisions in politically controversial areas involving vexatious moral dilemmas and issues of complex science-policy in which it possesses no special expertise. Nevertheless, it does not necessarily follow that judges have usurped decision-making authority and power in an entrepreneurial fashion. On the contrary, as Judge Frank Johnson underscored at his confirmation hearing, courts have "nothing to do with the creation of the case or controversy that forms the basis for [a] lawsuit." To be sure, judicial decisions and the way in which they are communicated may invite further or related litigation. Still, courts—and especially trial courts—do not set their own agendas. The judiciary is not a self-starter or, as Justice Benjamin Cardozo observed, a "roving commission" initiating lawsuits.

"Our Litigious Society"

In the last decade, besides charges of "an imperial judiciary," criticism has also centered on "our litigious society." In 1980–1981, for instance, there were 180,576 civil and 31,287 criminal cases filed in federal courts, for a total of 211,863 filings. By comparison, a decade earlier 125,423 cases were filed—87,321 civil and 38,102 criminal cases—and in 1960 there was a total of 87,421—or 59,284 civil and 28,137 criminal—filings in federal courts. The federal judiciary, of course, handles but a small percentage of the total litigation in the United States. In 1980—1981, state courts faced over 25 million filings—some 13,689,450 civil and 12,145,623 criminal cases. Litigation rates, in the view of A.E. Dick Howard, reflect "the 'judicialization' of an ever widening variety of issues." . . .

Somewhat ironically, however, criticisms of "an imperial judiciary" and "our litigious society" are never quite joined . . .

The propensity to rely on the judicial forum to settle disputes—disputes ranging from those that pose profound moral-political issues to those that are ostensibly "frivolous"—[Alexis de] Tocqueville. . . suggested, is more appropriately attributed to the practice of rights and to the influence of the legal community than to "an imperial judiciary." No less than judges and juries, lawyers are the vehicle for extending the practice of rights and introducing legalese into our everyday discourse and life. The legal profession "adapts itself with great flexibility to the exigencies of the social body," Tocqueville observed, "extend[ing] over the whole community and penetrat[ing] into all classes which compose it; it acts upon the country imperceptibly. . . ."

Tocqueville thus anticipated "our litigious society" as well as an association between increasing litigation and the growing number and influence of members of the bench and bar. The number of federal trial judges has grown markedly. In the first 50 years of this century, the number only slightly more than doubled, rising from 102 in 1900 to 237 in 1960, but more than doubled again in the last 20 years, growing to 483 in 1980. In relative terms, that amounts to a growth from 1.2 to 2.2 federal trial judges per million citizens in the total population and represents an 83% increase since 1960. Besides the increasing number of judges, there has been a corresponding growth in support staff, and hence in the size of the entire federal judiciary. . . .

In the last 20 years the size of the legal profession has also increased—at a much faster rate than the total population. . . . In 1980, 70% of the legal profession was engaged in private practice, but there has been a movement toward larger law firms, larger corporate legal staff and more government employment. Hence, there is a corresponding trend toward more organizational and policy-oriented litigation. . . .

There is no need to pretend greater precision in linking increased litigation, and the size of the federal judiciary or legal profession, with judicial expansionism. Perhaps, a kind of law of supply and demand operates: more lawyers, more filings and more judges. Lawyers certainly facilitate the expanding number and kind of lawsuits, but the availability of judges may also encourage litigation. Indicators of "our litigious society" and broader socio-economic and legal trends nonetheless appear more closely associated with judicial expansionism than does the charge of a conspiring, entrepreneurial judiciary.

In historical perspective, along with the above trends, the business of the state and federal judiciaries has also rather dramatically changed during the past century. . . .

The business of federal district courts . . . evolved during the last century but, in contrast to the state courts, toward less criminal and more civil litigation. Here, again, trends appear more closely associated with socio-economic developments than with judicial usurpation of political power. In 1876, only 39% of the workload of federal trial courts involved criminal cases, but by 1890 that figure had reached 61%, and criminal cases predominated the dockets of federal district courts until the mid-1930s. The filing of criminal cases rapidly increased during the 1920s and early 1930s when it leveled off until a surge in the late 1960s, and then gradually declined from 1975 through the end of the decade. In 1980, criminal cases constituted only 15% of the business of federal district courts—a decline of 24.5% since 1975.

The changing business of federal district courts is attributed more to socio-economic and legal policy changes than to the policy preferences of federal judges. Apart from jurisdictional changes, the workload of federal trial courts was significantly affected by the decriminalization of internal revenue cases and the abolition of prohibition in the early part of the 20th century, a subsequent shift in prosecutorial policy on immigration, and in the 1970s and 1980s by the Department of Justice's attempt to divert criminal cases to state courts. The increase in civil litigation, especially since the 1960s, also largely reflects changing governmental policies involving governmental contracts after World War II, suits under the Federal Tort Claims Act, and in the 1970s, the federal government's attempt to recover defaulted student loans and overpaid veterans' benefits. By 1982, the government was a plaintiff in no less than 64.9% of all civil government cases, compared with 51% in the early 1970s. Private civil suits, however, do figure prominently in the noncriminal business of federal district courts. Beginning in the 1960s a trend continues toward the filing of more federal question cases—those involving labor disputes, civil rights and prisoners' claims—and diversity contract cases. Notably, since the 1960s the filing of class action suits also contributed to the changing business of federal district courts: in 1976 the filing of class action cases reached a high of 3,584, but declined by 1980 to 1,568, less than half that number.

In the last 20 years, as Glazer and others contend, public law litigation—perhaps epitomized by class action suits—invited judicial intervention in the operation of public institutions. Still, that increase occurs within the context of the increasing and changing nature of litigation in both state and federal courts. Most cases do not present novel points of law or complex factual circumstances. Class action suits—although time-consuming for judges, disruptive of the organizational life of public institutions, and disproportionately represented in media coverage of the courts—constitute less than one-tenth of one percent of all filings in federal courts, and average about five cases per federal judge.

Class action suits, furthermore, epitomize the trend of both government and private individuals or groups toward the politically strategic use of litigation to fashion and implement public policy....

In responding to the rise of interest group liberalism, Congress increased the procedural complexity of agency rulemaking, enlarged the opportunities for interested individuals to participate in or otherwise challenge agency regulations, and heightened the standards for judicial review of administrative decisions. In other words, as the administrative state has expanded, litigation has come to play an ever more critical role in regulatory politics, with agencies defending all major regulatory action in the judicial arena....

In short, the argument that judicial expansionism has created "an imperial judiciary," in the strong, entrepreneurial sense of that charge, focuses on isolated and relatively few of the total number of cases adjudicated. Moreover, socio-legal indicators of "our litigious society" appear to support a case for judicial expansionism and "an imperial judiciary" only in the weak, nonentrepreneurial sense of that charge. As J. Woodford Howard notes, it is "hard to prove ...that an oligarchy of judicial activists is more responsible for expanding judicial roles and swollen dockets than other branches of government...."

Interest-Group Pluralism and Constitutional Politics

The rise of the administrative state and the increasing and changing nature of litigation appear in important ways linked to judicial expansionism....

In American politics, the political use of litigation has a long history. Yet, in the last few decades the politics of litigation have become more self-conscious and more prominent with the rise of interest-group pluralism. Occasionally, as in *Buckley* v. *Valeo*, for instance, representatives of the entire political spectrum join together in seeking judicial resolution of a public policy dispute. When challenging the Federal Elections Campaign Act, New York conservative and former Senator James Buckley was joined by former Senator and liberal presidential candidate Eugene McCarthy, as well as by the New York State Conservative Party, the Mississippi Republican Party, the Libertarian Party, the New York Civil Liberties Union and the American Conservative Party.

In other words, more crucial in understanding the contemporary judiciary than even the general trends identified above with the administrative state and "our litigious society," are fundamental political changes; in particular, the ascendence of interest-group pluralism and the greater political recourse to litigation and courts....

... [J]udicial expansionism appears not unrelated to interest-group pluralism and to the decline in voter participation in electoral politics over the last two decades, during which both the size of the voting population and the number of lawsuits filed grew. Interest-group pluralism contributes to the erosion of the moderating influence *cum* discipline associated with a competitive two-party political system, as special interest groups exercise greater independent influence in regulatory politics and the administrative state. At the same time, interest-group pluralism contributes to judicial expansionism through legislative enactments increasing the opportunities for interest representation in, and heightened judicial review of, regulatory politics, as well as through the strategic use of litigation in formulating and challenging public policies....

THE SUPREME COURT: FROM THE LEAST DANGEROUS TO A CO-EQUAL BRANCH OF GOVERNMENT

Critics such as Glazer typically single out the Supreme Court for special approbation. When one considers only that court, the case for "an imperial judiciary" in the strong sense of judicial usurpation and entrepreneurship has special attraction. This is so because the modern Supreme Court has greater control over its docket and agenda-setting than any other court, and because the nine justices ostensibly decide cases in a collegial fashion. Still, critics of "an imperial judiciary" often neglect the significance of socio-economic and political changes for the contemporary role of the Supreme Court. This section briefly sketches how these broader trends—specifically, the increasing and changing nature of judicial business, caused by socio-economic and political changes such as the rise of interest-group pluralism and the administrative state, as well as the inflation of constitutional politics and the proliferation of specialized theories of judicial review—are related to the Supreme Court and the claim of "an imperial judiciary."

The Supreme Court has proven to be neither "the least dangerous" branch nor aquiescent under "the chains of the Constitution." Just as the contemporary presidency is vastly different from the presidency in the 19th century, so too the Court is quite a different institution from what it was during the founding, the late 19th century, or even the early 20th century. "The great tides and currents which engulf the rest of men," in Justice Benjamin Cardozo's memorable words, "do not turn aside in their course, and pass judges by." The socio-economic and political trends that contributed to the increasing and changing nature of judicial

business in lower federal and state courts had a similar impact on the role and business of the Supreme Court. The contemporary Court is no longer primarily concerned with resolving disputes per se but with providing uniformity, stability and predictability to the law—primarily through constitutional and statutory construction. . . .

The modern Supreme Court, therefore, perhaps inevitably plays an important role in the national political process. Congress so expanded the Court's discretionary jurisdiction that the justices may now largely define their own agenda and respond to the inexorable necessity, brought on by competing special interest groups and "our litigious society," of deciding primarily issues of national importance. "The function of the [modern] Supreme Court," as Chief Justice Taft envisioned when commenting on the passage of the Judiciary Act of 1925, has indeed become "not the remedying of a particular litigant's wrong, but the consideration of cases whose decision involves principles, the application of which are of wide public or governmental interest, and which should be authoritatively declared by the final court.". . .

The inflation of constitutional politics and the Supreme Court's intervention in an ever-growing range of areas will not likely decrease, but not for the reasons suggested by Glazer and others. Retrenchment is unlikely, precisely because the Court's expanded discretionary jurisdiction enables it to set its own agenda, selecting only issues of a national importance from a growing number and range of cases. Prior to the 1983 ruling in *INS* v. *Chadha*—striking down a one-house veto provision for federal regulations, and thereby throwing into question the validity of more than 200 other statutes with similar provisions—the Court had invalidated over 110 congressional statutes and 1,050 state laws or municipal ordinances. In the last 30 years the Court, *regardless* of its composition, has increasingly asserted the power of judicial review, whether in overturning its prior decisions, congressional and state legislation, or municipal ordinances.... Institutional norms and practices of collegial decision-making have changed. More specifically, as the Court has acquired greater discretion in deciding what to decide, it has confronted more constitutional controversies. The increase in the amount and complexity of constitutional adjudication perhaps has made it more difficult for the justices either to abide by stare decisis or to reach agreement on an institutional opinion justifying any particular decision.

In the last 30 years there has been a concomitant trend toward more divisiveness within the Court. While the percentage of unanimous opinions remains at about 30%, the number of dissenting votes cast each term has increased.... Similarly, there has been a greater increase in the frequency, and hence cumulative number, of plurality decisions and cases decided by a bare majority of the Court....

Not unrelated is the fact that the justices also tend to issue more specialized justifications for their votes and decisions. Since 1939 the total number of opinions—including opinions announcing the Court's decision and concurring, separate and dissenting opinions—issued each term has rather steadily increased....

There are a number of possible explanations (none of which by itself is entirely persuasive) for these trends, including: the increasing complexity and proportion of constitutional cases decided by the Court; changes in the process of assigning, drafting and circulating opinions; a greater propensity for justices "to state their views their own way;" and the relative influence of employing a greater number of law clerks. The only explanation advanced here is, as suggested above, that these trends are not unrelated to the inflation of constitutional politics and the proliferation of specialized theories of judicial review. In any event, these trends indicate, contrary to what Glazer and other critics of "an imperial judiciary" claim, that the justices do not conspire to exercise judicial review in an entrepreneurial fashion or to usurp the power of other political branches. Rather, Congress has expanded the bases and opportunities for access to the judiciary and enlarged the Supreme Court's discretionary jurisdiction. The justices now confront increasing and more vexatious issues of public law and policy, and tend to be less inclined to agree with each other on either the basis for or the outcome of their votes when deciding those issues.

CONCLUSION: JUDICIAL EXPANSIONISM AND "AN IMPERIAL JUDICIARY"

On reconsidering the claim of judicial expansionism as advanced by Glazer and others, that claim appears too abstract and unempirical. The claim of "an imperial judiciary" in a strong and provocative sense is too difficult to prove. Critics often fail to distinguish different kinds of intervention by trial and appellate judges in the various state and federal courts. More importantly, when focusing on particular cases of judicial intervention in public policy and affairs, they fail to pay sufficient attention to broader yet more fundamental legal, socio-economic, and political changes. Specifically, those trends are associated with the expansion of the administrative state, "our litigious society," the rise of interest-group pluralism, and the proliferation of specialized theories of judicial review. The judiciary and, in particular, the Supreme Court, has evolved, for better or worse, with the evolution of free government and American politics throughout the bicentenary.

CHAPTER 12

Courts as Small Groups

In viewing judicial decision making we have seen how several factors influence judicial behavior. Analysts of the judicial role attempt to link individual and institutional characteristics in explaining judicial behavior. Others interested in what affects judicial behavior have chosen to direct attention to a variety of structural considerations beyond those embodied in the concept of judicial role. Among these considerations are the number of judges with decisional responsibility in a particular case, that is, whether decisions are made by one judge or by a group of judges.

In the United States today, both types of decision-making structures are used. However, for the most part, the single-judge structure is found in the trial courts while the collegial court apparatus is common to appellate tribunals. But even this dichotomy between trial and appellate courts is misleading as suggested in the reading by Herbert Jacob. The everyday working relationship of trial judges, prosecutors, and defense lawyers is in reality a functioning small group.[1] Nevertheless, the focus of court oriented small group research is on courts whose formal institutional apparatus is that of collegial courts. In the federal system the judicial institutions that provide for collegial court decision making are, with some exceptions (such as the very infrequently used three-judge federal district court), appellate courts. These include the eleven numbered regional courts of appeals, the Court of Appeals for the District of Columbia, the United States Court of Appeals for the Federal Circuit (with specialized jurisdiction over fiscal claims against the federal government, patent appeals, and customs or trade issues), and, of course, the United States Supreme Court. Collegial courts are also found in the state systems, primarily at the intermediate level (the majority of states have them) and at the highest appellate levels.

The fact that decisions are made by a group rather than by an individual requires us to examine the dynamics of the group process and to seek to discover what difference it makes that decisions are a *group* and *not* an individual product. Social psychologists have utilized small experimental decision-making groups (composed of paid subjects, usually college students, who are unobtrusively observed by researchers) to study group behavior and to generate as well as to test hypotheses. One common-sense proposition about group decision making is that leadership will be exercised within a group. Consequently, leadership roles have been carefully examined by researchers. The concepts of task leadership and social leadership, discussed in the Danelski readings, have resulted from this research.

Other hypotheses have also been formulated and put to the test. A number of findings have emerged.[2] For example, in a small group there are strong pressures to conform to the majority position (that is, deviance is discouraged). Small groups have been found to be more accurate than individuals acting alone in solving certain kinds of problems. Small groups have also been found by some (but not all) researchers to take greater risks than individuals.[3] The literature also suggests that the quantity and quality of communication within the small group may in themselves affect the decisional behavior of the group.

It is a fair question to ask how these and other small-group findings by social psychologists relate to collegial court decision making. We further can and should ask how we can test small group hypotheses when we obviously cannot bring the judges to the small-group laboratory or otherwise observe the conference deliberations of collegial courts. In other words, even if we think the small-group concepts are relevant for court behavior, how can we objectively determine if indeed they are, and what data *can* be collected to test the hypotheses?

First let us consider the question of relevance. We can observe that the small-group leadership concepts directly relate to how collegial courts go about their business. In the first selection by David Danelski these leadership concepts are developed with reference to the United States Supreme Court, and a convincing argument is made that the role of Chief Justice is the one that best permits the exercise of both task leadership and social leadership, although it does not necessarily follow that all Chief Justices will assume these leadership roles. The study by David and Jeanne Danelski follows through the analysis of leadership with a focus on the Warren Court, utilizing objective indicators of leadership.

The concepts of conformity and deviance are obviously applicable to the study of dissent behavior of members of collegial courts. It has been found that, with the exception of the United States Supreme Court since 1943,[4] the large majority of the decisions of state and federal collegial courts have been unanimous. Although the dissent rates have varied,[5] it appears that the pressures to conform are there and that it is these pressures and not necessarily the characteristics of the cases that has led to so much consensus.[6] When dissents occur, they tend to reflect attitudinal and value commitments rather than a deviant type of personality.[7] Studies of consensus (conformity) and conflict (deviance) on collegial courts reflect a continuing research interest on the part of judicial behavior scholars,[8] and the small-group literature is certainly suggestive of hypotheses to test.

We may infer from the article by J. Woodford Howard, Jr., "On the Fluidity of Judicial Choice," that the accuracy of judgment finding of social psychologists may be applicable to collegial courts. Howard demonstrates that in some of the more complex and controversial cases decided by the Supreme Court, the small-group context has facilitated some justices changing their initial perceptions of the issues involved; that is, had these justices not had the benefit of interchange with their fellow justices in the small-group context of Supreme Court decision making, their judicial decisions would have been different. But, as Saul Brenner's research demonstrates, the number and proportion of decisions in which fluidity is found are small, with the overwhelming majority of cases not demonstrating the phenomenon described by Howard. Furthermore, the importance of the accuracy of judgment small group concept for Supreme Court decision making may be called into question because it is difficult to objectively determine that the majority view on thorny issues is necessarily more accurate than the view of the dissenters or, in the case of a unanimous court, that even a solid consensus represents the most accurate representation of reality. Because of the dynamics of the small-group interchange, Justice Douglas may indeed have been led to a more accurate perception than he had at first concerning the issues in the Terminiello case, but it is difficult to objectively demonstrate that his final view and that of the majority indeed reflected more accurate judgment than his earlier and the dissenting views.

Another small-group hypothesis that has found its way into the judicial behavior literature raises the question whether a collegial court will take more risks, that is, will be more willing to make decisions that the judges believe will provoke significant criticism, than a single-judge court. One political scientist, Thomas Walker, explored this question with reference to federal district court judges. He took advantage of the fact that although district court judges usually sit as single-court judges, on some occasions they have sat as members of three-judge federal district courts. Walker assumed that a pro-civil liberties decision would tend to be more controversial than a decision limiting the scope of civil liberties. This assumption may be problematic, but it is nonetheless of interest to note that Walker examined the civil liberties decision making of the same judges in the single-judge and collegial court contexts and found that the judges were more likely to decide in favor of civil liberties, that is they made more controversial decisions and thus took greater risks, in the group context.[9] Walker also conducted a survey of the judges and found that although a majority expressed no preference as to court context for deciding controversial cases, a large majority of those who did express a preference favored the group over the single-judge setting.[10]

The group context of appellate court decision making is conducive to negotiation, bargaining, and the utilization of a variety of strategies of persuasion. Walter Murphy, in a classic work of political analysis, *Elements of Judicial Strategy*,[11] demonstrated the workings of these processes within the Supreme Court. The Danelski and Howard readings also offer insight into the negotiation process.[12]

Unlike social psychologists, students of collegial court behavior cannot directly observe the group in action, but the group is real and not experimental. Researchers must rely on accounts of group deliberations or draw inferences from the voting records of judges. Accounts of collegial court deliberations are found in the diaries and other private papers of judges and sometimes in memoirs, interviews, articles, or speeches of judges and their close relatives or associates. The Danelskis, Howard, and Brenner drew from the private papers including the docket books of deceased justices and found data to permit analyses of small-group processes.

To be sure, some small-group concepts are not readily applicable to collegial court decision making, but even those that are offer formidable problems of data collection.[13] Nevertheless, as the selections in this chapter demonstrate, insights into judicial decision making are to be gained from an examination of the dynamics inherent in the structural context of decision making. Although the evidence is not massive, there appears to be justification for asserting that the group condition makes a difference in judicial decision making.

NOTES

1. Also see Peter F. Nardulli, James Eisenstein, and Roy B. Flemming, "Unraveling the Complexities of Decision Making in Face-to-Face Groups: A Contextual Analysis of Plea

Bargained Sentences," *American Political Science Review*, 78 (1984), 912–928 and James Eisenstein, Roy B. Flemming, and Peter F. Nardulli, *The Contours of Justice* (Boston: Little, Brown, 1988).

2. This discussion draws heavily on the review of the small group literature in S. Sidney Ulmer, *Courts as Small and Not so Small Groups* (New York: General Learning Press, 1971).

3. See "'Risky Shift' Baffles Social Scientists," *ISR Newsletter*, 3 (Autumn 1975), 2–3.

4. C. Herman Pritchett, *The Roosevelt Court: A Study in Judicial Politics and Values, 1937–1947* (Chicago: Quadrangle, 1969), p. 25; Glendon Schubert, *The Judicial Mind* (Evanston, Ill.: Northwestern University Press, 1965), p. 45; and the statistical tables in the November issues of the *Harvard Law Review*.

5. In general, see the studies in Sheldon Goldman and Charles M. Lamb, eds., *Judicial Conflict and Consensus: Behavioral Studies of American Appellate Courts* (Lexington, Kentucky: The University Press of Kentucky, 1986), and in particular Table 9.1 by Henry R. Glick and George W. Pruett, Jr., on pp. 202–203.

6. See, for example, Robert J. Sickels, "The Illusion of Judicial Consensus: Zoning Decisions in the Maryland Court of Appeals," *American Political Science Review*, 59 (1965), 100–104; Sheldon Goldman, "Voting Behavior on the United States Courts of Appeals, 1961–1964," *American Political Science Review*, 60 (1966), 374–383; Sheldon Goldman, "Conflict and Consensus in the United States Courts of Appeals," *Wisconsin Law Review*, (1968), 476–480; Burton M. Atkins and Justin J. Green, "Consensus on the United States Courts of Appeals: Illusion or Reality?" *American Journal of Political Science*, 20 (1976), 735–748; Donald R. Songer, "Consensual and Nonconsensual Decisions in Unanimous Opinions of the United States Courts of Appeals," *American Journal of Political Science*, 26 (1982), 225–239. In general, see Goldman and Lamb, *op. cit.*, pp. 1–18 and Steven A. Peterson, "Dissent in American Courts," *Journal of Politics*, 43 (1981), 412–434.

7. Burton M. Atkins, "Judicial Behavior and Tendencies Towards Conformity in a Three Member Small Group: A Case Study of Dissent Behavior on the U.S. Court of Appeals," *Social Science Quarterly*, 54 (1973), 41–53; Peterson, *op. cit.;* and Goldman and Lamb, *op. cit.*

8. See, for example, the studies in Goldman and Lamb, *op. cit.*

9. Thomas G. Walker, "Judges in Concert: The Influence of the Group on Judicial Decision-Making," Ph.D. dissertation, University of Kentucky, 1970.

10. *Ibid.*, pp. 99–104. Note that in 1976 Congress enacted legislation restricting the use of three-judge district courts.

11. (Chicago: University of Chicago Press, 1964).

12. Inferences about the negotiations process may be drawn from the statistical analysis found in Saul Brenner and Harold J. Spaeth, "Majority Opinion Assignments and the Maintenance of the Original Coalition on the Warren Court," *American Journal of Political Science*, 32 (1988), 72–81.

13. See the discussion in Sheldon Goldman and Thomas P. Jahnige, *The Federal Courts as a Political System*, 3rd ed. (New York: Harper & Row, 1985), pp. 157–158.

Trial Courts in the United States

Herbert Jacob

. . .

Three models most frequently compete for the attention of trial court researchers. One is an organizational model; the second is a role model; the third is a decisional model. Each targets a particular element of the world of trial courts; none is holistic.

The organizational model became prominent through the pathbreaking book, *Criminal Justice* (1967), in which Abraham Blumberg argued that the criminal process in trial courts more nearly resembled a bureaucratic than an adversarial model (see also Packer, 1968). James Eisenstein and I (1977), Peter Nardulli (1978; 1979), and others (e.g., Clynch and Neubauer, 1981) have since tried to elaborate on this model. But as Lawrence Mohr (1976)—an organizational theorist more than a legal researcher—has pointed out, not all elements of the conventional organizational model apply comfortably to courts. What the organizational model does best perhaps is to call attention to the interactional elements of trial court proceedings. Both trials and out-of-court settlements involve interactions among various members

of the courtroom work group. That work group is characterized by continuing relationships of varying intensities. The fact that work group members interact with varying frequencies over a long period of time affects the ways in which they deal with one another. It especially affects their communication patterns by allowing them to develop shorthand ways of transmitting information and by building trust or distrust among the work group. Since the heart of trial court decisions is the communication of information, organizational links are presumed to have important consequences for the work of courts.

Ideally, the organizational model would lead us to look for structured interactions and for the effects of those interactions on communications. This, however, requires intense observation of a relatively fragmented structure. A trial court is composed not just of the judge and clerks who are located in the courtroom and its adjacent chambers. Other important members of the work group, especially the attorneys who practice there, move in and out of the courtroom. No small team of researchers can shadow all of those who are important to a case. Criminal courtrooms are relatively well structured and almost all organizational studies look at them rather than at civil court-

"Trial Courts in the United States," Herbert Jacob. *Law & Society Review* , Vol. 17, No. 3, 1983. Reprinted by permission of the Law and Society Association. Some references omitted.

rooms. Much more of the business of the civil courts is done in lawyers' offices, and the number of attorneys practicing in a particular civil court is often far greater than what one finds in its criminal counterpart. Thus, studying the civil side is more difficult. Perhaps for this reason we have almost no studies that attempt to utilize the organizational perspective for civil courts.

Role theory has been invoked by others—notably James Gibson. . .—as an alternative perspective (see also Flango et al., 1975; Ish, 1975; Ungs and Baas, 1972; Galanter et al., 1979). This stream of research is heavily influenced by research on appellate judges, where the role concept was first applied (Glick and Vines, 1969; Glick, 1971). In trial court research it has been applied principally to characterizations of judges, although Heumann (1978) examines not only the socialization of judges to their roles but also that of prosecutors and public defenders. Role theory focuses more on individuals than on groups even though roles are by definition the consequence of perceptions by others that come to have behavioral significance for the role player. Although role-focused analyses are frequently presented as alternatives to the organizational model, the two are quite compatible. The link, however, has not been effectively made, and the role model by itself has not guided enough studies to produce comprehensive results.

The third type of model is the decisional model. Such models reflect the judge orientation of appellate court studies. The empirical research here attempts to examine the degree to which criminal court judges show biases of various sorts—toward women, toward blacks, toward various classes of defendants. Most of the research has concentrated on the sentencing decision, as if the judge made it alone. There are also a handful of studies which attempt to relate judges' backgrounds or the political

context in which they work to their decisional propensities. Peltason's (1961) study of how judges handled southern school desegregation cases in the 1950s is an early example of this genre; another is Martin Levin's (1977) comparison of Pittsburgh and Minneapolis judges. A more recent example is the study by Kuklinski and Stanga (1979) of the relationship between judges' decisions on marijuana use and local voting on this question. Once again, this approach has been applied to civil cases less frequently than to criminal ones, but it has figured in studies of civil cases that involve important policy questions.

The organizational, role, and decisional models may be seen as complementary to one another rather than as mutually exclusive. Organizational models are the most comprehensive of the three. They readily incorporate the concept of role and in some versions focus quite explicitly on the conditions governing decision-making. However, they have not been so used. Rather than being employed to guide research by identifying critical problems that might substantially enhance our understanding of trial courts, these models are more frequently used after the fact to understand data that have been collected with different questions in mind. My own research with Jim Eisenstein illustrates this weakness. We began our investigation with questions about the prevalence of plea bargaining and were not guided by a theoretical model. We elaborated our organizational model after we had begun collecting our data when we realized that we could best understand what we were observing if we adopted the organizational framework. As a consequence, we failed to collect some data that were critical to an organizational understanding of trial courts.

The theoretical perspectives that I have been discussing are limited in that they relate largely to only one of the four aspects of trial courts...the "how" of the judicial process. They have little to say about the characteristics of outputs, the distribution of outcomes, or the timing of adjudication. For such matters, we need to turn to still other theoretical perspectives.

.   .   .

REFERENCES

Blumberg, Abraham S. (1967) *Criminal Justice*. Chicago: Quadrangle Books.

Clynch, Edward J. and David W. Neubauer (1981) "Trial Courts as Organizations: A Critique," 3 *Law and Policy Quarterly* 69.

Eisenstein, James and Herbert Jacob (1977) *Felony Justice: An Organizational Analysis of Criminal Courts.* Boston: Little, Brown and Co.

Flango, Victor E., Lettie McSpadden Wenner and Manfred W. Wenner (1975) "The Concept of Judicial Role: A Methodological Note," 19 *American Journal of Political Science* 277.

Galanter, Marc, Frank S. Palen and John M. Thomas (1979) "The Crusading Judge: Judicial Activism in Trial Courts," 52 *Southern California Law Review* 699.

Glick, Henry R. (1971) *Supreme Courts in State Politics: An Investigation of the Judicial Role*. New York: Basic Books.

Glick, Henry R. and Kenneth N. Vines (1969) "Law Making in the State Judiciary: A Comparative Study of the Judicial Role in Four States," 2 *Polity* 142.

Heumann, Milton (1978) *Plea Bargaining*. Chicago: University of Chicago Press.

Ish, Joel S. (1975) "Trial Judges: Their Recruitment, Backgrounds, and Role Perceptions." Paper delivered at the annual meeting of the American Political Science Association.

Kuklinski, James H. and John E. Stanga (1979) "Political Participation and Governmental Responsiveness: The Behavior of California Superior Courts," 73 *American Political Science Review* 1090.

Levin, Martin A. (1977) *Urban Politics and the Criminal Courts*. Chicago: University of Chicago Press.

Mohr, Lawrence B. (1976) "Organizations, Decisions, and Courts," 10 *Law & Society Review* 621.

Nardulli, Peter F. (1978) *The Courtroom Elite.* Cambridge, MA.: Ballinger Publishing Co.

———(1979) "Organizational Analysis of Criminal Courts: An Overview and Some Speculation," in Peter F. Nardulli (ed.), *The Study of Criminal Courts: Political Perspectives*. Cambridge, MA: Ballinger Publishing Co.

Packer, Herbert L. (1968) *The Limits of the Criminal Sanction*. Stanford, CA: Stanford University Press.

Peltason, Jack W. (1961) *Fifty-Eight Lonely Men*. New York: Harcourt, Brace.

Ungs, Thomas D. and Larry R. Baas (1972) "The Judicial Role Perception: A Q Technique Study of Ohio Judges," 6 *Law & Society Review* 343.

On the Fluidity of Judicial Choice

J. Woodford Howard, Jr.

...It has long been known, of course, that judges change their votes and permit their opinions to be conduits for the ideas of others....

Walter F. Murphy's excellent *Elements of Judicial Strategy* is replete with examples of how Justices work such changes via internal bargaining. Yet it may come as some surprise to political scientists how commonplace, rather than aberrational, judicial flux actually is. The recently opened papers of Justice Murphy, which contain fairly extensive conference notes for the years 1940–49, as well as docket books for the 1947 term, give a much more plastic impression of judicial choice in the making than the rigidly stratified bloc warfare by which most of us have characterized the Roosevelt and Vinson Courts. Indeed, when meshed with the Stone and Burton papers, which overlap the same period, the Murphy papers tempt one to say that hardly any major decision in this decade was free from significant alteration of vote and language before announcement to the public. Neither was the phenomenon confined to Justices whose overt allegiances

Reprinted by permission from *American Political Science Review* 62 (1968), 43–57. Most footnotes have been omitted.

were to professional ideologies of law as reason or to philosophies of self-restraint. One of the most striking aspects of the decade is that the most important instances of judicial flux, from the doctrinal standpoint, occurred precisely among those Justices most suspected of ideological automation and in cases that stand as highpoints of their libertarian commitment. From the very human tendency to change one's mind under pressure, no one, and certainly no "libertarian activist," was immune.

Examples of fluctuating options are legion; but for convenience of illustration, certain types of flux may be distinguished from among well-known civil liberties decisions of the day. Without pretending to offer the following categories as a unified theoretical construct, we may classify fluid choices according to certain intervening variables which appear to have been at work. First is the "freshman effect"—i.e., unstable attitudes that seem to have resulted from the process of assimilation to the Court. It is not uncommon for a new Justice to undergo a period of adjustment, often about three years in duration, before his voting behavior stabilizes into observable, not to mention predictable, patterns. Biographical materials suggest the generality of this experience, irrespective of prior background and ranging from Justices as dissimilar as Cardozo and Murphy. Justice Cardozo, according to one clerk's recollection of the docket books, registered surprisingly unstable options as a newcomer. Frequently voting alone in conference before ultimately submerging himself in a group opinion, Cardozo himself confessed discomfort in adjusting from the common law world of the New York Court of Appeals to the public law orientation of the federal Supreme Court. Elsewhere I have documented a similar instability on the part of Justice Murphy. During his freshman years on the high bench, Murphy swung from the wing of Justice Frankfurter, whom he had assumed would be his intellectual mainstay and ally, to substantial agreement with Justice Black, whose views regarding the First Amendment and state criminal procedure, it should be remembered, were also shifting ground at the time. In the process of adjustment, however, Murphy had problems of craftsmanship in the picketing cases and, along with other members of the Court, groped for a coherent position regarding free speech. He drowned a dissent in *Gobitis*; he cast a decisive turnabout vote at the last minute in *Bridges* v. *California*; and he also switched sides in *Hines* v. *Davidowitz*. However contrary to preconceptions, it was the libertarian Justice Murphy who had to be talked out of publishing a concurrence in *Cantwell* v. *Connecticut* (in return for different language) which criticized Justice Roberts' Court opinion for inadequately protecting state power to preserve the peace from clashing religious sects.

Eloise Snyder's pioneering study of the Court as a small group supports the hypothesis that the "freshman effect" has been a continuing phenomenon.[1] Parallels in other decision-making groups, e.g., the socialization of freshman Senators, also indicate that the Court is not alone in creating assimilation problems for new members. What occurs is a sort of hiatus between the norms of the individual's belief system and new institutional norms which must be internalized as role expectations unfold. Still, the aggregate effects of such freshman transitions are probably more difficult to trace in the judiciary. Using the concept of cliques, Snyder hypothesized that the high court assimilates its new members through a "pivotal clique" in the ideological center, with the implication that uncommitted newcomers on stratified courts are likely to maximize influence at the outset of their judicial careers, before attitudes and bloc alignments jell. The experience of Justices Cardozo and Murphy suggests the need of refining this concept, however, especially the suggestion that fledgling judges with unstable or inchoate attitudes are more influential than senior, committed members. While a pivotal Justice may have a controlling vote in a given five-four situation, the very reasons for the "freshman effect"—inexperience, feelings of inadequacy, hesitation about premature bloc identification, low seniority in assignments, strategies of playing safe, etc.—all point to the opposite direction of freshmen Justices following rather than leading. . . .

A second cluster of fluctuating choices may be grouped around the familiar strategic variables of massing the Court and of institutional loyalties. Justices frequently compromise personal opinion in order to maximize their collective force and to safeguard the power and legitimacy of the Court. . . . That personal ideology may be qualified or even defined by organizational perspectives is by no means unique to the judiciary. . . . The evidence of the 1940's suggests that all of the Justices, at one time or another, were constrained by group and institutional interests. Not only was it common for them to offer helpful suggestions and advice to adversaries, according to the official theory of collective responsibility, but they also sacrificed deeply felt views. For example, Justice Murphy stifled a powerful lone dissent in the first Japanese Relocation Case under the badgering and patriotic appeals of Justice Frankfurter; and Justice Douglas did the same in the second. After finding himself alone, and probably under advice from Justice Rutledge, Murphy also withheld an elaborate dissent in the case of runaway spy Gerhard Eisler, with the result that he left stillborn the first known assault by a Justice upon the House Un-American Activities Committee for violating the First Amendment. Similarly, Justice Rutledge swallowed personal opinion in order to avoid stalemate in *Screws* v. *United States*, an important civil rights decision which held off an attack on expansive concepts of state action at the price of enfeebling federal statutory power to punish police brutality in the states....

More difficult to analyze is a third class of fluctuating options, those which appear to have resulted from the changing factual perceptions of a particular judge. In some cases, the reasons for such a shift may be indistinguishable from pressures to coalesce. Thus, Justice Douglas' acquiescence in *Korematsu* v. *United States* probably was made easier by Chief Justice Stone's continuing reminders that opportunity to challenge relocation orders still remained open to petitioners so long as orders to report to control centers and actual detention were separable. Lack of opportunity for individuals to prove their loyalty was what had troubled Douglas all along. In other cases, shifting perspectives appear to have been a function of additional thought and homework, by a clerk or a Justice, into issues that were only partially perceived at first because of inadequate argument, briefs, or time. The Supreme Court does not follow the practice in some state supreme courts of assigning

cases by lot and of infrequent dissent. But it is not uncommon for a Justice assigned to express one consensus to reverse field after further analysis, and then persuade his colleagues to follow suit. Justice Murphy did so with unanimous approval in the complex Chickasaw-Choctaw land claim controversy.[2] An even neater example occurred in *Lawson* v. *Suwannee Fruit & Steamship Co.*, in 1949. There, after independent research by a clerk in a poor record showed that a workmen's compensation award for the particular petitioner might jeopardize statutory rights of longshoremen as a class, Murphy turned tail, reworked the opinion without asking the Court's leave, and won quick, eight-to-one approval at conference. Justice Frankfurter, at that point, could not resist the "dig":

> It seemed to me a compelled conclusion if due respect is to be given to legislation—if, that is, we let Congress make laws and not re-make them.
>
> This opinion (and change of Conference vote) ought to be a lesson that merely because a particular case is to be decided for a particular employee the result on a fair and long view may be a great disservice to labor and to Law. I could 'document' this truth.[3]

The difficulty is that the reasons for changing perceptions are not usually so obvious. One may argue that flux of this sort is inevitable in the cross-pressures of a collegial court of last resort whose main business lies at the frontier of legal development. One may speculate further about the competing values, the strategies of avoidance, the problems of obtaining linguistic consensus, the rush of business, and the just plain difficulties of substance which induce perceptual change. Occasionally, one may even suspect Justices of doing the unexpected just to confound bloc identification....

But no outsider really knows why judges

change their minds. Seldom do they admit, as Jackson hinted in *Everson* v. *Board of Education*, to having switched their votes.... Nor, it must be stressed, should judges be faulted either for changing their minds or for lack of complete candor. A major objective of the adversary system, after all, is prevention of premature classification and judgment. That judges may shift position between conference and final voting is not only well understood among themselves, but a testament to the limitations of conference and the effectiveness of the argumentation system. And it is hardly "robism" to suggest that a cloak of secrecy may be just as necessary for judges as for diplomats in making such accommodations possible.

Whatever their causes, however, shifting individual perceptions can significantly affect public policy and the ideological complexion of courts. Consider, for example, the changing positions of Justices Black and Douglas in three of the most ideology-charged decisions of the decade: *Martin* v. *Struthers, Colegrove* v. *Green,* and *Terminiello* v. *Chicago.*[4]

In *Struthers*, the Court faced the question whether an anti-doorbell ringing ordinance designed to protect sleeping night-shift workers in an industrial town violated the First Amendment rights of proselyting Jehovah's Witnesses. Although he too expressed sympathy in conference for the Sunday sleepers of Struthers, Chief Justice Stone at first was unable to attract a majority in support of "preferred freedoms." Justice Black, who saw the scales tipping toward privacy of the home and local control, expressed prophetic fears in conference that the next case might be Jehovah's Witnesses invading Roman Catholic services if no restraints were approved. That view was accepted by a five-four vote; and, after assigning himself the majority opinion, Black circulated a hard-hitting memorandum to the effect that such a

community reasonably could forbid doorbell ringing altogether in order to protect privacy. Then, after answering objections in a second circulation, Justice Black suddenly reversed himself. The ordinance was overturned by a five-four vote, and the Chief Justice graciously permitted Black to write a new majority opinion which in effect invited the town to try again with a more carefully drafted ordinance that accommodated privacy and free speech. After all, as Stone argued behind the scenes, some room for accommodation remained before community action, at least until homeowners had an opportunity to listen or object.

Justice Black's about-face in *Struthers* goes far toward explaining some of the puzzles in the opinions. For one thing, it accounted for Justice Murphy's emotional concurrence which replowed the same terrain but had originated as a Murphy-Douglas-Rutledge dissent against their colleague's failure to balance interests. It also made more sense of the Frankfurter-Jackson complaints that the Court was "wanting in explicitness" and attempting to resolve tough practical issues by a "vague but fervent transcendentalism." What the Court had decided was a narrow question of judgment—whether it was possible for a community to accommodate colliding interests by more carefully framed time, place, and manner regulations. What the public read, on the other hand, were heavily rhetorical outpourings from both sides which obscured the precise rights involved and exaggerated the doctrinal split over "preferred freedoms." No one could have guessed until twenty-five years later that privacy of the home and local control loomed so high in Justice Black's scale of values. No one could have guessed that the attitudes he expressed in the sit-in and racial picketing cases of the 1960's represented, not a switch attributable to advancing age, but constancy to prime values which, for two decades, the course of litigation had left unexposed.

Likewise, from reading the opinions in *Colegrove* v. *Green*, no one could have fathomed that Justice Black, author of the three-man opinion which viewed congressional reapportionment as a justiciable issue, had initially expressed contrary conclusions in conference, along with every other Justice but one.[5] Who could have guessed that Justice Black had not only echoed the general fears about entering the apportionment thicket, but himself had attempted to express those sentiments for the Court before he once again changed his mind and wrote the powerful minority opinion which structured a fateful enlargement of judicial power as a supervisor of the electoral process? The answer, of course, is that no one could have inferred such flux from votes or opinions. Having resolved his own misgivings, Justice Black simply advanced his conclusions unencumbered by his previous doubts.

The majority opinion in *Terminiello* v. *Chicago* also provided no clue that its author, Justice Douglas, had followed a parallel course. Nevertheless, both the Murphy and Burton papers indicate that Justice Douglas had initially perceived Terminiello's speech at a volatile political rally of Gerald L. K. Smith forces in Chicago as throwing a lighted match into an explosive situation and had cast his vote accordingly. Then, after reversing position and thus the result, Justice Douglas was assigned the majority opinion and defended the choice by arguments that many contemporaries regarded as the apogee of libertarian dogma.

These examples may be extreme because the opinions acknowledged none of the doubts which had been resolved. Yet they serve to make the point. Votes can be a crude measure of attitude. So can opinions, and even the lack of them. The ideological

commitments seemingly manifest in both may be lower and the basis of choice far more pragmatic than either imply on their face. Certainly that was true of the 1940's. The disparity between the rigid ideological appearance of opinions and the fluid choices behind them was sufficiently widespread as to pose genuine problems for anyone making ideological inferences, whether by analyzing opinions or by aggregating votes. After all, if it is true that even the most libertarian of Justices sweated so hard over their options, what are we to make of interpretations, advanced by both quantitative analysts and their critics, which explain libertarian judicial behavior as simply attitudinal automatism? Plainly, the data point to a deflation of the ideological component in the decision-making of this period.

. . . [T]he fluidity of choice on the Roosevelt and Vinson Courts serves as a reminder that judging, like most American decision-making, is situational and that causation is apt to be more complex than the simple mirroring of precedent or principle or personal belief systems.

This observation has particular bearing on the controversy between "quantifiers" and "qualifiers" regarding the accuracy of attitude measurement. All doubtless would agree that attitudes affect action. All probably would agree with Justice Frankfurter's aphorism that general propositions do decide concrete cases if a judge's convictions are strong enough. The main issue is how to determine attitudes and to chart their effects, and that touches again upon the question whether influence should be measured by doctrines or by votes. This question, of course, has close parallels to an older conflict between aggregationists and survey researchers in the study of voting behavior. An inherent problem of voting analysis generally is that votes, of themselves, do not distinguish underlying variations of intensity, issue perception, and certainty of response among voters. Opinion sampling and scaling techniques were designed to unravel these variables in mass electoral behavior, and today few scholars would seriously dispute their efficacy or rich potential. Guttman scaling, content analysis, and other quantitative techniques were adapted to judicial behavior as surrogates for opinion sampling. But while sampling poses problems enough in mass populations, there is little doubt that the surrogate methods of attitude analysis face rougher sledding in the Supreme Court. The principal reason is that the universe is a collegial elite whose members not only make decisions in a highly structured and secret process but also must offer persuasive collective reasons to the public. While scaling of judicial votes in split decisions has the virtue of stressing relationships among the decision-makers, the method excludes unanimous decisions and the power considerations which help produce them. Further, the unit of analysis itself is under collegial influences. The very reliance on votes to infer attitudes points to the essential problem of identifying the intervening variables which affect those votes.

. . . [T]he intervening variables of strategy and style, in my judgment, are so critical in judicial decision-making that they cannot be excluded from any stimulus-response model without distorting results and reducing the reliability of the most carefully constructed attitudinal inferences. . . .

If the foregoing argument is persuasive that greater fluidity of choice prevailed in the Supreme Court of the 1940's than is commonly assumed, the evidence presented has several implications for the empirical and normative concerns of the discipline. First, assuming that the experience of this decade can be projected, the data point to a potential disparity between a highly complex and fluid "input" stage and a relatively simplistic

official "output" in the judicial process. This disparity between choice and explanation aggravates a general analytical problem of reliably classifying hard data, votes and opinions, whether classification proceeds by a single observer or risks are cut by panel techniques. The disparity also points to the complexity of conversion processes, since presumably they too are affected by group interaction. The disparity likewise suggests the need of refining popular concepts about blocs, cliques, and attitudinal automatism which sometimes pass for causal explanations in both quantitative analyses and normative critiques of Supreme Court behavior. By no means do I conclude that the above examples of fluctuating options *refute* the findings of socio-psychological measurement, particularly the more sophisticated and careful versions as exemplified by Schubert's *The Judicial Mind*, or by Ulmer's suggestive work on the theory of sub-groups. Indeed, a surfacing latent attitude may be the very reason for the flux described; and aggregate analysis may be the most effective safeguard against the hazards of classification, particularly in the nonreplicable and highly impressionistic form in which findings such as mine are usually presented. The point is, however, *not necessarily*. Quantifiers must classify no less than qualifiers, and both should face squarely the probability and effect of fluid choices on their modal categories and attitudinal inferences. Because group theory focuses upon such variables while drawing from both behavioral and traditional resources, that approach offers a rich potential source of synthesis for analysis of judicial behavior.

Second, the evidence of the 1940's lends greater support to the lawyer's ideal of the judicial process as a system of reasoning than many legal realists would accept. Clearly, judges of all ideological persuasions pondered, bargained, and argued in the course of reaching their decisions, and they compromised their ideologies, too. No one can plow through the papers of a Stone or a Murphy without coming out with renewed respect for the give-and-take or without appreciation for the multiplicity of variables and constraints, including that old whipping-post, Law, that went into the decision-making of the era. . . .

NOTES

1. Eloise Snyder, "The Supreme Court as a Small Group," *Social Forces* 36 (March, 1958), 236–238.
2. *Choctaw Nation* v. *United States and Chickasaw Nation*, 318 U.S. 423 (1943). . . .
3. 336 U.S. 198 (1949). The conference vote was 5–4 in favor of reversal, with Vinson, Black, Douglas, Rutledge, and Murphy in the majority, but the last three Justices apparently had misgivings because the clerk noted question marks by their votes. The final outcome was an affirmance, Douglas, J., dissenting without opinion.
4. 319 U.S. 141 (1942); 328 U.S. 549 (1946); 337 U.S. 1 (1949).
5. On first impression, only Justice Douglas voted to intervene. Justice Murphy passed, and Justice Rutledge echoed general doubts about the political implications of the case. Rutledge later changed his mind on the justiciability issue, but cast the decisive vote against intervention because of difficulties perceived in equitable remedies. . . .

Fluidity on the United States Supreme Court: A Reexamination

Saul Brenner

At least since the late 1950s behavioral students of the Supreme Court have claimed that the justices' attitudes toward public policy issues are key determinants of their voting (see, for example, Schubert, 1965, 1974). The evidence in support of this claim has been derived mainly from Guttman scales of judicial voting on the final vote on the merits. In a bold article, published in 1968, Howard challenges the attitudinal explanation, arguing that: (1) it is "commonplace" for justices on the Supreme Court to "change their votes and permit their opinions to be conduits for the ideas of others.... Fluidity of choice is...extensive"; (2) "intervening variables operating in a collegial court mediate significantly between individual attitude and behavior"; and (3) "if a vote or an opinion has changed in response to a multiplicity of intracourt influences before its public exposure, how reliable is that vote or opinion as an indicator of attitude, ideology, or if one pleases, predilection?" (1968, pp. 43–44).

"Fluidity of the Supreme Court: A Reconsideration," Saul Brenner. An earlier version of this selection appeared in the *American Journal of Politics*, Vol. 24 (1980), 526–535 and in Vol. 26, (1982), 388–390. This version was written in July 1987. By permission of the University of Texas Press.

As evidence of his first two points Howard offers examples of Supreme Court behavior. ... Nevertheless, Howard's article is valuable because it suggests interesting theoretical questions that can be tested with more precise tools. To measure fluidity on the Court it would be useful both to do a content analysis of its opinion drafts and internal memos and to compare systematically the votes cast by the justices. This study will focus only upon the votes. More specifically, it will compare the original vote on the merits (also called the conference vote) with the final decision vote. These two votes are the only ones that pertain to the same decision by the Court, that is, whether to affirm or reverse the decision of the lower court. A comparison of these two votes offers a simple, if partial, measure of fluidity on the Court.

What kinds of questions ought to be asked when comparing these two votes? First, we want to know how much fluidity there is on the Court. We are interested both in *strong* fluidity, *i.e.*, a shift from affirm to reverse or from reverse to affirm, and in *weak* fluidity, *i.e.*, a switch from nonparticipation to reverse or affirm. Nonparticipation in a particular case occurs when a justice is absent from the Court's conference or when he is present but chooses not to vote.

Second, we want to find out if there are more vote changes for major decisions than for nonmajor ones. Howard argues that examining the private papers of several justices who served on the Court in the 1940s "tempt[s] one to say that hardly any major decision in. . .[that] decade was free from significant alteration of vote and language before announcement to the public" (1968, p. 44). Is the same conclusion also appropriate for nonmajor decisions?

Third, we are concerned not only with the extent of fluidity in voting on the Court but also with its impact. One way of measuring impact is to compare the number of votes received by the majority at the final vote on the merits with its tally at the original vote. If vote alterations were necessary for the minority to become the majority, then the vote changes are of significance. If, on the other hand, the vote shifts merely modified the size of a majority that was already winning at the original vote, then they are less important.

DATA AND PROCEDURE

I will attempt to answer these three questions regarding the full opinion cases of the Vinson Court. The Vinson Court lasted seven terms (i.e., from October term 1946 through October term 1952).

I chose to investigate the Vinson Court because I wished to use highly reliable original vote data. These data were collected by Jan Palmer of Ohio University who obtained them from the docket books and conference lists of seven justices who served on that Court. Palmer also gathered final vote data by examining the *United States Reports*.

In comparing the original and final votes I followed several rules. First, when there was more than one original vote on the merits, a condition present in a small number of cases, I used the last original vote.

Second, votes to "vacate" or to "modify" were treated as votes to "reverse." Third, if any vote could not be classified as either a vote to "affirm," "reverse," or "nonparticipation," its pair was excluded. There were 738 cases in Palmer's data set, of which 686 were usable. I was able to use 5840 pairs of votes.

Major, as opposed to nonmajor, cases were identified by using Slotnick's "important case" list.[1] In the Vinson Court era thirty-six cases were cited in at least three of Slotnick's five sources, of which thirty-three were usable.

FINDINGS

Amount of Fluidity

A comparison of the original and final votes reveals strong fluidity in ten percent of the pairs of votes (N=590), weak fluidity in three percent (N=204), and no fluidity in 86 percent (N=5046). Different results, of course, are obtained when cases are inspected, instead of pairs of votes. In 59 percent of the 686 cases (or in 402 cases) there was at least one strong or weak change in vote (see Table 1). In 74 percent of the cases in which there was an alteration of vote (or in 297 cases) only one or two justices shifted positions (see Table 1).

Fluidity in Major and in Nonmajor Cases

Whether one inspects pairs of votes (see Table 2) or cases one discovers that there are slightly more vote switches in nonmajor cases than in major cases. In nonmajor cases ten percent of the pairs of votes constitute strong fluidity, four percent weak fluidity, and 86 percent no fluidity. The equivalent statistics for major cases are six percent, three percent, and 91 percent (GAMMA= .22). There was at least one strong or weak

TABLE 1
Number of Vote Changes on the Vinson Court[a]

Weak Vote Changes	Strong Vote Changes								
	0	1	2	3	4	5	6	7	8
0	284	113	61	29	17	7	3	1	1
1	81	28	16	10	1	1	2	0	0
2	14	8	2	1	0	0	1	0	0
3	5	0	0	0	0	0	0	0	0

[a] N of Cases = 686

TABLE 2
Comparison of Fluidity in Major and in Nonmajor Cases in the Vinson Court

	Major Cases	Nonmajor Cases
Strong Fluidity	6% (18)[a]	10% (572)
Weak Fluidity	3% (8)	4% (196)
No Fluidity	91% (253)	86% (4793)
	100% (279)	100% (5561)
	Gamma = .22	

[a] N's of pairs of votes in parentheses

change in vote in 59 percent of the nonmajor cases (or in 386 cases) and in 48 percent of the major ones (or in 16 cases) (Q=.21).

IMPACT OF FLUIDITY: CONVERTING A MINORITY INTO A MAJORITY

In 15 percent of the cases in which vote changes occurred (that is, in 59 cases) the shifts in vote either transformed a minority at the original vote into a majority at the final vote (48 cases) or created a majority after the original vote was tied (11 cases). In 13 of the 59 cases (22 percent) there were four votes for a particular outcome at the original vote

and five votes for that outcome at the final vote.

In 85 percent of the cases in which fluidity took place (343 cases) the majority at the final vote was already winning at the original vote. The majority increased its size in 78 percent of these cases (313 cases), lost votes in 10 percent, and remained the same size in 12 percent (see Table 3).

These findings suggest that the justices are more likely to switch from the minority or nonparticipation position at the original vote to the majority position at the final vote than to shift in the opposite direction. The vote changes that occurred conformed to this pattern, for 79 percent of the strong fluidity votes (306 votes) and 69 percent of the weak

TABLE 3
Comparison of the Original Vote Size with Final Vote Size in Cases Where Fluidity Occurred on the Vinson Court[a]

Size of Majority in Original Vote	Size of Majority at Final Vote						
	4	5	6	7	8	9	Total
0	0	0	0	0	1	0	1
1	0	1	1	0	0	1	3
2	0	1	1	0	1	3	6
3	2	3	1	3	2	2	13
4	0	18	14	7	8	5	52
5	0	27	51	17	8	14	117
6	1	15	15	42	14	19	106
7	0	5	5	4	30	19	63
8	0	2	6	3	3	24	38
9	0	0	0	2	1	0	3
Total	3	72	94	78	68	87	402

[a] N = 402, N of non-fluidity cases = 284

fluidity votes (118 votes) moved toward consensus, while only 21 percent of the strong and 31 percent of the weak fluidity votes moved in the opposite direction.[2]

CONCLUSION AND DISCUSSION

The findings of this study suggest that the justices usually vote at the final vote in the same way as they voted at the original vote. This pattern occurs in 86 percent of the situations. The justices strive to vote "correctly" at the original vote because that vote not only decides which group of justices is in the majority for the purposes of the initial assignment of the Opinion of the Court, but also determines which group of justices will almost always be in the majority at the final vote. Too many alterations in votes would disrupt the Court's proceedings (Goldman, 1969, p. 219; Spaeth, 1979, p. 22), necessitating the reassignment of the Court's opinion

or a substantial redrafting of it. As a consequence the Court's output would decline.

But, as Court procedures allow, justices do modify their votes. A strong or weak change in vote took place in 13 percent of the votes and in 59 percent of the cases. Only in 15 percent of the cases, however, did the shifts in vote convert a minority at the original vote into a majority at the final vote or create a majority after the original vote was tied. In the other 85 percent of the cases the fluidity merely affected the size of a majority that was already winning at the original vote, mostly by increasing its size. Clearly, some of the justices, once they have lost at the original vote or failed to participate at that vote, are willing to conform to the opinion of the Court's majority and vote with them at the final vote. Indeed, over three-quarters of the vote changes moved in a consensus direction. In this respect the Supreme Court is similar to almost all other small groups.

What insight does this study provide about

the reliability of the final vote scales as a measure of judicial attitudes? The finding that in 86 percent of the votes the justices voted the same way at both stages supports the contention that the final vote scale is a good index of attitudes, although voting consistency can be explained on other grounds as well.[3] On the other hand, the great amount of consensus voting between the original and final vote on the merits suggests that the final vote scale may be a product not only of attitudes but also of consensus voting. In view of this possibility it is strongly recommended that when original vote data are available they should be used in interpreting the final vote scales.

One final caveat: this study, of course, only pertains to the Vinson Court. We do not know to what extent the patterns observed here can apply to Courts in which consensus norms or work loads differ substantially from this Court.

RESEARCH POSTSCRIPT

Howard (1968) speaks of extensive fluidity in vote and language on the U.S. Supreme Court. In my earlier analysis, I compared the original vote on the merits in conference with the final decision vote in the 1946 to 1952 period and found considerable stability in voting. I examined both *strong* fluidity (*i.e.*, a shift from reverse to affirm or from affirm to reverse) and *weak* fluidity (a switch from nonparticipation to affirm or reverse). Now that the University of Texas Law Library has opened Justice Tom Clark's docket books, I can test whether the results of my earlier study hold for the 1956 to 1967 period.[4]

Amount of Fluidity

Eighty-seven percent of the time in the 1956 to 1967 era the justices voted the same way at the final vote that they had voted in the

original vote (N = 7,150). Strong fluidity took place in 10 percent of the situations (N = 791), while weak fluidity occurred in 3 percent (N = 206). In 55 percent of the cases there was at least one strong or weak change of vote. These results are virtually the same as those reported for the 1946 to 1952 period. . . .

Fluidity in Major and Nonmajor Cases

There were 770 pairs of votes in major cases and 7,377 pairs in nonmajor cases.[5] No significant differences were found between the vote changes in these two kinds of cases (Gamma = .14). The results for major cases were 8 percent (strong fluidity), 2 percent (weak fluidity), and 90 percent (no fluidity), and for nonmajor cases 10 percent (strong fluidity), 3 percent (weak fluidity), and 87 percent (no fluidity). A similar pattern emerges when one focuses upon cases instead of votes. In 56 percent of the nonmajor cases, and in 44 percent of the major ones, was there at least one strong or weak change in vote (Q = .25). Both these findings closely parallel those obtained. . .for the Vinson Court.

Impact of Fluidity: Converting a Minority into a Majority

In 16 percent of the cases in the 1956 to 1967 era in which vote changes took place (that is, in 85 cases) the shifts in vote between the original and final vote transformed a minority at the original vote into a majority at the final vote (see Table 4). In the remaining 84 percent of the fluidity cases (or in 339 cases) the majority at the final vote was already winning at the original vote. The majority increased its size in 68 percent of the fluidity cases (or in 298 cases), lost votes in 24 percent (105 cases), and remained the same size in 8 percent (26 cases).

TABLE 4
Comparison of the Original Vote Size With Final Vote Size in Cases Where Fluidity Occurred (Supreme Court)

Size of Majority In Original Vote	Size of Majority at Final Vote						Total
	4	5	6	7	8	9	
0	1	0	0	1	2	0	4
1	0	0	1	1	1	0	3
2	0	0	2	2	1	0	5
3	2	5	6	3	1	3	20
4	0	17	18	9	2	7	53
5	2	11	42	21	6	11	93
6	0	21	11	44	16	26	118
7	0	7	28	9	35	38	117
8	0	2	7	17	5	57	88
9	0	0	3	2	16	0	21
Total	5	63	118	109	85	142	522

N = 522.
N of non-fluidity cases = 427

These results are comparable to those found for the Vinson Court period. The only difference worth noting is that in the 1956 to 1967 time span there was slightly less conformity voting than in the Vinson Court era and slightly more shifting away from the majority position at the original vote.

Thus, three fluidity patterns found for the 1946 to 1952 period continued in the 1956 to 1967 era. It appears, therefore, that certain aspects of internal decision making on the Court were remarkably stable in a twenty-one year period, under two chief justices, in a Court in which eleven new justices started their careers, and during a time in which the work load of the Court was continuously increasing. . . .

NOTES

1. Slotnick's "important case" list is derived from Constitutional Law texts. Us-ing these texts to identify major decisions can be defended on grounds of convenience only, for what is actually isolated is major *constitutional* decisions, not major decisions. Nevertheless, there is probably a substantial overlap between major decisions and major constitutional decisions in modern Supreme Courts. [See Elliot E. Slotnick, "Who Speaks for the Court? Majority Opinion Assignment from Taft to Burger," *American Journal of Political Science* 23 (1979), p. 62.]

2. In computing these statistics the votes in the 59 cases mentioned above are un-counted.

3. The final vote can be based upon attitude even if it differs from the original one. A justice may, for example, have been absent at the original vote or may have been too rushed to study the case and may only later, at the final vote, cast

a ballot that mirrors his attitudes. Or a justice may switch from affirm to reverse because by the second vote he has a different understanding of the issues. Both votes may reflect his attitudes.

4. The original vote on the merits was obtained from Clark's docket books, while the final vote was secured from *U.S. Supreme Court Reports—Lawyer's Edition*. Companion cases in which all the original and final votes were the same were counted as one case with one set of votes. Excluded from the data set were: (1) cases for which most or all of the votes were not recorded by Clark, (2) cases which could not be classified as affirm, reverse, or nonparticipation at either the original or final vote, (3) the few cases in which more than one original vote was cast (usually as a consequence of a rehearing), and (4) the twenty-seven votes from the 1961 term of the Court in which Justice Frankfurter voted at the original vote on the merits but failed to vote at the final vote. In contrast to the first study, all other votes in which a justice voted to affirm or reverse at the original vote and did not participate at the final vote were counted as weak fluidity. There were few votes of this kind. There were 949 cases and 8,147 pairs of original and final votes in the data set.

5. Major cases were secured by using Slotnick's "important case" list. One hundred twenty-one cases in the 1956 to 1967 era were cited in at least three of Slotnick's sources, of which eighty-seven were usable.

REFERENCES

Goldman, Sheldon. 1969. Backgrounds, Attitudes and the Voting Behavior of Judges: A Comment on Joel Grossman's Social Backgrounds and Judicial Decisions. *Journal of Politics*, 31 (February 1969): 214–222.

Howard, J. Woodford, Jr. 1968. On the fluidity of judicial choice. *American Political Science Review*, 62 (March 1968): 43–56.

Schubert, Glendon. 1965. *The Judicial Mind: Attitudes and Ideologies of Supreme Court Justices*, 1946–1963. Evanston: Northwestern University Press.

———. 1974. *The Judicial Mind Revisited: Psychometric Analysis of Supreme Court Ideology*. New York: Oxford University Press.

Spaeth, Harold J. 1979. *Supreme Court Policy Making: Explanation and Prediction*. San Francisco: W.H. Freeman.

The Influence of the Chief Justice in the Decisional Process of the Supreme Court

David J. Danelski

In theory, the relationship among the Justices of the Supreme Court of the United States is one of equality, and frequently the Chief Justice is referred to as first among equals. Rarely, however, is there equality in practice. Some Justices are more able, more persuasive, or more personable than their associates, and, in the calculus of influence which lies behind every decision of the Court, these are the important factors. The Chief Justice, by virtue of his office, has a unique opportunity for leadership. He is the key figure in the Court's *certiorari* practice. He presides in open court and over the secret conferences where he usually presents each case to his associates, giving his opinion first and voting last. He assigns the opinion of the Court in virtually all cases when he votes with the majority, and, as a practical matter, he decides when the opinion will be announced. But the Chief Justiceship does not guarantee leadership. It only offers its incumbent an opportunity to lead. Optimum leadership inheres in the combination of the

office and an able, persuasive, personable judge.

The Chief Justiceship has lived and grown in the shadow of judicial secrecy. Data cannot be obtained about it for purposes of analysis by direct observation of the Chief Justice's participation in the decisional process of the Court. Manuscripts, memoirs, interviews, and the Court's official reports are the chief available sources of data. Although one must be wary of coming too close to the present, lest disclosures embarrass Justices still on the bench, a study of the Chief Justiceship, to be worthwhile, must be close enough to the present to yield generalizations useful in understanding the office as it is today. In an effort to avoid both difficulties, the period 1921 to 1946—the era of Chief Justices Taft, Hughes, and Stone—was selected for analysis.

SOME THEORETICAL CONSIDERATIONS

Leadership in the Supreme Court is best understood in terms of influence: CJ influences J to do x to the extent that CJ performs some activity y as a result of which J chooses to do x. Explicit in this definition

Paper delivered at the 1975 annual meeting of the American Political Science Association. Reprinted with the permission of the author. Most footnotes have been omitted.

are the two concepts, activity and interaction. Activity simply refers to things Court members do, for example, voting and writing opinions. Interaction refers to activity by one member of the Court to which another member responds, for example, conference discussion and opinion assignment. Interaction is indispensable to influence, for if J does not respond to CJ's activity, J cannot choose to do x as the result of y. Influence, however, implies more than surface activity and interaction, for frequently underlying these phenomena are expectations, values, and attitudes of CJ and J.

Expectations are evaluative standards applied to an incumbent of a position, such as the Chief Justice, and a set of those expectations defines his role. The term "expectation" is used in the normative sense (CJ *should* do y) rather than in the predictive sense (CJ *will* do y). Role is an important concept in the analysis of judicial behavior because the expectations the Chief Justice and Justices hold for themselves and each other affect their activity. Conversely, activity affects expectations. The Chief Justice, by his activity, can create new expectations and to some extent thereby redefine his role and even the roles of the Justices. Chief Justice Hughes, for example, did this when he established the "special list" for disposing of unmeritorious *certiorari* cases without conference discussion. Thereafter, the Chief Justice was expected to determine initially which *certioraris* should be considered in conference, and if a Justice wanted a case transferred from the "special list" so that it might be discussed and voted upon, the Chief Justice was expected to do so upon request.

Likability is an important dimension of influence. Like other men, Court members tend to like some of their associates more than others, to be indifferent to some, and perhaps even to dislike others. Chief Justice

Taft, for example, regarded Justice Van Devanter as "the closest friend [he had] on the Court...," and when he was fatally ill in January, 1930, Van Devanter was the only member of the Court who was allowed to see him.[1]...As this paper will show, the social structure of the Court is significant in the decisional process, and likability is an important variable in influence, for it is related to the degree and kind of interaction between Court members. Thus, the more the Chief Justice is liked, the greater is his influence potential.

Esteem is another important dimension of influence. The member who is regarded as having the best ideas in conference and being best able to handle the tough cases assigned him for opinion is ordinarily highly esteemed by his associates. Of course, there may be differences of opinion as to who is the most able member of the Court, the next most able, etc., but there is no doubt that such ranking occurs.[2] Esteem within the Court may rest on, or be increased by, prestige he carries over from previous high status positions, such as President, presidential candidate, Secretary of State, etc. The position of Chief Justice in itself, however, probably adds only a little to the esteem of its incumbent in the eyes of his associates. In the Court his esteem depends more upon his over-all ability and how well he fulfills his role as Chief Justice.

In terms of influence, then, the ideal Chief Justice is a persuasive, esteemed, able, and well-liked judge who perceives, fulfills, and even expands his role as head of the Court. One might ask: influence for what? The more important objects of influence are the attainment of: (1) a majority vote for the Chief Justice's position, (2) written opinions satisfactory to him, (3) social cohesion in the Court, and (4) unanimous decisions. In the close case, where a Justice is wavering in his vote, influence may be the difference between a decision one way or another. Since the Chief Justice assigns opinions in cases in which he votes with the majority, the content of an opinion is to some degree determined by his selection of the Court's spokesman. Unless there is minimum social cohesion among the Justices, collegial decision-making is virtually impossible. And where there is such cohesion, unanimous decisions tend to be prevalent, for unanimity arises from the give and take of compromise. Thus, the main objects of influence go to the heart of the Court's decisional process.

THE DECISION TO MAKE A DECISION

Today, the appellate jurisdiction of the Court is almost entirely discretionary. Therefore, the threshold decision to take or not to take a case for review is crucial; six out of seven cases go no further in the Court's decisional process. Standing at the throat of the Court's discretionary jurisdiction is the Chief Justice. All the justices examine the petitions for *certiorari* and jurisdictional statements, but the Chief Justice's examination must be particularly careful, for it is his duty to present them in conference. Chief Justice Taft's preparation of *certioraris* was like Holmes's: not done so thoroughly as to decide the cases, but thoroughly enough to decide whether or not they should be brought before the Court.[3] Chief Justice Hughes, however, made very complete and thorough preparation, usually going into the merits of each case and often deciding it "then and there in his own mind."[4] Apparently Chief Justice Stone, who was prone to defer judgment for days and even weeks after cases were argued, usually prepared the *certioraris* and jurisdictional statements only to determine whether the Court should exercise its jurisdiction.[5]

Until the middle 1930's, every petition for *certiorari* was presented in conference by the Chief Justice and voted upon by the Court. At the beginning of a term, some 250 to 300 *certioraris* would be awaiting disposition. Taft scheduled daily conferences to dispose of them, taking up about 50 to 60 cases a day. At first, Hughes followed Taft's procedure, presenting and disposing of as many as a hundred petitions for *certiorari* in a single afternoon.[6] Then he established a unanimous consent procedure in which the Chief Justice was the key figure. If the Chief Justice decided that a petition for *certiorari* was frivolous or ill-founded and therefore did not merit conference discussion, he placed it on a "special list" which was circulated to the Associates. Upon request, any case on the special list would be transferred to the regular take-up list, but cases remaining on the special list were automatically denied *certiorari* without discussion. Hughes disposed of about 60 per cent of the petitions for *certiorari* via the special list, and rarely did a Justice challenge his lists. Challenges were also relatively rare during Stone's Chief Justiceship.[7]

The innovation of the speical list increased the influence potential of the Chief Justice. Petitions he wants discussed in conference are taken up automatically, but petitions are not so easily transferred from the special to the regular list. The Justice who challenges the special list must be well prepared and willing to disagree openly with the Chief Justice. To the extent, therefore, that a Justice does not prepare thoroughly or is hesitant to disagree with the Chief Justice, because he likes or esteems him or for some other reason, the Chief Justice's influence increases proportionately.

The Chief Justice's second opportunity for influence during this phase of the decisional process arises when he presents the petitions for *certiorari* and jurisdictional statements to the conference, for he gives his views first and usually speaks longer than any of his associates. The influence of the Chief Justice in conference is considered later, but a word as to the time spent on petitions for *certiorari* and jurisdictional statements is in order here. Frequently when Hughes finished his presentation of those cases, his associates had nothing to add, and when there was a discussion, he limited it. In the Hughes Court, the average time devoted to the discussion of a *certiorari* case was 3.6 minutes. During Taft's Chief Justiceship, the average *certiorari* case received about 10 minutes, but Taft felt that too much time was devoted to such cases, thus limiting discussion of argued and submitted cases. During Stone's Chief Justiceship, "petitions for *certiorari* and jurisdictional statements," said Justice Douglas, "were never more fully or carefully discussed."[8]

Taft admitted that his conference activity in regard to *certioraris* was not very influential: when the Court votes on *certioraris*, he said, "I'm usually in the minority...."[9] Hughes was more influential partly because of his rigorous control of discussion. In the three and one-half minutes allowed each *certiorari* petition, there could be little discussion, for usually it would take that long to present the case and vote. Thus, by virtually monopolizing the time available, he greatly influenced the *certiorari* and probable jurisdiction decisions. Conversely, Stone's influence was probably less than Hughes's because of the expanded discussion of *certioraris* and jurisdictional statements during his Chief Justiceship.

ORAL ARGUMENT

When the Court hears oral argument, the Chief Justice is only in a little better position than his associates to influence the deci-

sional process. As presiding officer, he has some discretion in extending counsel's time for argument, but beyond that, his influence depends primarily upon his esteem and interaction. For oral argument is a period of deliberation in which Court members frequently arrive at tentative decisions that usually accord with their final votes....

IN CONFERENCE

In conference, the Chief Justice is in a favorable position to influence his associates. In order to explain the nature of his influence at this stage of the decisional process a theory of conference leadership is necessary. Relying principally upon the empirical studies of decision-making groups by Bales, Slater, and Berkowitz, the following theory has been constructed: The primary task of the conference is the decision of cases through interaction. In making decisions, some Court members initiate and receive more interaction than others. Usually one member makes more suggestions, gives more opinions, orients the discussion more frequently, and successfully defends his ideas more often than the others. Usually, he is regarded as having the best ideas for the decision of cases and is highly esteemed by his associates. Thus, he emerges as *task leader* of the conference. He is apt to be an intense man, and, in concentrating on the Court's decisions, his response to the emotional needs of his associates is apt to be secondary. The interaction involved in deciding cases tends to cause conflict, tension, and antagonism, which, if allowed to get out of hand, would make the intelligent decision of cases virtually impossible. The negative aspects of interaction are counterbalanced by members of the conference who initiate interaction relieving tension and showing solidarity and agreement. One member usually performs more such activity than the others. He invites orientation, opinions, and suggestions, and, in general, attends to the emotional needs of his associates by affirming their value as individuals and Court members. Typically, he is the best-liked member of the conference and emerges as its *social leader*. Not only is he well liked; usually he wants to be well liked. He is apt to dislike conflict, and its avoidance may be a felt necessity for him. Thus, it is difficult for him to assume task leadership of the conference.

Yet it is possible for the Chief Justice to be both task and social leader. Although his task leadership is not primarily derived from his office, the fact that he speaks first in conference tends to maintain such leadership if he has an independent claim to it. Also his control of the conference process puts him in a favorable position to exercise social leadership, for he can minimize exchanges which contribute toward negative feelings among Court members and perform other activity which favorably disposes his associates toward him. Assuming he performs both aspects of leadership well and fulfills the important expectations of his role, his influence in conference tends to be high. Other important consequences, stated as hypotheses, are: (1) Conflict in conference tends to be minimal. (2) Court members tend to be socially cohesive. (3) Court members tend to be satisfied with the conference. (4) The conference tends to be productive in terms of the number of decisions made for the time spent. Rarely, however, are both aspects of leadership combined in a single individual. Typically, leadership is shared in conference. If it is positively shared, that is, if a Chief Justice who is social leader forms a coalition with a Justice who is task leader and they work together, a situation prevails which is similar to the one in which both aspects of leadership are combined in the Chief Justice. Such coalitions ordinarily occur where the personal relations between the Chief Justice and the task leader are fairly close. However, if leadership is negatively shared, that is, if the Chief Justice and the task leader do not work together and even compete against each other, then not only does the Chief Justice's influence in conference tend to decrease, but conflict tends to increase, and cohesion, satisfaction, and production tend to decrease.

There was positive sharing of leadership during Taft's Chief Justiceship: Taft was social leader and his good friend and appointee, Van Devanter, was task leader. Evidence of Van Devanter's esteem and task leadership is abundant. Taft, time and time again, asserted that Van Devanter was the most able Justice on the Court. If the Court were to vote, he said, that would be its judgment, too. The Chief Justice admitted that he did not know how he could get along without Van Devanter in conference, for Van Devanter kept the Court consistent with itself, and "his power of statement and his immense memory make him an antagonist in conference who generally wins against all opposition." The impression Van Devanter's contemporaries had of him was: "Here is a man with great physical vigor, a powerful intellect and a driving and dominant personality."[10] Though he was absorbed by his work, he had a sense of humor, "not of the frivolous or merry sort," but "always dignified." At times, Van Devanter's ability actually embarrassed Taft, and the Chief Justice wondered if it might not be better to have Van Devanter run the conference himself. "Still," mused the former President, "I must worry along until the end of my ten years, content to aid in the deliberation when there is a difference of opinion." In other words, Taft was content to perform the functions of social leadership. Clearly, he was the best liked member of his Court, and he wanted to be liked. His friendship with Van Devanter was especially close, but he valued the friendship of each Justice with whom he served, even that of McReynolds, whom he characterized as a "grouch." "I am old enough to know," he wrote to one of his sons after an incident with McReynolds, "that the best way to get along with people with whom you have to live always is to restrain your impatience and consider that doubtless you have peculiarities that try other people."

Discussion in the Taft-Van Devanter conference was described in 1928 as being of "the freest character," and naturally this led to some conflict. But when the Justices disagreed, it was usually, as Brandeis said, "without any ill feeling"; it was "all very friendly."

. . . During his Chief Justiceship, the Justices were satisfied with the conferences. "Things go happily in the conference room," Brandeis remarked. "The judges go home less tired emotionally and less weary physically than in White's day." Despite differences of opinion, there was compromise and teamwork among the liberal and conservative Justices alike. And there was production. The Court under Taft, for the first time in more than 50 years, came close to clearing its docket. Taft's influence in conference was probably as great as it could have been, for his coalition with Van Devanter gave him power he would not have had otherwise.

Task and social leadership were combined in Hughes. Overall, he was the most esteemed member of his Court.[11] His prior high positions undoubtedly contributed to his high esteem, but primarily it was due to his performance in conference. His associates could always be sure that he was well prepared. Blessed with a photographic memory, he would summarize comprehensively and accurately the facts of each case. When he was finished, he would look up and say with a smile: "Now I will state where I come

out." Then he would outline his views as to how the case should be decided. Sometimes that is all the discussion a case received, and the Justices proceeded to vote for the disposition suggested by the Chief. Where there was a discussion, the Justices gave their views in order of seniority without interruption, stating why they concurred or dissented from the views of the Chief Justice. After the Justices had their say, Hughes would review the discussion, pointing out the agreement and disagreement with the views expressed. Then he usually called for a vote. In terms of interaction, Hughes was the key figure of the conference. He made more suggestions, gave more opinions, and oriented the conference more than any other member. He not only did most of the talking; his associates' remarks were usually addressed to him, and they discussed the views he initially presented. Clearly, Hughes was conference task leader. His personality was in some respects similar to Van Devanter's. "The Chief Justice was an intense man," said Justice Roberts. "When he had serious business to transact he allowed no consideration to interfere with his operations. He was so engrossed in the vital issue that he had no time for lightness and pleasantry."

Yet Hughes's relationship with his associates was genial and cordial, and he was regarded as being "considerate, sympathetic, and responsive." Never in the eleven years that Roberts sat with Hughes in conference did he see him lose his temper. Never did he hear him pass a personal remark or even raise his voice. Never did he witness him interrupting or engaging in controversy with an associate. Despite his popular stereotype, Hughes had a "keen sense of humor" which aided in keeping differences in conference from becoming discord. On the whole, he was well liked. . . .

Justice Stone's attitude toward Hughes, however, was ambivalent. From the beginning of Hughes's Chief Justiceship, he thought Hughes did not allow adequate time for discussion in conference. Stone was also critical of Hughes' presentation of cases. The Chief Justice, he said, would greatly over-elaborate "unimportant details" and then dispose of the vital questions "in a sentence or two." Stone referred to a portion of Hughes's presentation of the AAA case as "painful elaboration." Oddly enough, Hughes was not aware of Stone's attitude, for Stone never openly challenged Hughes' methods, even when he had strong feelings about them. Why did not Stone speak out? If he had pressed his views in conference, Hughes could not have stopped him. It might be suggested that Hughes' esteem among his associates tended to inhibit discussion generally; for, as Frankfurter said, the "moral authority" exerted by the Chief "inhibited irrelevance, repetition, and fruitless discussion." It might have inhibited relevant and fruitful discussion as well. Stone's ambivalence toward Hughes might be also traced to his conception of the Chief Justice's role in conference which he learned during Taft's Chief Justiceship. Since leadership was shared in the Taft Court, the Chief Justice was a more permissive presiding officer, and Stone apparently felt that Hughes should have presided in a similar manner.

Although there was some conflict in the Hughes conference, the Chief Justice used his position as presiding officer to cut off discussion that showed signs of deteriorating into wrangling. Socially, the Hughes Court was fairly cohesive. Justice Roberts said that though the Court was divided on constitutional policy, there was a feeling of "personal cordiality and comradeship" among the Justices.... Unquestionably, Hughes's influence in conference was great.

During Stone's Chief Justiceship, conference leadership was negatively shared.... Stone departed from the conference role cut

out for him by Hughes. When he presented cases, he lacked the apparent certitude of his predecessor, and, at times, his statement indicated that he was still groping for a solution. In that posture, the case would be passed down to his associates. Justices would speak out of turn, and Stone did little to control their debate. Instead, like his younger associates, he would join in the debate with alacrity, "delighted to take on all comers around the conference table." "Jackson," he would say, "that's damned nonsense." "Douglas, *you* know better than that." In other words, Stone was still acting like an Associate Justice, and in the free and easy interaction of the conference, his presumptive task leadership began to slip from his grasp.

Eventually, Justice Black emerged as leading contender for task leadership of the conference. Although Stone esteemed Black, he distrusted his unorthodox approach, and no coalition occurred as in the Taft Court. Most of the Justices, having served under Hughes, probably expected that Stone should lead in conference much in the same manner as his predecessor. When he did not, a problem arose which is similar to the one studied by Heyns. Heyns's study suggests that when a designated leader of a conference group does not perform the task functions expected of him, the group will tend to accept leadership from one of its other members. But if the designated leader performs his task functions, members who act like leaders will tend to be rejected by the group. Stone's case was ambiguous, for Stone performed some task functions. That may explain why some Justices accepted Black's assertion of task leadership and others did not. Douglas, Murphy, and Rutledge esteemed and liked Black and went along with his leadership which, as senior Associate, he was able to reinforce by usually speaking before them in conference and by assigning opinions when Stone dissented. Roberts, Frankfurter, and Jackson, however, rejected Black's leadership, regarding him as a usurper of functions which were properly Stone's. Reed, who was inclined toward Black, stood in the middle as did Stone. Since Black asserted task leadership, a word might be said about his personality. His former law clerk, John P. Frank, described him in the following terms: "...Black is a very, very tough man. When he is convinced, he is cool hard steel.... His temper is usually in close control, but he fights, and his words may occasionally have a terrible edge. He can be a rough man in an argument."

Debates in conference were heated in the Stone Court and a social leader was needed to sooth ruffled tempers, relieve tensions created by interaction, and maintain solidarity. Stone was liked and respected by all of his associates and could have performed this function well, but he did not. He did not use his control over the conference's process, as Hughes did, to cut off debate leading to irreconcilable conflict. He did not remain neutral when controversies arose so that he could be in a position to mediate them. As Professor Mason said, "He was totally unprepared to cope with the petty bickering and personal conflict in which his Court became engulfed." In sum, he did not provide the conference with effective social leadership.

The combination of negative sharing of task leadership and the failure of social leadership increased conflict in conference during Stone's Chief Justiceship. The conflict was not friendly as in Taft's day; rather it was acrimonious, and, at times, descended to the level of personalities. On one occasion, even Stone's integrity was challenged. Cohesion in the Court decreased. Satisfaction with the conference also decreased. Frankfurter warned Stone about the dangers of Justices speaking out of turn after the first confer-

ence, and a year later he was appalled at the "easy-going, almost heedless way in which views on Constitutional issues touching the whole future direction of this country were floated...." Extended discussion meant extended conferences, and frequently they lasted until after six in the evening and sometimes had to be continued on Monday, Tuesday, or even Wednesday of the following week. "On more than one Saturday," Frankfurter noted, "the discussion after four-thirty gave evidence of fatigued minds and occasionally of frayed nerves." He longed for the taut four-hour conference of the Hughes Court and felt that the justices of the Stone Court were not always well prepared for conference and discussion was not duly focused. Production decreased. The Court under Stone decided as many cases as the Hughes Court did, but the time spent in conference to do this was just about double. It is probably safe to say that Stone's influence in conference was no greater than that of some of his associates.

Hughes was probably the most influential conference leader in modern times because he was able to perform both the task and social functions of leadership. These functions are to some degree incompatible and ordinarily a Chief Justice will be predisposed to perform either the task or social function, but not both. It is possible that Taft's strong dislike of conflict and his desire to be liked would have prevented him from becoming task leader even if he had the ability and esteem of Van Devanter. This, too, may have been the reason for Stone's failure as task leader. For Justice Jackson said, "Stone dreaded conflict" and the description of Black as "a very, very tough man" could not be applied to Stone. Stone, it would seem, was made of the intellectual, but not of the emotional, stuff that task leaders are made of. By comparison, it would seem that these elements were magnificently combined in

Hughes. But there was more to Hughes' success as conference leader than that. He had all the advantages of both Taft and Stone and few of their disadvantages. He apparently had more esteem than Taft when he came to the Court as Chief Justice, and on the Court he had more esteem than either Taft or Stone. Like Stone, he had the advantage of having been a Court member; but he did not have the disadvantage of disassociating himself from his former role of Associate Justice. The principal thing he learned during his service with Chief Justice White was how not to preside in conference. He felt White did not give the leadership he should have in conference and did not control and focus the discussion of the Justices. As Chief Justice, Hughes intended to act otherwise. He had a clear conception of his role in conference and acted accordingly. One might well conclude that Hughes understood the task and social functions of leadership and rationally sought to perform them to maintain his position in conference.

ASSIGNMENT OF THE COURT'S OPINION

In all cases in which the Chief Justice votes with the majority, he may write the Court's opinion or assign it to one of his associates who voted with him.[12] The making of assignments is significant in terms of influence because the selection of the Court's spokesman may be instrumental in:

(1)   Determining the value of a decision as a precedent, that is, depending upon the writer, an opinion may be placed on one ground rather than another or two grounds instead of one, or deal narrowly or broadly with the issues.

(2)   Making a decision as acceptable as possible to the public.

(3)   Holding the Chief Justice's majority

together in a close case.

(4)   Persuading dissenting associates to join in the Court's opinion.

The Chief Justice has an opportunity to exercise such influence in a high percentage of cases. Taft and Hughes assigned more than 95 per cent of the Court's opinions during their Chief Justiceships. Stone's assignment average was slightly better than 85 per cent. Usually assignments by the Chief Justice are accepted without question by the Justices.

The Chief Justice has maximal control over an opinion if he assigns it to himself, and undoubtedly Chief Justices have retained many important cases for that reason. The Chief Justice's retention of "big cases" is generally accepted by the Justices. In fact, the expectation is that he should write in those cases so as to lend the prestige of his office to the Court's pronouncement. In varying degrees, Chief Justices have fulfilled this expectation. Taft wrote opinions in 34 per cent of the "important constitutional cases"[13] decided while he was Chief Justice. Hughes' and Stone's percentages were 28.9 and 17.9, respectively.

When the Chief Justice does not speak for the Court, his influence lies primarily in his assignment of important cases to associates who generally agree with him. From 1925 to 1930, Taft designated his fellow conservatives, Sutherland and Butler, to speak for the Court in 50 per cent of the important constitutional cases assigned to Associate Justices. From 1932 to 1937, Hughes, who agreed more with Roberts, Van Devanter, and Sutherland than the rest of his associates, assigned 44 per cent of the important constitutional cases to Roberts and Sutherland. From 1943 to 1945, Stone assigned 55 per cent of those cases to Douglas and Frankfurter. During that period, only Reed agreed more with Stone than Frankfurter, but Douglas agreed with Stone less than any other

Justice except Black. Stone had high regard for Douglas' ability, and this may have been the Chief Justice's overriding consideration in his assignments to Douglas.

It is possible that the Chief Justice might seek to influence dissenting Justices to join in the Court's opinion by adhering to one or both of the following assignment rules:

Rule 1: Assign the case to the Justice whose views are the closest to the dissenters on the ground that his opinion would take a middle approach upon which both majority and minority could agree.

Rule 2: Where there are blocs on the Court and a bloc splits, assign the case to a majority member of the dissenters' bloc on the ground that he would take a middle approach upon which both majority and minority could agree and that the minority Justices would be more likely to agree with him because of general mutuality of agreement.

There is some evidence that early in Taft's Chief Justiceship he followed Rule 1 occasionally and assigned himself cases in an effort to win over dissenters. An analysis of his assignments from 1925 to 1930, however, indicates that he apparently did not adhere to either of the above rules with any consistency. Stone's assignments from 1943 to 1945 show the same thing. In other words, Taft and Stone did not generally use their assignment power to influence their associates to unanimity. However, an analysis of Hughes' assignments from 1932 to 1937 indicates that he probably did. He appears to have followed Rule 1 when either the liberal or conservative blocs dissented intact. When the liberal bloc dissented, Roberts, who was then a center judge, was assigned 46.5 per cent of the opinions. The remaining 53.5 per cent were divided among the conservatives, apparently according to their degree of conservatism: Sutherland, 25 per cent; Butler, 17.8 per cent; McReynolds, 10.7 per cent.

When the conservative bloc dissented, Hughes divided 63 per cent of the opinions between himself and Roberts.

Hughes probably also followed Rule 2 to some extent. When the left bloc split, Brandeis was assigned 22 per cent of the cases he could have received, compared with his 10 per cent assignment average for unanimous cases. When the right bloc split, Sutherland was assigned 16 per cent of the decisions he could have received, compared with his 11 per cent average for unanimous cases. He received five of the six cases assigned the conservatives when their bloc was split. One of those cases was *Powell* v. *Alabama* which, it has been said, was assigned Sutherland "probably in the hope that he could bring over Justices Butler and McReynolds while some of the more 'liberal' Justices could not."

If the Chief Justice is to be well liked, he must appear to be generous, considerate, and impartial in assigning cases, particularly the important cases. Taft was considered generous in his assignments, and undoubtedly this contributed to his likeability. Hughes said he tried to assign each Justice the same proportion of important cases and especially took into account the feelings of the senior Justices. Justice Roberts thought Hughes' assignments were generous and considerate, and Justice Frankfurter believed that no Chief Justice equalled Hughes in the "skill, wisdom, and disinterestedness" with which he assigned opinions. Justice Stone, however, thought otherwise. During the early and middle Thirties, he felt that Hughes was not assigning him as many important cases as he should have received. Just as Stone felt slighted by Hughes in the matter of assignments, so did Justices Murphy and Rutledge during Stone's Chief Justiceships. Stone was aware of this, but he did little about it.

How often the Chief Justice uses his assignment power to influence activity of his associates cannot be determined with certainty. Besides influence, there are other reasons underlying opinion assignments such as equality of case distribution, ability, and expertise. Nonetheless, every assignment presents the Chief Justice with an opportunity for influence.

THE FINAL PHASE: PERSUASION AND UNANIMITY

In the last stage of the decisional process, opinions are written, circulated, discussed, and approved or disapproved. Final decision near, Court members have their last chance to persuade each other. The results of interaction during this period can be highly significant: opinion modification, increase or decrease in the size of a majority, and even the reversal of a conference decision. Again the Chief Justice is in a favorable position for purposes of influence. Standing at the center of intra-Court communication, he ordinarily knows better than any of his associates the status of each case—who is having trouble writing an opinion, who is overworked, who is wavering in his vote, etc.—and if he is so inclined, he can play an active role in reconciling differences, seeking compromises, and attaining unanimity. Since, as a practical matter, he decides when an opinion will be announced, he can delay the announcement in hope of augmenting the Court's majority. What the Chief Justice actually does greatly depends upon how he views his role in this final phase of the decisional process.

Seldom has a Chief Justice had a more definite conception of his role than Taft. The Chief Justice, he said, is "expected to promote teamwork by the Court so as to give weight and solidarity to its opinions." He believed his predecessor, White, earnestly sought to avoid divisions by skillfully reconciling differences among the Justices, and he intended to do the same. His aim was unanimity, but he was willing to admit that at times dissents were justifiable and perhaps even a duty. Dissent was proper, he thought, in cases where a Court member strongly believed the majority erred in a matter involving important principle or where a dissent might serve some useful purpose, such as convincing Congress to pass certain legislation. But in other cases, a Justice should be a good member of the team, silently acquiesce in the views of the majority, and not try to make a record for himself by dissenting.

Taft's conception of the function of the dissent was shared by most of his associates, and when he sought to unite them, his efforts were accepted as proper and consistent with his role as Chief Justice. Justices joining the Taft Court were socialized in the no-dissent-unless-absolutely-necessary tradition, and most of them learned it well. Justice Butler gave it classic expression on the back of one of Stone's slip opinions:

> I voted to reverse. While this sustains your conclusion to affirm, I still think reversal would be better. But I shall in silence acquiesce. Dissents seldom aid in the right development or statement of the law. They often do harm. For myself I say: "lead us not into temptation."

Even Stone, who was not so sure about the no-dissent tradition, usually went along with it, acquiescing in the appropriate cases.

Taft enjoyed moderate success in his efforts to attain unanimity. During his first year as Chief Justice, he united the Court in a number of [controversial] cases.... Usually he would assign himself such cases and try to write an opinion which would bring in the dissenters. This meant he had to make concessions to Justices like Brandeis, but he was willing to exchange concessions for votes. When there were divisions in cases he assigned to others which could be reconciled, Taft would try to mediate between majority and minority (at times with the help of Van Devanter) in an effort to attain unanimity. If there was a possibility of winning over a dissenter, Taft would frequently let the case go over a few conferences with hope that time would work in his favor.

Hughes easily assumed the role of Court unifier that Taft had cut out for him, for he believed that unanimity should be sought where it could be attained without sacrificing strongly held convictions. Like Taft, he distinguished two types of cases, those involving matters of important principle and those of lesser importance. The former were dissentworthy; the latter were not. As to the cases of lesser importance, Hughes felt it was better to have the law settled one way or the other regardless of his own ideas as to the correct disposition of the case; and if the majority voted contrary to his view, he would change his vote. For example, in a case involving statutory construction, Hughes wrote to Stone: "I choke a little at swallowing your analysis; still I do not think it would serve any useful purpose to expose my views."

Like Taft, Hughes mediated differences of opinion between contending factions, and in order to get a unanimous decision, he would try to find common ground upon which all could stand. He was willing to modify his own opinions to hold or increase his majority, and if this meant he had to put in some disconnected thoughts or sentences, in they went. In cases assigned to others, he would suggest the addition or subtraction of a paragraph if by doing so he could save a dissent or concurring opinion. According to Justice Roberts, dissents were thus avoided in some cases in which agreements seemed impossible. But unlike Taft, Hughes apparently seldom held up the delivery of an opinion in an effort to secure another vote or two. He made his attempt to secure unanimity, and if it failed, the case was usually handed down as soon as the opinions were ready.

Hughes' efforts to attain unanimity were fairly successful. During his Chief Justiceship, there was no radical increase in the number of dissents. Even in the cases that invalidated New Deal legislation, the Court was fairly intact. Of the eleven such cases, five were unanimous, and two were decided 8 to 1. The no-dissent-unless-absolutely-necessary tradition continued, and in a host of lesser cases Court members acquiesced in silence. The Roosevelt appointees, particularly, showed remarkable restraint in the matter of dissents while serving under Hughes. Frankfurter, who had the best record, registered only seven dissents in his three years with Hughes. The New Deal Justices were baptized in the old tradition concerning dissent, but whether they would retain the faith after Hughes left the Court was another matter.

As an Associate Justice, Stone prized the right to dissent and occasionally rankled under the no-dissent-unless-absolutely-necessary tradition of the Taft and Hughes Courts. As Chief Justice, he did not believe it appropriate for him to dissuade Court members, by persuasion or otherwise, from dissenting in individual cases. A Chief Justice, he thought, might admonish his associates generally to exercise restraint in the matter of dissents and seek to find common ground for decision, but beyond that he should not go. Stone usually went no further. His activity or lack of it in this matter gave rise to new expectations on the part of his associates as to their role and the role of the Chief Justice regarding unanimity and dissent. A new tradition of great freedom of individual expression displaced the tradition of the Taft and Hughes Courts. This explains in part the unprecedented number of dissents and separate opinions during Stone's Chief Justiceship.

Chief Justice Stone, nonetheless, exercised some influence in the final phase of the decisional process. In *Edwards* v. *California*, one of the first cases heard by the Court after he became Chief Justice, he persuaded Justice Byrnes to change his conference vote, and the switch resulted in a decision based on the commerce clause rather than on the privileges and immunities clause of the Constitution. He also influenced the content of many opinions, especially those of Justice Murphy, by suggesting additions and deletions. Although Justices who voted against Stone in conference would occasionally go along with his opinions, he usually made no concerted effort to attain unanimity. He recognized, however, that unanimity in certain cases was desirable, and in a few cases he sought it....

The unprecedented number of dissents and concurrences during Stone's Chief Justiceship can be only partly attributed to the displacing of the old tradition of loyalty to the Court's opinion. A major source of difficulty appears to have been the free and easy expression of views in conference. Whether the Justices were sure of their grounds or not, they spoke up and many times took positions from which they could not easily retreat, and given the heated debate which sometimes occurred in the Stone conference, the commitment was not simply intellectual. What began in conference frequently ended with elaborate justification as concurring or dissenting opinions in the United States Reports. This, together with Stone's passiveness in seeking unanimity, is probably the best explanation for what Professor Pritchett characterized as "the multiplication of division" in the Supreme Court.

CONCLUSION

The task of the political scientist, said John Morley, is not simply to describe governmental institutions, but to penetrate to the secret of their functions. In regard to the Chief Justiceship, that is difficult, for complex relationships among the Chief Justice and Justices are involved. The office provides the Chief Justice with an opportunity for influence, but it does not guarantee it. To exercise influence, he must perform activity that results in his associates choosing to do what he wants them to do; and in this regard, his success depends largely upon his likability and esteem in the Court and upon how he perceives and fulfills his role....

NOTES

1. Taft to Charles Taft, June 8, 1927; Taft to Horace D. Taft, June 29, 1927; Taft to Van Devanter, Jan. 7, 1930, William Howard Taft Papers, Manuscript Division, Library of Congress.

2. See Henry F. Pringle, *The Life and Times of William Howard Taft* (New York, 1939), II, pp. 968–972; Alpheus Thomas Mason, *Harlan Fiske Stone: Pillar of the Law* (New York, 1956), p. 793; Charles Evans Hughes, Biographical Notes, 1930–1941, p. 12, Hughes Papers, Manuscript Division, Library of Congress; Steven T. Early, Jr., *James Clark McReynolds and the Judicial Process*, Unpublished Ph.D. dissertation, Department of Political Science, University of Virginia, 1954, p. 90....

3. Holmes to Lewis Einstein, May 19, 1927, Oliver Wendell Holmes, Jr., Papers, Manuscript Division, Library of Congress.

4. Edwin McElwain, "The Business of the Supreme Court as Conducted by Chief Justice Hughes," *Harvard Law Review*, Vol. 63 (1949), p. 13. McElwain is a former law clerk of Chief Justice Hughes.

5. See Mason, *op. cit.,* p. 792; William O. Douglas, "Chief Justice Stone," *Columbia Law Review*, Vol. 46 (1946), p. 693; Alfred McCormack, "A Law Clerk's Recollections," *ibid.*, p. 716; Bennett Boskey, "Mr. Chief Justice Stone," *Harvard Law Review*, Vol. 59 (1946), p. 1200.

6. Hughes to Stone, Oct. 1, 1931, Harlan F. Stone Papers, Manuscript Division, Library of Congress; Hughes to Brandeis, Oct. 1, 1931, Louis D. Brandeis Papers, University of Louisville Law School; McElwain, *op. cit.,* p. 15.

7. Stone's papers indicate that his special lists were challenged less than 10 times in five years.

8. Douglas, *op. cit.,* p. 695.

9. Taft to McKenna, April 20, 1923, Taft Papers.

10. Remarks of former Attorney General William D. Mitchell, 316 U.S. xvii (1941).

11. Frankfurter has said that if Hughes "made others feel his moral superiority, they merely felt a fact.... All who served with him recognized the extraordinary qualities possessed by the Chief Justice...." *Of Law and Men* (New York, 1956), p. 148. Hughes was the only member of the Court to whom McReynolds would defer. Early, *loc. cit.* Black said he had "more than impersonal and detached admiration" for Hughes' "extraordinary intellectual gifts." Black to Hughes, June 3, 1941. Hughes Papers.

12. One minor exception to this rule is that a newcomer to the Court is entitled to select his first case for opinion. This is a tradition of long standing. Matthews to Waite, Oct. 5, 1881, Morrison R. Waite Papers, Manuscript Division, Library of Congress.

13. The "important constitutional cases" decided by the Court from 1921 to 1946 were determined by examination of four leading works on the Constitution: Paul A. Freund, Arthur E. Sutherland, Mark De Wolfe Howe, and Ernest J. Brown, *Constitutional Law* (Boston, 1954); Alfred H. Kelly and Winfred A. Harbison, *The American Constitution: Its Origins and Development* (New York, 1948); Alpheus T. Mason and William M. Beaney, *American Constitutional Law* (Englewood Cliffs, N.J., 1959); and C. Herman Pritchett, *The American Constitution* (New York, 1959). If a case was discussed in any two of these works, it was considered an "important constitutional case."

Leadership in the Warren Court

David J. Danelski
Jeanne C. Danelski

This paper explores and attempts to explain leadership in the Warren Court. Principal data for the study are from the papers of Earl Warren at the Library of Congress. We selected six terms of the Warren Court for our analysis—the first two terms (1953 and 1954), two middle terms (1962 and 1963), and the final two terms (1967 and 1968). We focused particularly on all divided decisions in conference as shown in Warren's docket books and on intra-Court communications during those terms. Our analysis builds on the judicial leadership literature that began in the early 1960's. We assume that leadership in the Supreme Court is important because it often determines the outcome of cases, the size of majorities, and the content of opinions. We define leadership as a process in which the actions of justices contribute either to decisional outcomes (task leadership) or to the maintenance of social-emotional conditions necessary for efficient decisionmaking (social leadership).

. . .

Warren began his chief justiceship as an observer. Soon after he was sworn in on October 4, 1953, he attended his first confer-

Reprinted from a paper delivered at the 1986 Annual Meeting of the American Political Science Association, pp. 1–2, 9–24. Reprinted with permission of the authors. Most footnotes omitted.

ence. At Warren's request, Justice Hugo L. Black presided over that conference and a few others thereafter.... Within six weeks, Warren had experienced all the phases of the Court's decisional process—case selection, oral argument, conference on the merits, opinion assignment, and opinion writing and circulation. He could not help noticing the competition for leadership among some of his colleagues, especially Frankfurter and Black, and he probably also noticed that as chief justice he had special opportunities to lead the Court in confernce, where he spoke first, and in opinion assignment....

POST-CONFERENCE LEADERSHIP AND ACQUIESCENCE: AN EMPIRICAL ANALYSIS

Leadership in the Supreme Court is difficult to measure, but a rough estimate can be made in the post-conference phase of the decisional process. The measure requires three observations at different points in time. *Hernandez* v. *Texas* provides an apt illustration. At t^1, (January 16, 1954), seven justices agreed to reverse Hernandez's conviction, with Minton dissenting and Clark either passing or dissenting. At t^2, (April 29, 1954),

Warren circulated his opinion for the Court. At t^3 (May 3, 1954), the Court announced that it had unanimously reversed Hernandez's conviction. We know from Warren's papers that Minton and Clark had been persuaded by Warren's opinion. Without such evidence, we cannot be sure that the change of vote was the result of leadership behavior. But it is reasonable to assume that often it is. Acting on that assumption, we have aggregated data recording events at t^1, t^2, and t^3 for cases decided during the six terms covered by this study, and we then calculated acquiescence scores for justices who changed their conference dissenting or pass votes to majority votes and leadership scores for assigned opinion writers who received those dissenting and pass votes or who lost majority conference votes. Those scores and the data upon which they are based are shown in Tables 1, 2, and 3.

Before presenting our analysis, we offer these comments. First, leadership scores hypothetically measure task leadership, but they probably also reflect elements of social leadership and perhaps even feelings of friendship or hostility. Second, acquiescence scores hypothetically measure social leadership because changes of dissenting and pass votes to majority votes show solidarity and are almost always satisfying to opinion writers and those who voted with them. Acquiescence scores also hypothetically measure the adequacy of social leadership, for they reflect social cohesion among the justices, which is a major consequence of adequate social leadership. Third, in certain cases involving important legal or constitutional issues, justices are less likely to join majority opinions than in other cases. If all justices are assigned roughly the same proportion of important cases, that would not be a problem, but complete equality of assignments seldom occurs. Fourth, it is more important in policy terms to hold the fifth

vote than to gain the sixth, seventh, eighth, and ninth votes, which the leadership score primarily measures, but, of course, holding majority members and persuading dissenters are related. Finally, leadership scores measure only post-conference behavior. Justices who are successful in persuading colleagues in other phases of the decisional process may have low leadership scores because they are content with victory however narrow and make few concessions in their opinions to gain dissenting votes, or they may be so aggressive in securing majorities that dissenters respond negatively to them and thus are disinclined to consider changing votes when those aggressive justices write for the Court.

1953 and 1954 Terms

Jackson had a heart attack late in the 1953 term and died early in the 1954 term. Justice John Marshall Harlan took his place on March 28, 1955. Neither justice participated sufficiently in conference decisionmaking to be included in this analysis. Table 1 presents the remaining eight justices' leadership and acquiescence scores for the 1953 and 1954 terms.

It should be noted at the outset that Warren's leadership score probably should be adjusted upward, for he did not record the Court's conference vote in the Segregation Cases [*Brown* v. *Board of Education*] in the 1953 term, and hence it is not reflected in Table 1. Had a vote been taken on December 12, 1953, it is almost certain that Reed would have dissented, and it is quite probable that Jackson would have passed. Thus Warren's leadership score actually is almost as high as Clark's. Warren's post-conference leadership success was not the result of one-on-one attempts to persuade dissenters, for his papers indicate that he seldom engaged in such behavior. An exception is his successful efforts in persuading Reed to make the

TABLE 1
Leadership and Acquiescence, 1953 and 1954 Terms

	Warren	Black	Reed	Frankfurter	Douglas	Burton	Clark	Minton	Leadership Score	%
		(−1)			(−1)				(−2)	
Warren	—	0/0	2/7	1/2	0/1	1/3	4/4	5/9	13/26	42
Black	3/3	—	2/11	6/8	1/5	0/8	3/3	1/5	16/43	37
				(−1)					(−1)	
Reed	1/5	1/8	—	1/3	2/11	1/1	1/2	2/4	9/34	24
					(−1)		(−1)		(−2)	
Frankfurter	0/5	0/10	1/8	—	0/10	2/5	2/6	3/11	8/55	11
		(−1)				(−1)			(−2)	
Douglas	1/1	2/4	5/6	0/3	—	0/2	1/1	2/3	11/20	45
Burton	0/0	0/5	0/3	4/6	1/11	−	0/0	1/2	6/27	22
				(−1)					(−1)	
Clark	4/4	2/7	4/8	4/7	4/8	3/7	—	3/10	24/51	45
					(−1)				(−1)	
Minton	1/2	0/2	0/2	1/4	0/3	1/2	1/3	—	4/18	17
									(−9)	
Totals:									91/274	30
Acquiescence Scores:										
	10/20	5/36	14/45	17/33	8/49	8/28	12/19	17/44	91/274	
%	50	14	31	52	16	29	63	39	33	

Rows indicate conference dissenting and pass votes received and conference majority votes lost (−) by justices assigned opinions. Columns indicate conference dissenting and pass votes given by justices to majority opinion writers and conference majority votes changed to dissenting votes (−).

Leadership score = $\dfrac{d + p - mc}{n}$ where d is a dissenting vote and p is a pass vote in conference that later became a majority vote in a decision assigned to a justice for opinion; mc is a majority vote in conference that later became a dissenting vote; and n is total number of dissenting and pass votes in conference in all decisions assigned for opinion to that justice.

Acquiescence score = $\dfrac{c}{n}$ where c is a dissenting or pass vote in conference that later became a majority vote and n is the total number of dissenting and pass votes in conference for each justice.

Standard deviation for leadership scores = 13%.
Standard deviation for acquiescence scores = 17%.
☐ = one standard deviation above or below the mean.

Court's decision in the Segregation Case unanimous. Because Warren was known as an effective social leader of his Court, his high acquiescence score was expected.

Some may find Clark's high leadership score surprising. The fact that Clark did not write in important constitutional cases during the 1953 and 1954 terms may partly explain why he received more dissenting and pass votes than any of his colleagues. Another explanation is Clark had far more ability than most commentators gave him credit for. Bernard Schwartz, after examining Clark's papers at the University of Texas, wrote: "Clark may not have been the intellectual of his more brilliant brethren, but he developed into a more competent judge than any of the other Truman appointees. In fact,

Clark has been the most underrated justice in recent Supreme Court history."[1] If Clark's leadership score is surprising, his acquiescence score is not. One of his clerks said of him: "He doesn't like dissent for the sake of dissent. Where he has no absolute convictions, he will be inclined to go with the majority." Clark acquiesced in every case in which he had dissented or passed in conference when Warren, Black, or Douglas wrote for the Court.

Douglas' pattern of scores—high leadership and low acquiescence—suggests task leadership. But Douglas, like Warren, seldom sought votes after he wrote an opinion. "(I)n my long service," he wrote in his autobiography, "I never tried to persuade any justice that I was right and he was wrong. I was probably the one justice in the long history of the Court never to proselytize."[2]

Black's leadership score is not as high as Douglas', but it is well above the mean, and his leadership and acquiescence scores have the same pattern as Douglas' scores, thus suggesting task leadership.

Frankfurter was more effective as a task leader than his low leadership score indicates, but the score is no fluke. He had similar low leadership scores during the Hughes and Stone Courts. It isn't that he did not try to lead; his attempts at post-conference leadership were probably rejected because he tried too hard. His high acquiescence score probably reflects his satisfaction with decision making in the Court during the early years of Warren's chief justiceship. His willingness to change his dissenting votes even for Black appear to be a gesture in celebration of harmony.

Minton's low leadership score and considerably higher acquiescence score might be explained by Frankfurter's comment about him: "Minton will not go down in history as a great jurist, but he was a delightful colleague."[3]

1962 and 1963 Terms

After Harlan replaced Jackson in 1955, William J. Brennan, Jr., succeeded Minton the following year, and Potter Stewart replaced Burton two years later. Charles E. Whittaker succeeded Reed in 1957 but remained on the Court for only five years. Byron R. White took his place in 1962, the same year that Arthur J. Goldberg succeeded Felix Frankfurter. The Court had radically changed both in membership and ideological orientation. Warren, who voted with Clark and Frankfurter more than 70 per cent of the time in the 1953 and 1954 terms, shifted his ideological orientation and began voting regularly with Black and Douglas, and Brennan joined them to make a liberal bloc of four. Goldberg provided the fifth liberal vote. As a result, several important cases that had been reargued in the 1962 term were decided differently than they would have been if Frankfurter had remained on the Court. Although the liberals usually prevailed, the vote was often 5 to 4, which meant that dissenting votes in those cases did not change after the conference.

Table 2 presents the leadership and acquiescence scores for the 1962 and 1963 terms. Clark's leadership score for those terms is virtually the same as it was in the 1953 and 1954 terms, but his acquiescence score is lower by more than 50 per cent. The reason for this also appears to be the reason for Harlan's low acquiescence score. Both Clark and Harlan found themselves frequently outvoted in conference, and because they regarded the cases as important, they refused to change their votes. Brennan and Warren often wrote for the Court in those cases, and thus their leadership scores are low. If Clark's and Harlan's dissenting and pass votes are not used in computing Brennan's and Warren's leadership scores, those scores would be, respectively, 35 and 33 per cent, both above the mean. Thus, except for

TABLE 2
Leadership and Acquiescence, 1961 and 1962 Terms

	Warren	Black	Douglas	Clark	Harlan	Brennan	Stewart	White	Goldberg	Leadership Score	%
				(−1)						(−1)	
Warren	—	0/2	1/1	1/6	0/11	1/1	3/10	1/5	1/2	8/38	18
				(−2)			(−1)	(−1)		(−5)	
Black	0/0	—	0/1	1/3	3/7	0/0	6/8	3/4	1/2	14/25	36
				(−1)					(−1)	(−2)	
Douglas	3/5	3/5	—	2/9	2/17	2/3	5/15	3/7	4/7	24/68	32
							(−1)			(−1)	
Clark	1/4	0/3	7/10	—	5/9	4/8	3/10	2/5	5/10	27/59	44
	(−1)						(−1)			(−2)	
Harlan	4/7	4/10	0/8	2/4	—	2/5	4/5	1/1	1/4	18/44	36
	(−1)	(−2)	(−4)					(−2)	(−1)	(−10)	
Brennan	1/4	2/7	2/3	3/10	3/20	—	5/15	3/9	1/2	20/70	14
	(−1)								(−1)	(−2)	
Stewart	1/2	2/8	3/8	2/6	3/6	2/3	—	3/5	1/5	17/43	35
		(−1)			(−3)				(−1)	(−5)	
White	2/3	2/6	1/9	1/5	4/9	1/1	7/10	—	1/2	19/45	31
				(−2)	(−1)		(−1)	(−1)		(−5)	
Goldberg	3/3	2/4	3/4	2/9	4/15	1/1	9/17	2/9	—	26/62	34
										(−33)	
Totals:										173/454	31
Acquiescence Scores:											
	15/28	15/45	17/44	14/52	24/94	13/22	42/90	18/45	15/34	173/454	
%	54	33	39	27	26	59	47	40	44	38	

For an explanation of this table and the calculation of leadership and acquiescence scores, see Table 1.
Standard deviation for leadership scores = 9%.
Standard deviation for acquiescence scores = 11%.
□ = one standard deviation above or below the mean.

Clark's high leadership score and Brennan's and Warren's high acquiescence scores, which are important because they indicate considerable social leadership, Table 2 tells us only that there are no great differences in leadership and acquiescence among the justices in the 1962 and 1963 terms. But there is one statistic in Table 2 that stands out—the Court's acquiescence mean of 38 per cent, which is precisely the acquiescence mean of the late Hughes Court.

1967 and 1968 Terms

Only two justices came to the Court between 1963 and 1967—Abe Fortas, who replaced Goldberg in 1965, and Thurgood Marshall, who replaced Clark in 1967. Marshall and Fortas generally voted with the liberal bloc, and both of their votes were often necessary for the bloc to prevail, for beginning in 1964, Black no longer regularly voted with it.

Table 3 shows the leadership and ac-

TABLE 3
Leadership and Acquiescence, 1967 and 1968 Terms

	Warren	Black	Douglas	Harlan	Brennan	Stewart	White	Fortas	Marshall	Leadership Score	%
Warren	—	(−1) 3/5	(−1) 1/2	1/7	0/0	3/6	2/3	0/0	0/0	(−2) 10/23	35
Black	1/1	—	(−1) 2/3	(−2) 2/7	1/1	(−1) 2/8	(−1) 2/4	(−1) 2/4	1/2	(−6) 13/30	23
Douglas	2/4	0/7	—	(−1) 5/14	3/6	3/15	4/12	1/1	3/5	(−1) 21/64	31
Harlan	2/7	(−1) 0/5	5/9	—	0/0	(−1) 3/6	(−2) 0/3	(−1) 4/5	2/3	(−5) 16/38	29
Brennan	0/2	(−1) 5/10	3/7	3/9	—	(−2) 4/7	1/4	(−1) 2/4	1/2	(−4) 19/45	33
Stewart	1/1	3/11	1/8	9/14	1/1	—	(−1) 3/7	(−1) 3/6	1/1	(−2) 22/49	41
White	2/3	(−1) 2/7	4/9	(−1) 0/6	2/4	(−1) 1/8	—	(−2) 2/6	2/2	(−5) 15/45	22
Fortas	3/3	3/9	2/4	5/9	2/2	5/7	3/6	—	0/0	23/40	58
Marshall	1/2	2/6	(−1) 1/5	(−3) 5/10	2/5	(−1) 3/9	2/6	0/1	—	(−5) 16/44	25
Totals:										(−30) 155/378	33
Acquiescence Scores:											
	12/23	18/60	19/47	30/76	11/19	24/66	17/45	14/27	10/15	155/378	41
%	52	39	40	39	58	36	38	52	67	41	

For an explanation of this table and the calculation of leadership and acquiescence scores, see Table 1.
Standard deviation for leadership scores = 10%.
Standard deviation for acquiescence scores = 12%.
☐ = one standard deviation above or below the mean.

quiescence scores for the 1967 and 1968 terms. The most remarkable score in the table is Fortas' leadership score of 58 per cent—the highest leadership score in this six-term analysis. Only Justice Black changed less than half of his dissenting and pass votes to majority in cases when Fortas wrote for the Court. The reason appears to be that Black did not hold Fortas in as high esteem as the rest of his colleagues. Nonetheless, there is little doubt that Fortas was one of the most persuasive justices in the sixteen years of the Warren Court. Not

only his opinions for the Court elicite changes of votes; his dissenting opinions, more than those of any other member of the Warren Court, persuaded members of the majorities to join him in dissent, and when he defected from majorities, which he did six times in the 1967 and 1968 terms, he never joined another justice's dissenting opinion but instead wrote for himself. That was not the case for the rest of the justices.

The leadership scores of Black, White, and Marshall are low because they lost relatively large numbers of majority votes. Had they not lost those votes, their leadership scores would have been above the Court mean.

Brennan's and Marshall's pattern of changing their dissent and pass conference votes to majority votes is similar, and their acquiescence scores are the highest in the period. Warren's and Fortas' acquiescence scores are also quite high. Most important, the acquiescence mean for the Court reached 41 per cent. Such acquiescence had not occurred in the Court for at least 30 years.

Consequences of Leadership

Besides identifying certain justices as task or social leaders—particularly Warren, Brennan, and Fortas—what does the above analysis show? We believes it shows that task and social leadership were generally in balance during the period of the Warren Court after years of imbalance during the Stone and Vinson Courts. Adequate performance of social leadership, which was largely Warren's contribution, achieved the balance. As a result, interpersonal conflict in the Court declined and satisfaction, efficiency, and social cohesion increased. These are largely impressionistic findings based on the papers of the justices and their comments, but there is some quantitative support for the findings. From the 1953 term to the 1968 term, the number of cases on the Court's docket rose from approximately 1,500 to 3,500, and, with exception of the 1956 term, the Court always adjourned each year in June, which suggests increased efficiency. If we use the Court's mean acquiescence score as a measure of social cohesion among the justices and the acquiescence score of the early Stone Court as a bench mark, we see the following progression in social cohesion: 1942 and 1943 terms, 29 per cent; 1953 and 1954 terms, 33 per cent; 1962 and 1963 terms, 38 per cent, and 1967 and 1968 terms, 41 per cent.

Thus we conclude that balanced leadership in the Warren era strengthened the Supreme Court as an institution. This is important because a constitutional revolution occurred within the Warren Court that led to considerable criticism outside it, and it was able to accomplish the former while surviving the latter.

WARREN'S LEADERSHIP: A PRELIMINARY ASSESSMENT

Soon after Warren's death in 1974, Abe Fortas wrote an article for the Yale Law Journal entitled "Chief Justice Warren: The Enigma of Leadership."[4] Fortas acknowledged that Warren amply deserved the title of "Super-Chief." "We know this; we feel it," he said. "But," he continued, "when we attempt to identify the ingredients—the particulars—of Warren's leadership, we find great difficulty. He made no apparent effort to impress his views upon his brethren. He was no more emphatic than some of them in stating his conclusions. He did not attempt to persuade by one-to-one, off-the-record sessions. He did not convert his fellow Justices by the kind of penetrating, irresistible, jugular stroke which is so often the contribution of Mr. Justice Douglas. He did not press his brethren against a stone wall of logic and stern assurance in the manner that characterized the formidable Hugo Black. His effectiveness did not stem from the kind of calm and impressive scholarship that was the contribution of John Harlan." Yet, "(b)y some process short of the occult," Fortas concluded, "Warren was a great, powerful leader." If Fortas had great difficulty in explaining Warren's leadership, we social scientists will have just as much or more difficulty. An adequate explanation of Warren's leadership requires far more data than we have used in this study. Nonetheless, enough is known about Warren's leadership to make at least a preliminary assessment of it. But we stress our assessment is preliminary.

Social Leadership

To explain Warren's leadership in the Supreme Court one must begin with his personality. When Fortas said he knew Warren was "Super-Chief" because he felt it, he was, we submit, reacting to Warren's personality, and that personality suited Warren well for social leadership. "Always at ease with others," Pollack wrote, "he was an attentive listener who radiated simple humility and a benign desire to do and say the right thing. He had a talent for being both affable and dignified in a way that most persons found comfortable and reassuring. . . ."[5]

Evidence of Warren's social leadership in the decisional process is abundant. . . . [I]n case selection he frequently contributed the crucial fourth vote to review a case three of his colleagues wanted to hear, and he seldom dissented by himself to a grant or denial of review.

During oral argument, he was polite and helpful to counsel and confined his remarks usually to brief questions. Unlike Hughes, he was not a stickler for holding counsel to the precise time allotted them. He usually remained above the fray when fellow justices squabbled on the benches, but there were a few instances in open court when he lost his temper with Frankfurter or counsel.[6]

In conference, Fortas said that "Warren was an immensely attractive, considerate and diplomatic leader. He was never divisive, impatient, short-tempered or abrasive. He created an atmosphere of comradeship, even within strongly felt and sharply stated disagreements. No one differed with him personally, even if sharply differing with his convictions and conclusions."[7] Fortas, however, had served on the Court after Frankfurter retired. Douglas, who served

with Frankfurter during Warren's chief justiceship, recalled that "most of the time Warren was polite, considerate and friendly, handling the conference with consummate skill."[8] But Warren had problems with Frankfurter, and on a few occasions spoke in anger to the justice.[9] During conferences over which Warren presided every justice had his full say, including Frankfurter, who tended to hold forth. Rarely did Warren contradict a colleague, and, as White said, Warren "never felt he had to get the last word in."[10]

"In assigning opinions, Warren," Brennan recalled, "bent over backwards . . . to assure that each Justice, including himself, wrote approximately the same number of opinions and wrote a fair share of the more undesirable opinions."[11] Stewart agreed. "I remember," he said, "the Chief Justice typically and invariably would take more than his share of (the "dogs,") you know. So that if you got assigned one you wouldn't resent it."[12]

Finally, Warren was a model of collegiality in the post-conference phase of decision-making. As the analysis in the previous section showed, he changed more than half his dissenting and pass votes to majority votes, and in the six terms studied, he defected from a majority only once.

Task Leadership

Warren's leadership was an enigma for Fortas because Warren was not an intellectual leader. Stewart, who felt Warren's leadership as strongly as Fortas, agreed that the Chief "did not lead by intellect, and he did not greatly appeal to other's intellects."[13] If intellect was not a part of Warren's task leadership, then what were its ingredients? We suggest the following:

1. His affability and dignity. These are elements of social leadership, but for Warren they opened the way for the exercise of task leadership. They put

his colleagues at ease and emotionally disposed them toward him and his views.

2. His rectitude. His first question in deciding a case was: "Is it right or wrong?" "His answer," said Fortas, "was always rooted in a profound sense of justice and human dignity, and in a simple and uncomplicated conception of the essential, noble meaning of our Constitution's precepts."[14] One gets the impression in reading his colleagues' comments about his leadership that when he spoke they often felt his moral sense as well as his personality.

3. His decisiveness. He seldom had difficulty reaching a decision, and once he reached it, he generally stuck with it. "Warren," said White, "was quite willing to listen to people at length...but, when he made up his mind, it was like the sun went down, and he was very firm about it."[15] But in cases where Warren had no strong feelings, he was flexible. "About one in a hundred cases," recalled Stewart, "there would be some tax case in which there would be some conflict in the circuits, and...he would say, 'Look, our duty is to resolve this conflict. I'm not a tax lawyer. I'll go whichever way you want to go on this, just go with the majority and get this conflict resolved.'"[16]

4. His courage. "He was fearless," said Fortas, "and his calm courage and steady course in face of vicious assault clarified and simplified his like-minded colleagues."[17] As Hughes pointed out in discussing influence in the Court, "courage of conviction" commands respect of one's colleagues.[18]

5. His presiding skill. Brennan said right after Warren's death: "It is incredible how efficiently the Chief would conduct the Friday conferences, leading the discussion of every case on the agenda, with a knowledge of each case at his fingertips."[19]

6. His willingness to share leadership with others. An avid fan of team sports, Warren was a team player. Early in his chief justiceship, he shared some task leadership with Frankfurter; later he shared it with Brennan....

The full extent of Warren's task leadership in the decisional process is yet to be measured. In the case selection process, we know he asked his clerks to find a case to overrule *Betts* v. *Brady*, and they came up with Clarence Earl Gideon's petition for certiorari. And research on Warren's opinion assignments reveals that he sought to influence policy in areas that concerned him—for example, reapportionment, censorship, and electronic surveillance. Although he usually made no special efforts to persuade others to join his opinions, the analysis in the previous section of this paper shows he won over as many dissenting and pass votes as most of his colleagues.

Shared Leadership

As mentioned in the previous section, Warren's success as a leader can be attributed in part to sharing leadership with his colleagues. When he came to the Court in 1953, he needed someone to play the part that Willis Van Devanter had played for Taft in the 1920's—someone who was a close and loyal friend, an experienced judge, an intellectual leader, and an ideological soulmate.... On the Court, Warren enjoyed a friendly relationship with Clark from the beginning, and during the 1953 term he agreed with him more than any other justice, including Black and Douglas, but Warren did not share leadership with Clark as much as he did with other members of the Court, especially Frankfurter.

Warren and Frankfurter worked together in securing unanimous decisions in both *Brown I* and *Brown II*, and Frankfurter had advised Warren in other cases as well. If Warren was seeking a special partner, Frankfurter was more than willing, but in fact it was Frankfurter who courted Warren. Warren was not the first justice to be courted by Frankfurter. Burton, among others, had received the same treatment—a warm welcome to the Court, books and articles to read, flattering handwritten notes, memoranda on Court practices, and so forth. Frankfurter was genuinely enthusiastic about Warren and had high hopes for him as chief justice.... [But] the differences betwen the two men were enormous. Yet at least until the end of the 1956 term, when Warren was already voting more frequently with Black and Douglas than with Frankfurter, relations between Warren and Frankfurter were still quite cordial.

It may have been only coincidental, but personal relations between Warren and Frankfurter began to deteriorate within a year of Brennan's coming to the Court. Brennan was the special partner Warren wittingly or unwittingly was seeking and within a few years their agreement on decisions reached the 90 per cent level.

Schwartz described the Warren-Brennan relationship as follows:

> Warren was more comfortable with Brennan than with any of the other Justices, and an intimacy developed between them of a type that never took place between Warren and Black or Warren and Douglas, however close

the latters' views may have been to his. The Chief would turn to Brennan when he wanted to discuss a case or some other matter on which he wanted an exchange of views. The two would usually meet on Thursday when Warren would come to Brennan's chambers to go over the cases that were to be discussed at the Friday conference.[20]

Brennan and Warren were similar: both were gregarious persons, committed to liberal values; both were deeply interested in politics.... In intellect, he [Brennan] could hold his own with Frankfurter. Frankfurter also reacted negatively to Brennan, and that probably strengthened the bond between Brennan and Warren. Brennan became Warren's architect and technician supplying rationales for Warren's decisions and devising constitutional theories that would provide the foundation for the transformation of constitutional law during the Warren era in such landmark cases as *Cooper* v. *Aaron*, *Baker* v. *Carr*, *Roth* v. *United States*, *New York Times* v. *Sullivan*, *Sherbert* v. *Verner*, and *Malloy* v. *Hogan*.

Because Brennan is still on the Court, a full analysis of his sharing of leadership with Warren is premature. But it is clear that such sharing occurred, and it appears that it differed from the sharing of leadership in the Taft Court, where Taft was the social leader and Van Devanter was the task leader. Warren and Brennan appear to have shared both task and social leadership. How they did this and what it meant for constitutional policy-making in the Warren Court are fascinating questions for future research.

NOTES

1. Bernard Schwartz, *Super Chief* (New York: New York University Press, 1983), p. 58.

2. William O. Douglas, *The Court Years,*

1939–1975 (New York: Random House, 1980), p. 88.

3. Quoted in Schwartz, *Super Chief*, p. 59.

4. Abe Fortas, "Chief Justice Warren: The Enigma of Leadership", *Yale Law Journal* 84 (1975), pp. 405–12.

5. Jack Harrison Pollack, *Earl Warren* (Englewood Cliffs: Prentice Hall, 1979), p. 357.

6. Schwartz, *Super Chief*, pp. 114, 253–55, 289.

7. Fortas, "Chief Justice Warren," p. 412.

8. Douglas, *The Court Years*, p. 228.

9. *Ibid.*; Schwartz, *Super Chief*, pp. 261–63.

10. Quoted, *ibid.*, p. 144.

11. William J. Brennan, "Chief Justice Warren," *Harvard Law Review*, 88 (1974), p. 5.

12. Quoted in Schwartz, *Super Chief*, p. 46.

13. Quoted, *ibid.*, p. 144.

14. Fortas, "Chief Justice Warren," p. 411.

15. Quoted in Bernard Schwartz, *The Unpublished Opinions of the Warren Court* (New York: Oxford University Press, 1985), p. 7.

16. Quoted in Schwartz, *Super Chief*, p. 143.

17. Fortas, "Chief Justice Warren," p. 411.

18. Charles Evans Hughes, *The Supreme Court of the United States* (New York: Columbia University Press, 1928), p. 57.

19. Quoted in *The New York Times*, July 16, 1974, p. 24.

20. Schwartz, *Super Chief*, pp. 205–06.

PART FOUR

Problems of Compliance and Impact

CHAPTER 13

Who Gets What

The results of the judicial process can be analyzed by asking three questions. The first is the question of who wins and who loses. As the article by Kritzer et. al. shows, identifying winners and losers in litigation is often very difficult. Thus it may be hard to determine whether there are consistent patterns of winning and losing that are associated with particular characteristics of the parties and the situations in which they are involved. The second question is a question of reaction. How do those directly affected by court policy decisions respond to them? The third question is, simply, what difference do court decisions make to the parties involved in a dispute and to others? The second and third questions will be considered in chapter fourteen.

In the Introduction to this book we argued that there has been a gradual increase in the scope of the American legal system. This increase, whose origins date back at least to the 1930s, means that the law now regulates or reaches almost everything in American life. The scope and reach of law in turn determines the role and significance of our courts. The greater the former, the greater the latter. As new and different kinds of rights and remedies are created, new and different kinds of disputes reach courts, thus providing more opportunities to make and shape policy. Although courts decide lawsuits between particular litigants, the significance of any court decision often reaches far beyond those immediately involved. The decision may set a precedent for future litigation, and its effect may be to distribute, either directly or indirectly, tangible or intangible resources throughout society. When the Supreme Court ordered the Board of Education of Topeka, Kansas, to end de jure (required by law) segregation, the "defeat" was borne not only by that city but also by the entire Southern region (including the Border States).[1] When the Court found that Roe had a constitutionally protected right to an abortion, all women found themselves with a newly recognized right.[2] Patterns of victory and defeat may have the broadest political and social ramifications.

Patterns of victory and defeat may also be important in addressing the issue of the distinctiveness of the courts as dispute-processing institutions. Unlike some types of dispute-processing institutions, courts are expected to provide impartial judgment; courts are supposed to decide disputes by reference to the facts of who did what to whom and by identifying, interpreting, and applying appropriate norms. This requires that judges remain neutral with regard to both the issues of the case and its result. We have already discussed the extent to which American judges allow themselves to be influenced by their own political attitudes and values when they feel free to exercise their discretion in making decisions.

In this chapter we present two selections that examine patterns of court decisions. Both emphasize the difficulty of utilizing a simple calculus of winning and losing. Both suggest that who wins is often ambiguous and controversial.

One can, however, examine court decisions to determine the extent to which cases are decided independently of the personal attributes of the parties involved. We assume that impartiality is displayed when both parties to a case are given the same opportunities and shown the same consideration. Equality of consideration requires that the judge be influenced neither by a personal interest in the outcome of a case nor by positive or negative attitudes toward the people and the particular situation involved.[3] Impartiality in result cannot be determined, we believe, by analyzing a single decision. Rather, it is necessary to examine a series of decisions involving similar situations to ascertain whether, over time, different kinds of parties are equally likely to gain favorable results. If the results were perfectly impartial, then the pattern of decision should be random and should not consistently favor one type of litigant over another. If, for example, courts in custody cases sometimes rule for the mother and sometimes rule for the father, the conclusion may be drawn that they show equal regard for both sexes. If, on the other hand, courts were to favor mothers over fathers regardless of the facts or the applicable law, then their results would not be impartial.[4]

The problem with this way of determining result impartiality is that it does not take into account the several factors responsible for variations from the standard of randomness that go beyond the attitudes and values of the judges. The first, and most obvious, is that even if courts are impartial in their procedures, they may still produce biased results if the laws applied favor one type of litigant. This is certainly true in our example of custody cases, since in most states divorce laws embodied a strong presumption in favor of the mother until recently. No matter how even-handed the application of such laws, the pattern of results is predetermined by the bias in their substance. Other factors producing deviations from the standard of randomness are the costs of using courts, the fact that they operate in accord with complex legal rules and procedures, and the fact that they tend to be passive in the manner in which they acquire cases.

As we have suggested several times, dispute processing by American courts is costly. The major cost affecting the result of litigation is the time it takes to obtain a judicial decision. Delay, according to Marc Galanter, favors parties who are better organized and who have more expendable resources.[5] Delay favors such parties in three ways. First, by complicating the task of challenging ongoing activities, delay advantages parties who derive benefits from the existing rules. Second, delay tends to protect the "possessor," that is, those who have resources that might be endangered in the course of litigation. Third, delay means that courts cannot efficiently protect all of the rights that are formally recognized by law. Since there are priorities in the allocation of judicial resources, judges tend to favor the more organized and the more attentive among their clientele. In each instance, delay benefits the well organized and the economically powerful.

The fact that courts operate in accord with legal procedures puts a premium on the ability of parties to obtain expert legal counsel. Since not all lawyers are equally skillful or committed, resource differentials result in an unequal distribution of legal talent. In addition, the reactive organization of courts gives advantage to those parties with information and a sense of legal efficacy. The passivity of courts means that the burden of instituting a lawsuit remains on the parties themselves. Parties are treated as if they were equally capable of marshaling the resources and legal skills needed to effectively present a case. When they are in fact not equally capable of doing so, the pattern of results will be imbalanced. Finally, the lack of impartiality in the results of the judicial process may be a function of the personal biases of judges. To the extent that judges are selected from among particular groups or interests, they may be expected to sympathize with the attitudes and values associated with those groups or interests when making decisions.

The Dolbeare article suggests that parties who are better organized and wealthier fare considerably better in all types of cases than those who act on their own with little in the way of organization and resources. This suggests that the results produced in many American courts are not impartial and that those results tend to be predictable on the basis of the characteristics and configurations of the litigants and the situation or context.[6] Courts, then, in terms of the pattern of results they produce, cannot be said to differ greatly from other more overtly political institutions.

NOTES

1. *Brown* v. *Board of Education*, 347 U.S. 483 (1954).
2. *Roe* v. *Wade*, 410 U.S. 113 (1973).
3. Torstein Eckhoff, "Impartiality, Separation of Powers and Judicial Independence," *Scandinavian Studies in Law* 9 (1965), 9.
4. See Martha Fineman, "Implementing Equality," *Wisconsin Law Review* 1983 (1983), 789; see also Robert Mnookin, "Child Custody Adjudication," *Law and Contemporary Problems* 39 (1975), 226; Nancy Polinkoff, "Why Mothers Are Losing," *Women's Rights Law Reports* 7 (1982), 235.
5. Marc Galanter, "Why the 'Haves' Come Out Ahead: Speculations on the Limits of Legal Change," *Law and Society Review* 9 (1974), 98–101. Also see Stanton Wheeler, Bliss Cartwright, Robert A. Kagan, and Lawrence M. Friedman, "Do the 'Haves' Come out Ahead? Winning and Losing in State Supreme Courts, 1870–1970," *Law and Society Review* 21(1987), 403.
6. Marc Galanter, "Afterword: Explaining Litigation," *Law and Society Review* 9 (1975), 357.

Winners and Losers in Litigation: Does Anyone Come Out Ahead?

Herbert M. Kritzer
Austin Sarat
David M. Trubek
William L. F. Felstiner

An enormous literature which surveys, discusses, and analyzes the so called litigation explosion has been generated over the past several years.... Considerable attention has been devoted to trying to understand why people use the courts, whether there has been an increase in popular reliance on judicial dispute resolution, and whether the volume of litigation poses special problems for courts. At the same time much less attention has been devoted to the question of what difference litigation makes and to an examination of the outcomes and consequences of ordinary litigation.

. . .

This paper takes up the question of who gets what in ordinary civil litigation at the trial court level; that is, who wins, who loses, and how much is gained and/or lost? Ordinary civil litigation involves neither high principle nor complex legal issues; instead it typically involves the question of whether money should be transferred, because of some violation of state norms or individual rights, from one party to another. In this sense ordinary litigation involves an effort by one party to obtain resources as compensation, remedy or redress from an alleged wrong doer. Litigation is, thus, a form of redistributive activity and courts provide a forum in which the justification for redistribution and its appropriate amounts become the object of bargaining and negotiation, or, in the last instance, official *governmental* decision.

. . .

THE PROBLEM OF "WINNING"

The problem of ascertaining who wins and who loses in the litigation process is nicely illustrated by the recently concluded Westmoreland-CBS libel case. In the wake of the abandonment of the trial, both sides proclaimed victory. No one made it clear what was meant by "victory" in this context, and in fact, some observers declared both CBS and Westmoreland to be "losers". However, the complexity of the question of evaluating who wins and who loses is not unique to the big, flashy case.

. . .

... [F]rom the Westmoreland case, we can see the difficult problem of establishing an appropriate baseline against which out-

Paper presented at the 1985 annual meeting of the Midwest Political Science Association, Chicago, Ill. Footnotes & most references omitted.

comes can be assessed. Only with such a baseline could we begin to make statements about who wins and who loses. In establishing the baseline, we must recognize that civil litigation is part of an ongoing process of bargaining and negotiation. Litigation alters the bargaining arena...and may change the stakes, but it rarely ends the bargaining (though it sometimes plays an important role in getting serious negotiations underway). Thus one way of thinking about the results of civil litigation is to assess them against the results that could have been achieved earlier in the bargaining process, before the formalities of litigation are begun. It is possible that the outcome achieved through litigation is no better (and perhaps considerably worse) than that which could have been achieved without ever involving the court or lawyers.

Thus, from the plaintiff's viewpoint, one possible image of victory is relative to what is *really* at stake, not what is nominally at stake as reflected in court documents. But the concept of stakes in civil litigation is often expressed in terms that are extremely ambiguous: "the best interests of the child" (in child custody cases), or defending a trademark, or vindication of one's position. Even in cases where the stakes are clearly monetary (e.g., personal injury), there is no scientific way of ascertaining what a "case is worth" particularly when factors like compensation for "pain and suffering" are included.

.   .   .

This discussion suggests several points regarding the idea of "winning" and "losing" in litigation. First, there is an important distinction between the individual case and how it might have fared depending upon the choices the participants made and the role of the judicial system of conflict resolution. That is, while it may be true that for any given

case, one side or the other, or both, might have "done better" if they had avoided going to court or going to trial, the "shadow" of the courthouse...sets the terms by which the processes outside the courthouse operate. Second, the assessment of success must usually be made in relative terms.... While success in litigation must be evaluated relative to some base, there are often several bases from which to choose for a given actor (not all of which are necessarily susceptible to measurement). Moreover, the appropriate base will usually be different for each of the "players" in a particular case. As we consider the results of ordinary litigation, it may be useful to distinguish between "winning" and "prevailing". Often in litigation one hears reference to the "prevailing" party; this is usually meant to refer to which side receives a favorable judgment from the court; however, most civil cases never get to the point of a judgment, and even for those that do a party can "win" even if it does not "prevail"...And third, in considering outcomes in litigation, one must consider not only cases that went through the process all the way to a court judgment, but also cases in which a negotiated settlement is reached. Ultimately, one should look at both cases that were filed in court and cases that never even got to that stage; our analysis, however, will be limited to cases in which a lawsuit was actually filed.

DATA

...The data that we analyze is drawn from interviews with 1382 lawyers; these lawyers represented parties in 1649 court cases selected randomly from twelve courts (seven state and five federal) in five federal judicial districts around the country (Eastern Wisconsin, Eastern Pennsylvania, South Carolina, New Mexico, and Central California). The interviews, which averaged one hour in length, covered all facets of the sampled cases; additional data were obtained from the court records for each of the cases. Since we are concerned about results from the viewpoint of the "players" as reported by their attorneys, we will use the attorney as the unit of analysis.

Given that we have previously shown that stakes in ordinary civil cases tend to be modest (Trubek et al., 1983a, 1983b), it should not be surprising that the *outcome* in the typical, everyday court case is modest. Table 1 provides a basic description of the outcomes in the cases in our sample, both for all cases and for federal and state cases separately. Note that the cases represented in the table are only those for which the outcome was monetary in nature; we did not ask our respondents to monetize the non-monetary aspects of settlements and judgments, and thus cases where the outcomes were wholly or partially nonmonetary are not used in the analysis.

The median outcome (recovery for plaintiffs or payment for defendants) was only $3,500 in state courts; as one would expect,

the figure is higher in federal courts: $6,500. Both of these figures are lower than the median stakes of $4,500 and $15,000 for the state and federal courts respectively. . . .

WINNING AND LOSING FROM THE PLAINTIFF'S PERSPECTIVE

There are at least two ways that one might go about assessing winning and losing from the plaintiff's perspective. First, one might take an approach resembling a cost-benefit analysis by comparing fees paid to amount recovered. The difficulty with this approach is that for most plaintiffs the ratio of fees to recovery is fixed by the percentage (contingent) fee agreement; thus the cost-benefit approach is applicable only to the relatively small group (around 20% in our sample) of plaintiffs who paid their lawyer on some basis other than a contingent fee.

The second approach is to assess the outcome, net of transaction costs, against the amount at stake. We assessed stakes

TABLE 1
Case Outcomes by Court

Amount	Unadjusted Outcomes Percent of Cases			Adjusted Outcomes Percent of Cases		
	All	*State*	*Federal*	*All*	*State*	*Federal*
Less than $0[a]	—	—	—	6%	5%	7%
$0–2500	38%	41%	35%	26	64	19
2501–5000	17	23	10	18	23	12
5001–10000	13	16	12	17	19	16
10001–25000	18	15	21	17	14	21
25001–50000	6	5	8	8	4	11
50000 & up	8	1	13	8	1	14
Median	$4,289	$3,500	$6,500	$5,069	$3,081	$8,946
(n)	(767)	(372)	(395)	(676)	(333)	(343)

[a] These are plaintiffs only (who paid out more in legal fees and expenses than they recovered).

by asking plaintiffs' lawyers how much they felt their client should have been willing to accept to settle the case; if the lawyer indicated that the evaluation of stakes changed over the course of the case, we used the highest value. The underlying assumption here is that we are assessing success against no recovery at all. One might argue, as we suggested previously, that in some cases a more appropriate base would be the amount that could have been recovered without resort to litigation. We assume that without at least the potential of litigation there is a substantial probability that no recovery would have been possible in many cases; this makes no recovery (and thus the overall stakes value) the appropriate base for comparison.

The formal definition of plaintiff's success is a ratio of the form:

$$\frac{\text{Plaintiff}}{\text{Success}} = \frac{\text{Recovery} - \text{Fees}}{\text{Plaintiff's Highest Stakes Estimate}}$$

The higher this ratio, the better the plaintiff has done in relation to expectations. Since

the stakes question elicited the amount of money the case should settle for, not what the client should get after paying the attorney, success ratios above 1.0 would be exceptional. In a contingent fee case where the lawyer's fee equalled one third of the recovery, and the recovery was exactly the same as the stakes estimate, the ratio would be .67 or two-thirds.

Table 2 shows separate win/loss statistics for plaintiffs who used hourly and contingent fee lawyers. As the table shows, the patterns for those who used hourly and for those who were represented by contingent fee lawyers are quite similar. There is one difference worth noting: the fact that the contingent fee lawyer always gets a percentage of the recovery serves to limit the level of success that can be achieved; thus, for cases over $10,000, plaintiffs with hourly fee lawyers achieve success ratios of .8 to .9, while those with contingent fee lawyers typically achieve ratios in the .5 to .6 range. The table also shows that success improves as the size of the recovery goes up. In some

TABLE 2
Plaintiffs' Success

| | All Cases | Size of Recovery | | | Court | |
		<$10,000	$10,000–$50,000	>$50,000	Federal	State
			Hourly Fee Lawyers			
Median	.60	.38	.78	.93	.71	.54
First Quartile	.19	.00	.71	.68	.06	.31
Third Quartile	.95	.56	.95	1.00	.94	.95
(n)	(57)	(32)	(13)	(12)	(30)	(27)
			Contingent Fee Lawyers			
Median	.49	.44	.57	.52	.39	.56
First Quartile	.23	.11	.28	.37	.11	.33
Third Quartile	.67	.64	.68	.74	.66	.67
(n)	(256)	(155)	(79)	(22)	(117)	(139)

of the smaller cases, the ratio is actually negative because fees exceed recovery. Thus, the figures suggest something resembling a threshold effect: in all cases certain costs must be incurred regardless of the stakes. This effect can be seen in the dramatic improvement in success ratios as outcomes go from under $10,000 to the $10,000 to $50,000 (from .38 to .71 for plaintiffs with hourly fee lawyers and from .44 to .57 for those with contingent fee lawyers). Success changes only slightly when we move from the $10,000–$50,000 range to over $50,000, and in fact it actually goes down from .57 to .52 for contingent fee plaintiffs; it goes up from .78 to .93 for clients plaintiffs represented by hourly fee lawyers.

What do we find when we look at the impact of other factors on the success ratio for plaintiffs? Given the generally similar behavior of the ratio for plaintiffs with contingent and hourly fee lawyers, we have ignored that distinction in looking at the impact of variables like lawyers activities, experience, expertise, etc. When we examined the effect of lawyer activities (i.e., how much they concentrated their efforts on client conferences, discovery, other factual investigation, settlement discussions, pleadings and motions, and/or legal research), the results suggest that the return from a settlement oriented strategy is better than from a "fight it out" strategy. For each activity we divided the lawyers into those who spent a "large" proportion of their time on that activity and those who spent a "small" proportion of their time; we also computed the correlation (Kendall's tau b) between the proportion of time spent on each activity and the success ratio. Table 3 shows the relationship between the lawyer's activities and success: success goes up as lawyers concentrate their time on settlement activities (.59 versus .44) and factual investigation other

TABLE 3
Plaintiff Success by Lawyer Activities

Activity	Below "Median"	Above "Median"	Kendall's tau b
Conferring with Client (n)	.50 (164)	.56 (148)	.09**
Discovery (n)	.62 (123)	.47 (190)	−.13***
Factual Investigation other than Discovery (n)	.49 (168)	.58 (144)	.07*
Settlement Discussions (n)	.44 (180)	.59 (132)	.16***
Pleadings and Motions (n)	.49 (168)	.58 (144)	.04
Legal Research (n)	.58 (165)	.43 (147)	−.17***

  * p < .05 (one-tailed)
 ** p < .01 (one-tailed)
*** p < .001 (one-tailed)
NOTE:
The above and below "median" groups are defined by the median proportions of time devoted to each activity for the complete sample of lawyers (not just for hourly plaintiff's lawyers).

than discovery (.58 versus .49), and success goes down as time on discovery (.47 versus .62) and legal research (.43 versus .58) goes up. One interesting caveat (shown in Table 4) is that there is a slight tendency for success to go down as the amount of lawyer effort goes up (Kendall's tau b = −.11) and as the number of events goes up (tau b = −.14); this suggests that the most success tends to be achieved when a resolution is obtained relatively easily.

There is additional evidence that plaintiffs do better by pursuing a strategy of "bargained" justice. First, the success ratio for cases that went to trial (.23) was significantly lower than for those that did not go to trial (.54). Second, plaintiffs who make an initial demand substantially above their evaluation of stakes, achieve a higher success ratio (tau b = .18) between success ratio and ratio of stakes to first demand).

Does a "better" lawyer produce a "better" result? There are some very, very slight relationships between plaintiff success and the variables that one might expect to be associated with lawyer productivity (i.e., experience and specialization) but none of the variables have enough influence to suggest that a client would gain meaningfully by seeking out a very experienced lawyer. Table 4 shows the correlations between these (and other) variables and our success ratio for plaintiffs. At least for plaintiffs in ordinary litigation the chances of winning are not increased substantially by using more experienced and specialized counsel. This may simply reflect the fact that there is not enough latitude in these cases for expertise and experience to make a difference, or it may be that there is not enough variation in experience and specialization among our lawyers for us to uncover a notable relationship. It might also be that whatever gains are accrued from specialization and experience are not passed onto the client but, at

TABLE 4
Correlations of Plaintiff Success with Lawyer and Case Characteristics

Variable	Kendall's tau b
Years of practice	.06*
Specialization	.08**
Self-ranked expertise	.05
Craftsmanship	−.06*
Percent of time on litigation	−.03
Amount of lawyer time	−.11**
Duration	−.06*
Number of pretrial events	−.14***
Ratio of first demand to stakes	.18***

* $p < .05$ (one-tailed)
** $p < .01$ (one-tailed)
*** $p < .001$ (one-tailed)

least for hourly fee lawyers, are absorbed by the higher fees which older and more specialized lawyers are able to charge.

WINNING AND LOSING FROM THE DEFENDANT'S PERSPECTIVE

Having looked at winning and losing from the plaintiff's perspective, how can we assess whether litigation "pays" for the defendant? It makes little sense to compare the fees defendants pay their lawyers to the amount they must pay plaintiffs (recoveries). These ratios could be (and often are) very high. Yet defendants could (and do) still consider that their litigation investment "paid off" handsomely. Assume a case in which the plaintiff expects to recover $100,000 but in the end the defendant pays only $10,000 and the defendant's lawyer receives a fee of $20,000. In that situation, the recovery to fee ratio would be very low (.5). Yet as long as the original claim had some merit and there was some real risk that the plaintiff could recover most or all of the amount at issue, the defendant's lawyer has been quite effective; the defendant has spent $20,000 in legal fees to save $90,000 in payment to the plaintiff. As suggested by this example, the defendant's litigation investment works to reduce or eliminate an expenditure the defendant would otherwise have to incur. When presented with a claim, a defendant sees the expenditure on lawyer's fees as a way to avoid paying some or all of the amount claimed. If the lawyer's work reduces the claim by an amount greater than her fees, the defendant's investment has been successful.

This leaves the problem of measuring the amount of the "claim" against which to assess the result of the lawyer's work. One could identify a variety of indicators that might be used in this regard. One might use the amount that the defendant thought he might have to pay based on what the plaintiff initially demanded ("exposure"); however, this is likely to overestimate the potential benefit because the plaintiff for tactical reasons will often ask for more than he expects to get. Alternatively, one could use the plaintiff's (highest) estimate of what was at stake. While the defendant will not usually be aware of this figure, it is a more accurate indicator of the potential loss to the defendant than is a possibly exaggerated demand. . . . In our analysis we rely upon the second of these indicators (the plaintiff's estimate of stakes); we have information from the plaintiff's lawyer for 143 defendants, and this group forms the basis of our analysis. The specific indicator of defendant's success that we will report on below is:

$$\text{Defendant Success} = \frac{\text{Plaintiff's Stakes}}{\text{Recovery} + \text{Fees}}$$

This index is always positive, with values greater than 1.0 indicating "success" (i.e., less was paid out in fees and recovery than the plaintiff had sought) and values less than 1.0 indicating "failure" (the defendant would have been better off simply paying to the plaintiff the plaintiff's estimate of stakes—if the defendant had known what that figure was).

In some ways, this index parallels the measure of success used for plaintiffs in that if we rewrite the two equations using "adjusted outcomes" in place of "recovery + fees" or "recovery − fees", the two formulas are the inverse of one another:

$$\text{Plaintiff Success} = \frac{\text{Adjusted Outcome}}{\text{Plaintiff's Stakes}}$$

$$\text{Defendant Success} = \frac{\text{Plaintiff's Stakes}}{\text{Adjusted Outcome}}$$

However, there is one important asymmetry between the equations for plaintiffs and defendants—only the plaintiffs can have negative values. Let us now turn to the results of our analysis of success from the defendant's perspective.

Table 5 shows summary information for defendants' success. For two-thirds of the defendants, their lawyer saved more in reduced payments to plaintiffs than the lawyer was paid in fees. Thus, for most defendants, litigation was "successful". This does not necessarily mean that two-thirds of the defendants "won" while that proportion of plaintiffs lost; rather, for both plaintiffs and defendants, retaining a lawyer is *usually* not a "losing" proposition. Relative to what they might lose, defendants' positions are improved by the work of the lawyer, and relative to getting nothing, the plaintiff comes out ahead by litigating.

The seond thing to be noted in Table 5 is the lack of variation in level and likelihood of success for different groups of cases: Defendants do just as well in state and federal

TABLE 5
Defendant Success

	All Cases	Size of Recovery			Court	
		<$10,000	$10,000–$50,000	>$50,000	Federal	State
Median	1.44	1.56	1.27	1.47	1.35	1.44
First Quartile	.90	.89	.95	.99	.84	.96
Third Quartile	2.58	3.11	1.88	2.03	2.58	2.50
Percent Successful[a]	67%	67%	66%	67%	65%	69%
(n)	(143)	(93)	(41)	(9)	(75)	(68)

[a] This is the percent of respondents with a success ratio exceeding 1.0.

courts, and in big and small cases. In fact, when we looked at the various factors we considered in the sections on outcomes from the plaintiff's perspective, we found, with one exception, no relationships worth noting. That is, the success of defendants is not improved by the lawyer concentrating her attention on certain activities, it is not improved by going to trial or by settling short of trial, and it is not improved by using a lawyer with more experience or expertise. We did find very, very slight relationships between defendant's success and duration (success goes up as duration goes up), and between success and numbers of court events (success goes up as number of events goes up), but these relationships are so weak that little would be gained (in terms of success as we have measured it here) by a defendant who intentionally delayed settling or filed nonessential motions or discovery requests. The one exception to the pattern of nonrelationships concerns negotiation strategy: those who take a tough bargaining stance (by making a low offer relative to the plaintiff's evaluation of stakes) do better than those whose initial offer is closer to the opponent's stakes evaluation (tau b = .41).

.   .   .

The conclusion to be drawn from our analysis of defendants' success is clear: defendants usually come out ahead from the litigation process in that they save more than they pay out in expenses to their legal counsel. We should note that this does not take into account the "internal costs" that are incurred, i.e., the value of the time of the people who are directly affiliated with the defendant (such as the defendant him or herself if it is an individual or the employees of the defendant if it is an organization); however, much, if not most, of these costs would be incurred regardless of whether or not the dispute was taken to court. Even though most defendants come out ahead, a sizeable proportion (about one-third) do not, and there is a substantial amount of variation in the degree to which defendants profit or lose by litigation; interestingly, with the exception of bargaining strategy, none of the variables that we looked at, primarily case characteristics and lawyer productivity indicators, accounts for this variation.

.   .   .

REFERENCES

Trubek, David M., Austin Sarat, William L.F. Felstiner, Herbert M. Kritzer, and Joel B. Grossman (1983a) "The Costs of Ordinary Litigation," 31 *UCLA Law Review* 72.

Trubek, David M., Joel B. Grossman, William L.F. Felstiner, Herbert M. Kritzer, and Austin Sarat (1983b) *Civil Litigation Research Project: Final Report* (2 volumes). Madison, Wisconsin. University of Wisconsin Law School.

The Federal District Courts and Urban Public Policy

Kenneth M. Dolbeare

This paper reports some beginning steps toward two still distant goals: assessment of the policy outcomes of federal court activity and comprehensive evaluation of the political role and policy impact of such courts. At this early stage, the focus of inquiry extends no further than a quantitative account of the decisional output of federal District Courts concerning selected public policy matters in twenty large cities of the United States. Even with this limited scope, and despite certain serious data limitations, some useful potential seems to inhere in an output focus, stemming from the fact that analysis is projected in both directions around the now-familiar systems theory circle. First, taking output as the dependent variable in the usual manner, some additional insight may be gained into the significance of particular decision-making patterns from identification of the nature and objects of the burdens and benefits allocated by the courts. Second, taking output as the independent

Reprinted by permission of John Wiley & Sons, Inc., from Kenneth M. Dolbeare, "The Federal District Courts and Urban Politics: An Exploritory Study (1960–1967)," in Joel B. Grossman and Joseph Tanenhaus, eds., FRONTIERS IN JUDICIAL RESEARCH. Copyright © 1969 by John Wiley & Sons, Inc.

variable, it may be possible to identify patterns of differential policy impact, reactions, and resultant feedback associated with particular policy outputs. Placing policy content at the center of theoretical interest (rather than decision making), leads, in effect, to collection of data which outline a different and as yet undefined set of causes and effects. I do not suggest that such an output-impact focus is necessarily more fruitful than one which takes the behavior of the judge as its focus, but merely that it is a useful complement in that it projects empirical inquiry toward relatively unexplored areas which are of perhaps equal importance to the building of a comprehensive theory of the part played by judges as actors and courts as institutions in the larger political system.

.   .   .

THE NATURE OF THE INQUIRY AND THE CHARACTER OF THE DATA

Three limits were imposed on the scope of this preliminary inquiry in order to maximize explanatory potential from a manageable and relevant body of data. These included *political contexts* (twenty large cities), *policy areas* (urban public policy problems), and *cases employed* (decisions made between January 1, 1960 and March 31, 1967, which are reported in the *Federal Reporter* or *Federal Supplement* series). Each category requires further elaboration.

Political Contexts

The settings selected for this inquiry included seven of the nation's ten largest cities, plus thirteen others of more than 150,000 population. Urban settings were chosen because of the range and multitude of their public policy problems, as well as their social and political importance. These particular cities were included because they were the ones which had been the subject of relatively systematic published analyses by political scientists; it was my original intention to explore relationships between the part played by the federal courts and the political (as well as socioeconomic) characteristics of the cities in which they are located.

Policy Areas

The kinds of public policy problems selected for inclusion are those which are generally perceived as such by urban scholars, publics, and public officials—and which have been acted upon by the federal government or the cities themselves. Law enforcement, civil rights, urban renewal, public housing, pollution, poverty, and transportation make up the major policy areas of urban concern which meet this standard. Not included are such general federal court matters (bearing no special relevance to the urban character of the setting) as bankruptcy, admiralty, tax, workmen's compensation, federal law enforcement, or ordinary diversity cases. The focus is the city's local urban problems—its policy practices, segregation in its schools, its slums, and air and water pollution—with

regard to which it, as a political entity, has at least potential capacity to act.

Cases Employed

District Court output which meets the geographic and policy criteria of the foregoing paragraphs is only a small proportion of the total workload of such courts, although it is of important political relevance. Not all of such cases, however, are publicly reported. This inquiry includes only those cases decided between January 1, 1960 and March 31, 1967, which were reported in the *Federal Supplement* or could be reconstructed from the opinions of the Courts of Appeals as reported in the *Federal Reporter*. This limitation may be a major weakness, but several factors suggest that the resultant body of cases still may be employed, with appropriate care in certain respects, for the purposes of this inquiry.

First, the publisher of the *Federal Supplement*, the West Publishing Company of St. Paul, Minn., exercises no independent judgment as to which cases should be reported. The practice is to publish all decisions for which opinions should have been written, except for those few which are not released for publication. This means that the trial judge's decision to write an opinion or to simply render a judgment without an opinion essentially controls the content of the *Federal Supplement*. Because public bodies or officials are frequently involved in the cases of concern for this study, and because these cases are those which carry public significance, it seems likely that there is a high incidence of opinion writing in cases which fit our criteria. At the very least, it would appear that the resultant body of cases would include most of the *major* policy decisions made by federal district judges.

Second, although the reports of District Court activity emanating from the Administrative Office of the U.S. Courts do not contain detailed breakdowns in classifications reflecting our public policy concerns, it is possible to use those statistics to develop rough estimates of the total number of cases decided per year in some of our areas for some of our cities. In the case of New York, Chicago, and Philadelphia, for instance, it appears that the cases included within this study constitute between 40 and 50 percent of all those falling within our criteria which were actually decided by the relevant District Courts. Thus, while no claim can be made as to representativeness of this body of cases, the proportion is probably substantial.

. . .

Table 1 details the major classifications of subjects of these cases for the cities involved. The small number of cases in the "all other" category indicates that District Court public policy actions are relatively narrowly confined to those areas which rest upon constitutional interpretations or statutory extensions of constitutional rights— principally the post-Civil War Civil Rights Acts. The "all other" category includes public housing, urban renewal, and slum clearance (a total of 8 cases), city tax and regulatory powers (20 cases), and a miscellaneous remaining group of 12 cases. Few of the several federal programs for aid to urban areas, such as mass transportation, poverty, and air pollution, are included among these cases, probably as a result of the fact that they are based chiefly on grants-in-aid and potential opponents normally lack standing to challenge them in court. As might be expected, the number of cases rises in the latter years of the study. An average of 28 cases per year was decided in 1960 through 1962 while the average for the remainder of the period was nearly 60 per year. The increase, however, was due almost entirely to a rise in habeas corpus petitions, and

there is very little change in any other category.

. . .

THE SUBJECTS AND RESULTS OF DISTRICT COURT DECISIONS

The subjects with which the District Courts are engaged, and hence the areas in which they may have policy effects, are shaped by their jurisdiction, the substance of "federal questions," and the litigiousness of actors in the various urban political contexts—itself a product of both cultural factors and the characteristics of the particular subject areas involved. The former is both well known and relatively fixed in effect, requiring little comment. The latter two factors present empirical questions. Some extensions of the definition of a "federal question" occur from time to time as new constitutional interpretations are made or new federal statutes are passed, and considerable variability inheres in the local propensity to invoke the courts as a means of advancing one's policy goals. Thus, it is helpful to first establish the grounds on which the District Courts were called upon, the forms of action which were employed, the parties who came to court, and the purposes which animated them.

The scope of District Court policy action is practically coterminous with the reach of constitutional limitations. In more than 90 percent of the cases, a constitutional provision was the ultimate basis of the claim. In 90 of these cases (30 percent), the action was based on a federal civil rights statute which, in effect, extended legal enforceability of constitutional rights. Only 17 cases invoked provisions of the Civil Rights Act of 1964, and all the rest employed one or more provisions of the post-Civil War Civil Rights Acts to seek injunctions or damages from

TABLE 1
District Court Cases per City, Major Classifications

City	Total Number of Cases	Major Classifications							
		Civil Rights-Race Relations		Civil Rights-Free Speech and Due Process in Police Practices		Habeas Corpus-State Prisoners vs. City Police Practices		All Others	
		Number	Percent of City Total	Number	Percent of City Total	Number	Percent of City Total	Number	Percent of City Total
New York	85	3	4	25	29	48	56	9	11
Philadelphia	41	2	5	14	34	21	51	4	10
Chicago	39	1	3	19	48	12	31	7	18
Los Angeles	36	0	—	23	64	11	31	2	5
New Orleans	30	14	47	4	13	9	30	3	10
Houston	17	4	23	0	—	10	59	3	18
St. Louis	13	1	8	8	61	4	31	0	—
Pittsburgh	12	0	—	5	42	5	42	2	16
Denver	12	0	—	6	50	5	42	1	8
Atlanta	11	8	73	1	9	0	—	2	18
Detroit	8	1	12	3	38	1	12	3	38
Nashville	5	2	40	1	20	2	40	0	—
Boston	4	0	—	2	50	2	50	0	—
Cleveland	4	1	25	2	50	0	—	1	25
Miami	4	2	50	0	—	0	—	2	50
Milwaukee	4	0	—	2	50	2	50	0	—
All others	10	2	20	6	60	2	20	0	—
(Salt Lake City 2, Seattle 2, Minneapolis 3, Kansas City 3)									
	335	41	(12)	121	(36)	134	(40)	39	(12)

state officials who allegedly denied complainants their federally secured rights. This may be a result of the broadly inclusive nature of the applicable sections of those statutes, together with expanding definitions of constitutional rights produced by the Supreme Court. In any event, it is a fact that these Civil Rights Acts were almost the only federal statutes which came before the District Courts in these cases. Only five cases involved other statutes, and in 240 cases there was no substantive federal statute involved.

The forms of action in which these policy questions arose reflect the constitutional and statutory grounds just described. A large number (134 or 40 percent of the total number of decisions) were habeas corpus petitions in which a state prisoner contested a contemporary city police practice. The next largest proportions (20 percent and 16 percent respectively) were injunctions against present or prospective deprivations of constitutional rights or suits for damages for past violations of civil rights. Other forms of action, in order of incidence, included motions to suppress allegedly illegally obtained evidence about to be used in a state trial, actions for damages arising without statutory grounds, and miscellaneous declaratory judgment and other actions. In those areas where constitutional limitations may be applicable, at least, the District Courts are offered opportunities for varying forms of policy applications.

Those who invoke the federal courts are, not surprisingly, those who are apparently low in influence within their communities—Negroes, prisoners, marginal businessmen, and individuals whose claims have been unsuccessful elsewhere. Table 2 presents a composite "who sues whom" summary of the parties to these cases. About half of all cases were brought by state prisoners contesting actions of city police. The remaining

cases were brought by white individuals (chiefly suits for damages against police and city officials for violations of civil rights) and Negro individuals or groups (injunctions against segregation in school districts or city facilities, plus some damage suits for violations of civil rights). Suits by businesses were for declaratory judgments as to invalidity of city tax or regulatory laws. Even if the large proportion of prisoner-generated cases is excluded, the share of cases initiated by groups is comparatively low, despite a generous definition of "group," indicating that assumptions as to group sponsorship of litigation may not hold true at the trial court level. The nature of the litigants and their goals, of course, is in part a product of the jurisdictional and state-of-the-law qualifications for access to the courts, but in part it is the product of the local environment and political structure.

This complex of forces produces a specialized set of policy issues for the District Courts. We have already seen that these issues are almost entirely reflections of constitutional limitations, and thus, our question is one of the particular distribution of subjects among the various possible constitutional dimensions. Table 3 presents a detailed breakdown of the actual subjects of cases before the District Courts in these cities. The preponderance of police practice-due process issues is again emphasized.

The policy actions of the District Courts are not the same in each of these subject areas. For purposes of analysis, we may include the race relations cases as a single category. Habeas corpus petitions, given their number and special character, deserve independent classification, but the remaining civil rights issues show sufficient consistency to permit consolidation. Such organization of the case classifications facilitates analysis of the *direction* of District Court policy making in a way which highlights the

TABLE 2
Plaintiffs and Defendants: A Composite Summary of Who Sues Whom in the District Courts[a]

Defendants / Plaintiffs	School Districts	City Government	Public Officials (Not Police) Personally	Policemen, Sheriffs	Custodians of Prisoners	Law Enforcement Officials	Other Officials, Boards, Governments	Individuals	Businesses, Groups	Others	Total Suits by: Number	Percent of Total
Negro individuals	4	1	0	4	2	1	2	1	0	0	15	5
Negro groups	7	2	1	0	0	0	2	0	1	0	13	4
Businesses	0	12	2	0	0	4	2	1	0	0	21	7
State prisoners, before and after state trial	0	0	2	4	133	10	3	1	0	0	153	49
White individuals	1	15	8	19	1	8	5	0	1	1	59	19
White groups	1	1	1	0	0	0	5	0	1	0	9	3
Governments	0	0	0	0	0	0	0	33[b]	4	1	38	12
Others	0	0	0	0	0	0	1	0	2	1	4	1
Total suits against by number	13	31	14	27	136	23	20	36	9	3	312	
Total suits against by percent of total	4	10	4	9	44	7	6	12	3	1		100

[a] A total of 23 cases were unclassifiable for this purpose, either because of multiple plaintiffs or defendants, uncertainty as to character, or the preliminary nature of a motion.
[b] This category is potentially misleading: in most instances, governments were only nominal plaintiffs, such as in actions to suppress evidence or quash subpoenas, allegedly unlawfully secured by city police.

TABLE 3
Subjects of Cases, District Courts

Subjects	Number of Cases	Percent of Total
Civil rights—race relations—education	22	7
Civil rights—race relations—all others	19	6
Civil rights—other noncriminal due process (free speech, church/state, etc.)	38	11
Criminal law—police practices (search and seizure, confessions, interrogation, counsel, wiretap, etc.) (includes habeas corpus)	194	58
Criminal law—other issues (practices of city officials, judges, prosecutors, etc.)	23	7
Urban renewal, slum clearance, other housing	8	2
City tax and regulatory policy	20	6
All other issues	11	3
	335	100

uniqueness of the courts' actions in the race relations area, as is indicated by the data in Table 4. In each major area, the District Courts support local city policy a high proportion of the time—with the sole exception of race relations, where the proportion is 45 percent, about half that of other areas.

For two important reasons, then, District Court policy making is narrowly channeled. The kinds of issues in which they may develop significant impact are few, and in most of these areas their role is essentially supportive of local city policy and police practices. This is not to suggest that the areas or instances of District Court action are not consequential; qualitative analysis might indicate that they have substantial effects even where they modify city policy infrequently, and federal court effects on race relations can hardly be overlooked. . . .

.   .   .

THE POLICY IMPACT OF THE FEDERAL DISTRICT COURTS

The concept of the "policy impact" of authoritative decisions made by the institutions of a political system, or by any particular institution of that system, is broadly inclusive of a variety of factors. Each of these factors is closely related to the characteristics of the ongoing political context and process; none is under the sole control of the decision-making institution, not even the substance of the policy which it produces. I shall attempt to identify several of these factors which together would comprise the policy impact of trial court decision making. Although the data developed in this preliminary inquiry are sufficient to provide empirical evidence in only a few of these areas, I shall try to identify a larger number of them in order to lay a base for some inordinately speculative extractions yet to follow. If data were available in each, they should add up to a characterization of the part played by the federal District Courts in the urban political system.

Preliminary to the study of policy impact, of course, is the classification of the subjects of cases on which the court makes decisions. Detailed specification of those areas in which the courts had an opportunity to

TABLE 4
District Court Action, Major Classifications, All Cities (Percent)

District Court Action	Total[a]		Civil Rights— Race Relations	Civil Rights— Free Speech and City Police Practices	Habeas Corpus— City Police Practices	All Others
	Number	Percent				
Supports present city policy or practice	224	81	45	88	84	81
Modifies or prohibits present city policy or practice	44	16	33	11	14	19
Supports present private policy or practice	6	2	12	—	2	—
Modifies or prohibits present private policy or practice	4	1	10	1	—	—
	278	100	100	100	100	100
			N = 33	N = 107	N = 106	N = 32

[a] 57 cases were unclassifiable for these purposes and are omitted from this table. Some of these involved preliminary or procedural issues which did not bring the court to the point of taking a stand for or against basic city policy, while others involved mixed results.

develop policy effects, *and of those in which they did not*, are essential to an opening perspective on policy impact. That different subjects are brought to court in different types of political contexts may be anticipated, and considerations of policy impact must allow for varying impact in different contexts. Outcome patterns—in the sense of the results of decisions, not the effects as yet—are also an early component of policy impact. Such questions as who wins and who loses in the decisions of the courts in each of the contexts and in each of the subject areas in which the courts are active must be answered in order to establish a sense of the nature and objects of the allocations of various kinds of benefits and burdens of public policy. The results in cases may also be expressed, as we have done, in terms of the policy changes required; this is short of policy effects or impact... but it is a first step which permits identification of

probable differing results in various contexts and subjects areas....

. . .

Table 5 summarizes the proportions of success enjoyed by various plaintiffs and defendants. Negro groups prove to be the most successful complainants; almost every instance reflects a court order to desegregate some governmental facility. Businesses trail Negro groups but are still ahead of all others. Their achievements are in the area of preventing city regulatory and taxing efforts and in voiding ordinances that would license or prevent the sale or showing of books and films. State prisoners, both before and after trial (civil actions, injunctions, and habeas corpus petitions), are no more successful than the average of all other cases in the District Courts, which casts some light on the charge that the federal courts are opening the state jails. Similar implications may be seen

TABLE 5
"Success Ratios" of Various Plaintiffs and Defendants in the District Courts[a]

Plaintiffs	Success Ratio (Percent)	Total Cases	Defendants	Success Ratio (Percent)	Total Cases
Negro individuals	14	16	School districts	69	13
Negro groups	42	12	City governments	69	26
Businesses	24	21	Public officials (not police) personally	100	11
State prisoners (before and after trial)	14	125	Policemen, sheriffs	81	21
White individuals	11	46	Custodians of prisoners	84	107
White Groups	17	6	Law enforcement officials	96	23
Others[b]	0	9	Other officials, boards, and governments	78	18
			Individuals	90	33
			Businesses, groups	75	4
			Others	67	3

[a] "Success Ratios" represent the proportion of cases in which the party emerged with substantially what he had sought from the litigation. Some close questions arose where plaintiffs received only a small part of their goals, and in some instances cases had to be eliminated from the classification.
[b] Cases in which governments were only nominal parties were eliminated.

from the fact that law enforcement officials are almost always successful in defending themselves in these courts. Only school districts and city governments are required to change their policies more than 30 percent of the time, and this reflects the winners and effects outlined above.

.   .   .

We lack the data to fulfill the requisites for understanding of the stages of policy impact subsequent to patterns of winners, losers, and differential policy results in varying types of cases. If possible, it would have been profitable to examine qualitative effects, political accommodations, compliance, employment of alternative means and shifts in goals, functional implications, and feedback and support effects. Even without such inquiry, however, it is possible to draw some speculative extractions out of our data and apply them to the problem of defining the

part played by the federal District Courts in the political system and thereby moving toward building a more comprehensive theory of the judicial subsystem's linkage to the larger political system. In particular, it is possible to suggest some comparisons with the part played by the state trial courts in at least four respects.[1]

Users of the Courts and Their Purposes

Those who invoked the federal courts were chiefly individuals (and among them, predominantly state prisoners and Negroes), with some cases brought or sponsored by voluntary associations and a few by businesses. Their motives were *offensive*, in that they sought to use the federal courts to prevent action or negate action already taken by the state or local machinery, or (frequently) to force the urban government to take action in a manner contrary to its existing polices. On the other hand, those who invoked the state courts as plaintiffs were individuals and businesses in nearly equal proportions. Their motives were more likely to be *defensive* and chiefly economic in character. They sought to defend the status quo and themselves against limitations of one form or another on the profitability of their use of their property; only a small proportion of litigants sought to force modification in established government policies. In both instances, however, the proportion of litigation initiated by organized interest groups was slight, in contrast to the assumptions of some students of higher courts.

Subject Areas of Court Activity

District Court cases were shown to be confined to narrow areas related to constitutional rights and statutory extensions therefrom. But the subjects of state trial courts are quite different: they include zoning and land use, the powers and organization of local governments, and the property rights of businessmen and others who seek to avoid local regulation. Few constitutional issues and almost no civil rights issues were litigated in the state trial courts examined.

Many important issues and problems of the urban political arena never are the subject of decision making by either set of courts. The federal courts are limited by the criteria of their jurisdiction and the fact that such federal statutes as exist are likely to be grant-in-aid or other kinds of statutes which do not give rise to standing to sue. The state courts are limited by the insulation which state legislatures frequently provide for such intimate state functions as education, welfare, utility and rate regulation, and public improvements. In many states, these functions are discharged through elaborate administrative structures which can be challenged, if at all, only in specialized courts

and after exhaustion of remedies within the agency structure itself.

Policy Impact of the Courts

We have seen that the policy-change ratios of the federal courts were low, with the single exception of the race relations area. The District Courts modified local government policies less than 20 percent of the time in every area of their activity, and there was very little variation between the different subject areas in this respect. Race relations cases were the sole exception, and the ratio in these cases was 43 percent. But the policy-change ratio of the state courts was much higher overall—amounting to nearly 50 percent of all cases. And there was much greater variability between areas: in cases involving education or elections, for example, the policy-change ratio was no higher than in the federal courts, but in taxation and business regulation cases it was 67 and 57 percent respectively. If the number and proportions of reversals of local government policies are a valid measure, the state trial courts are much more intimate participants in the policy-making complex of local institutions.

Overall Effects and Functions

Each set of courts is narrow in the range of impact, though the state courts are the broader of the two and also the heavier in impact (at least in quantitative terms) in those areas where they are active. The areas of impact of the federal courts are too few and their impact too limited to do more than intimate that they are highly relevant to the content of urban public policy in the two basic areas of police practices and race relations. For the state courts, because of the larger number of areas and heavier impact (as well as a more extended and comprehensive analysis), it was possible to identify three major policy functions performed by courts within the local political system. They were found to have a "constitutional" function, in which they regularly determined the powers and legitimated the forms of local governments; a "rules of the game" function, in which they maintained the openness of the political process in a variety of ways, thereby enabling new groups to rise to power in the other arenas of politics; and an "economic rights" function, in which they defended businessmen's investments in the status quo and continuously limited local governments' efforts to regulate the uses of property in the social interest.

In Summary

Neither set of courts really overlaps the other in any frequent or recurring way, for the subjects with which they deal are demonstrably independent, except in rare instances. The state trial courts were found not to engage in any substantial number of civil rights issues but to be regularly involved in land use, regulation, taxation, and other economic rights matters. The federal courts, on the other hand, touched upon these matters rarely (except for some regulation or taxation issues, and these may be the inevitable product of the law's concern for property rights in all forms) and concentrated instead on race relations and criminal due process problems, almost never touching the structure or powers of local government.

The federal courts, not unexpectedly, appear to be less fully integrated into the ongoing political processes of the urban polity. They are relevant chiefly to certain limited (and output) areas of the urban political process, while the state trial courts had functions at the formative (and input) stages of that process as well as on the output side. The integration of the state trial courts did not depend entirely on the number of areas of activity and weight of the impact which they had in each, but also on the intimacy of engagement of local judges with the day-to-day activity of the political system and their interaction with the political parties and other decision-making elements. In neither instance, however, did the courts exercise a major influence on the ultimate shape of public policy: there are too many areas in which they are not involved—too many alternatives to the routes that their actions do foreclose for other political actors to be bound by their decisions.

The intimation that the federal courts are involved in the civil rights-law enforcement sets of policy-making actors, institutions, and processes, and that the state trial courts are in the property rights-regulation-local governments bodies of actors, institutions, and processes, could be an important cue toward theories of linkage of these courts to elements of the larger political system. If we posit disparate groupings of actors, institutions, and processes for each major policy area, or at least different distributions of power and goals among them regarding various policies, the part played by courts might be more readily defined along the lines suggested earlier in this section. From this point, comparisons of the role of courts in other contexts and with other institutions might facilitate the kind of more general theory that has so far not been achieved.

. . .

NOTE

1. All findings regarding state trial courts are drawn from Kenneth M. Dolbeare, *Trial Courts in Urban Politics: State Court Policy Impact and Functions in a Local Political System* (New York: Wiley, 1967).

CHAPTER 14

Compliance and Policy Impact

Specific problems involving particular parties come before courts, and judges seek to resolve those disputes. Appellate courts, notably the highest state courts and the U.S. Supreme Court, consider the broader public policy implications of the resolution of the initial dispute (of course, so may lower courts as well). Technically and legally the resolution of a legal dispute at every court level binds only the parties to that particular case (or, when government officials are involved, their successors in office). Therefore, compliance in its basic sense means adherence by the parties to the rulings and orders of the court, be it a trial court, an appeals court, or a supreme court. However, scholarly concern with compliance must go beyond the immediate parties because courts, in resolving particular disputes, frequently make broad policy declarations that are applicable to many others in society. A court, for example, may declare that certain programs, procedures, or actions of governmental authorities (within the jurisdiction of the court) are against the law and that any cases involving them will be decided accordingly if brought to that court. Compliance here is a matter of those who are not parties to a dispute following the court's policy statement and voluntarily doing or not doing whatever the court has said.

Compliance generally has a negative quality to it. A court says, in effect, "no, this should not be done—you should do this instead" (although the court may then take steps to implement a new policy). Students of compliance then examine what happens following such a public policy ruling by the court. Of course the "thou-shalt-not" decisions of courts are only part of the picture. Courts also say "yes," but these decisions are permissive in that they allow ongoing practices to continue and thus require no change in behavior.

The focus on the thou-shalt-not decisions means that we are concerned with court rulings that something violates *the law*. But rulings of a trial court that can be appealed to a higher court need not necessarily be obeyed while an appeal is in progress. Certainly those who are within the court's jurisdiction but are not a party to the suit need not comply with the court's decision (even though it has policy implications relevant for their behavior) as long as the possibility remains that a higher court may reverse the lower court. Thus when compliance is studied, it is compliance to the authoritative rulings in cases that have run the course of appeal. These authoritative rulings may be interpretations of state or federal statutes, state constitutions, or the United States Constitution.

Because the U.S Supreme Court is the ultimate expounder of constitutionality in our political system, the compliance-to-court-decisions literature emphasizes compliance with Supreme Court decisions. Although it can be persuasively argued that such attention to the Supreme Court has resulted in the neglect of the federal circuit courts, the highest state courts, and both federal and state trial courts, many of whose policy decisions are never reviewed, it is likely that the kinds of variables and processes that affect compliance are common to most, if not all, courts. Also, in terms of compliance with Supreme Court decisions, other courts are frequently among those to whom the decision is applicable, thus *they* are examined from the standpoint of *their* compliance.[1]

When the United States Supreme Court announces its thou-shalt-nots, it is of interest to observe who are the intended recipients or the target population of its message. The study of compliance, in the broader public policy sense and not in the narrower parties-to-the-dispute sense, then becomes largely the study of how public officials and governmental institutions respond to the Court's determination of legality. Concern is focused on compliance by the police, local prosecuting attorneys, school boards, public school teachers, administrative officials, state legislatures, and so on. It can then be noted that the study of compliance includes the study of the extensiveness of the rule of law in the United States, and the extent to which lower-court judges and other public officials and public employees adhere to the law as determined by the highest legal authority in the land.

Research on the subject of compliance has concentrated on two main areas. The first, which is the one we are concerned with, is the narrower area of compliance with *court decisions*. The second area is compliance with the *law*. Research conducted in the first area has examined courts as a source of law. Research in the second, broader area has examined *all* law regardless of source; for example, statutory law (legislature as source), executive orders (President and governors as source), and administrative regulations (bureaucracy as source). The broader area of research on compliance focuses on the behavior of individuals, private organizations, and government employees acting in their public capacity. Much research effort has been spent studying compliance with criminal law, and the field of criminology has developed a rich literature.

The study of compliance with court decisions, we have observed, centers on the U.S. Supreme Court, the source of the most authoritatively pronounced constitutional thou-shalt-nots, which are often aimed at the official actions of public employees. This leads us to an important question: how are those decisions communicated to the intended recipients of the Court's message?

The first link in the chain of compliance with Court policy is the communication to the intended recipients of that policy. The characteristics of the decision in which the policy is announced—such as the clarity with which the policy is presented, its complexity in terms of what is or is not to be done, and the nature of the target group at whom the policy is aimed—are among the variables that are thought to ultimately affect compliance. A broad overview of compliance and the impact of court policies is offered in the reading by Charles Johnson and Bradley Canon.

Why do people obey or not obey court rulings? Don Brown and Robert Stover argue persuasively that compliance is a phenomenon that can best be understood in terms of utility theory—that is, people will or will not obey Court decisions when the benefits of compliance or noncompliance outweigh the costs. Assuming the accurate communication of the Court's policy decision, those who constituted the target population will behave rationally and will act in their own self-interest. For the Court to have its policies complied with, the costs of disobedience must outweigh the benefits, or the benefits of compliance must outweigh the costs.

We do not include in this chapter considerations of compliance by Congress and the presidency, although on occasion one or the other faces a Court decision requiring that something be done or not be done by either branch of government. More usual are Court decisions that stimulate some reaction from either or both branches even though neither may be a disputant in that particular issue area. The reactions may be positive and may facilitate implementation of Court policy, or they may be negative and may stimulate resistance. (For example, note the treatment by Congress and the President of the abortion issue in terms of federal funding of the abortions of poor women and federal financing of family planning centers in which abortion information is disseminated). Yet these reactions of Congress and the President do not squarely fall under the term "compliance" in the sense we use it here. Nonetheless, the reader should be aware that the actions and reactions of these two branches of government may have a profound effect on compliance with Court decisions.

When our focus turns to implementation of Supreme Court policy and its impact, a number of concerns come to mind. We are concerned with both short and long-range consequences, for the Court and for the nation, of the Court's having acted in that particular policy area.

For example, with the Court's school desegregation decisions we can ask, first of all, what have been the consequences for public education over the long run? Has the intent of the Supreme Court been realized or have unanticipated problems emerged? What have been the consequences for the Supreme Court itself, both in terms of broader race relations policy such as affirmative action and in terms of the Court's political standing? What have been the broader societal consequences of the Court's destruction of the legal basis of racism and its furtherance of the continuing struggle of racial minorities to have carried out the promises of the Declaration of Independence and the Constitution? Can we point to an event or a series of events that the Court's policy decisions set in motion? In other words, our concern with impact is a concern with the question "so what?" What difference has it made that the Court ruled as it did?

As should be obvious, the sorts of questions just raised are infinitely easier to ask than to answer. Some of them lend themselves to systematic empirical investigation. But the broader questions are more difficult to answer. For example, it is possible to examine the consequences of the original school desegregation policy announced in 1954 in *Brown* v. *Board of Education* in terms of the extent of desegregated education some three plus decades after the policy was first announced. It is also possible to examine the effect of racially integrated education on the performance and abilities of school children of both races. On a broader scale, it is not difficult to demonstrate the logical connection between the end of racism in public education and the end of racism in other aspects of public life and publicly sponsored activities. By taking the major step it did in *Brown*, the Court became involved in all aspects of the law of race relations and thus established the legal basis for the civil rights revolution. Ultimately *Brown* led to an assault on officially sponsored racism in all its guises throughout the country. One can suggest, then, that the *Brown* policy ushered in the civil rights revolution in political, social, and economic terms, and that the long-run impact of *Brown* has been and continues to be immense. However, this last assertion is more difficult to demonstrate conclusively. Charles Bullock and Charles Lamb focus their attention on the implementation of the broad array of civil rights policies set in motion by the Supreme Court and then by Congress with the enactment of various statutes.

The final selection in this chapter by Bradley Canon and Lawrence Baum concerns the highest state courts and is not devoted to compliance with, or the implementation or impact of U.S. Supreme Court policy. Yet it raises certain questions that are important to the central issues discussed in this chapter. Canon and Baum analyze the correlates of the pace of acceptance of innovative legal doctrines or policies in the realm of tort law over a century (1876–1975). These court policies can be considered liberal because they favored the plaintiffs (workers, tenants, consumers, others who are personally injured). The Canon and Baum study, although an exploratory one, implies that the implementation of new policies by the highest state courts, whether in response to the rulings of the Supreme Court or the rulings of other state high courts, is more complex than common sense might suggest and has varied significantly over time.

NOTE

1. In general, see the analysis and citations to the vast literature in Charles A. Johnson and Bradley C. Canon, *Judicial Policies: Implementation and Impact* (Washington, D.C.: C.Q. Press, 1984). Also see Phillip J. Cooper, *Hard Judicial Choices: Federal District Court Judges and State and Local Officials* (New York: Oxford University Press, 1987).

Responses to Judicial Policies

Charles A. Johnson
Bradley C. Canon

...[J]udicial policies are not self-implementing, and implementing judicial policies is a political process. In virtually all instances, the courts that formulate policies must rely on other courts or on nonjudicial actors to translate those policies into action. Inevitably, just as making judicial policies is a political process, so too is the implementation of the policies—the issues are essentially political, and the actors are subject to political pressures....

The best way to illustrate the political nature of the events that follow a judicial decision is to review the implementation and impact of a recent decision that remains controversial. We will use the Supreme Court's 1973 abortion decision in *Roe* v. *Wade* to show what may happen after a judicial policy is announced. Later...we will suggest a conceptual scheme by which the events following any judicial decision may be effectively organized and compared with the events following other judicial decisions.

Reprinted from Charles A. Johnson and Bradley C. Canon, *Judicial Policies: Implementation and Impact* (Washington, D.C.: C.Q. Press, 1984), pp. 2, 4–25. All notes and one table omitted.

The Decision

On Monday, January 22, 1973, Associate Justice Harry Blackmun announced the decision of the Court in two cases concerning the rights of women to end unwanted pregnancies with legal abortions, *Roe* v. *Wade* and *Doe* v. *Bolton*. According to Bob Woodward and Scott Armstrong's revealing account in *The Brethren*, this decision was the result of considerable conflict and compromise within the Court. The decision came after almost a full year of research by Justice Blackmun, and the justices fully expected a public outcry after the decision was announced. They were not disappointed.

The cases before the Court challenged the laws prohibiting abortion in Texas and Georgia. The Court decided in favor of the plaintiffs in both cases—women who were identified only as Jane Roe and Mary Doe. The direct effect of the decision was to void the antiabortion laws in Texas and Georgia. Indirectly, of course, the Court also voided laws in every state that prohibited or limited abortion....

In effect, the Supreme Court had given women the right to abortion on demand during the first two trimesters of pregnancy and had allowed the state to regulate abortions only to protect the mother's health during these two trimesters. The Court held that during the third trimester the state could regulate or even prohibit abortions, except where the life or the health of the mother was endangered.

Immediate Responses

On the day the Court announced the abortion decision, former president Lyndon B. Johnson died of a heart attack, and a few days before the Court's announcement, President Richard Nixon had announced the end of American military participation in the Vietnam War. These two events diminished the newsworthiness of the Court's decision in *Roe* and *Doe*. Instead of being the lead story in the weekly news magazines, the abortion decision received only limited coverage. Nevertheless, the reactions from several corners of the political system were immediate, and they were mostly negative. . . .

But not all reactions were negative. The president of Planned Parenthood, Alan F. Guttmacher, called the decision a "courageous stroke for right to privacy and for the protection of a woman's physical and emotional health." A similar reaction came from women attorneys at the Center for Constitutional Rights, who cited the decision as a "victory for [the] women's liberation movement.". . .

Reactions also came from members of Congress. A week after the Supreme Court's decision, Rep. Lawrence J. Hogan, R-Md., introduced the first of several "right to life" amendments to the U.S. Constitution. By November 1973 over two dozen resolutions to overturn some aspect of the Court's decision were introduced in Congress. Two of the proposals eventually enacted into law were added to the Health Programs Extension Act of 1973, which was amended to permit institutions receiving federal funds to refuse to perform abortions, and the 1973 Foreign Assistance Act, which was amended to prohibit the use of U.S. funds to pay for abortions overseas.

Response was also immediate from women who sought abortions. In the first three months of 1973, 181,140 abortions were performed in the United States; and during the first year following the Supreme Court's decision a total of 742,460 abortions were performed nationwide. The overwhelming majority of abortions occurred in metropolitan areas, and 41 percent occurred in Middle Atlantic states. The variation in the number of abortions from state to state was considerable; the greatest number of abortions was performed in New York, a state that had previously liberalized its abortion law, while two states—Louisiana and North Dakota—reported no abortions during 1973. Data from the first year of nationwide legal abortions suggest that almost one of every five pregnancies was terminated with an abortion. . . .

A national survey by the research division of Planned Parenthood, the Alan Guttmacher Institute, in 1973 revealed that less than one-third (30.1 percent) of the non-Catholic short-term general hospitals in the United States provided abortion services. Another survey revealed that 75 percent of the hospitals providing abortion services were privately controlled, rather than publicly controlled or government operated. In the year following the abortion decision, a relatively small number of nonhospital clinics provided abortion services (178 nationwide), and only a few physicians reported performing abortions in their offices (168 nationwide). Nonetheless, in the first year after the decision, the largest percentage of abortions occurred in clinics (44.5 percent), and most of the remaining abortions (41.1 percent) were performed in private hospitals.

The Alan Guttmacher Institute concluded

that in the 12 months following the Supreme Court's abortion decision, "the response of health institutions in many areas to the legalization of abortion in 1973 was so limited as to be tantamount to no response at all." This widespread nonresponse had a considerable effect on *Roe* v. *Wade's* impact—after being granted the *constitutional* right to an abortion, many women could not exercise that right because medical facilities in their communities refused to provide the services necessary to secure an abortion.

Later Responses

One year after the Supreme Court's announcement of the abortion decision, the first annual "March for Life" was held in Washington, D.C., to protest that decision. The demonstration gave direct evidence of political divisions created by the abortion decision. Battle lines were drawn by proponents and opponents of the Court's policy in several political arenas.

. . . There were also moves in Congress to limit the federal government's support of abortions. Much of the activity centered on the federal funding of abortions under existing Medicaid programs. In 1974 and 1975 antiabortion forces unsuccessfully attempted to amend the annual appropriations bills for the Department of Labor and the Department of Health, Education and Welfare with restrictions on the use of federal funds for elective abortions. However, in 1976 Congress approved a restriction on Medicaid funding for abortions known as the Hyde Amendment (for its sponsor, Rep. Henry J. Hyde, R-Ill.). The amendment was the subject of considerable debate and political maneuvering; it passed easily in the House, but the Senate voted to kill it. After 11 weeks of stalemate in the conference committee, both houses finally compromised on language barring federal funding of abortions

except where the life of the mother would be endangered if the fetus were carried to term. The provision came under attack immediately in the courts, and its implementation was delayed almost a full year, until August 1977.

Congress was not the only legislative body acting to restrict the implementation of the Supreme Court abortion decision. From 1973 through 1976, 34 states adopted laws relating to abortions. Some of the laws concerned regulations that the Court indicated states could pass to protect the health of the mother—for example, requiring that abortions be performed by licensed physicians—and others called for reporting abortions to a state agency. Such laws were not considered to be restrictive or aimed at limiting the availability of abortions. Other laws, however, were clearly intended to limit the impact of the Court's decision or to discourage the use of abortions by women with unwanted pregnancies. Several states passed consent requirements under which the husband of a married woman or the parents of an unmarried minor would have to give their written approval before an abortion could be performed. A few states also required consultation or certification by a second physician during the third trimester. A majority of the states (29) adopted laws protecting physicians from discriminatory, disciplinary, or recriminatory actions if they refused to perform abortions, and 31 states adopted "conscience clause" laws specifically authorizing physicians to refuse to perform abortions. . . .

In spite of intense opposition and various legal restrictions, the number of abortions performed in the United States continued to grow. By 1980 over 1.6 million legal abortions were performed annually. In contrast, the number of illegal abortions had shrunk from nearly 750,000 in 1969 to around 10,000 in 1980. Moreover, the increased emphasis on this issue had led to other gynecologic health improvements and to lower-cost services.

As before, the overwhelming percentage of abortions were performed in metropolitan areas; one survey found that there were no facilities in 80 percent of the counties in the United States. Significantly, although the number of abortions continued to increase, the number of hospital facilities offering abortion services remained relatively constant. More and more, however, abortions were performed in clinics—the number of which nearly doubled during the three years following the Court's abortion decision. . . .

THE CONTROVERSY CONTINUES

The controversy over the abortion policy announced by the Supreme Court in 1973 and over how that policy was to be implemented continued unabated four years after the decision was announced. . . . After compromising with the Senate in 1976, the House in 1977 adamantly insisted that no federal funds be used in any abortion procedures, even if the life of the mother was in danger. After five months of battling between the House and the Senate (whose version was less restrictive), Congress adopted an appropriations bill prohibiting federal expenditures for any *elective* abortion. The same language was adopted in 1978; in 1979 that language was altered to allow federal funding for abortions only to save the life of the mother or in cases of rape or incest, thus dropping the 1976 compromise provision allowing funding if two physicians agreed that the physical health of the mother would be damaged if the pregnancy continued. In addition, antiabortion riders were attached to six other appropriations bills and to two authorization bills in 1979. Although Congress had not passed a constitutional amendment to overturn the 1973 Supreme Court decision, it had gone quite far to limit the impact of the original abortion decision.

. . . In 1977 the Court held that states and municipalities could refuse to fund nontherapeutic abortions, even if they funded all other medical services (*Maher* v. *Roe*, 1977). And in 1980 the Court upheld by a five-to-four vote the constitutionality of the Hyde Amendment's prohibition of federal expenditures for elective abortions (*Harris* v. *McRae*, 1980). . . .

Because the operation of the Hyde Amendment had been enjoined pending the outcome of this suit, the effect of the Court's decision was almost immediate. The Department of Health and Human Services announced a fund cutoff date which, by their estimate, would reduce the projected number of federally funded abortions from 470,000 to less than 2,000 per year. It appears, however, that there was a far smaller reduction in the actual number of abortions obtained by poor women.

Following *Harris*, which was considered to be a victory for the antiabortion forces, the Court moved in 1983 to underscore its commitment to its original decision in *Roe* v. *Wade*. At issue were several sections of an Akron, Ohio, ordinance aimed at setting roadblocks to the provision and use of abortion services in that community. . . .

The embattled nature of the law and the Court in this area was perhaps best revealed by Justice Lewis Powell's majority opinion in the *Akron* case. In the opening paragraph of his opinion, Powell argued that *Roe* was now established law and that the doctrine of *stare decisis* ("let the decision stand," meaning that a precedent established in an earlier case is considered authoritative in the case at hand) required that the Court overturn the Akron ordinances, in spite of the continued arguments that the Court "erred in interpreting the Constitution."

The continuing controversial nature of the abortion issue is also revealed in the general public's attitude on abortion. A Gallup poll on the abortion issue immediately prior to the Supreme Court's decision in 1973 found that 46 percent of the respondents favored permitting a woman "to go to a doctor to end pregnancy at any time during the first three months." Almost exactly the same percentage of the respondents, 45 percent, opposed granting such a right. After the Court announced its decision, there was a slight jump in the proportion of the population favoring abortion, although the comparison is difficult to make precise because a different question was asked by the Gallup organization. However, a strong division in public opinion on abortion remained. . . .

In 1980 political conflict over abortion entered directly into the presidential campaign. While both Jimmy Carter and Ronald Reagan were personally opposed to abortion, their parties took opposing stands on the issue. The Republican platform recognized "differing views" on the abortion issue but supported a constitutional amendment "to restore protection of the right to life for unborn children." The platform also supported "congressional efforts to restrict the use of taxpayers' dollars for abortion." The Democratic platform took the opposing point of view, expressing support for the 1973 decision "as the law of the land and opposing any constitutional amendment to restrict or overturn that decision." Reagan's landslide victory—accompanied by a significant increase in the number of Republican representatives and the first Republican majority in the Senate in 26 years—gave renewed vigor to efforts to outlaw abortion. . . . For various reasons, such as divisions within the antiabortionist ranks over strategy, the threat of a filibuster by senators favoring *Roe v. Wade*, and the press of other "Reagan reform" proposals, [proposals is to overturn

Roe failed] . . . . The opponents of abortion, however, are still very strong politically, and in the second decade after *Roe* it seems clear that the controversy it raised is not going to go away any time soon.

A MODEL OF THE IMPLEMENTATION AND IMPACT OF JUDICIAL POLICIES

Chronicling the events that followed the Supreme Court's abortion decision gives some idea of the range of reactions and actors that may become involved in the implementation of a judicial decision. Similar case histories could be supplied for other court decisions. But our aim is not to study the aftermath of *every* judicial decision; instead, we want to make general statements about what has happened or may happen after *any* judicial decision. That is, we hope to move away from idiosyncratic, case-by-case or policy-by-policy analyses toward a general theoretical understanding of the events that may follow a judicial decision. . . .

The first step in understanding any political process is to develop a conceptual foundation upon which explanations may be built. We will organize our presentation of what happens after a court decision around two major elements: the *actors* who may respond to the decision and the *responses* that these actors may make. Focusing on these two elements enables us to define more precisely who is reacting and how. In studying the responses to judicial policies we describe and attempt to explain the *behavior* following a court decision— specifically, what the behavior is, its antecedents, and its consequences. Hence, when we discuss "impact," we are describing general reactions following a judicial decision. When we discuss "implementation," we are describing the behavior of lower courts, government agencies, or other affected parties as it relates to enforcing a judicial decision. When we discuss what many would call "compliance/noncompliance" or "evasion," we are describing behavior that is in some way consistent or inconsistent with the behavioral requirements of the judicial decision.

Figure 1 presents a schematic diagram of the different sets of actors, referred to as *populations*, that may respond to a judicial policy. The organization of these populations is essentially a functional one, in which their roles in shaping the impact of judicial decisions and their influence on the ultimate impact of judicial policy differ. In addition to the four populations, Figure 1 also presents two broadly defined categories of responses in the response process: (1) acceptance decisions, which include attitude changes or nonchanges, and (2) behavioral responses, which include responses to the decision in terms of maintaining or changing policies

and informal norms, as well as other types of actions. These include what is often termed *feedback behavior*—actions directed at the judiciary or other policy makers in the system and designed to alter or reinforce the judicial decision. We now turn to a discussion of these populations and their responses, illustrated with examples drawn from the events after the Supreme Court's abortion decision as well as other recent Supreme Court decisions.

The Interpreting Population

For any appellate court decision, the actor most often charged with responding to a decision is a particular lower court, often a trial court. Moreover, in our common law system many appellate court decisions become policies used in deciding future cases. In a general sense, therefore, a higher court's policy affects all lower courts within its jurisdiction. This set of courts (and in some instances government officials such as attorneys general) is known as the *interpreting*

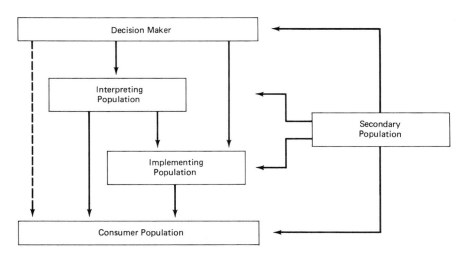

FIGURE 1 Populations and lines of communication involved in the implementation and impact of judicial policies. (Adapted from Charles A. Johnson, "The Implementation and Impact of Judicial Policies: A Heuristic Model," in *Public Law and Public Policy*, ed. John A. Gardiner [New York: Praeger, 1977], 107–126.)

population. The interpreting population, as the name implies, responds to the policy decisions of a higher court by refining the policy announced by the higher court. Such refinements could have the effect of enlarging or of limiting the original policy. This population, in other words, interprets the meaning of the policy and develops the rules for matters not addressed in the original decision. Of course, all populations must "interpret" the decision in order to react to it. Interpretations of lower courts, however, are distinguished from the interpretations of others since theirs are viewed as authoritative in a legal sense by others in the political system. Hence, this population provides "official" interpretations of a court policy applicable to the other populations under their jurisdiction.

The Supreme Court's abortion decision launched the judiciary into a new area of the law, which required considerable refining before complete implementation. Shortly after the decision was announced, lower state and federal courts began hearing cases presenting issues that had not been directly addressed in the *Roe* or *Doe* opinions. In Florida, for example, the issue of a father's rights were raised by a father who brought legal action to restrain the mother of his unborn child from obtaining an abortion. The lower court denied relief and the Florida Supreme Court affirmed that decision, arguing that the Supreme Court's abortion decision was based on the mother's "right of privacy" (*Jones* v. *Smith*, 1973). The decision to terminate a pregnancy was, therefore, purely the right of the mother and could not be subject to interference by the state or private individuals.

Meanwhile, in Arizona, another matter was before the courts. Arizona law prohibited the advertisement of any medicine or procedures that facilitated abortions. New Times, Inc., a local publisher, was convicted under this

statute and appealed to the state supreme court. The conviction was reversed, since the Arizona abortion statutes were found to be similar to the Texas statute struck down in *Roe* v. *Wade*, even though the issue before the court was different from that decided in the original abortion cases (*State* v. *New Times, Inc.*, 1973).

In each of these instances the issue before the court had not been addressed directly in the original decision. Consistent with the common law tradition, the lower courts had the responsibility of making authoritative interpretations of policy in light of the original Supreme Court decision. In their interpretations these courts could limit the application of the original policy, as did the Arizona trial court in convicting the publisher, or could facilitate its implementation, as did the Florida courts. . . .

The Implementing Population

The lower courts usually apply a higher court's policy only in cases coming before them. Higher court policies and their interpretation by lower courts quite often affect a wider set of actors. We refer to this set of actors as the *implementing population*. In most instances, this population is made up of authorities whose behavior may be reinforced or sanctioned by the interpreting population. The implementing population usually performs a policing or servicing function in the political system—that is, implementors apply the system's rules to persons subject to their authority. Prominent examples of this population are police officers, prosecutors, university and public school officials, and welfare and social security workers. In many instances, the original policy and subsequent interpretations by lower courts are intended to set parameters on the behavior of the implementing population. A clear example of this activity involves decisions concerning police behavior with regard to the rights of criminal suspects.

Occasionally, the implementing population is composed of private individuals or institutions. This is the case when services provided by private concerns are the subject of a judicial policy. The best example of such a circumstance involves the Supreme Court's abortion decision, for which physicians and hospitals were the actual implementors. When the implementing population falls into this private classification they are usually under a different obligation from most public implementing populations. In the case of public implementing agencies, the court ordinarily *requires* that the agencies change behavior, stop a particular type of service, or provide some new service. Such was the obligation for school systems with regard to *Brown* v. *Board of Education* and the police with regard to *Miranda* v. *Arizona* (1966) and *Mapp* v. *Ohio* (1961). On the other hand, when private concerns are the implementing population, the compulsion to act affirmatively is substantially weaker, if it exists at all. For example, the abortion decision gave women the right to an abortion; hospitals could provide abortions, but hospitals and physicians were not obliged to provide abortion services against their will. Thus, affirmative action implementing a judicial policy by private implementing groups is most often voluntary.

The implementing population may vary from decision to decision. For criminal justice decisions, prosecutors, police officers, and defense attorneys are the primary implementors. For school prayer or busing decisions, the implementors are largely public school officials. Reapportionment decisions usually involve legislators as the implementing population. When judicial decisions require no action by government agencies, nongovernmental service agencies

may implement decisions; alternatively, there may be no implementing population at all. As we mentioned in our earlier discussion, hospitals and individual physicians composed the primary implementing population for the abortion decision, although few of those capable of implementing the abortion decision actually did so by offering abortion services. And in a case such as *New York Times Co.* v. *Sullivan* (1964), which significantly decreased the applicability of libel law to public officials, there is no implementing population.

The degree to which a court decision actually benefits those it was intended to benefit depends on the actors and institutions who police the activities or provide the services called for in the decision. Women in communities where there were no physicians or hospitals willing to provide abortion services were effectively denied their newly granted right or were forced to go elsewhere to benefit from the judicial policy. As another example, where school officials sanctioned prayers after 1963, they often persisted for years.

. . .

The Consumer Population

Those for whom the policies are set forth by the court are identified as the *consumer population*. This population is the set of individuals (usually not affiliated with the government) who would or should receive benefits or suffer disabilities as a result of a judicial decision; that is, they gain or lose desired rights or resources. Criminal suspects, for example, benefit from judicial policies announced by the Supreme Court in *Miranda*, and black students in newly desegregated schools benefit from the *Brown* decision. In other instances, some consumer populations may not benefit from a judicial policy. For example, juvenile court defendants suffer from not being extended the right of trial by jury; stockholders may suffer when their corporation is split up as a result of an antitrust ruling. And there are decisions under which members of the consumer population may either benefit or suffer, depending on their attitudes toward the policy. Under the *Schempp* decision on prayer in public schools, children who want to pray in public school suffer limitations and children who do not want to pray there gain benefits.

The consumer population, depending on the policy involved, may include the entire population of the political system, as with judicial decisions concerning general tax legislation. On the other hand, a very limited population may be directly involved, such as criminal suspects under arrest. When the policy affects a specific sector but supposedly is for the public good (for example, antitrust decisions), a distinction between direct and indirect consumption must sometimes be made.

Specifying the consumer population exactly may be troublesome in some cases. For example, few would dispute that women with unwanted pregnancies are the consumers for the Supreme Court's abortion decision. Those opposed to abortion would likely argue that unborn children are also consumers and receive negative benefits from the abortion decision. Others might argue that fathers of unborn children or parents of underaged, pregnant girls are part of the consumer population.

In studying the reactions of consumers to judicial policies, several questions need to be addressed. Do the potential consumers of a judicial policy know of the policy? If they know of the policy, why and how do they modify their attitudes or behavior because of it? What effect, if any, does the policy have on the attitudes and behavior of the consumer with regard to the judiciary or other political institutions? . . .

The Secondary Population

The populations we have discussed so far are those directly affected by a judicial policy or its implementation. The *secondary population* is a residual one. It consists of everyone who is not in the interpreting, implementing, or consumer population. Members of the secondary population are not directly affected by a judicial policy; however, some may react to a policy or its implementation. This reaction usually takes the form of some type of feedback directed toward the original policy maker, another policy maker, the implementing population, or the consumer population.

The secondary population may be divided into four subpopulations: government officials, interest groups, the media, and the public at large. First, there are *government officials*. This subpopulation includes legislators and executive officers who are not immediately affected by the decision. Though usually unaffected directly, these individuals are often in a position to support or hinder the implementation of the original policy. This subpopulation is distinguished from other secondary subpopulations in that its members have direct, legitimate authority in the political system, and they are often the recipients of political pressure from the public. The second subpopulation is *interest groups*, which are often activated by court policies even when they are not directly affected by them. Subsequent actions by these groups may facilitate or block effective implementation of the judicial policy. The third subpopulation is the *media*, which communicate the substance of judicial policies to potentially affected populations. Included here are general and specialized media, which may affect implementation by editorial stance or simply by the way of reporting judicial policies. Media attention to a policy, descriptions of reactions to it, and support or criticism of it can play a large role in determining the amount and direction of feedback behavior. The fourth subpopulation consists of members of the *public at large*, insofar as they do not fall within the consumer population. The most important segment of this subpopulation is attentive citizens— those who are most aware of a judicial policy. This segment includes individuals who may be related to the consumer population (for example, parents of students affected by school prayer decisions), politically active individuals (for example, political party workers), and perhaps knowledgeable or alert individuals.

For the Supreme Court's abortion decision, the secondary population is large and quite varied. Recall from our chronicle of the events following *Roe* that although there were apparently some minor moves in public opinion regarding abortions, most of the reaction came from interest groups and government officials. As to the former, existing institutions or groups such as the Catholic church and many Protestant denominations vigorously denounced the decision, while organizations such as Planned Parenthood, the National Organization for Women, and the American Civil Liberties Union supported it. New groups on both sides devoted solely to the abortion issue also developed quickly. The efforts of these groups produced additional litigation, intensive lobbying, electoral maneuvering, and attempts to mobilize public opinion. Government officials also reacted to the abortion decision by passing restrictive laws, issuing restrictive orders, or, in a few cases, adopting policies that provided opportunities for women to obtain abortions. A fundamental issue for some government officials after *Roe* was whether the government should aid in the implementation of the policy by funding the abortions of poor women. With the eventual approval of the Supreme Court, Congress and several states restricted funding for elective abortions for poor women.

Legislative and executive officials may have considerable influence on the implementation of a judicial policy, even though they are not members of the implementing population (that is, they do not provide policing or implementing services). Legislatures, for instance, may be generous or stinting in appropriating money to carry out a policy, as in funding legal services for the poor. The president and state governors may use their appointing authority to select officials with power over members of the implementing population; or they may use their personal or official influence to encourage either maximum or minimum cooperation in the implementing process, as well as to mobilize public opinion. . . .

Fluidity and Linkage among Populations

The basis for the foregoing classification of populations is primarily functional. We may, therefore, on some occasions find that particular individuals are members of different populations in different circumstances. For example, it is entirely possible for an attorney general to be an interpreter for one judicial policy and an implementor for another. In the former instance, the attorney general would be issuing an authoritative, legally binding statement interpreting a judicial decision; in the latter instance, the attorney general would be charged with the responsibility of applying a judicial policy to some consumer population or of carrying out some order of the court. It is also possible that courts as members of the interpreting population may occasionally be in a position to direct the implementation of judicial policy. Such may be the case when a judge takes direct charge of the implementation of a school desegregation order, as happened in Boston in the 1970s. Teachers are implementors of the prayer decision and consumers of decisions affecting funding levels of public schools. Obviously, private citizens are in both consumer and secondary populations, depending on the nature of the judicial policy.

Attorneys constitute a special set of participants whose function may vary from one setting to another. By and large, this subpopulation is composed of lawyers who practice before various judicial bodies. These attorneys may insist that other participants follow or implement rules promulgated by a higher court. When they assert the rights of criminal suspects or protect citizens whose constitutional rights have been violated, attorneys are playing a role as quasi-members of the implementing population.

Perhaps even more often, attorneys are called upon to give their interpretations of judicial policies for potential consumers, implementing groups, and, occasionally, secondary groups such as interested citizens or legislative bodies. Such interpretations are not official like those of the interpreting population; however, on many occasions these interpretations are likely to be final, since paying clients assume that the attorneys give a reasoned and fair interpretation of a court decision. Unfortunately, we have no way of knowing how frequently attorneys are called upon to interpret judicial decisions or how frequently their interpretations are accepted and effectively become final, but it is reasonable to assume that such interpretations play an important role in accounting for the reactions of others to judicial policies. Attorneys also serve as interpreters of judicial policies for courts themselves. Because judges cannot read and interpret all higher court policies, they frequently rely on attorneys' briefs to inform them of relevant cases and, sometimes, rival interpretations of those cases.

In a broad sense, attorneys performing these functions serve as linkages between various populations. They provide a link for the communication of decisions downward from higher courts to relevant actors as well as being unofficial interpreters of these decisions. Their linkage activities may also prompt new litigation or feedback to the courts or other agencies, which, in turn, may affect the implementation of a decision.

Acceptance Decisions and Behavioral Responses

We are interested in the responses to judicial policies by all of the populations identified above. We may observe a large variety of responses to judicial decisions, so precise distinctions are difficult to make. Nonetheless, we believe two general categories of responses are captured in the concepts of acceptance decisions and behavioral responses.

The *acceptance decision* involves psychological reactions to a judicial policy, which may be generalized in terms of accepting or rejecting the policy. The acceptance decision is shaped by several psychological dimensions: intensity of attitude, regard for the policy-making court, perceptions of the consequences of the decision, and the respondent's own role in society.

The intensity of a person's *attitude toward the policy* prior to the court's decision can be important. Most white southerners, for example, were extremely hostile toward policies of racial integration before *Brown*; thus their unwillingness to accept the decision was not surprising. Many people had similarly intense attitudes about abortion and about prayers in the public schools. Many blacks, feminists, and civil libertarians, respectively, had equally intense attitudes in favor of these policies. For most policies, though, feelings are not so intense. Few people feel strongly about such issues as the size and composition of juries, new doctrines in libel law, or the application of the First Amendment guarantees to commercial advertising. In such instances the acceptance decision is less likely to be governed by prior attitudes.

Another dimension involves *regard for the court* making the decision. People who view the Supreme Court favorably may be more inclined to accept a decision as legitimate and proper. Those who generally view the Court negatively or who believe it has usurped too much authority may transfer these views to particular decisions that the Court makes.

A third dimension relates to a person's *perception of the consequences* of a decision. Those who may not quarrel with a decision in the abstract but believe it will have a serious and detrimental effect on society may be reluctant to accept it. In the 1950s, for example, many citizens feared that the Supreme Court's decisions granting due process to suspected subversives dismissed from government employment would aid the spread of Communism; more recently, many people were disturbed about the exclusion of illegally seized evidence from criminal trials, fearing that criminals might often go without punishment.

Finally, acceptance decisions are shaped by a *person's own role in society*. An ambitious judge or attorney general may be reluctant to accept (publicly, at least) an unpopular judicial policy for fear that it will harm his or her career. Corporate officers or citizens may be unwilling to accept a decision if they think it will reduce their profits or cause them great inconvenience. Conversely, people may accept quite willingly decisions that are popular with the public or that bring them financial or other benefits.

Behavioral responses involve reactions that may be seen or recorded and that may determine the extent to which a court policy is actually realized. These responses are often closely linked to acceptance decisions. Persons who do not accept a judicial policy are likely to engage in behavior designed to defeat the policy or minimize its impact. They will interpret it narrowly, try to avoid implementing it, and refuse or evade its consumption. Those who accept a policy are likely to be more faithful or even enthusiastic in interpreting, implementing, and consuming it. Of course, nonacceptors may not always be in a position to ignore a decision or refuse completely to comply with it. Some behavioral responses may be adjusted to meet the decision's requirements while other, less visible, behavioral responses may more truly reflect their unwillingness to accept the decision. Conversely, acceptors may for reasons of inertia never fully adjust their behavioral responses to a new judicial policy.

Policy changes concern changes in rules, formal norms within an organization, or even informal rules regarding behavior within an organization. Police departments may, for example, adopt formal policies against illegal searches, but may informally wink at violations. Schools may devise strategies to comply with the letter but not the spirit of the Supreme Court's school prayer decision in *Schempp*. Policy changes may also include changes in organizational structure or function. As indicated previously, the delivery of health care services related to abortion changed after *Roe* v. *Wade* to the extent that currently most abortion services are provided by clinics, not hospitals.

Another dimension of behavioral responses is the activities involved in carrying out the policy. These actions by interpreting and implementing populations may benefit or disadvantage the consumer population; in turn, the consumer population may respond by using, ignoring, or avoiding the policy. (The behavioral responses of the secondary population are usually manifest in the form of feedback behavior, which is discussed below.) We must examine these actions, in addition to such formal responses as written policies, because written policies sometimes bear little relation to a population's behavior.

Feedback behavior is another behavioral response to a judicial policy. It is directed toward the originator of the policy or some other policy-making agency. The purpose of feedback behavior is usually to provide support for or make demands upon other political institutions regarding the judicial policy. Almost immediately after the Supreme Court announced its abortion decision, feedback in the form of letters to the justices began. Also, some members of Congress let the Court know of their displeasure with the abortion decision by introducing amendments to the Constitution to overturn *Roe*. Frequent manifestations of displeasure, as well as some of support, by various interest groups have been directed at the Court and other political institutions, such as Congress and state legislatures. In varying degrees, these attempts at feedback have led to modifications of the policy—as we can see in the Court's approval of the Hyde Amendment passed by Congress, which terminated federal payment for abortions for poor women. . . .

Compliance with Court Directives:
A Utility Approach

Don W. Brown
Robert V. Stover

... [S]ome scholars have suggested the potentially broad usefulness and integrative capacity of treating individuals' compliance decisions as though they were made on the basis of a cost-benefit or utility analysis (Rodgers and Bullock, 1972; Krislov, 1965: Ch. 6)....

According to utility theory, human behavior is motivated by a desire to maximize positive gratification and minimize negative gratification of *subjectively* defined wants, needs, desires, and drives. The utility of any action is simply the net gratification which an individual expects from it.[1] This will be determined by the individual's *value* (conceived so as to encompass all wants, needs, desires and drives and the relative intensity with which they are felt) and *expectations* (perceived probabilities) that performing the action will positively or negatively gratify these values. Positive gratification of values can be thought of as *benefits* and negative gratification as *costs*. Thus the utility of any action is the sum of its expected benefits (a non-negative number) and its expected costs (a non-positive number).

Utility theory, as we are using it, does not imply that human beings are always rational, in the sense of being willing or able to calculate those actions which in fact would maximize net gratification. Nor does it imply that subconscious motives are unimportant or that a person's values are constant over time. It simply says that people act so as to try to satisfy their desires, regardless of the source, "rationality," or stability of those desires.

A person with the physical capacity either to comply or not comply with a given legal directive will not comply when the utility of noncompliance is greater than the utility of compliance....[2] Utility theory treats compliant and noncompliant behavior as *each* having a set of costs and benefits associated therewith.

Numerous factors might contribute to the total expected costs and benefits summarized in...the...above inequality, which we will refer to as the *utility inequality*. For example, the expected benefits of noncompliance for a white school board member directed to implement a court-ordered busing plan might include the political payoffs

Don W. Brown and Robert V. Stover, "Compliance with Court Directives: A Utility Approach," from "Court Directives and Compliance: A Utility Approach," American Politics Quarterly, Vol. 5, No. 4 (October 1977), pp. 465–480. Copyright © 1977 by Sage Publications, Inc. Reprinted by permission of Sage Publications, Inc. Most footnotes and references have been omitted.

of taking a position popular with his constituency, the symbolic and psychological gains of sending his own and his white friends' children to a white "neighborhood" school, and the social rewards of acting in accord with the norms of his friends and peers. The expected costs of noncompliance might include the guilt or discomfort felt from working to subvert a court order, the possibility of being cited for contempt of court and of receiving the subsequent sanctions, and the likelihood of being involved in further litigation. The expected benefits and costs of compliance probably would be multi-faceted, as well.

Finally, it is important to recognize that utility theory does *not* imply simply that individuals will engage in noncompliant activity whenever its expected benefits exceed its expected costs.... For example, a hypothetical person for whom only considerations of monetary gain were important might find himself able to earn $10,000 a year through illegal activity with an extremely low probability of detection but still not do it because of the opportunity to earn $20,000 over the same period by devoting the same time and resources to some legal activity. On the other hand, a person might perform an illegal act of negative utility if the utility of compliance was even more negative.... [O]ne [ought not] to think [simply] in terms of punishing noncompliance and to disregard rewarding compliance as a means of influencing behavior....

COMPLIANCE AND NONCOMPLIANCE WITH THE DIRECTIVES OF COURTS

The utility approach postulates that the extent of compliance with a legal directive depends on the values and expectations of the individuals to whom the directive is addressed. To affect levels of compliance, a source of law must influence either of these two variables. The low levels of compliance with many court decisions[3] can be explained in large part by the important limitations on the ways in which courts can affect the values and expectations of target populations. In exploring the court's ability to influence values and expectations, our discussion will be limited to their ability to affect compliance with their own legal directives.

Terminology

Understanding the capacity of courts to affect values and expectations can be facilitated by developing a set of terms classifying the tools available to the courts and the types to whom they may be applied. First, the term *target population* is applied to the individuals and institutions whose behavior a court wishes to influence in a given manner by making a decision....

Second, target populations can consist of *primary* and *secondary recipients* of court directives. Primary recipients are the participants in a case (e.g., litigants, jurors, witnesses, etc.) for whom a directive issued by the court prescribes or proscribes a particular behavior. Secondary recipients are individuals not participants in a case, for whom certain behavior is proscribed or prescribed by a court directive....

The term *sanction* is applied to the benefits and costs which a source of law may deliver to those who comply or fail to comply with its directives. For example, courts impose sanctions when they: (1) use their contempt power to fine or throw someone in jail, (2) suppress illegally obtained evidence to "punish" noncomplying police and prosecutors, and (3) reprimand a noncomplier or praise a complier in an opinion. By their very nature, sanctions are administered *after* complying or noncomplying behavior takes place. Only when a source of law can *respond* to such behavior has it the capacity to apply sanctions. However, having this capacity allows the source of law to affect expectations regarding the likelihood that it will apply the sanctions at its disposal in the future. Thus the *potential* imposition of sanctions may influence compliance through the effect it has on the expected costs and benefits of the utility inequality.

Influence through the Threat of Judicial Sanction

. . . [T]he range of sanctions available to courts is limited. They (unlike legislatures) must rely almost exclusively upon what commonly would be called "punishments" rather than "rewards." In terms of the utility inequality, courts have the ability to increase the costs of noncompliance (as through their contempt power) and to decrease the benefits of noncompliance (as through use of the exclusionary rule) but have very little opportunity to decrease the costs of compliance, or to increase the benefits of compliance.

Courts can administer most of the sanctions at their disposal only to the primary recipients of their directives. . . .

The limited arsenal of judicial sanctions, and the narrow scope within which courts may apply them, lead to our first hypothesis:

> **H₁:** Holding other factors constant, the level and rapidity of compliance with any court directive will vary with the proportion of the target population comprised of primary recipients.

Nevertheless, secondary recipients are not immune totally from the *threat* of judicial sanctions. Under some conditions, second-

ary recipients will feel that if they do not alter their behavior so as to conform to a court ruling they might become primary recipients of the same directive in some future case in which a court could fine or imprison them for contempt. The fear of being sued and losing may stimulate their compliance. In any case, the important question is. . . "When will secondary recipients tend to feel a *threat* of judicial sanctions?"

We identify two factors: the total number of noncomplying secondary recipients in the target population and the number of persons willing to bring suit against such noncompliers. Therefore,

> **H₂:** The smaller the total number of noncomplying secondary recipients, the greater will be their individual expectations of being sued, and the greater will be their frequency of compliance

and,

> **H₃:** The greater the number of parties willing to bring suit against secondary recipient noncompliers, the more will secondary recipients feel a threat of judicial sanctions and the greater will be their frequency of compliance.

The first factor is important because a given number of potential litigants with finite resources will be able to only bring suit against a limited number of noncompliers. To exemplify this relationship, one can compare the reaction of state legislatures to the Supreme Court's reapportionment decisions with the response of segregated local districts to desegregation decisions or of local officials to obscenity rulings which appear to make unconstitutional their obscenity ordinances. The state legislatures, a set of secondary recipients to Reynolds v. Sims (377 U.S. 533, 1964) which numbered no more than forty-nine, complied relatively promptly with the reapportionment decisions. Had they not, most, and perhaps all, soon would have found themselves pushed into the role of primary recipients of similar rulings. Their response contrasted with the slow move toward desegregation by the over four thousand school districts in southern and border states which imposed racial segregation by law in 1955.

The second factor (number of persons willing to bring suit) will be affected by the way in which courts act as "gatekeepers" on relevant litigation and by the separate cost-benefit concerns of potential plaintiffs or appellants. The courts' gatekeeper role is exercised through rulings on standing, justiciability, and jurisdiction, which, although variable in application, have an important effect on the likelihood that potential litigants will bring, and successfully complete, legal action.

Cost-benefit considerations are important because potential plaintiffs and appellants will litigate more frequently when they feel they have the most to gain and the least to lose in terms of their own values. . . .

Influence without the Threat of Judicial Sanctions

In many instances, the circumstances which surround and follow an initial court directive do not allow the use or even the threatened use of judicial sanctions. Nevertheless, courts can still affect the values and expectations represented in the utility inequality.

Influencing Expectations. Courts can affect expectations by at least two important routes, neither of which is linked to the use of judicial sanctions. First, they can influence expectations of individuals in target populations regarding the imposition of sanctions by *other* groups. Some studies have found that courts can do this by serving a scapegoat function. Peltason, for example, argued that by taking a harder line in *Brown* the Supreme

Court could have promoted compliance by allowing lower court judges and school board members wanting desegregation to justify their actions on the grounds that they had no choice; *Brown II*, of course, clearly gave them a great deal of choice (Peltason, 1961; 245–246). Had the Court permitted them little or no discretion they would have found it easier to blame their complying behavior on the nine justices and thereby to insulate themselves from some of the political and social consequences of more rapidly implementing desegregation of educational facilities.

Returning to the language of the utility inequality we have

> **H$_4$:** When courts fill a scapegoat function by writing opinions that precisely proscribe or prescribe behavior, they tend to increase compliance by reducing the expected costs of compliance for target populations.

Second, the influence courts have on expectations can be totally unrelated to any kind of sanction. Perhaps the primary way in which courts can affect expectations is by convincing members of the target population that implementation of a decision will gratify positively their pre-existing social goals and more personal values or that failure to implement it will negatively gratify them. Of course most of a target population may either be already convinced or virtually beyond convincing. . . . Courts might significantly affect compliance with their decisions by using their opinions to address the empirical questions crucial in determining a target population's expectations about the consequences of compliance. Hence,

> **H$_5$:** As courts more effectively show that compliance tends to fulfill positively, and noncompliance negatively, important values held by members of a target population, levels of compliance will tend to increase.

Influencing Values. Influencing the values of individuals may be a good deal more difficult than influencing their expectations about empirical outcomes. Such deep-seated predispositions as a bigoted school-board member's attitudes toward racial equality, a fundamentalist teacher's views on separation of church and state, or a law-and-order policeman's orientation toward defendants' rights are not likely to be changed by any arguments a court might make in handing down an opinion.

Even so, two important ways in which courts may influence values are (1) by increasing the intensity of people's commitment to values which specific decisions or sets of decisions are seen as advancing, such as racial equality in desegregation decisions and (2) by increasing their desire to comply with court decisions as an end in itself, apart from the goals which the decisions advance.

With regard to the first, a court can use its written opinions to argue in favor of certain values, perhaps relying on its own moral authority as a source of influence. Single opinions are unlikely to have an effect on deep-seated convictions, but a consistent line of decisions handed down over a period of years might help modify the moral climate within a community. One could argue for instance, that this was the case with the Supreme Court's decisions concerning racial equality.

Courts can increase people's desire to comply as an end in itself by acting in ways that serve to increase court legitimacy. Such actions might include handing down large numbers of substantively popular decisions and conforming to existing norms of court behavior to build up a reservoir of legitimacy on which a court may draw when issuing substantively unpopular decisions (Wasby, 1970:265).

RESEARCH DIRECTIONS

Two general sets of research directions are suggested by the foregoing discussion. The more specific set arises from the hypotheses proposed and the more general set from the utility framework that stimulated the hypotheses. First, how might researchers proceed to employ the five hypotheses empirically? Hypotheses one and two should be the easiest to handle. The most difficult task is to operationalize compliance, a task which is complicated by the fact that the legal directives of courts are sometimes quite ambiguous. Once the meaning of the legal directive has been determined, the target population can be specified and the level and rapidity of compliance and the number of noncompliers can be measured, subject to the everpresent restrictions that data availability impose.

The other hypotheses may prove more difficult to operationalize, yet they should still prove fruitful guides. For hypothesis three, survey techniques would probably be necessary to determine directly the number of parties willing to bring suit against secondary recipient noncompliers, although reasoned estimates at a lower level of measurement could also be made. The fourth hypothesis requires that the researcher classify the precision with which a court directs the behavior of a target population; ordinal rankings may be the most that can be expected; few analysts would disagree that the directive in Brown II was less precise than those in Miranda, but a determination of exactly how much less would surely be more arguable. With regard to the fifth hypothesis, to know *effectively* a court shows how compliance positively fulfills important values held by a target population would require measurement of the population's perceptions, a difficult and expensive task. But a researcher should be able to determine whether a court *overtly* tries to demon-strate that compliant behavior would be of greater utility in positively fulfilling the recip-ients' values or simply issues a command largely unsupported by such an argument....

CONCLUSION

Despite its present skeletal form, a utility theory approach to the study of compliance has several important virtues. First, it pro-vides a degree of conceptual and analytical rigor that the study of compliance has often lacked....

Second, utility theory serves as a frame-work for analyzing the variable capacity of courts to affect compliance with their own directives and gives rise to a number of hypotheses about levels of compliance with such directives.

Finally, utility theory provides a guide for research which we believe increases the likelihood that studies of compliance will be more fruitful and more cumulative.

NOTES

1. It must be emphasized that *gratification*, as we are using the term, can be either positive or negative, or in other words, can involve either "pleasure" or "pain."

2. Compliance and noncompliance, as we use them, refer simply to behavior which respectively conforms and does not con-form to legal directives....

3. For a review of the literature on decision-al areas in which compliance rates have been low see Wasby (1970): 126–135, 147–185.

REFERENCES

Krislov, S. (1965) The Supreme Court in the Political Process. New York: Macmillan.

Peltason, J. (1961) Fifty-Eight Lonely Men: Southern Federal Judges and School Desegregation. New York: Harcourt, Brace and World.

Rodgers, H.R., Jr. and C.S. Bullock, III (1972) Law and Social Change: Civil Rights Laws and Their Consequences. New York: McGraw-Hill.

Wasby, S. (1970) The Impact of the United States Supreme Court. Homewood, Ill.: Dorsey.

Toward a Theory of Civil Rights Implementation

Charles S. Bullock, III
Charles M. Lamb

Civil rights research by political scientists has tended to be primarily descriptive. It has typically depicted the plight of minorities in the areas of education, voting rights, housing, employment, and public accomodations. It has also usually provided a summary of relevant provisions of legislation, court decisions, administrative regulations, and executive orders which set forth policy goals. While useful, these descriptive studies have not provided a theoretical framework through which findings can be classified and integrated. Such a framework could be employed to direct us to aspects of the implementation process that have generally been ignored.

The purpose of this article is to develop the contours of a theory of civil rights implementation. In developing such a theory, we emphasize why policies succeed or fail primarily in terms of administrative implementation. After very briefly surveying how successes and failures have characterized civil rights implementation since the 1950's, we present ten hypotheses derived from substantive and theoretical literature which

Reprinted from *Policy Perspectives* 2 (1982), pp. 376–393. Reprinted with permission of the authors. Footnotes and references have been omitted.

will move us closer to a theory of civil rights implementation.

During the 1950's and 1960's, there was a widespread hope among civil rights activists and their politically placed supporters that a combination of legislative enactments, judicial decisions, and federal enforcement activities would breach the barricades of traditional discrimination. In civil rights as well as other policy areas, the belief that new laws, court orders, or enforcement measures will produce substantial change is encouraged by leading public officials. Presidents, legislators, and candidates for public office frequently promise that problems will be resolved by the adoption of their proposals.

Yet such promises are fraught with difficulties. We only delude ourselves by thinking that there is an easy solution or a quick fix for deeply-rooted problems like discrimination. Experiences of the 1970's, which have been replicated many times over, strongly suggest that a pattern of behavior once embarked on has a trajectory which is not readily deflected by a single statutory, judicial, presidential, or bureaucratic decree. For example, contrary to the promises of the supporters of the War on Poverty, obviously the anti-poverty legislation passed in the mid-1960's did not eliminate want from the American social lexicon.... Similarly, the environmental legislation of the early 1970's has not resulted in the full attainment of clean air and water objectives in many areas of the country.... Nor have Supreme Court decisions holding various religious practices in public schools to be unconstitutional led to their universal discontinuation.... This is not to deny that these policy statements have had some effect. Yet they have not lived up to the high, at times unrealistic, expectations of their proponents.

Extensive evidence that policy decisions often fail to produce anticipated outputs forces us to pay more attention to the policy implementation process.... Interest in implementation has grown as evidence has mounted that problems at this stage quite regularly account for policies not achieving expectations. Good intentions alone are insufficient to change social realities. For policy statements to overcome the status quo, it is essential that careful attention be paid not only to what is included in terms of policy but also the environment in which implementation will occur. Attention to circumstances surrounding policy implementation has thus spawned attempts such as this one to help explain the conditions under which policy goals are not achieved and the reasons for such failures.

CIVIL RIGHTS IMPLEMENTATION: SUCCESSES AND FAILURES

The implementation of civil rights policy has encountered some of the same pitfalls as other reform efforts of the 1960's and 1970's. For example, although equal employment opportunity programs have opened some previously closed jobs to minority workers, the distribution of minorities across job and income categories is skewed, with minorities overrepresented in less prestigious and poorer-paying classifications.... Minorities still have significantly lower incomes than whites,...and minority unemployment is much higher than that of whites.... Fair housing efforts provide another illustration of the failure to attain civil rights policy objectives. Although federal legislation has increased the housing options for minorities, residential segregation remains the rule rather than the exception....

On the other hand, there has been considerable success in achieving certain civil rights objectives. Some of the more notable changes have occurred in school desegregation and voter registration. To be sure, for many years there was deeply-rooted opposition to racial equality in these areas.... Yet by the early 1970's most southern school districts had been desegregated, and the registration and participation of blacks in the political process had risen substantially.... In fact, the South is now ahead of the rest of the country in school desegregation.

Beyond variations in program progress among policies, there have been variations across time even for the more successful policies. During the first half-decade after Brown v. Board of Education (1954), which held de jure school segregation to be unconstitutional, very little changed in the South, and in six southern states not a single black child attended public schools with whites. ... The impact of early legislation aimed at reducing impediments to black registration in the South resulted in only a four percentage point increase between 1956 and 1962 in the proportion of eligible blacks registered to vote.... Therefore, even for policy decisions which ultimately had notable impacts, there was a delay between policy promulgation and meaningful changes in the behavior of those subject to regulation....

HYPOTHESES FOR INTEGRATING PAST AND FOCUSING FUTURE RESEARCH

We have sought to keep the administrative process in mind in developing ten hypotheses necessary to move toward a theory of civil rights implementation. Others could be presented, but these seem to be the most critical. Generally speaking, we begin by presenting the most elementary hypotheses and then proceed to others which have received less attention, with elaboration and illustrations. While there is some literature, either substantive or theoretical, on most of the hypotheses, the fourth, seventh, ninth, and tenth have been the focus of comparatively little research. Although some hypotheses may naturally be more easily operationalized than others, most implicitly or explicitly suggest the type of data essential for testing. More importantly, they also suggest how facets of the political system may be mobilized to provide solutions to ineffective civil rights implementation.

Hypothesis 1: Active Federal Involvement Is a Basic Prerequisite for Successful Civil Rights Implementation.

The level of federal involvement in promoting equal opportunity for minorities and women is crucial for successful policy implementation. Prior to the 1960's, state human rights commissions or related state agencies were principally responsible for insuring the rights of minorities. But to think that state governments would effectively perform this function, particularly in the South, was highly questionable from the beginning. To secure successful civil rights implementation, the federal government was thus forced to intervene at the state and local levels in the 1960's, and a lasting pattern was emerging.

The nation ultimately witnessed the creation of such activist agencies as the U.S. Commission on Civil Rights, and later the Equal Employment Opportunity Commission, as well as such governmental subunits as the Office of Civil Rights at HEW. These and other federal entities would ultimately accept the challenge of civil rights effectuation that could only be met through active federal involvement.

Nevertheless, frequently in the past, when a new right has been established, executive branch agencies have been largely passive in implementation. . . . Under these conditions, the federal government recognizes the existence of a right, but enforcement rests largely with private parties who must sue to force compliance by the reluctant. It is not surprising that when private individuals bear the burden of initiating litigation, change comes very slowly, as was the case for voting rights and school desegregation during the 1950s. . . .

If Congress decides to have the federal government play a more active role in implementing civil rights policy, it can, of course, authorize the Justice Department to file suits on behalf of persons who are being denied their rights. Congress may create or designate a bureaucracy responsible for more complete implementation and to monitor compliance. All other things being equal, active bureaucratic involvement increases the likelihood of implementation more in line with what was expected by those who advocated adoption of the policy, and it speeds up the compliance process considerably.

One effective means through which federal authorities can promote the likelihood that policy objectives will be achieved is to supplant the authority of local or state officials who would otherwise implement the policy. Footdragging by local voter registrars ceased to be an obstacle when federal agents were sent to selected southern counties to enroll eligible blacks.... Supplanting of state and local authority is, however, an extreme step and is usually unnecessary once federal administrative agencies have demonstrated a commitment to enforcing civil rights policy. As a second example, the discretion of some employers, particularly public employers, has been circumscribed by court orders which have prescribed that minorities and women must constitute a specific proportion of all new hirees until the employer's labor force ceases to be disproportionately made up of white males....

Hypothesis 2: Federal Civil Rights Enforcement Agencies Are Essential for Effective Implementation.

Policy decisions may be enunciated by several sources—the courts, Congress, the chief executive, or the bureaucracy. Policies made through congressional action or executive decree are dependent on bureaucratic implementation. Court decisions may also be carried out by the bureaucracy. A serious problem arises, however, when there is no administrative structure responsible for executing a policy. For example, during the first decade after the Supreme Court's Brown decision (1954), there was no federal agency responsible for monitoring progress in the elimination of segregated schools....

Without an agency responsible for seeing that program objectives are accomplished, the desired changes rest precariously on voluntary compliance. This situation most often occurs when the policy is based on a court decision which has not been endorsed by the other branches of government. It is, of course, possible that private plaintiffs who observe an absence of voluntary compliance will bring suit. Yet, when noncompliance is pervasive and there are few private parties

having the resources needed to sue, relatively little change is likely to occur in the direction sought by the policy.... Moreover, when the policy goal is generally unpopular, as has been typical with many civil rights objectives, voluntary compliance is rare. A federal agency is clearly needed to implement civil rights policy under such circumstances.

The focus of implementation research must center on bureaucratic activities when responsibility for attaining policy goals is assigned to a federal agency. Indeed, the exploration of bureaucratic behavior is absolutely essential in developing a theory of civil rights implementation. While other decisionmakers, such as Congress, may alter an agency's responsibilities, it is the agency itself which attends to the day-to-day decisions affecting implementation. An agency responsible for a program will define policy intent, elaborate standards, and issue regulations which will be used when evaluating the behavior of those subject to the policy. Agency employees then seek to apply these standards and guidelines when dealing with those who are being regulated. The agency may conduct investigations, seek to negotiate with those being regulated, or assess penalties against the noncompliant. Because it is less dependent on voluntarism, administrative enforcement holds greater potential than judicial enforcement for securing compliance with unpopular policies.

Hypothesis 3: Civil Rights Implementation Is More Successful Where Policy Goals Are Clearly Stated.

While scholars who have written on policy implementation have suggested numerous variables which seem to be related to policy success, a point on which there is near unanimity is the importance of having policies clearly stated....

First, there should be a categorically clear pronouncement of policy goals. This becomes particularly crucial when Congress has sketched out the policy, but left it up to administrators or judges to flesh out the skeletal directives. Due to uncertainty about legislative intent, judges and bureaucrats play a critical role in determining the extent and conditions under which a piece of legislation is applied. Judges do this as they decide cases; bureaucrats do it in the course of drafting regulations, applying the law in administrative hearings, and undertaking various enforcement steps.

. . .

Beyond intent, a second component of clarity important for understanding implementation involves the specificity of the standards to be used in evaluating compliance with the legislation. In the absence of a measure against which to mark progress, it is impossible to determine whether the law is being adequately executed. For example, if quantitative standards for judging the adequacy of a school desegregation plan are lacking, a school district might be able to argue successfully that it is no longer segregated once a token black enrolls in a previously all-white school.

Even when the decision-makers seek to clarify their intent and to define precisely the standards used in assessment, problems may occur in accurately transmitting this information to those regulated. Reports on legislative, administrative, and especially judicial decisions may be garbled since those being regulated may learn of the policy from intermediaries who do not fully understand it. . . . Thus, we expect that maximum progress toward the objectives of civil rights policy-makers will occur when it has been made explicit what the objectives of the policy are, what is expected of those whose behavior is being regulated, and when quan-

titative standards have been established for measuring compliance. . . .

Hypothesis 4:   A Precondition for Full Civil Rights Implementation Is Having Monitoring Agencies.

Progress toward civil rights policy goals cannot be guaranteed since most legislation and court decisions are not self-executing. While we can usually count on some degree of voluntary compliance, it is necessary to provide for monitoring of performance by federal executive branch agencies to achieve anything approaching full realization of policy objectives. When objectives are as unpopular as those in civil rights policy have been in some quarters, monitoring is essential to achieve more than token compliance. The Supreme Court's Brown v. Board of Education decisions (1954 and 1955), which were not accompanied by systematic monitoring of progress (although federal district courts were directed to oversee implementation), triggered massive resistance rather than compliance in the South. . . . Substantial changes in the South's dual system of black and white schools were not achieved until a monitoring mechanism was established in the wake of the 1964 Civil Rights Act.

Monitoring is more likely to produce desired changes in policy when there are quantifiable standards with which to measure performance. To be effective, this requires the collection of data. . . . When a monitoring agency can numerically assess progress, or its absence, some disputes with those subject to the policy are eliminated, and others can be more easily resolved. . . .

An additional component of effective monitoring is on-site inspection of a sample of those subject to the policy. . . . In the sphere of civil rights policy, it has not been unusual for the regulated to file less than wholly accurate reports on their performance. On-site visits provide an opportunity to determine the quality of the reports received and to identify emerging problems not tapped by current data collection. Another pay-off of on-site inspections is the ripple effect on those not visited. If it is known that the monitor periodically drops in to inspect the records and performance of those being regulated, this will induce compliance with the law's requirements. Effective monitoring further requires adequate training of those who carry out on-site inspections. . . . These people must be able to discern not only what behavior is in violation of the law, but also be sensitive to omissions in formal reports or oral interviews which may indicate that some requirements are not being implemented.

> **Hypothesis 5:** Administrative Personnel Responsible for Implementation Must Be Committed to Promoting Civil Rights.

Perhaps of greater significance than the presence of monitors are the attitudes of those responsible for monitoring. Agency personnel who are not strongly committed to promoting equality may only haphazardly look into complaints alleging discrimination or not rigorously apply standards when reviewing the behavior of those subject to the policy. Commitment to achieving policy goals takes on increased importance as the range of administrative and judicial discretion broadens. When uncertainty exists about what the policy requires and what administrators or judges must do to carry it out, enforcement officials have the option of ignoring all but the most flagrant abuses. For instance, some southern judges interpreted evidence that no blacks were registered to vote in a county with a sizable black population as indicative not of discrimination but of a lack of political interest by blacks.

·   ·   ·

When civil rights duties are assigned to existing bureaucracies, a different impediment to enforcement may exist. Agency personnel are well settled into a routine and have priorities which do not include the new responsibility. The new program may be subordinated to the older responsibility, which is seen as the agency's primary mission. Thus, when HEW's Office for Civil Rights was directed to oversee the establishment of bilingual education programs, this was accorded a lower priority than the agency's initial job of desegregating the schools. . . . Or, rather than assigning a lower priority to the new policy, an agency's modus operandi may ·conflict with its new obligatons. The U.S. Office of Education, which for almost a century had provided assistance and advice to schools, was unprepared to play a civil rights enforcement role and deny federal funds to schools which refused to desegregate. . . . There are, then, a number of potential factors which may dissuade those to whom implementation is entrusted from vigorously discharging their responsibilities. When this occurs, policy objectives are less likely to be realized.

Yet, if the enforcers are dedicated to using the tools available to maximize compliance, they may constitute a potent force indeed, especially when standards and goals are clear, and when there is periodic monitoring. Some federal agents involved in early attempts at securing black suffrage and school desegregation performed well beyond what was expected of them, withstanding abusive language, harassment, and threats while working long hours during extended periods away from home. . . .

> **Hypothesis 6:** The Commitment of the Enforcer's Superiors May Be Critical and Affects the Behavior of Those Responsible for Implementation.

The degree to which the personnel of federal agencies pursue policy goals entrusted to them will in part depend on the cues which they pick up from those to whom they are subordinate. If the administrative enforcers perceive that the President and Congress support their efforts, then they will be encouraged to apply standards rigorously. On the other hand, if the Congress and the president oppose the objectives of the policies assigned to an agency, this can become a powerful incentive not to apply the law forcefully.

The President, as head of the executive branch, is of course ultimately responsible for implementation of the law. High-ranking officials who actually oversee the carrying out of civil rights guarantees by federal agencies are his appointees. The more dedicated the President is to civil rights, the more likely his administration will be to place a high priority on civil rights implementation. A President who opposes an agency's program can severly impede implementation.

Congress may additionally impede administrators from implementing, unpopular programs. Funds may by denied—e.g., for busing or abortions—and administrators who persist in supporting unpopular policies which have not been repealed may be badgered when appearing as witnesses before congressional committees. Another ploy is to assign an agency new responsibilities so that it has little time in which to pursue unpopular policies. An illustration is the assignment of responsibility for reviewing applicants for emergency school aid to the Office for Civil Rights, thereby deflecting it from its desegregation efforts....

When an agency encounters continuing negative feedback from the White House and Congress, prudent administrators begin searching for reasons not to enforce the letter of the law. Persistent pursuit of what has become a politically sensitive objective will lead to a rising tide of opposition and job frustration for the beseiged bureaucrats. This happened regarding HEW's civil rights responsibilities during the Nixon Administration...as well as to the fair housing enforcement duties of the Department of Housing and Urban Development....

Hypothesis 7: Administrative Coordination is Important if Civil Rights Laws Are to Be Successfully Implemented.

A common obstacle to effective policy implementation, which has received relatively little attention,... is the failure of federal agencies with overlapping responsibilities to coordinate enforcement activities. The basic problem may be traced to the statutes themselves. When the same type of discrimination is addressed by different statutes, this piecemeal approach may create widely varied coverage and overlapping remedies. For instance, several laws, including the Fair Housing Act of 1968, Title VI of the Civil Rights Act of 1964, and the Housing and Community Development Act of 1974, prohibit housing discrimination. A number of federal agencies have subsequently been assigned the duty of enforcing these laws with virtually no coordination. Therefore, implementation occurs in a haphazard manner....

In an effort to overcome similar coordination problems which have existed among agencies with equal employment opportunity enforcement duties, President Carter shifted many of the responsibilities of the Civil Service Commission, the Department of Labor, and the Equal Employment Opportunity Coordinating Council to the Equal Employment Opportunity Commission in 1978.... In areas outside of equal employment opportunity, however, few steps have been taken to resolve coordination problems.

Hypothesis 8: Benefits of Complying with Civil Rights Policies Must Outweigh Related Costs.

While a number of the items discussed earlier could be subsumed under a full blown cost/benefit approach,... a narrower perspective can also be adopted in developing a theory of civil rights implementation. The kinds of costs of interest here are the penalties assessed for failing to comply with the law. The perspective of those who would use such sanctions is that once the cost of noncompliance becomes too great, the regulated will conform and the program will be implemented. The costs may involve a loss of funds, the threat of punishment, or loss of standing in the eyes of one's reference group. While sanctions directed at funding were instrumental in southern school desegregation,...it is often politically unacceptable to use this tool to force compliance....

Theoretically, inducements may also be strong motivators of behavior. Offering a reward for carrying out a program in some instances suffices to secure compliance. Grant programs operate on the premise that if funding is made contingent upon prescribed behavior, the desired behavior can be obtained. Apropos to civil rights, federal grants and contracts now regularly include a provision in which the recipient agrees not to discriminate on the basis of race, color, religion, sex, or national origin as a condition for funding.

Whether sanctions or incentives are used to prompt compliance, it may prove necessary for federal authorities to adjust the terms to elicit the desired response from those subject to the regulation. For example, when termination of federal funds failed to secure desegregation in some southern schools, the ante was raised, and segregated districts were threatened with loss of state education money.... Or an offer of additional grant funds arguably may induce suburban communities to accept more units of low-income housing which might produce a more racially heterogeneous population.... Most civil rights policies, however, have relied more on sanctions than incentives to promote implementation. In the absence of either, compliance becomes highly problematic.

Hypothesis 9: The Attitudes and Actions of Those Who Benefit from Civil Rights Implementation Affect Whether There Will Be Forceful Enforcement in the Future.

In light of the foregoing discussion of elements which may operate to thwart implementation, a potentially significant counterweight are those who would benefit from the policy. Support of the policy by the potential beneficiaries may provide critical psychological reinforcement for agency personnel who want to continue faithful implementation but are encountering strong opposition from the agency's superiors.

A second function of beneficiaries is more coercive, that is, to monitor the enforcers. Sometimes this involves collusion between the beneficiaries and the enforcers in an attempt to hold the influence of the agency's sovereigns in check. At other times minority monitoring of civil rights implementation has been designed to force improved performance by the implementer. A coalition of civil rights groups published an outspoken criticism of the way in which emergency aid was distributed to desegregating school districts.... Similarly, civil rights groups have repeatedly chided the Justice Department for not enforcing voting rights more aggressively.... Some civil rights groups, by pointing out administrative deficiencies, have sued the federal agencies responsible for implementation....

Beneficiaries may additionally play a role

at the local level where they can augment the monitoring capability of the enforcement agency. They can bring local deficiencies to the regulator's attention either through informal means or by filing a complaint with the agency charging local decision-makers with violating civil rights requirements. And, as has often been the case since the 1950's, they have testified before the U.S. Commission on Civil Rights which has travelled around the country to investigate civil rights conditions.

For beneficiaries to be most effective, it is axiomatic that there be some organizational structure. An organization purporting to speak for the beneficiaries will receive more attention from the regulator, local officials being regulated, and the press than will an aggrieved individual. To overcome opposition from Congress or a local school or zoning board, it is probably necessary that the beneficiaries be united in their demand that corrective action be taken. When there is disunity among the beneficiaries, as for example the conflict among Hispanics over which should have priority, bilingual education programs or a reduction in the ethnic isolation of Hispanic students,... the regulators are able to ignore in large part the politically more sensitive issues.

Hypothesis 10: The Influence of Interest Groups, the Mass Media, Public Opinion, and the Legal Profession Affects Civil Rights Implementation.

Certain groups—particularly college students, organized labor, and church groups— have supported the civil rights movement. This was most evident during the nonviolent protests of the early 1960's and the "March on Washington" in the summer of 1963 which ultimately contributed to the passage of the Civil Rights Act of 1964 and the Voting Rights Act of 1965. To some extent the mobilization of these groups was due to the coverage of the mass media.... Yet relatively little research has been devoted to the study of the impact that interest groups, other than those specifically created to promote civil rights, and the mass media have had on full civil rights implementation....

The same can be said for the effect of public opinion and the legal profession on the implementation process. The course of popular passions may change the implementation environment much as the force of nature can reshape the physical environment. In the 1960's, many whites joined minorities to protest pervasive discriminatory practices. Congress responded to widespread public preferences and enacted sweeping new legislation. But during the process of implementation, as the full consequences of these new policies became evident, public preferences shifted. Once it became clear, for instance, that school desegregation was not unique to the South, support in the North for the changes needed to eliminate racial isolation declined appreciably. By the early 1970's public opinion polls found that a substantial proportion of white respondents were willing to accept educational, employment, and especially housing discrimination.... Shifts in public attitudes thus may prompt re-evaluations among members of Congress, the president, and his enforcement bureaucracy regarding civil rights implementation. Such shifts were reflected in the fact that Richard Nixon and Gerald Ford considered civil rights to be a second-order priority....

Finally, certain segments of the legal profession, especially during the 1960's, came to the aid of minorities seeking to have their legal rights translated into political realities. An active role by lawyers and legal aid societies may clearly improve the chances for successful civil rights implementation. Dedicated legal assistance may underscore the fact that minorities and women do indeed have rights which can be enforced through the courts and the federal bureaucracy. While litigation is a useful means for mobilizing enforcement, relatively little research has focused on this aspect of the implementation process. . . .

CONCLUSIONS

Civil rights implementation, like implementation in any other policy field, has had its ups and downs, its successes and failures. In moving toward a theory of civil rights implementation, it is essential that future research test the above hypotheses in all fields of civil rights: equal education, employment, and housing opportunity, as well as the enforcement of voting rights. We have suggested that necessary conditions for effective implementation hinges on direct federal involvement, the presence of federal enforcement agencies, clearly stated policy goals, precise standards for measuring compliance, civil

rights personnel fully committed to their enforcement responsibilities, the support of the enforcer's superiors, adequate administrative coordination, the advantages of compliance outweighing its costs, and active support from those who benefit from successful implementation, from other interest groups, the mass media, the public, and the legal profession. Systematic examination of these hypotheses will enable future studies to determine why civil rights implementation has met with the fate that it has and why greater compliance came when it did rather than earlier. Particularly useful will be research which uses multivariate techniques. Only through this kind of overarching research design will it be possible to develop a parsimonious model of the civil rights implementation process. When this research agenda is met, generalizations for the conditions under which civil rights policy is most likely to be fully carried out will be forthcoming, and a theory of civil rights implementation will be within our grasp.

Patterns of Adoption of Tort Law Innovations: An Application of Diffusion Theory to Judicial Doctrines

Bradley C. Canon
Lawrence Baum

...This study concerns the diffusion of 23 plaintiff-oriented tort doctrines among the state court systems in the 1876–1975 period....

We chose tort law for two reasons. First, it has undergone enormous development over the last century. As a result, we were able to find a reasonably large number of doctrinal innovations scattered over a long period. In contrast, doctrine has been much more static in other traditional areas of law such as property law and contract law. Second, we preferred to focus on interaction among the states without contamination from federal action. While federal laws or decisions have affected many diffusion patterns at the state and local levels,... tort law has developed virtually without federal guidance or interference.

All 23 doctrines that we analyze are plaintiff-oriented. That is, they improve the legal position of plaintiffs by such means as creating new rights, easing burdens of proof, and eliminating or weakening certain defenses. Both the plaintiffs who benefit

Reprinted from *American Political Science Review* 75 (1981), pp. 975–987. Reprinted with permission of the authors. Footnotes, most references, and some tables omitted.

from the doctrines and the defendants who are disadvantaged constitute fairly distinct groups in society. The plaintiffs are usually individuals who have suffered physical injury. By contrast, the defendants are often business corporations, government agencies, or other institutions. When this is not the case, an insurance carrier is often the real if not the nominal defendant.

The choice of plaintiff-oriented doctrines was virtually dictated by the direction of change in tort law over the last 100 years. For much of the nineteenth century, innovations in tort were largely defendant-oriented, aimed at protecting the accumulation of capital for use in industrial development.... But subsequently courts—along with other agencies—became more concerned with the social costs of the industrial revolution for injured workers and consumers. As a result, they fashioned doctrines shifting these costs to the more solvent elements of society....

Selection of Doctrines

We began with the common definition of an innovation as a program or policy which is new to the adopting unit, regardless of how old the idea may be or where it originated.... While courts make new law regularly in the course of their work of resolving new factual situations, we limited our concern to those changes which involved major departures from past policies and which sooner or later had a significant impact on the real world. We identified these with the aid of legal encyclopedias, treatises, and casebooks, particularly Prosser and Wade (1971). Of those so identified, our ultimate selections were based upon several criteria.

The first was the scope of the adoption. To be included, an innovation had to be adopted in a minimum of 18 states and could not be explicitly rejected, following the first adoption, in as many states as had adopted it. In other words, it had to be an emergent or dominant doctrine in the law while being diffused. Second, we excluded doctrines in whose development state legislatures played a large role. The relatively few tort law innovations that were adopted by the legislature or were rejected legislatively without prior judicial adoption in more than eight states were not considered. The third criterion was temporal. Doctrines were excluded if a significant part of their adoption process occurred prior to 1876.

Identification of Adoptions

Our identification of adoptions of doctrines was fairly straightforward. We examined the system of regional reports of state court opinions published by the West company for potential adoptions. We considered an adoption to have occurred whenever a state court said or implied that the doctrine was now the law in that state. We focused only on the initial adoption and did not consider subsequent "disadoptions" by the same court or legislative action to override the adoption. Such occurrences, however, were infrequent. We included partial adoptions (e.g., adoptions made with reservations or adoptions of

only one element of a doctrine) so long as they constituted significant departures from the previous state of the law.

The vast majority of the adoptions came from the states' highest courts, which we will label "supreme courts." A few came from lower courts. A lower court adoption was not included if the supreme court superseded the decision through either adoption or rejection of the doctrine in the next five years, or if a court of equal authority in the state explicitly refused to follow the doctrine within that five-year period.

DATA AND ANALYSIS: INNOVATIVENESS

Rankings of the States

We created a composite innovation score for each state based on the timing of its courts' adoptions of the 23 individual doctrines. For each doctrine each state was given a score corresponding to the proportion of the "adoption period" that remained when that state adopted the doctrine; the adoption period begins with the first adoption of a doctrine and ends one year after its last adoption. For a doctrine whose last "counted" adoption occurred in 1975, that year was treated as the year of last adoption. Thus the first adopter would receive a score of 1.000 and the last adopter a score slightly above .000. Nonadopters received scores of .000. This formula is similar to that used by Walker (1969, pp. 882–83). Where the state courts were preempted by federal court adoption or state legislative action, the state was not given a score for that doctrine. The composite score for each state is simply the mean of the individual scores it received for each doctrine. These are shown in Table 1.

The rankings are interesting. It is not surprising that states such as Minnesota and California rank high, because they have reputations for progressivism and innovative-

TABLE 1

State Innovation Scores for 23 Plaintiff-Oriented Doctrinal Innovations in Tort Law

1.	Minnesota	.509	26.	Colorado	.284
2.	Texas	.458	27.	New Hampshire	.258
3.	Kentucky	.457	28.	Florida	.251
4.	Washington	.433	29.	Alabama	.237
5.	California	.419	30.5	Arkansas	.229
6.	Missouri	.400	30.5	South Dakota	.229
7.	Louisiana	.388	32.	Nebraska	.227
8.	New Jersey	.375	33.	Arizona	.226
9.	Connecticut	.374	34.	Montana	.216
10.	Oklahoma	.360	35.	Maryland	.202
11.	Illinois	.354	36.	Delaware	.198
12.	Tennessee	.353	37.	North Dakota	.189
13.	Pennsylvania	.343	38.	Idaho	.173
14.	Michigan	.341	39.	Utah	.172
15.	Iowa	.339	40.	West Virginia	.159
16.	Ohio	.335	41.	Rhode Island	.147
17.	Oregon	.332	42.	Virginia	.112
18.	Wisconsin	.331	43.	New Mexico	.108
19.	North Carolina	.323	44.	Nevada	.105
20.	Georgia	.320	45.	Massachusetts	.096
21.	South Carolina	.309	46.	Alaska	.078
22.	New York	.307	47.5	Maine	.074
23.	Kansas	.295	47.5	Vermont	.074
24.	Mississippi	.293	49.	Hawaii	.053
25.	Indiana	.288	50.	Wyoming	.019

SOURCE:
Collected and compiled by the authors.

ness. Similarly, some low-ranking states such as West Virginia and New Mexico have the opposite reputation. The low rankings of states with small populations, such as Alaska and Wyoming, also might have been expected. But the rankings of many states do not comport very well with conventional wisdom about innovativeness—either in general or as it relates to judicial doctrines. It is almost shocking to see Texas, Kentucky, and Louisiana among the top ten and Massachusetts near the bottom.

Because changing conditions over time in the states may bring about new patterns of innovativeness in judicial decisions, rankings for a century-long period may obscure as much as they show. Consequently, we created separate innovation scores for the early and late segments of our study period by dividing the doctrines into two groups. One consists of 9 doctrines whose median adoption date occurred between 1902 and 1938 (the pre-World War II group); the other consists of 14 doctrines with median adoption dates between 1950 and 1970 (the postwar group)....

There is some similarity between the two sets of scores, as indicated by the correlation between them (r = .450). But . . . some dramatic changes took place between the two periods. New Hampshire and New Jersey climbed over 30 places, Louisiana and Michigan over 20 places. Meanwhile, Kansas, Montana, Nebraska, North Carolina, and Tennessee all dropped more than 20 places. Twenty-four states shifted at least 10 ranks in one direction or the other, and only three states were in the top 10 in both periods. The mean shift in rank for a state was 12.0.

Table 2 summarizes the states' rankings by census region. In the prewar period, the most innovative appellate courts came largely from relatively rural states of the South and the great plains farm belt. By contrast, most of the heavily industrialized states of the Northeast and North Central regions were in the lower half of the rankings. In the postwar period the patterns shifted somewhat. Many of the southern and plains states lost their penchant to adopt innovative tort doctrines early, and the more industrialized states of the Middle Atlantic and East North Central regions became much more innovative as a group. The regional patterns suggest some correlates of innovativeness related to state characteristics. . . .

Characteristics of States

. . . The most important demographic characteristic probably is *population*. The level of a state's population will be reflected in the volume of litigation. This is significant because innovation is dependent upon the existence of appropriate cases. A sparsely populated state such as Wyoming simply may generate too few cases to allow its

TABLE 2
Average Tort Law Innovation Scores and Rankings by Census Region

	Whole Period		Prewar Period		Postwar Period	
	Average	*Rank*	*Average*	*Rank*	*Average*	*Rank*
Northeast						
New England	.171	8	.201	9	.152	8
Middle Atlantic	.342	2	.283	7	.382	1
North Central						
East North Central	.330	4	.371	4	.302	3
West North Central	.313	5	.437	2	.233	6
South						
South Atlantic	.234	7	.328	5	.174	7
East South Central	.335	3	.444	1	.260	4
West South Central	.359	1	.392	3	.338	2
West						
Mountain	.163	9	.212	8	.134	9
Pacific	.263	6	.293	6	.245	5

NOTE:
The composition of the regions is as follows. *New England:* Maine, N.H., Vt., Mass., R.I., Conn.; *Middle Atlantic:* N.Y., N.J., Pa.; *East North Central:* Ohio, Ind., Ill., Mich., Wisc.; *West North Central:* Minn., Iowa, Mo., N.D., S.D., Neb., Kansas; *South Atlantic:* Del., Md., Va., W. Va., N.C., S.C., Ga., Fla.; *East South Central:* Ky., Tenn., Alab., Miss.; *West South Central:* Ark., La., Okla., Texas.; *Mountain:* Mont., Idaho, Wyo., Colo., N.M., Ariz., Utah, Nevada; *Pacific:* Wash., Oregon, Calif., Alaska, Hawaii.
SOURCE: Collected and compiled by the authors.

courts to adopt doctrines before most other states. In contrast, courts in a heavily populated state such as California may receive rapid demands for the adoption of innovative doctrines.

Urbanization and *industrialization* may affect innovation in several ways. They increase interactions of the sort that lead to litigation. Urban-industrial areas are likely to be relatively sophisticated and cosmopolitan, and these characteristics in individuals render them more receptive to innovations.... Finally, attorneys in urban-industrial states may well be better trained and more aware of developments in the law than their rural counterparts.

We tested the relationships between our innovation scores and these three characteristics for the two periods....

[O]nly population was positively related to innovation during both periods. That relationship was moderately high and statistically significant in both periods, and it remained significant when controls for the other demographic variables were introduced. In the postwar period all three demographic variables had highly significant positive relationships with innovation; the introduction of controls establishes that population was the most important of the variables and that urbanization had little independent effect. The change in the relationship between industrialization and innovation over time suggests that the level of industry in itself has not been important for innovation. Urbanization appears to be uniformly unimportant. Certainly the most important implication of these findings is support for our speculation that sparse population reduces opportunities for judicial innovation.

.   .   .

Innovativeness in tort law also might be related to two political characteristics of

states: prevailing ideology and political culture. The regional patterns seen in Table 2 make political ideology particularly promising. In the prewar period the Populist and Progressive movements might have encouraged the adoption of legal doctrines favoring individuals over corporate interests. In the postwar period New Deal liberalism might be associated with the adoption of liberal tort rules.

To test the impact of political ideology we analyzed the relationship between innovation scores and voting patterns. In the prewar period we used the proportions of votes obtained by three Populist and Progressive candidates for president (Bryan in 1896, Roosevelt in 1912, and La Follette in 1924) and the success of Progressive party candidates in state elections in the 1910–1912 period.... In the postwar period we used the proportions of votes obtained by Democratic candidates in 1936 and 1964 and the combined support for Truman and Wallace in 1948. We included the 1936 election, even though it occurred in the prewar period, because the divisions in that election reflected ideological coalitions that were typical of the postwar period.

The results suggested a lack of impact for ideology. While the relationships between party voting and innovation generally were in the posited direction, in no case were they statistically significant. Controls for the impact of demographic variables and exclusion of southern states in the postwar period did not change this pattern. It may be that dominant state ideologies have had an effect on some state court systems. But state political ideology—at least as measured by general election results—was not reflected systematically in the innovativeness of state courts in tort law.

...We tested the relationship between tort innovation and political culture; our measure of culture was Sharkansky's quantification of

Elazar's state cultures, which ranks states from moralistic to traditionalistic (1969). The results were entirely nonsignificant. No meaningful relationship appeared between culture and innovation for the whole period or for the two subperiods, with or without controls for population.

Characteristics of Courts

Attributes of courts and court systems might have a stronger effect on innovation than attributes of states because their effect is more direct. One cluster of court attributes which may be significant is judicial professionalism. Scholars and practitioners concerned with judicial administration have argued that certain kinds of "professional" features enhance the capacity of courts to function effectively.... Among the features referred to as professional are the presence of professional administrators, the existence of an intermediate appellate court, and "merit selection" of judges. In the aggregate, these features may create conditions that are favorable for innovation. Professional administrators and intermediate appellate courts may give supreme court justices more time to become aware of innovative doctrines and to consider their implications. Merit selection procedures may produce judges who are more sensitive to needs for doctrinal change....

The relationship between innovation and professionalism is moderate ($r = .274$, significant at the .05 level). But judicial professionalism is strongly related statistically to population, industrialization, and urbanization, and controlling for any of them reduced the relationship to virtually zero. Thus professionalism seems not to have an independent effect on innovation.

A second type of court characteristic that may be related to a court's readiness to adopt innovations is the backgrounds of its judges. Because of the weakness of political pressures for change in common law fields and the absence of major resource needs for innovation, judges' decisions whether to adopt innovations may be based chiefly on their personal preferences. Those preferences in turn may reflect and be reflected in their background characteristics.

Three background characteristics seem most likely to be linked with inclination to innovate in tort law. The first is *party affiliation*. Democratic judges as a group take more liberal positions than do Republicans, and one component of this liberalism is a sympathy for plaintiffs in tort cases.... A second is judges' *legal education*. Judges with law degrees from prestigious, top-quality law schools are likely to have greater knowledge of legal developments and more confidence about adopting innovations than judges from other institutions. The third is the *locale* of judges' last private *law practice*. Judges who practiced in metropolitan areas may be more likely than other judges to have entered communication networks that make them aware of innovations in other states, and they may be less resistant to legal change....

We analyzed the impact of these three characteristics in the postwar period with the data collected by Canon and Jaros (1970) on the backgrounds of state supreme court justices who served between 1960 and 1968. These data are not ideal, because they cover only a small part of the postwar period. But the long service of many justices and the stability that probably exists in background characteristics in many states made it reasonable to use these data at least for exploratory purposes.

We found little relationship between the

states' innovation scores and the number of justices with prestigious law degrees ($r = .192$), and the relationship with the number of Democrats was even weaker ($r = .066$; $.064$, with the South excluded). But the correlation between number of justices with metropolitan practices and innovation scores was a dramatically significant $.543$. Even with controls for all three demographic variables, the partial correlation for metropolitan practice and innovation remains moderately high at $.318$, considerably higher than for any of the demographic variables and innovation with an equivalent set of controls.

The absence of a relationship between justices' party affiliations and judicial innovativeness is consistent with the unimportance of party voting patterns as an explanation for states' receptivity to judicial innovations. The complexity of the relationship between party and ideology at the individual and state levels undoubtedly contributed to these negative findings. It also may be that ideological liberalism is less closely related to support for innovations that favor tort plaintiffs than we had posited.

Because of the limitations of our data, the relationship between metropolitan law practice and innovation should not be emphasized. The relationship may be limited to a particular period, and it might be largely spurious because of the impact of variables that we did not analyze. But we think that it makes intuitive sense for the reasons that we suggested. Urban judges, like urban residents generally, are most likely to have the information and orientations that support innovation. Moreover, the urban or rural background of the bench should have a much more direct effect on judicial behavior than the urbanization of the state as a whole. . . .

DATA AND ANALYSIS: THE PATTERN OF DIFFUSION

Regionalism in the Diffusion Process. . . .

We cannot investigate the role of regionalism in the process by which state judges learn of innovations and choose to adopt them. But we can investigate regionalism in the patterns by which innovations spread. To do so we have adopted Walker's methodology: a varimax factor analysis with the states as variables and doctrines as cases. As in Walker's analysis, consistent patterns of diffusion within a region will be reflected in a clustering of the states in that region on a single factor.

The results of the analysis. . . offer a mixed picture. There is some evidence of regionalism in the first two factors, both of which have a majority of southern and border states among the highest loaders. But factor 1 is perhaps best seen as a clustering of nonindustrial states. None of the remaining factors has a strong regional cast. Factor 6 is of interest because it includes four of the five leading innovators, all except Kentucky.

We also undertook separate factor analyses for the prewar and postwar periods. The patterns that emerged must be interpreted with great caution because of the small numbers of doctrines that we analyzed in each period. But generally we found that the effect of regionalism was even weaker in these subperiods than it was in the entire study period.

Certainly our findings indicate that regionalism plays a far weaker role in defining factors for judicial tort innovations than was the case for Walker's legislative innovations. To the extent that we can identify regional elements in the factors, they are not very strong. Our findings suggest that state appellate courts are open to influence from other courts regardless of location.

More generally, the factor analysis discloses a weak structure to the tort diffusion pattern.... [T]he pattern of adoption for tort doctrines is largely idiosyncratic.

The Speed of Diffusion

It is difficult to say whether innovative policies generally diffuse more rapidly among courts than among legislatures. Diffusion among legislatures is slowed by several factors that should be less important in the courts, including communication weaknesses, the existence of multiple decision points, and the need to weigh political pressures. But this advantage may be offset by courts' dependence on litigants for action. Moreover, judicial acceptance of innovations frequently is slowed by adherence to precedent and deference to the legislature as the appropriate source of major legal change.

Once again we may use Walker's study for comparison. Walker (1969, p. 895) found that the first 20 adoptions of legislation required an average of around 20 years, declining slightly from 23 years in the late nineteenth century to 18 years in the mid-twentieth century. The rate of diffusion for our tort innovations was markedly slower. For the entire set of doctrines (excluding one that was adopted by fewer than 20 states), the average time required for 20 adoptions was 37.1 years. For the 12 doctrines first adopted prior to 1920, the mean period was 46.5 years; for the 10 adopted later, the mean declined to 25.9 years. Even that figure is 8 years greater than the rate for legislation in the most comparable period.

Because these findings are based on a single limited comparison, they do not allow firm conclusions. But they do suggest the importance of judicial passivity and restraint

in delaying the adoption of innovations.

The growing speed of diffusion for the tort law that we found in the past half century is in part an artifact of our selection of doctrines. A doctrine that was first adopted in 1950 and that has diffused fairly slowly would not have met our criterion for inclusion. But there have been real changes as well. Of the six doctrines that were adopted by 20 states in fewer than 20 years, for instance, five were first adopted in 1950 or later. It is much more common for large numbers of courts to adopt a doctrine quickly than it used to be.

This change can be traced to both litigants and courts. The growing volume of litigation has reduced the time that an appellate court must wait for a chance to act. Moreover, professionalization and improved communication within the personal injury bar have given plaintiffs greater capacity to argue for the adoption of innovations.

Probably more important are changes in the courts. Judges have become more aware of doctrinal developments in other states' appellate courts and in law review commentaries; this growing awareness is reflected in an increasing self-consciousness with which innovations are discussed and adopted in judicial opinions. In addition, the traditional nineteenth-century view that law was a permanent entity has gradually eroded. Many modern judges have adopted the view that the law should be flexible and responsive to social needs, and in doing so they have developed a more favorable attitude toward doctrinal innovation.

CONCLUSION

The most important implication of our findings for the study of state judicial systems concerns the dramatic shift in the geographical locus of doctrinal innovativeness over time. Our analysis of this change in conjunction with Populist, Progressive and New Deal voting patterns revealed little ideological linkage. Unfortunately, we have few insights into other causes of this shift because scholars who have studied state court policy making longitudinally have largely passed over the first half of the twentieth century.... Nonetheless, the geographical and social nature of the shift in judicial innovativeness in tort law is both striking and unconventional and calls for further study to determine what has caused it and whether it is part of a more general phenomenon.

Our findings have two noteworthy implications for diffusion theory. First, the reactive position of the courts is an important explanatory consideration. Because courts are dependent upon litigants' demands, a strong element of idiosyncracy governs the diffusion of tort doctrines. Moreover, it is doubtful that this idiosyncracy is peculiar to one branch of the law.

The courts' reactive role contrasts with the initiatory powers of legislatures and administrative agencies. While policy making in these institutions is often responsive to external events, they are usually aggregate events. The courts' lack of control over the timing of the adoption of innovations is reflected in the considerable difference between the relatively systematic diffusion patterns that Walker (1969) and others have found outside the judiciary and the seemingly unstructured patterns we have found.

This difference is important to diffusion theory because courts are by no means the only reactive policy makers in our political and social systems. Other institutions must on occasion adopt policies in response to relatively random events. For instance, state and local governments must respond to natural disasters or urban disorders, business firms to new competitive products or attempts at corporate takeovers. Our findings suggest that conventional explanations for the diffusion of innovations have limited application in such situations.

The second implication stems from our finding little evidence of regionalism in the diffusion of tort doctrines. This is in considerable contrast with Walker's data about diffusion in the legislative arena. While geographical proximity is undoubtedly an important aspect of diffusion, we suspect that a process which transcends regionalism is the wave of the future. The legal system developed rather early a method for communicating court decisions that is both formally structured and geographically unlimited. Only in the current era are many other political and social systems developing social and technological avenues of information exchange which override geographical barriers. This is perhaps reflected in Walker's having noted a diminution of regionalism in the diffusion of new laws since the 1930s (1969, p. 896). We would expect this trend to continue so that the pattern of diffusion that we found in the judiciary will become common in the legislature as well as in other institutions....

REFERENCES

Canon, Bradley C., and Dean Jaros (1970). "External Variables, Institutional Structure and Dissent on State Supreme Courts." *Polity* 3: 175–200.

Prosser, William L., and John W. Wade (1971). *Cases and Materials on Torts*, 5th ed. Mineola, N.Y.: Foundation Press.

Sharkansky, Ira (1969). "The Utility of Elazar's Political Culture: A Research Note." *Polity* 2: 66–83.

Walker, Jack L. (1969). "The Diffusion of Innovations among the American States." *American Political Science Review* 63: 880–99.

PART FIVE

The Special Place of the Supreme Court

CHAPTER 15

The Role of the Supreme Court in the American Political System

The United States Supreme Court, by its exercise of judicial review, has long been thought to have a distinctive impact on the American political system. It is the exercise of this power to determine the constitutionality of any act or action of any governmental official or agency, federal or state, that has continually captured the attention of scholars. This power has provided a fertile source of scholarly and public controversy throughout American history.[1] In particular there has been periodic controversy about what has been considered the "counter-majoritarian" status of judicial review.[2] It is often argued that judges, because they are not elected, must be restrained in the exercise of their power. They must interpret the Constitution in light of the intention of its Framers and defer to the popularly elected branches.[3] Others suggest that judicial activism is both inevitable and desirable. For them judges properly play a role in defining and elaborating public values.[4] The first two selections in this chapter (Meese and Brennan) provide a recent example of this debate.

Beyond the argument about judicial activism and restraint scholars have tried to assess the implications of judicial review for the functioning of American democracy. Robert Dahl, in an article that has achieved the status of a "classic" in the literature (and is included in an updated version), suggests that the Supreme Court has historically been part of the national governing coalition and has rarely been out of step (and even then, only for the short run) with the popularly elected components of that coalition. He argues that judicial review over congressional legislation has rarely been used to substitute judicial judgments for those of stable and substantial popular majorities. Rather, he feels that the most important function of judicial review is to legitimize national policy, that is, to confer legitimacy on controversial policies fashioned by the popularly elected branches of government.

The article by Jonathan Casper focuses on the Warren Court years of the 1960s. Casper notes that judicial review negating the actions of government was vigorously exercised, particularly when the states were concerned (and Casper stresses that Dahl's assessment was weakened because he ignored judicial review over the actions of the states).[5] Thus the Court's exercise of judicial review is not as benign as Dahl's analysis would lead us to believe. Casper also views the Court's record differently than Dahl when considering judicial review over congressional legislation.

Is judicial review justifiable? Does the Court's use of judicial review to confer legitimacy on controversial policies make the institution of judicial review an essential prop for the legitimacy of the entire political system? The Adamany reading cautions us about the basic assumption that underlies these questions—that the Court has a legitimacy-conferring function. Adamany can find no hard evidence demonstrating the so-called legitimacy-conferring capability of the Court. (Adamany bases this conclusion on a review of public opinion-and-the-Court literature such as that presented in Part One, Chapter Five). Adamany examines the Court during major party-realigning periods of American history and indeed finds the Court at odds with the popularly elected governing majorities. Far from legitimizing the actions of the regime, the Court does quite the reverse. The Court once again becomes part of the new governing structure only after at least some of the old justices have beaten a strategic retreat (usually as a consequence of attacks against the Court itself) and new justices, appointed by the new administration, have come to the Court. During the realigning periods the Court flexes its judicial muscles. Despite majority opposition to the Court's policies, judicial review always has remained intact because the opponents of the Court typically become divided when the issue becomes one of whether or not to fundamentally alter Court power. The Court's legitimacy as an institution of government thus saves the day.

In some respects Casper's article can be taken as further evidence in support of Adamany's argument. The 1960s was a decade of political and partisan flux and gave many indications that the party configuration that came into being with the New Deal in the 1930s had come to an end. It was precisely during that decade that the Warren Court, with its concern for civil rights and liberties not unlike many of the concerns of the old liberal Democratic majority, was in conflict with the emerging, considerably more conservative, new governing majority. After the Nixon appointees came to dominate the Supreme Court, the Court retreated—most noticeably in the criminal procedures area, but in some others as well—and once again came to terms with the new majority. Only the incredible events of "Watergate," and the severely troubled national economy, prevented the Republicans from winning the presidency in 1976 and fully exploiting an apparent shift to a more conservative, and less party oriented, electorate.

Four years later saw the election of a popular Republican president, reelected in 1984, philosophically committed to reorienting judicial priorities. President Ronald Reagan placed three new justices on the Supreme Court and elevated Justice Rehnquist to the chief justiceship. How those appointments reshape the direction of the Court is a still unfolding story, although Table 2 in the introductory essay for Chapter Ten offers some hints. That they will reshape the Court is a foregone conclusion. The Supreme court has, throughout our history, had a broad impact on the political system and the political system has in turn affected the Court. Judicial review is a power that is inherent in our judicial institutions. How that power should be exercised is an important question but one that cannot be definitively answered. How courts in general should exercise their powers is a question that is equally difficult to answer but one that is worth considering.

NOTES

1. See for example, Henry Steele Commager, *Majority Rule and Minority Rights* (New York: Peter Smith, 1943).

2. Alexander Bickel, *The Least Dangerous Branch* (Indianapolis: Bobbs-Merrill, 1962).

3. See Henry Monaghan, "Our Perfect Constitution," *New York University Law Review* 56 (1981), 353; see also Raoul Berger, *Government by Judiciary* (Cambridge: Harvard University Press, 1977) and Robert Bork, "Neutral Principles and Some First Amendment Problems," *Indiana Law Journal* 47 (1971), 1.

4. Michael J. Perry, *The Constitution, The Courts, and Human Rights* (New Haven: Yale University Press, 1982) and Owen Fiss, "The Forms of Justice," *Harvard Law Review* 93 (1979), 1.

5. Also see John Gates, "Partisan Realignment, Unconstitutional State Policies, and the U.S. Supreme Court, 1837–1964," *American Journal of Political Science* 31 (1987), 259 and William Lasser, "The Supreme Court in Periods of Critical Realignment," *Journal of Politics* 47 (1985), 1174.

Toward a Jurisprudence of Original Intention

Edwin Meese III

The Supreme Court's 1984–85 term was once again characterized by a nearly crushing workload. There were 4,935 cases on the docket this past year; 179 cases were granted review; 140 cases issued in signed opinions, 11 were *per curiam* rulings. Such a docket lends credence to Alexis de Tocqueville's assessment that in America, every political question seems sooner or later to become a legal question.

In looking back over the work of the court, I am struck by how little the statistics tell us about the true role of the court. In reviewing a term of the court, it is important to reflect upon the proper role of the Supreme Court in our constitutional system.

THE FOUNDERS' VIEW OF THE SUPREME COURT

The intended role of the judiciary generally and the Supreme Court in particular was to serve as the "bulwarks of a limited consti-"fundamental law" and would "regulate their tution." The judges, the founders believed,

would not fail to regard the Constitution as decisions" by it. As the "faithful guardians of the Constitution," the judges were expected to resist any political effort to depart from the literal provisions of the Constitution. The text of the document and the original intention of those who framed it would be the judicial standard in giving effect to the Constitution.

Alexander Hamilton, defending the federal courts to be created by the new Constitution, remarked that the want of a judicial power under the Articles of Confederation had been the crowning defect of that first effort at a national constitution. Ever the consummate lawyer, Hamilton pointed out that "laws are a dead letter without courts to expound and define their true meaning."

The anti-Federalist *Brutus* took him to task in the New York press for what the critics of the Constitution considered his naivete. That prompted Hamilton to write his classic defense of judicial power in *The Federalist*, No. 78. An independent judiciary under the Constitution, he said, would prove to be the "citadel of public justice and the public security." Courts were "peculiarly essential in a limited constitution." Without them, there would be no security against "the encroachments and oppressions of the representative body," no protection against "unjust and partial" laws.

Hamilton, like his colleague Madison, knew that *all* political power is "of an encroaching nature." In order to keep the powers created by the Constitution within the boundaries marked out by the Constitution, an independent—but constitutionally bound—judiciary was essential. The purpose of the Constitution, after all, was the creation of limited but also energetic government institutions with the power to govern, but also with structures to keep the power in check. As Madison put it, the Constitution enabled the government to control the governed, but also obliged it to control itself.

But even beyond the institutional role, the court serves the American republic in yet another, more subtle way. The problem of any popular government, of course, is seeing to it that the people obey the laws. There are but two ways: either by physical force or by moral force. In many ways the court remains the primary moral force in American politics.

By fulfilling its proper function, the Supreme Court contributes both to institutional checks and balances and to the moral undergirding of the entire constitutional edifice. For the court is the only national institution that daily grapples with the most fundamental political questions—and defends them with written expositions. Nothing less would serve to perpetuate the sanctity of the rule of law so effectively.

But that is not to suggest that the justices are a body of Platonic guardians. Far from it. The court is what it was understood to be when the Constitution was framed—a political body. The judicial process is, at its most fundamental level, a political process. While not a partisan political process, it is political in the truest sense of that word. It is a process wherein public deliberations occur over what constitutes the common good under the terms of a written constitution.

As Justice Benjamin Cardozo pointed out, "the great tides and currents which engulf

the rest of men do not turn aside in their course and pass the judges by." Granting that, Tocqueville knew what was required. As he wrote:

> The federal judges therefore must not only be good citizens and men of education and integrity,...[they] must also be statesmen; they must know how to understand the spirit of the age, to confront those obstacles that can be overcome, and to steer out of the current when the tide threatens to carry them away, and with them the sovereignty of the union and obedience to its laws....

A RETURN TO A JURISPRUDENCE OF ORIGINAL INTENTION

The Bill of Rights came about largely as a result of the demands of the critics of the new Constitution, the unfortunately misnamed Anti-Federalists. They feared, as George Mason of Virginia put it, that in time the national authority would "devour" the states. Since each state had a bill of rights, it was only appropriate that so powerful a national government as that created by the Constitution have one as well. Though Hamilton insisted a Bill of Rights was not necessary and even destructive, and Madison (at least at first) thought a Bill of Rights to be but a "parchment barrier" to political power, the Federalists agreed to add a Bill of Rights.

Though the first ten amendments that were ultimately ratified fell far short of what the Anti-Federalists desired, both Federalists and Anti-Federalists agreed that the amendments were a curb on national power.

When this view was questioned before the Supreme Court in *Barron* v. *Baltimore* (1933), Chief Justice Marshall wholeheartedly agreed. The Constitution said what it meant and meant what it said. Neither political expediency nor judicial desire was sufficient to change the clear import of the language of the Constitution. The Bill of Rights did not apply to the states—and, he said, that was that. Until 1925, that is. Since then a good deal of constitutional adjudication has been aimed at extending the scope of the doctrine of incorporation. But the most that can be done is to expand the scope; nothing can be done to shore up the intellectually shaky foundation upon which the doctrine rests. And nowhere else has the principle of federalism been dealt so politically violent and constitutionally suspect a blow as by the theory of incorporation.

In thinking particularly of the use to which the First Amendment has been put in the area of religion, there is much merit in Justice William Rehnquist's recent dissent in *Wallace* v. *Jaffree*. "It is impossible," Justice Rehnquist argued, "to build sound constitutional doctrine upon a mistaken understanding of constitutional history." His conclusion was bluntly to the point: "If a constitutional theory has no basis in the history of the amendment it seeks to interpret, it is difficult to apply and yields unprincipled results."

The point is that the establishment clause of the First Amendment was designed to prohibit Congress from establishing a national church. The belief was that the Constitution should not allow Congress to designate a particular faith or sect as politically above the rest. But to argue, as is popular today, that the amendment demands a strict neutrality between religion and irreligion would strike the founding generation as bizarre. The purpose was to prohibit religious tyranny, not to undermine religion generally.

In considering these areas of adjudication —federalism, criminal law, and religion—it seems fair to conclude that far too many of the court's opinions are, on the whole, more policy choices than articulations of constitutional principle. The voting blocs, the arguments, all reveal a greater allegiance to what the court thinks constitutes sound public policy than a deference to what the Constitution—its text and intention—demand.

It is also safe to say that until there emerges a coherent jurisprudential stance, the work of the court will continue in an *ad hoc* fashion. But that is not to argue for *any* jurisprudence. In my opinion a drift back toward the radical egalitarianism and expansive civil libertarianism of the Warren court would once again be a threat to the notion of limited but energetic government.

What should the court's constitutional jurisprudence actually be? It should be a Jurisprudence of Original Intention. By seeking to judge policies in light of principles, rather than remold principles in light of policies, the court could avoid both the charge of incoherence *and* the charge of being either too conservative or too liberal.

A jurisprudence seriously aimed at the explication of original intention would produce defensible principles of government that would not be tainted by ideological predilection. A Jurisprudence of Original Intention also reflects a deeply rooted commitment to the idea of democracy. The Constitution represents the consent of the governed to the structures and powers of the government. To allow the court to govern simply by what it views at the time as fair and decent, is a scheme of government no longer popular; the idea of democracy has suffered. The permanence of the Constitution is weakened. A Constitution that is viewed as only what the judges say it is, is no longer a constitution in the true sense.

Those who framed the Constitution chose their words carefully; they debated at great length the most minute points. The language they chose meant something. It is incumbent upon the court to determine what that meaning was. This is not a shockingly new theory; nor is it arcane or archaic. Joseph Story, who was in a way a lawyer's Everyman—lawyer, justice, and teacher of law—had a theory of judging that merits reconsideration. Though speaking specifically of the Constitution, his logic reaches to statutory construction as well.

> In construing the Constitution of the United States, we are in the first instance to consider, what are its nature and objects, its scope and design, as apparent from the structure of the instrument, viewed as a whole and also viewed in its component parts. Where its words are plain, clear and determinate, they require no interpretation. . . . Where the words admit of two senses, each of which is conformable to general usage, that sense is to be adopted, which without departing from the literal import of the words, best harmonizes with the nature and objects, the scope and design of the instrument.

A Jurisprudence of Original Intention takes seriously the admonition of Justice Story's friend and colleague, John Marshall, in *Marbury* v. *Madison* (1803) that the Constitution is a limitation on judicial power as well as executive and legislative. That is what Chief Justice Marshall meant in *McCulloch* v. *Maryland* (1819) when he cautioned judges never to forget it is a constitution they are expounding.

.   .   .

The Constitution of the United States

William J. Brennan, Jr.

...It will perhaps not surprise you that the text I have chosen for exploration is the amended Constitution of the United States, which, of course, entrenches the Bill of Rights and the Civil War amendments, and draws sustenance from the bedrock principles of another great text, the Magna Carta. So fashioned, the Constitution embodies the aspiration to social justice, brotherhood, and human dignity that brought this nation into being. The Declaration of Independence, the Constitution and the Bill of Rights solemnly committed the United States to be a country where the dignity and rights of all persons were equal before all authority. In all candor we must concede that part of this egalitarianism in America has been more pretension than realized fact. But we are an aspiring people, a people with faith in progress. Our amended Constitution is the lodestar for our aspirations. Like every text worth reading, it is not crystalline. The phrasing is broad and the limitations of its provisions are not clearly marked. Its majestic generalities and ennobling pronouncements are both luminous and obscure. This ambiguity of course calls forth interpretation, the interaction of reader and text. The encounter with the constitutional text has been, in many senses, my life's work.

My approach to this text may differ from the approach of other participants in this symposium to their texts. Yet such differences may themselves stimulate reflection about what it is we do when we "interpret" a text. Thus I will attempt to elucidate my approach to the text as well as my substantive interpretion.

Perhaps the foremost difference is the fact that my encounters with the constitutional text are not purely or even primarily introspective; the Constitution cannot be for me simply a contemplative haven for private moral reflection. My relation to this great text is inescapably public. This is not to say that my reading of the text is not a personal reading, only that the personal reading perforce occurs in a public context, and is open to critical scrutiny from all quarters.

The Constitution is fundamentally a public text—the monumental charter of a government and a people—and a Justice of the Supreme Court must apply it to resolve public controversies. For, from our beginnings, a most important consequence of the constitutionally created separation of powers

Reprinted from *The Great Debate* (Washington, D.C.: The Federalist Society, 1986), pp. 11, 13–18, 24–25.

has been the American habit, extraordinary to other democracies, of casting social, economic, philosophical and political questions in the form of law suits, in an attempt to secure ultimate resolution by the Supreme Court. In this way, important aspects of the most fundamental issues confronting our democracy may finally arrive in the Supreme Court for judicial determination. Not infrequently, these are the issues upon which contemporary society is most deeply divided. They arouse our deepest emotions. The main burden of my twenty-nine terms on the Supreme Court has thus been to wrestle with the Constitution in this heightened public context, to draw meaning from the text in order to resolve public controversies.

Two other aspects of my relation to this text warrant mention. First, constitutional interpretation for a federal judge is, for the most part, obligatory. When litigants approach the bar of court to adjudicate a constitutional dispute, they may justifiably demand an answer. Judges cannot avoid a definitive interpretation because they feel unable to, or would prefer not to, penetrate to the full meaning of the Constitution's provisions. Unlike literary critics, judges cannot merely savor the tensions or revel in the ambiguities inhering in the text—judges must resolve them.

Second, consequences flow from a Justice's interpretation in a direct and immediate way. A judicial decision respecting the incompatibility of Jim Crow with a constitutional guarantee of equality is not simply a contemplative exercise in defining the shape of a just society. It is an order—supported by the full coercive power of the State—that the present society change in a fundamental aspect. Under such circumstances the process of deciding can be a lonely, troubling experience for fallible human beings conscious that their best may not be adequate to the challenge. We Justices are certainly aware that we are not final because we are infallible; we know that we are infallible only because we are final. One does not forget how much may depend on the decision. More than the litigants may be affected. The course of vital social, economic and political currents may be directed.

These three defining characteristics of my relation to the constitutional text—its public nature, obligatory character, and consequentialist aspect—cannot help but influence the way I read that text. When Justices interpret the Constitution they speak for their community, not for themselves alone. The act of interpretation must be undertaken with full consciousness that it is, in a very real sense, the community's interpretation that is sought. Justices are not platonic guardians appointed to wield authority according to their personal moral predilections. Precisely because coercive force must attend any judicial decision to countermand the will of a contemporary majority, the Justices must render constitutional interpretations that are received as legitimate. The source of legitimacy is, of course, a wellspring of controversy in legal and political circles. At the core of the debate is what the late Yale Law School professor Alexander Bickel labeled "the counter-majoritarian difficulty." Our commitment to self-governance in a representative democracy must be reconciled with vesting in electorally unaccountable Justices the power to invalidate the expressed desires of representative bodies on the ground of inconsistency with higher law. Because judicial power resides in the authority to give meaning to the Constitution, the debate is really a debate about how to read the text, about constraints on what is legitimate interpretation.

There are those who find legitimacy in fidelity to what they call "the intentions of the Framers." In its most doctrinaire incarnation, this view demands that Justices discern exactly what the Framers thought about the question under consideration and simply follow that intention in resolving the case before them. It is a view that feigns self-effacing deference to the specific judgments of those who forged our original social compact. But in truth it is little more than arrogance cloaked as humility. It is arrogant to pretend that from our vantage we can gauge accurately the intent of the Framers on application of principle to specific, contemporary questions. All too often, sources of potential enlightenment such as records of the ratification debates provide sparse or ambiguous evidence of the original intention. Typically, all that can be gleaned is that the Framers themselves did not agree about the application or meaning of particular constitutional provisions, and hid their differences in cloaks of generality. Indeed, it is far from clear whose intention is relevant—that of the drafters, the congressional disputants, or the ratifiers in the states?—or even whether the idea of an original intention is a coherent way of thinking about a jointly drafted document drawing its authority from a general assent of the states. And apart from the problematic nature of the sources, our distance of two centuries cannot but work as a prism refracting all we perceive. One cannot help but speculate that the chorus of lamentations calling for interpretation faithful to "original intention"—and proposing nullification of interpretations that fail this quick litmus test—must inevitably come from persons who have no familiarity with the historical record.

Perhaps most importantly, while proponents of this facile historicism justify it as a depoliticization of the judiciary, the political underpinnings of such a choice should not escape notice. A position that upholds constitutional claims only if they were within the specific contemplation of the Framers in effect establishes a presumption of resolving textual ambiguities against the claim of constitutional right. It is far from clear what justifies such a presumption against claims of right. Nothing intrinsic in the nature of interpretation—if there is such a thing as the "nature" of interpretation—commands such a passive approach to ambiguity. This is a choice no less political than any other; it expresses antipathy to claims of the minority rights against the majority. Those who would restrict claims of right to the values of 1789 specifically articulated in the Constitution turn a blind eye to social progress and eschew adaptation of overarching principles to changes of social circumstance.

Another, perhaps more sophisticated, response to the potential power of judicial interpretation stresses democratic theory: because ours is a govenment of the people's elected representatives, substantive value choices should by and large be left to them. This view emphasizes not the transcendant historical authority of the framers but the predominant contemporary authority of the elected branches of government. Yet it has similar consequences for the nature of proper judicial interpretation. Faith in the majoritarian process counsels restraint. Even under more expansive formulations of this approach, judicial review is appropriate only to the extent of ensuring that our democratic process functions smoothly. Thus, for example, we would protect freedom of speech merely to ensure that the people are heard by their representatives, rather than as a separate, substantive value. When, by contrast, society tosses up to the Supreme Court a dispute that would require invalidation of a legislature's substantive policy choice, the Court generally would stay its hand because the Constitution was meant as a plan of government and not as an embodiment of fundamental substantive values.

The view that all matters of substantive policy should be resolved through the majoritarian process has appeal under some circumstances, but I think it ultimately will not do. Unabashed enshrinement of majority will would permit the imposition of a social caste system or wholesale confiscation of property so long as a majority of the authorized legislative body, fairly elected, approved. Our Constitution could not abide such a situation. It is the very purpose of a Constitution—and particularly of the Bill of Rights—to declare certain values transcendent, beyond the reach of temporary political majorities. The majoritarian process cannot be expected to rectify claims of minority right that arise as a response to the outcomes of that very majoritarian process. As James Madison put it:

> The prescriptions in favor of liberty ought to be levelled against that quarter where the greatest danger lies, namely, that which possesses the highest prerogative of power. But this is not found in either the Executive or Legislative departments of Government, but in the body of the people, operating by the majority against the minority. (1 Annals 437).

Faith in democracy is one thing, blind faith quite another. Those who drafted our Constitution understood the difference. One cannot read the text without admitting that it embodies substantive value choices; it places certain values beyond the power of any legislature. Obvious are the separation of powers; the privilege of the Writ of Habeas Corpus; prohibition of Bills of Attainder and *ex post facto* laws; prohibition of cruel and unusual punishments; the requirement of just compensation for official taking of property; the prohibition of laws tending to establish religion or enjoining the free exercise of religion; and, since the Civil War, the banishment of slavery and official race discrimination. With respect to at least such principles, we simply have not constituted

ourselves as strict utilitarians. While the Constitution may be amended, such amendments require an immense effort by the People as a whole.

To remain faithful to the content of the Constitution, therefore, an approach to interpreting the text must account for the existence of these substantive value choices, and must accept the ambiguity inherent in the effort to apply them to modern circumstances. The Framers discerned fundamental principles through struggles against particular malefactions of the Crown; the struggle shapes the particular contours of the articulated principles. But our acceptance of the fundamental principles has not and should not bind us to those precise, at times anachronistic, contours. Successive generations of Americans have continued to respect these fundamental choices and adopt them as their own guide to evaluating quite different historical practices. Each generation has the choice to overrule or add to the fundamental principles enunciated by the Framers; the Constitution can be amended or it can be ignored. Yet with respect to its fundamental principles, the text has suffered neither fate. Thus, if I may borrow the words of an esteemed predecessor, Justice Robert Jackson, the burden of judicial interpretation is to translate "the majestic generalities of the Bill of Rights, conceived as part of the pattern of liberal government in the eighteenth century, into concrete restraints on officials dealing with the problems of the twentieth century." *Board of Education* v. *Barnette*, [319 U.S. 624, 639 (1943),].

We current Justices read the Constitution in the only way that we can: as Twentieth Century Americans. We look to the history of the time of framing and to the intervening history of interpretation. But the ultimate question must be, what do the words of the text mean in our time. For the genius of the Constitution rests not in any static meaning it might have had in a world that is dead and gone, but in the adaptability of its great principles to cope with current problems and current needs. What the constitutional fundamentals meant to the wisdom of other times cannot be their measure to the vision of our time. Similarly, what those fundamentals mean for us, our descendants will learn, cannot be the measure to the vision of their time. This realization is not, I assure you, a novel one of my own creation. Permit me to quote from one of the opinions of our Court, *Weems* v. *United States*, [217 U.S. 349,] written nearly a century ago:

> Time works changes, brings into existence new conditions and purposes. Therefore, a principle to be vital must be capable of wider application than the mischief which gave it birth. This is peculiarly true of constitutions. They are not ephemeral enactments, designed to meet passing occasions. They are, to use the words of Chief Justice John Marshall, 'designed to approach immortality as nearly as human institutions can approach it.' The future is their care and provision for events of good and bad tendencies of which no prophesy can be made. In the application of a constitution, therefore, our contemplation cannot be only of what has been, but of what may be.

Interpretation must account for the transformative purpose of the text. Our Constitution was not intended to preserve a preexisting society but to make a new one, to put in place new principles that the prior political community had not sufficiently recognized. Thus, for example, when we interpret the Civil War Amendments to the charter—abolishing slavery, guaranteeing blacks equality under law, and guaranteeing blacks the right to vote—we must remember that those who put them in place had no desire to enshrine the status quo. Their goal was to make over their world, to eliminate all vestige of slave caste. . . .

If we are to be as a shining city upon a hill, it will be because of our ceaseless pursuit of the constitutional ideal of human dignity. For the political and legal ideals that form the foundation of much that is best in American institutions—ideals jealously preserved and guarded throughout our history—still form the vital force in creative political thought and activity within the nation today. As we adapt our institutions to the ever-changing conditions of national and international life, those ideals of human dignity—liberty and justice for all individuals—will continue to inspire and guide us because they are entrenched in our Constitution. The Constitution with its Bill of Rights thus has a bright future, as well as a glorious past, for its spirit is inherent in the aspirations of our people.

The Supreme Court's Role in National Policy-Making

Robert A. Dahl

...In the course of its one hundred and sixty-seven years, in eighty-five cases, the Court has struck down ninety-four different provisions of federal law as unconstitutional, and by interpretation it has significantly modifed a good many more. It might be argued...that in all or in a very large number of these cases the Court was...defending the legitimate constitutional rights of some minority against a "tyrannical" majority. There are, however, some exceedingly serious difficulties with this interpretation of the Court's activities.

To begin with, it is difficult to determine when any particular Court decision has been at odds with the preferences of a national majority. Adequate evidence is not available, for scientific opinion polls are of relatively recent origin; and, strictly speaking, national elections cannot be interpreted as more than an indication of the first choice of about 40 to 60 per cent of the adult population for certain candidates for public office. The connection between preferences among candidates and preferences among alternative public policies is highly tenuous. On the basis of an election, it is almost never possible to adduce whether a majority does or does not support one of two or more *policy* alternatives about which candidates are divided. For the greater part of the Court's history, then, there is simply no way of establishing with any high degree of confidence whether a given alternative was or was not supported by a majority or a minority of adults or even of voters.

In the absence of relatively direct information, we are thrown back on indirect tests. The ninety-four provisions of federal law that have been declared unconstitutional were, of course, initially passed by majorities of those voting in the Senate and in the House. They also had the President's formal approval. One could, therefore, speak of a majority of those voting in the House and Senate, together with the President, as a "law-making majority." It is not easy to determine whether a law-making majority actually coincides with the preferences of a majority of American adults, or even with the preferences of a

PLURALIST DEMOCRACY IN THE UNITED STATES, Robert Dahl. © 1967 Rand McNally & Company, Chicago, pp. 155–164. Reprinted by permission of author. This excerpt is an updated version of "Decision-Making in a Democracy: The Supreme Court as a National Policy Maker," Journal of Public Law, Vol. 6 (1957), 279–295.

majority of that half of the adult population which, on the average, votes in congressional elections. Such evidence as we have from opinion polls suggests that Congress is not markedly out of line with public opinion, or at any rate with such public opinion as there is after one discards the answers of people who fall into the category, often large, labeled "no response" or "don't know." If we may, on these somewhat uncertain grounds, take a law-making majority as equivalent to a "national majority," then it is possible to test the hypothesis that the Supreme Court is shield and buckler for minorities against tyrannical national majorities.

Under any reasonable assumptions about the nature of the political process, it would appear to be somewhat naive to assume that the Supreme Court either would or could play the role of Galahad. Over the whole history of the Court, one new Justice has been appointed on the average of every twenty-three months. Thus a President can expect to appoint two new Justices during one term of office; and if this were not enough to tip the balance on a normally divided Court, he would be almost certain to succeed in two terms. For example, Hoover made three appointments; Roosevelt, nine; Truman, four; Eisenhower, five; Kennedy in his brief tenure, two. Presidents are not famous for appointing Justices hostile to their own views on public policy; nor could they expect to secure confirmation of a man whose stance on key questions was flagrantly at odds with that of the dominant majority in the Senate. Typically, Justices are men who, prior to appointment, have engaged in public life and have committed themselves publicly on the great questions of the day. As the late Mr. Justice Frankfurter pointed out, a surprisingly large proportion of the Justices, particularly of the great Justices who have left their stamp upon the decisions of the Court, have had little or no prior judicial experience. Nor have the Justices—certainly not the great Justices—been timid men with a passion for anonymity. Indeed, it is not too much to say that if Justices were appointed primarily for their 'judicial' qualities without regard to their basic attitudes on fundamental questions of public policy, the Court could not play the influential role in the American political system that it does in reality play.

It is reasonable to conclude, then, that the policy views dominant on the Court will never be out of line for very long with the policy views dominant among the law-making majorities of the United States. And it would be most unrealistic to suppose that the Court would, for more than a few years at most, stand against any major alternatives sought by a law-making majority. The judicial agonies of the New Deal will, of course, come quickly to mind; but President Franklin D. Roosevelt's difficulties with the Court were truly exceptional. Generalizing over the whole history of the Court, one can say that the chances are about two out of five that a President will make one appointment to the Court in less than a year, two out of three that he will make one within two years, and three out of four that he will make one within three years (Table 1). President Roosevelt had unusually bad luck: he had to wait four years for his first appointment; the odds against this long interval are about five to one. With average luck, his battle with the Court would never have occurred; even as it was, although his "court-packing" proposal did formally fail, by the end of his second term in 1940, Roosevelt had appointed five new Justices and he gained three more the following year: Thus by the end of 1941, Mr. Justice Roberts was the only remaining holdover from the pre-Roosevelt era.

It is to be expected, then, that the Court would be least successful in blocking a determined and persistent law-making majority

TABLE 1
The Interval Between Appointments to the Supreme Court, 1789–1965

Interval in Years	Number of Appointments	Percentage of Total	Cumulative Percentage
Less than 1 year	38	41	41
1	22	24	65
2	10	11	76
3	9	10	86
4	6	6.5	92.5
5	6	6.5	99
12	1	1	100
Total	92	100	100

NOTE:
The table excludes six Justices appointed in 1789. It includes only Justices who were appointed and confirmed and served on the Court. All data through 1964 are from *Congress and the Nation*, 1452–1453.

on a major policy. Conversely, the Court is most likely to succeed against "weak" law-making majorities: transient majorities in Congress, fragile coalitions, coalitions weakly united upon a policy of subordinate importance or congressional coalitions no longer in existence, as might be the case when a law struck down by the Court had been passed several years earlier.

An examination of the cases in which the Court has held federal legislation unconstitutional confirms these expectations. Over the whole history of the Court, about half the decisions have been rendered more than four years after the legislation was passed (Table 2). Thus the congressional majorities that passed these laws went through at least two elections before the decision was handed down and may well have weakened or disappeared in the interval. In these cases, then, the Court was probably not directly challenging current law-making majorities.

Of the twenty-four laws held unconstitutional within two years, eleven were measures enacted in the early years of the New Deal. Indeed, New Deal measures comprise nearly a third of all the legislation that has ever been declared unconstitutional within four years of enactment.

It is illuminating to examine the cases where the Court has acted on legislation within four years of enactment—where the presumption is, that is to say, that the law-making majority is not a dead one. Of the twelve New Deal cases, two were, from a policy point of view, trivial; and two although perhaps not trivial, were of minor importance to the New Deal program. A fifth involved the NRA, which was to expire within three weeks of the decision. Insofar as the unconstitutional provisions allowed "codes of fair competition" to be established by industrial groups, it is fair to say that President Roosevelt and his advisors were relieved by the Court's decision of a policy that they had come to find increasingly embarrassing. In view of the tenacity with which FDR held to his major program, there can hardly be any doubt that, had he wanted to pursue the policy objective involved in the NRA codes, as he did for example with the labor provisions, he would

TABLE 2
Supreme Court Cases Holding Federal Legislation Unconstitutional: By Time Between Legislation and Decision

Number of Years	Supreme Court Cases Involving:					
	New Deal Legislation		Other		All Federal Legislation	
	N.	%	N.	%	N.	%
2 or less	11	92	13	17.5	24	28
3–4	1	8	13	17.5	14	16
5–8	0	0	20	27	20	24
9–12	0	0	10	14	10	12
13–16	0	0	7	10	7	8
17–20	0	0	2	3	2	2
21 or more	0	0	8	11	8	10
Total	12	100%	73	100%	85	100%

not have been stopped by the Court's special theory of the Constitution. As to the seven other cases, it is entirely correct to say, I think, that whatever some of the eminent Justices might have thought during their fleeting moments of glory, they did not succeed in interposing a barrier to the achievement of the objectives of the legislation; and in a few years most of the constitutional dogma on which they rested their opposition to the New Deal had been unceremoniously swept under the rug.

The remainder of the thirty-eight cases where the Court has declared legislation unconstitutional within four years of enactment tend to fall into two rather distinct groups: those involving legislation that could

reasonably be regarded as important *from the point of view of the law-making majority* [15 cases] and those involving minor legislation [11 cases].... We would expect that cases involving major legislative policy would be propelled to the Court much more rapidly than cases involving minor policy, and, as the table ... shows, this is in fact what happens (Table 3).

Thus a law-making majority with major policy objectives in mind usually has an opportunity to seek ways of overcoming the Court's veto. It is an interesting and highly significant fact that Congress and the President do generally succeed in overcoming a hostile Court on major policy issues (Table 4). It is particularly instructive to examine the

TABLE 3
Number of Cases Involving Legislative Policy Other Than Those Arising Under New Deal Legislation Holding Legislation Unconstitutional Within Four Years After Enactment

Interval in Years	Major Policy	Minor Policy	Total
2 or less	11	2	13
3 to 4	4	9	13
Total	15	11	26

TABLE 4

Type of Congressional Action Following Supreme Court Decisions Holding Legislation Unconstitutional within Four Years after Enactment (Other Than New Deal Legislation)

Congressional Action	Major Policy	Minor Policy	Total
Reverses Court's Policy	10[a]	2[d]	12
Changes Own Policy	2[b]	0	2
None	0	8[e]	8
Unclear	3[c]	1[f]	4
Total	15	11	26

[a] *Pollock* v. *Farmers's Loan & Trust Co.*, 157 U.S. 429 (1895); *Employers' Liability Cases*, 207 U.S. 463 (1908); *Keller* v. *United States*, 213 U.S. 138 (1909), *Hammer* v. *Dagenhart*, 247 U.S. 251 (1918); *Bailey* v. *Drexel Furniture Co.*, 259 U.S. 20 (1922); *Trusler* v. *Crooks*, 269 U.S. 475 (1926); *Hill* v. *Wallace*, 259 U.S. 44 (1922); *Knickerbocker Ice Co.* v. *Stewart*, 253 U.S. 149 (1920); *Washington* v. *Dawson & Co.*, 264 U.S. 219 (1924).
Washington v. *Dawson & Co.*, 264 U.S. 219 (1924).
[b] *Ex parte Garland*, 4 Wall. (U.S.) 333 (1867); *United States* v. *Klein*, 13 Wall. (U.S.) 128 (1872).
[c] *United States* v. *Cohen Grocery Co.*, 255 U.S. 81 (1921); *Weeds, Inc.* v. *United States*, 255 U.S. 109 (1921); *Eisner* v. *Macomber*, 252 U.S. 189 (1920).
[d] *Gordon* v. *United States*, 2 Wall. (U.S.) 561 (1865); *Evans* v. *Core*, 253 U.S. 245 (1920).
[e] *United States* v. *Dewitt*, 9 Wall. (U.S.) 41 (1870); *Monongahela Navigation Co.* v. *United States*, 148 U.S. 312 (1893): *Wong Wing* v. *United States*, 163 U.S. 228 (1896), *Fairbank* v. *United States*, 181 U.S. 283 (1901); *Rasmussen* v. *United States*, 197 U.S. 516 (1905); *Muskrat* v. *United States*, 219 U.S. 346 (1911); *Choate* v. *Trapp*, 224 U.S. 665 (1912); *United States* v. *Lovett*, 328 U.S. 303 (1946).
[f] *Untermyer* v. *Anderson*, 276 U.S. 440 (1928).

cases involving major policy. In two cases involving legislation enacted by radical Republican Congresses to punish supporters of the Confederacy during the Civil War, the Court faced a rapidly crumbling majority whose death knell as an effective national force was sounded after the election of 1876. Three cases are difficult to classify and I have labeled them "unclear." Of these, two were decisions made in 1921 involving a 1919 amendment to the Lever Act to control prices. The legislation was important, and the provision in question was clearly struck down, but the Lever Act terminated three days after the decision and Congress did not return to the subject of price control until the Second World War, when it experienced no constitutional difficulties arising from these cases (which were primarily concerned with the lack of an ascertainable standard of guilt). The third case in this category suc-

cessfully eliminated stock dividends from the scope of the Sixteenth Amendment, although a year later Congress enacted legislation taxing the actual income from such stocks.

The remaining ten cases were ultimately followed by a reversal of the actual policy results of the Court's action, although not necessarily of the specific constitutional interpretation. In four cases, the policy consequences of the Court's decision were overcome in less than a year. The other six required a long struggle. Workmen's compensation for longshoremen and harbor workers was invalidated by the Court in 1920; in 1922, Congress passed a new law which was, in its turn, knocked down by the Court in 1924; in 1927, Congress passed a third law, which was finally upheld in 1932. The notorious income tax cases of 1895 were first somewhat narrowed by the Court itself; the Sixteenth Amendment was recommended by

TABLE 5
Type of Congressional Action after Supreme Court Decisions Holding Legislation Unconstitutional within Four Years after Enactment (Including New Deal Legislation)

Congressional Action	Major Policy	Minor Policy	Total
Reverses Court's Policy	17	2	19
None	0	12	12
Other	6*	1	7
Total	23	15	38

* In addition to the actions in Table 4 under "Changes Own Policy" and "Unclear," this figure includes the NRA legislation affected by the *Schechter Poultry* case.

President Taft in 1909 and was ratified in 1913, some eighteen years after the Court's decisions. The two child labor cases represent the most effective battle ever waged by the Court against legislative policy-makers. The original legislation outlawing child labor, based on the commerce clause, was passed in 1916 as part of Wilson's New Freedom. Like Franklin Roosevelt later, Wilson was somewhat unlucky in his Supreme Court appointments; he made only three appointments during his eight years, and one of these was wasted, from a policy point of view, on Mr. Justice McReynolds. Had McReynolds voted "right," the subsequent struggle over the problem of child labor need not have occurred, for the decision in 1918 was by a Court divided five to four, McReynolds voting with the majority. Congress moved at once to circumvent the decision by means of the tax power, but in 1922, the Court blocked that approach. In 1924, Congress returned to the engagement with a constitutional amendment that was rapidly endorsed by a number of state legislatures before it began to meet so much resistance in the states remaining that the enterprise miscarried. In 1938, under a second reformist President, new legislation was passed twenty-two years after the first; this a Court with a New Deal majority finally

accepted in 1941, and thereby brought to an end a battle that had lasted a full quarter-century.

The entire record of the duel between the Court and the law-making majority, in cases where the Court has held legislation unconstitutional within four years after enactment, is summarized in Table 5.

A consideration of the role of the Court as defender of minorities, then, suggests the following conclusions:

First, judicial review is surely inconsistent with democracy to the extent that the Court simply protects the policies of minorities from reversal or regulation by national majorities acting through regular law-making procedures.

Second, however, the frequency and nature of appointments to the Court inhibits it from playing this role, or otherwise protecting minorities against national law-making majorities. National law-making majorities —i.e., coalitions of the President and a majority of each house of Congress— generally have their way.

Third, although the court evidently cannot hold out indefinitely against a persistent law-making majority, in a very small number of important cases it has succeeded in delaying the application of a policy for as long as twenty-five years.

The Supreme Court and National Policy Making

Jonathan D. Casper

The role of the Supreme Court in national policy making has long been a subject of debate among students of the Amercian legal system and of democratic theory. The relative influence of the Court vis-à-vis other political institutions and the implications of its activities for principles of majority rule and democracy have been central issues in this discussion. One of the most influential treatments of this issue in recent years is the argument advanced by Robert A. Dahl in 1957.[1] Dahl offers a sophisticated "political" view of the role played by the Court, arguing that it is an active participant in the ruling national coalitions which dominate American politics but that the Court does not perform the task of protecting fundamental minority rights that is often attributed to it. The Court, like other political institutions, says Dahl, is a member of such ruling coalitions, and as such its decisions are typically supportive of the policies emerging from other political institutions. Dahl's account has endured so well because it frames the questions precisely and brings to

bear a carefully selected body of evidence upon a dispute long characterized by anecdote and example.

I argue here that Dahl's account is not adequate for understanding the role of the Supreme Court in policy making. Consideration of the way he interprets his own evidence and of other relevant evidence that is excluded from his analysis suggests that the Court participates more significantly in national policy making than Dahl's argument suggests....

THE SUPREME COURT AND FEDERAL LEGISLATION, 1958–1974

Dahl's article was published in 1957, appearing at the end of a decade that had seen one of our periodic episodes of national political repression. Fear of internal subversion by Communists and fellow-travelers had produced not only intense public concern but a variety of federal and state programs aimed at control of the thought, expression, and behavior of allegedly subversive elements in our society. The rulings of the Supreme Court in this period did not mark it as a bastion of

Reprinted by permission from *American Political Science Review* 70 (1976), 50–63. Most footnotes have been omitted.

individual rights standing against a fearful and repressive national majority. The Court vacillated on the civil liberties issues raised by the loyalty-security programs and generally placed the imprimatur of legitimacy upon a variety of constitutionally questionable governmental activities (e.g., prosecutions under the Smith Act, employee loyalty-security screening programs, legislative investigations.) In this partly salient issue area, then, the Supreme Court did follow the deferential path suggested by Dahl's analysis.

Since then, we have witnessed the work of the Warren Court and are currently in the midst of the emergence of the Burger Court. The Warren Court, by general reputation at least, was quite different from most of its predecessors. Indeed, one associates with it precisely the characteristics that Dahl found lacking in the Supreme Court—activism and influence in national policy making and protection of fundamental rights of minorities against tyrannical or indifferent majorities. The first step, then, in examining Dahl's thesis is to look at what has happened since he wrote. Do events since that date suggest the possibility of a different pattern of Supreme Court participation in policy making?

With respect to the dimensions of frequency, decisiveness, and direction, the data since 1957 are somewhat mixed. During this period, the Supreme Court declared 32 provisions of federal law unconstitutional in 28 cases. In the entire previous 167-year period, 86 provisions had been declared unconstitutional in 78 cases. Putting the two sets together, we note that more than a quarter of all cases involving a declaration of unconstitutionality (28 of 106) have occurred since 1957. In terms of frequency, the Supreme Court proved more active in recent years than it typically had been in the past.

But Dahl's argument does not rest simply upon the frequency of Supreme Court holdings that federal statutes are unconstitutional. Since he focuses upon the relation of policy emerging from the Court to policy emerging from the "lawmaking majority," particular attention is paid to the period of time that occurs between passage of legislation and the declaration that it is unconstitutional. Dahl lays great stress upon declarations of unconstitutionality occurring within four years of enactment—"where the presumption is . . . that the lawmaking majority is not necessarily a dead one." Table 1 reproduces his findings about the time intervals between enactment and Court decisions and also brings them up to date. Recent decisions seem to follow the same pattern as before—the bulk of cases involve a Court decision somewhat removed in time from the passage of the legislation. In sum, the data suggest that although the period since 1957 did involve a substantial amount of Supreme Court activity in declaring legislation unconstitutional, only about a fifth of the cases involved clashes between what Dahl would call "live" national majorities and a Court bent upon pursuing other policy alternatives.

Dahl also pays attention to the decisiveness dimension—what happened *after* the Court declared laws unconstitutional within four years of enactment. Especially in matters involving what he calls "major policy," Dahl found that the Court policy has typically been reversed, either by legislation, constitutional amendment, or a change of heart by the Court itself. In the six cases during the 1958–74 period in which the Court held legislation unconstitutional within four years after passage, one seems clearly "major" and was reversed by a quickly passed constitutional amendment (*Oregon* v. *Mitchell*,[2] holding that the provision of the 1970 Voting Rights Act lowering the voting age in state and local elections to 18 was beyond the power of Congress). Since Dahl does not offer a definition of "major" and "minor"

TABLE 1
Cases in Which Federal Legislation Was Held Unconstitutional, Arranged by Time Intervals between Legislation and Decision

Time Interval (in years)	1789–1957[a]	1958–1974	1789–1974
2 or less	30%	7%	25%
3 to 4	18	14	17
5 to 8	24	11	20
9 to 12	11	21	13
13 to 16	6	21	10
17 to 20	1	7	3
21 or more	10	18	12
	100%	99%	100%
	(N = 78)	(N = 28)	(N = 106)

[a] See Dahl, p. 290.

policy, it is difficult to classify the other five cases. They involved the residency requirement for welfare recipients in the District of Columbia, military trials for civilian dependents and employees stationed abroad with servicemen and a form of censorship of mail from Communist countries.[3] The Court's decision was not followed by reversal or a change of mind in any of these cases. The same was true with the 22 cases holding federal statutory provisions unconstitutional more than four years after enactment—all were followed either by positive congressional acceptance (e.g., amending the law to conform to the Court's holding or formal repeal) or by acquiescence. Thus, the evidence appears to support the view that the Court intervened decisively in these 22 cases holding federal legislation unconstitutional. In the next section, however, we will discuss a peculiar feature of the way in which Dahl treats his evidence—he considers the decisiveness dimension only for cases occurring within four years of enactment. Those occurring more than four years after enactment are excluded on the ground that we cannot be sure that the law-making majority continues

to be "alive" and hence that the clash of preferences required to judge relative influence exists. As a result, it is not clear how to interpret the 22 cases during the 1958–1974 period. For some—particularly those dealing with internal security matters—the view that the law-making majority was no longer "alive" seems plausible; for others—those dealing with the administration of justice, citizenship rights, and welfare programs—an account attributing influence to the Court seems more plausible.

Thus, because of the nature of Dahl's coding rules, evaluation of the Court's recent work on the decisiveness dimension is difficult. Given that there has been only one instance of reversal in 28 cases, one must conclude either (1) that the ambiguity in Dahl's coding rules makes the issue unanswerable for the recent period (and, it is argued in the next section, for the period Dahl himself covers); or (2) that the recent experience does not support the Dahl thesis.

On the dimension of direction, the pattern of decisions since 1958 is clearly at variance with Dahl's findings. With the exception of *Oregon* v. *Mitchell*, all of the 28 decisions were based upon provisions of the Bill of Rights (primarily the First and Fifth Amendments) and the Fourteenth Amendment. In addition to furthering the interests of all in the society in greater freedom of expression, equal application of the laws, and procedural fairness, the decisions had special impact upon such groups as aliens, communists and other alleged subversives, criminal defendants, war protesters, and poor people. The Court attempted to extend to these groups rights and privileges that the law-making majorities had not chosen to extend. For example, a series of decisions struck down statutes that took away citizenship for such activities as voting in foreign elections, desertion from armed forces, leaving the country to avoid military service, and extended residence in country of origin. By the same token, the heart of the McCarran Act—its registration provisions and restrictions upon employment in sensitive industries for members of Communist action organizations—was struck down on Fifth and First Amendment grounds.

We have now examined the recent decisions in terms of Dahl's three dimensions. The results, while not wholly conclusive, do not tend to support Dahl's thesis. The Supreme Court has, in recent years, struck down federal legislation more frequently than in the past. The Court's decisions, with one exception, were not met with reversal by legislation, constitutional amendment, or a reversal by the Court itself (though a few have occurred sufficiently recently that this outcome may still occur). By the same token, however, the bulk of the decisions did not involve legislation passed shortly before the Court intervened, so one cannot, under Dahl's rules, be sure that the lawmaking majority on the issue was still alive. Finally, in terms of direction, the recent cases demonstrate a concern for and protection of basic liberties and rights of minorities that is

different from the picture Dahl draws from past cases. With the exception of *Oregon* v. *Mitchell*, none can be adequately interpreted as protecting the privileged at the expense of the poor or a majority at the expense of an insular minority.

It would be somewhat improbable—in either a statistical or substantive sense—for the Court in 16 years to erase a pattern that had stood for nearly 170 years before. My updating of Dahl's argument does not render his conclusions invalid or totally inapplicable to more recent events. By the same token, recent experience does suggest that the Court may operate differently from the way in which Dahl suggests it has and, even more important, from the way he suggests it must.

THE EVIDENCE CONSIDERED

One of the most appealing aspects of Dahl's argument is his careful specification and gathering of evidence. In dealing with an issue that has long been the subject of discussion and argument based upon impression and example, Dahl offers a carefully developed specification of the question and of the evidence that he believes is required for an informed resolution of the conflicting views that have been offered. Yet analysis of what Dahl has done and what he has not done reveals problems both in his mode of analysis and his conclusions. The issues I wish to raise in this section deal with both the way in which he treats his own evidence and with relevant evidence that is excluded from his analysis.

Dahl considers only cases in which federal legislation has been declared unconstitutional, and offers two justifications for casting his evidentiary net in this way. The first centers around the proposition that relative influence in policy making can be determined only when there are disagreements among participants[4] and upon his selection of the "lawmaking majority" as the most useful criterion for majority preferences. The second is based upon the assertion that it is *national* (for which he substitutes *federal*) issues that defenders of the importance of the Court in policy making have in mind....

Both of these justifications are plausible, but they produce a very narrow evidentiary net. Later in this section, I shall suggest a variety of relevant evidence that is excluded. First, I shall discuss the way in which Dahl analyzes the data that he does utilize.

Dahl's Evidence and Coding Rules

Dahl asks three questions about Supreme Court decisions declaring federal legislation unconstitutional: what has been their frequency, their decisiveness, and their direction? In analyzing the cases to determine whether they support the view that the Court plays an influential role in national policy making, he relies almost exclusively upon the decisiveness dimension. Thus, in dealing with two typical sequences of events, he codes them as follows on the dimension of relative influence of Court and law-making majority:

Type I (Court Influential)

1. Law-making majority acts
2. Court reverses policy within 4 years
3. Court's policy stands

Thirty-eight of the 78 cases he discovered fell into one of these two categories, and, of these, 19 fell into what I shall call Type II (law-making majority influential). Moreover, applying a distinction between what he calls "major policy" and "minor policy" cases, 17 of 23 "major policy" cases fell into Type II.

He takes special note of the fact that in some of these Type II situations the overriding of the Court's policy has taken a period of many years (e.g., those dealing with child labor legislation, the federal income tax, and workman's compensation for longshoremen). But his analysis of the decisiveness dimension concludes that, particularly in cases involving "major policy" issues, the Court has not generally succeeded in resisting the law-making majority. This finding is the linchpin for his conclusion that the Court does not play the significant role in national policy making that many of its defenders have suggested.

Type II (Law-making Majority Influential)

1. Law-making majority acts
2. Court reverses policy within 4 years
3. Court's policy reversed

Yet Dahl considers the decisiveness dimension *only for cases in which the Court declares federal legislation unconstitutional within four years of the enactment of the statute*. What of the forty cases in which the Court's decision came more than four years after enactment? His analysis of this group of cases—which comprises more than half of his data—is restricted to a discussion of the *direction* of the Court's policy. He notes that the bulk of the Court decisions were neither based upon provisions of the Bill of Rights nor protective of fundamental rights of minorities. He provides neither data nor discussion of the decisiveness of these decisions.

Dahl's reasons for this approach are discussed only casually. He obliquely asserts that in situations involving a period of more than four years between enactment and Court decision, the law-making majority cannot be assumed to be still viable, and hence we cannot judge relative influence. For example, he introduces his discussion of what

I call here "Type I" and "Type II" cases (declarations of unconstitutionality *within* four years) by saying that in these cases "the presumption is...that the lawmaking majority is not necessarily a dead one." In his discussion of the cases that occurred more than four years after enactment (what I will call Type III), he asks, "Do we have evidence in these [cases] that the Court has protected fundamental or natural rights and liberties against the *dead hand of some past tyranny* by the lawmakers?" If more than four years have passed, then, we lack the evidence necessary to judge relative influence.

Type IIIa

1. Law-making majority acts
2. Court reverses policy more than 4 years later
3. Court's policy stands

There is logic to this argument, but it has implications that are largely unexamined. Not only do we lack data relevant to assessing the decisiveness of Court action in nearly half the cases, but the logic of Dahl's argument seems to load the dice strongly against the possibility of discovering influence by the Court if we *did* gather such data. Consider the following sequences of events:

Type IIIb

1. Law-making majority acts
2. Court reverses policy more than 4 years later
3. Court's policy reversed

Common sense would suggest that Type IIIb is one in which the law-making majority should be judged to have been influential. By the same token, Type IIIa is one in which the Court ought to be judged to have exercised influence. Assume, for example, that the Court declares an act of Congress uncon-

stitutional more than four years after its enactment. Assume that there is no move to reverse the Court or that there is a move to reverse the decision by further legislation or a constitutional amendment but that such an effort is defeated. What are we to make of the relative influence of the Court under such circumstances? The Court appears to have played a decisive role: without its intervention, the original policy would presumably have been continued. Yet Dahl's coding scheme asserts that the law-making majority was "dead" by the time the Court acted and hence we cannot judge relative influence (and cannot conclude that the Court has intervened in an important fashion). If we did gather data on cases occurring more than four years after enactment and most of them fell into Type IIIb—if the bulk of such decisions were reversed by the law-making majority—it would be reasonable to conclude that they, like those of Type II, support Dahl's conclusion that the Court has not been able to intervene decisively against the law-making majority. But suppose most of them fell into Type IIIa? Dahl seems to assert that this would not be evidence for decisive intervention by the Court because we cannot assume that the law-making majority is still viable. Under such a view the Court *cannot* be judged to be influential in circumstances that compose more than half of his evidence. If the Court's policy is reversed, it has clearly not been influential; if the Court's policy stands without discussion or is debated but not reversed, again the Court has not been influential. With such coding rules, heads and the law-making majority wins; tails and the Court loses.

This feature may assume increasing importance as the workload of the Court becomes heavier. The time required for the typical case to get to the Supreme Court for resolution is now on the order of two to three years and seems to be growing. As a result, the probability that an issue will reach the Court in time to fall within the category when we can, under Dahl's rules, assess relative influence, is decreasing.

In sum, more than half the cases Dahl dicovered fall into a category in which under his coding rules it is not possible to conclude that the Court (or law-making majority) has been influential. Not only does he fail to provide the relevant data, but he seems tacitly to assert that if such data were gathered and appeared to indicate decisive interventions by the Court (Type IIIa), such data would not be interpreted in this fashion. This feature of his treatment of the evidence suggests that the conclusions based upon his analysis, though by no means disproved, are potentially a product of an asymmetry in the coding rules as well as of the nature of the evidence itself.

THE EVIDENCE EXCLUDED

Dahl limits his consideration to cases in which the Court held federal legislation unconstitutional. Yet cases involving tests of constitutionality of federal legislation compose only one segment of the work of the Court. Two other types of activities also stand out as particularly important arenas in which the Court contributes to national policy making. The first deals with statutory construction and the second with federal constitutional issues arising out of state and local legislation or practice.

Statutory Construction

The Court is frequently called upon to interpret the meaning of federal statutes, and in the course of doing so, important policy choices must be made. If we adopt for the moment the notion that influence in policy making is most accurately judged in situa-tions in which various participants conflict with one another, it is clear that the interpretations that are made by the Court—even when they are based on "legislative intent"—are often quite different from those that members of Congress and the President had in mind when the legislation was passed. The Court's doctrine that it will, if at all possible, interpret a statute in such a way as to "save" it from being declared unconstitutional means that the Court will often significantly twist and change the ostensible provisions of a statute. Thus, in interpreting statutes the Court often makes important policy choices, and these choices are at least arguably quite contrary to the preferences of the law-making majority that passed the legislation. The more influence the Court exercises by virtue of statutory construction, the less influence it will appear to have in terms of Dahl's coding rules. When the Court "saves" a law by interpreting it rather than declaring it unconstitutional, its contribution to the course of public policy is excluded from consideration under Dahl's rules. . . .

Recent years have seen a variety of . . . instances of important policy making by the Court in the context of statutory construction. The extension of conscientious objector status to those without formal religious training, restrictions upon the use of delinquency provisions against opponents of the Vietnam War, restrictions upon residency requirements for welfare recipients, limitation upon the power to use surveillance techniques without a warrant, elimination of the "man-in-the-house" rule for welfare recipients, and freedom for broadcasters to refuse to sell air time to individuals and groups wishing to speak out on public issues have all been based wholly or in important measure upon interpretations of various federal statutes.

In some of the examples cited, especially those in which attempts by Congress to reverse the interpretation offered by the Court failed to pass, the mode of Dahl's analysis might suggest that the law-making majority was no longer viable, and hence the influence of the Court not significant. Yet this argument has the peculiar implication discussed above: if the Court acts and Congress overrides, then the Court has not been influential; yet if the Court acts and Congress *fails* to override, then again, the Court has not been influential for we assume the law-making majority no longer exists.

In sum, then, one must consider the work of the Court in the area of statutory construction in any discussion of its role in policy making. Dahl's exclusion of this activity in his consideration of the role of the Court constitutes a serious omission, and its inclusion will significantly increase the scope of Court influence that one is likely to observe.

The State and Local Cases

The second major area of the Court's work that is excluded from Dahl's analysis involves constitutional issues arising in cases involving state and local statutes or practice. As suggested above, this exclusion is justified on the grounds that we lack evidence about the preferences of the lawmaking majority in such cases and that these cases have not been typically cited by defenders of the Court as the basis of their view that the Court plays a significant role in national policy making. Although there are, to be sure, difficulties in establishing the preferences of the national majority in these cases, a review of them suggests that many do indeed involve the Court in important issues of national policy.

To use the schematic device introduced above, the state and local cases deal with situations in which the Court may be conceived of as speaking first and in which the law-making majority is placed in the position

of responding to the policy promulgated by the Court. Applying the type of coding rules that Dahl follows, one might code the following sequences of events in terms of relative influence:

Type IV (Law-making Majority Influential)

1. Court promulgates policy
2. Law-making majority reverses policy
3. Law-making majority's policy stands

The decision in *Chisholm* v. *Georgia*[5] asserting federal jurisdiction in diversity suits against state governments and the subsequent passage of the Eleventh Amendment is an example of a Type IV sequence.

Type V situations are more significant for our purposes. Here the Court speaks "first," and its policy is not followed by reversal by the law-making majority. In the various cases discussed below, this appears to have been the pattern followed, despite frequent attempts at reversal by legislation or constitutional amendment. After a brief review of these cases, we shall return to the problem of whether they are consistent with the argument that Dahl presents and what they suggest about the role of the Court in national policy making.

In the nineteenth century, a long line of important Supreme Court decisions dealt with the development of interstate commerce and relations between the national and state governments. Cases like *McCulloch* v. *Maryland*,[6] *Gibbons* v. *Ogden*,[7] and *Cooley* v. *Board of Wardens*[8] are merely the landmarks in a gradual development of a set of rules designed to produce a national government and economy. In citing the power of Congress via the supremacy and interstate commerce clauses, the Court was not simply legitimizing assertions of power by the national government via-à-vis the states but took the initiative in offering its own theory of the nature of the union and of the most satisfactory distribution of powers among the various levels of government. Such cases are excluded from Dahl's analysis.

In the area of individual rights and liberties during the second half of the twentieth century, the contributions of the Court are equally striking. A simple catalogue of the issue areas in which the Court has become involved suggests the breadth of its contributions to national policy that emerged in the context of state and local cases.

In the area of reapportionment, the line of decisions beginning with *Baker* v. *Carr*[9] and proceeding through *Reynolds* v. *Sims*[10] and on to the recent decisions in *Mahan* and *Gaffney*[11] have produced significant changes in the districting of local, state, and congressional districts in nearly all the states.

Type V (Court Influential)

1. Court promulgates policy
2. Law-making majority fails to reverse policy
3. Court's policy stands

Although questions have been raised about the impact of such changes upon party competition and policy outputs of legislatures, it seems clear that such widespread reform in legislative apportionment would not have occurred without the Court's intervention.

In the religion cases, especially the *Engel* and *Schempp*[12] decisions, the Court set forth a policy toward devotional exercises in public schools that affected all schools, not just those in particular localities. Though the decisions were by no means greeted with total compliance, they have not been reversed and still stand as national policy. By the same token, a string of decisions dealing with aid to parochial schools has restricted the nature and types of aid that states and the federal government have been permitted to offer. Though the decisions have not cut off such aid, they have shaped these programs in ways that run contrary to the directions that they would have gone without such intervention.

A long line of confusing and confused decisions emerged as the Court attempted to define obscenity and thus to determine what enjoyed the protection of the First Amendment and what did not. Though the Court is still grappling with this problem...the upshot of this line of cases has been to expand greatly the range of materials available to the society.

In the area of race relations, the Supreme Court played a vital role in the development of national policy. Its decisions in the 1950s and 1960s placed a stamp of legitimacy upon claims for equality on the part of black citizens that was crucial to the development of organizations and activities that eventually succeeded not only in the streets but in the Congress as well. Though a solid consensus against *de jure* segregation did subsequently emerge, the Court played a crucial role in this process rather than merely reflecting developments in other political arenas.

In the areas of criminal procedure, the Court developed a federal constitutional code of criminal justice, ranging from initial contacts of suspects with police, through the development of evidence, the adjudication of guilt or innocence, the imposition of penalties, the appellate process, and the treatment of offenders by probation and correction agencies. From a wealth of cases reflecting the diverse policies of various jurisdictions the Court produced a series of rules aimed at vindicating the adversary system and vouchsafing substantive and procedural rights ignored in many localities. Surely uniformity of treatment has not been achieved in doctrinal, much less behavioral, terms. Yet the Court has moved us toward policies that were not emerging from state legislatures or Congress. The criminal justice cases illustrate an issue area in which the Supreme Court itself took up the burden of being the major advocate for a group in the society that was politically powerless and subject to deprivation of basic procedural rights.

This brief review of some of the Court's work in the area of state and local statutes and practice suggests several issues relevant to Dahl's analysis. First and most important, the policy questions at stake in these cases are not narrow, local or regional issues. In all of these areas the policy promulgated by the Court, although emerging in the context of cases arising out of states or localities, was directly aimed at and had an effect upon governmental activities throughout the nation. *Miranda* v. *Arizona, Gideon* v. *Wainwright, Reynolds* v. *Sims, Abington Township* v. *Schempp, Cooley* v. *Board of Wardens, Memoirs* v. *Massachusetts, Brown* v. *Board of Education* all came from cities or states. Yet the policies that were enunciated had relevance to the whole nation in ways much more manifest than many of the cases involving federal legislation with which Dahl deals.

Did the Court prevail? Was it reversed by a subsequent act of the law-making majority? Did the Court itself take back what it had said? In some areas, these questions are difficult to answer at this time, for a few of the decisions are recent. In terms of one crude indicator, the Court has not been substantially reversed in any of these areas by the passage of legislation or constitutional amendment. In some areas, though, the pattern Dahl suggests does not seem apposite: unpopular decisions became part of the country's political agenda, and changes in political regimes affected recruitment to the Court. The replacement of the Warren Court by the Burger Court is to some extent verification of his thesis. Recent decisions in the areas of obscenity, reapportionment, and criminal justice suggest modifications in policy to some extent congruent with the demands of Court opponents. So the thrust of this argument is not that new evidence unambiguously indicates a role for the Court that is radically different from the one that Dahl suggests. The Court *is* a member of ruling alliances and does respond to others. But examination of the state and local cases does reveal that the arena in which the Court makes policy is substantially broader than the limited area Dahl selects for discussion. Moreover, it suggests that the Court can and does get its way a good deal more frequently than his analysis implies.

Assuming that the Court has not been reversed and has not reversed itself in several important issue areas arising out of state litigation—a plausible account of the areas of civil rights, religion, and the basic thrust of policy in criminal justice and reapportionment—what are we to make of this fact in assessing the relative influence of the Court in our political system? One of the problems with dealing with such cases—and one of the reasons why they were excluded from Dahl's analysis—is that it is, to be sure, difficult to make the determination of the preferences of the national majority that Dahl says is necessary in order to decide whether the Court's policy was influential. Yet these cases did involve issues of broad national significance, and none of the decisions was struck down by legislation or constitutional amendment, even though such efforts were attempted. Thus, in formal terms the Court seems to have "won" (setting aside for the moment the possibility that new appointments may lead the Court to step back to some degree in some issue areas). On the other hand, Dahl's analysis might suggest that the very lack of overriding legislation indicates that the Court was not acting contrary to the preferences of a law-making majority. The difficulty with this argument, of course, is that it places the Court in a no-win situation: if it acts first, regardless of what happens subsequently, it is judged not to have exercised influence.

Another facet of Dahl's argument is relevant to this issue. He suggests that, in general, the major function of the Court, as a member of the ruling alliance at any particular time, is to "confer legitimacy on the fundamental policies of the successful coalition." He goes on to note that at certain periods—when the ruling coalition in an issue domain is weakened and decaying or when a stable coalition has not emerged in the issue area—the Court may "at great risk to its legitimacy powers" intervene and even "succeed in establishing policy." The Court, in such situations, is likely to be successful only when its "action conforms to and reinforces a widespread set of explicit or implicit norms held by political leadership." Dahl refers to the work of the Court in dealing with civil rights as an example of this ability of the Court to intervene when stable coalitions do not exist.

The areas in which the Court has been particularly active in recent years—civil rights, reapportionment, criminal justice, religion, obscenity, privacy—do seem to have been characterized by substantial division both within the political stratum and in the society at large about the most preferable policy alternatives. The Court's intervention has been followed by substantial controversy and attempts to modify its policy as well as attacks on its institutional powers. Both types of opposition have been unsuccessful, and the activities of other members of the political leadership stratum have been of great importance. Lyndon Johnson's activities as majority leader during the late 1950s were crucial in thwarting attempts to modify deci-

sions dealing with loyalty-security programs and to punish the Court for its libertarian decisions in the 1956–57 terms. John F. Kennedy's support for the bible-reading and school prayer decisions was, again, an important element in cooling off attacks on the Court as an institution and attempts to reverse its policy by constitutional amendment.

Assuming, though, that many of the Court's most important contributions to public policy in recent years have involved situations in which the Court was appealing to norms implicitly held by other influential policy makers and that the ability of the Court as an institution and the policies it has promulgated to survive have required support by others, what are we to make of these facts? Dahl's argument stresses the importance of the values and activities of other policy makers rather than the influence exercised by the Court. In one sense he is of course correct, for no institution can successfully carry the day when others are cohesively arrayed against it. But the overall impression that his analysis yields is somewhat misleading. He argues that the Court's activities are best understood by examining the constellation of other political interests willing to support its policies even though they were not united and powerful enough to promulgate such policies on their own. An equally plausible interpretation of such events would suggest that the crucial role was played by the Court, by its willingness to set forth policies that other state and federal institutions were unwilling or unable to promulgate. To be sure, support for such policies by others, or at least their grudging acquiescence, was crucial to the viability of the Court's policies (just as the Court's acquiescence is often crucial to the success of policies promulgated by the law-making majority). But if we are to identify the crucial participants in the policy-development process, to minimize the role of the Court, as Dahl is inclined to do, provides a view of policy making that does not do justice to the potential or actual contributions of the Court.

In sum, there are several difficulties with the evidence that Dahl gathers and the ways in which he utilizes it. The coding rules he employs have a certain asymmetry such that much of his own evidence is excluded from analysis and if further relevant information were gathered it would not be possible to conclude that the Court has been influential. He also excludes from consideration a large body of evidence that seems highly relevant to determining the Court's role in national policy-making. Consideration of this evidence indicates a substantially more influential role than Dahl's argument admits.

THE COURT
AND POLICY MAKING

Dahl's analysis is based upon the premise that policy making is most fruitfully analyzed in terms of concepts like influence or power, a view that the crucial questions deal with winners and losers. The argument that Dahl sets out to confront and evaluate—the view of the Court as a protector of fundamental minority rights against majority tyranny—is itself framed in terms of influence. Moreover, Dahl's article was written at a time when he was developing and conducting his research on community power. In his article dealing with the "ruling elite model" published in 1958, Dahl asserts that "one cannot compare the relative influence of two actors who always perform identical actions with respect to the group influenced. What this means as a practical matter is that ordinarily one can test for differences in influence only where there are cases of differences in initial preferences."[13]

If one can judge relative influence of various individuals, groups, and institutions only when there are disagreements among them, focus upon Court declarations that federal legislation is unconstitutional appears to make sense. From this basic posture about the way in which to study influence, Dahl moves to a view of the policy-making process that focuses upon disputes among policy makers and determines who prevails and who does not. His view of the way to measure influence shades into a conception of policy making that stresses its zero-sum characteristics.

There are several difficulties with Dahl's account of policy making and the role of the Court in it. Some deal with his specific conclusions about the role of the Court; others center about the relatively narrow conception of policy making that underlies his argument.[14]

To begin, let us assume that the winners and losers view that Dahl utilizes is a reasonable way to conceive of the policy-making process. Dahl's basic conclusion is that, except for its important role as a legitimator, the Court does not play an especially influential role in national policy making. There are three major difficulties with this view, the first two of which may be disposed of briefly. First, as argued above, the exclusive focus upon cases in which federal statutes are declared unconstitutional ignores a good deal of what the Court in fact contributes to national policy making. Second, Dahl does not place sufficient emphasis upon those cases in which the Court succeeded in delaying policies for periods of up to 25 years. He focuses upon the dénouement—upon the ultimate rejection of the Court's policy—while an equally salient feature of these examples is the extensive period of time in which the law-making majority was prevented from working its will.

The third and most important objection to

Dahl's characterization of the influence of the Court—assuming that we accept the winners and losers approach—is that he engages in a somewhat misleading contrast in comparing the influence of the Court to that of the law-making majority. Dahl concludes that the Court does not typically play a decisive role in national policy making. "Acting solely by itself with no support from the President and Congress, the Court is almost powerless to affect the course of national policy." He essentially stops here, contenting himself with an effective antidote to the mythology that the Court stands as a lonely bastion single handedly thwarting tyrannical majorities from trampling upon the rights of despised minorities.

Although he does not address the question in detail, at this level of generality such a proposition is true of all institutions of government as well as other groups and individuals in the society. Certainly this comports with Dahl's emphasis upon the building of coalitions, upon the notion of minorities' rule, and upon the great restraints that such stable coalitions place upon the policy choices that may be made at any point in time. But because he frames the question in terms of who wins or loses—Court versus President and Congress—and because he does not in this article emphasize the degree to which *no* institution is really capable of the decisive role he argues the Court fails to possess, the impression of the Court's relative insignificance is cemented. Thus, the framing of the question as one of relative influence produces a view of policy making in which such influence seems to be the touch-stone of significant participation, and this produces a view that the Court, except in its legitimizing role, simply is not a particularly important participant in national policy making.

The arguments offered above suggest that even within the framework for analyzing

policy making that Dahl adopts, there is room for disagreement with his basic conclusion that the Court does not frequently exercise an important influence on the national political outcomes. There is another set of objections that center about the rather narrow conception of policy making that seems to inform Dahl's analysis.

The policy-making process involves more than clashes among political coalitions and institutions, more than winners and losers.[15] The winners-and-losers view implies that there are decisive outcomes to disputes about issues—that among the variety of policies that might be selected, one outcome ultimately prevails. It implies (1) that when interests or institutions clash, the position of one side or another prevails; (2) that the outcomes in policy making that occur as a result of such disagreements somehow "settle" disputes; and (3) that the crucial contributions to policy making consist in promulgating policies that prevail. All of these are implicit in the conception of policy making that informs Dahl's approach to the Supreme Court, and none is adequate.

Dahl argues that when the Court clashes with the law-making majority we can assess its significance in policy making by examining whose policy prevailed. The consistent "winner" in such clashes is judged to be influential and the loser to be a less significant contributor to the policy-making process. This view assumes that when such clashes occur the policy of the "winner" is adopted and the policy of the "loser" is discarded. In fact, when such clashes occur, the policies that eventually emerge are affected by the interaction among institutions that takes place.

For example, when we examine the role of the Court in policy making in the area of economic regulation in the first third of this century, Dahl's view suggests that the Court, although delaying certain policies, was ultimately not influential because its laissez-faire policy was discarded. But one could argue that the Court played a particularly important role in this episode of policy development. Not only for the period in which its decisions thwarted the law-making majority, but also for its role in leading other groups and interests in society to come to grips with laissez-faire economic policy and the interests that supported it. The laissez-faire decisions contributed to the development of the coalition that led to the election of Roosevelt, the legislation of the New Deal, and the eventual discarding of the Court's policies in favor of a conception of public welfare policy that had not heretofore enjoyed the political base it subsequently developed. In this way, both the nature of subsequent policies—their breadth, their statutory and administrative form—and the constellation of political forces in the society were shaped by the activities of the Court. What emerged at the "end" of this struggle was quite different from what had been proposed by the law-making majority at its beginning.

To suggest another example, suppose that changes in Court decisions or a constitutional amendment were to "reject" the Supreme Court's policies since 1957 dealing with the freedom to distribute and possess "obscene" materials. Two features of this hypothetical case suggest difficulties with the notion of examining winners and losers in policy making. First of all, it is hard to imagine what the supposed "winning" policy might be that we could compare with the "losing" policy of the Court. Because there was almost no federal constitutional doctrine on the subject of obscenity before 1957, almost any new "winning" policy would produce a policy outcome different from the pre-1957 status quo.

Second, suppose the new "winning" policy permitted states and localities a substantially greater discretion to restrict the dissemination of such materials. Surely events of the past 18 years affect what types of material would remain available. Experience with the availability of pornography—for example, the fact that substantial numbers of people in the society have come to enjoy it or to believe that it is less harmful than they once believed—would probably produce policies permitting substantially greater availability than existed in the pre-1957 period. Moreover, the political and economic interests with an investment in protecting the freedom to distribute and profit from such materials have greatly increased in recent years and would also operate to dampen to some degree the ability of the "anti-obscenity" interests to impose restrictive policies. In this fashion, the very enunciation of a policy by one institution is likely to affect future policies, even if the original policy is "reversed." The notion of a "winning" and a "losing" policy when institutions clash imposes an artificial distinction that obscures a dynamic process in which even "losers" contribute importantly to outcomes that eventually emerge.

The second objection is related to the first, and it simply states that many of the issues in which national political institutions become involved are not "settled" but continue to recur. Conflicts among political institutions produce not "winning" and "losing" policies, but rather tentative solutions that themselves become the basis for future policy making. Consider, for example, recent developments in national policy dealing with racial equality, legislative apportionment, the relationship between church and state, and criminal procedure. All of these were issues that had long smoldered beneath the surface of American politics. Regardless of the decisions of the Warren Court, these issues have surely not been resolved: we have not succeeded in defining, much less in embracing, racial equality; malapportionment remains a disputed issue; religious practices continue in many schools; and the typical criminal defendant does not enjoy the rights that the Court has doctrinally afforded. Yet all of these issues have become increasingly salient features of the national political agenda in the past twenty years; what was latent conflict has become manifest, and both the general public and political institutions have been forced to confront the policy questions involved. The dénouement is not clear, any more than it was twenty years ago, for these are questions that our society presumably will always have to confront. Though at various times one position or another may carry the day, ultimate resolutions are not discovered, and the Court, like other political institutions, has and will continue to make important contributions to the "solutions" that carry the day, become the subject for further debate, and are modified or rejected.

This suggests a third point. The policy-making process—and the exercise of influence within it—involves more than producing outcomes that prevail. Providing effective access to participants who wish to take part in decision making, placing issues on the agenda of public opinion and of other political institutions, providing an imprimatur of legitimacy to one side or another that may affect its ability to attract adherents, mobilize resources, and build institutions—these are all important parts of the policy-making process that may get lost if we pay attention only to winners and losers. One reason that courts may have particular importance in placing issues on the agenda of other political institutions and in development of interest groups is that "success" in a court requires only that a party convince a relatively small number of decision makers. At the trial level, success requires only a favorable decision from a single individual;

at the Supreme Court level, success requires the approval of five of nine. Thus, interests that lack resources for effective influence in legislative, executive, or administrative arenas may find the legal system an attractive spot in which to attempt to influence public policy. "Success" in a court then becomes useful in participation in these other arenas—the court's decision may require other institutions to come to grips with an issue they have ignored; the legitimacy conferred by victory in court may be useful in attracting members and resources and mobilizing others. For example, the civil rights decisions culminating in *Brown* contributed to the growth of civil rights organizations like SCLC, CORE, and SNCC that became active in the streets as well as in the Congress. The right-to-counsel decisions contributed to the development of a more respectable criminal bar and widespread use of organizations like Public Defender offices that have become active in behalf of criminal defendants not only in trial courts but in appellate courts, the legal community, and legislative settings as well.

The burden of this section, then, is that the view of policy making that informs Dahl's analysis is too narrow. Even in Dahl's own terms, he does not take account of the Court's influence on public policy. Moreover, the winners-and-losers approach leads to a view of policy making that diverts attention from a variety of ways in which the Supreme Court makes significant contributions to national policy making.

NOTES

1. Robert A. Dahl, "Decision-Making in a Democracy: The Supreme Court as a National Policy-Maker," *Journal of Public Law* 6 (Fall 1957), 279–295. Dahl integrated and somewhat revised this

article as a chapter in two editions of his American government text. See Robert A. Dahl, *Pluralist Democracy in the United States* (Chicago: Rand McNally & Company, 1967), Chapter 6; in the 1972 edition, called *Democracy in the United States*, see chapter 16. Because the original is the clearest and most widely read version of his arguments, I shall focus upon it here.

2. 400 U.S. 112 (1970).
3. *Washington* v. *Legrant*, 394 U.S. 618 (1969). *Grisham* v. *Hagan*, 361 U.S. 278 (1960); *McElroy* v. *Guargliardo*, 360 U.S. 281 (1960); *Kinsella* v. *Singelton*, 361 U.S. 234 (1960). *Lamont* v. *Postmaster General*, 381 U.S. 301 (1965).
4. Dahl's "ruling elite model" article, published in 1958, argues that influence can only be measured effectively in such situations. See "A Critique of the Ruling Elite Model," *American Political Science Review* 52 (June 1958), 463–69.
5. 2 Dall, 419 (1793).
6. 4 Wheat 316 (1819).
7. 9 Wheat 1 (1824).
8. 12 How. 299 (1852).
9. 369 U.S. 186 (1962).
10. 377 U.S. 533 (1964).
11. *Mahan* v. *Howell*, 410 U.S. 315 (1973); *Gaffney* v. *Cummings*, 412 U.S. 735 (1973).
12. *Engel* v. *Vitale*, 370 U.S. 421 (1962); *Abington Township* v. *Schempp*, 374 U.S. 203 (1963).
13. Dahl, "A Critique of the Ruling Elite Model," p. 464.
14. I shall not discuss here the problem of taking account of "anticipated reactions" in discussing the relative influence of the Court in the policy-making process. It seems plausible to argue, though, that just as the Court in its decisions may take account of the breadth and intensity of support for various policies, members of Congress may take into account their predictions of potential rulings by the Court in making choices about what legislation to pass. For a discussion of the role of constitutional considerations in the legislative decision-making process, see Donald G. Morgan, *Congress and the Constitution* (Cambridge, Mass.: Harvard University Press, 1966); and Paul Brest, "The Conscientious Legislator's Guide to Constitutional Interpretation," *Stanford Law Review* 27 (February 1975), 585–601.
15. Much of Dahl's work is consistent with this view and has added to our understanding of the ways in which these processes operate. Yet in the article under consideration here, a narrower view of the nature of the policy-making process emerges from the fashion in which he formulates the question and gathers his data.

Legitimacy, Realigning Elections, and the Supreme Court

David Adamany

...The symbolic quality of the Constitution and the Supreme Court has...long ago become a commonplace in the literature of law and political science. But the hands of creative scholars have recently bent it to new purposes. Jerome Frank and Thurman Arnold intended to strip away the mystery of law so that people might govern themselves free of its irrational appeals. Edward S. Corwin and Max Lerner exposed and dispelled the myth of Constitution and Court to open the way for the New Deal vehicle of popular, as opposed to judicial, will. Karl Llewellyn wanted "an intelligent reconstruction of our constitutional law theory"[1] around the view that the Constitution was an operating contemporary institution, subject to popular controls. And Alpheus T. Mason's pleas were for open criticism and debate of the merit of judge-made policy rather than awe-stricken acceptance of judicial decisions.

The unmasking of judicial power—so ardently sought by these friends of popular policymaking—has for Robert A. Dahl ...revealed an entirely new justification for judicial review. Dahl...concedes that the Supreme Court is a national policymaker; dismisses on grounds of both logic and history the claim that the Court is a "democratic" vehicle for safeguarding minority rights; finds that virtually all "important" congressional policies struck down by the Court within four years of enactment, and thus presumably while the sponsoring lawmaking majority was still intact, subsequently are vindicated by further congressional action or judicial reversal; ascribes this mainly to the President's appointment power, noting that on the average a new justice is appointed every 22 months; and concludes finally that "the policy views dominant on the Court are never for long out of line with the policy views dominant among the lawmaking majorities of the United States."

This line of reasoning is not entirely free from difficulty, however. If judicial review cannot be theoretically squared with democracy and if the Court is defended mainly because it quickly harmonizes its policies with the preferences of lawmaking majorities, then why have judicial review at all? The American polity would be different without judicial review only to the extent that lawmaking majorities would never, as happens now, be delayed or, in a handful of cases, obstructed in effecting major policies.

Dahl responds in several directions. "National politics in the United States,..." he says, "is dominated by relatively cohesive alliances that endure for long periods of time." The Supreme Court could not, except in rare cases, sustain policies at odds with those of the dominant coalition. It might, however, occasionally take policy initiatives when the coalition is so unstable on key issues that no lawmaking majority can be assembled for any policy option, or when there is adequate support to sustain the Court's decision against attempts to override it. Why judicial enactment of policies which cannot garner a lawmaking majority is appropriate in a democracy remains unanswered. Even where the conflict over policy is a struggle only among minorities, a situation Dahl suggests is typical, Supreme Court policymaking cannot be viewed as democratic, for it neither advances majority aspirations nor necessarily promotes the position of the most numerous minority.

The Supreme Court, Dahl goes on to say, "is an essential part of the political leadership and possesses some bases of power of its own, the most important of which is the unique legitimacy attributed to its interpretations of the Constitution." It is this special legitimacy that defines the Court's role as a national decisionmaker. "The main task of the Court is to confer legitimacy on the fundamental policies of the successful coalition." It does this, presumably, by declaring presidential and congressional actions constitutional.

But the Court's role does not stop there.... If...the Court's role [is] as a defender of minorities or an agent of external standards of justice, then there is a contradiction with Dahl's earlier concession that "no amount of tampering with democratic theory can conceal the fact that a system in which policy preferences of minorities prevail over majorities is at odds with the traditional criteria of distinguishing a democracy from other political systems."

Furthermore, Dahl's own analysis of judicial vetoes of congressional legislation does not support the proposition that the Supreme Court legitimizes basic rights....

Dahl's survey, made in 1958, does not take into account the Court's recent role as a defender of disadvantaged minorities. But the minority-rights activism of the Warren Court is already fading; that one 15 year period will not counterbalance the whole of the Court's historical record recited by Dahl; and even in this modern role, judicial review will still not square with democratic theory as Dahl postulates it.

It is difficult to know, then, what Dahl means when he defends the Court as a legitimator of rights, liberties, restraints, and obligations which are fundamental to a democracy. These issues come to the Court's attention in only two situations. First, the lawmaking majority expands such rights by legislation (for example, the Voting Rights Act of 1965), in which case the Court's approval is indistinguishable from its usual legitimization of legislation and its disapproval, as Dahl himself concedes, has been substantially damaging to the cause of liberty throughout history. Second, minorities may seek judicial protection from legislation which trammels rights but "legitimization" of rights, liberties, restraints, and obligations in such instances means striking down legislation to protect freedom, which Dahl concedes is not justified by democratic theory and which has not been the Court's usual conduct in history.

Thus, neither Dahl's assertion that the Court may exercise leadership in an unstable coalition nor his admonition that the justices legitimize rights or liberties will square with his own definition of democracy and his own rendering of the Court's historical use of the power of judicial review. All that remains is Dahl's bare assertion that the Supreme Court's special role in American democracy is freighting majority policies with the special legitimacy it derives from the public reverence for its guardianship of the Constitution. Thus does the much assailed myth of Constitution and Court become the handmaiden of majority rule. . . .

WHAT IS LEGITIMACY?

Central to the modern resurrection of that myth is the concept of legitimacy. . . .

Seymour M. Lipset defines legitimacy in political systems as "the capacity. . .to engender and maintain the belief that the existing political institutions are the most appropriate ones for the society."[2] He distinguishes this from "effectiveness," the system's performance in satisfying societal expectations. Legitimacy, then, is not instrumental, but evaluative. It lies in the eye of the beholder, who believes the Supreme Court is endowed with the "right" to make decisions because it follows the Constitution, has traditionally exercised authority, and is therefore an appropriate decisionmaking institution for his society.

This definition sets aside the content of decisions. . .which is conceptually distinct. Content legitimacy rests on agreement with the substance of policies rather than awe of the source of decision. It therefore lies between symbolic legitimacy and effectiveness. Agreement with its policy may heighten regard for an institution's "right" to act. At the same time, approval of policy may contribute to a perception that an institution is effective, that it meets felt needs.

But content legitimacy is not the "legitimacy" expounded by Black, Dahl, or Bickel, for they anticipate that the Court's legitimacy-conferring power will create acceptance of policy among those who oppose or are neutral about its substance and heighten acceptance among those already committed to its content. Robert G. McCloskey captured the distinction, saying that:

> the Supreme Court has historically been blessed with two kinds of supporters—those who venerate it and are prepared to defend it as the symbol of continuity and fairness who are attached to the idea of the rule of law; and those who happen to be gratified by the course of policy the judges are pursuing at the moment.[3]

It is the former attitude, symbolic legitimacy, rather than the latter, content legitimacy, that is the foundation upon which the elegant judicial mansions of Black, Dahl, and Bickel have been so carefully constructed.

Distinguishing these concepts—symbolic legitimacy, content legitimacy, and effectiveness—should not, however, obscure their interplay. An institution's overall influence depends on all of them. Lipset suggested this relationship when he said that " . . . prolonged effectiveness over a number of generations may give legitimacy to a political system."[4]

We might say, then, that levels of symbolic legitimacy are affected by the content and effectiveness of constitutional decisions. The individual who strongly or consistently disapproves policies of a legitimate institution may reconcile this conflict by asserting that the institution has forsaken its traditional function or that it has broken loose from the rules that gave it "legality." Similarly, an institution which is consistently ineffective in meeting deeply felt needs may ultimately be discredited as no longer appropriate for the society.

Dahl stresses the potential for such trade-offs when the Court advances its own preferences rather than legitimizing policies established by the lawmaking majority. "There are times when the coalition is unstable with respect to certain key policies; *at very great risk to its legitimacy powers*, the Court can intervene in such cases and may even succeed in establishing policy." Certainly the *Dred Scott Case* illustrates the point: So repugnant was the decision to many Northerners that the Court's "right" to make decisions was eroded in their minds.

Although they do not precisely define the concept of legitimacy on which their arguments turn, it is plain from their texts that a special kind of legitimacy—that is, symbolic legitimacy—is the Atlas holding up the constitutional worlds of Charles Black, Robert Dahl, and Alexander Bickel....

Thus symbolic legitimacy—an evaluative perception by the people that Supreme Court mandates should be accepted because the justices, as guardians of the Constitution, act by legal right, because they exercise a traditional authority, and because they constitute an appropriate societal institution— coincides with the sometimes thinly, sometimes fully elaborated concept of legitimacy advanced by Black, Dahl, and Bickel....

CAN THE COURT LEGITIMIZE?

Whether the legitimacy-conferring function justifies judicial review or judicial self-restraint, it rests on an assumption about the facts: That the Supreme Court has the capacity to and does throw the cloak of legitimacy over governmental actions. Yet none who bottom their arguments on the Court's legitimacy-conferring capacity offer the slightest empirical basis for its reality....

Without assuming the burden of disproof, ...review [of] the bits and pieces of evidence...reenforce doubt and, indeed, suggest the Court's *incapacity* to legitimize governmental action....[Here follows the public opinion evidence concerning support for the Court.]....

THE LEGITIMIZING FUNCTION AND REALIGNING ELECTIONS

Let us suppose arguendo that scholars pondering speculatively in their studies have better insight into the public mind than do survey researchers, that the Supreme Court does indeed have a legitimacy-conferring capacity. Such a concession in no way frees the legitimacy-conferring function from theoretical and practical difficulties, especially as it is advanced by Charles Black and Robert Dahl as a stabilizing force in a democratic society. These troublesome elements become most evident when judicial review is placed in the framework of American election cycles.

Political scientists now recognize that most voters hold long-term party allegiances which create stable party divisions during long periods of American history. Elections are classified to acknowledge continuity and change in party alignments in the electorate and in party control of government. Maintaining elections are those in which the majority party retains the loyalty of its electorate and wins the presidency. A deviating election sees long-term voter allegiance unchanged but witnesses a defeat for the majority party because of short-term factors such as temporarily persuasive issues or candidate personalities. Converting elections are characterized by substantial shifts in party allegiance in the electorate, but the majority status of the dominant party is preserved and it wins at the polls. Realigning elections, finally, occur when voters revise their party loyalties in such a way as to create a new majority party and to give it control of the government.

It is realigning elections that create the gravest theoretical and historical difficulties for the asserted legitimacy-conferring function of the Supreme Court. Such elections ordinarily occur in response to major social upheavals that discredit old regimes and cause voters to shift their allegiances to an alternate set of party leaders. Those swept into office by such electoral tides attempt to respond to popular discontents by bold programs addressing the sources of unrest. At the onset of a realigning period, which may actually take several elections as groups of voters break former party ties and give their allegiances elsewhere, the effectivenss of government in meeting deeply felt public needs is low. This ineffectiveness corrodes to some extent the legitimacy of governmental arrangements and institutions; and stability is, as Seymour M. Lipset points out, endangered. The actions of the new regime are ordinarily designed to consolidate electoral gains by responding to public concerns, and they simultaneously have the result, by actual or apparent effectiveness, of increasing public confidence in government.

It is at such critical moments in history that the Supreme Court, according to its defenders, most importantly plays a legitimacy-conferring role. Charles Black points out that the Court's endorsement of the New Deal after 1937 was essential for reconciling that large minority whose reservations went beyond the merits of Rooseveltian policy to the constitutionality of the program.[5] A similar task fell to the justices in other great periods of governmental change. Dahl's analysis emphasizes the Court's legitimization of rising party coalitions....

This interpretation of history in support of the legitimacy-conferring function seems flawed. I concede that eventually a new majority coalition will win control of the Court. But the moment of crisis, when stability is most impaired, occurs during the realigning period itself. The newly instituted regime is challenged to meet public needs and restore public confidence because both the effectiveness and the legitimacy of government are in doubt. Yet at precisely this moment the Supreme Court is most likely to impose a barrier to both goals. A new political coalition usually inherits a Court fully staffed by the opposition party....

Even if vacancies occur at average intervals of 22 months, as calculated by Dahl, the President who leads the newly emergent majority party does not win working control on a nine member Court during the period of most severe crisis. Furthermore, there might be fewer opportunities than usual for presidential appointments if justices of the displaced majority party tend to cling to their seats, echoing the sentiment of Chief Justice William Howard Taft, expressed during Herbert Hoover's presidency, that "[A]s long as...I am able to answer in my place, I must stay on the Court in order to prevent the Bolsheviks from getting control...."[6] And, finally, does not the new coalition find that, to respond to the turmoil in society, it must attempt to overcome the judicially created barriers, even if compelled to assail the Supreme Court itself?

The Court, then, might easily be viewed as blocking the effectiveness of government in periods of crisis by the exercise of its "checking" power. But it has an even more subtle role which implicates its presumed legitimizing capacity. Charles Black has insisted that the legitimizing function can be carried out only if the Court has and occasionally uses the power to declare laws unconstitutional.... But is it not also true that the capacity to legitimize is the capacity to delegitimize? And it follows that at moments of crisis and realignment, the Court's opposition to the popular branches may reach beyond checking their actions to undermining their legitimacy. Too narrow is

Black's view that the Supreme Court legitimizes only when it validates actions of the popular branches, for expressions other than validation may express legitimacy.... And the converse is also true: It is not mere checking that delegitimizes, but any conflict which shows the guardians of the Constitution in a posture hostile to the politicians who man the elected branches:

Humpty Dumpty, once shattered, may not be so easily put back together; and it would not be surprising if fragile legitimacy too, once smashed, is difficult to repair. The new coalition's eventual appointment of a majority of the justices and their validation of its policies may not so quickly restore the legitimacy withdrawn by the Court in its conflict with the popular branches in the immediate aftermath of a realigning election. Indeed, since the legitimacy-conferring function necessarily assumes a reasonably alert electorate and because the popular branches may often be compelled in realigning periods to assail a recalcitrant judiciary, the eventual coming around of the Court—its eventual validation and other approvals of popular branch policies—may have more the appearance of surrender to superior force than of legitimization.

In the main, these speculations, rather than those advanced by Professor Black, seem more nearly consistent with the history of relations between the Court and majority coalitions in realigning periods. Although electoral realignments occur during a series of elections rather than in a single balloting and despite some scholarly contentiousness about just which elections constituted realignments, the best analyses cite the election of Jefferson in 1800, of Jackson in 1828, of Lincoln in 1860, and of Franklin Delano Roosevelt in 1932 as the moments in realigning periods at which the leadership of new majority coalitions actually took public office.[7]

Thomas Jefferson swore the oath of office facing a Supreme Court of six unsympathetic Federalists. Lincoln found seven Democrats, one Whig, and one vacant seat on the high Bench. Roosevelt inherited a Court divided between five Republicans, including one unwilling to interpose judicial power against New Deal policies (Justice Harlan F. Stone) and four Democrats, of whom Pierce Butler and James C. McReynolds were steadfast conservatives. Thus he counted an unfavorable margin of six to three. Jackson was greeted by a less clear situation because the three Democratic-Republicans were not necessarily sympathetic and the three Federalists not necessarily hostile—party lines being fluid and increasingly meaningless in the period before Jackson's inauguration. It cannot be doubted, however, that the justices were not in tune in style, ideology, or regional orientation with the new "popular" coalition that Jackson was building. In each instance, therefore, new presidents correctly perceived the Court as dominated overwhelmingly by opposition partisans.

Jefferson named three justices, the third in 1807 to fill a newly created seat, never winning a Republican majority on the Court. Jackson was more fortunate; he appointed five members of a seven man bench. But three of his appointments were in the last two years of his tenure and his first, John McLean, in 1829, was a Whig. Lincoln was also fortunate: He named Samuel Miller to a vacancy existing at his inauguration, replaced three of the eight sitting justices, and named War Democrat Stephen Field to a new tenth seat. Five justices in five years constitutes an heroic exception to the ordinary pace of appointments....

Democratic Justices Samuel Nelson, Robert Grier, Nathan Clifford, and, until 1865, John Catron, constituted a potential bloc which, in concert with Field and Lincoln's politically ambitious Chief Justice Salmon P.

Chase, menaced the policies of lawmaking majorities, especially the Radical Congress, until 1870. In his first two terms Franklin Roosevelt actually appointed five justices, but not a single one until after the old Court's obstruction of the New Deal had led to the court-packing fight of 1937.

These "realigning presidents" actually had greater appointment opportunities than the average, but because vacancies occurred slowly and because the pre-existing membership of the Court was so dominated by the other party, their appointees constituted majorities, if at all, only very late in their second terms. Furthermore, because some justices—estimated by Robert Scigliano as one in four[8]—stray far from the general ideological position of their appointing presidents, even a slim majority attained late in the second term could not be counted upon to validate and thus legitimize the new majority's program....

There is, finally, slight evidence that justices are more reluctant to resign after a realigning election. Of the 92 cases in which men have left the highest bench, 44 (48 percent) were retirements or resignations. Ten justices vacated their chairs under Jefferson, Jackson, and Lincoln, but only three (30 percent) by resignation or retirement. Roosevelt by contrast, had three resignations and one death during his first two terms; but the first retirement (Willis Van Devanter) did not occur until 1937, after the Hughes-Roberts switch that reversed the Court's policy toward the New Deal, and it was followed rapidly by the retirements of Justices Sutherland and Brandeis and the death of Justice Butler. Thus, when the President represented a newly forged majority coalition, justices have seemed somewhat more reluctant to leave the bench, at least before the point when judicial resistance to the new regime has been overwhelmed.

Command of the Court by men of the old majority, slow turnover on the bench, and the added reluctance of justices to resign after a new lawmaking majority is inaugurated all set the stage for conflict between the Supreme Court and the new, dominant electoral coalitions. There is nothing to be gained by rehearsing here all the scenes and subplots in those struggles. But a broad rendering of the scenarios... [shows] that each realigning election has been followed by conflict which somewhat discredited and sometimes checked the lawmaking majority. And each scenario's dénouement was a clash that left doubtful the Court's capacity ultimately to legitimize the new regime and its policies.

[The author presents detailed analyses of the Court during the realignments of 1800, 1828, 1860, and 1932.]...

What conclusions are fairly drawn from these historical vignettes? First, each new party coalition took office in a condition of tension with the judiciary. Prior judicial decisions were repugnant to the ideology of the new regime. The Court—indeed, the entire judiciary—was drawn mainly from the ranks of partisan and ideological opponents. There is no evidence that "realigning presidents" were denied the same opportunity to make appointments as other chief executives; and only the scantiest support can be drummed up for the proposition that justices of the old coalition held more tenaciously to their posts after realigning elections than did other justices in other times. Nonetheless, the adherents of the repudiated party so dominated the Court that the new coalition's chief executive either was unable to appoint a majority of friendly justices or at least was unable to do so until well into his term.

Second, after two realigning elections—those of 1860 and 1932—the Court used its checking power to thwart significantly the policies of the new coalition. In all four realigning election periods the executive and legislative leadership firmly believed that the

Court would disrupt their program. Certainly in the former two cases, and perhaps in all four, the capacity of the newly elected majority effectively to undertake actions they deemed necessary to relieve the national crisis and preserve the stability of our democratic system was impaired.

Third, after each realigning election there was intense and highly visible conflict between the Court and the lawmaking majority. Professor Black measures legitimization by judicial validation of popular branch programs; but it must also follow that the checking function involves "delegitimization" of the popular branches and their policies. Nor does the legitimizing aspect of judicial review end with the validating and checking activities of the Court. There are other relations between the elected branches (or the States) and the Supreme Court—not every expression of agreement or hostility need be manifested in finally adjudicated cases. And if legitimacy inheres in any of the Court's actions it inheres in them all—just as the President's ceremonial role as chief of state is implicated whenever he acts as legislative leader, administrative chief, party politician, and so forth. Thus, any conflict, whether in litigation or otherwise, between the justices and elected officials brings into play the Court's unique standing as arbiter of the Constitution, its potential to legitimize or delegitimize policies and regimes. The recurring clashes between the Court and the popular branches in realigning periods therefore erode regime legitimacy, the appearance that the popular branches are meeting the crisis within their constitutional mandate.

Finally, in each case the clash between the justices and the lawmaking majority rose to such fury that elected officials felt compelled to assail the Court. Sometimes this involved defiance, either in fact or appearance. At others it spawned attempts, twice successful, to alter the Court's size, jurisdiction, or decisional process. In 1805 it led to the only impeachment of a Supreme Court justice. I will return shortly to the diversion of energies and resources of new coalitions that accompanies these battles over judicial power. But it is enough to conclude here that the legitimacy conferring capacity of the Supreme Court is vastly reduced by these battles. When the Court finally comes into line with the new majority, it appears to capitulate to overpowering force rather than freely to legitimize. And those who disagree with the new regime's policies, who must be persuaded of its legitimacy, and who would be attentive enough to comprehend legitimizing action by the justices must certainly also be counted intelligent enough to draw the common inference that the Court has been taken by storm rather than by persuasive constitutional argument. Little legitimization is likely in such circumstances.

Thus, even conceding the dubious proposition that the Court has a legitimacy-conferring capacity, the history of realigning election periods more readily supports the view that the justices check and delegitimize popular government and constitute a force for instability than the conclusion advanced by Black and Dahl that the Court legitimizes the actions of the elected branches, reconciling recalcitrant minorities to the constitutionality of new regimes and their policies.

CONCLUSIONS

Now briefly to recapitulate. The symbolic qualities of law, especially constitutional law and the Supreme Court, were expounded by the Legal Realists in the 1920's and 1930's. This was not only the development of a legal philosophy, but in the 1930's a strategem in the assault upon the old Court. The purpose was a better understanding of law and a freeing of popular government from the restraints of judicial power.

Modern constitutional scholars, however, have stood the Realists on their heads. The symbolic quality of Supreme Court adjudication is recognized as a fact, but not for the purpose of debunking. It becomes in the hands of Charles Black and Robert Dahl a justification for judicial review. The Supreme Court, because of its identification as the oracle of the Constitution, serves a valuable function in American democracy by legitimizing the actions of popular government and regime changes.

What strikes one about these arguments is the absence of evidence. Not one of these commentators advances any factual support for the Supreme Court's legitimacy-conferring capacity, the linchpin in their lawyerly arguments. Indeed, a survey of the available public opinion studies suggests quite another conclusion: That the public has sufficient knowledge about neither the Court's actions nor its function to meet the conditions necessary in an operationalized definition of legitimization. Even an attempt to save the commentators from themselves, by limiting their theory of legitimization to opinion molding elites is not promising, despite the bits of evidence that might lay a foundation for such a revised approach.

But, even if the legitimacy-conferring function is conceded, it will not sustain the argument of those, especially Black and Dahl, who have put it at the center of their vision of the Supreme Court's role in American politics. At the critical moments of economic and social crisis in American history, when both government effectiveness and legitimacy are impaired, the Supreme Court is a barrier to majorities, operating through the medium of realigning elections, as they attempt to meet the emergency. This is not simply because life tenure and partisan-ideological appointments combined with the power of judicial review make the Court "the check of a preceding generation on the present one; a check of conservative legal philosophy upon a dynamic people, and nearly always the check of a rejected regime on the one in being."[9] More important, the symbolic status of the Supreme Court has the effect, when the justices and the popular branches are thrown into conflict, not simply over specific cases but in the fullness of philosophical debates and political maneuvering, of "delegitimizing" the elected branches, thus casting doubt not only on politics enacted but also on the "rightness" of the regime. And when the justices are finally brought into line, usually following bitter assaults on the Court itself, those disaffected from the new regime's substantive policy, among whom the Court might well legitimize the new leadership, certainly see that the constitutional citadel has been taken by force and that the legitimizing voices come from justices installed by the new regime or at least intimidated by it. . . .

Finally, then I venture a speculation. . . . The Court may not, in fact, have a legitimacy-conferring capacity; but it may nevertheless command the same reverence as a constitutionally sanctioned branch that the others do. It may, in short, have legitimacy as an institution in a legitimate political system, to which it in a small way contributes, as do other institutions and centers of opinion formation. And might it also be true that the Court commands some additional reverence because of the American devotion to "law" and to the Constitution.

May not this more modest legitimacy of the Supreme Court, then, cast it in realigning election periods as the reef upon which the vessel of reform is shattered? In the early stages of each new electoral coalition party majorities tend to be inflated. Spurred by the ideological zeal common among those long out of power and by the national crisis, these large majorities move toward sweeping reform. But the Supreme Court, because of its composition and its checking power, stands in the way or seems to. Finally the new coalition's leadership, often its most reformist wing and usually the Executive, concludes that it must curb the Court.

It is at this moment that the Court's legitimacy is important, for elements of the coalition's elected elite and of its electoral base now hold back in reverence to a constitutional institution, whose actions and function they may or may not fully understand or approve. The coalition is thus divided over an issue of constitutional structure; the energies, resources, and zeal of the reformist wing of the coalition are diverted to that struggle; the leadership's hold over the loosely joined alliance is weakened; and the momentum for substantive policy change is slowed or stopped.

One can only idly speculate about the history of race relations in America if the Radical Republicans had not been diverted from their Reconstruction program by their attacks first on the Court and then on an Executive branch which had been lost to their party by assassination rather than election. Similarly, what measures toward social welfare and redistribution of wealth might have been enacted by the New Deal coalition if it had not splintered in the court-packing fight? Might poverty, again a visible issue in the 1960's but without any effective legislative response, have been mainly alleviated by more sweeping legislation in the 1930's?

Finally, one is entitled to speculate whether a large, younger electorate, just now coming of age politically, might be the stuff from which a new political coalition will be made. Restoration of the natural environment, dramatic redistribution of wealth, sternly enforced rules against discrimination by race or sexual identity, and medical care for all citizens—to select only four examples requiring massive new governmental "regi-mentation" of the conduct of individuals and of such collectivities as corporations, unions, and medical associations—might be goals of such a coalition. The ideological predilections and the age of recent judicial appointees certainly presage another "old Court" which would block such reform, first by checking legislation and then by itself becoming an issue which diverts reform energies and divides a political coalition.

But this is simply speculation, an alternative definition and interpretation of Supreme Court legitimacy. Whatever the merit of this different model, there seems no question that the widely asserted legitimizing function of the Supreme Court cannot summon adequate empirical support from public opinion studies, does not square with the history of relations between the justices and the popular branches, and will not withstand a searching analysis of its assumptions. Such a formulation cannot be the foundation for elaborately structured theories about the worth, justification, or scope of judicial review in a democracy.

NOTES

1. Llewellyn, *The Constitution As An Institution*, 34 COLUM. L. REV. 1, 3 (1934).
2. S. Lipset, POLITICAL MAN 77 (1959).
3. R. McCloskey, THE AMERICAN SUPREME COURT 72 (1960).
4. S. Lipset, at 82.
5. C. Black, THE PEOPLE AND THE COURT 56–69 (1960).
6. H. Pringle, THE LIFE AND TIMES OF WILLIAM HOWARD TAFT 955 (1939).
7. With two exceptions, these demarcations follow the analysis of Thomas P. Jahnige. Jahnige, *Critical Elections and Social Change*, 3 POLITY 468, 469 n. 11 (1971). I have marked 1800 as the onset of the Jeffersonian party system; Jahnige

more vaguely describes the period 1789–1828 as the Federalist-Jeffersonian party period. And I have adopted Pomper's view that 1896 was a converting election, which strengthened the preexisting Republican majority, rather than a realigning election. Pomper, *Classification of Presidential Elections*, 29 J. POL. 533, 562 (1967) . . . .

8. R. Scigliano, THE SUPREME COURT AND THE PRESIDENCY 125–48 (1971).

9. R. Jackson, THE STRUGGLE FOR JUDICIAL SUPREMACY (1941) at 315. After this paper was in draft, an additional commentary bearing on its historical thesis became available. Sheldon Goldman and Thomas P. Jahnige compare the nation's realigning election cycles with the successful "court-curbing" periods discovered by Stuart S. Nagel. There is a distinct coincidence, with these court-curbing periods occurring on the eve of and during realigning election periods. This seems added confirmation that conflict between the Judiciary and the popular branches accompanies these electoral upheavals, threatening effectiveness by checking programs of the new coalition and delegitimizing the new regime by subjecting it to judicial disapproval. S. Goldman & T. Jahnige, THE FEDERAL COURTS AS A POLITICAL SYSTEM 261–68 (1971); cf. S. Nagel, THE LEGAL PROCESS FROM A BEHAVIORAL PERSPECTIVE 260–279 (1969).